THE FINANCIAL MARKETPLACE
THIRD EDITION

S. Kerry Cooper
Texas A&M University

Donald R. Fraser
Texas A&M University

ADDISON-WESLEY PUBLISHING COMPANY
Reading, Massachusetts ■ Menlo Park, California ■ New York ■ Don Mills, Ontario

Sponsoring Editor: *Barbara Rifkind*
Production Administrator: *Loren Hilgenhurst Stevens*
Associate Editor: *Christine A. O'Brien*
Managing Editor: *Mary Clare McEwing*
Copy Editor: *Barbara Willette*
Cover and Text Design: *Vanessa Piñeiro*
Illustrators: *Terry Presnall, George Nichols*
Manufacturing Supervisor: *Roy Logan*

Library of Congress Cataloging-in-Publication Data

Cooper, S. Kerry.
    The financial marketplace/S. Kerry Cooper, Donald R. Fraser.—
3rd ed.
      p.   cm.
    Bibliography: p.
    Includes index.
    ISBN 0-201-50848-6
    1. Finance. 2. Finance—United States.   I. Fraser, Donald R.
II. Title.
HG173.C675 1990   89-34010
332.1—dc20   CIP

BCDEFGHIJ-HA-943210

For our wives, Maryvonne
Lyn
and kids, Chris and Danielle
Eleanor

Preface

This third edition of *The Financial Marketplace* appears at the end of a decade of sweeping change in the financial system of the United States and the world. Throughout the 1980s, financial innovation and deregulation were at center stage in the economic arena, and virtually all financial markets and institutions were affected in varying degrees. These changes are incorporated into the discussion of each of the chapters in the new edition. This edition also features a "postscript" describing the Financial Institutions Reform, Recovery, and Enforcement Act of 1989. The "postscript" not only reflects the authors' desire to have the new edition of the book as up-to-date as possible, but also is symbolic of the rapid pace of change in the financial marketplace in recent years.

MAJOR CHANGES IN THE THIRD EDITION

Developments such as continuing financial innovation, economic change, and regulatory and legislative developments required the addition of new material and the reorganization of entire chapters. All tables, charts, and other data have been updated as much as possible. Other changes have been made to improve exposition and to enhance treatment of especially significant material. Brief descriptions of some of the major changes, by chapter, follow.

Chapter 1, "An Overview of the Financial System," has been completely rewritten to make it much more substantive and to expand the conceptual treatment of saving, investment, and the role of the financial marketplace. The new Chapter 2, "Financial Assets: Income and Value," now focuses on the principles of valuation of financial instruments. Chapter 6, "The Level of Interest Rates," has been revised to reflect more fully the major role that foreign capital inflows now play in U.S. financial markets. Chapter 9, "The Financial Services Industry: Depository Institutions," has been rewritten to include functions of financial service organizations, size and market shares of financial service firms, and a discussion of major factors determining the size and market shares of financial service firms. Chapters 11 and 12, which focus on the federal government's role as financial regulator and lender, have been revised to include discussion of the crises relating to the Farm Credit System, the Federal Home Loan Bank System, and the regulatory (and deregulatory) difficulties of recent years. Indeed, recent developments in regulatory issues have been incorporated into all the chapters concerned with financial institutions, particularly Chapters 9 through 14. Chapter 14, "Issues in the Regulation and Deregulation of Financial Institutions," includes a more extensive treatment of the deposit insurance issue.

The treatment of financial theory in Chapter 15, "Risk, Return, and the Efficiency of Financial Markets," has been expanded to cover arbitrage pricing theory and other theoretical developments. All the chapters concerned with financial markets have been completely updated. Chapter 21, which is concerned with the stock market, features full discussion of the 1987 stock market crash and its implications for market efficiency. Chapter 22, "Futures, Options, and Swaps," has been completely rewritten and offers expanded treatment of these instruments and markets. Chapters 24 and 25, which focus on the international monetary-financial system, have been thoroughly updated to reflect such developments as the trade and external debt problems of the United States, the burgeoning financial power of Japan, and the continuing problem of Third World debt (including a discussion of the Brady plan). Finally, the last three chapters of the book, which are concerned with economic policy, have been updated to reflect both theoretical and institutional developments. Chapter 27, "Fiscal Policy: Federal Taxing, Spending, and Borrowing," includes an updated treatment on the federal budget deficit problem and a thorough discussion of the 1986 federal income tax "reform."

New Applications

To help focus the reader on the most significant innovations and issues, we have added special-interest boxes in most chapters to illuminate significant topics, including "Money, Money, Money" (page 60), "CARs and CARDs: The Securitization of Practically Everything" (page 221), "Property Held by the Deposit Insurance Agencies: The Disposable and the Nondisposable" (page 342), "The Explosion of Junk" (page 453), and "Europe '92: European Economic Integration" (page 567).

USE OF THE BOOK

As with previous editions, *The Financial Marketplace* is designed primarily for use in junior, senior, and MBA courses concerned with the financial system—its components, functions, economic roles, and significance. In such macrofinancial courses, the book is designed to serve as the primary textbook. The book is also suitable for use as a companion or supplemental text in courses concerned with microfinancial decision-making, such as commercial bank management and financial institutions management courses.

The Financial Marketplace covers the entire spectrum of the financial system in the economy, with special emphasis on financial markets. The sequence and selection of chapters can be easily adapted to suit the background of students, the emphasis and orientation of the instructor, and the course in which the book is used. For example, coverage of Chapter 4, "Money and the Financial System," and Chapter 5, "The Structure and Role of the Federal Reserve System," may be of marginal value for students with a strong background in economics. Also, instructors wishing to devote maximum attention to private-sector financial markets, instruments, and institutions (and less to monetary policy and other macro-economic influences), may choose to omit or minimize coverage of Chapters 4, 5, 26 ("Monetary Policy: Formulation, Implementation, and Impact"), 27 ("Fiscal Policy: Federal Taxing, Spending and Borrowing"), and Chapter 28 ("The Record of Economic Policy").

As in previous editions, the text material is presented with minimal mathematics and only limited integration with the original literature. Technical terms are carefully defined when introduced and, on occasion, redefined when employed in a subsequent chapter. This facilitates altering the chapter sequence and also helps the student develop a thorough grasp of the terminology of the financial marketplace. A careful balance of description and analysis is attempted for all subjects. It is intended that students using this text will find the descriptive content complete and the analytical aspect useful.

ACKNOWLEDGMENTS

We have received a great deal of help from many individuals on all editions of this book. We are very grateful for their assistance and regret that we cannot acknowledge them all. We are particularly indebted to the following individuals who have served as reviewers on one or more editions: Fuad A. Abdullah, University of Nebraska, Omaha; James C. Baker, Kent State University; William Christiansen, Florida State University; Lawrence Conway, University of Toledo; Inayat U. Mangla, Western Michigan University; David Nawrocki, Villanova University; and Daniel White, Georgia State University.

Finally, we wish to thank the staff at Addison-Wesley Publishing Company, especially Barbara Rifkind, Senior Editor, Christine O'Brien, Associate Editor, and Loren Hilgenhurst Stevens, Production Administrator. We also extend our thanks to Vanessa Piñeiro, text designer, and Terry Presnall, illustrator.

We welcome any suggestions and comments on this text from both students and faculty.

S.K.C.

College Station, Texas   D.R.F.

Contents

PART **II**

INTEREST RATES 127

6 THE LEVEL OF INTEREST RATES 129

7 THE TERM STRUCTURE OF INTEREST RATES 155

8 INFLATION AND OTHER INFLUENCES ON THE STRUCTURE OF INTEREST RATES 185

PART IV
GOVERNMENT REGULATION AND THE FINANCIAL SYSTEM 273

17   THE MONEY MARKET: U.S. TREASURY AND FEDERAL AGENCY SECURITIES, FEDERAL FUNDS, AND REPURCHASE AGREEMENTS   401

18   THE MONEY MARKET: DOMESTIC AND EURODOLLAR CERTIFICATES OF DEPOSIT, BANKERS ACCEPTANCES, AND COMMERCIAL PAPER   423

19   THE CAPITAL MARKET: BONDS   441

27   FISCAL POLICY: FEDERAL TAXING, SPENDING, AND BORROWING   661

28   THE RECORD OF ECONOMIC POLICY   687

PART I

THE STRUCTURE AND ROLE OF THE FINANCIAL SYSTEM

CHAPTER **1**

An Overview
of the Financial System

The financial system of the United States and other developed nations performs a number of functions that are essential for a modern private enterprise economy. Two of the most important of these functions are providing the means by which (1) payments for transactions are accomplished and (2) savings are accumulated and channeled into investment uses. Paying for goods and services, saving, lending, borrowing, and investing are all activities that are carried out in the framework of instruments, institutions, and markets that constitute the financial system. Included in this framework are the financial agents of the central government, which in the United States include the Treasury and the Federal Reserve System, as well as numerous private institutions and agents. A complex and sophisticated financial system is an integral and essential component of the economic system of any advanced, industrialized society.

The financial system's components can be defined as **financial instruments,** documentary evidences of obligations underlying the exchange of resources among contracting parties; **financial markets,** the arenas or mechanisms by which financial instruments are traded; and **financial institutions,** which create and trade financial instruments and otherwise facilitate the flow of resources among market participants. Financial instruments include, but are not limited to, bank deposits, debt securities, and shares of stock issued by corporations. Financial markets include the capital market (in which long-term securities are traded), the "money market" (in which short-term debt securities are traded), and markets in foreign currencies and futures and options. Financial institutions include various types of financial intermediaries such as commercial banks, savings and loan associations, credit unions, insurance companies, and brokerage firms.

Knowledge of the nature and significance of the financial system is best attained by understanding these various financial instruments, markets, and institutions and the manner in which the financial requirements of a modern economy are satisfied by their interaction. This book focuses primarily on financial markets, for it is in these markets that financial institutions, savers, and investors come together to effect exchanges of financial instruments. The financial marketplace is the core of the financial system.

The purpose of this chapter is to develop an overview of the role, structure, and operation of the financial system. In addition, a brief discussion of this book's organization and content is included.

THE ROLE OF THE FINANCIAL SYSTEM

Economic activity is characterized by many exchange transactions—the buying and selling of goods, services, and productive resources. Economists often find useful a distinction between the "real" and "financial" aspects of these transactions. In a sales transaction, for example, a buyer takes physical possession of goods in exchange for a payment of money or a promise to pay in the future. The former aspect of the transaction is "real"; the latter is "financial." The goods are "real assets"; the payment is with a "financial asset." In a barter system, goods are exchanged for goods; the introduction of money as a medium of exchange adds the "financial" element to economic transactions.

As the "real" aspects of transactions become more complex, involving exchanges over time as well as at a point in time, their "financial" aspects necessarily become more involved. The "real" aspect of a loan, for example, is the postponement by the lender of the opportunity to consume now (buy something with the funds instead of lending them) with the expectation of consuming more in the future. The "financial" aspect of a loan involves the creation of a financial instrument, which may range from an IOU between friends, through the execution of a bank note indicating due date, interest, and so on, to the rather complex process of the issuing of debt securities by a corporation.

There are important relationships between the financial system of the domestic and international economy and the enormously varied and complex activities of individuals and businesses working, buying, and selling as part of the ordinary course of human affairs. The financial system includes both markets for financial instruments and those institutions that are concerned with financial transactions, just as the "real" component of the economic system includes both markets for goods and services and those institutions that bring together people and resources to produce goods and services. The financial system is a vital component of the total economic system, greatly increasing its capacity to satisfy the needs and wants of individuals for goods.

The economic role of the financial system can be mainly characterized as one of facilitating real and financial transactions. Figure 1.1 depicts the relationship between the financial system and the various real and financial flows in the economy. In this simplified view the economic system consists of a **business** sector, a

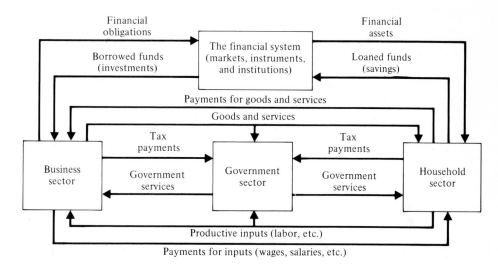

FIGURE 1.1 Exchange Flows in an Economic System

household sector, and a **government** sector. In terms of **real flows,** the business sector produces goods and services, which are purchased by the household sector for consumption purposes. The household sector provides labor and other necessary productive inputs to the business sector in exchange for wages, salaries, and other compensation. (We shall say more about these "other" inputs and compensation shortly.) The government sector collects tax payments from the household and business sectors and uses these receipts to buy goods, services, and productive inputs, which are then used to supply government services (roads, law enforcement, and so on) to the other sectors.[1]

Turning to the role of the financial system (other than the payments function) in this simple model of the economy, we may note that the financial system is interposed between flows of saving, investment, and financial instruments (financial assets of savers and financial obligations of investors). We may note further that these flows reflect exchanges of resource use over time, rather than exchanges of real resources at points in time ("spot" exchanges). Exchanges of resource use over time (lending and borrowing) is made possible by some economic participants' forgoing current consumption in favor of future consumption. This postponement of consumption—saving—is encouraged by the prospect that future consumption opportunities will be enlarged as the result of the

---

[1]For the sake of simplicity, Fig. 1.1 assumes a "balanced budget" in the government sector. Actually, of course, the government sector is a frequent participant in financial markets, borrowing funds by issuing financial obligations.

productive use of the resources currently made available for investment purposes.[2]

The existence of saving in an economic system provides an opportunity for the business sector to expand the means of production. In a private enterprise economy, households can use saved receipts to lend to business firms or to purchase ownership shares in business firms. Such transfers of purchasing power supply the business sector with **money capital,** the financial resources that enable firms to gather and use real resources for investment and thereby increase output of goods and services. The investment of these funds in turn provides the means of paying a return on savings—**interest** in the case of loaned funds and **dividends** in the case of purchases of ownership shares. The flow of saved resources to the business and government sectors from the household sector is a productive input into these sectors, just as is labor. Interest and dividends are the compensation for this flow of saved resources, just as wages are the compensation for labor provided. (These are the "other" inputs and compensation mentioned previously.)

Economic units, whether in the household, business, or government sector, that spend less than their net receipts are called **surplus economic units.** This excess of net receipts over expenditures for a period of time is called **saving** when it occurs in the household sector, **retained earnings** in the business sector, and a **budget surplus** in the government sector. (The term "saving" is used for all instances of surplus receipts in the following discussion.) An economic unit in any of the economy's sectors may also elect (voluntarily or involuntarily) to spend more than its net receipts by drawing on past saving (**dissaving**) or by borrowing. These economic units are called **deficit economic units.** Dissaving is made possible by the conversion of past saved funds into currently spendable funds.

The financial system—the framework of instruments, markets, and institutions—facilitates the transfer of saved funds from surplus (savers) to deficit spending units (borrowers).[3] A deficit spending unit may borrow from a surplus unit by exchanging a financial instrument (a promise to make future payments) for the latter's saved funds. The issuer of the instrument (the borrower) thus incurs a **financial obligation.** The recipient of the instrument (the lender) obtains a **financial asset.** Such exchanges of saved funds for financial assets are readily and efficiently accomplished in financial markets. The important contribution to this process made by the third component of the financial system—financial

---

[2]**Saving** is a flow, an amount for some period of time equal to the difference between two other flows for that period: income and consumption spending. **Savings** is a stock, the accumulated quantity of saved funds at a point in time.

[3]A deficit spending unit need not be a borrower if it has saved resources from prior periods. In this case, dissaving is possible by expending these saved resources. If, as is likely, the saved resources are held in the form of financial instruments, they can be readily converted into money for spending purposes.

institutions—is made through their role as **intermediaries** between lenders and borrowers. The financial intermediation process is of great significance for the channeling of saved funds into investment uses. Financial intermediation involves financial instrument creation and acquisition and financial market activities, as well as financial institutions, and warrants some additional introductory discussion.

SAVING, INVESTMENT, AND FINANCIAL MARKETS

Fundamental to understanding the role of financial markets in the economy is some understanding of saving and investment. Decisions to save and invest strongly influence the level of employment, production, and income. Moreover, the long-term economic growth of a society depends on the saving and investments habits of its population. It is often argued that the relatively rapid economic growth rate in Japan in recent years reflects the high rate of saving and investment in that country.

Saving

Saving refers to the act of postponing current consumption, that is, of consuming less than current income. As such, saving is sometimes referred to as **abstinence**—abstaining from using all of one's current income to purchase goods and services. Saving releases resources for the consumption of other economic units or for investment by the saver or others. It is in saving for investment purposes that the act of saving has its paramount economic significance. Through investment an economy both broadens and deepens its productive capacity. Investment involves the business sector expanding its equipment and other productive facilities and financing inventories as production expands.

The decision to save—to postpone current consumption—and the decision about where to place these savings—a savings account, Treasury securities, stocks, or other types of financial assets—are quite distinct and fundamentally different decisions. The decision to save is essentially nonfinancial in nature and depends on the individual's preference for present consumption compared with future consumption and on the real (inflation-adjusted) return expected on that saving. In contrast, the decision to add to a savings account, buy stocks, or purchase other types of financial assets is a financial transaction determined by the relative return/risk characteristics of the different assets.[4] It is the former decision—to postpone current consumption—that makes resources available for investment purposes and thus is essential for economic growth.

---

[4]The saving habits of individuals tend to be relatively stable, but the particular type of financial outlet for savings shifts substantially as relative rates on different financial instruments change.

Investment

Investment refers to the acquisition of new productive equipment, buildings, and inventory—that is, the purchase of real assets. Such increases in capital are a means of expanding the productive capacity of an economy. Economic growth is fundamentally dependent on investment. Increases in real productive assets add to the output capacity of the economy and can be achieved only in conjunction with the act of saving. Real resources can be used to expand the capital base of the economy only if those real resources are not being used to produce consumer goods. In contrast, buying common stock or bonds does not add directly to the quantity of equipment and plant.

The foregoing discussion is not meant to imply that transactions in the financial markets are unimportant. Indeed, much of this book is devoted to explaining why these financial transactions are important to economic stability and growth. But it is necessary to note the crucial distinction between real investment and the acquisition of financial instruments. Throughout this chapter, unless otherwise noted, the term "investment" will refer to the purchase of real assets, such as plant, equipment, and inventory.

The Importance of Saving and Investment

The volume of saving and investment is important from at least two perspectives. First, the amount of saving and investment has a profound impact on the economic growth potential of an economy. Although economic growth is a complex issue involving social, political, and cultural characteristics of nations, as well as the availability of natural resources and various other economic factors, one of the most significant influences is investment. Additions to plant and equipment incorporating new technology and other types of investment are at the base of an expanding economy. It is no accident that nations that devote a large proportion of their resources to investment also tend to have rapid economic growth. Such investment cannot occur without saving. Many observers view the relatively slow growth in productivity in the United States in recent years as attributable to policies that have encouraged consumption at the expense of saving and discouraged productivity-expanding investment.

Saving and investment are also important because of their influences on economic stability and the business cycle. The balance between the amount that people desire to save and the amount that they wish to invest is a basic factor affecting the short-run economic stability of the economy. If the volume of **desired saving** (*ex ante*) exceeds the volume of **desired investment** (*ex ante*), there will be insufficient demand for the total output of the economy. As a result, production will be cut, income and employment will fall, and indeed, actual saving will decline. (The Great Depression of the 1930s has been explained by some scholars as resulting from an excess of desired saving compared with desired investment.) In contrast, if desired investment exceeds desired saving, there will be an excessive amount of demand for the current level of output.[5] At output levels at which substantial amounts of unused labor and capital resources are available, the result of the imbalance of desired investment over desired saving is an expansion in total output. As the economy comes closer to full employment of resources, however, the result is increases in prices for goods and services. Ultimately, at the point at which no further resources are available, the excess of desired investment simply results in higher prices for a constant quantity of goods and services.

FINANCIAL INTERMEDIATION

Our discussion of financial intermediation has focused so far on the nature of saving and investment and their importance. The relationship of financial markets to the saving and investment process stems from an important aspect of this process: saving and investing in most advanced economies are done by different groups. Most saving is done by individuals (households), and most investing is done by business.[6] As a result, individuals provide funds to business to hire labor and capital and expand the productive capacity of the economy. But there must be some mechanism by which saved funds (which represent released real resources) are made available to those who need the funds (command over real resources) to accomplish their investment goals. This mechanism is provided by the financial marketplace.

Table 1.1 provides lists of the major participants and instruments in the saving–investment process. At the core of the process are the basic economic sectors of our economy: business, government (federal, state, and local), and households. These economic sectors are connected with one another, and saving is channeled to investment through the financial system, often through the intermediating function of financial institutions. For example, households may deposit saved funds with a commercial bank, savings and loan association, or other similar type of financial institution. The command over real resources that these funds represent is thus transferred to the financial institution, and the individual

---

[5]This discussion is in terms of desired or *ex ante* saving and investment. After the fact, realized or *ex post* saving and investment must be equal. Changes in production and income that occur as the result of the differences in desired saving and investment produce the equality *ex post* between saving and investment.

[6]This does not mean that business does not save, nor does it mean that individuals do not invest. Obviously, through the act of retaining earnings, business saves a substantial amount, and through their purchase of homes and other real assets, individuals invest large sums. But on balance, households save more than they invest, and businesses invest more than they save. Furthermore, the government sector must be included, although over a long period, government varies from being a net saver to a net investor.

TABLE 1.1   Participants and Instruments in the Financial Markets _____

Fundamental (Nonfinancial) Participants	Financial Institutions	Financial Instruments
Business	Commercial banks	Transactions accounts
Government	Savings and loan	Savings accounts
Households	associations	Certificates of deposits
	Savings banks	Loans
	Credit unions	Government bonds
	Life insurance companies	Mortgages
	Property and casualty	Corporate bonds
	insurance companies	Stocks
	Mutual funds	
	Pension funds	

receives a financial asset—a savings account—which is commonly referred to as an **indirect security.** As the second step in this process, the financial institution may loan funds to a business to buy a machine. The debt instrument issued by the business is usually referred to as a **primary (direct) security.**[7] This process is illustrated in more detail in Table 1.2. In step 1 the individual exchanges a real resource claim for a savings account, and the financial institution obtains the real resource claim. In step 2 the real resource claim is transferred to the business, and the financial institution acquires an interest yielding note. Therefore through the use of the financial institution and the securities market the claim on real resources has been transferred from an economic unit with surplus resources to a unit with deficient resources.

This illustration of the role of financial markets in the saving–investment process is the typical case in which the flow of funds from saver to investor is intermediated; that is, a financial intermediary has been interposed between the saver and investor. It would, of course, have been possible for funds to be transferred from the household sector to the business sector without the intervention of the financial intermediary. The possibility, illustrated in Table 1.3, is often referred to as **direct finance** (as opposed to **indirect finance,** in which a financial intermediary is involved). In this instance the claim on real resources is transferred directly from the business sector to the household sector. The household sector holds the note (a primary, or direct, security), an asset in Table 1.3 rather than the savings account (an indirect security) in Table 1.2.

Tables 1.2 and 1.3 look fairly similar from the perspective of the business and household sectors. The question might be raised as to whether one funds transfer procedure is preferable to the other. If not, we would expect to find

---

[7]Primary or direct securities are those issued by the basic nonfinancial sectors of the economy such as businesses, households, and governments.

TABLE 1.2 Saving/Investment without Financial Institutions

Business	Financial Institutions			Household
(2) + Real resource claim	(2) + Note	(1) + Real resource claim (2) − Real resource claim + Note	(1) + Savings account	(1) + Savings account − Real resource claim

direct finance to be at least as prevalent as indirect finance. In fact, however, the overwhelming proportion of the flow of funds in the United States and other advanced economies is indirect and involves the interposition of financial inter-mediaries between savers and investors. This suggests that the indirect transfer of funds has some significant advantages, especially since these advantages must be sufficient to offset the costs involved in the intermediation by financial institu-tions.

The very fact that financial intermediaries exist in such large numbers and varieties and have such a high degree of economic significance is prima facie evidence that the indirect securities they issue are greatly desired by households and other owners of savings. Surplus economic units always have the option of acquiring primary securities and, indeed, do purchase and hold large amounts of these obligations. The purchase of primary securities, however, has certain disadvantages, particularly to the individuals and entities whose savings tend to be relatively small in amount.

Disadvantages of Primary Securities

One disadvantage of acquiring primary securities is **search costs**—the costs in time and out-of-pocket outlays of identifying and analyzing securities that are

TABLE 1.3 Saving/Investment without Financial Institutions

Business		Household	
(1) + Real resource claim	(1) + Note	(1) + Note − Real resource claim	

candidates for possible acquisitions. Households, for example, can be expected to have limited information about the availability of borrowers and little expertise in evaluating risk and return characteristics of primary securities. Another disadvantage of primary securities is **transactions costs**—brokerage commissions and other costs of buying and selling securities. An example is the cost of "odd-lot" purchases of corporate stock (fewer that 100 shares). Further, trades of large blocks of shares that involve many round lots are subject to substantially lower commission costs per share traded than is a single round lot. Still another disadvantage of acquiring primary securities is that a large amount of funds may be required to reduce the overall risk of holding primary securities by practicing **diversification** (holding various types of securities, the fortunes of which are not all likely to be affected in the same way by economic events). Finally, the desired degree of **liquidity** (ease of converting assets to cash quickly without appreciable losses) is difficult to achieve with holdings of primary securities unless, again, a relatively large sum is involved.

These various disadvantages of direct securities do not generally hold for indirect securities, and therein lie the advantages of the latter. With a minimum of search and transactions costs, a saver can find a financial institution that will accept a deposit (issue an indirect security). The indirect securities thus obtained are likely to be quite low-risk and to be as liquid as the depositor desires. The advantages of indirect securities relative to primary securities (and thus of indirect finance relative to direct finance) can be summed up by their relative denomination, risk, and liquidity aspects. Indirect securities, such as savings accounts, are available in small denominations (the saver may have only a small amount of funds), whereas primary securities (such as mortgages) are available only in relatively large denominations. This denomination advantage for indirect securities has been especially important in recent years with the large growth in the number of savers of relatively modest means. Second, the perceived risk to the household sector is likely to be less with an indirect security than with a primary security. With such indirect securities as savings accounts, the household sector is acquiring the liability of a financial institution that can reduce risk through skilled management and diversification among a larger number of assets. Moreover, in some financial institutions, government has further reduced risk to the saver through deposit insurance. Third, indirect securities have attractive liquidity features. The saver may obtain the return of principal at virtually any time without concern about receiving less than was invested. On the other hand, a primary security such as a mortgage can be difficult to sell prior to its maturity and then perhaps only at a substantial loss.

The financial intermediary itself is an acquirer of direct securities. By pooling relatively small individual amounts of funds obtained by the issue of indirect securities the intermediary acquires a large aggregate sum that effectively minimizes the disadvantages of direct security acquisition. Enjoying what are called

economies of scale, financial intermediaries are able to spread search, analysis, and transactions costs over a large volume of diverse security purchases and sales. Because of their large holdings of direct securities, financial intermediaries are able to achieve the desired degree of diversification and liquidity at low unit costs. These various economies in the holding of direct securities and the advantages they entail for the management of liquidity make it possible for financial institutions to issue indirect securities tailored to the needs of their customers. In a sense, depository intermediaries transform relatively illiquid direct securities into highly liquid indirect securities.

The motive of financial intermediaries in performing the intermediation function is, of course, an adequate rate of return on investment. These institutions anticipate that the net returns on the financial obligations they acquire will exceed the net costs of the obligations they issue by a satisfactory margin. Returns on the former type of obligations (direct securities) are likely to be higher than returns on the latter (indirect securities) because of the relatively greater risk and lesser liquidity associated with direct securities.

FINANCIAL INTERMEDIARIES AND INSTRUMENTS
Types of Financial Intermediaries

Depository Institutions. These include commercial banks, savings and loans, savings banks, and credit unions. Taken together, the assets of depository institutions comprise about one half of the assets of all financial service organizations (as shown in Table 1.4).

Commercial Banks. Commercial banks, perhaps the most familiar type of intermediary, issue "indirect securities" in the form of demand deposits (checking accounts) and time deposits (savings accounts). Time deposits called certificates of deposit (CDs) have become increasingly important in recent years. Demand deposits are payable to the depositor (or for the depositor) on demand, but time certificates have a stipulated time to maturity (ranging up to several years, interest rates generally increasing with maturity). "Passbook" savings accounts are generally paid on demand, although banks can legally require a notice-of-withdrawal period.

Commercial banks acquire direct securities by lending to business firms and consumers and by purchasing various types of securities (mostly federal, state, and local government securities) in the securities markets.

Operating distinctions between commercial banks and other depository institutions (savings and loan associations, savings banks, and credit unions) have been narrowed and blurred in recent years by the rapid pace of financial innova-

TABLE 1.4   Total Financial Assets and Market Shares of Different Financial Service Firms (September 30, 1988)

	Value (Billions of Dollars)	Percent of Total
Commercial banks	2850.5	30.7
Savings and loans	1335.5	14.3
Savings banks	275.4	3.0
Credit unions	195.0	2.1
Life insurance companies	1096.6	11.8
Private pension funds	1085.6	11.7
State and local government employee retirement funds	587.3	6.2
Other insurance companies	435.0	4.7
Finance companies	476.1	5.0
Real estate investment trusts	11.6	0.1
Mutual funds	483.9	5.2
Money market funds	326.5	3.5
Securities brokers and dealers	129.5	1.7
	$9288.5	100.0

Source: *Federal Reserve System,* Flow-of-Funds Accounts, *September, 1988.*

tions and regulatory changes. In particular, the fact that banks no longer have a "monopoly" on their liabilities (demand deposits) as a means of payment had a considerable impact.

Savings and Loan Associations.   Like commercial banks, savings and loan associations are depository institutions, and the indirect securities they issue have essentially the same characteristics as the time deposits of commercial banks. In the case of mutual savings and loan associations, depositors are technically owners, and deposit claims are often called shares, but the distinction has no operational significance. Savings and loan associations' principal holdings of direct securities have historically been mortgages on residential dwellings, though they have diversified their portfolios considerably in recent years.

Savings Banks.   Savings banks are very similar to savings and loan associations in the types of indirect securities issued and direct securities acquired. However, they are much less numerous (fewer than 1000 are in operation) and have historically been geographically concentrated in the northeastern United States.

Credit Unions.   Credit unions are cooperatively owned associations, membership usually exhibiting some particular institutional or professional affiliation. Their indirect securities are member deposits (shares), and their direct securities are generally loans to members (consumer loans).

Nondepository Financial Institutions

Insurance Companies. Insurance companies are nondepository intermediaries of considerable significance. The "indirect securities" issued by insurance firms are various types of life, asset protection, and annuity policies. The premium payments on these policies are used to acquire a wide variety of direct securities, including corporate stocks and bonds, real estate mortgages, and government securities.

Mutual Funds. Although nondepository in nature, mutual funds constitute a form of "pure" intermediation. Investors buy ownership shares (indirect securities) of the mutual fund, which in turn purchases direct securities. Mutual funds differ somewhat in organization form and vary quite widely in terms of the type of direct securities purchased. Mutual funds provide investors with considerable diversification, liquidity, and professional security analysis and selection, irrespective of the amount of the sum invested.

Pension Funds. The indirect securities issued by pension funds are the obligations to the covered employees for retirement pensions. The contributions to the fund—by either employers, employees, or both—are used to purchase various types of direct securities, including corporate stocks and bonds, government securities, and real estate mortgages.

The list above is not exhaustive, but it does include the most important privately owned financial intermediaries. A number of government agencies serve a significant financial intermediation function, but discussion of their nature and role will be deferred to a later chapter.

Types of Financial Instruments

A financial instrument is generally defined as an obligation, in money terms, of a borrower of funds (the issuer of the instrument) to the holder of the instrument (Table 1.5 provides an interesting perspective on the magnitude of the principal financial instrument). For the holder it is a financial asset; to the issuer it is a financial obligation. Financial instruments may be issued by economic units within the private sector or the public sector (federal, state, or local governments). In the case of the private sector, financial instruments may be either **debt** instruments or **equity** instruments. Debt instruments may be either **short-term** (all payments of interest and principal occur within one year) or **long-term** (all other obligations). This one-year distinction is obviously arbitrary, but it is commonly employed.

Government Debt Instruments. The U.S. Treasury issues enormous numbers of **Treasury bills** with maturities ranging up to one year. Various other U.S. govern-

TABLE 1.5   Amounts Outstanding of Principal Financial Instruments (September 30, 1988)

Financial Instrument		Value (Billions of Dollars)
Money Market		
Bankers acceptances		58.3
Certificates of deposits		579.4
Commercial paper		425.1
Federal funds		368.6
Treasury bills		398.8
	Total	1,830.2
Capital Market		
Bonds		
Corporate		755.0
Foreign		86.7
State and local government		553.7
U.S. Treasury		1,389.5
	Total	2,784.9
Mortgages		
Home mortgages		2,056.6
Multifamily residential		286.7
Commercial		694.6
	Total	3,037.9
Stocks		3,088.9

Source: Data on U.S. Treasury Securities taken from Federal Reserve Bulletin, April 1989, A 30. All other data from Federal Reserve System Flow-of-Funds Accounts, September 1988.

ment agencies also issue short-term debt instruments. The federal government is also a principal supplier of longer-term debt securities: **Treasury notes** (one to ten years in maturity), **Treasury bonds,** and issues of various agencies with maturities up to 30 years.

State and local governments are not major issuers of short-term debt instruments, but they borrow large sums via the issuance of long-term municipal bonds.

Private Debt Instruments.   The business sector's extensive borrowing is accomplished by a large variety of debt instrument. Firms with strong credit ratings issue short-term **commercial paper,** unsecured notes with maturities of nine months or less. The negotiable **certificates of deposits** issued by commercial banks are also a notable short-term financial instrument. **Bankers acceptances** are another type of short-term debt instrument and usually originate in the financing of international trade. They obtain their name from the guarantee of payment by a bank.

Long-term private debt instruments include **corporate bonds,** of which there are many varieties. In general, corporate bonds are issued in denominations of

AUCTIONS

In market economies, prices of products, services, and financial assets are set by supply and demand. Perhaps the most direct circumstance in which this is true is the case of the **auction.** Auctions have been used to set prices and sell goods (and sometimes slaves) for at least 2500 years. In his book *Auctions and Auctioneering,* Ralph Cassady, Jr., offers an account of various ancient auctions, including one involving bidding for wives in Babylon circa 500 B.C.

Prices for products and services are generally set either by a practice of posted prices, negotiated prices, or an auction process. In the United States and in most advanced economies, retail prices are generally posted prices, and buyers must take or leave the product at that price. Negotiated prices—as are generally set for cars and houses—involve interaction between the buyer and the seller in which an initially high price and low offer are adjusted until a mutually acceptable selling price is reached (or else no sale occurs). Auctions involve elements of both posted and negotiated prices. Sellers do not set the price nor haggle with potential buyers. Instead, sellers set the rules of the auction, and buyers determine the selling price within the rules of the auction.

Auctions may be conducted by sealed bids or by oral statements of price offers. Potential buyers obviously have more information in the latter case to use in formulating an offer. There are two types of oral auctions: the English auction and the Dutch auction. The English variant is the most common and involves the auctioneer raising the price until only one bidder (the buyer) remains. The Dutch auction is conducted by the auctioneer starting at a high price and lowering it until a bidder (the buyer) stops him and buys the goods at that price.

In the case of the sealed bid auction there are also two basic types. In the discriminatory sealed bid auction the winning (highest) bidder pays the price that he or she bid. In the uniform sealed bid auction, all winning (highest) bidders pay the same price, which is the highest *rejected* bid.

Adapted from Loretta J. Mester, "Going, Going, Going, Gone: Settling Prices With Auctions," Federal Reserve Bank of Philadelphia *Business Review* (March/April 1988), pp. 3–13.

$1000 per bond, have fixed maturity dates, and pay a stated amount of interest per bond at designated dates. **Mortgages,** loans secured by real property, represent another major long-term financial instrument.

Equity Instruments. In addition to bond issues, corporations obtain external long-term capital by issuing shares of stock. Stockholders have ownership rights, including a claim to dividends, rather than creditor status. Corporations must always have shares of common stock outstanding, which represent the ultimate (residual) ownership of the firm. **Preferred stock** may also be issued. The "preferences" of preferred stock include priority as to dividend payment and claims to assets in the event of liquidation. The dividends on preferred stock are usually "cumulative"; that is, any dividends "passed" (not paid) in any period must be paid before any dividends can be paid to the common stockholders. Unlike debt instruments, equity instruments do not have a fixed maturity. A stockholder can generally recover his or her investment only by selling shares.

ORGANIZATION AND STRUCTURE OF FINANCIAL MARKETS

Financial instruments are traded by financial institutions and other economic agents in financial markets. Financial markets provide a facility in which funds are transferred, financial risk is reduced, and the prices of financial instruments are determined. Financial markets also provide a mechanism for the transfer of resources from lenders to borrowers and the management of the financial assets (portfolios) of individuals and institutions in their role as economic agents. A salient aspect of financial markets is their role in the collection, analysis, and dissemination of financial information; the latter is an integral aspect of the functioning of the financial marketplace.

Financial markets, as a principal component of the financial system, facilitate economic specialization and accommodate individual differences among economic agents regarding consumption time preferences and behavior toward risk. The trading of financial assets in financial markets makes some of these economic benefits possible. The degree to which financial markets contribute to these ends may be gauged, in large measure, by liquidity, that is, the depth, breadth, and resiliency of asset trading in these markets. **Depth** refers to the range of viable buy-and-sell orders above and below the prevailing market price. If such trading orders exist in large volume and stem from diverse trading groups, the market is said to have **breadth.** The market possesses **resiliency** when asset price changes trigger a wave of new trading orders. Broad, deep, and resilient markets are necessarily highly competitive markets in which transactions costs are a small proportion of aggregate value exchanged.

Financial markets can be divided and classified in a number of different ways. Although some of the distinctions are arbitrary, attention to the various classifications is useful in further assessing the role and structure of financial markets.

Classifications of Financial Markets

Although all financial markets involve the process of transferring funds from savers (lenders) to borrowers, the precise role played by different financial markets varies widely. These differences may be characterized by classifying the financial markets in a variety of ways. The most common classification is the distinction made between the money market and the capital market. This distinction, though somewhat arbitrary, is based on the maturity of the financial assets purchased and sold in the financial market. Short-term financial assets (usually with a maturity of one year or less) are involved in the money market. Examples are Treasury bills, commercial paper, bankers acceptances, and other short-maturity financial assets. These types of financial instruments are used by individuals, businesses, and governments primarily to adjust their liquidity. (See Chapter 17 for a more complete discussion of the role of money market instruments.) In contrast, longer-term instruments traded in the capital market include such financial claims as corporate bonds and stocks, mortgages, and U.S. government and municipal bonds.

Another classification distinguishes between **intermediated** and **nonintermediated** financial markets. Intermediated financial markets include the financial instruments that are created by financial intermediaries (so-called indirect securities). For example, in the federal funds market the reserves held by member banks in the Federal Reserve are bought and sold by financial intermediaries. Similarly, the market for large certificates of deposit is an intermediated market, since the asset bought and sold is the liability of a financial institution. Nonintermediated financial markets involve exchanges of primary, or direct, securities. For example, the market for corporate bonds (a primary security) is essentially a nonintermediated market, since most corporate bonds are issued by nonfinancial rather than financial institutions. An important function of financial intermediaries is to transfer funds from savers to investors. In this process, financial intermediaries not only transfer funds but also transform primary into indirect securities. Financial intermediation thus results in the creation of new financial assets.

Another classification of the financial markets may be made in terms of the legal obligation of the issuer of a security. In this classification the fundamental difference is between debt and equity securities. **Debt** represents a creditor's interest, while **equity** represents an ownership interest in a business. The money market is entirely a market for debt instruments, whereas the capital market includes trading in both debt and equity instruments. Intermediated financial markets are primarily (though not exclusively) debt markets, but nonintermediated financial markets include both debt and equity instruments.

A fourth classification, one that is especially important in understanding the specific use made by market participants of the different financial markets, relates to the nature of the financial market. This classification provides for the differentiation of the market into two segments, primary and secondary. The **primary market** is the market for new securities.[8] For example, when General

---

[8]The "primary market" should not be confused with "primary securities." A primary security, such as a share of stock, remains a primary security even when it is traded in the secondary market.

Motors sells additional stock, the relevant market is the primary market. Similarly, when a large bank borrows by issuing a certificate of deposit, the relevant market is the primary market. It is, of course, through the primary market that the financial markets play their essential role of transferring funds from savers to investors. Yet the **secondary markets,** in which existing securities are bought and sold, also play an important role in the funds transfer process. Without an adequate secondary market providing liquidity for the financial instruments, investors would be less willing to purchase stocks and bonds in the primary market. Funds would be less available to investors, and the cost of such funds would be higher.

Auction Versus Over-the-Counter Financial Markets

Another classification division of financial markets may be made in terms of the structure of the market, as either **auction** or **over-the-counter** (OTC) markets. In an auction market, financial asset trading is accomplished by a process of open, competitive bidding in a unified trading facility. Trading in an OTC market is not unified and is based on a network of dealers who buy and sell financial assets among themselves and with other market participants.

In an auction market the unified trading facility consolidates information relevant to financial asset trading. All trades are priced and executed centrally, and the central trading facility makes publicly known all price and trade information on a continuous basis. This significant function can be performed whether or not the central trading facility is a particular physical location (such as the floor of a stock exchange); the important element is that all trades be executed centrally. As noncentralized trading increases, the nature of the market shifts from an auction to an OTC framework.

OTC markets are characterized principally by the absence of centralized trading and by the dominant role of dealers. Dealers differ from brokers, who do not buy and sell securities themselves but rather act as agents for buyers and sellers, because dealers buy, sell, and maintain inventories of securities. Dealers differ from financial intermediaries, which acquire securities with the proceeds of securities they issue, because dealers do not create securities but only buy and sell securities issued by other economic entities.

Both auction and OTC markets are important in the U.S. financial system. The primary Treasury bill market, for example, is a pure auction market, but the secondary Treasury bill market is OTC. Equity shares of the largest corporations are traded in auction markets—the stock exchanges—but there is also a large volume of corporate equity trading in the OTC market. The market for corporate debt securities is predominantly an OTC market. In general, this country's financial markets are regarded as the most highly developed, sophisticated, and efficient in the world.

THE EFFICIENCY OF THE FINANCIAL SYSTEM

It has been asserted that the financial system makes the functioning of the economic system—the production and distribution of goods and services—more efficient. To better assess this contribution to economic efficiency, it is useful to recognize two types of efficiency: operational (or transactional) efficiency and allocational efficiency. **Operational efficiency** is attained by the minimization of the amount of resources required for the performance of the volume of exchange transactions (trading of goods, services, and productive resources) necessary for allocational efficiency. **Allocational efficiency** is attained when the maximum quantity of output of goods and services, in the optimal composition, is achieved from a given level of available productive resources (an achievement that in turn implies an optimal combination of these resources). These two types of efficiency are obviously interrelated, and their attainment requires a "joint solution." Allocational efficiency requires some optimal volume and pattern of exchange, which is in turn governed by the amount of search and transactions costs required for exchanges to take place. Correspondingly, the gains available from potential exchanges (the reallocation of resources), in conjunction with the costs of these exchanges, will determine the volume of exchanges that will be affected. As long as benefits from exchange exceed the costs of exchange, exchange will occur. The minimization of exchange costs thus implies the maximization of exchange gains, subject to the condition that resources devoted to the consummation of exchanges are made unavailable for other productive purposes. Exchange transactions do, of course, consume resources in the form of the time and efforts of the individuals involved in trading activities, the real assets (land, equipment, and so on) devoted to trading activities, and the materials and supplies used in identifying, analyzing, monitoring, and recording exchanges.

The financial system contributes to operational or transactional efficiency by providing a payments mechanism for effecting exchanges. Sellers of goods, services, and productive resources can exchange them for money, a means of "generalized purchasing power" that enables these sellers, in turn, to buy the particular goods, services, and productive resources they most desire. Buyers and sellers are spared the onerous search and transactions costs that a barter system entails. Producers and suppliers of productive resources are able to specialize, and specialization and division of labor contribute to both operational efficiency and allocational efficiency (by increasing the amount of output that can be attained with a given amount of resources). The payments mechanism embodied in the financial system facilitates the establishment of markets for goods, services, and productive resources and the formation of prices, which serve as a "signaling" function in the allocation process. The information conveyed by relative prices (and other market information) is an operationally efficient means of achieving allocational efficiency.

The payments mechanism also facilitates the transfer of resources from surplus to deficit economic units, an aspect of the financial system that contributes to operational efficiency and is essential to allocational efficiency. Further, just as the payments mechanism facilitates the formation of markets for the exchange of goods, services, and productive resources (and the establishment of prices for them), it makes possible the development of financial markets for the exchange of resource use over time (borrowing and lending). Financial markets establish relative "prices" for the financial obligations (financial instruments) that are used to effect such exchanges and thus channel the savings of surplus economic units to those deficit economic units that are the "highest bidders." This ensures the flow of available funds into the most productive uses, consistent with the wants and needs of society. In other words, deficit units that are willing to pay the highest returns to units forgoing consumption (and thus making resources available for other purposes) are the units expecting to realize the highest returns from the investment of these resources. Thus it is possible for productive resources made available for investment by savers to be efficiently allocated among competing possibilities.

The intermediation function of the financial system further facilitates the transfer of funds from surplus to deficit economic units. Financial intermediaries, by issuing indirect securities to savers, pool the savings of many economic units into an aggregate sum that is sufficiently large to realize many economies of scale in the purchase of direct securities by these intermediaries. The effect of intermediation is to enhance operational efficiency via these economies and to improve allocational efficiency by channeling savings into appropriate investment uses.

The saving–investment process, whether direct or intermediated, is an exchange of the use of resources over time and, as an exchange, is subject to the test of operational efficiency. The contribution of financial intermediaries to the operational efficiency of these exchanges is apparent from our previous discussion of their role, since they offer saving units an efficient alternative to the acquisition of direct securities. The financial markets in which saving units, borrowing units, and intermediaries exchange financial obligations constitute an operationally efficient process of the allocation of saved funds.

SUMMARY

The financial system is a vital component of a modern economy. It is the framework of instruments, markets, and institutions in which exchanges of resources at points in time and over time are accomplished. More specifically, the financial system facilitates payments for goods, services, and productive resources (the exchange of real assets) and provides means for the efficient accumulation of saved funds and their allocation into investment uses. The financial system includes such private institutions as commercial banks, savings and loan associations, and insurance companies, as well as such government institutions as the U.S. Treasury and the Federal Reserve System. Financial markets include such markets as the stock market, bond market, money market, and mortgage market. Financial instruments used in the financial system (other than money) include such financial obligations as shares of stocks, debt securities, and mortgages.

Saving and investment are essential for economic growth, and facilitating the process by which the savings of surplus economic units (savers) are channeled to deficit economic units (investors) for investment purposes is a vital role of the financial system. In addition to the instruments, markets, and institutions that the financial system provides to accomplish the efficient transfer of saved funds, the financial system facilitates the saving–investment process through financial intermediation. Financial intermediaries acquire the financial obligations of deficit spending units (primary securities) and issue their own financial obligations to surplus spending units (indirect securities). Such intermediated flows of funds are predominant in the financing of investment spending.

Financial instruments are traded by financial institutions and other economic agents in financial markets. Efficient financial markets accomplish such trading with low transactions and allocation costs, establish financial asset prices that reflect all available information pertinent to risk and returns, and evidence breadth, depth, and resiliency in trading behavior. Financial markets can be classified in a variety of ways, stemming from their multiple functions and differences in structure and organizations.

QUESTIONS

1. Define the term "financial system." What economic functions are performed by the financial system?

2. Name and define the major components of the financial system, and give examples of each.

3. What is the distinction between "real" assets and "financial" assets? Why are financial assets so important to the exchange of the use of real resources over time (borrowing or lending)?

4. Define financial intermediation, primary securities, and indirect securities, and describe their relationships.

5. Name and describe five possible classifications of types of financial markets.

6. Describe the relationship between "allocational" and "operational" efficiency.

REFERENCES

Benston, George J., and Clifford W. Smith, Jr., "A Transactions Cost Approach to the Theory of Financial Intermediation," *Journal of Finance* (May 1976), 215–232.

Campbell, Tim S., *Money and Capital Markets* (Chicago, Ill.: Dryden Press, 1988).

Dougall, Herbert E., and Jack E. Gaumnitz, *Capital Markets and Institutions,* 4th ed. (Englewood Cliffs, N.J.: Prentice-Hall, 1980).

Garbade, Kenneth, *Securities Markets* (New York: McGraw-Hill, 1982).

Gurley, John, and Edward Shaw, *Money in a Theory of Finance* (Washington, D.C.: Brookings Institution, 1960).

Light, J.O., and William L. White, *The Financial System* (Homewood, Ill.: Richard D. Irwin, 1979).

Moore, Basil J., *An Introduction to the Theory of Finance—Assetholder Behavior Under Uncertainty* (New York: Free Press, 1968).

Polakoff, Murray E., et al., *Financial Institutions and Markets,* 2nd ed. (Boston: Houghton Mifflin, 1981).

Pyle, David H., "On the Theory of Financial Intermediation," *Journal of Finance* (June 1971), 737—747.

Simpson, Thomas D., "Development in the U.S. Financial System Since the Mid-1970's," *Federal Reserve Bulletin* (January 1988), 1–13.

Smith, Paul F., *Economics of Financial Institutions and Markets* (Homewood, Ill.: Richard D. Irwin, 1971).

CHAPTER 2

Financial Assets: Income and Value

Financial markets establish prices (i.e., values) for financial assets. These prices (or values) are determined by the expected cash flows from the asset and the risk of these cash flows. Once the values of the financial instruments are established in the market, the income or yield per dollar of investment to the holder of the asset is also determined. Conversely, given the income or yield per dollar of investment from an asset and the market's required rate of return for the asset, the price or value of the asset (representing the asset's capitalized income) is determined. Thus financial markets in their fundamental role of providing for the exchange of claims for assets (such as stocks and bonds) simultaneously determine incomes and prices.

This chapter discusses both the income and price (or value) dimension of financial assets. It begins with a treatment of the various measures of the flow of cash from an asset. This is followed by a treatment of the concept of asset valuation and the determination of values in financial markets. Knowledge of these two topics is fundamental to gaining a thorough understanding of the operation of financial markets.

MEASURING THE INCOME STREAM FROM A FINANCIAL ASSET

A number of measures of income from financial assets are in common usage. The most widely used of these are the following.

Coupon Rate

The **coupon rate** is the contractual rate that the security issuer (i.e., borrower) agrees to pay at the time the security is sold. The total amount of interest that the security issuer has agreed to pay to the lender or provider of funds is obtained by taking the coupon rate and multiplying it by the par or stated value of the instrument. These relationships are illustrated in Equations (2.1) and (2.2):

$$\text{Coupon rate} = \frac{\text{Total dollar payment}}{\text{Par value of instrument}} \qquad (2.1)$$

or

$$\text{Total dollar payment} = \text{coupon rate} \times \text{Par value of instrument} \qquad (2.2)$$

For example, assume a bond in which the issuer promises to pay $70 per year until the maturity of the bond after ten years and a par value of $1000. The coupon rate is thus 7 percent or $70/$1000. However, except at the initial creation of the security, its market value will seldom equal par (generally $1000 for a bond). The coupon rate is a meaningful measure of the rate of return on a debt instrument only if the market price of the security is at or near par.

Current Yield

The **current yield** may be obtained by taking the interest paid on a debt security and dividing it by the market price of the security, as shown in Eq. (2.3):

$$\text{Current yield} = \frac{\text{Total dollar payment}}{\text{Market price of the security}} \qquad (2.3)$$

The current yield as a measure of return is preferable to the coupon rate, since it takes into account the probability that the market value or price of the security will differ from par. In the above example, if the market price of the security was $700, then the current yield of 10 percent ($70/$700) would be more meaningful as a measure of the return on the security than the coupon rate of 7 percent. ($70/$1000). However, the current yield is still deficient in that it ignores the price at which the investor can redeem the security at par (if the security is a bond or note). For example, the investor in the security just discussed not only receives a 10 percent current yield on a purchase price of $700 but also a $300 gain (the difference between the purchase price of $700 and the par or maturity value of $1000) if the security is held until maturity. Since the current yield ignores this gain (or loss) at maturity, it understates the interest yield when the security is bought at a price below par (and overstates it when the security is bought at a price above par).

Yield to Maturity

The yield to maturity is probably the most widely used measure of the rate of return on a bond, note, or other fixed income security. It is preferable to the coupon rate and the current yield in that it recognizes the amount and the timing of all cash flows from a security and adjusts for the time value of money. The **yield to maturity** is the rate of interest that equates the present value of all cash flows from a security with the market price of the security. It may be expressed as in Eq. (2.4):

$$P = \frac{CB_1}{(1 + r)^1} + \frac{CB_2}{(1 + r)^2} + \ldots + \frac{CB_N}{(1 + r)^N} \tag{2.4}$$

where r is the yield to maturity, CB is the cash benefit from the security, and P is the market price. For a bond the cash benefits in the years prior to maturity are the interest payments, while the cash benefits at maturity include both interest and principal. In the earlier example the yield to maturity on a 7 percent coupon rate bond, with a ten-year maturity, selling at a price of $700 is that rate of discount that makes the present value of $70 per year for ten years plus $1000 at the end of the tenth year equal to $700. The yield to maturity on this bond is about 12 percent (assuming annual interest payments).

Holding Period Yield

The **holding period yield** is essentially the same as the yield to maturity except with the assumption that the security is sold prior to maturity. The holding period yield is particularly relevant for securities such as common stocks for which there is no stated maturity. This concept may be expressed as in Eq. (2.5):

$$P = \frac{CB_1}{(1 + r)^1} + \frac{CB_2}{(1 + r)^2} + \ldots + = \frac{CB_N}{(1 + r)^N} \tag{2.5}$$

where all terms are as in Equation (2.4) except for CB_N, which is the amount of the cash flow realized at the sale of the asset (rather than at the maturity of the asset).

The holding period yield and the yield to maturity are, of course, equal if the security is held until maturity. However, if the security is sold prior to maturity, the holding period yield may be above or below the yield to maturity.

As an example of the difference between the holding period yield and the yield to maturity, suppose that the bond just discussed was purchased at a price of $700 and sold two years later at $900. (Recall that the yield to maturity on that bond was approximately 12 percent.) The holding period yield on the bond exceeds 16 percent.

Bank Discount Basis Yield

Many money market securities carry no coupon (i.e., they are zero coupon instruments, sold at a discount, and quoted by the bank discount basis yield method. The **bank discount basis yield** is calculated by subtracting the price of the security from par in order to obtain the discount (D), dividing the discount by par (p), and annualizing the discount on the basis of a 360-day year. For example, assume a 147-day Treasury bill selling at a price of $97.55 per $100 face value. The bank discount basis yield on the security may be obtained through the use of Eq. (2.6):

$$\text{Bank discount basis yield} = \frac{D}{PR} \times \frac{360}{DM} \times 100 \tag{2.6}$$

where D is the dollar value of the discount, PR is the par value of the security, and DM is the number of days until maturity. In the above example the bank discount basis yield is 6 percent ($2.45/100 \times 360/147$).

Although widely used, the bank discount basis yield obviously understates the "true" yield on the security, since it divides the discount by par rather than price and annualizes the discount on the basis of a 360-day year rather than a 365-day year. The bond equivalent yield may be calculated with the use of Eq. (2.7):

$$\text{Bond equivalent yield} = \frac{D}{\text{Price}} \times \frac{365}{DM} \times 100 \tag{2.7}$$

In the example above, the 6 percent bank discount basis yield is, in reality, a 6.24 percent bond equivalent yield $\left(\frac{2.45}{97.55} \times \frac{365}{147} \times 100 \right)$.

Simple Interest and Compound Interest

These measures of return are commonly used on deposits at commercial banks and on loan contracts. **Simple interest** is the interest charged or paid for exactly one year and paid at the end of the year. The coupon rate on a single payment security is simple interest. With **compound interest,** in contrast, interest is earned on interest. For example, the coupon rate on a security that matures in exactly one year but that pays semiannual or quarterly interest would be less than the compound interest rate on that security. Assuming a 12 percent security and a par value of $1000, with a single payment at maturity, the simple interest paid (and received) would be $120. With monthly payments, though, which allow for compounding (i.e., interest paid on interest), the total interest paid is $127, so the compound interest rates is 12.7 percent. For a given simple interest rate, the more frequent the compounding, the higher the coupon interest rate.

Add-on Interest, Discount Interest, and the Annual Percentage Rate

Lending rates are frequently stated according to the "add-on" or "discount" method. With the **add-on method** the total amount of interest is added to the loan, and the sum of the interest and principal is divided by the total number of payments to obtain the dollar amount of each payment. For example, again assuming a 12 percent coupon or stated rate and a $1000 par value, the total interest paid on the security is $120. If the security was to be paid off in equal maturity installments, the amount of each payment would be $1120/12, or $93.33. Note that if the security pays only once (at maturity), the add-on interest and the simple interest are the same. However, if the security pays more than once, then the effective interest rate is higher than the simple interest rate.

With a **discount loan,** the interest is deducted from the amount advanced on the loan. In the 12 percent coupon rate, $1000 par value illustration, the interest of $120 is deducted at the time of the loan. The lender advances only $880 to the borrower, but the borrower repays $1000 at maturity. The effective interest rate for a one-year single-payment discount note may be calculated as the ratio of interest paid to the net funds advanced multiplied by 100 or 120/880 × 1000 = 13.6 percent. Most discount loans are single payments and thus do not call for intermediate payments.

Neither the add-on nor the discount method provides an accurate measure of the yield (or cost) of a loan. For this reason, in 1968 the U.S. Congress passed the Consumer Credit Protection Act, requiring lenders to inform borrowers of the "true" rate. This rate is known as the **annual percentage rate (APR).** An approximation to the APR is given in Eq. (2.8):

$$\text{APR} = \frac{2 \times \text{number of payment periods in a year} \times \text{annual interest cost in dollars}}{(\text{total number of loan payments} + 1) \times (\text{principal of the loan})} \times 100 \qquad (2.8)$$

In the 12 percent single-payment example the APR can be obtained from Eq. 2.9:

$$\text{APR} = \frac{2 \times 1 \times 120}{2 \times 1000} = \frac{240}{2000} = 12\% \qquad (2.9)$$

If the loan were to be repaid in monthly installments, the APR would be given by Eq. (2.10):

$$\text{APR} = \frac{2 \times 12 \times 120}{13 \times 1000} = \frac{2880}{13,000} = 22.15 \qquad (2.10)$$

VALUATION OF FINANCIAL ASSETS

Financial markets establish the prices or values of financial assets (such as stocks and bonds) that are traded in financial markets. At the same time that the values of the assets are determined (i.e., simultaneously), the yields or rates of return are also established. The value of an asset and its yield are thus two sides of the same coin: Once the value of an asset is set, its yield is determined; once the yield is determined, the value is set. Value is a stock concept (that is, an amount at a particular point of time), while yield is a flow concept (an amount over some time period such as a day, a week, or a year). An asset may be discussed in either stock or flow terms.

Determinants of Value

The value of an asset is determined fundamentally by the cash benefits (dividends or interest payments) that the holder (or potential holder) of the asset *expects* to receive. One method of determining the value of a particular asset is to calculate the present value of the expected cash benefits discounted at some particular required rate of return. This is known as **capitalizing** the income from the asset. This approach may be expressed as in Eq. (2.11):

$$V_0 = \frac{CB_1}{(1 + r)^1} + \frac{CB_2}{(1 + r)^2} + \frac{CB_N}{(1 + r)^N} \tag{2.11}$$

where

V_0 = the present value of the asset at time zero

CB = the expected cash benefits that accrue to the owner of the asset during the owner's holding period

r = the required rate of return, or discount rate, or yield to maturity

N = the amount of time the asset is held (or is expected to be held)[1]

By this approach the value of an asset may increase either because the expected cash benefits from the asset increase (notice that the discussion is of expected rather than known benefits, since the determinants of value are future rather than past benefits) or because the discount rate used to find the present value of those cash benefits decreases. Conversely, the value of an asset may decrease either because the expected cash benefits from the asset decrease or because the required rate of return increases. For example, if the asset is a share of common stock, the value of that share would increase with growing earnings for the firm and the expectation of rising future dividends. Similarly, if there were a downward revision in the required rate of return (due to less perceived risk, for example) from an investment in the stock, the market value would increase.

---

[1]There are, of course, different estimates by different market participants of both the expected cash benefits from an asset and the required rates of return. Hence market participants will value the assets differently. These market participants interact as buyers and sellers in the market to determine market price. It is the buyer and seller at the margin that determines market price, where the marginal buyer is the one that has paid his or her highest price and the marginal seller is the one who has sold at the minimum acceptable price.

If the asset valuation were for a U.S. Treasury bond, however, for which the cash benefit to be received by the holder was fixed for the life of the bond, the changes in value would result only from changes in the required rate of return (with an inverse relationship between value and the required rate of return).

An example of the determination of value for a financial asset and of changes in value may add to the understanding of this concept. Assume that the cash benefits from holding a particular financial asset for five years is $100 per year. Further assume that the holder expects to be able to sell the asset at the end of the fifth year at $1000 and that the required rate of return is 12 percent. Then the value of the asset, according to Eq. (2.12), is

$$V_0 = \frac{100}{(1 + 0.12)^1} + \frac{100}{(1 + 0.12)^2} + \frac{100}{(1 + 0.12)^3} + \frac{100}{(1 + 0.12)^4} \quad (2.12)$$

$$+ \frac{100}{(1 + 0.12)^5} + \frac{1000}{(1 + 0.12)^5} = \$927.5.$$

The value of the asset can be determined easily with the use of present value tables such as Taole 2.1.

The present value of a financial asset that offered $100 per year for five years with the expectation of receiving $1000 at the end of the fifth year is $927.50. If the market requires a 12 percent return for this type of risk in an investment, then the current equilibrium market value would be $927.50 (Table 2.1).

The formula given in Eq. (2.11) and the calculations shown in Eq. (2.12) and Table 2.1 are perfectly generalizable and apply to any asset whose benefits are cash benefits. This includes all types of financial assets—such as bonds, preferred stocks, and common stocks—as well as real assets such as real estate. The value of an asset today is determined jointly by its expected cash benefits and the required rate of return used to discount or capitalize those benefits. Although the approach is common to all assets, minor modifications are often made for financial assets with particular types of cash benefit characteristics.

TABLE 2.1 Present Value of Cash Benefits

Time	Cash Benefit	Present Value Interest Factor $(1/1 + r)$	Present Value
1	100	$0.893 = (1/1.12)$	$ 89.30
2	100	$0.797 = (1/1.12)^2$	79.70
3	100	$0.712 = (1/1.12)^3$	71.20
4	100	$0.636 = (1/1.12)^4$	63.60
5	100	$0.567 = (1/1.12)^5$	56.70
5	1000	$0.567 = (1/1.12)^5$	567.00
		$V_0 = $ Present value	$927.50

Bonds

For bonds (and other fixed income instruments) the analysis is quite similar to that shown in the above example, since a bond normally pays a fixed coupon cash benefit during the life of the asset and then returns principal at maturity. In this case, Eq. (2.11) can be simplified as in Eq. (2.13):

$$P_0 = \sum_{t=1}^{n} \frac{CB_N}{(1 + r)^t} + \frac{PAR}{(1 + r)^N} \tag{2.13}$$

The first term in Eq. (2.13) represents the present value of an annuity of coupon payments (or cash benefits) during the life of the bond, and the second term is the present value of the repayment of principal at the maturity of the bond. By using the information from the above example the value of the bond may be expressed as in Table 2.2 using a 12 percent discount or required rate of return.

By using the present value factor for an annuity for five years at 12 percent (3.605) the value of the cash benefits deriving from the coupon payments is $360.50, as shown in Table 2.2. Add to that the present value of the principal of $1000 at the end of five years ($567) and the total present value of the bond is $927.50, the same as in the previous example.

Since the cash benefits from bonds are virtually ensured (at least for high-quality bonds), it is obvious from the equation that the value of bonds moves with changes in the required rate of return and moves inversely to changes in the required rate of return.

The required rate of return can be thought of (as in Eq. 2.14) as being composed of some basic real rate plus a premium for risk. The risk premium itself reflects three various types of risk: default, inflation, and price risk. **Default risk** refers to the prospect that the cash benefits will not occur as promised. **Inflation or purchasing power risk** refers to the possibility that the cash benefits will purchase less tomorrow than today. **Price volatility risk** is the risk of loss due to the potential price changes that occur on bonds and other financial assets.

$$\begin{matrix} \text{Required} & & & \text{Premium} & \text{Premium} & \text{Premium} \\ \text{rate of} & = & \text{Real rate} + & \text{for default} + & \text{for inflation} + & \text{for price} & (2.14) \\ \text{return} & & & \text{risk} & \text{risk} & \text{risk} \end{matrix}$$

While it may be argued that the real rate is relatively constant (this argument is developed in Chapter 8), the other factors that affect the risk premium may change substantially for individual bonds and for bonds as a group. For example, suppose in the example discussed above that the required rate of return increased from 12 to 14 percent. In that instance, as shown in Table 2.3, the value of the bond would fall to $862.3, a decline of almost 8 percent. Similar but opposite changes would occur if the required rate of return were to fall.

TABLE 2.2 Present Value of a Bond

Time	Cash Benefit	Present Value Interest Factor	Present Value
1–5	$ 100	3.605*	$360.5
5	1000	$0.567 = 1/(1.12)^5$	567.0
			927.5

*$1/1.12 + 1/(1.12)^2 + 1/(1.12)^3 + 1/(1.12)^4 + 1/(1.12)^5$.

Stocks

Although in principle the valuation of common stocks is similar to the valuation of bonds, the uncertainty surrounding the receipt of cash benefits from equities makes analysis of common stock prices more difficult. For bonds, of course, the cash benefits to the holder—interest and principal—represent a legal obligation of the issuer. But for common stocks there is no legal obligation to pay dividends, nor in many cases any real expectations that dividends will be paid in the near future. Also, with common stock there is no maturity value. Yet fundamentally, the cash benefits discounted at some required rate of return reflecting risk must determine the value of equity instruments just as they do the value of debt instruments.

The valuation of common stock can be explained also with the use of Eq. (2.11), in which the cash benefits during the life of the financial instruments (CB_1, CB_2, and so on) are expected future dividends. CB_n, the principal value of the bond example, can be thought of as the expected market price at which the stock could be sold at the end of the investor's holding period. In this case the value of the security may be shown as in Eq. 2.15:

$$V_0 = \frac{D_1}{(1 + r)^1} + \frac{D_2}{(1 + r)^2} + \ldots + \frac{EP_N}{(1 + r)^N} \qquad (2.15)$$

where D represents cash dividends and EP is the expected price at the time of sale. The immediate question that arises is what determines EP. Of course, the answer is that the expected price at which the stock can be sold at the end of

TABLE 2.3 Present Value of Bond with Rising Required Rate of Return

Time	Cash Benefits	Present Value Interest Factor	Present Value
1–5	100	3.433*	$343.30
5	1000	$0.519 = 1(1.14)^5$	519.00
		Present value =	$862.30

*$1/(1.14) + 1/(1.14)^2 + 1/(1.14)^3 + 1/(1.14)^4 + 1/(1.14)^5$.

period n is determined by the expected future dividends after period n. Mathematically, this is shown in Eq. 2.16:

$$PR_N = \sum_{t=n+1}^{\infty} \frac{D_t}{(1 + r)^{t-n}}, \qquad (2.16)$$

which shows that the value of the stock at the end of period n is determined by all dividends from period $n + 1$ forward. Substituting Eq. (2.16) into (2.15) produces Eq. (2.17):

$$V_0 = \frac{D_1}{(1 + r)^1} + \frac{D_2}{(1 + r)^2} + \ldots + \sum_{t=n+1}^{\infty} \frac{D_t}{(1 + r)^{t-n}} \qquad (2.17)$$

or

$$V_0 = \sum_{t=1}^{n} \frac{D_t}{(1 + r)^t} + \sum_{t=n+1}^{\infty} \frac{D_t}{(1 + r)^t}, \qquad (2.18)$$

which can be further simplified into

$$V_0 = \sum_{t=1}^{\infty} \frac{D_t}{(1 + r)^t}. \qquad (2.19)$$

This is commonly referred to as the general dividend valuation model. It shows once again that the value of the financial asset—in this case a share of stock—is determined by the cash benefits and the required rate of return and that increases in cash benefits increase the value of the stock and increases in the required rate of return decrease the value.[2]

INTEREST RATE CHANGES AND PRICE VOLATILITY FOR FINANCIAL INSTRUMENTS

As we discussed above, the present value of a financial asset such as a bond or stock varies inversely with changes in the required rate of return. Also, the required rate of return is determined by taking the real rate and adding to it a premium for default, purchasing power, and other types of risk. Those relationships provide a framework for analyzing the effects of interest rate changes on the value of bonds and stocks. The focus of the analysis is on bonds (and other

---

[2]This model treats dividends as a perpetuity, which may be an unreasonable assumption for many firms. There are many variants of the general dividend valuation model that are designed to adapt it to particular dividend patterns, such as constant growth of dividends, increasing growth of dividends, declining growth of dividends, or some other pattern such as no growth in dividends. Further specificity of these models is beyond the scope of this book, though references at the end of the chapter provide additional information on these models.

TABLE 2.4 Value of 12 Percent, $1000 Par Bonds at Various Required Rates of Return

Required Rate of Return	Value of 20-Year Bond	Value of 5-Year Bond
16	$ 762.9	869.0
14	867.5	931.3
12	1000.0	1000.0
10	1170.3	1075.8
8	1392.7	1159.7

fixed income instruments) rather than on stocks, since the connection between bond values and changes in interest rates is much more direct for these securities.

Our example is in terms of increases in interest rates, though the illustration is equally valid for declines in interest rates. The increases in interest rates may reflect higher expected inflation, greater default risk expectations, a rising real rate, or other factors. In any case the result is an increase in the required rate of return on financial (and other) assets. The effect of the higher required rate of return on the value of bonds is illustrated in Table 2.4.

Table 2.4 shows the present value of two bonds that are identical in coupon at 12 percent and in principal value at $1000 but differ in their maturities, one being at twenty years and the other at five years. It should be noted that at a required rate of return of 12 percent, both bonds have a value of $1000. As the required rate of return (or interest rate) increases, the values of both bonds decline; however, the value of the 20-year bond declines much more than the value of the 5-year bond. Conversely, as the required rate of return declines, the values of both bonds increase, although the value of the long-term bond increases much more than the value of the short-term bond. This relationship leads to one of the most important generalizations about relationships in the financial markets: *For identical changes in interest rates, long-term bonds change in price more than short-term bonds.*

This generalization indicates that the price variability (for example, the standard deviation or variance) of long-term bonds exceeds that of short-term bonds. Hence price volatility risk is greater for long-term bonds than for short-term bonds. (Note that price volatility risk is only one type of risk.)

PRICE VOLATILITY AND DURATION

Although the above discussion of the effects of interest rate changes on bond values has been in terms of the different maturities of bonds, in fact the maturity of a bond is only a rough measure of the life of the bond. Maturity measures only the date on which the last payment (the maturity date) on a bond is made and ignores all payments during the life of a bond in the form of interest. A better measure of the length of bond's life is its **duration,** which is the weighted average time at which all payments are made on a bond or other financial instrument.[3]

In its simplest form, duration is computed by multiplying the length of time to each scheduled payment by the ratio of the present value of that payment to the total present value or price of the security and then summing the result as shown in Eq. (2.20):

$$
D = \frac{\sum\limits_{t=1}^{L} t \cdot PVF_t}{\sum\limits_{t=1}^{L} PVF_t}
\tag{2.20}
$$

where

D = duration

t = length of time (number of years, etc.) to the date of payment

PVF_t = present value of the payment (F) made at (t) or $F_{t/(1+i)t}$

Σ = a summation from the first (1) to the last payment (L)

Duration is thus a single number that is measured in units of time such as months or years. For securities that make only one payment at maturity (such as zero coupon bonds), duration is equal to maturity; for all other securities, duration is shorter than maturity.

While bond price volatility and maturity are only roughly related, price volatility and duration are very closely related and can be expressed as in Eq. (2.21):

$$
\frac{\Delta S}{S} = -D \frac{\Delta i}{(1 + i)} \approx -D\Delta i
\tag{2.21}
$$

where

S = price of a security

i = yield to maturity

Δ = change from previous value

By Eq. (2.21) the percentage change in the price of a financial asset is equal to its duration (with a negative sign) multiplied by the change in interest rates, divided by 1 plus the interest rate. This is approximately the same as duration

---

[3]The duration concept was first proposed by Frederick R. Macaulay in 1938. See Frederick R. Macaulay, *Some Theoretical Problems Suggested by Movements of Interest Rates, Bond Yields, and Stock Prices in the United States Since 1856* (New York: National Bureau of Economic Research, 1938).

multiplied by the change in interest rates. Hence for a given change in interest rates, the decline in price for a 10-year duration bond will be double that of a 5-year duration bond (though the decline in price might not be twice as great for a 10-year maturity bond as for a 5-year maturity bond).

It might be useful in understanding the duration concept to illustrate the calculation of duration for two different types of bonds: (1) a zero coupon, 5-year maturity bond and (2) a high coupon (8 percent), 5-year maturity bond. Assuming an 8 percent required rate of return, the durations of the two bonds are as follows:

$$D \text{ (zero coupon)} = \frac{\dfrac{(1000)\,(5)}{(1.08)^5}}{\dfrac{1000}{(1.08)^5}} = 5 \text{ years}$$

$$D \text{ (high coupon)} = \frac{\dfrac{80(1)}{(1.08)} + \dfrac{80(2)}{(1.08)^2} + \dfrac{80(3)}{(1.08)^3} + \dfrac{80(4)}{(1.08)^4} + \dfrac{80(5)}{(1.08)^5} + \dfrac{1000(5)}{(1.08)^5}}{\dfrac{80}{(1.08)^1} + \dfrac{80}{(1.08)^2} + \dfrac{80}{(1.08)^3} + \dfrac{80}{(1.08)^4} + \dfrac{80}{(1.08)^5} + \dfrac{1000}{(1.08)^5}} = 4.3 \text{ years}$$

The duration of the zero coupon bond is the same as its maturity. However, the duration of the 8 percent coupon bond is less than its maturity, as is true for all positive coupon bonds.

SUMMARY

Financial markets simultaneously determine the yields and prices of financial assets. The yield or rate of return on financial assets may be measured in various ways. These include coupon rate, current yield, yield to maturity, holding period yield, bank discount basis yield, simple and compound interest, add-on and discount interest, and the annual percentage rate.

Prices of financial instruments are determined in financial markets. The principal determinants of these prices are the expected return (usually measured as cash flow) for holding the asset and the risk associated with the asset. Other things being equal, increases in cash benefits produce an increase in the price of a security, while increases in risk lead to a decrease in the price of a security. For bonds the cash benefits are the coupon interest payments plus the return of principal at maturity, both of which are fixed. Hence changes in required returns that reflect changing risk levels or changing levels of interest rates are the principal factors that cause changes in prices. In contrast, for equities, price changes also reflect changes in uncertain cash benefits due to changes in anticipated dividends.

The present value or price of a financial instrument varies inversely with the required rate of return. For identical changes in interest rates, while all bonds decline in price, long-term bonds fall in price more than short-term bonds. However, price volatility is more correctly related to duration than to maturity.

QUESTIONS

1. What is the coupon rate? How does it compare to the current yield? How do both compare to the yield to maturity?

2. Why is the holding period yield especially relevant for common stocks?

3. What is the bank discount yield? How does it compare to the coupon equivalent yield?

4. Calculate the present value of a bond with a 14 percent coupon, $1000 principal value, and 20-year maturity at (a) 10 percent required return; (b) 16 percent required return.

5. What is meant by duration? What is the duration of a zero coupon, 10-year bond? What is the duration of a 10 percent coupon, 10-year bond, with a required return of 12 percent?

6. Assuming that interest rates increase from 6 to 8 percent, what will be the percentage change in the price of a 10-year duration bond? Of a 5-year duration bond?

REFERENCES

Bierwag, Gerald, *Duration Analysis: Managing Interest Rate Risk* (Boston, Mass.: Ballinger Press, 1987).

——, George Kaufman, and Alden Toevs, "Duration: Its Development and Use in Bond Portfolio Management," *Financial Analysts Journal* (July/August 1983), 15–35.

Fama, Eugene F., and Merton H. Miller, *The Theory of Finance* (New York: Holt, Rinehart and Winston, 1972).

Henning, Charles, William Pigott, and Robert Scott, *Financial Markets and the Economy,* 5th ed. (Englewood Cliffs, N.J.: Prentice-Hall, 1988).

Kaufman, George, "Measuring and Managing Interest Rate Risk: A Primer," Federal Reserve Bank of Chicago, *Economic Perspectives* (January/February 1984), 16–29.

Trainer, Richard, *The Arithmetic of Interest Rates* (New York: Federal Reserve Bank of New York, 1983).

Van Horne, James, *Financial Market Rates and Flows,* 2nd ed. (Englewood Cliffs, N.J.: Prentice-Hall, 1984).

CHAPTER 3

Historical Development of the United States Banking and Financial System

The U.S. financial system (and indeed the financial system of the entire world) is complex and ever changing. The financial system is in a continual state of evolutionary change in response to changes in the overall economic system, to statutory and regulatory change, and to new technological developments. This pattern of innovative response is apparent from an examination of the history of the financial system. In this chapter we will trace the historical evolution of the banking and financial system, with emphasis on the basic economic factors that have produced this evolution.

The history of the banking and financial system of the United States can be conveniently, though somewhat arbitrarily, divided into the following periods: the colonial period, during which financial institutions and markets were few in number and primitive in function; the early national period from the American Revolution to the Civil War, during which many of the financial institutions that we know today were founded and financial markets began to develop; the period from the Civil War to the founding of the Federal Reserve in 1913, during which an explosion took place in the size and functions of the U.S. financial institutions and markets; and the period from the founding of the Federal Reserve to the present, during which the complex financial system that we know today developed.

THE COLONIAL PERIOD

Financial institutions and markets as we know them today did not exist in the colonial period because investors and savers at that time were one and the same—farmers, merchants, artisans, and others. These individuals were generally self-employed and financed the expansion of their businesses by retaining the earnings from their operations. It is only when savers and investors are different groups that a strong need exists for complex financial markets and institutions.

There were, of course, some financial institutions in the colonies. Among the most prominent were the **land banks,** which issued paper money against mortgages or agricultural land, the principal source of wealth in the colonial period. Though called "banks," these organizations neither accepted deposits nor discounted commercial notes. The success of these largely government-owned ventures was limited, partly because of poor credit policies. In addition to the emergence of land banks serving as pseudofinancial intermediaries, gambling lotteries' operations were employed in the financing of hospitals, manufacturing companies, roads, charitable institutions, and schools and colleges. It has been estimated that by 1815 there was at least one lottery office in every town with a population of 1000 or more; in the early 1800s there were more than 200 lottery offices in Philadelphia alone. Fortunately or unfortunately (depending on your point of view), lotteries fell into disrepute with middle-class Americans and by the mid-1800s were prohibited in most states. In recent years state governments have established lotteries to raise funds for numerous public purposes, including support of the arts in Massachusetts and expanding public parks in Colorado.

Commercial banks failed to develop in the colonial period for a variety of reasons. The largely agriculturally based economy relied heavily on barter rather than on money (commodity or paper). Hence the demand for traditional banking services was not great. Moreover, there was intense hostility toward banking as an alleged arm of the privileged, wealthy segments of society. But perhaps equally important was the domination of the credit supply by English merchants who, in effect, provided some of the financial services that are today associated with commercial banks. The U.S. economy exported agricultural products and imported finished goods from (primarily) English merchants. These English merchants sold their goods on credit to U.S. merchants who, in turn, sold the goods to their local customers. Hence the merchants played a commercial banking role. Occasionally, U.S. merchants were financed directly by British banks. The financial service role of some merchants sometimes became so lucrative as to cause them to abandon the sale of goods in favor of total concentration on their financial services role. Indeed, a number of U.S. banks eventually evolved out of this earlier merchant-finance role.

Financial transactions did, of course, take place in the colonial period. Savers could try their luck at lotteries, buy local mortgages either directly or through a land bank, make loans directly to individuals, or buy British securities through a London financial institution. Similarly, individual borrowers could obtain funds directly from savers for the purchase of houses, and businesses could obtain financing from merchants. Governments generally covered any budget deficit by printing paper money.[1] Yet this method of finance was cumbersome and ineffi-cient, and while sufficient for a primitive, agriculturally based economy, it was clearly inadequate for the rapidly developing commercial economy that followed the Revolutionary War. A more sophisticated financial system evolved after U.S. independence.

FROM THE REVOLUTION TO THE CIVIL WAR

Commercial Banks

The financial structure of the United States became much more complex in the period from the Revolutionary War to the Civil War. The first commercial (as opposed to land) bank was founded in 1781 in Philadelphia as the Bank of North America. And by 1790 the four major cities of the new nation—Philadel-phia, New York, Boston, and Baltimore—each had at least one bank. Commercial banks quickly spread to other states so that by 1800 only four states were without commercial banks. Indeed, as Table 3.1 shows, by 1820 there were over 300 com-mercial banks. They were all state banks (banks chartered by a state government) and performed a variety of functions including safekeeping of valuables, provid-ing deposits against which checks could be written, issuing notes, making short-term loans to merchants and manufacturers, and making longer-term real-estate related loans. They also bought government bonds. In many ways they were simi-lar to modern commercial banks, but they generally ignored consumer lending and often focused primarily on short-term lending following the "real bills" doc-trine that argues a commercial bank should confine its lending to short-term, self-liquidating credits, such as inventory financing. It is also interesting to note that many state governments—including Vermont, Illinois, South Carolina, Ten-nessee, Alabama, Georgia, and Arkansas—formed their own banks in this period. Moreover, other state governments held equity positions in privately owned com-mercial banks.[2]

Other Financial Institutions

The unwillingness of many commercial banks to provide consumer credit and longer-term business credit, as well as their unwillingness to accept small-

---

[1]By 1712, Massachusetts, New Hampshire, Rhode Island, Connecticut, New York, New Jersey, and South Carolina were issuing paper currency. Pennsylvania, Maryland, Delaware, Virginia, and Georgia were also issuing paper currency by 1760.

[2]See Benjamin Klebaner, *Commercial Banking in the United States: A History* (Hinsdale, Ill.: The Dryden Press, 1974) for further information on this topic.

TABLE 3.1   Number and Total Assets of Commercial Banks _____

Year	Number of Banks	Total Assets (Millions of Dollars)
1811	88	42
1820	307	103
1834	506	419
1866	1,931	1,673
1880	3,355	3,399
1900	13,053	11,388
1920	30,909	53,094
1930	24,273	74,290
1940	15,076	79,729
1950	14,676	179,165
1960	13,999	230,046
1970	14,199	518,220
1980	15,120	1,704,000
1987	14,004	2,854,973

Sources: U.S. Bureau of the Census, Historical Statistics of the U.S., Colonial Times to 1970, *Bicentennial Edition, Part 2, September, 1985; U.S. Bureau of the Census,* Statistical Abstract of the United States; *Board of Governors of the Federal Reserve System,* Federal Reserve Bulletin, *various issues.*

denomination time deposits, provided an opportunity for the development of other financial institutions in this postrevolutionary but preindustrial period. In particular, **mutual savings banks** were founded in the early nineteenth century and experienced considerable growth. There is some disagreement about the first savings bank. One mutual savings bank was formed in New York under De Witt Clinton in 1817, but it was unable to receive a charter from the state legislature. A successor, however, was chartered in 1819 as the Bank for Savings. Another savings institution was founded in Philadelphia in 1816 as the Philadelphia Savings Fund Society. Still a third organization was founded in Boston in the same year as The Provident Institute For Savings.[3] These organizations were founded by wealthy individuals as devices to assist the "new immigrants," who were attempting to improve their financial position. The principal emphasis of these institutions was on offering an outlet for savings in small denominations from individuals of modest means. Indeed, some mutual savings banks placed a maximum limit on the size of any deposit in order to discourage deposits by the wealthy. The principal use of funds for mutual savings banks was the purchase of mortgages.

---

[3]See H. Kroos and M. Blyn, *A History of Financial Intermediaries* (New York: Random House, 1971) for more information on the development of the mutual savings bank industry.

The period between the Revolutionary War and the Civil War also witnessed the founding of building and loan associations (now commonly called savings and loan associations), mutual life insurance companies, and investment companies. The first building and loan association—The Oxford Provident Building Association—was founded in Philadelphia in 1836. Similar in many ways to the mutual savings banks, the building and loan associations were cooperative ventures in which individuals pooled their funds to make home ownership possible. Unlike mutual savings banks, however, which were established principally to offer small-denomination time deposits to individuals, the building and loan associations were established primarily to provide financing for home ownership. Following their organization, savings associations grew more rapidly and extensively throughout the United States than did mutual savings banks.

The founding of the Massachusetts Hospital Life Insurance Company (referred to by some as the most unusual financial institution founded in the nineteenth century) in 1818 represents the beginning of the mutual life insurance industry in the United States. Organized in a manner similar to a trust company (but with comingled funds), the Massachusetts Hospital Life Insurance Company actually insured few lives. In fact, between 1823 and 1831 it insured only ninety-four individuals.[4] Of importance also was that the Massachusetts Hospital Life Insurance Company was a model for the development of the trust industry, including a number of trust companies that later evolved into commercial banks.

Of the other types of insurance companies in the pre-Civil War period, most were associated with protection of property rather than with life insurance, and many were offshoots of English insurance companies. Because of the large volume of exports and imports between the United States and England, there existed a substantial need for marine insurance. With wood construction for most buildings and primitive fire protection there was a decided need for fire insurance. By the early 1830s there were more than seventy marine and fire insurance companies in New York and Boston alone, though the number shrank dramatically after a major fire in New York City in 1835 resulted in bankruptcy among many of these financial institutions.

The beginnings of the securities industry and the origins of the nation's money and capital markets may be traced to the 1783–1860 period. To some extent the origins of the securities markets could be traced to trading in U.S. government bonds in 1791. Much early trading of equity securities was concentrated in bank stocks. In 1800 a stock exchange was organized in Philadelphia. The New York Stock Exchange was formed in 1817. Listed securities encompassed banks, insurance companies, and a variety of U.S. government bonds. In

---

[4] See H. Kroos and M. Blyn, *A History of Financial Intermediaries* (New York: Random House, 1971) for a more complete discussion of the Massachusetts Hospital Life Insurance Company in the United States.

PRESIDENT JACKSON AND THE "BANK WAR"

When Andrew Jackson, the seventh president of the United States, was a young man, he exchanged 6000 acres of Tennessee soil for bank notes that proved to be worthless. This bitter experience, combined with other adversarial episodes with eastern banks, made Jackson even more antibank than most of the small farmers, craftsmen, and frontiersmen that he represented. When Jackson once told Nicholas Biddle, the president of the Second Bank of the United States, that "I do not dislike your bank any more than all banks," he meant that he disliked the Bank a very great deal. When Biddle, taking the advice of Jackson's political opponents to seek confrontation, applied for a new charter in 1832 (four years before the old one expired), Jackson said, "The Bank is trying to kill me, but I will kill it."

Jackson did, indeed, kill the Bank. Although the Congress readily passed a bill to recharter the Bank, Jackson vetoed it. The message of Jackson's veto was one of politics, not economics. The President maintained that the Bank was unconstitutional, represented a dangerous concentration of power, had too much foreign ownership, and was foul in a variety of other un-American ways. However demogogic and lacking in economic logic Jackson's message might have been, Jackson used "the Bank War" to his advantage in the election of 1832. Henry Clay, Jackson's Whig opponent, had believed that the President's anti-Bank position would work against Jackson; the contrary proved to be the case. Jackson won by a landslide. He was perhaps not the last incumbent president to demonstrate that bad economics is often good politics.

The "Bank war" continued after Jackson's reelection, however. Jackson pulled federal deposits out of the Bank and placed them in state banks that were owned by his friends and supporters (and were thus called "pet banks"). The President was obliged to fire two Secretaries of the Treasury before he got one willing to cooperate in this scheme. The weakened Bank's charter expired in 1836, with Jackson thus the clear victor in the "Bank War." The Bank operated as a Pennsylvania-chartered bank until 1841, when that year's depression drove it and many other state banks into failure.

an economy that was still essentially agrarian it is not surprising that equity securities of manufacturing firms were generally absent from such trading.

The First and Second Banks of the United States

The importance of the First and Second Banks of the United States (both of which were organized and liquidated in the period between the Revolutionary and Civil Wars) is so great that it warrants a special section. Not only did these banks play an important role in the financial history of the period, but they also represent the origins of a central bank in the United States. Indeed, the First and Second Banks of the United States may be viewed together as the first central bank in the United States.

The Revolutionary War had been financed by printing money, a process that led to an excess of paper money and rapid inflation. With U.S. independence from Britain it was realized that a strong federal government required a sound money system and that a sound money system required a national bank. As a result, Secretary of the Treasury Alexander Hamilton pushed strongly for the chartering of a national bank of the United States.

The First Bank of the United States was chartered in February 1791 for a period of twenty years with a total capitalization of $10 million—a very large sum for the time. Its principal functions were to increase the amount of money (since it operated on a fractional reserve system), to assist the U.S. government in its borrowing needs, and to assist in the tax collection process. Fundamentally, the First Bank of the United States was designed to contribute toward a restoration of a sound money system and a reduction in the inflation rate brought about, in part at least, by excessive issuance of notes by state banks.

The bank was opposed by the Jeffersonians on constitutional grounds. Moreover, agrarian interests who wanted "cheap" money (that is, inflation) in order to pay off their debts with depreciated dollars were opposed to the bank. In addition, state banks opposed the Bank of the United States, fearing (correctly, as it turned out) that it would curtail the ability of these banks to issue notes that circulated in place of "specie" (gold and silver).[5] The influence of these groups was so substantial that the charter of the First Bank of the United States was allowed to expire in 1811, and the bank went out of existence.

Following the termination of the First Bank of the United States, an explosion occurred in the number of state banks; the number of commercial banks tripled in the following five years, and their notes outstanding and other liabilities almost quadrupled. While perhaps undesirable from the perspective of price stability, this expansion of commercial banks in the period firmly established the commercial banking industry as the largest group of financial institutions in the nation, a position it has retained to this day.

Not surprisingly, the excesses of bank expansion in the years after the death of the First Bank of the United States produced a call for controls over the ability of state banks to expand and issue bank notes and for pressure to charter a new Bank of the United States. Such pressure was successful in 1816, when Congress chartered for another twenty-year period the Second Bank of the United States. This bank was similar in structure and role to the First Bank, though much larger in size. Again, for a brief period at least, the nation had a central bank and some control over the ability of state banks to expand money. Yet this power was again

---

[5]In this pre–checking account era, state banks made loans by issuing their own notes, supposedly backed by (and redeemable in) specie. The Bank of the United States could amass a large number of notes from an individual state bank and present them for redemption in specie. The fear of such demands for payment in specie was a restraining element in the lending activities of individual state banks.

to be its undoing. Moreover, the Second Bank suffered initially from vacillating and inept leadership, which resulted in severe financial difficulties for the state banks (almost one half of the banks chartered in the period from 1810 to 1820 had failed by 1825). As a result, bank notes outstanding declined drastically, and the economy plunged into a severe depression.

The Second Bank finally was stabilized under the strong leadership of Nicholas Biddle. Throughout the 1820s and 1830s the Second Bank constrained the ability of state banks to create credit and inflate the money supply, but these restrictive policies again gained the enmity of agrarian interests and other cheap money advocates. Thus the charter of the nation's central bank was again not renewed (because of the determined opposition of President Andrew Jackson) when it expired in 1836. And once again, following the demise of the Second Bank, state banks embarked on a rapid expansion of credit and bank notes outstanding.

FROM THE CIVIL WAR TO THE FOUNDING OF THE FEDERAL RESERVE

The roughly fifty-year period from the Civil War to the founding of the Federal Reserve was one of exceptional expansion and change in both the U.S. economy and the U.S. monetary system. The Industrial Revolution that had begun earlier in England was transmitted to the United States despite attempts by England to confine its technology within its own borders. The economy changed from being predominantly agrarian to having a very strong manufacturing orientation. With the shift toward manufacturing came a change in the location of the population from rural to urban areas. Large cities grew around large businesses. A working class developed that did not have the alternative of reinvesting its savings in its own businesses; savers and investors increasingly became different individuals. All these trends created the need for a more complex financial system. It was in this period that the financial system as we know it today began to take shape.

Developments in the commercial banking sector of the economy were especially significant in this era. Following the cessation of the Second Bank of the United States in 1836 and during the era of "free banking," the United States once again experienced an excessive number of commercial banks, many of which were not financially sound.[6] Indeed, the poor quality of many banking organizations gave rise to the term "wildcat banking" to describe the fact that

---

[6]Before 1837, obtaining a bank charter required a special act of a state legislature. However, in 1837 the state of Michigan introduced "free banking," whereby a charter would be granted to an individual or group of individuals who met certain specified requirements, most of which were easily satisfied.

many banks were located in isolated, rural locations that were more agreeable to wildcats than to individuals trying to redeem their bank notes.[7] The problem with bank safety and soundness was one reason for the creation of an "independent Treasury system" of regional offices of the U.S. Treasury, at which federal payments were made in specie. The system made it unnecessary for the U.S. government to use the banking system, but it also constituted a destabilizing influence for the latter (as government receipts and payments resulted in corresponding changes in the banking system's specie reserves).

The National Banking System

The U.S. government financed a substantial part of the Civil War with paper money popularly called "greenbacks" (because of their color, of course). The need to use greenbacks arose from difficulties encountered in the sale of Union bonds. Concern with the financing requirements of the war was the major element resulting in the creation of a new banking system—the **national banking system.** Between 1863 (passage of the National Banking Act) and 1865, Congress passed a number of bills that, in combination, created the national banking system. Under these laws the U.S. government began to charter national banks through the newly established Office of the Comptroller of the Currency within the Treasury Department. These national banks were required to hold substantial reserves (which state banks generally did not do) and also to hold a portion of their reserves in U.S. government bonds. With these two provisions the U.S. government improved the safety and soundness of the banking system. (The major intent of Congress in passing the National Banking Acts—to aid the financing of the Civil War by providing an incentive for the purchase of U.S. bonds by banks—was less successful).

The National Banking Act was expected to persuade state banks to convert to national charters. However, to accomplish this, Congress had to place a 10 percent tax on the bank notes of state chartered banks (which did not apply to the **national bank notes** issued by national banks). Initially, this tax appeared to be effective, since most state banks converted to national charters in order to be in a position to issue national bank notes. Such conversions substantially reduced the problems associated with the numerous different bank notes that had been issued by the state banking system. Yet while partially successful in creating a uniform, circulating paper currency, the national banking system did not elimi-

---

[7]Rolnick and Weber make a distinction between free banking and wildcat banking. **Free banking** refers to the ease of entry into banking during the 1837–1863 period, while **wildcat banking** refers to fraudulent practices followed by the management of many of these banks. They present evidence that the large number of bank failures during this period were caused not by banks cheating their noteholders but rather by losses produced by the declining value of bonds. See Arthur J. Rolnick and Warren E. Weber, "Free Banking, Wildcat Banks, and Shinplasters," Federal Reserve Bank of Minneapolis *Quarterly Review* (Fall 1982).

nate state banks. As demand deposits began to supplement note issuance by banks as a way of providing funds to borrowers, state banks lost their disadvantage, and the number of state banks once again began to expand. The net result was the creation of a **dual banking system** that still exists and is composed of both state and nationally chartered commercial banks.

The national banking system constituted substantial improvement in the U.S. monetary system. Yet it too had a number of problems that were aggravated by the lack of a central bank (recall that the Second Bank of the United States had gone out of existence in 1836). In particular the quantity of money was "inelastic"; that is, the quantity did not rise and fall automatically with the need for money by commerce. This inelasticity of the money supply reflected a number of different considerations. Under the national banking system a portion of a bank's reserves could be held as "correspondent" bank deposits at other banks, resulting in a pyramiding of deposits, with New York banks as the focal point. During seasonal peaks in the demand for money, country banks would draw down their deposits at the New York banks, which would then be forced to call (liquidate) their loans, sometimes producing a financial crisis. Indeed, periodic liquidity crises associated with the pyramiding of reserves were quite common during this era. This problem was further intensified by the legal requirement that the volume of bank notes outstanding be determined by the number of government bonds held by commercial banks—a requirement that did not allow for seasonal movements in the demand for money.[8]

These defects of the national banking system and their associated financial panics finally led to the permanent establishment of a central bank—the Federal Reserve System—in 1913. The purposes, organization, and power of the Federal Reserve are discussed in Chapter 5. The Federal Reserve has become one of the nation's most powerful economic organizations. For now, however, it is important only to recognize that the Federal Reserve (or the Fed, as it is commonly called) was established (among other things) to create an elastic currency supply through its lending to member banks. (The Fed's lending operations were expected to accommodate seasonal and cyclical increases in the demand for money and credit.)

Reflecting the expansion of the U.S. economy in the period from the Civil War to the founding of the Federal Reserve, the commercial banking industry grew remarkably in terms of both number of banks and total assets. But growth in the financial institutions sector was not limited to commercial banks. In some cases the growth of nonbank financial institutions was even greater than it was for commercial banks. Moreover, important changes were taking place in the

---

[8]Timberlake points out that clearinghouse associations provided a quasi–central banking function during this period. See Richard Timberlake, "The Central Banking Role of Clearinghouse Associations," *Journal of Money, Credit, and Banking* (February 1984), 1–15.

nation's financial markets as these markets became broader in terms of securities traded and in regional scope.

Other Financial Institutions

Mutual savings banks experienced rapid growth in the period surrounding the Civil War. However, as the population and economic activity of the United States moved westward into states that did not provide for chartering of these types of thrift institutions, the growth of mutual savings banks diminished considerably. Also, the periodic liquidity crises of the late nineteenth century affected the mutual savings bank industry to a particularly large extent, causing failures among a number of the organizations. To some extent the time deposits that the mutual savings banks lost went to commercial banks. To a much greater extent these deposits were lost to savings and loan associations, which experienced phenomenal growth late in the nineteenth century. During the latter period the purpose of savings and loan associations changed from temporary provision of home financing for those involved in the cooperative to a more permanent structure with emphasis on offering savings and time accounts to the general public.

Life insurance companies also experienced rapid growth in this period, the most rapid growth in the history of the industry. To a considerable extent this growth reflected the aggressive marketing by life insurance firms. New policy types were developed and aggressively marketed to new customers, particularly blue-collar workers. Moreover, there was a substantial reduction in government regulation of the life insurance industry during this period.

Securities markets and firms such as investment bankers that operated in these markets also developed substantially. Trading in securities listed on the New York Stock Exchange increased dramatically in the late nineteenth century. With the growth of manufacturing enterprises, new companies went public and were traded on organized exchanges. Financial markets generally became better integrated. Not the least of the reasons for these developments was the growth of powerful investment banking firms like those led by Jay Cooke and J. Pierpont Morgan. These organizations created some of the giant businesses that we know today (U.S. Steel and American Can, for instance) and, in the process, gave the era a name that is still commonly used: **finance capitalism.**

FROM THE FOUNDING OF THE FEDERAL RESERVE TO THE PRESENT

The Federal Reserve (the Fed) was founded in 1913. Originally designed to provide "elasticity" to the currency (a limited but attainable objective for a central bank), the Fed has gradually taken on much more ambitious and difficult objectives, as we will discuss in more complete detail in Chapter 5. The period since the founding of the Fed has been one in which enormous changes have occurred in the nature of the economy and in the role of different financial institutions. The Great Depression of the 1930s, the First and Second World Wars, the rapid economic expansion following these wars, and the persistence of high inflation and high interest rates in the late 1960s and throughout the decade of the 1970s also substantially affected the role of individual financial institutions. As a general rule (though with some notable exceptions), financial institutions became less specialized and more competitive during this era. Moreover, the nation's financial markets became incredibly sophisticated and highly integrated with financial markets throughout the world.

Commercial Banks

The commercial banking industry experienced some noticeable deterioration in its relative position vis-à-vis other financial institutions during this period. While the economy was generally prosperous throughout the 1920s, the agricultural sector experienced a severe depression that had a substantial impact on the profitability of rural banks. Moreover, the boom in stock prices and increased use by business of new stock issues to obtain funds rather than borrowing from banks also contributed to the declining position of the commercial banking industry. Large numbers of banks failed during the 1920s, as shown in Table 3.2. This fact principally reflects substantial financial problems in agriculturally oriented banks. As the prosperity of the 1920s gave way to the depression of the 1930s, the incidence of bank failure accelerated. Finally, in a nationwide radio address on March 12, 1933, President Franklin Roosevelt announced a "bank holiday," during which the soundness of individual banks could be assessed.

The bank holidays of March 1933 marked the beginning of a fundamental change in the nature of commercial bank management and regulations. New laws were passed, particularly the Banking Acts of 1933 and 1935, that were designed to reduce the risk of bank failures. Chartering of new banks was made more difficult. Interest payments on demand deposits were prohibited on the grounds that excessive payments on deposits forced banks to make excessively risky loans. Substantial restrictions were placed on the portfolio management policies of commercial banks. For the first time, commercial banking and investment banking (underwriting of securities) were separated to prevent the possibility that unsuccessful underwritings would lead to the sale of the underwritten securities to the commercial bank. But perhaps most important, the Federal Deposit Insurance Corporation (FDIC) was created to insure the depositors against loss from the collapse of an insured commercial bank.

Since the establishment of the FDIC, the incidence of bank failure has diminished considerably. Depositors have refrained from mass withdrawals from banks

TABLE 3.2   Bank Suspensions, 1890–1987 ____

Year	Number of Bank Suspensions
1890–1899	1294
1900–1909	797
1910–1919	849
1920	168
1921	505
1922	367
1923	646
1924	775
1925	618
1926	976
1927	669
1928	499
1929	659
1930	1352
1931	2294
1932	1456
1933	4004
1934–1940	313
1941–1950	73
1951–1960	43
1961–1970	63
1971–1980	83
1981–1983	100
1984–1986	344
1987	184

Sources: U.S. Bureau of the Census, Historical Statistics of the U.S., Colonial Times to 1970, *Bicentennial Edition, Part 2, September 1985; U.S. Bureau of the Census,* Statistical Abstract of the United States; *Board of Governors of the Federal Reserve System, Federal Reserve Bulletin, various issues.*

suspected of being in financial difficulty because they feel secure in the expectation that their funds would be returned by the FDIC if there were bank failures. In fact, there have been only a small number of bank failures each year during the past fifty years, though the incidence of failures increased sharply in the 1980s.

The commercial banking industry, like the rest of the economy, recovered gradually during the late 1930s and then rapidly during the 1940s with the prosperity that came with the Second World War. However, the nature of commercial banking after the Second World War (and particularly after 1960) changed markedly. Banks became much more aggressive in their portfolio management, soliciting new funds through time deposits and making different kinds of loans in direct competition with other financial institutions. Moreover, banks began to expand internationally through extensive foreign operations and domestically through bank holding company structures.

The banking system experienced especially rapid change in the 1980s with falling profitability for many banking organizations and a large increase in financially distressed and failed organizations. These changes reflected the combined effects of instability in the domestic and international economies—evidenced by the international debt crisis, the real estate "bust" in Texas, and problems in the agricultural sector—and legislative and regulatory deregulation. As the 1980s came to a close, serious questions were being raised about the viability of the banking system in its traditional form.

Other Financial Institutions

The various other financial institutions experienced similar trends in this era, though the impact of the Great Depression of the 1930s was generally less severe than for the commercial banks. Savings and loan associations expanded rapidly in the 1920s but retrenched during the 1930s. (These patterns are shown in Table 3.3.) Following the Second World War, the savings and loan industry expanded markedly in response to the baby boom and the huge demand for housing. Indeed, the period from the end of World War II to the mid-1960s was perhaps the most profitable in the history of the savings and loan associations. A large demand existed for their principal product (single-family mortgage loans), and it was also relatively easy and inexpensive for the industry to raise funds through savings acounts. As a result, the share of total assets of financial institutions held by savings and loans expanded substantially. A similar, though somewhat less favorable, experience was shared by the mutual savings bank industry. Yet the persistence in recent years of high interest rates and inflation has seriously eroded the financial viability of these organizations.

The profitability of the savings and loan industry, which had been eroded substantially in the early 1980s by high interest rates, was further affected by significant credit quality problems in residential and commercial real estate lending. The sharp increase in defaults in real estate loans, especially those made on property in Texas, caused the failure of hundreds of savings and loans and drained the insurance fund of the Federal Savings and Loan Insurance Corporation. By the end of the 1980s the "thrift crisis" had become a problem of national significance encompassing both the need for billions of dollars to restructure the industry and also the issue of what role savings and loans would play in the financial marketplace of the future. In early 1989 President Bush proposed a thrift rescue plan that would involve investing over $100 billion in federal government money and a reorganization of the industry.

TABLE 3.3 Total Assets of Major Financial Institutions, 1900–1988
(Billions of dollars)

	1900	1922	1929	1933	1945	1952	1960	1970	1980	1988
Commercial banks	10.0	47.5	66.2	46.1	160.3	188.6	179.1	504.9	1386.3	2850.5
Savings banks	2.4	6.6	9.9	10.8	17.0	25.2	41.4	79.7	171.5	275.4
Life insurance companies	1.7	8.7	17.5	20.9	44.8	73.4	115.8	200.9	469.8	1096.6
Private pension funds	—	0.1	0.5	0.7	2.9	9.0	38.1	110.4	286.8	1085.6
State and local governments' pension funds	—	0.1	0.5	0.8	3.0	7.5	19.7	60.3	198.1	587.3
Property and casualty insurance companies	0.5	2.3	4.7	3.5	7.7	15.9	26.2	49.9	180.0	435.0
Savings and loan associations	0.5	2.8	7.4	6.2	8.6	22.5	71.5	176.2	629.8	1335.5
Credit unions	—	—	—	—	0.4	1.5	6.3	18.0	69.2	195.0
Investment companies	—	0.1	3.0	1.3	2.7	6.1	17.1	47.6	63.7	483.9

Note: Data for open-end investment companies excludes money market funds.

Source: Data from Raymond W. Goldsmith, Financial Intermediaries in the American Economy Since 1900, (Princeton, N.J.: Princeton University Press, 1958), p. 75; Board of Governors of the Federal Reserve System, Flow of Funds Accounts: Assets and Liabilities Outstanding.

Life insurance companies experienced substantial prosperity during the 1920s and even through the 1930s. Of those financial institutions that we have already discussed, life insurance companies were least affected by the Great Depression—a perhaps not surprising discovery, considering the nature of the services offered by life insurance companies. Total assets under management expanded throughout the 1920s and 1930s, and the share of total assets held by life insurance companies of all financial institutions was significantly higher in 1940 than in 1920. Yet the inflationary period that began in 1966 has also had a substantial impact on life insurance companies. Inflation has produced a difficult environment for life insurance corporations to sell their principal product—whole life policies in which premium payments are made throughout the life of the insured. Instead, consumers are increasingly purchasing term policies.

Three new types of financial institutions—credit unions, pension funds, and investment companies—have been created since the founding of the Federal Reserve. Credit unions were founded by employers as cooperative organizations to provide consumer credit to workers at a time when such credit was generally unavailable at other financial institutions. Growth has been rapid and essentially uninterrupted. Though their total assets remain quite small, credit unions have been among the most rapidly growing financial institutions in percentage terms.

The growth of pension funds is primarily a post–World War II phenomenon. Indeed, the expansion of the volume of assets under pension funds management has been remarkable in the last thirty-five years. Similarly, investment companies (in quantitative terms at least) represent primarily a post–World War II development. Common-stock–oriented investment companies, better known as mutual funds, grew rapidly with the upward surge in stock prices in the 1950s and 1960s. However, these types of investment companies grew more slowly after the late 1960s as common stock returns became less attractive to many investors. The investment company industry was transformed in the late 1970s by the phenomenal growth of money market mutual funds—a development that has fundamentally altered the role of many financial institutions. More will be said of this remarkable development in later chapters.

Securities markets also developed markedly in this area. Trading volume increased sharply, particularly in the 1920s and later in the 1960s and 1970s. Both the financial instruments traded in the securities markets and the markets themselves became much more complex, elaborate, and sophisticated.

SUMMARY

The historical evolution of the U.S. banking and financial system can be conveniently divided into four eras:

1. *The colonial period:* In this period, financial intermediaries and markets were rudimentary. The economy was essentially agricultural, and there was limited need for finan-

cial institutions and markets. Most financing was done through English financial institutions and merchants.

2. *From the Revolution to the Civil War:* In this period the nation's financial institutions and markets began to develop considerable sophistication. The first commercial bank—The Bank of North America—was founded in Philadelphia in 1781. Moreover, commercial banking organizations became common throughout the major cities. Mutual savings banks and savings and loan associations were founded and experienced a good deal of growth. Also, life insurance companies and investment companies were established. Indeed, one life insurance company was the largest financial institution in the United States in the early nineteenth century. This era also witnessed the first attempts to establish a central bank with the First and Second Banks of the United States, neither of which achieved permanence, largely because of the political influence of agrarian interests that favored easy money.

3. *From the Civil War to the founding of the Federal Reserve:* This era saw a remarkable expansion of both the U.S. economy and the U.S. monetary and financial system. Indeed, the U.S. financial system as we know it today may be traced to developments in this period. The national banking system was established, which ultimately, though not by design, led to the present dual-banking system of both state and nationally chartered banks. Nonbank financial institutions continued to develop. Following a series of money panics associated with the inelasticity of the money supply, the United States finally established a central bank, the Federal Reserve System.

4. *From the founding of the Federal Reserve to the present:* The Federal Reserve has been successful in creating an elastic currency, but this success has not eliminated all economic and financial problems. The Great Depression of the 1930s had a profound impact on the evolution of the financial system, as did the depression in the agricultural sector during the 1920s. Commercial banks failed by the thousands in the 1920s and 1930s. As a result, legislative changes—especially the Banking Acts of 1933 and 1935 and the establishment of the Federal Deposit Insurance Corporation—substantially altered the "rules of the game" for the financial system. Moreover, there has been a virtual revolution in the roles of different financial institutions in the post–World War II period, especially in the high inflation/high interest rate environment that began in the late 1960s.

QUESTIONS

1. Why didn't commercial banks develop extensively in the colonial period? Why did commercial banks develop extensively after the colonial period?

2. Briefly discuss the history of central banking in the United States. What functions do central banks perform? How did the First and Second Banks of the United States perform these functions? How does the Federal Reserve perform these functions?

3. Trace the historical evolution of savings and loan associations, mutual savings banks, and insurance companies.

4. What is meant by the term "free banking"? "Wildcat banks"? The National Bank Act? The dual banking system? How are these related?

5. Why were the Banking Acts of 1933 and 1935 enacted? What were they designed to accomplish? Why was the Federal Deposit Insurance Corporation created?

REFERENCES

Dewey, Davis R., *Financial History of the United States* (New York: Augustus M. Kelley, 1968).

Goldsmith, Raymond, *Financial Institutions* (New York: Random House, 1968).

———, *Financial Intermediaries in the American Economy Since 1900* (Princeton, N.J.: Princeton University Press, 1958).

Gorton, Gary, "Private Clearinghouses and the Origins of Central Banking," Federal Reserve Bank of Philadelphia *Business Review* (January/February 1984), 3–12.

Klebaner, Benjamin, *Commercial Banking in the United States: A History* (Hinsdale, Ill.: The Dryden Press, 1974).

Kroos, Herman E., and Martin R. Blyn, *A History of Financial Intermediaries* (New York: Random House, 1971).

McCarthy, F. Ward, Jr., "The Evolution of the Bank Regulatory Structure: A Reappraisal," Federal Reserve Bank of Richmond *Economic Review* (March/April 1984), 3–21.

Perkins, Edwin J., "The Divorcement of Commercial and Investment Banking: A History," *The Banking Law Journal* (June 1971), 483–528.

Polakoff, Murray E., et al., *Financial Institutions and Markets,* 2nd ed. (Boston: Houghton Mifflin, 1981), Ch. 2.

Rolnick, Arthur J., and Warren E. Weber. "Free Banking, Wildcat Banking, and Shinplasters," Federal Reserve Bank of Minneapolis *Quarterly Review* (Fall 1982), 10–19.

Studenski, Paul, and Herman E. Kroos, *Financial History of the United States* (New York: McGraw-Hill, 1963).

Timberlake, Richard H., Jr., "The Central Banking Role of Clearinghouse Associations," *Journal of Money, Credit, and Banking* (February 1984), 1–15.

Veazey, Edward, "Evolution of Money and Banking in the United States," Federal Reserve Bank of Dallas, *Business Review* (December 1975), 1–12.

CHAPTER **4**

Money
and the
Financial System

Money is an integral and essential part of the financial system of any country. Whether called dollars, pesos, pounds, or francs, money is necessary to serve as a means of payment, a store of value, and a unit of account in all but the most elemental economic systems. In this chapter we are concerned with the nature of money, its economic significance, the process by which it is created, and the factors that determine its quantity (supply). Since the Federal Reserve System is the ultimate arbiter of the U.S. money supply, this institution is given special attention.

Increases and decreases in the supply of money are both cause and effect of events in the "real" sector of the economy. Because money is the means by which spending is accomplished, the quantity of money is of great significance for the level of prices, interest rates, and the employment of productive resources to produce goods and services. The economic significance of monetary change is so great that economic policy focuses largely on controlling money growth.

Thus the institutions and process involved in money creation and the control of its quantity are vital elements of the financial system. Banks continue to play the principal role in the creation (and destruction) of money, and we will examine banking with regard to this aspect of its activities. Actions of the public, the U.S. government, and the Federal Reserve System (the Fed) also affect the quantity of money, and these aspects of change in the potential money supply also receive attention. Indeed, the Fed's responsibility for monetary control gives this agency special significance in the financial system.

THE NATURE OF MONEY

Money is anything that is generally accepted as payment for goods, services, and debts. Money is a **medium of exchange;** people accept money in exchange for the goods or services they provide in the expectation that they can subsequently exchange the money for goods and services they wish to acquire. Without such a medium of exchange, people must resort to **barter**—the direct exchange of goods and services for other goods and services—a very inefficient means of affecting exchange. Barter involves finding another party who has what you want and wants what you have to exchange. It requires searching out all the possible exchange partners necessary to supply one's needs and wants for goods and services and then reaching agreement on the terms of the exchange. Barter thus results in very high **search and transactions costs,** as the costs of affecting exchanges are called. In other words, bartering obliges people to spend a great deal of time searching, negotiating, and otherwise incurring considerable costs in their trading activities.

Money also serves as a **unit of account,** or a "standard of value." Money's role as a "measuring rod" allows the use of established prices for transactions. Money's unit-of-account function allows measuring economic values in a universally (almost) understood fashion. In addition to serving as a **medium of exchange** and a **unit of account,** money is both a convenient way to save (a **store of value**) and a convenient way to borrow (a **standard of deferred payment**). In its store-of-value function, money facilitates saving by providing a means of securing future purchasing power from present income. In its standard-of-deferred-payment function, money facilitates borrowing (and lending) by providing a measure of the purchasing power that is being borrowed and loaned. Money is unique in its immediacy as a means of making payment for goods and services; it is the most liquid of assets.

MEASUREMENT OF THE MONEY SUPPLY

Money is ordinarily defined as a generalized means of purchasing power that is acceptable as payment for goods and services. Currency, coin, and all checkable deposits obviously qualify as "money," since they serve as an immediate means of payment. **Noncheckable** deposits and similar liquid assets are not money in terms of this definition, since they must first be converted into checkable deposits or currency before being used for payment. Such highly liquid assets, because of the ease with which they can be converted into money, are often referred to as "near monies."

Measurement of the amounts of money and liquid assets ("monetary aggregates") is important for economic policy purposes. Monitoring of these various quantities is accomplished by the Federal Reserve. Table 4.1 indicates the measures of money and liquid assets employed by the Fed and the amounts of these monetary aggregates.

Prior to discussing the rationale for the various monetary aggregates, shown in Table 4.1, a brief description of their components is useful.

TABLE 4.1 Measures of Money and Liquid Assets, January 1989 _____

M1	Components	
	Currency and coins held by the nonbank public	211.8
	Traveler's checks	7.0
	Demand deposits owned by the nonbank public	290.5
	Other checkable deposits	283.7
	M1 Total	793.0
M2	Components	
	M1	793.0
	Savings deposits	422.8
	Small-denomination time deposits	1041.8
	Money market deposit accounts	495.1
	Money market mutual funds for individuals	242.0
	Overnight repurchase agreements issued by commercial banks	65.3
	Overnight Eurodollar deposits held by U.S. nonbank residents at foreign branches of Federal Reserve System member banks	16.6
	M2 Total	3,076.3
M3	Components	
	M2	3,076.3
	Large-denomination time deposits	545.1
	Term repurchase agreements and term Eurodollars	220.0
	Money market mutual funds for institutions	89.3
	M3 Total	3,930.7
L	TOTAL (M3 plus nonbank public holdings of U.S. savings bonds, short-term U.S. Treasury securities, commercial paper and bankers acceptances, net of money market mutual fund holdings of these assets)	4,708.3

Source: Board of Governors of the Federal Reserve System.

Components of the Monetary Aggregates

Currency. "Currency" refers to coins as well as paper money. Currency and coin are "manufactured" by the U.S. Treasury Department's Bureau of Engraving and Printing and Bureau of the Mint. The Treasury transfers printed currency (Federal Reserve notes) and minted coin to the Federal Reserve System as required to replace worn-out currency (which is destroyed) and to satisfy growth in the public's demand for cash holdings. Depository institutions obtain the currency they need from the Fed (the nature of this transfer is described at a later point). In monetary measurement, only "currency in circulation"—currency out-

MONEY, MONEY, MONEY ...

Most of the money in industrialized, economically advanced nations like the United States exists only in the form of computer records in banks. But money's interesting history reveals that a great many interesting types of money have been used in the past. A few historical facts about money that you might find of interest include the following:

1. The word "money" stems from the use by the ancient Romans of the temple of the goddess Juno Moneta as a workshop in which to make coins. (If this seems disrespectful, it should be recalled that the ancient Romans had gods and goddesses in such quantity as to view them rather cavalierly.) In due time, all the places in which coins were made came to be called *moneta.* The English version of this word is "mint." The French version of *moneta* is *monnaie,* and this word gave rise to the English word "money."

2. Coins themselves have been around for about 2500 years, but they were preceded by a variety of objects that served the purposes of money as we know it. Ancient Egyptian wall-paintings show gold rings being weighed on a balance-scale. The earliest written records (from long-ago Mesopotamia) indicate the use of weighed metal as money. Cowrie shells, the shells of a species of Indian Ocean mollusk, were used as money in China at least 3000 years ago. (Some North American Indians also used mollusk shells as money, which they called "wampum.") There is also evidence that stones were used as money in primitive societies thousands of years ago. Indeed, the Yap islanders—inhabitants of one of the Caroline Islands in the Pacific Ocean—were still using massive, unmovable stones as a medium of exchange and store of wealth when Europeans first visited them in the last century.

3. Paper money had antecedents in documents promising payments in gold, silver, or other valuable commodities. But the first circulating bank notes known to history were issued by Chinese bankers in the eleventh century. (Banks and bankers had already been around for many centuries when the first bank notes appeared.) Early bank notes were backed by coin, and their acceptability as money stemmed from that fact. By the seventeenth century, paper money was being circulated in a very limited degree in a few nations. Bank of England notes began to be issued in 1694, the year in which that venerable institution was established.

side the Treasury, Federal Reserve Banks, and the vaults of commercial banks—is included. Currency constitutes roughly one third of the M1 measure of money, but the amount of currency in circulation fluctuates seasonally, increasing, for example, during the Christmas shopping period and decreasing thereafter.

Demand Deposits.   The monetary aggregates include all demand deposits at all commercial banks other than those which represent deposits of domestic banks, the U.S. government, foreign banks, and foreign official institutions. Currently, depository institutions are not permitted to pay interest on demand deposits. Demand deposits presently account for more than half of checkable deposits, and their importance is especially great for business firms.

Other Checkable Deposits. This category includes all deposit accounts due from depository institutions other than demand deposits of commercial banks. Included in this category are negotiated order of withdrawal (NOW) accounts and automatic transfer service (ATS) accounts (which allow for immediate transfer of funds from a savings account to a checking account to cover checks drawn on the latter). NOW and ATS accounts can be offered by all depository institutions. Also included in this category are credit union share draft (CUSD) accounts (essentially checking deposits held with credit unions) and demand deposits at mutual savings banks. NOW, ATS, and CUSD deposits are interest-bearing checking accounts.

Noncheckable Deposits. This category includes both savings and time deposits and thus ranges from passbook savings accounts and money market deposit accounts to certificates of deposit holdings. Time deposits are separated into "small-denomination time deposits" (accounts issued in less than $100,000 amounts) and "large-denomination time deposits" (greater than $100,000) for purposes of measuring the monetary aggregates. Further, large-denomination time deposits are measured net of the holdings of depository institutions, the U.S. government, foreign official institutions, and money market mutual funds.

Money Market Mutual Fund Shares. Shares in money market mutual funds (MMMFs) are not deposit claims but rather represent ownership rights in the assets held by the funds. MMMF shares nonetheless have monetary characteristics. Certainly, such shares, like noncheckable deposits, constitute a highly liquid asset that can readily be converted to spendable form in order to exercise purchasing power. Further, most MMMFs offer check-writing privileges, albeit only in large minimum amounts ($250 and $500 minimums are typical).

Repurchase Agreements (RPs). Repurchase agreements are arrangements by which individuals or institutions secure funds by selling a financial instrument while, at the time of sale, agreeing to buy the instrument back at a specified price and specified time. (In essence, RPs are collateralized loans.) RPs are often "overnight" (one-day) arrangements but are also executed for longer terms. RPs issued by commercial banks to parties other than depository institutions and MMMFs are included in the M2, M3, and L monetary aggregates, as shown in Table 4.1.

Eurodollars. Eurodollars are U.S. dollar-denominated deposits outside the United States. Certain Eurodollar deposits held by nonbank U.S. residents are included in the M2, M3, and L monetary aggregates.

The Monetary Aggregates

The Federal Reserve's measures of monetary aggregates are labeled M1, M2, M3, and L. M1 is a measure of money as conventionally defined—a means of payment used in effecting transactions. M1 consists of the following items: currency and coins in circulation, traveler's checks, demand deposits (except interbank deposits, federal government deposits, and deposits of foreign banks and official institutions), and other checkable deposits. "Other checkable deposits" include NOW accounts and ATS accounts with depository institutions, and credit union share draft accounts. Thus the components of M1 are financial assets that are acceptable as a means of payment and are held for the purpose of making payments. For this reason, holdings of M1 are often referred to as "transactions balances."

The use of monetary measures other than M1 (M2, M3, and L) reflects the fact that spending units in the economy hold large amounts of "near-money" liquid assets, which can quickly be converted to M1 and then used to make payments. Indeed, some liquid asset holdings often represent temporarily "parked" money, which is not currently required for payments purposes but which will soon be returned to the spending stream. As indicated in Table 4.1, certain liquid asset items are included with M1 to develop these broader monetary aggregates. The characteristic that distinguishes M2, M3, and L from one another is that each successive measure includes less liquid assets; the incremental components of M3 are less liquid than those of M2, and the incremental components of L are in turn less liquid than those of M3. The concept underlying the definitional boundaries of these various measures is that M2 is more nearly "money" than M3, and M3 is closer to being "money" than L. The choice of liquid assets to be included in a given monetary aggregate is, of course, necessarily a matter of judgment and is arbitrary to some degree.

The rationale for developing measures of the monetary aggregates in this fashion is a corollary of the reason for attempting to measure "money" at all. The latter reason stems from the fact that the quantity of money (and particularly changes in the supply of money) has great economic significance. Because of money's economic significance, central governments seek to control the money supply to pursue economic policy objectives; in the United States the Federal Reserve system has this responsibility. Thus the quantity of "money" must be monitored, and the monetary aggregates to be measured and monitored are the ones that are most relevant for such economic policy variables as price level changes, aggregate output, and the level of interest rates. The conventional (although not universally held) view is that changes in the quantity M1, M2, M3, and L have important effects on the levels of prices, output, employment, and interest rates, and that the immediacy of the apparent linkage is in that order.[1] Thus the

---

[1]Until the early 1980s, most economists regarded M1 as the monetary measure most closely associated with economic activity. However, the deregulation of deposit interest rates that began in 1981 resulted in the inclusion of interest-bearing balances in M1. In turn, this appeared to loosen the linkage between changes in M1 and changes in the economy.

EXHIBIT 4.1 ▰
The Money Supply

THE EMINENT M

More than a letter of the alphabet, it is watched continuously by economists, investors and analysts. But this illustrious letter also represents a major function of the Federal Reserve System. For most of us, it represents the thirteenth letter of the alphabet. For those who follow the Fed and monetary policy, however, "M" is also the symbol of the nation's money supply.

Each nation has its own money supply, and in the United States it is the responsibility of the Federal Reserve System to monitor that supply and see to it that its long-run growth is conducive to achieving low unemployment, price stability, and moderate interest rates. Members of the Federal Open Market Committee—the arm of the Federal Reserve with responsibility for setting money supply target ranges—study the level of funds available for use. These funds, together with the number of times funds change hands (velocity), are what help determine prices (the level of inflation) and the expansion of economic activity.

The money supply has been broken down into three Ms, which also are known as monetary aggregates. M1 is the narrowest measure of the money supply. Basically, it is currency and coin in the hands of the public plus accounts that are used primarily for check-writing purposes. M2 is comprised of M1 plus funds in savings accounts and small time deposit accounts, including the new money market deposit accounts (MMDAs) held by financial institutions and money market mutual funds (MMMFs) held by organizations such as Merrill Lynch and Sears Roebuck and Co. M3 is the broadest measure of the money supply. It includes the funds in M1 and M2 and adds other assets such as Eurodollars held by U.S. residents, large time deposits ($100,000 or more), and repurchase agreements.

The Fed considers a number of factors when it defines the monetary aggregates. But what ultimately matters is how the public uses the different forms of money. For example, depositors can write checks on their MMDAs or their MMMFs. However, most people use these types of accounts primarily for savings and only secondarily for transactions. Therefore the Fed has placed these accounts in M2 along with savings and time deposit accounts because they also are used primarily as savings accounts. On the other hand, deposits in NOW, super NOW, and automatic transfer accounts are included in M1 because they are used mainly as transaction accounts even though they pay interest to the holder and depositors also use them for savings.

MONEY SUPPLY COMPONENTS

M1 consists of currency and coin in the hands of the public, traveler's checks, demand deposits (balances in checking accounts), balances in NOW and super NOW accounts, balances in automatic transfer service (ATS) accounts, and balances in credit union share draft accounts.

M2 consists of M1 plus savings and small time deposits (less than $100,000) at financial institutions (including MMDAs), overnight repurchase agreements at commercial banks, certain Eurodollar deposits, and shares in money market mutual funds held primarily by households and small businesses.

M3 consists of M1, M2, and large time deposits ($100,000 or more) at financial institutions, repurchase agreements with maturities longer than one day at commercial banks and savings and loan associations, and shares in money market mutual funds that are held by large financial institutions and corporations.

Source: Federal Bank of Dallas *Roundup* (March 1984).

Fed generally pays more attention to changes in M1 and M2 than to changes in M3 and L.

The importance of these various measures of monetary aggregates is thus due to the great significance of money in the economy. Indeed, the degree of refinement of any particular monetary measurement scheme is a function of how closely changes in the monetary aggregates are related to changes in economic variables. We turn now to a discussion of the role that the quantity of money plays in the performance of the economy.

THE ECONOMIC SIGNIFICANCE OF MONEY

Money's link to prices is inherent in money's role as a medium of exchange and a unit of account. It follows that the quantity of money is closely related to the level of prices, a relationship that has been recognized for centuries. Less apparent but equally real is the impact of the quantity of money on the employment of resources to produce goods and services.

The "circulation" of money in a market economy occurs in two channels. The producers of goods and services make payments to the suppliers of the resources necessary for production. Such payments include wages, salaries, interest, rents, and dividends. Payments for the factors of production thus constitute one channel of money flows in the economy. The other channel is the flow of payments to producers as goods and services are purchased from them. These receipts of producers supply the means of payment for factors of production to produce additional goods and services, and so on. This "circular flow" of money receipts and payments constitutes the aggregate money income stream for an economy.

The Velocity of Money

Money units can be used over and over again in the circular flow of income. The more often money units are used for payments in a given period—the faster money "turns over"—the smaller the required size of the supply of money for a given volume of real income at a fixed price level.[2] This rate of turnover of the money stock is called the income velocity of money, since it amounts to the rate at

---

[2]The distinction between "real" and "nominal" income is important to an understanding of the economic role of money. The concept of real income is the physical quantity of goods and services, independent of its monetary measurement. Nominal income is determined by both the level of real income and the level of prices. For a given level of real income, nominal income is a function of the price level. For example, if the price level doubles when real income is unchanged, nominal incomes will also double.

which money is spent on goods and services within a given time period. **Monetary velocity** is thus a measure of the frequency with which the average dollar is used to effect transactions during a given span of time.

Monetary velocity depends largely on established habits of payments. In our society, for example, workers are likely to be paid weekly, biweekly, or monthly, but not daily or annually. The frequency of wage and salary collection affects the amount of money workers hold from one payday to the next; their average money holdings will decrease as the frequency of their collection of wages and salaries increases, and vice versa. This inverse relationship between average money holdings and the frequency of receipts is true for other household income sources and for business firms' income as well. Thus for a given level of income, the smaller the average money holdings by the various economic units of an economy are, the larger monetary velocity will be, and vice versa.

Conventional patterns of receipts and payments largely determine the amount of average money holdings and thus the velocity of the money stock. Historically, such transaction patterns have changed rather slowly. In the United States, however, the velocity of M1 rose dramatically from the end of World War II to about 1980, rising about 3 percent a year in the past two decades of that era. This increase in M1 velocity was due to a combination of relatively rapidly occurring social, economic, and technological developments that reduced average cash balances in the economy. Higher interest rates produced an incentive for achieving reductions in holdings of noninterest-bearing M1, and technological developments made possible such reductions by allowing more rapid payments and collections. For example, the effects of various procedures employed by business firms in speeding up collections, the use of systems of electronic funds transfer, and the emergence of mass use of credit cards served to greatly reduce the amount of M1 required for a given transactions volume. This upswing in M1 velocity changed to a decline when the nature of M1 changed as the result of the Depository Institutions Deregulation and Monetary Control Act of 1980. From 1981 to 1986, M1 velocity fell 16 percent. Figure 4.1 shows the behavior of M1, M2, M3, and L velocity in recent years.

The postwar behavior of money velocity illustrates that, although slow-to-change conventional patterns of receipts and payments largely determine average cash holdings (and thus the income velocity of money), certain other economic variables also influence the average amount of money balances held by households and business firms. Income and wealth of economic units have an effect: holdings of cash balances tend to increase as income and total wealth increase. Interest rates also affect desired money holdings (and thus money velocity). The higher the rate of interest, the more expensive idle cash balances become, and vice versa. Thus we may expect velocity to increase (average holdings of cash balances to decrease) as interest rates rise and to decline as interest rates fall. The magnitude of the so-called **interest elasticity of the demand for money**

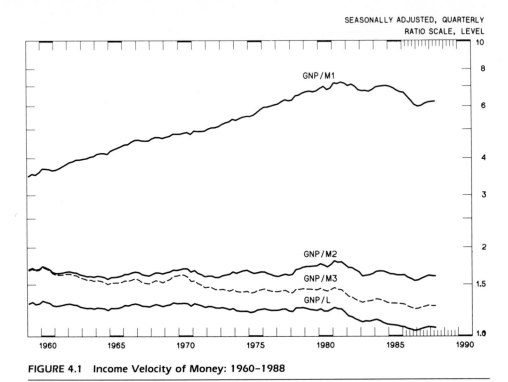

FIGURE 4.1   Income Velocity of Money: 1960–1988

Source: Board of Governors of the Federal Reserve System, Historical Chart Book, *1988.*

(the degree of sensitivity of the desired size of average money holdings to interest rate changes) is an unsettled issue, however.

Another significant factor regarding the amount of money balances people choose to hold is expectations regarding the future course of economic events. If a high rate of inflation is expected, for example, individuals will hold less cash, since the purchasing power of money is eroded by price increases.[3] On the other hand, expectations of declining prices and/or employment tend to result in increased money holdings. Expectations regarding the future course of interest rates may also affect desired cash balances. When interest rates are expected to rise, individuals may wait to lend until higher rates are available and thus hold larger cash balances.

---

[3]An extreme case of this phenomenon occurred in Germany during the "hyperinflation" of the 1920s. It is reported that workers paid one or more times daily would hurry home and distribute the money to all family members with instructions to go out and buy any item they could find available for sale—before prices rose further.

The Equation of Exchange

In a monetary economy it is obvious that all money payments spent for goods and services in a given time period must equal all money receipts of sellers of those goods and services during that time period. This is a useful notion when expressed as "the equation of exchange":

$$MV = PQ.$$

In this version, M is the total money stock, V is the income velocity of money, P is the weighted average price of all goods and services sold, and Q is the physical quantity of those goods and services. MV is thus total money payments to suppliers of goods and services, PQ is the total money receipts of these suppliers, and their equality is apparent.[4]

Though true by definition, the equation of exchange is a useful means of assessing the economic significance of money. It is a springboard for economic theorizing about the relationship of money supply to the price level and real income. For example, in its earliest (and simplest) version the Quantity Theory of Money is an extension of the equation of exchange. The **Quantity Theory of Money,** as originally formulated, holds that the money supply determines the price level; changes in the level of prices (P) are directly proportional to changes in the quantity of money (M). This result follows from the postulation of a constant V and a constant Q by the quantity theorists. We may note that a constant V is plausible only if habits and conventions of payment are the principal determinants of V and are very slow to change or, if other factors affect V, those factors are also constant. A constant Q is plausible if the equilibrating mechanisms of a market economy ensure full employment of all available resources (as the quantity theorists presumed) or if the central government successfully pursues economic policies that result in full resource employment.

The Quantity Theory is only one possible scenario. Another is that changes in the money supply are matched by exact inverse changes in the velocity of money; that is, P and Q are unaffected by changes in M. (This is the extreme "money does not matter" approach.) Also, it could be postulated that changes in M have a corresponding direct effect on Q, with V and P constant except when Q is at its maximum (at full employment of resources).

---

[4]As formulated here, PQ is the total income for an economy for a time period—the gross (or net) national product—and V is **income** velocity of money. An alternative formulation is to consider all exchanges of money (total transactions) rather than only spending on final goods and services. In this case, sales of intermediate goods, used items, and financial assets would also be included. When all spending is thus considered, V is the **transactions** velocity of money and is clearly much larger than income velocity. The equation of exchange was popularized by Irving Fisher, an American economist, in the early years of this century. An alternative version, discussed later in this chapter is called the "Cambridge equation" because of its association with various Cambridge University economics professors, particularly the great British economist Alfred Marshall.

One plausible scenario is that changes in M will generally impact on V, P, and Q, and the magnitude of the relative effects on each will be a function of the present levels of V and Q (which, unlike P, have practical maximums in the short run) as well as of expectations and the present level of interest rates (since rates of interest affect spending and perhaps desired money holdings). For example, an increase in the money supply during a severe economic recession would be likely to impact primarily on Q. With large quantities of unemployed resources, increases in Q resulting from increased M should not generate significant upward pressure on P. On the other hand, increases in M when the economy is enjoying full employment of available resources will almost certainly result in higher P (and perhaps a somewhat lower V).

The "Cambridge Equation"

The economists who formulated the equation of exchange and the Quantity Theory of Money believed that the quantity of money *in the long run* determined only the level of prices. The so-called Cambridge equation, an alternative expression of the equation of exchange, makes this evident. The Cambridge equation amounts to taking the equation of exchange,

$$MV = PQ$$

dividing PQ by V, or

$$M = PQ/V$$

and labeling $1/V$ as k; thus

$$M = kPQ$$

So what? The significance lies in the behavioral connotation of k. It expresses the demand for money (how much money the public wishes to hold) as a fraction of money income. This formula substitutes a behavioral variable (k) for V, which *in appearance* (in reality, V is only $1/k$) is a mechanical one. Since the purpose of money is to make payments, the value of k can be viewed as determined by the pattern of payments in an economy, a pattern that tends to be both highly regularized and slow to change. The demand for money is thus tightly (even totally) linked to the volume of payments or, what is the same thing, the level of money income (PQ). A constant k means that the public persists in holding only the amount of money equal to kPQ. Money supplied in excess of kPQ will quickly be spent on goods and services, driving up the level of prices until the new kPQ equals the money supply, and vice versa. If changes in the money supply were to be perceived as having an impact on Q (output and employment), the case had to be made that Q and k were not economic constants.

Until the Great Depression of the 1930s there was little demand for such a case to be made. The quantity theorists believed in the equilibrating capacity of the "real" marketplace to maintain full employment and maximum output. Until the 1930s the periods of interruption of this condition were either of such short duration or so obviously related to such disturbances as war and famine as to make economists comfortable with the notion. But worldwide economic collapse in the 1930s engendered a demand for some new notions about the economic order. The result was the economic theory called Keynesianism.

The Rise of Keynesian Economics N|A

John Maynard Keynes's 1936 book, *The General Theory of Employment, Interest, and Money,* is generally recognized as having launched the beginning of a new era of economic interventionism by governments and as having provided a rationale for fiscal policy (the deliberate use of government spending and taxing powers to affect economic conditions) as a principal tool of such government "management" of the economy. Keynes rejected the argument of the classical economists that full employment was a natural and "automatic" condition of a market economy and argued that government intervention in the form of fiscal policy and discretionary monetary policy was needed for economic stabilization. Keynes regarded management of the quantity of money to be a potential stimulant for output and employment, as well as a means of controlling the price level.

In Keynes's view, increases in the quantity of money generally result in decreases in the rate of interest, thus encouraging borrowing and investment (and other) spending. In the Great Depression, however, Keynes suggested that interest rates were already so low that an increased money supply would have little or no stimulative effect (the "liquidity trap"). Thus Keynes's original analysis suggested that fiscal policy measures (deficit spending by governments) would be needed for economic recovery in the 1930s.

Keynes's ideas won rapid acceptance among many economists and government policy makers. In their fascination with the now intellectually respectable tool of fiscal policy, many of Keynes's disciples (Keynes died in 1946) neglected monetary policy. As Keynesianism was generally practiced and preached in the 1940s and 1950s, little significance was attached to the money supply. (Keynes himself would have doubtless disapproved.) To a large degree, Keynesianism became synonymous with "fiscalism"—the belief that fiscal policy, not monetary policy, was the most effective way to "manage" the economy.

Monetarism

Emerging as the opponents of fiscalism were the latter-day quantity theorists—"monetarists"—led by Milton Friedman. The monetarists' attack on fiscal policy (and their touting of monetary policy, insofar as the monetarists favored any form of discretionary economic policy) was primarily an empirical effort.

N/A

In a plethora of studies the quantity of money was repeatedly shown to be of considerable economic significance, with fiscal variables showing poorly, if at all.[5] The ascendancy of monetarism in the late 1960s and 1970s was, however, probably due more to the replacement of unemployment by inflation as the principal economic bugaboo than to the labors of the monetarists. The fiscal remedy for inflation is increased taxes and/or reduced government spending (the reverse is true for unemployment)—actions likely to give even the boldest of politicians pause. The monetary remedy, tightening the money supply, is more politically palatable because it is less visible and less understood and can always be blamed on the central bankers.

On the intellectual front the last decade saw a rediscovery of Keynes as a monetary economist and the growing acceptance by Keynesians of monetary policy as an equal partner of fiscal policy. Ironically, some monetarists were having no part of such détente and rapprochement in the realm of economic theory. Instead, the old Quantity Theory notion that money can affect only the level of prices, not output, was resurrected. One limb of this new branch of monetarism is the notion, advanced most notably by Milton Friedman, that employment is a function of the "natural rate of unemployment." This natural rate is the fraction of the labor force that will be jobless even when the real wage rate is in equilibrium. At this level of unemployment the quantity of labor demanded is in line with the quantity of labor supplied, the real wage rate will not decline to permit any expansion of employment, and efforts to trigger such expansion (whether by monetary or fiscal policy) will only result in inflation. Still another offshoot of monetarist theorizing, the so-called "rational expectations" theory, holds that monetary or fiscal policy cannot affect output and employment (but only prices) because such measures are fully anticipated by business and consumers and are fully offset by their anticipatory responses. (These issues are treated further in Chapters 26 and 27.)

How much does money matter for the economy's health and well-being? The foregoing discussion makes the point that there exists no general agreement as to *how* or *to what degree* variations in the rate of growth in the money supply affect output, employment, and prices. We do know that changes in quantity of money are of great economic importance and that the actions of the Federal Reserve System in controlling the money supply do, indeed, matter to a very significant

---

[5]See, for example, Milton Friedman and David Meiselman, "The Relative Stability of Monetary Velocity and the Investment Multiplier in the U.S.," *Stabilization Policies,* The Commission on Money and Credit (Englewood Cliffs, N.J.: Prentice-Hall, 1963); Leonall C. Andersen and Jerry Jordan, "Monetary and Fiscal Actions: A Test of Their Relative Importance in Economic Stabilization," Federal Reserve Bank of St. Louis *Review* (November 1968); Michael W. Keran, "Monetary and Fiscal Influences on Economic Activity—The Historical Evidence," Federal Reserve Bank of St. Louis *Review* (November 1969); and Leonall C. Andersen and Keith M. Carlson, "A Monetarist Model for Economic Stabilization," Federal Reserve Bank of St. Louis *Review* (April 1970), 7–25.

degree for the economy. We turn now to a description of how changes in the quantity of money occur.

start again

MONEY CREATION IN A MODERN ECONOMY

Our description of the money creation process focuses on demand deposit expansion in the commercial banking system. Although it must be recognized that demand deposits are only a portion (albeit the largest portion) of total check-able deposits, that nonbank depository institutions also play a role in monetary expansion and contraction, and that other components of the monetary aggre-gates are also important, our focus is on the most important element of the mone-tary system: commercial bank demand deposits.

It is useful to describe the process of demand deposit expansion by the com-mercial banking system in a "balance sheet" framework. Demand deposits ap-pear on the balance sheets of banks as **liabilities** (debts). Banks accept these de-posits (and thus incur an obligation to the depositor for the amount deposited) to obtain the means of acquiring interest-earning **assets**—loans to individuals and business firms and interest-bearing securities. A restriction of this use of deposits by banks to obtain interest-earning assets is the **reserve requirement** set by the Federal Reserve that limits use of deposits for bank lending and investing purposes to a specified fraction of total deposits. Banks (and all depository insti-tutions) must hold such required reserves as deposits with a Federal Reserve Bank or as vault cash. (Required reserve holdings are assets of depository institutions but earn no interest at the present time.)

The Commercial Bank Balance Sheet

Under the double-entry system of accounting, the financial position of an economic entity is depicted in a "balance sheet." The fundamental balance sheet equation for any business entity (including banks) is

$$\text{Assets} = \text{Liabilities} + \text{Capital}$$

Assets are things of value belonging to the entity for which the balance sheet is prepared. In the case of a bank, assets typically include such items as vault cash, loans (receivables), securities, and the bank's deposits with its Federal Re-serve Bank (to satisfy reserve requirements). **Liabilities** are debts, and the princi-pal obligations of banks are to its depositors. In addition to demand deposits, a bank is likely to have sizable amounts of time and savings deposits among its deposit liabilities. **Capital** is the sum of the owners' funds that have been paid into the entity (contributed capital) plus past earnings that have been retained in the business rather than paid to owners as dividends (retained earnings).

In the double-entry accounting model, asset accounts are increased with debits and decreased with credits. Liability and capital accounts are also increased with credits and decreased with debits. These debit–credit rules, in conjunction with the requirement that all changes in assets, liabilities, and capital be recorded so that debits equal credits, keep the balance sheet "in balance."

A typical condensed balance sheet for a commercial bank in "T-account form" is shown below. Note that deposits with the Federal Reserve consist of "required reserves" and "excess reserves." The amount of required reserves is determined by the amount of deposit liabilities of the bank.

BANK BALANCE SHEET (THOUSANDS OF DOLLARS)

Assets		Liabilities and Capital	
Cash in vault	$1000	Demand deposits	$3500
Deposits at Federal		Time and savings deposits	4500
Reserve Bank:		Other liabilities	500
Required reserves	200	Capital	550
Excess reserves	50	Total	$9050
Loans	5000		
Securities	2000		
Building and equipment	500		
Other assets	300		
Total	$9050		

In reviewing the process of demand-deposit expansion by commercial banks, it is useful to assume the following simplified situation.

1. Only loans, securities, and reserves are considered on the asset side, and only demand deposits on the liabilities side. Effects of currency in circulation, time deposits, and so on, are ignored.

2. The legal reserve requirement for demand deposits is assumed to be 20 percent. All bank reserves, including those necessary to meet the legal reserve requirement (required reserves) and any excess reserves, are held with a Federal Reserve Bank. (In practice a bank's vault cash is part of its legal reserves.)

3. The banking system initially has zero excess reserves.

Deposit Expansion for a Single Bank

The initial question is what amount of deposits can be created by an individual bank on a given reserve base. Suppose the Federal Reserve purchases $1000 of securities from Bank A (at a later point we will examine the motivation for such a purchase). The Fed pays for securities by crediting Bank A's account with a Federal Reserve Bank. To simplify the analysis, our discussion is in terms of *changes* in balance sheet items. The effect on Bank A's balance sheet is:

BANK A

Changes in:	$	
Securities	− 1000	
Excess reserves	+ 1000	

How much can Bank A lend, and how much money can Bank A create in the process of lending? Of course, the limiting constraint is the amount of reserves. Bank A may, if it wishes as management policy, maintain excess reserves (though at the cost of lost income on the potential investment of those noninterest-earning reserves), but it cannot maintain deficit reserves; that is, excess reserves may be positive but they may not be negative. Deficient reserves lead to the assessment by the Fed of a penalty on the bank or more severe action if the deficiency continues.

In making its decision on how much to lend, Bank A is faced with the knowledge that it is one among many (actually around 15,000) commercial banks in the country. As such, when it makes a loan and creates a demand deposit and when borrowers spend the proceeds of the loan (as they are likely to do, since few individuals borrow simply to increase the amount in their checking account), it is probable that the check written by the borrower will be deposited at another bank and that the other bank will demand payment from Bank A. This is known as an **adverse clearing balance;** that is, when the checks written against banks are presented for payment (are cleared), there is a net drain of funds from Bank A.

Given the potential of an adverse clearing balance, how much do you think Bank A can lend? Take a few examples. Suppose Bank A makes a loan of $500, exactly 50 percent of its excess reserves. The initial impact on the balance sheet of Bank A will be:

BANK A

Changes in:	$	Changes in:	$
Loans	+ 500	Demand deposits	+ 500
Excess reserves	− 100		
Required reserves	+ 100		

The loan shows up as an asset on the balance sheet of Bank A and also as a liability—a demand deposit—since the bank simply credits the demand deposit account of the borrower. At this point, Bank A has no reserve requirement problem. Its excess reserves have been reduced from $1000 to $900 (because $500 in demand deposits increases required reserves by $500 × 0.2, or $100) but remain positive. Now further suppose (as seems likely) that the borrower writes a check against the demand deposit and the check is deposited at another bank (any bank). When the check clears, Bank A will lose $500 in deposits and reserves. Thus the changes in the balance sheet of Bank A would be:

BANK A

Changes in:	$	Changes in:	$
Excess reserves	− 400	Demand deposits	− 500
Required reserves	− 100		

In this instance the bank still has no cause for concern; its excess reserves remain large ($500), though down from the $1000 that resulted from the purchase of securities by the Fed. More generally, an individual bank can safely extend new loans as long as it holds excess reserves without fearing a reserve deficiency due to an adverse clearing balance.

Suppose that Bank A, with its $1000 of excess reserves, lends $1200. In that case the net changes in the balance sheet after the loan is made and the proceeds are spent (a check is written against the demand deposit created by the loan and is deposited at another bank) would be:

BANK A

Changes in:	$	Changes in:	$
Loans	+ 1200	Demand deposits	+ 1200
Excess reserves	− 1200		− 1200

In this case, Bank A management has a problem, since reserves with the Federal Reserve are below required levels. Excess reserves are − $200 (the $1000 created by the initial Fed purchase and the − $1200 resulting from the adverse clearing balance). More generally, an individual bank cannot safely lend any amount above the volume of its excess reserves without fearing a reserve deficiency due to an adverse clearing bank balance.

As a final illustration, suppose that Bank A lends exactly the amount of its excess reserves. In that case, changes in the balance sheet of Bank A after the clearing process is complete would be as follows:

BANK A

Changes in:	$	Changes in:	$
Loans	+ 1000	Demand deposits	+ 1000
Excess reserves	− 1000		− 1000

In this case, Bank A ends up with neither excess nor deficient reserves. The purchase of securities by the Fed from Bank A created $1000 of excess reserves. Those $1000 of excess reserves were fully used up by Bank A as it sought to profit from a lending opportunity. Lending in excess of $1000 would result in a reserve deficiency. This leads to an important generalization: *An individual bank cannot safely make loans in excess of its excess reserves.* It is this generalization that is the basis for the statement often attributed to bank managers: "We don't create money, we just lend out the money left with us." From the perspective of the individual bank in a banking system made up of many banks this statement has considerable validity. However, as we next demonstrate, banks taken as a *group* can create loans and deposits equal to a multiple of any given amount of excess reserves. What is generally true for an individual bank is not true of the banking system.

Deposit Expansion: The Banking System

Again we begin with Bank A and consider for this bank and other banks in this example only changes in its balance sheet—not total amounts. Suppose once again that the Fed purchases $1000 of securities from Bank A. The Fed pays for the securities by crediting Bank A's account with a Federal Reserve Bank. The effect on Bank A's balance sheet is:

BANK A

Changes in:	$	
Securities	−1000	
Excess reserves	+1000	

Bank A now has on deposit with the Federal Reserve $1000 of excess reserves that can be used to acquire interest-earning assets.[6] Unless Bank A uses some or all of these new excess reserves for this purpose, there will be no change in the money supply (demand deposits) as a result of this purchase of securities by the Federal Reserve. Banks do not generally hold significant amounts of excess reserves, however, so we may assume that Bank A uses its new reserves of $1000 by lending that amount to a customer, Mr. One. It accomplishes this by increasing Mr. One's account by $1000 and recording a new asset (a loan) on its books:

BANK A

Changes in:	$	Changes in:	$
Loans	+1000	Demand deposits	+1000
Excess reserves	− 200		
Required reserves	+ 200		

---

[6]Suppose that the Fed had purchased the securities from a nonbank dealer. What would the effect be in this case? The answer is that the bank at which the dealer firm held its account would receive both a new deposit (in the amount of the Fed's purchase) and new reserves, but a portion of the new reserves would be required reserves rather than excess reserves. In this particular example a purchase of $1000 of securities by the Fed from a nonbank dealer would supply the dealer's bank with a new $1000 deposit, $800 of excess reserves, and $200 of required reserves. Unlike the case of a sale of securities by a bank to the Fed, the bank does not reduce its assets in exchange for the new reserves.

When Bank A creates the demand deposit of $1000 by using its excess reserves in that amount, the money supply increases by $1000. For the bank its excess reserves shrink (and its required reserves expand) by 0.20 ($1000) = $200. Immediately after the loan is made, Bank A has $800 of excess reserves ($1000 − $200).

Now assume that Mr. One writes a check on his account at Bank A in favor of Ms. Two. Further assume that Ms. Two deposits the check in her account at Bank B. After the check is cleared, the changes in the balance sheets of Banks A and B would appear as follows:

BANK A

Changes in:	$	Changes in:	$
Excess reserves	− 800	Demand deposits	− 1000
Required reserves	− 200		

BANK B

Changes in:	$	Changes in:	$
Excess reserves	+ 800	Demand deposits	+ 1000
Required reserves	+ 200		

At this point, Bank A has no more excess reserves, whereas Bank B has $800 of excess reserves.[7] Bank B can now make new loans in the amount of its excess reserves. We may therefore assume that it lends $800 to Mr. Three, another of its customers. As before, the balance sheet effect of the loan is:

BANK B

Changes in:	$	Changes in:	$
Loans	+ 800	Demand deposits	+ 800
Excess reserves	− 160		
Required reserves	+ 160		

Mr. Three subsequently writes a check to Mrs. Four, who banks at Bank C and deposits the check there. Bank C thus acquires excess reserves of $640, which is (1.00 − 0.20)$800, and Bank B loses reserves in that amount:

BANK B

Changes in:	$	Changes in:	$
Excess reserves	− 640	Demand deposits	− 800
Required reserves	− 160		

---

[7]The Federal Reserve Bank, as part of the check-clearing process, will reduce Bank A's total reserves by $1000 and increase Bank B's total reserves by $1000.

BANK C

Changes in:	$	Changes in:	$
Excess reserves	+640	Demand deposits	+800
Required reserves	+160		

Bank C will now be in a position to lend $640, the amount of its excess reserves. Such lending will result in new excess reserves of $(1 - 0.20)\$640$, or $512, being supplied to Bank D, which it can then lend. This process will continue, the amount of excess reserves being transferred from bank to bank diminishing by 20 percent (the reserve requirement ratio) each time; at each step in the lending progression, 20 percent of excess reserves are "used up" by becoming required reserves. Each individual bank lends (and thus creates new demand deposits) in the amount of the excess reserves it receives, which is 80 percent of the amount of new demand deposits created by the preceding bank in the series. Table 4.2 summarizes this process of new lending and demand deposit expansion.

In mathematical language the simplified demand deposit expansion process as described constitutes an example of an infinite geometric series, which is a sequence of amounts such that each amount after the first can be determined by multiplying the preceding amount in the series by a fixed number called the common ratio. The sum of an infinite geometric series is determined by the formula:

$$\frac{1}{(1 - \text{The common ratio})} \times \text{The first amount in the series}$$

In our demand deposit expansion case the "common ratio" is 80 percent, and the "first amount in the series" is the initial increase in excess reserves of $1000. Thus the formula for the sum of new demand deposits created in this simplified case is

$$\frac{1}{\text{Reserve requirement ratio}} \times \frac{\text{Excess}}{\text{reserves}} = \begin{array}{l}\text{Maximum amount}\\\text{of new demand}\\\text{deposits created}\end{array}$$

or

$$\frac{1}{0.20} \times \$1000 = \$5000$$

Thus while each individual bank lends (creates demand deposits) only in the amount of its excess reserves, all the banks taken together have created demand deposits in an amount that is a multiple of the original increase in excess reserves of $1000. If the new demand deposits are summed, we add $1000, $800, $640, $512, and so on, and approach a sum at the limit of the process of $5000. Matching this increase in demand deposits of $5000 is an increase in required reserves

TABLE 4.2 Summary of Demand Deposit Expansion Illustration

Bank	Receives Excess Reserves in the Amount of:	Lends (Creates Demand Deposits) in the Amount of:	Retains New Demand Deposits in the Amount of:	Required Reserves Increase in the Amount of:
A	$1000.00	$1000.00	$ 0.00	$ 0.00
B	800.00	800.00	1000.00	200.00
C	640.00	640.00	800.00	160.00
D	512.00	512.00	640.00	128.00
E	409.60	409.60	512.00	102.40
F	327.68	327.68	409.60	81.92
G	262.14	262.14	327.68	65.54
H	209.72	209.72	262.14	52.43
I	167.77	167.77	209.72	41.94
J	134.22	134.22	167.77	33.55
K	107.37	107.37	134.22	26.84
L	85.90	85.90	107.37	21.47
Other banks	68.72	343.60	429.50	85.90
Total	$1000.00	$5000.00	$5000.00	$1000.00

of $1000—all the original injection of excess reserves has become required reserves.

In our simplified example the "deposit expansion multiplier" (or **monetary multiplier**) for this multiple expansion of deposits is the reciprocal of the reserve requirement ratio, that is, of $1.0/0.20 = 5$, in the above example. Stated as an equation,

$$\Delta D = \Delta R / r_d$$

where ΔD is the total potential change in demand deposits resulting from an injection of new (excess) reserves, ΔR is the dollar amount of such an injection, and r_d is the reserve requirement for demand deposits.

Note that ΔD is described as the *potential* change in demand deposits. Actually, the expansion in demand deposits is likely to be considerably less because of factors not considered in the above case but discussed later in this chapter. (In practice the deposit expansion multiplier is much smaller than $\Delta R / r_d$.) We should also note that banking *assets* expand by the amount of the increase in demand deposits.

Deposit Contraction

It is important also to note that the process works in reverse; a withdrawal of reserves from the banking system (in this simple case) would force a contraction in the amount of demand deposits potentially equal to $\Delta R / r_d$. Indeed, the ability of the Fed to contract the amount of demand deposits is much stronger than its ability to expand the volume of demand deposits. Banks are not permitted to have reserve deficiencies, while they may choose to hold excess reserves. In the contraction case, assuming that the banking system has no excess reserves, sales of securities by the Fed force a contraction of demand deposits, regardless of the desires and behavior of the commercial banking system. In the expansion case the Fed provides excess reserves, but no new demand deposits are created unless commercial banks use those reserves to make loans and to purchase securities. Under most circumstances it is a reasonable assumption that banks will prefer earning assets like loans and securities to nonearning assets like excess reserves. However, under some conditions, such as a period of great uncertainty or financial turmoil, banks may prefer the safety of excess reserves.

Exactly how does the Fed force a contraction in demand deposits? Suppose that the Fed sold (rather than purchased) $1000 in securities to Bank A at a time when Bank A had no excess reserves.[8] In this situation the balance sheet of Bank A would change as follows:

BANK A

Change in:	$	
Securities	+1000	
Excess reserves	−1000	

Assuming that Bank A did not have excess reserves, this transaction creates a reserve deficiency, which the bank must find some way to cover. One way would be to reduce its loans through, for example, refusing to renew maturing loans. But in this case, loans would have to fall not by $1000 but rather by $5000 to increase excess reserves by $1000. This reduction in loans reduces demand deposits by an equal amount, which thereby reduces required reserves by 20 percent (the reserve requirement ratio) of the change in deposits. In this case, Bank A's balance sheet would change as follows:

BANK A

Change in:	$	Change in:	$
Required reserves	−1000	Demand deposits	−5000
Excess reserves	+1000		
Loans	−5000		

[8]One might wonder why Bank A would purchase securities at a time when such a purchase would create a deficiency in its reserve position with the Fed. In practice, it is unlikely that a bank would do this. However, the Fed can and does sell securities to *customers* of banks. These buyers of securities from the Fed pay for their purchase with checks drawn on their banks. When the Fed collects the checks, it reduces the reserves of the buyers' banks. Thus the effect on bank reserves is the same as in the example; the difference is that Bank A would have reduced deposits as well as reduced reserves (and, of course, it would not have a reduction in its holdings of securities).

Although this strategy is possible, such behavior is likely to harm the long-run profitability of the bank by driving away customers. A more likely occurrence is that Bank A would sell the securities to another investor, perhaps to another commercial bank. In that case, Bank A's balance sheet would change as follows:

BANK A

Change in:	$
Securities	− 1000
Excess reserves	+ 1000

Suppose that the securities were sold to a customer of Bank B and that the customer paid for the securities by writing a check on Bank B. After the check was cleared, the balance sheet of Bank B would change as follows:

BANK B

Change in:	$	Change in:	$
Excess reserves	− 800	Demand deposits	− 1000
Required reserves	− 200		

This transaction eliminates the reserve deficiency at Bank A, but only by creating a reserve deficiency for Bank B. Bank B must now eliminate its reserve deficiency, and it faces the same alternatives as Bank A: Either reduce its loans and thereby its deposits by a multiple of the reserve deficiency, or sell securities, in which case its reserve deficiency will again be eliminated, but only at the expense of creating a reserve deficiency at another bank. In any case the ultimate outcome in this simplified case will be the same: Demand deposits must decline by an amount equal to $\Delta R/r_d$. (As in the expansion case, *actual* contraction will be less than $\Delta R/r_d$.) Assets of the banking system will decline by the amount of the decrease in demand deposits. In the present example of a $1000 sale of securities by the Fed to a bank the effect on all banks (the entire banking system) can be depicted as follows:

ALL BANKS (THE BANKING SYSTEM)

Change in:	$	Change in:	$
Securities	+ 1000	Demand deposits	− 5000
Loans	− 5000		
Required reserves	− 1000		

The Fed can thus force a contraction of bank reserves and demand deposits by selling securities. Compared to the simplified example above, the money contraction multiplier will be lower than the reciprocal of the reserve requirement (and sales will be to securities dealers), but the Fed can reduce the money supply just as the example illustrates.

Primary and Derivative Deposits

As discussed above, the elements of money creation and contraction are simple. When a bank obtains new excess reserves, it can make loans (or buy securities) simply by increasing the borrower's (or seller's) demand deposit. As these funds are spent, they become excess reserves for other banks, and the process is repeated. While simple, the process involves an apparent paradox—banks create deposits in the act of lending, but they can lend only if they have deposits in sufficient amounts. Reconciling this paradox is best accomplished by identifying two different types of deposits: primary and derivative.

Primary deposits supply reserves to banks and thus make new lending possible. They generally arise from customer deposits of currency or checks drawn on other banks. As excess reserves resulting from primary deposits are used to make loans, **derivative deposits** are created. For instance, in the example in the preceding section, Bank B received a primary deposit of $1000 (a check drawn on Bank A) and subsequently created a derivative deposit of $800, which in turn became a primary deposit for Bank C. Derivative deposits, both in existence and in magnitude, are a function of primary deposits. (In our deposit expansion illustration we assumed that banks retained all primary deposits but lost all derivative deposits to other banks; what is a derivative deposit for one bank becomes a primary deposit for the next bank in the deposit expansion process.) Thus demand deposit expansion is essentially the cumulative result of a chain of derivative deposits.

SOURCES OF CHANGE IN BANK RESERVES

While the reserves of an individual bank are increased by receipt of a primary deposit, the banking system as a whole can gain reserves only from some nonbank source. Similarly, the banking system as a whole can lose reserves only when they are withdrawn by a nonbank agent (although an individual bank loses reserves as deposits are transferred to another bank). There are three possible sources of change in the quantity of reserves held by the banking system: the public, the U.S. Treasury, and the Federal Reserve System.

Actions of the public that have a potential impact on bank reserves stem from changes in public preference regarding the composition of their liquid financial asset holdings—specifically, the desired mix of currency holdings, time and savings deposits, and demand deposits. (The public does not *seek* to alter the quantity of bank reserves.) The Treasury can affect the quantity of bank reserves primarily by altering the proportion of its cash balances held with depository institutions and with the Fed, but in practice the Treasury seeks to minimize such disturbances of the monetary system. It is only the Federal Reserve that actively and consciously seeks to control the quantity of bank reserves (and thus the money supply), and the Fed has by far the greatest discretionary powers to pursue such control. For this reason we separately consider the Fed's impact on the quantity of bank reserves after reviewing the potential effects of actions of the public and the Treasury. (The latter actions are only *potential*, since the Fed can, and often does, offset them.)

The Public

The public's demand for currency may change. If the public increases its holdings of currency by reducing demand deposit holdings, reserves of the banking system will decline. Since bank reserves support a multiple of demand deposits, this occurrence (if not offset by other changes in reserves) would reduce the money supply. The reverse holds for decreases in the amount of currency in circulation. If more currency is deposited in banks by the public, the banking system gains reserves, thus making possible an expansion of demand deposits. Currency holdings by the public are quite seasonal, increasing sharply, for example, shortly before holiday periods and diminishing sharply after holiday periods.

Changes in the public's desired holdings of other types of assets can also affect the quantity of **excess reserves** held by the banking system, even when **total reserves** do not change. This is true essentially because reserve requirements for time and savings deposits differ from reserve requirements for demand deposits. Since reserve requirements for time and savings deposits are lower than those for demand deposits, increased holdings of the former relative to the latter increase excess reserves. On the other hand, a shift in the public's portfolio preference toward demand deposits (or toward financial assets that are exchanged for demand deposits) and out of time and savings deposits with commercial banks will result in a reduction of excess reserves (an increase in required reserves) in the banking system (since reserve requirements for demand deposits are higher than for time deposits).

The Treasury

Though its primary role is to serve as the payments and collection agent for the federal government, the U.S. Treasury also has a part in the monetary system. In the past the Treasury was a significant issuer of paper currency (particularly so-called "silver certificates"), but at the present time its currency production is limited to coins. The Federal Reserve "buys" coins from the Treasury by crediting (increasing) the Treasury's account with the Federal Reserve Bank and then provides coins to depository financial institutions on request, reducing the institutions' reserve deposit account in the amount of coin provided. The effect on the balance sheet of the Federal Reserve is:

FEDERAL RESERVE BANKS

Changes in:	$	Changes in:	$
Treasury currency	+5000	Treasury deposits	+5000
Treasury currency	−5000	Deposits of financial institutions	−5000

As with paper currency (Federal Reserve notes), banks will return any undesired number of coins to the Federal Reserve for deposit credit.

Even though Treasury transactions in gold have been rare in recent years, we may note the effects of a gold purchase. When the Treasury purchases gold, it writes a check drawn on its account with the Federal Reserve. When the check is deposited with a commercial bank, the reserves of the banking system increase. The Treasury is then likely to replenish its account with the Federal Reserve by issuing a gold certificate to the Federal Reserve in exchange for deposit credit. The net effect on the balance sheet of the Federal Reserve of a $10,000 gold purchase (and gold certificate issue) by the Treasury is:

FEDERAL RESERVE BANK

Changes in:	$	Changes in:	$
Gold certificates	+10,000	Treasury deposits	−10,000
		Treasury deposits	+10,000
		Deposits of financial institutions	+10,000

This sequence of events results in an increase in the quantity of commercial bank reserves (unless offset by an open market sale of securities by the Federal Reserve or some other action that decreases reserves). However, a gold purchase by the Treasury need not affect bank reserves. If the Treasury does not issue a gold certificate to replenish its account for the amount of a gold purchase, but instead sells securities in that amount, the gold is "sterilized," and there is no monetary effect.

The Federal Reserve serves as the principal bank of the U.S. Treasury, and Treasury deposits are a major component of Federal Reserve liabilities. The Treasury also maintains accounts, called **tax and loan accounts,** in thousands of commercial banks across the country. These accounts are "collection points" for payments of federal taxes by individuals and business firms. Further, the accounts are often the source of funds for purchases of Treasury securities by banks for themselves or for their customers (thus the word "loan" as part of the name). Tax and loan (T & L) accounts are periodically transferred to the Treasury's balance with the Federal Reserve for purposes of federal disbursements. While the transfer of the funds from T & L accounts to the Federal Reserve account drains reserves from the banking system, their subsequent disbursement by the Treasury restores the reserves (as recipients of government payments deposit the funds in their banks). Nonetheless, time lags between such transfers, collections in the T & L accounts, and Treasury expenditures frequently impact sharply on individual bank reserves and can create a degree of disturbance for the banking system as a whole.[9]

The influence of Treasury tax and loan accounts on bank reserves may be illustrated with the following T accounts. In step 1 a check written by the public (to pay taxes, for example) is deposited to the account of the Treasury at a commercial bank. This has no impact on bank reserves. In step 2 the Treasury transfers these funds to the Federal Reserve. This transaction reduces bank reserves. In contrast, if the Treasury were to transfer funds from its account at the Fed to its tax loan accounts at commercial banks, this transaction would increase bank reserves (step 3).

FEDERAL RESERVE		COMMERCIAL BANKS	
Changes in: (1)	Changes in:	Changes in:	Changes in: Deposits of public — Deposits of Treasury +

FEDERAL RESERVE		COMMERCIAL BANKS	
(2)	Deposits of financial institutions (reserves) — Deposits of Treasury +	Deposits at Fed (reserves) —	Deposits of Treasury —

---

[9]The purpose of tax and loan accounts is to minimize fluctuations in bank reserves from Treasury receipts and payments. By keeping receipts in the general location of their collection (in T & L accounts) until needed for Treasury disbursement the Treasury avoids draining reserves from banks every time tax payments are made. See Chapter 26 for additional discussion of T & L accounts.

FEDERAL RESERVE		COMMERCIAL BANKS	
(3)	Deposits of financial institutions (reserves) + Deposits of Treasury −	Deposits at Fed (reserves) +	Deposits of Treasury +

THE FED AND THE MONEY SUPPLY

The Federal Reserve System exercises by far the greatest influence on the quantity of bank reserves and thus the supply of money. The Fed has responsibility for monetary policy generally, a role of enormous economic significance. Chapter 5 describes the Fed's role and organization, and Chapter 26 explores the nature and significance of monetary policy (and the Fed's role in formulating and implementing it) in some detail. At this point we limit our discussion to the mechanics of the Fed's operations as they affect the quantity of bank reserves.

Tools of Monetary Control

The Fed can increase or decrease the amount of bank reserves directly by means of its **open market operations** (buying and selling securities in the open market) and **discount window lending** to banks. The Fed (within statutory limits) can also change the proportion of total reserves required by **changing the reserve requirement ratio**. The latter action will not change the amount of total reserves but will change the amount of credit that the banking system can extend and thus the amount of deposits that can be created by a given amount of reserves.

The effect of the Fed's open market operations on the quantity of bank reserves is straightforward. As indicated in the foregoing examples of deposit expansion and contraction, a purchase of securities by the Fed creates new bank reserves, and a sale of securities by the Fed reduces bank reserves. The Fed can (and does) offset any undesired change in reserves with an appropriate open market transaction. The Fed can (and does) initiate credit and monetary expansion by an active program of (net) open market securities purchases. The Fed can (and does) restrict credit and monetary expansion by pursuing a policy of (net) open market sales of securities. Open market operations, which impact on lending volume and monetary expansion as previously illustrated, are by far the Fed's most important instrument of monetary control.

Much less important as a tool of monetary policy, but nonetheless affecting the quantity of bank reserves, is Fed lending to banks. This aspect of Fed operations is described in detail in Chapter 26. We need note here only that total bank reserves will include at any time the amount of reserves borrowed from the Fed (generally less than 2 percent of total reserves). The Fed manages (and limits) such lending quite carefully. If, however, the volume of such lending were to rise to undesired levels (perhaps to forestall a widespread "liquidity crisis"), the Fed could offset the undesired expansion in total reserves with open market security sales.

Changes in reserve requirements change the proportions of total reserves that are "required" and "excess." A reduction in reserve requirements increases the amount of excess reserves, thus allowing the banking system to expand credit and deposits. Such a reduction also increases the amount of deposits (and credit) that can be created from a given amount of reserves—a decrease in the reserve requirement ratio increases the deposit expansion (monetary) multiplier. Conversely, an increase in the reverse requirement ratio will increase the proportion of total reserves required. The banking system must respond by reducing total deposits unless existing excess reserves are sufficient to meet the increase in required reserves (which is unlikely). Further, an increase in the reserve requirement ratio reduces the deposit expansion (monetary) multiplier. In sum, reserve requirement *increases* will *reduce* the amount of deposits (money), and reserve requirement *decreases* will *increase* the amount of deposits (money).

Other Monetary Activities of the Fed

In addition to its discretionary use of open market operations, bank lending, and setting of reserve requirements to control the supply of money and credit, the Fed also performs other activities that affect the composition and size of the money stock. To describe these activities (and review previously described Fed operations), it is useful again to take a "balance sheet approach."

The following condensed balance sheet for the Federal Reserve Banks shows the major categories of the Fed's assets and liabilities:

FEDERAL RESERVE BANKS
(Amounts in Billions of Dollars as of February 22, 1989)

Assets		Liabilities	
Cash	$ 0.5	Federal Reserve notes	$223.0
Gold certificates	11.1	Deposits of financial institu-	
Loans to depository financial		tions (reserves)	33.4
institutions	2.0	U.S. Treasury deposits	6.3
Cash items in process of		Foreign deposits	0.3
collection	11.1	Deferred-availability cash items	8.9
U.S. government securities	224.7	Capital	4.6

Cash is mostly coins issued by the Treasury and held by the Federal Reserve. Monetary gold holdings of the federal government are the responsibility of the U.S. Treasury, but the Federal Reserve has ownership claims on the gold stock via **gold certificates.** The dollar amount relating to these gold certificates is quite large, but their significance for the money supply is minor.

Cash items in process of collection (shown as an asset) and **deferred-availability cash items** (shown as a liability) relate to **float,** which is the monetary effect of time lags in the clearing of checks. For example, suppose that a check drawn on Bank X is deposited with Bank Y, and Bank Y sends the check to a Federal Reserve Bank for clearing. On receipt of the check the Federal Reserve Bank debits (increases) "cash items in process of collection" and credits (increases) "deferred-availability cash items." The check proceeds will be credited to Bank Y's account within two days, at which point the "deferred-availability cash items" account is debited (reduced) for that amount. The corresponding "cash items in process of collection" account is not credited (reduced), however, until Bank X receives the check for payment. During this time lag, both Bank X and Bank Y have the check amount in their deposit account with the Federal Reserve. In terms of the balance sheet, reserves (**deposits of financial institutions**) will always be greater by the amount that the balance of "cash items in process of collection" exceeds the balance of "deferred-availability cash items," which is Federal Reserve float. Federal Reserve float thus constitutes a net source of reserves for member banks. In the past its magnitude for any time period was a function of how efficiently the transportation and communication systems normally used to clear checks functioned during that time. However, since passage of the Depository Institutions Deregulation and Monetary Control Act of 1980, the Federal Reserve has attempted to reduce sharply the amount of float, primarily by reducing the time needed to clear checks.

The creation of float is shown by the following example:

FEDERAL RESERVE

Changes in:		Changes in:	
(1) Cash items in process of collection	+	Deferred-availability cash items	+
(2)		Reserves of Bank Y	+
		Deferred-availability cash items	−

FEDERAL RESERVE

(3) Cash items in process of collection	–	Reserves of Bank X	–

The initial check deposit by Bank Y produces an increase in "cash items in process of collection" and "deferred-availability cash items" (step 1). Following a set schedule (which is usually in advance of the collection of the check), the Federal Reserve increases the reserves of Bank Y (as shown in step 2) without reducing the reserves of Bank X. This creates a difference between "cash items in the process of collection" and "deferred availability cash items"—float. Of course, when the check is cleared (step 3), the float is eliminated.

When banks borrow from the Fed, they create an asset for the Fed called **loans to depository financial institutions.** However, the so-called federal funds market (in which banks lend reserves to other banks) has supplanted the direct lending function of the Federal Reserve to a large degree, so that borrowing from the Federal Reserve is not a significant source of reserves in its aggregate amount.

The **U.S. government securities** held by the Federal Reserve are an asset item of special importance. These security holdings make possible the "open-market operations" of the Federal Reserve: the buying and selling of government securities in the marketplace. As was previously noted, such purchases and sales of securities by the Federal Reserve impact directly on reserves. When, for example, the Federal Reserve *buys* securities, it pays with a check drawn on itself, which is credited to the reserves of the seller's bank when that institution sends it to the Federal Reserve Bank. The effect on the Federal Reserve's balance sheet of a $1000 purchase of securities is:

FEDERAL RESERVE BANKS

Changes in:	$	Changes in:	$
U.S. government securities	+1000	Deposits of financial institutions (reserves)	+1000

If the Fed were to purchase securities from a bank, the increase in excess reserves would be equal to the amount of the purchase. When (as in the example above) the Fed buys securities from, say, a government securities dealer who deposits the Fed's payment in a bank, the amount of the increase in excess reserves is reduced by the amount of the reserve requirement for the new deposit. Thus a $1000 purchase by the Fed from a nonbank dealer results in an increase in excess reserves of $(1 - \text{Reserve requirement ratio}) \times \$1000$, since a $1000 deposit is created in favor of the seller of the securities.

When the Fed *sells* securities, bank reserves are decreased. A sale of securities to a bank would reduce bank reserves by the amount of the sale. The sale of securities by the Fed to a nonbank dealer reduces both bank deposits and bank reserves. When the seller's check is paid to the Fed, member bank deposits at the Fed are reduced:

FEDERAL RESERVE BANKS

Changes in:	$	Changes in:	$
U.S. government securities	−1000	Deposits of financial institutions (reserves)	−1000

Again, the change in the amount of excess reserves depends on the reserve requirement ratio and whether the purchaser of the securities is a bank or a nonbank party. Open market operations are the principal tool of the Federal Reserve in pursuing its monetary policy objectives. The Fed buys securities to increase reserves of the banking system and sells securities to reduce reserves.

While the U.S. Treasury continues to produce the coin component of currency in circulation, the Federal Reserve is now the sole issuer of all new paper currency. **Federal Reserve notes** account for most (and all new) currency.[10] The Federal Reserve supplies Federal Reserve notes to banks on demand and reduces the banks' deposits at Federal Reserve Banks by the amount of currency sent. For example, a $100,000 transfer would have this effect:

FEDERAL RESERVE BANK

		Changes in:	$
		Federal Reserve notes	+100,000
		Deposits of financial institutions (reserves)	−100,000

As long as the currency provided to the banks remains in the bank vaults, it remains part of bank reserves. As discussed previously, an increase in the amount of currency in circulation *outside* banks will reduce bank reserves.

When banks find themselves holding excessive amounts of currency, they return the undesired amount to the Federal Reserve for deposit credit, an action that, in itself, does not affect total reserves. If the amount of currency in circulation outside banks decreases, however, the reserves of the banking system are increased as currency flows into deposit accounts.

---

[10]New coins are minted at the Treasury's Bureau of the Mint facilities in Philadelphia, Denver, and San Francisco. Federal Reserve notes are printed for the Federal Reserve by the Treasury's Bureau of Printing and Engraving in Washington, D.C.

THE MONETARY BASE
AND THE MONETARY MULTIPLIER

The total amount of depository institution reserves plus currency in circulation (not held in banks or government vaults) is called the **monetary base.** Because of the deposit expansion process, the total money supply is a multiple of the monetary base. Changes in the amount of the monetary base will result in changes in the money supply. The monetary base is, in a sense, the foundation on which the money supply is built.

Figure 4.2 shows the amount of the adjusted monetary base (adjusted for changes in reserve requirements) as well as its growth rate during 1988 and early 1989. The growth of the monetary base is extremely important. Increases in the growth rate of the base lead (though sometimes with a lag) to increases in the

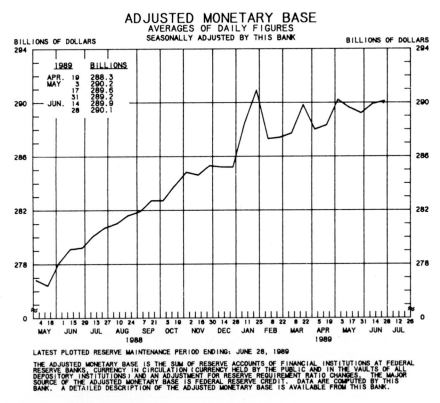

**FIGURE 4.2   Adjusted Monetary Base
(Averages of Daily Figures Seasonally Adjusted by This Bank)**

Source: Federal Reserve Bank of St. Louis, U.S. Financial Data *(May 11, 1989).*

growth rate of the money supply. In contrast, decreases in the growth rate of the monetary base lead (though again sometimes with a lag) to decreases in the growth rate of the money supply. The monetary base and the money supply are linked together by the monetary multiplier.

The Monetary Multiplier

The simple **deposit expansion multiplier,** $1/r_d$, the reciprocal of the reserve requirement ratio, does not hold in practice. Rather, the actual magnitude of the **monetary multiplier** (ΔMoney/ΔReserves) is much less as a result of the various "leakages" in the deposit expansion process. The principal leakages are changes in the amount of currency in circulation and the conversion of new demand deposits into nontransactions accounts (noncheckable time and savings deposits). Further, it is useful to view the money expansion process in terms of the monetary base—reserves of depository institutions plus currency in circulation— rather than in terms of reserves alone. Both reserves and currency in the hands of the public (by virtue of its redeposit capability) have the potential to generate multiple expansion of deposits.

To develop a more realistic formula for the monetary multiplier, we may add the following symbols to those previously employed (r_d = reserve requirement for demand deposits, R = reserves, and D = demand deposits):

$$C = \text{Currency in circulation}$$
$$c = \text{Ratio of currency to demand deposits} = C/D$$
$$B = \text{Monetary base } (R + C)$$

The "currency drain" is easily incorporated into the deposit multiplier formula. Recall that

$$\Delta D = \Delta R / r_d$$

We can then substitute $B - C$ for R in the equation (since $B = R + C, B - C = R$), or

$$\Delta D = \Delta(B - C)/r_d$$

Since $C = cD$, we can restate the equation as

$$\Delta D = \frac{\Delta B - c\Delta D}{r_d}$$

and then, performing some algebraic manipulation,

$$r_d\Delta D = \Delta B - c\Delta D$$
$$r_d\Delta D + c\Delta D = \Delta B$$
$$\Delta D(r_d + c) = \Delta B$$
$$\Delta D = \frac{\Delta B}{r_d + c}$$

The equation $\Delta D = \Delta B/(r_d + c)$ reflects the fact that increases in currency holdings by the public will absorb increases in the monetary base (as do reserve requirements) and therefore will limit deposit expansion. Since an increase in currency in circulation will add to the money supply (ΔM), just as does new deposit creation,

$$\Delta M = \Delta D + \Delta C$$
$$\Delta M = \Delta D + c\Delta D = \Delta D(1 + c)$$

and since

$$\Delta D = \Delta B/(r_d + c)$$

then

$$\Delta M = \frac{\Delta B(1 + c)}{r_d + c}$$

To illustrate the dampening effect of the currency drain on deposit expansion, suppose that $r_d = 0.10$. The simple deposit multiplier would thus be 10. However, if currency in circulation amounts to 30 percent of demand deposits ($c = 0.3$), the revised monetary multiplier is only $[(1 + 0.3)/(0.1 + 0.3)]$, or 3.25.

The money multiplier is reduced further to the extent that new nontransactions deposits (noncheckable time and savings accounts) are created during the money expansion process. To show this mathematically, we may define

t = Ratio of time and savings deposits to demand deposits
r_t = Reserve requirement for time deposits

The monetary multiplier now becomes $(1 + c)/(r_d + c + r_t t)$. Suppose that the amount of time and savings deposits is double the amount of demand deposits, or $t = 2$, and that the reserve requirement for time and savings deposits is 3 percent. Using the above values for r_d and c, we have

$$\frac{1 + 0.3}{0.1 + 0.3 + 0.03(2)} = \frac{1.3}{0.46} = 2.826$$

Thus the money supply is determined as

$$M = \frac{1 + c}{r_d + c + r_t t}(R + C)$$

This formulation reflects a composite "decision model," which determines how much money will exist. The decisions and actions of the public, the Treasury, and the Federal Reserve determine the amount of reserves and currency in circulation (the monetary base), as well as the size of the monetary multiplier. The magnitude of reserve requirements (on both checkable and noncheckable deposits) and the demand of the public for currency largely determine the value of the money multiplier. Changes in reserve requirements, in the demand for currency relative to deposits, and in the ratios of checkable to noncheckable deposits (and also the amount of U.S. government deposits relative to other deposit amounts, in a manner similar to the currency drain) will result in shifts in the magnitude of the money multiplier. Stability of the monetary multiplier is very important for the Fed in its conduct of monetary policy. Predictable changes in the quantity of money from any given injection or withdrawal of reserves depends on a relatively stable (predictable) monetary multiplier.

THE FEDERAL RESERVE SYSTEM'S ROLE IN THE FINANCIAL MARKETPLACE

The special significance of the Federal Reserve System in the monetary system is evident from the foregoing discussion. Chapter 26 offers further, more detailed discussion of how the Fed formulates and implements monetary policy. But the Fed's role in the financial system extends beyond the exercise of its monetary authority. It is the most important participant in the nation's money markets, as described in Chapter 17. It has major responsibilities for the supervision and regulation of the commercial banking system, as described in Chapter 12.

Like most central banks, the Fed acts as the principal fiscal agent for the national government. It is the federal government's main bank, since the Treasury keeps its "checking account" with the Fed. The Fed also handles new issues of Treasury securities and pays interest on outstanding Treasury issues. The Federal Reserve Bank of New York acts as the Treasury's agent in the latter's activities in the foreign exchange market. In addition, the Fed frequently acts as an agent for foreign central banks and otherwise maintains close relations with foreign official financial institutions in matters of mutual interest and in pursuit of common goals of international financial order.

The Fed's presence in the financial system is thus pervasive and of vital importance. It is the most important single participant in the U.S. financial system. As a result, other participants in the financial marketplace pay keen attention to the activities and attitudes of the Fed. The frequent references to the role of the Fed in subsequent chapters of this book reflect the great significance of this institution in our financial system.

SUMMARY

Though a variety of items have served as money over the centuries, modern money consists of currency and demand deposits in commercial banks and other depository financial institutions. The operations of commercial banks through their lending activities result in the expansion of demand deposits. To understand the deposit expansion and contraction process, it is necessary to distinguish between the individual banks and the banking system; an individual bank may safely make loans and create deposits only in the amount of its excess reserves. In contrast, the banking system can make loans and create deposits in the amount of a multiple of its excess reserves. Actions by the public and the government also affect the quantity of money.

The money supply is determined by the size of the monetary base—currency in circulation plus bank reserves—and size of the money multiplier. In the United States the Federal Reserve System controls the size of the money supply largely by controlling the amount of bank reserves via its open-market sales and purchases of securities. The Federal Reserve also affects the size of the money multiplier by its power to set reserve requirements. Other influences on the magnitude of the money multiplier include the amount of currency in circulation, relative demand for noncheckable and checkable deposits, and the amount of Treasury deposits with commercial banks. While the public, the Treasury, and the commercial banks can all have a significant impact on the money supply, the Federal Reserve System is our economy's final arbiter concerning the amount of money in existence. The Federal Reserve has the ability to impact critically on both the money multiplier (via reserve requirements) and bank reserves (via open market operations). More important, the Fed has the mandate to control the supply of money, a mandate based on the fact that changes in the quantity of money have great significance for the economy. Ultimately, the Federal Reserve System can determine the size of the money stock, although its control may be less timely and precise than desired. The monetary authority vested in the Fed, along with its other responsibilities and activities, give the Fed a special and very powerful role in the financial marketplace.

QUESTIONS

1. What are four basic functions of money? Describe the contribution of each to the economic system.

2. The equation of exchange is a tautology, that is, true by definition. Why is it nonetheless a useful analytical device?

3. Explain "monetary velocity." What are the principal determinants of the velocity of money?

4. What are the major items in a commercial bank's balance sheet?

5. How are demand deposits created by the banking system? Can an individual bank create money? Use the concepts of "primary" and "derivative" bank deposits in your answer.

6. What is meant by an "adverse clearing balance" for a bank? Are the implications of an adverse clearing balance different from those of a positive clearing balance?

7. Give an example of an action by each of the following that will change the amount of reserves held by commercial banks:

   a. the public.
   b. the Federal Reserve.
   c. the U.S. Treasury.

8. What is the "monetary base"? How is it related to the magnitude of the money supply?

9. Name the principal determinants of the "monetary multiplier."

10. What are "monetary aggregates"? Why are they measured? How are M1, M2, M3, and L related?

11. What is the fundamental point of disagreement between the "Keynesian" and "monetarist" schools of economic thought? How is their dispute related to money velocity?

REFERENCES

Burger, Albert E., *The Money Supply Process* (Belmont, Calif.: Wadsworth, 1972).

Crick, W. F., "The Genesis of Bank Deposits," *Economica* (1927). Reprinted in American Economic Association, *Readings in Monetary Theory* (Homewood, Ill.: Irwin, 1951), 41–53.

Friedman, Milton, *A Program for Monetary Stability* (New York: Fordham University Press, 1960).

Galbraith, John Kenneth, *Money: Whence It Came, Where It Went* (Boston: Houghton Mifflin, 1975).

Jones, Frank L., *Macrofinance: The Financial System and the Economy* (Cambridge, Mass.: Winthrop, 1978), Ch. 3–6.

Jordan, Jerry L., "Elements of Money Stock Determination," Federal Reserve Bank of St. Louis *Monthly Review* (October 1969), 10–19.

Keran, Michael W., "Monetary and Fiscal Influences on Economic Activity—The Historical Evidence," Federal Reserve Bank of St. Louis *Monthly Review* (November 1969), 5–27.

Nichols, Dorothy M., *Modern Money Mechanics: A Workbook on Deposits, Currency, and Bank Reserves* (Chicago: Federal Reserve Bank of Chicago, 1979).

Ritter, Lawrence L., "The Role of Money in Keynesian Theory," in Deane Carson (Ed.), *Banking and Monetary Studies* (Homewood, Ill.: Richard D. Irwin, 1963), 134–148.

Sellon, Gordon H., Jr., "The Instruments of Monetary Policy," Federal Reserve Bank of Kansas City *Review* (May 1984), 3–20.

Thornton, Daniel L., "Why Does Velocity Matter?" Federal Reserve Bank of St. Louis *Review* (December 1983), 5–13.

Tobin, James, "Commercial Banks as Creators of Money," in Deane Carson (Ed.), *Banking and Monetary Studies* (Homewood, Ill.: Richard D. Irwin, 1963).

CHAPTER **5**

The Structure and Role of the Federal Reserve System

In Chapter 4 we discussed the nature of money, its economic and financial role, and the contemporary framework for its creation and control. The role of the commercial banking system in money creation was described, and the factors that determine the limits of deposit expansion by banks were identified and discussed. The importance of the money supply in the economy and the role that financial institutions and markets play in determining the quantity of money and credit make it inevitable that the central governments of modern nations will seek to control the money stock and will regulate the private institutions that, in their role as financial intermediaries, have such an enormous economic influence.

Most nations have institutions called **central banks,** which are instruments of governmental policy regarding money and credit conditions and which exercise regulatory authority over financial institutions and markets. The Bank of England, established in the late seventeenth century, performs these functions, as do the Bank of France (established in 1800) and the Bank of Canada (established in 1935). In the United States they are performed by the Federal Reserve System (the Fed), established by an act of Congress in 1913. In this chapter we are concerned with the origins, organization, and operating characteristics of the Fed. While the Fed's role as ultimate arbiter of the money supply is emphasized, detailed consideration of the formulation and implementation of monetary policy is deferred to Chapter 26.

ORIGINS OF THE FED

As was noted in Chapter 3, the establishment of the Federal Reserve System by congressional approval of the Federal Reserve Act in 1913 stemmed from concerns about the recurring instability of the nation's financial system. After the financial crisis of 1907, Congress established the National Monetary Commission to formulate and recommend reform measures. Most of the commission's recommendations (presented in a 1910 report) were incorporated into the Federal Reserve Act. The title of the Act reads as follows:

> *An Act to provide for the establishment of Federal reserve bank, to furnish an elastic currency, to afford means of rediscounting commercial paper, to establish a more effective supervision of banking in the United States, and for other purposes.*

The monetary commission viewed the fundamental problem of the pre-Fed monetary system as its inability to match currency and credit availability to the needs of the economy—its "inelasticity."[1] Further, the reserve framework of the national banking system, in which banks held reserves with other banks, was destabilizing because it led to rapid (and amplified) transmission of liquidity problems among banks.

The Federal Reserve System, it was hoped, would provide a mechanism for ensuring that the quantity of available credit would be appropriate for the economy's needs. Now, as business activity expanded and business borrowing from banks increased, banks could borrow from the Fed by using their own business loans as collateral ("rediscounting" the notes received from business borrowers). Federal Reserve notes became available as currency, and deposits in Federal Reserve Banks became the principal form of bank reserves.[2]

The Federal Reserve System was formulated as a uniquely U.S. institution, its organization reflecting much of what the people of the day believed appropriate in terms of decentralization versus centralization, private versus public enterprise, and small versus large institutions. Rather than a single central bank (as most European nations had previously established), the Federal Reserve System was organized as twelve regional Federal Reserve Banks and a Board of Governors in Washington, D.C. Though all national banks were required to join the system (become "member banks"), state banks were permitted, but not forced, to join. Ownership of the various Federal Reserve Banks was vested in the member banks.

The present role and functions of the Federal Reserve System are quite different from those envisioned by its founders. Some of these changes are the result of the Banking Act of 1933 and 1935, which, in turn, were enacted as a consequence of the economic depression of the 1930s and the weaknesses in the

---

[1] Indeed, the volume of national bank notes outstanding (which was based on the amount of U.S. government securities outstanding) tended to vary *inversely* with the level of business activity. During the upswing of the business cycle, federal government revenues rose, and government bonds were retired. Since national bank note issue was tied to bank holdings of government bonds, declines in the latter led to reductions in the former.

[2] It should be noted that, when the Fed was established, it was not intended that the Fed would control the *quantity of money*. Since the United States was then on the gold standard, the money supply was determined by the amount of gold in the banking system.

country's financial system that it exposed. Other changes have come about as an evolutionary consequence of economic change and as a product of shifting attitudes toward centralization and government intervention in the economy.

For our purposes the present structure, function, and operating characteristics of the Federal Reserve System are most relevant. In the following sections of this chapter we will focus on the modern framework, making reference to discarded past arrangements only when such discussion is useful for understanding the present system.

STRUCTURE OF THE FEDERAL RESERVE SYSTEM

The major components of the Federal Reserve System are member banks, the twelve Federal Reserve Banks, the Board of Governors, the Federal Open Market Committee, and the Federal Advisory Council. Figure 5.1 offers a schematic representation of the system's organization.

Member Banks

National banks, but not state banks, are required to be members of the Federal Reserve System. Of the roughly 6000 banks that belong to the system, about 83 percent are nationally chartered, and 17 percent are state chartered. Federal Reserve member banks thus comprise less than 40 percent of all commercial banks. However, since larger banks are more likely to be members than smaller banks (partly because larger banks are likely to be national banks), member banks hold about 70 percent of total deposits.

Prior to enactment of the Depository Institutions Deregulation and Monetary Control Act of 1980 (DIDMCA), the relative costs and benefits of Fed membership versus nonmembership were rather sharply defined for a bank. Fed membership entitled a bank to such Fed services as the check-clearing, wire-transfer, and securities-safekeeping facilities of the system. Further, membership provided a ready source of currency and coin and, of particular importance, entitled a bank to request loans from the Fed. Along with these various privileges, membership entailed (and still entails) a number of obligations. These include subscribing to capital stock of the bank's district Federal Reserve Bank, complying with Federal Reserve rules and regulations, paying checks presented at par (face value), and, in the case of state member banks, being examined and supervised by the Federal Reserve Banks. The most significant obligation (and cost) of membership, however, was adherence to the Fed's reserve requirements. Before DIDMCA mandated uniform reserve requirements for all banks, this obligation often resulted in member banks bearing heavier costs from holding reserves than those borne by nonmember banks, whose reserve requirements were then established by the various states of charter.

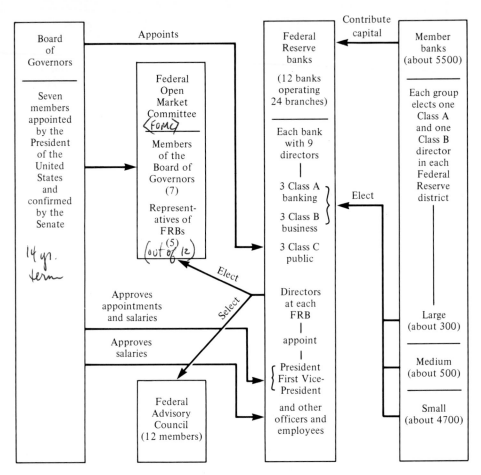

FIGURE 5.1   Organization of the Federal Reserve System

Source: Board of Governors of the Federal Reserve System, Federal Reserve System: Purposes and Functions, *6th ed. (Washington, D.C.: September 1984), 18.*

Fed Membership

The fact that membership in the Federal Reserve System declined steadily after World War II until 1980 indicates that, for many banks, the pre-DIDMCA costs and benefits of membership favored nonmembership.[3] During this period

---

[3]Further, nonmember banks were frequently able to secure the same types of service offered by the Fed from their large city correspondent banks and also some services not offered by the Fed, such as loan participation and investment assistance.

the percentage of all banks holding system membership fell from more than 50 percent to less than 40 percent. The percentage of bank deposits held by members dropped from almost 90 percent to less than 70 percent. The Federal Reserve Board of Governors became quite concerned about this decline in membership because of its implications for the effectiveness of monetary policy. Since the Fed had no control over reserve requirements of nonmember banks, declining membership implied (at least to the Fed) declining ability of the Fed to control the money supply.

Indeed, the principal reason for the decline in bank membership between 1945 and 1980 was the magnitude and nature of the Fed's reserve requirements relative to those imposed by the various states on nonmember banks. Not only was the Fed's reserve requirement ratio frequently higher than those of many states, but it also immobilized that percentage of member bank deposits in nonearning form, since Fed reserve requirements mandate that reserves must be held as either vault cash or deposits with the district Federal Reserve Bank. State reserve requirements for nonmember banks allowed correspondent accounts (interbank deposits) to be counted as reserves, and a number of states allowed reserves to be held in interest-earning assets. These differences between Fed and state reserve requirements amounted to the imposition of a significant cost for membership in the system.

At the urging of the Fed, Congress mandated in 1980 the elimination of differential reserve requirements between member and nonmember banks. This provision was part of the wide-ranging, watershed banking legislation that the DIDMCA of 1980 constituted. As discussed earlier, this act called for the phased establishment of uniform reserve requirements for all depository institutions. These reserve requirements were initially set at 3 percent on transactions balances (checkable deposits) up to $25 million and 12 percent on transactions balances of more than $25 million at all depository institutions. Reserves on nonpersonal time deposits with original maturities of less than four years were set at 3 percent of such deposits. (This reserve requirement structure was altered somewhat in 1983 and 1986; see Table 5.2.) The Fed was empowered to alter the reserve requirement ratio on checkable deposits above $25 million within a range of 8 percent to 14 percent and on nonpersonal time deposits from 0 percent to 9 percent. The Fed could also require additional reserves equal to as much as 4 percent of checkable deposits, but interest would be paid on these reserves. The Act provided that these requirements would be phased in for nonmember depository institutions over an eight-year period.[4] Member bank reserve requirements were to be reduced to the new levels over a four-year period.

DIDMCA also made the various services of the Fed available to nonmember

---

[4]Nonmember institutions were allowed to hold reserves directly with the Fed or indirectly through "pass-through" arrangements with a correspondent bank, a Federal Home Loan Bank, or the National Credit Union Administration Central Liquidity Facility.

depository institutions, as well as to member banks. Further, beginning in 1981 these services were provided on an explicit-fee basis rather than as a privilege of Fed membership. Also, all depository institutions subject to reserve requirements were made immediately eligible by the act to request loans from the Fed.

It is apparent that this highly significant banking legislation greatly narrowed the difference between being a member and not being a member of the Federal Reserve System. The DIDMCA of 1980 checked the decline in Fed membership, but the proportionate size of such membership is no longer of great significance for the financial system, since the act's reserve requirements apply to both member and nonmember banks.

The Federal Reserve Banks

The 12 regional reserve banks, each of which has a "district," are located in the cities of Boston, New York, Philadelphia, Cleveland, Richmond, Atlanta, Chicago, St. Louis, Minneapolis, Kansas City, Dallas, and San Francisco.[5] Figure 5.2 provides further information on the geographical location of the Federal Reserve districts. Each bank has a president, who is elected by the Board of Directors but is subject to review by the Board of Governors of the Federal Reserve System. Of the nine-member Board of Directors of each Federal Reserve Bank, three are appointed by the Board of Governors of the Federal Reserve, and the other six are elected by the member banks in each region. Three members represent the banking community, three the general business community, and three the general public.

The various reserve banks are "owned" by member banks in the sense that each member bank must subscribe to stock in its district bank in the amount of 3 percent of its total capital. Member banks are paid dividends at a rate of 6 percent per annum on their stock "purchase." This arrangement is an artifact of the 1913 Federal Reserve Act (the Fed's architects were opposed to government ownership of banks) and has no real significance; the stock ownership carries no private property rights. Member banks have little influence on Fed policy. Moreover, if a member bank relinquishes its membership, the Federal Reserve stock must be returned—it cannot be sold.

The principal source of revenues for the Federal Reserve System is interest earnings on holdings of securities and on loans to member banks. These revenues are used to pay operating expenses and pay the statutory 6 percent dividend on Federal Reserve stock held by member banks. The remainder (less any required additions to Federal Reserve Bank capital) is paid to the Treasury, as a matter of Fed policy.

---

[5]This regionalization was established because of the widespread fear that a powerful centralized bank would be dominated by Wall Street financial interests.

FIGURE 5.2 The Federal Reserve System
(Boundaries of Federal Reserve Districts and Their Branch Territories)

Source: Federal Reserve Bulletin.

The Federal Reserve regional banks are the principal operating arm of the Federal Reserve System. They provide currency and coin to depository institutions, clear checks, and provide other service functions.

Board of Governors

The Board of Governors consists of seven members appointed for fourteen-year terms by the President of the United States. The appointments (which must be approved by the U.S. Senate) are staggered so that one governor's term expires every two years. A governor who serves a full term cannot be reappointed. A chairman and vice-chairman of the board are designated by the president for four-year terms and can serve in this capacity for an additional term, subject to the general limitation on time in service on the board. The board is the focus for the formulation and conduct of monetary policy within the entire Federal Reserve System.

The Board of Governors is located in Washington, D.C. Its functions, broadly stated, are formulating and executing monetary policy, overseeing the operations of the Federal Reserve Banks, and exercising various regulatory and supervisory powers over member banks. More specifically, the major responsibilities of the board are to:

1. Set reserve requirements on the deposits of all depository institutions within the limits mandated by Congress. (As discussed previously, uniform reserve requirements now apply to *all* depository institutions.)

2. Determine the rate of interest (discount rate) to be charged for borrowing from the Federal Reserve Banks.[6]

3. Participate in planning the nature and magnitude of Federal Reserve open market operations (the buying and selling of securities by the Fed) via membership of the seven governors on the Federal Open Market Committee.

4. Appoint three directors on each Federal Reserve Bank board of directors and approve the appointment of the president of each regional bank.

5. Provide for periodic audit of regional Federal Reserve Banks.

6. Review and approve or disapprove applications by bank holding companies to acquire banks and other firms.

7. Review (for possible approval) applications for merger of two or more banks into a state member bank.

8. Provide for supervision and examination policies and procedures for state-

---

[6]Technically, the discount rate is determined by the various reserve banks and is subject to review and approval by the board. In fact, the board has now assumed the power to determine the discount rate for all Federal Reserve Banks.

chartered member banks. (Bank examinations are actually conducted by the staffs of the various Federal Reserve Banks.)

The Board of Governors thus possesses considerable economic power, and since its chairman generally dominates the board, the Chairman of the Board of Governors has come to be viewed as a principal figure in the formulation of U.S. economic policy. This development is attributable to a number of factors, including the great increase in the perceived importance of monetary policy (relative to fiscal policy) in recent years, the personalities of recent chairmen, and a number of political factors relating to the degree of power that can be effectively wielded by the President and by congressional leaders in economic matters.

The Federal Open-Market Committee

The Chairman of the Board of Governors is also chairman of the Federal Open-Market Committee (FOMC), the organization within the Fed that has primary responsibility for monetary policy. The voting members of the FOMC are the seven board governors and five of the twelve Federal Reserve Bank presidents. The president of the New York Fed is a permanent voting member (and also vice-chairman), but the other four reserve bank positions on the FOMC (one-year terms) are rotated among the other presidents. The seven other Federal Reserve Bank presidents also generally attend the meetings of the committee along with a number of senior staff personnel.

Further discussion of the role of the FOMC is included in Chapter 26, which is concerned with the formulation and implementation of monetary policy. At this point, however, note that the Fed's open market operations (described later in this chapter) are guided by FOMC decisions.

The Federal Advisory Council

The Federal Advisory Council is by far the least important of the constituent parts of the Federal Reserve System. Yet it is not without influence both within the Fed and as a significant factor in affecting the relationship between the Fed and its critics. The Federal Advisory Council consists of twelve members, one from each Federal Reserve District. The members are selected annually by the Board of Directors in each district. Many come from the banking community, though professors and representatives from the general business community also are frequently members of the council. The principal function of the council, which meets in Washington, D.C., is to provide advice to the Fed about the conduct of monetary policy and about other matters over which the Fed legally has influence, though the Federal Advisory Council has no direct decision-making power.

We turn now to a discussion of the Fed's various policy instruments and the means of their employment in the Fed's pursuit of monetary goals.

TOOLS OF MONETARY POLICY

Chapter 4 includes a discussion of how the Federal Reserve can affect reserves, the monetary base, the money multiplier, and thus the supply of money. The Fed can expand or contract reserves by buying or selling securities (open market operations) and by increasing or decreasing the volume of its lending to depository institutions. The Fed can increase or decrease the magnitude of the money multiplier by lowering or raising the reserve requirement ratio, an action that also changes the proportions of required and excess reserves (which constitute total reserves). When the Fed wishes to stimulate economic activity, it will take action to increase the quantity of excess reserves held by banks and other depository institutions. When excess reserves increase, these institutions have the means and incentive to acquire additional interest-earning assets (make loans and acquire securities), which results in an expansion of deposits and currency in circulation. If the Fed instead seeks to restrain economic activity, its policy actions will be aimed at reducing reserves. A reduction in reserves is likely to force depository institutions to cut back on lending and investing, thereby resulting in a decrease in deposits and currency in circulation. The Fed can thus affect the availability of credit, the money supply, and interest rates by its policy actions. Changes in these variables in turn impact considerably on economic activity. The Fed also has a considerable degree of influence with depository institutions, and it employs "moral suasion" through letters, telephone calls, and speeches in order to steer these institutions toward behavior that is consistent with Fed policy. We will now discuss each of the Fed's major policy instruments.

Open-Market Operations

Open-market operations are by far the most frequently used policy tool of the Fed because of their flexibility and effectiveness. Open-market operations impact directly on reserves; reserves increase when the Fed buys securities and decrease when the Fed sells securities. Uses of this technique are often **defensive** in nature—designed to offset undesired temporary changes in reserves due to currency flows and other factors over which the Fed has no control. For example, currency in circulation outside depository financial institutions increases during the period immediately before Christmas. This occurrence reduces bank reserves and, if reserves were not injected into the financial system by the Fed to offset it, would result in a multiple contraction of demand deposits. Such injection is accomplished by Fed purchases of Treasury securities in its open-market operations. When Christmas is over and currency flows back into banks, the Fed reverses its field, selling securities to avoid an undesired expansion of reserves. Other short-run disturbances that call for these defensive open-market opera-

PAUL VOLCKER

The post of Chairman of the Board of Governors of the Federal Reserve System is unquestionably a powerful one. The Fed has had a number of strong, competent chairmen who have unquestionably had a decisive impact on the economic history of this country. Marriner S. Eccles is remembered as the chairman who restored the good name of the Fed after its loss of reputation in the Great Depression of the 1930s. William McChesney Martin, who served from the Truman presidency to that of Richard Nixon, shaped postwar Federal Reserve policy. However, the reputation of a more recent chairman (named to the post in 1979), Paul Volcker, is likely to loom as large as any of his predecessors.

As an undergraduate economics major at Princeton University in 1949, Paul Volcker wrote his senior thesis on the subject of the problems of postwar Federal Reserve policy. Young Volcker correctly reported that the Fed—because of its World War II–induced policy of supporting Treasury borrowing—had lost its ability to control the money supply and thus inflation. He argued for an end to the Fed's policy of supplying whatever quantity of bank reserves was necessary to fix Treasury security interest rates. (The accord between the Fed and the Treasury in 1951 eventually led to the independent Fed that Volcker argued was necessary to prevent inflation.) Thirty years later, when President Carter elevated him from the presidency of the Federal Reserve Bank of New York to Chairman of the Board of Governors of the Federal Reserve System, Paul Volcker found himself in the role of the principal architect of monetary policy in the United States.

A towering figure at six feet, seven inches (despite a slight stoop in his posture), the balding, cigar-smoking Volcker brought an extraordinary record of experience in government and finance, unquestioned integrity, and enormous technical expertise to the Fed chairmanship. Volcker could be droll and charming when he chose to be and was a master of the art of Congressional testimony.

Volcker tightened monetary policy soon after becoming Fed chairman. As the economy slid into the severe 1981–1982 recession, he became a controversial figure. But when economic recovery commenced and inflation and interest rates subsided, the Fed chairman's prestige rose rapidly. A 1983 Gallup survey among top executives of the nation's largest corporations found Volcker to be much more highly regarded among this group than President Reagan. The international financial community held Volcker in equally high regard. President Reagan had no real choice but to reappoint Chairman Volcker for another term in 1983, despite resentment of Fed policies on the part of some of the administration's principal figures. There was to be no third term, however. Volcker was succeeded by Alan Greenspan in 1987.

tions include cyclical changes in Federal Reserve float, new Treasury issues of securities, seasonal variations in the demand for credit, and change in the Treasury's balance with the Fed.

The Fed employs so-called **dynamic** open-market operations in its pursuit of longer-run objectives. When inflation is the foremost economic problem, the Fed is likely to pursue a policy of monetary stringency—slowing money supply growth and allowing interest rates to rise. In this case the Fed's dynamic open-market operations would amount to net sales of securities and the corresponding reduction in reserves. On the other hand, depressed economic activity is likely to result in open-market operations that inject reserves into the financial system to permit monetary expansion and an easing of interest rates. To some extent, dynamic operations can be augmented by not using the usual defensive operations to offset an extraneous reserve change in the desired direction. On the other hand, the Fed must often employ defensive measures in the course of conducting dynamic operations for the latter to proceed smoothly.

Open-market operations are conducted by the Open-Market Trading Desk of the Federal Reserve Bank of New York under the direction of the Manager of the System Open-Market Account, who, in turn, is guided by the policy directives of the Federal Open-Market Committee. The Fed conducts open-market operations virtually every business day, and the Open-Market Trading Desk is a very busy place. In addition to trading activities the account manager and the account staff must continually monitor a wide range of information about conditions in the financial markets, Treasury activities, and the reserve positions of depository institutions. The staff is in constant contact with the dozen or so large government bond dealers with whom the trading desk does most of its business. Daily contact is also generally maintained between the trading desk and the Board of Governors and the various presidents of the Federal Reserve Banks. Such contact is generally accomplished by telephone discussions between trading desk officers and senior members of the board's staff (and sometimes the governors themselves) and the bank presidents. These discussions focus primarily on developments in the securities markets, the reserve positions of depository institutions, and the actions taken and to be taken by the trading desk.

Most of the Fed's security trading is done in Treasury bills, which are short-term U.S. government securities. The New York government security dealers with whom the Fed trades hold large inventories of Treasury bills. The dollar volume of Fed trading is enormous. Table 5.1 indicates the amount, by major type of financial instrument, of Federal Reserve purchases and sales in recent years.

Two items in Table 5.1 warrant explanation: A **repurchase agreement** ("repo") involves an agreement between the Open-Market Trading Desk and a security dealer to buy securities from the dealer subject to dealer repurchase at the end of a specified time period (perhaps as short as a single day). Similarly a

TABLE 5.1   Federal Reserve Open Market Transactions[1]
Millions of dollars

Type of transaction	1986	1987	1988
U.S. TREASURY SECURITIES			
Outright transactions (*excluding matched transactions*)			
Treasury bills			
1 Gross purchases	22,604	18,983	8,223
2 Gross sales	2,502	6,051	587
3 Exchange	0	0	0
4 Redemptions	1,000	9,029	2,200
Others within 1 year			
5 Gross purchases	190	3,659	2,176
6 Gross sales	0	300	0
7 Maturity shift	18,674	21,504	23,854
8 Exchange	−20,180	−20,388	−24,588
9 Redemptions	0	70	0
1 to 5 years			
10 Gross purchases	893	10,231	5,485
11 Gross sales	0	452	800
12 Maturity shift	−17,058	−17,975	−17,720
13 Exchange	16,985	18,938	22,515
5 to 10 years			
14 Gross purchases	236	2,441	1,579
15 Gross sales	0	0	175
16 Maturity shift	−1,620	−3,529	−5,946
17 Exchange	2,050	950	1,797
Over 10 years			
18 Gross purchases	158	1,858	1,398
19 Gross sales	0	0	0
20 Maturity shift	0	0	−188
21 Exchange	1,150	500	275
All maturities			
22 Gross purchases	24,081	37,170	18,863
23 Gross sales	2,502	6,803	1,562
24 Redemptions	1,000	9,099	2,200
Matched transactions			
25 Gross sales	927,999	950,923	1,168,484
26 Gross purchases	927,247	950,935	1,168,142
Repurchase agreements[2]			
27 Gross purchases	170,431	314,621	152,613
28 Gross sales	160,268	324,666	151,497
29 Net change in U.S. government securities	29,988	11,234	15,872

(continued)

TABLE 5.1   (Continued)
Millions of dollars

Type of transaction	1986	1987	1988
FEDERAL AGENCY OBLIGATIONS			
Outright transactions			
30 Gross purchases	0	0	0
31 Gross sales	0	0	0
32 Redemptions	398	276	587
Repurchase agreements[2]			
33 Gross purchases	31,142	80,353	57,259
34 Gross sales	30,521	81,350	56,471
35 Net change in federal agency obligations....	222	−1,274	198
36 **Total net change in System Open Market Account**	**30,212**	**9,961**	**16,070**

[1]Sales, redemptions, and negative figures reduce holdings of the System Open Market Account; all other figures increase such holdings. Details may not add to totals because of rounding.
[2]In July 1984 the Open Market Trading Desk discontinued accepting bankers acceptances in repurchase agreements.

Source: Federal Reserve Bulletin, May 1989.

matched sale–purchase agreement ("reverse repo") is accomplished by a sale of securities to a dealer concurrent with Fed agreement to buy them back at the end of the agreed period. The trading desk uses repurchase agreements to supply reserves to the market for a short time period and matched sale–purchase agreements to withdraw reserves for a limited time. Repos and reverse repos are convenient instruments for defensive open-market operations. Both the Fed's frequent use of repurchase agreements and matched sales–purchase transactions and the significance of day-to-day "defensive operations" are evidenced by the fact, as shown in Table 5.1, that the dollar amount of these transactions is about ten times that of outright purchases and sales of securities by the Fed.

Table 5.1 also shows, as indicated above, that the Fed deals primarily in Treasury bills and does comparatively little trading in long-term securities. The market for short-term securities (the money market) has greater breadth and depth than the capital market (the market for securities having a maturity of more than one year). This fact, along with the nature of the role of time-to-maturity to the security price/interest rate relationship makes the money market an attractive arena for Fed operations. By primarily confining its trading to Treasury bills, the Fed reduces the likelihood of undue disturbances in the bond market and minimizes interest rate fluctuations related to its operations.

Finally, note in Table 5.1 that the net change in the Fed's holdings of securities was positive—the Fed increased the amount of its holdings of U.S. government securities and federal agency obligations—over this time period. This is hardly surprising, for as the economy expands, the money supply is likely to expand also. Monetary expansion in turn requires an expansion of the monetary base—currency in circulation and reserves. Such long-term expansion in reserves can be accomplished in whole or in part by secular increases in the Fed's holdings of securities. In Chapter 26 we will discuss the process by which the Fed establishes monetary growth goals for given time periods, which in turn determine the nature and scope of its policy actions during these periods.

Federal Reserve Lending

When the Federal Reserve System was established, its role as lender to member banks was considered one of its principal functions, and this was indeed the case during its early years of operation. The provision of facilities for the "discounting" (selling) of "commercial paper" (written instruments pertaining to business loans) to the Federal Reserve by member banks was regarded as the key element of the Fed's perceived role in supplying an "elastic currency." The theory ("real bills" doctrine) was that as business loan demand mounted during an economic upswing, banks would have more commercial paper to discount in order to obtain more loanable funds. As loan demand abated and outstanding business loans were paid, commercial banks would repay their indebtedness to the Fed. Thus the volume of outstanding Fed loans would expand and contract with the level of business activity, and so would credit availability. This notion of "elasticity" in available credit has largely been discarded. Instead, a phrase such as "leaning against the wind" (checking inflationary booms and deflationary slides) better characterizes modern-day Fed objectives than does the automatic accommodation of the business cycle. The notion of an "elastic currency" has thus been supplanted by more direct and purposeful management of money and credit conditions by the Fed, and open-market operations have made Fed lending very much a secondary instrument of Federal Reserve policy.

In the early years of the Fed's existence, bankers actually appeared at a Reserve Bank teller window to request loans from the Fed, and this gave the Fed's credit-granting role the figurative label "discount window." The interest rate charged on member bank borrowing from the Fed is still called the "discount rate," and the Fed's lending facilities are still referred to as the "discount window," but only a small portion of Fed loans to member banks are currently accomplished by the discounting of commercial paper. (And bankers are unlikely to appear at the teller window of a Federal Reserve Bank.) The general practice now is for banks to post government securities as collateral for direct advances from the Fed. Further, the Depository Institutions Deregulation and Monetary Control Act of 1980 made the privilege of requesting loans from the Fed available to all depository institutions required to hold reserves against deposits, not just member banks.[7] At the time of DIDMCA's enactment this amounted to extending the discount privilege to 15,000 additional institutions.

As currently conceived, the purpose of the discount window is to help depository institutions adjust to short-run reserve needs when they encounter difficulty securing needed reserves elsewhere.[8] The Federal Reserve frowns on continuous borrowings by institutions and uses "administrative counseling" of those borrowers that are judged to be inappropriately using the discount window privilege. From the perspective of a depository institution considering use of the discount window this attitude of the Fed constitutes a qualitative cost factor that must be weighed along with the discount rate on Fed loans for purposes of comparing the cost of this source to the cost of alternative reserve sources (federal funds, selling off securities, and so on).

Though the Fed views most borrowing through the discount window as appropriate only if it is short-term in nature, there are some longer-term discount window borrowings that are acceptable under an extended credit program. This extended credit program consists of three parts: seasonal credit, extended credit in exceptional circumstances, and other extended credit. Seasonal credit is designed to provide a longer-term source of funds to financial institutions with a strong seasonal loan demand and limited access to financial markets. The secondary category of extended credit provides funds to an institution experiencing liquidity difficulties that are specific to that institution rather than to financial institutions in general, such as an institution experiencing severe pressure because of rapid declines in the local economy. The third category—other extended credit—allows depository institutions experiencing industrywide liquidity pressures because, for example, of very high interest rates, to borrow for 60 days at the basic discount rate and for longer periods at higher rates (generally one to two percentage points above the basic discount rate).

Depository institution borrowing fluctuates very widely over the business cycle. Figure 5.3 indicates the magnitudes of member bank borrowings (and excess reserve positions) in recent years. As would be expected, when the Fed allows the discount rate to lag behind movements in money market rates, as it has frequently done, borrowing rises when interest rates rise and falls as credit conditions ease. When the Fed follows a practice of infrequent revision of the discount rate, it is ensured that both average borrowing and the range of magnitudes of borrowing would be much greater if the Fed did not exercise administrative restraint on use of the discount window.

---

[7]Nonmember depository institutions, however, are expected to turn first to special industry lenders (such as the Federal Home Loan Banks) for funds rather than to the discount window.

[8]The development of the so-called federal funds market, in which depository institutions with excess reserves lend (sell) them to institutions that need additional reserves, has greatly reduced their need to use the Fed's discount window. The Fed prefers that depository institutions turn first to the federal funds market to borrow reserves, partly because interinstitution loans of reserves, unlike its own, do not change the aggregate amount of reserves.

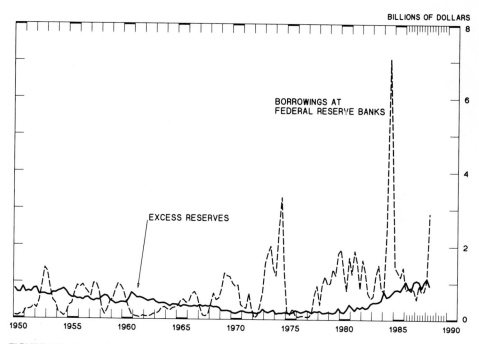

FIGURE 5.3 Excess Reserves and Borrowings
(Averages of daily figures, quarterly)

Source: Board of Governors of the Federal Reserve System, Historical Chart Book *(Washington, D.C.), 1988.*

It can be argued that the discount window, though to some extent an out-moded mechanism, is useful on grounds of equity, since its availability is impor-tant to many smaller institutions that lack the range and quantity of resources available to larger ones. This seems to be especially valid for the extended credit program. Further, the discount window can be (and has been) a stabilizing factor during periods of financial disturbances (such as the 1966 "credit crunch," the 1970 collapse of the Penn Central Railroad, which sent shock waves through the commercial paper market, and the 1987 stock market crash). Fed lending has also, on a few occasions, prevented (or deferred) failure of particular financially troubled banks. Thus the "lender of last resort" function continues to be of importance. It has also been argued that the Fed's power to set the discount rate is a useful signaling device for its monetary policy objectives (so-called announce-ment effects). It has, however, been rightly pointed out that many other means of communication are available to the Fed, none of which represent a source of disturbance in the level of bank reserves.

EXAMPLES OF DISCOUNT WINDOW TRANSACTIONS

Example 1: It is Wednesday afternoon at a regional bank, and the bank is required to have enough funds in its reserve account at its Federal Reserve Bank to meet its reserve requirement over the previous two weeks. The bank finds that it must borrow to make up its reserve deficiency, but the money center (that is, the major New York, Chicago, and California) banks have apparently been borrowing heavily in the federal funds market. As a result, the rate on federal funds on this particular Wednesday afternoon has soared far above its level earlier that day. As far as the funding officer of the regional bank is concerned, the market for funds at a price she considers acceptable has "dried up." She calls the Federal Reserve Bank for a discount window loan.

Example 2: A West Coast regional bank, which generally avoids borrowing at the discount window, expects to receive a wire transfer of $300 million from a New York bank, but by late afternoon the money has not yet showed up. It turns out that the sending bank had erroneously sent only $3000 instead of the $300 million. Although the New York bank is legally liable for the correct amount, it is closed by the time the error is discovered. To make up the deficiency in its reserve position, the West Coast bank calls the discount window for a loan.

Example 3: It is Wednesday reserve account settlement time at another bank, and the funding officer notes that the spread between the discount rate and federal funds rate has widened slightly. Since his bank is buying federal funds to make up a reserve deficiency, he decides to borrow part of the reserve deficiency from the discount window to take advantage of the spread. Over the next few months he repeats this until the bank receives an "informational" call from the discount officer at the Federal Reserve Bank, inquiring as to the reason for the apparent pattern in discount window borrowing. Taking the hint, the bank refrains from the practice on subsequent Wednesday settlements.

Example 4: A money center bank acts as a clearing agent for the government securities market. This means that the bank maintains book-entry securities accounts for market participants and that it also maintains a reserve account and a book-entry securities account at its Federal Reserve Bank, so that securities transactions can be cleared through this system. One day, an internal computer problem arises that allows the bank to accept securities but not to process them for delivery to dealers, brokers, and other market participants. The bank's reserve account is debited for the amount of these securities, but it is unable to pass them on and collect payment for them, a situation that results in a growing overdraft in the reserve account. As close of business approaches, it becomes increasingly clear that the problem will not be fixed in time to collect the required payments from the securities buyers. To avoid a negative reserve balance at the end of the day, the bank estimates its anticipated reserve account deficiency and goes to the Federal Reserve Bank discount window for a loan for that amount. The computer problem is fixed, and the loan is repaid the following day.

Example 5: Because of mismanagement, a privately insured savings and loan association fails. Concerned about the condition of other privately insured thrift institutions in the state, depositors begin to withdraw their deposits, leading to a run. Because they are not federally insured, some otherwise sound thrifts are not able to borrow from the Federal Home Loan Bank Board to meet the demands of the depositors. As a result, the regional Federal Reserve Bank is called upon to lend to these thrifts. After an extensive examination of the collateral the thrifts could offer, the Reserve Bank makes loans to them until they are able to get federal insurance and attract back enough deposits to pay back the discount window loans.

Source: David L. Mengle, "The Discount Window," Federal Reserve Bank of Richmond Economic Review *(May/June 1986), p. 3.*

On balance, the discount window is probably best viewed not as a tool of monetary policy but as (1) an "escape valve" to ease the pressures on banks and the economy while adjustment to more stringent credit conditions is being accomplished or (2) a "rapid rescue" mechanism when financial crisis threatens (for individual banks or for the entire banking system). In recent years, borrowing from the Federal Reserve, on the average, has constituted less than 2 percent of total bank reserves, hardly providing the Fed a significant degree of leverage in influencing monetary variables. Further, since changes in the discount rate are unlikely to have a major effect on the magnitude of borrowings, and unless the amount of reserves that exist because of the discount window increase significantly, the monetary effect of such changes is likely to remain small. Although the Fed has continued to make occasional symbolic use of discount rate changes in recent years, its periodic alteration is usually aimed only at keeping it in line with the money market rate structure. Such changes must be coordinated with other policy actions; the quantity of reserves supplied via the discount window must be taken into account in the Fed's task of managing total reserves.

Reserve Requirements

As a policy tool, changes in reserve requirements have been likened to an axe, and the same simile usually likens open-market operations to a scalpel. Changes in the reserve requirement ratio immediately affect both the legal reserve positions of depository institutions and the money multiplier, thus changing both the amount of reserves required against existing deposits and also the quantity of deposits that a given level of reserves can support. Decreases in the reserve requirement ratio thus free reserves and increase the monetary multiplier, with an increase in the volume of credit and the money supply likely to follow. The reverse holds for increases in the reserve requirement. Though an extremely powerful tool, reserve requirement changes can hardly be employed on a day-to-day basis (as can open-market operations) unless very small changes in reserve requirement ratios are to be used. Although the Federal Reserve changed the reserve requirement ratio on the average of almost once a year in the 1960s and 1970s, most of these changes were quite small, and some were related to a major structural overhaul of the reserve requirement structure by the Fed in 1972. As was discussed earlier, in 1980 the DIDMCA mandated a new structure of reserve requirements applicable to all depository institutions and to be phased in over a period of several years. These reserve requirements are shown in Table 5.2.

Whether reserve requirements are increased (to tighten the supply of money and credit when inflationary pressures exist) or decreased (to ease credit and expand the money supply as a counter to recessionary developments in the economy), the impact on depository institutions is immediate and universal. The effects of open-market operations, on the other hand, work their way through the economy more slowly, initially affecting institutions in money market centers and then being transmitted, with a lag, through financial markets to financial institutions around the country. The immediacy and magnitude of the effects of reserve requirement changes can be helpful to a stabilization program of the Fed. The same lack of subtlety, relative to open-market operations, that makes this policy instrument unsuitable for the mere smoothing of economic fluctuations renders

TABLE 5.2   Reserve Requirements of Depository Institutions[1]
Percent of Deposits

Type of Deposit, and Deposit Interval	Depository Institution Requirements After Implementation of the Monetary Control Act	
	Percent of Deposits	Effective Date
Net transaction accounts		
$0 million–$41.5 million	3	12/20/88
More than $41.5 million	12	12/20/88
Nonpersonal time deposits		
By original maturity		
Less than 1 ½ years	3	10/6/83
1 ½ years or more	0	10/6/83
Eurocurrency liabilities		
All types	3	11/13/80

[1]Reserve requirements in effect on Dec. 31, 1988. Required reserves must be held in the form of deposits with Federal Reserve Banks or vault cash. Nonmembers may maintain reserve balances with a Federal Reserve Bank indirectly on a pass-through basis with certain approved institutions.

Source: Federal Reserve Bulletin, *May 1988.*

it more effective when the Fed desires "announcement effects" to speed up the impact of its actions.

In any event the Fed must coordinate reserve requirement changes with open-market and discount window operations to cushion and smooth adjustment to the new level of required reserves. When reserve requirement ratios are increased, the Fed may temporarily ease its discount window posture and use open-market operations to supply reserves to depository institutions until an adjustment by the depository system is substantially accomplished. Such adjustment will involve depository institutions in the selling of securities, in bidding more aggressively for "federal funds," and in the curbing of lending. These actions put upward pressure on market interest rates, spread reserve pressures throughout the financial system, and slow the growth of the money supply. All these results, of course, are the Fed's objectives when it raises reserve requirements (unless a "structural change," rather than economic policy, is the impetus).

Credit Controls

The various "quantitative" instruments of Fed monetary policy—open-market operations, reserve requirements, and discount window policy—are intended to affect the **aggregate amount** of money and credit. At various times in the past the Fed has had the power to regulate the terms of credit granting in the economy, such as repayment periods and the minimum amount of down payments. One such direct credit control made available to the Fed in the 1930s was the margin for stock purchases, which amounts to a minimum down payment for securities purchased on credit. This control was intended to counter the use of credit to finance speculative booms in the stock market—a reaction to the excesses of the 1920s prior to the stock market's famous "crash" in 1929.

The Credit Control Act of 1969 permitted the president to authorize the Federal Reserve to "regulate and control any and all extensions of credit" when this was deemed necessary to control inflation. The Fed received such authorization in 1980 and took various actions, such as imposing marginal reserve requirements on increases in consumer credit, under authority of the act to curb lending. These actions were not universally popular, and Congress allowed the Credit Control Act of 1969 to expire in 1982.

Interest Rate Ceilings

The Fed's power (acquired in the 1930s) to set interest rate ceilings on savings and time deposits of member banks was a minor policy instrument that has been phased out as a result of the elimination of interest rate controls mandated by the Depository Institutions Deregulation and Monetary Control Act of 1980. Before DIDMCA the Fed specified these ceiling rates for member banks in the Board's Regulation Q. The Fed set the ceiling rates in consultation with the Federal Deposit Insurance Corporation, which exercised this power for nonmember insured banks, and the Federal Home Loan Bank Board, which set the ceiling rate on dividends paid by member and insured savings and loan associations. DIDMCA established a Depository Institutions Deregulation Committee to assume these scattered powers for all depository institutions and to proceed with phased elimination of interest rate ceilings on savings and time deposit accounts by 1986.

Few observers mourn the elimination of interest rate ceilings. These controls are of little policy value, introduced various distortions in the economy, and are inequitable for the "small" saver. Decontrol was resisted, however, by savings and loan associations because the old control structure allowed them to offer deposit rates that were one quarter of a percent higher than commercial banks. However, DIDMCA placated the savings and loans by permitting them to expand their lending powers into areas previously dominated by commercial banks and by allowing them to issue checkable deposits. Moreover, savings and loan associations, like all depository institutions, benefit from at least one aspect of the demise of rate ceilings: elimination of the tendency for "disintermediation" to occur when market interest rates surpass the ceiling rates by significant margins and savers withdraw (and withhold) funds from intermediaries in favor of direct security or mutual fund purchases.

PROBLEMS OF MONETARY CONTROL

The Federal Reserve System attempts to control money and credit in such a way as to achieve certain ultimate economic goals: an increase in the rate of economic growth, increase in employment, reduction in the rate of inflation, and so on. These are not easy tasks for two reasons: The linkage between changes in monetary and credit aggregates and "real" economic variables is only imperfectly understood; and there is an inevitable lag between Fed action and ultimate impact. These difficulties will be discussed in Chapter 26.

The Fed also has the problem of identifying an immediate target for its operations. Given the time lag before monetary changes affect the price level, employment, and so on, the Fed must aim at some growth rate of monetary and credit aggregates and/or some level of interest rates. Even the proper money supply measure is unsettled, as we indicated in Chapter 4. Further, the direction of changes in the money supply, amount of bank credit, and interest rates do not always signal the same economic message, a fact that continues to fuel a debate of long duration about which of these financial variables is most intimately related to "real" economic variables. The Fed's long-standing emphasis on such money market variables as the federal funds rate as targets (and indicators) of policy actions was the subject of severe criticism by "monetarist" economists, who urged an emphasis on monetary aggregates. In the early 1980's, the Fed shifted its emphasis from the money market variables to monetary aggregates. The Fed currently focuses its attention on the achievement of targeted growth paths for reserves—targets chosen to achieve growth of the monetary aggregates within a desired range—as well as money market conditions. Further discussion of the Fed's approach to monetary control is best deferred to Chapter 26. For the purpose of the ensuing chapters, however, it will be important to recall the Fed's pervasive and highly significant presence in financial markets.

THE FED AS FISCAL AGENT

Like most central banks the Federal Reserve System acts as the principal fiscal agent for the national government. The Fed is the federal government's main bank, since the Treasury also maintains "tax and loan" accounts at commercial banks. The Fed also handles new issues of Treasury securities. The reserve banks process applications from would-be purchasers of Treasury securities, allocate the securities among bidders, deliver the securities, and collect the purchase price from security buyers. The Fed also redeems Treasury securities, transfers securities by wire to other locations, pays interest on securities, and assists the Treasury and other government agencies in a number of other ways.

The Federal Reserve Bank of New York acts as the Treasury's agent in the latter's foreign exchange operations. The Fed also conducts such operations on its own in pursuit of the government's foreign economic policy objectives. Such operations include "dollar support" actions—the purchase of dollars (the selling of foreign currencies for dollars) in foreign exchange markets to increase or maintain the dollar's value in these markets. The Fed maintains close relations with foreign central banks in pursuit of common goals of international financial order.

REGULATION AND SUPERVISION OF MEMBER BANKS

The Fed performs important regulatory and supervisory functions regarding the structure of the banking system in the United States and its domestic and foreign operations. The regulatory function includes formulating and promulgating rules and regulations for the conduct of banking. The Fed's responsibilities also encompass overseeing measures to ensure the soundness of individual banks and the monitoring of actions that affect the structure of the banking system, specifically bank mergers and acquisitions.

The regulatory and supervisory structure of the U.S. banking system is unique in the world. There are three federal bodies and fifty state agencies concerned with this function. At the federal level, in addition to the Federal Reserve

System, the Federal Deposit Insurance Corporation (FDIC) and the Comptroller of the Currency have some measures of responsibility for supervising and regulating commercial banks. The obvious potential for inefficiency that such overlapping responsibilities create has been handled by various cooperative arrangements among the federal and state agencies. Thus the comptroller has primary responsibility for national banks, the Fed focuses on state member banks, and the FDIC has the principal supervisory responsibility for insured nonmember state banks. The examining function is allocated in this fashion among the federal agencies, with the Fed and FDIC coordinating examinations of state-chartered banks with the various state banking authorities.

THE FED AND BANKING STRUCTURE

The Federal Reserve Board of Governors has responsibility for reviewing and approving (or disapproving) certain bank merger proposals and all bank holding company acquisitions. In the case of proposed mergers, jurisdiction is established by the charter status of the resulting banks: if a national bank, the Comptroller of the Currency; if a state-chartered member bank, the Fed; and if a nonmember insured state bank, the FDIC. Merger review policy and procedures, as well as jurisdiction, are dictated by the Bank Merger Act of 1960.

The Fed's responsibility for **bank holding companies** is worthy of special note. In a 1970 amendment of the statute that gave the Fed this responsibility (the Bank Holding Company Act of 1956), a bank holding company was defined as any company that (1) directly or indirectly controls 25 percent of the voting shares of a bank; (2) controls the election of a majority of a bank's directors; or (3) controls the management or policies of a bank. This amendment limited bank holding company activities to those "closely related to banking" and gave the Fed authority to define the range of such activities.

Bank holding companies must register with the Fed and file periodic reports with the Board of Governors. Board approval must be obtained to acquire more than 5 percent of the share of either additional banks or nonbanking companies. In the case of nonbanking companies, only certain types of companies (those involved in designated banking-related activities) are eligible for acquisition by bank holding companies. In reviewing such requests the board considers the potential effect of the acquisition on present and future competition, the financial condition of the banks controlled by the holding company, and the impact on availability of banking and bank-related services to the public.

The board also has statutory responsibilities relating to international operations of member banks. The Fed must approve the establishment of foreign branches and subsidiaries, and it regulates their operations.

NATIONAL PAYMENTS SYSTEM

The Federal Reserve plays an integral role in establishing and maintaining an efficient payments system. Most paper money consists of Federal Reserve notes, a liability of the Federal Reserve. The total quantity of currency, as well as the denominations of the currency outstanding, is determined by the public. For example, around holiday and vacation periods the Fed provides additional currency to banks to meet the increased demands of the public. The Fed is also prepared to absorb the excess currency after holiday and vacation periods. In both instances—providing and withdrawing currency—the Fed works through depository financial institutions, principally commercial banks.

Although important, the Fed's role as a provider of currency has diminished as transactions have increasingly been accomplished with checks rather than currency. As this has occurred, the Fed's role in establishing and maintaining a national check-clearing mechanism has become more important. The Fed now clears checks for all depository institutions, though since DIDMCA, the clearing of checks, as with other Fed services, is performed on an explicit fee basis, either at the Federal Reserve Bank, at one of the branches of the Federal Reserve Banks, or through one of the Regional Check Processing Centers that the Fed has established. In this role the Fed acts as do clearinghouses that clear local checks, except that the Fed generally clears from banks located at considerable distances from one another. Also, the Fed has provided a leadership role in establishing and maintaining wire systems for the electronic transfer of funds throughout the country and, indeed, throughout the world.

THE INDEPENDENCE OF THE FED

One important topic concerning the structure of the Federal Reserve System is its independence. In contrast to most central banks of the world the central bank of the United States (the Federal Reserve) is not technically a part of the Treasury Department or any other part of government. Indeed, as was just discussed, the way in which the Fed has been structured internally—the diffusion of power among many different portions of the system, as well as its freedom from the budgetary process—creates a high degree of autonomy. This automony is there by design. The founders of the Federal Reserve were concerned that our central bank have independence from both Wall Street and the administration in power in Washington. Moreover, while the Federal Reserve was created by Congress and can be modified in structure by Congress, the day-to-day supervision of the Fed by Congress is minimal. Yet the "independence" of the Fed should not be overemphasized; at best, the Fed is independent *within* government, not independent *of* government. Moreover, there is serious debate not only about whether the Fed is independent, but also about whether it should be independent.

Arguments against Independence

The principal argument from those who are opposed to Fed independence stems from the view that monetary policy is too important to be isolated from the political process. Indeed, this argument is that an independent Fed is an undemocratic institution, and such an institution is undesirable in a democracy. By this view the President of the United States, as the only U.S. government official elected by all the people of the nation, is responsible for the performance of the economy, and that performance depends on the conduct of both fiscal and monetary policy. Yet the President has no direct control over the stance of monetary policy. As such, monetary and fiscal policy may be in conflict. These observers would bring the Fed under the direct control of the President. This could be done by making the term of office of the Board of Governors coterminous with that of the President, by eliminating the role of the Federal Reserve Bank presidents in the conduct of monetary policy, and by a number of other reforms.

Arguments for Independence

Those who favor independence also agree that monetary policy is extremely important. However, these groups argue that because it is so important, monetary policies must be isolated from the political process. National governments seem to have an inherent tendency to inflate the quantity of money and, through such inflation, reduce the value of money. Such inflation may be reduced, if not eliminated, by an independent monetary authority such as the Fed. Moreover, to the argument that the Fed is undemocratic, proponents of Fed independence would counter that the Fed is the creation of the elected legislative body of the U.S. government, the Congress. As such, since the Congress created the Fed, it can modify its organization in any way desired.

Arguments about how independent the Fed should be are essentially philosophical in nature. Yet the Fed is in fact a very political organization. Indeed, an understanding of the behavior of the Fed can perhaps best be gained by viewing the Fed as a political organization within the political process. By this view the Fed operates within the influence of a number of political pressures. These pressures emanate from the President, the Congress, the banking and financial community, and economists both within the academic community and in other organizations.[9] Each group attempts to sway the Fed in a particular way, though their

---

[9]See Edward Kane, "The Re-Politicization of the Fed," *Journal of Financial and Quantitative Analysis* (November 1974), 743–752, for a more extensive discussion of the Fed as a political organization.

pressures may be contradictory. The Fed, in turn, attempts to influence these groups in a number of ways. It engages in a good deal of direct publicity through press releases, speeches by officials of the Federal Reserve System, and other similar devices. Moreover, the Fed attempts to build a constituency for its actions in a number of ways. It has established, for example, the Federal Advisory Council in each Federal Reserve district. This group is composed of influential business people and bankers, and it is in a position to extend sympathetic political pressure in favor of a particular Fed position. Moreover, because of its extensive regulatory authority over banks and bank holding companies, the Fed has considerable extralegal power over commercial banking organizations.

SUMMARY

The Federal Reserve System performs functions of vital importance to the U.S. economy. As this nation's central bank, the Fed has the basic responsibility for maintaining money and credit conditions that are consistent with sustainable economic growth, price stability, and a strong dollar in the foreign exchange markets. The Fed controls monetary and credit aggregates by means of open-market operations and changes in reserve requirement ratios, and by controlling the cost and volume of its lending to depository institutions. The Fed also exercises various regulatory and supervisory powers over member banks with the objective of maintaining a sound and competitive banking system.

The major components of the Fed are the member banks (which technically "own" the Federal Reserve Banks), the twelve Federal Reserve Banks, the Board of Governors, and the Federal Open-Market Committee (FOMC). Fewer than two out of five U.S. banks are presently members of the system, but member banks account for about 70 percent of total bank deposits. All national banks must belong to the Federal Reserve System, but many state banks have chosen not to join because membership long entailed holding a significant portion of their assets in nonearning required reserves. The Depository Institutions Deregulation and Monetary Control Act of 1980 greatly changed the cost–benefit equation of membership versus nonmembership in the Fed. This law mandated uniform reserve requirements for all depository institutions while also making Fed services and the discount window available to nonmember institutions.

The Board of Governors, rather than the regional banks, is the seat of power in the Fed. The various banks in the system essentially carry out board policy, perform various operating functions, and serve as centers of economic information and research. The FOMC is also a highly significant entity in the Federal Reserve System because of the status of open-market operations as the principal tool of monetary policy.

The Fed makes extensive use of open-market operations to offset undesired temporary changes in the level of depository institution reserves. These so-called defensive operations minimize the effects on reserves of such disturbances as seasonal shifts in demand for credit and the amount of currency in circulation, cyclical changes in Federal Reserve float, and U.S. Treasury operations. Dynamic open-market operations, on the other hand, are the manifestation of an economic policy goal of the Fed: to restrict growth in money and credit aggregates when inflation is the target and to ease them when the objective is economic expansion.

Changes in reserve requirements (aside from "structural" changes, as in the 1972 and 1980 revisions) are used in the "dynamic" sense. Increases in reserve requirements tighten money and credit, both by increasing the amount of bank reserves that are immobilized as required reserves and by lowering the ratio. This is an extremely powerful policy tool, which is used sparingly and the implementation of which is eased by appropriate use of open-market operations.

The discount window is something of an anachronism, but it still provides the Fed with a ready and convenient means of serving as a "lender of last resort" during periods of financial stress for individual institutions and the financial system. In general, institutions are discouraged from using Fed borrowings as a continuing source of funds.

In its policy operations the Fed has employed a variety of "targets" at different times. It has recently shifted from a focus on the federal funds rate to reserves as "operating targets." In recent years the FOMC has increasingly emphasized the rates of growth in monetary and credit aggregates as public goals.

In addition to its function of monetary control, the Fed has the responsibility for monitoring the financial health of member banks (with the Comptroller of the Currency actually assuming this role for national banks), administering various regulations governing the financial system, and reviewing applications for bank mergers and for acquisitions by bank holding companies. The Fed also acts as fiscal agent for the U.S. Treasury and plays a key role in that nation's payments system.

The Fed's presence in the financial system is thus pervasive and of vital importance. It is the most important single participant in the U.S. financial system. As a result, other participants in the financial marketplace pay keen attention to the activities and attitudes of the Fed. The frequent references to the role of the Fed in subsequent chapters of this book reflect the great significance of this institution in our financial system.

QUESTIONS

1. What problems in the money and banking system of the United States led to the establishment of the Federal Reserve System?

2. Describe the organization and structure of the Federal Reserve System.

3. Why have many state banks in the past chosen not to be members of the Federal Reserve System?

4. What are the principal responsibilities of the Board of Governors of the Federal Reserve System?

5. Describe how the responsibility for bank regulation and supervision is assigned in the United States.

6. What are "open market operations"? Describe their nature and purpose.

7. Why does the Fed exercise "administrative restraint" on the use of the discount window?

8. Evaluate and discuss the following statement: "Open-market operations have emerged as the Fed's principal monetary policy tool because the discount mechanism is too weak and changes in reserve requirements are too powerful."

9. Should the Fed be independent?

10. What responsibilities does the Fed have in addition to the conduct of monetary policy?

REFERENCES

Black, Robert, "The Fed's Mandate: Help or Hindrance?" Federal Reserve Bank of Richmond *Economic Review* (July/August 1984), 3–7.

Board of Governors of the Federal Reserve System, *Federal Reserve System: Purposes and Functions* (Washington, D.C., 1984).

——, "Monetary Aggregates and Money Market Conditions in Open Market Policy," Federal Reserve *Bulletin*, 57 (February 1971), 79–104.

——, "The Depository Institutions Deregulation and Monetary Control Act of 1980," Federal Reserve *Bulletin* (September 1980), 444–453.

Burns, Arthur, *The Anguish of Central Banking* (Washington, D.C.: American Enterprise Institute, 1980).

Cacy, J. A., "Reserve Requirements and Monetary Control," Federal Reserve Bank of Kansas City, *Monthly Review* (May 1976), 3–13.

Johnson, Roger T., *Historical Beginnings . . . The Federal Reserve* (Boston: Federal Reserve Bank of Boston, 1977).

Kane, Edward, "The Re-Politicization of the Fed," *Journal of Financial and Quantitative Analysis* (November 1974), 743–752.

Nordhaus, William D., "The Political Business Cycle," *Review of Economic Studies* (April 1975), 17–26.

Prochnow, Herbert V. (Ed.), *The Federal Reserve System* (New York: Harper & Row, 1969).

"Record of Policy Actions of the Federal Open Market Committee" (published periodically), *Federal Reserve Bulletin.*

PART II

INTEREST RATES

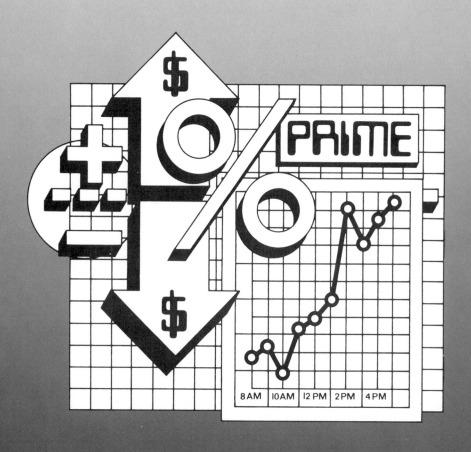

CHAPTER **6**

The Level of Interest Rates

The level and structure of interest rates are clearly of great importance to the economy. At any time there exists both a level of interest rates (high, low, or somewhere in between—relative to historical norms) and a structure (pattern) of the yields on the many different types of interest-bearing financial instruments. Changes in the level of interest rates act to equilibrate aggregate demand and supply for financial resources in the economy. The structure of rates directs (and also reflects) the allocation of financial resources and thus real resources. Changes in relative interest rates redirect financial resource flows, more funds being channeled into high-return (risk-adjusted) uses and away from low-return (risk-adjusted) uses.

In this chapter we are concerned with factors affecting the prevailing **level** of interest rates in the economy. In Chapter 7 we are concerned with the **term structure** of interest rates—the relationship between yields and maturities of financial instruments. Then in Chapter 8 we discuss how price level changes and various characteristics of financial instruments affect both the level and structure of interest rates.

THE REAL INTEREST RATE

The observed rate of interest (or yield) that exists for a given financial instrument at a given point in time is technically labeled a **nominal rate.** The nominal rate of interest can be conceptually disaggregated into a risk-free real rate of interest and various premiums. The **risk-free real rate of interest** is the term for the yield on a single-period maturity security in the absence of expected price level change, taxes, default risk, and uncertainty. The nominal interest rate thus consists of the risk-free real rate plus adjustments that reflect the influences of taxes, expected price level changes, and various risk factors. (The term "real rate" is often used to refer to the nominal interest rate less the expected or realized inflation rate; as the term is used in that case, the "real rate" excludes only the premium for price level change.)

Although not directly observable, the concept of the risk-free real interest rate is a useful device to aid understanding of the level and structure of nominal (observed) interest rates. Price level changes, taxes, and risk all play an important role in the determination of nominal interest rates. But even in the absence of these elements, it is evident that a rate of interest would exist, and this "real rate" is always a component of nominal rates. The real rate of interest was viewed by classical economists as being determined by the level of productivity and thrift in a society.

There is a well-developed "neoclassical" theory of the real rate of interest. Usually called Fisherian interest rate theory (in acknowledgment of the economist, Irving Fisher, who is responsible for much of the theory), this analysis focuses on the presumed principal economic determinants of a risk-free real interest rate: the marginal rate of **time preference** (the marginal rate of exchange between present and future consumption which emerges from individuals' choices in a free market) and the marginal **rate of return** on real capital investment projects. We now examine each concept and evaluate its significance for interest rate determination.

Time Preference

Saving represents the forgoing of present consumption of goods and services in exchange for future consumption. Why do individuals choose to save? One reason is simply to ensure future consumption—the proverbial "saving for a rainy day" motive. Saving motivated by such considerations of simple prudence can generally be expected to occur even if consumption is not augmented by its postponement. The motive for saving that is important in interest rate theory, however, is the attempt to enhance future consumption by forgoing present consumption. The textbook examples of saving seed corn rather than eating it and of a fisherman forgoing a day's catch with his or her fishing pole in order to construct a fishing net are classic illustrations of this motive for saving. (These examples also link the saving decision to the capital formation process.) The choice framework for decisions relating to the exchange of present for future consumption is called **time preference.**

The real, risk-free rate of interest essentially emerges from an act of saving that enlarges future consumption. The real rate of interest is the increment in consumption that results from saving. Suppose ten units of present consumption (of some good) are forgone to have eleven units of the consumption good at the end of some specified period. In effect, ten units of present consumption have

---

USURY: A MATTER OF INTEREST

The development of commercial credit and financial institutions in the Middle Ages was slowed by the opposition of the Christian church to usury, a word that has meant different things to different people for centuries. From the ninth to the thirteenth century the Church viewed all lending of money at interest as income without work and therefore sinful. Moneylending thus attracted some Jews, since they had no religious constraint and were barred from a number of other occupations. (However, Jews were at risk in lending both because of their persecution by Christians during the period and because of the general unenforceability of claims arising from moneylending.)

In the thirteenth century, as trade and commerce expanded, the Church modified its usury doctrine. The risk associated with putting one's capital on the line in a moneylending situation was accepted as a form of "work," and thus a fair interest return was acceptable as income for such "work." **Interest** thus became respectable. **Usury,** a payment for the lending of money when there was no risk to the lender (as when the loan was fully collateralized), remained wicked and was forbidden in many nations (including England) until the seventeenth century. By its most recent definition—an exorbitantly high rate of interest—usury remains illegal in many parts of the world, including a number of states in the United States. Much of the Islamic world still takes a dim view of lending money for interest.

---

been transformed into eleven units of future consumption. It is obvious that consumption has been increased by 10 percent for the period—the reward for the act of saving (which is the real rate of interest on the consumption forgone). In this case the saver preferred eleven units of future consumption to ten units of present consumption. The rates of time preference of other individuals might differ: they might require a greater increment in future consumption than 10 percent in order to be willing to forgo present consumption. And, of course, the opportunity to transform present into future consumption at a real rate of interest of 10 percent (or greater) might not be available. Such opportunities are called **capital investment projects,** and the returns on such projects, like the rate of time preference, is an element of real interest rate determination.

Capital Investment

Time preference theory concerns the choice made by individuals between present and future consumption. Capital investment theory concerns opportunities for trading present for future consumption. The rate at which future consumption can be enlarged by **investing**—the forgoing of present consumption in order to create capital goods—is the rate of return on capital investment projects.

If saving and investing had to be jointly conducted by the same individual, as in Robinson Crusoe's economic system, available investment opportunities would be quite limited. From this restricted set the individual investor–saver would save and invest in all projects that offered a rate of return at least equal to that individual's marginal rate of time preference. The volume of saving (quantity of present consumption forgone) would be equal to (and limited to) the aggregate resource requirements of these projects.

Real Interest Rate Determination

Suppose we move beyond this restricted scenario to a more realistic case in which the saving–investing individual is only one of many savers and investors in a society that also includes dissavers. Assume that borrowing and lending are possible. Consider investors who have attractive capital investment opportunities that, in the aggregate, require more saved resources than the investors can marshall or that offer rates of return less than the investor's marginal rate of time preference but greater than the marginal rate of time preference for some savers. Such investors can borrow from savers by offering to share the fruits of the capital projects with their lenders. Savers will lend if such "shared fruits," as a rate of return on the loaned resources, equal or exceed their marginal time preference rate. Savers will also lend to dissavers (who are, in effect, exchanging future consumption for current consumption) in exchange for future payment of the loaned resources plus interest. Borrowing and lending make possible a separation of individuals' consumption decisions and investment decisions (the Fisher separation theorem); they are linked only in the aggregate via the equilibrating mechanism of the real interest rate.

The point of all this is that the real interest rate in a society will reflect present versus future consumption time preferences of the individuals in that society and rates of return offered by available capital investment opportunities (productivity). In Fisherian interest rate theory the real interest rate is identical to the marginal rate of return on capital investment projects, which, in equilibrium, equals the marginal rate of time preference. In the market in which borrowing and lending occur (the use of productive resources is exchanged over time) a rate of exchange will be determined that equates borrowing and lending. This rate of exchange of present for future resources is, in turn, the real rate of interest.

What are the implications of this analysis for the level of interest rates? Consider the influence of time preference. A society that has a greater future consumption–present consumption preference ratio will generate more saved resources than a society that attaches relatively less importance to future consumption. All else being equal, the real rate of interest will be inversely related to the rate of saving. Further, an economy with a plethora of high-return capital investment projects (high marginal productivity of capital) will be characterized by a higher real rate of interest than would be the case if the economy were confronted with a dearth of attractive capital projects (low marginal productivity of capital). Further, the existence of well-developed and efficient markets for borrowing and lending will lower the real rate of interest.

Risk and uncertainty increase the real rate of interest. In practice, returns from proposed capital investment projects are expected, not assured. Repayment by borrowers is likewise uncertain. Thus risk premiums are incorporated into the process of determining the equilibrium real rate of interest. And since risk will vary across borrowers and capital projects, multiple real interest rates emerge. The fact that money is used to exchange and exercise control of real resources (and the fact that money's purchasing power is not constant) and the existence of taxation introduce elements into interest rate determination that are likely to remove further the observed rate from the underlying real rate of interest. (These influences are discussed in Chapter 8.) Before considering nominal interest rate determination in a monetary context, however, we note next the role of the real interest rate in equating saving and investment funds flows.

Savings and Investment

In Fisherian interest rate theory the real rate of interest equates desired borrowing and lending as an integral and essential part of the process by which consumption time preferences are satisfied and attractive capital investment projects are undertaken. On the other side of the same coin the real interest rate is the interest rate that results in equality between planned net saving and planned net investment. Figure 6.1 depicts this process.

Saving is shown in Fig. 6.1 to be a positive function of real income (y) and the level of the interest rate (r), or

$$s = s(y,r)$$

with $y_3 > y_2 > y_1$.

Saving will increase as the return to saving (the gain in the future consumption–present consumption forgone ratio) increases. Saving also increases as real income increases (which necessarily follows if consumption time preference is unchanged).

Investment is shown as an inverse function of the real rate of interest (r) or

$$i = i(r)$$

Since proposed capital investment projects will not be undertaken unless their expected returns exceed r, it follows that aggregate investment will decline as r rises and vice versa.

In equilibrium, $s = i$ at some r, as shown in Fig. 6.1. Why must investment and saving be identical amounts in equilibrium? First, note that real income arises from the production of goods and services—both consumption and investment goods—and that income is either spent for consumption or saved. Second,

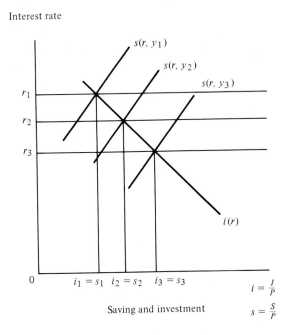

Interest rate

FIGURE 6.1   Saving, Investment, and the Rate of Interest

recognize that **planned investment** and **planned saving** are equal only when equilibrium is attained, but **actual** (or realized) saving and investment are always equal. Realized saving and realized investment are always equal because changes in business inventories are included in investment spending, and such changes will always equal any gap between planned saving and planned investment. If planned saving exceeds planned investment, people will spend less on consumption than the value of consumption goods produced. As a result, business firms will find themselves holding larger quantities of inventory than they had planned. As business firms subsequently trim production and reduce their labor force, income and saving will fall. The process will continue until the revised amount of planned saving (lower because of the decline in income) is equal to planned investment.

If, on the other hand, planned saving is less than planned investment, consumption purchases will exceed the output of consumption goods, and inventories will fall. Business firms respond by increasing output (to replenish their declining inventories), and income rises. Produced output and income will rise, and so will saving. Income and saving will increase until planned saving and planned investment are equal.

The saving–investment equilibrating process hinges on how income and the rate of interest affect saving and investment. In essence, when interest rates are low, investment is high (all else being equal). Income must be correspondingly high to bring forth saving in the amount necessary to achieve equilibrium. Similarly, high interest rates imply low levels of investment, so income must be low to bring saving down to those levels. To the extent that saving is responsive to the rate of interest, the process will be sensitized. High interest rates encourage saving at the same time that investment is discouraged, and vice versa.

THE LOANABLE FUNDS THEORY OF INTEREST RATE DETERMINATION

An understanding of the concept of the real interest rate and its determination is useful. Given the purposes of this book, however, a *monetary* theory of *nominal* interest rate determination warrants greater attention. Such a theory is the **loanable funds theory** of interest rate determination, which focuses on the nominal supply and demand for loanable funds. Like Fisherian real interest rate theory, loanable funds theory is only a short-run, partial equilibrium theory of interest rates that does not consider "feedback" effects of changes in real income stemming from initial interest rate changes. (A more general model would incorporate joint equilibrium conditions in which equilibrium levels of interst rates and real income are determined simultaneously.) Loanable funds analysis, however, is a very useful framework to assess the factors that give rise to the supply and demand for loanable funds and to understand the interaction of these factors in financial markets.

Supply of Loanable Funds

The supply of loanable funds provided to the financial markets is determined essentially by (1) the amount of saving by households, businesses, and governments; (2) the amount of capital inflows from foreign residents—the amount of foreign saving that flows into domestic financial markets from abroad; and (3) the amount of new money created by the banking system. The sum of these three items for a given period of time (say, one year) constitutes the supply of loanable funds for that period.

In our explanation of the supply of loanable funds and also of the demand for loanable funds we must keep in mind that we are dealing with supply and demand schedules. These schedules are "what if" relationships; that is, if the interest rate is at a certain level, then the quantity supplied or demanded is a certain amount. At a different interest rate, the quantity supplied (and quantity demanded) may be different, but we are moving along a given supply or demand curve, and the change in the quantities demanded and supplied result from the change in the rate of interest. In contrast, a change in supply or demand would involve a shift in the schedule whereby more or less would be supplied at all interest rate levels.

Saving.   As we discussed earlier, saving refers to the postponement of current consumption. The decision to save is the decision to forgo current consumption in order to have a larger quantity of consumption in the future. Households (individuals) save for a variety of reasons—the proverbial "rainy day," education of children, retirement, and other reasons—but little evidence suggests that the quantity of loanable funds supplied through saving is markedly influenced by the level of the interest rate. A higher interest rate represents a greater reward to the saver for postponing current consumption and thus might be expected to produce a higher quantity of savings for some individuals. Yet for the individual who has a target level of desired wealth, the higher interest rate might lead to a reduction in saving. In the view of most observers the quantity of savings supplied by individuals is principally determined by the level of income, and it is influenced to a lesser degree by the level of interest rates. (Of course, changes in the level of income will change the amount of desired saving at each level of interest rates.)

This relatively small impact of changes in interest rates on the quantity of saving by individuals is probably equally true for businesses and governments. Business saving refers to the net income after taxes of the firm, less any cash dividends—that is, retained earnings. Changes in business net income reflect changes in sales and costs, whereas the decision to distribute cash dividends reflects management judgment about internal investment opportunities, as well as management perceptions about the impact of dividend changes on the stock price of the firm. There is little reason to believe that the volume of saving at business firms is strongly influenced by the level of interest rates.

For governments, the volume of saving is defined as the difference between revenues and expenditures, such that saving exists when revenues exceed expenditures (a budget surplus). Completely separate from the fact that—at least at the federal level—governmental units in the United States have seldom had budget surpluses in recent years, there is again little reason to believe that the volume of saving is strongly influenced by the interest rate. At the federal level the budget surplus or deficit reflects the joint interaction of fiscal policy—changes in tax and expenditure policies designed to achieve broad macroeconomic objectives—and the level of economic activity. At the state and local levels the budget surplus or deficit is influenced by the demand for services by local residents, as well as by the strength of the local economy.

To summarize, saving (the postponement of current consumption) may be done by households, businesses, and governments. The volume of saving of each unit is influenced by various factors, of which the interest rate is only one. As a result, we might expect that the relationship between the interest rate and the volume of saving would appear as in Fig. 6.2—a mildly positive relationship between the interest rate and the volume of saving. For example, at an interest rate of r the volume of saving would be Q, whereas at the higher interest rate of r' the volume of saving would be only a slightly higher Q'. The responsiveness of saving to changes in interest rates is quite small. Relatively large increases in interest rates are required to produce modest increases in saving.

New Money.   Although the volume of saving is the principal source of loanable funds in financial markets, the supply of loanable funds may be increased through the creation of new money beyond the amount made possible by current saving. The amount of money created is determined jointly by the actions of the commercial banking system and the central bank—in the United States the Federal Reserve System. Commercial banks use any excess reserves to make loans, purchase securities, and create money (demand deposits) through the credit creation process. However, the ability of commercial banks to create money is limited by the Federal Reserve through the use of its monetary policy tools of open-market operations, reserve requirement changes, and discount rate changes.

Commercial banks are private, profit-seeking, business enterprises. In contrast, the Federal Reserve is a quasi-public organization whose primary function is to control the supply and cost of money in order to achieve broad macroeconomic goals. There is little evidence that either the Fed or the commercial banks are substantially influenced in the money creation process by the level of interest rates. The principal factor determining the volume of new money created by the

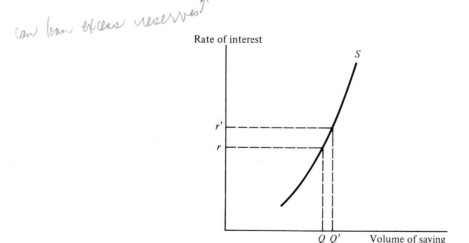

FIGURE 6.2   The Interest Rate and the Volume of Saving

banking system is the amount of reserves, and the principal factor that determines the amount of reserves is Federal Reserve monetary policy. Neither factor
should be directly influenced by the level of interest rates.[1]

Capital Inflows.   The supply of loanable funds in the United States is increased
when foreign residents acquire financial assets in the United States. Such capital
inflows have become quite significant for the United States in recent years. **Capital inflows** are, of course, a flow of loanable funds from other nations to the
United States. **Capital outflows**—the purchase of foreign financial assets by U.S.
residents—are a flow of loanable funds from this country to others. From World
War I to the late 1970s, capital outflows from the United States exceeded capital
inflows. But large trade deficits and federal budget deficits reversed this pattern
in the 1980s.

In summary, the amount of capital inflows is largely a function of yields of U.S. securities
relative to foreign securities, the proportion of total financial assets that foreign
investors wish to hold in U.S. dollars (which, in turn, is a function of a variety of
variables, including political risk), and the expected change in the foreign exchange value of the U.S. dollar. To a foreign investor the relevant expected yield
of an investment in U.S. securities is the nominal rate of interest (in U.S. dollars)
less any expected *decrease* in the value of the dollar relative to the investor's home
currency or *plus* any expected *increase* in the dollar's value. When this real return
on U.S. dollar investment becomes high in relation to what foreign investors can
earn in their own currency investment—as occurred in the early 1980s—capital
inflows rise. Thus unlike domestic savings and additions to the money supply,
capital inflows are quite sensitive to the level of interest rates, although the effect
of nominal rate levels may be offset by expected changes in the value of the
dollar in the foreign exchange market.

In summary, the supply of loanable funds is the sum of current domestic
saving, capital inflows, and the amount of new money created. It is convenient
for exposition to lump the saving of U.S. residents and capital inflows together
as "saving," and this will be done in the balance of this chapter. With this simplification, and recalling that additions to the money supply are not directly influ-

---

[1]This is something of an oversimplification. Higher interest rate levels encourage banks to use
their reserves more fully, so there may be some positive relationship between the interest rate
level and the quantity of money created on any given reserve base. Also, the amount of new
money created is relatively insensitive to the level of interest rates, but the amount of these funds
actually provided to the loanable funds market can be affected by the amount of **hoarding** or
dishoarding. At relatively low rates, economic participants may hoard a portion of the new money
(since the opportunity cost of holding money is low), whereas at high rates they may dishoard by
reducing their existing money balances (since the opportunity cost of holding money is high). As a
result, the supply of loanable funds may be less than the combined supply of savings and new
money at low interest rates and more than the combined supply in periods of high interest rates.

enced by the level of interest rates, we may depict the supply of loanable funds as shown in Figure 6.3.

Shifts in the supply of loanable funds function can occur for a variety of reasons. The most important cause of a shift of the supply of loanable funds schedule is a change in the rate of growth of the money supply. An increase in the rate of monetary growth increases the supply of loanable funds; since a greater amount of loanable funds at all interest rates is the result, this is depicted as a shift to the right of the supply of loanable funds schedule. A decrease in the rate of growth of the money supply reduces the supply of loanable funds; since a smaller amount of loanable funds at all interest rates is the result, this is depicted as a shift to the left of the loanable funds function. Similarly, changes in the saving rate or in the propensity of foreign residents to buy U.S. securities will shift the supply of loanable funds schedule. For example, it is obvious that if Americans began saving more at all rates of interest, the supply of loanable funds (all else being equal) would increase. In the case of capital inflows the supply of loanable funds would decrease if foreign investors reduced their holdings of U.S. securities because of fear of a sharp decline in the value of the U.S. dollar. Figure 6.4 depicts shifts in the supply of loanable funds schedule.

The Demand for Loanable Funds

The demand for loanable funds is composed of the demand by individuals, businesses, and governments. We will discuss each of these separately and then put them together to form the demand function for loanable funds.

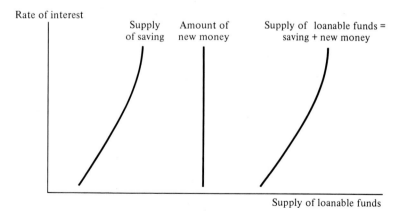

FIGURE 6.3   **The Interest Rate and the Supply of Loanable Funds**

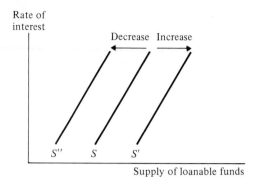

FIGURE 6.4   Shifts in the Supply of Loanable Funds Schedule

Consumer Demand.   Individuals desire to borrow for a variety of reasons.[2] Perhaps the most significant reason is to acquire homes, automobiles, and consumer durable goods. The reliance of consumers on funds borrowed through financial markets has become an accepted practice in the post–World War II period. The responsiveness of the quantity demanded of loanable funds by consumers to interest rate changes is generally thought to be relatively small, with sharp increases in rates being necessary to curtail consumer borrowing and spending (and vice versa).

Business Demand.   Business demand for loanable funds is influenced by a variety of factors but principally reflects investment spending for inventory and plant and equipment. Business investment in inventory holdings is highly volatile—rising by billions of dollars in some periods and falling by billions of dollars in others—and is primarily determined by the differences between expected (planned) sales and actual (realized) sales. In periods when actual sales are greater than expected sales, inventory holdings fall. In periods when actual sales fall short of planned or expected sales, inventory holdings rise. These undesired movements in inventory holdings must be financed, and it is usual to finance them by tapping the market for loanable funds (generally short-term funds). Not surprisingly, given the fact that many of these changes in inventory holdings do not reflect the plans of business management, the demand for loanable funds to finance changes in inventory levels is thought to be relatively insensitive to changes in the interest rate.

---

[2]Since households are the principal supply sector, it is also possible to subtract consumer borrowing from household savings and to talk about households only from a net supply perspective.

The other major determinant of business demand for loanable funds—expenditures for plant and equipment purchases—reflects more significantly the long-run planning function. Decisions to add to a plant or to install labor-saving equipment or other such plant and equipment decisions are important for the success or failure of most business organizations. Yet the profitability projections necessary to evaluate these potential purchases are subject to wide margins of error. Therefore the required return on investment used by many firms to justify the commitment of funds for plant expansion or other major investments is often quite high, substantially higher than the cost of borrowed funds. As a result, large movements in the interest rate are necessary to produce significant changes in the quantity of loanable funds demanded.

Government Demand.   The demand for loanable funds by government units is usually divided for discussion purposes into demand by the federal government and demand by state and local governments. This distinction is important, since the motives for state and local government borrowing tend to be similar to those of the private sector, whereas the motives underlying federal government borrowing decisions tend to be quite different. The demand for loanable funds by state and local governments is basically a function of population growth in the local area, which expands demands for local government services. For example, growth in population requires expansion of roads and sewage facilities. These expenditures, which are usually financed with borrowings from the loanable funds market, may be temporarily postponed if conditions in the credit markets are unfavorable, but they must be undertaken within a reasonably short time after the demand increases. As a result, even though there does appear to be responsiveness in the quantity of loanable funds demanded by state and local governments to changes in the interest rate, the impact of rising or falling interest rates is again thought to be quite small.

Federal government demand for loanable funds is thought to be completely insensitive to changes in the interest rate. The amount of funds the federal government must borrow is determined by the overall balance of the federal budget, which in turn reflects the fiscal policy of the nation. Fiscal policy itself is designed to achieve broad macroeconomic goals and is not thought to be affected in any direct way by the level of interest rates. In short, Congress determines the budget surplus or deficit (almost always a deficit in recent years), and the Treasury Department must finance that deficit, regardless of the level of interest rates.

To summarize, the demand for loanable funds is made up of the separate demands by consumers, businesses, and governments. Although the interest sensitivity of each basic component of the demand for loanable funds varies, it is generally accepted that the overall responsiveness of the quantity of loanable funds demanded to changes in interest rates is relatively small. This is shown in Fig. 6.5, where the demand for loanable funds is drawn as downward sloping, indicating that there is an increase in the demand for loanable funds as the inter-

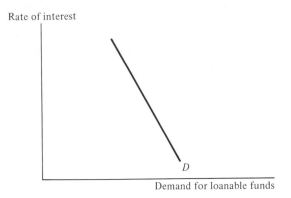

FIGURE 6.5   Demand for Loanable Funds

est rate declines, but the demand curve is drawn as relatively inelastic, indicating that the responsiveness of the quantity of loanable funds demanded to interest rate movements is fairly limited.

One other feature of the demand of loanable funds should be discussed: the volatility of the demand schedule. The quantity of loanable funds demanded is relatively insensitive to changes in interest rates, but the amount of loanable funds used by consumers, businesses, and governments varies widely. These large fluctuations reflect sharp changes (shifts) in the demand function itself. For example, in a period of rising inflationary expectations, businesses and consumers may desire to increase sharply their borrowings at any interest rate. This tendency is shown by the shift of the demand function from D to D' in Fig. 6.6. In periods of pessimism about the future of the economy, on the other hand, businesses and consumers may sharply curtail their borrowings at any given interest rate, as shown by D'' in Fig. 6.6. This immense volatility of the demand functions for loanable funds is of substantial importance in understanding movements in interest rates over the business cycle.

Supply and Demand for Loanable Funds.   We are now in a position to show how the supply and demand functions for loanable funds jointly determine the interest rate. Within the loanable funds perspective the interest rate (r) and the quantity of loanable funds bought and sold (Q) are determined by the interaction of the supply of loanable funds (lending) and the demand for loanable funds (borrowing). Given the demand and supply functions specified in Fig. 6.7, r and Q are equilibrium values. At an interest rate above r the quantity of loanable funds supplied would exceed the quantity demanded. Lenders seeking to get rid of their excess funds would lower their price (the interest rate) until the quantity supplied and quantity demanded were equal. At an interest rate below r the quan-

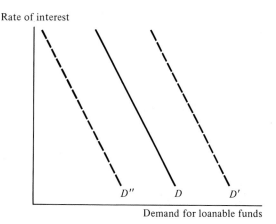

FIGURE 6.6 Shifts in the Demand for Loanable Funds

tity of loanable funds demanded would exceed the quantity supplied. Borrowers competing for scarce loanable funds would then drive the interest rate higher. Only at r are the quantity supplied and the quantity demanded in balance.

We can also explain changes in the interest rate through the loanable funds approach. For example, suppose that the demand for loanable funds shifted to D' in Fig. 6.8. This could occur because there was an increase in the demand for money at every interest rate level by consumers, businesses, or governments. In any case the equilibrium interest rate would rise to r'. Conversely, suppose that

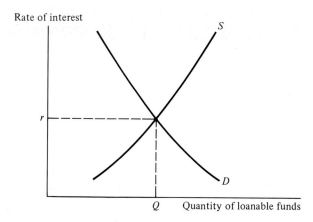

FIGURE 6.7 Supply and Demand of Loanable Funds

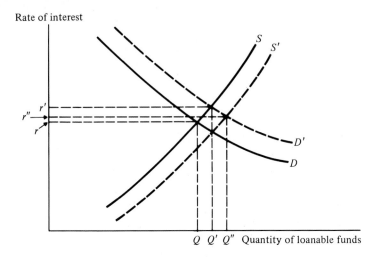

FIGURE 6.8   Changes in the Supply and Demand for Loanable Funds

the supply of loanable funds increased (a shift to the right of the supply schedule). This could result from a greater desire to save on the part of consumers,
businesses, and governments or an easy money policy by the Federal Reserve,
which allowed the banking system to expand the money supply. In this case, if
the supply curve shifted to S', the interest rate would fall to r''. Using the loanable
funds approach in this manner allows the financial analyst to predict and explain
the impact of many diverse factors on the interest rate.

Secondary Markets.   The discussion to this point has considered only *new* borrowing and lending taking place in *primary* markets for securities. However, the
role of the secondary markets for securities (and interest rates on previously
issued debt instruments) is easily incorporated into our analysis. Quite simply,
the equilibrium interest rate must be the same for the secondary market as for
the primary market. New securities and outstanding securities that are otherwise
identical will offer identical yields. New security issues (new borrowing and lending) constitute additions (flows) to the existing stock of securities, and supply–
demand shifts in the market for the latter will maintain equivalent yields for
equivalent securities.

Assessment of the Loanable Funds Theory

As we discussed above, the loanable funds explanation of interest rates emphasizes the significance of three factors that lead to increases and decreases
in "the" interest rate: (1) the volume of savings by individuals, businesses, and

governments; (2) the amount of new money created; and (3) the demand for funds by individuals, businesses, and governments. However, in any attempt to understand (or forecast) movements of interest rates over the business cycle it is important to determine whether any of these factors is a major influence in bringing about changes in interest rates. Evaluating this issue with the use of actual financial data is difficult. The loanable funds theory, like any theory, is an abstraction, since the theory deals with "what if" relationships, and since published financial data only approximate these abstractions. Yet many observers believe that the two dominant factors in explaining interest rate movements are changes in the demands for funds and changes in Federal Reserve monetary policy. Thus many interest rate forecasts focus on these factors, using projected funds flows in the economy. (Chapter 23 describes the use of flow of funds analysis to forecast financial developments.)

It should be noted that the loanable funds theory incorporates saving and investment flows and is thus in no way counter to the real interest rate theory discussed earlier in this chapter. Note also that there is an alternative monetary theory of interest rate determination, the liquidity preference theory (described in the appendix), which is essentially at variance with loanable funds theory only in the mode of formulation.

SUMMARY

The level of interest rates is clearly an economic variable of great significance. Thus an understanding of the process in which the magnitude and structure of interest rates are determined is very important. Such an understanding is facilitated by recognizing that the nominal interest rates observed at any point in time have several components. Conceptually, nominal rates consist of a real, risk-free component plus premiums that reflect the influences of risk, taxation, and expectations. The principal determinants of this real, risk-free rate are saving and investment flows, which in turn reflect patterns of thrift and productivity of capital in a society. In the Fisherian theory of interest the real interest rate is equal to the marginal rate of return on real capital investment, the marginal rate of consumption time preference, and the interest rate on borrowing and lending.

The loanable funds theory focuses on the determination of the nominal interest rate by the interaction of the supply of loanable funds (lending) and the demand for loanable funds (borrowing). This short-term, partial equilibrium explanation focuses on the supply of saving as the basic determinant of the supply of loanable funds, the roles of the Federal Reserve and the commercial banking system in creating additional loanable funds, and the demand for borrowed funds by households, businesses, and governments. The interaction of the supply of loanable funds with the demand for them determines the equilibrium interest rate. Changes in interest rate levels may then be analyzed by looking at changes in the supply and demand for loanable funds.

Understanding the basic determinants of "the" interest rate and of movements in "the" interest rate over time is not easy. Yet such an understanding is vitally important to participants in financial markets, since the prices of financial assets are affected greatly by changes in the level of interest rates. In this chapter we presented a conceptual framework for organizing the various factors that influence interest rates. Yet this conceptual framework is necessarily abstract and simplified. We turn our attention in the next two chapters to reducing the degree of abstraction in discussing the factors that influence interest rates. In Chapter 7 we will explain how the time to maturity of a financial instrument affects the yield on the instrument, and in Chapter 8 we will treat the influence of inflation, credit risk, and other factors.

QUESTIONS

1. The classical economists viewed real interest rate determination as a process of interaction between thrift (saving) and productivity (investment). How does the Fisherian theory of real interest determination constitute a refinement of the classical view?

2. Define the "real interest rate." How is it determined? Relate it to a "nominal" interest rate.

3. Explain the role of the real interest rate in equilibrating planned saving and planned investment.

4. In what way is the loanable funds theory a theory of borrowing and lending?

5. The interest elasticity of the demand for loanable funds is thought to be quite small. Of what significance is this for monetary policy?

6. Evaluate the interest sensitivity of each of the following.
   a. The supply of saving.
   b. The supply of new money.
   c. The demand for loanable funds.

7. Using the loanable funds theory, explain the impact of each of the following on the interest rate.
   a. A decrease in the desire to save.
   b. A shift to an "easy" money policy on the part of the Federal Reserve.
   c. Increased profit opportunities on business investments.

8. Demonstrate that the loanable funds model is consistent with the Fisherian theory of the real interest rate.

9. Explain the significance of capital inflows for the level of interest rates.

REFERENCES

Campbell, Tim S., *Financial Institutions, Markets, and Economic Activity* (New York: McGraw Hill, 1982).

Conard, Joseph, *An Introduction to the Theory of Interest* (Berkeley: University of California Press, 1959).

Fisher, Irving, *The Theory of Interest* (New York: Macmillan, 1930).

Gurley, John G., and Edward S. Shaw, *Money in a Theory of Finance* (Washington, D.C.: The Brookings Institution, 1960).

Haggio, Craig S., and Bryon Higgins, "Is the United States Too Dependent on Foreign Capital?" Federal Reserve Bank of Kansas City *Economic Review* (June 1985), 3–22.

Hirschleifer, Jack, *Investment, Interest and Capital* (Englewood Cliffs, N.J.: Prentice-Hall, 1970).

Homer, Sidney, *A History of Interest Rates* (New Brunswick, N.J.: Rutgers University Press, 1962).

——, and Richard I. Johanneson, *The Price of Money* (New Brunswick, N.J.: Rutgers University Press, 1969).

Lutz, Frederick A., *The Theory of Interest,* 2nd ed. (New York: Aldine Press, 1960).

Patinkin, Don, *Money, Interest and Prices: An Integration of Monetary and Value Theory,* 2nd ed. (New York: Harper & Row, 1965).

Van Horne, James C., *Financial Market Rates and Flows,* 2nd ed. (Englewood Cliffs, N.J.: Prentice-Hall, 1984).

APPENDIX
The Liquidity Preference Theory of Interest Rate Determination

The "loanable funds" approach to interest rate determination focuses on supply of and demand for loanable funds. An alternative approach, the "liquidity preference" view, focuses instead on the supply of and demand for money. It is assumed that individuals inherently prefer money among all financial assets. Wealth holders are persuaded to hold financial assets other than money only because these nonmoney assets offer an interest return greater than that yielded by money (with both explicit and implicit returns on cash holdings being considered). Further, the greater the spread between the yields on nonmoney financial assets and money, the less the demand for money holdings and the greater the demand for other financial assets, and vice versa. The demand schedule for money can thus be depicted as a function of the rate of interest, as shown in Fig. 6A.1.

The amount of money that people wish to hold is also a function of the level of their spending, since money is used for payments. In turn, spending is determined by income. Thus the greater the income, the greater will be the quantity of money demanded at a given rate of interest and vice versa. This relationship is depicted in Fig. 6A.2, where M_DY_1, M_DY_2, and M_DY_3 represent the demand for money at the successively higher income levels Y_1, Y_2, and Y_3, respectively.

Thus for a given income level, say Y_2, and a given money supply, the rate of interest (r_E) is viewed as determined by the supply–demand equilibrium depicted in Fig. 6A.3, where M_S is the supply of money.[3]

The equilibrium interest rate, r_E, is obtained by actions of individuals seeking to maintain desired levels of cash balances. Since the amount of desired money holdings is a function of the rate of interest, in only one rate of interest is the demand for money balances the same as the amount of the money supply. At a rate of interest higher than r_E, say r_H in Fig. 6A.3, individuals in the aggregate will be holding more money (M_S) than they desire (M_{D_H}) at that rate of interest (the total supply of money must be held by the public). To rid themselves of "excess" cash, individuals purchase interest-bearing financial assets, driving their prices up and their interest rates down. This occurs until the rate of interest falls to r_E, at which $M_{D_E} = M_S$.

The outcome, of course, is that the public still holds, in the aggregate, the same amount of money, but at the lower rate of interest this is now the desired

---

[3]The supply of money, as well as the demand for money, can be viewed as being responsive to the rate of interest. One reason for an interest-sensitive money supply function is the possibility that banks may hold smaller amounts of desired excess reserves as interest rates rise. However, the Fed can offset such a phenomenon (as it can do with any factor that induces money expansion) by use of its tools of monetary control.

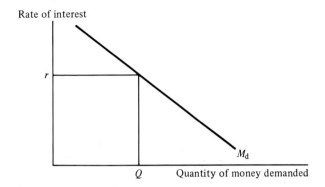

FIGURE 6A.1   The Demand for Money as a Function of the Rate of Interest

amount. On the other hand, if the interest rate is lower than r_E, say r_L in Fig. 6A.3, the public will be holding smaller money balances (M_S) than they desire (M_{D_L}) at that rate of interest. As a result, to obtain more cash in this situation, individuals sell interest-bearing securities, the aggregate effect of which is lower security prices and higher interest rates. The interest rate will thus rise to r_E, at which point desired cash holdings equal the supply of cash.

A principal aspect of the liquidity preference model is that changes in the money supply affect the rate of interest. In the liquidity preference framework, with income and price level assumed to be constant, an increase in the money supply will lower r_E, the equilibrium rate of interest (Fig. 6A.4), and a decrease in the money supply will raise r_E (Fig. 6A.5).

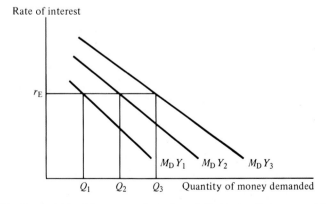

Figure 6A.2   The Demand for Money as a Function of the Rate of Interest and Level of Income

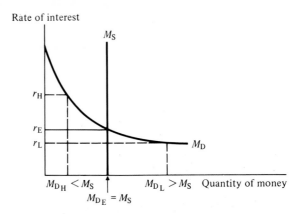

FIGURE 6A.3   Interest Rate Determination According to the Theory of Liquidity Preference

Figure 6A.6 serves as a summary depiction of interest rate determination according to the liquidity preference model. When the money supply is M_{S_1}, the rate of interest is r_1. As the money supply expands to M_{S_2} and M_{S_3}, the rate of interest falls to r_2 and r_3, respectively. The process by which interest rates fall as M_S expands can again be interpreted in terms of public preferences for money holdings relative to other financial assets, such as interest-bearing securities.[4] For example, as the money supply expands from M_{S_1} to M_{S_2}, individuals find themselves holding larger cash balances than they desire at interest rate r_1. As they seek to reduce money holdings by the purchase of securities, security prices rise and interest rates fall until a new equilibrium is established at interest rate r_2, where $M_D = M_{S_2}$.

This monetary view of interest rate determination, though having a measure of validity in the short run, ignores "feedback" from the real sector of the economy. Growth in the money supply has an impact on prices and production, although the manner and degree of impact are subjects of dispute. One "real" effect of lower interest rates due to an increased money supply is believed to be an increase in investment spending. The latter is likely to result in increased borrowing by investors (increase in supply of securities), which tends to raise interest rates. Further, if an increased money supply spurs inflation, inflationary pressures will cause interest rates to rise. Even more contrary to the liquidity preference model, if an increase in the money supply triggers expectations of inflationary pressures, an anticipatory rise in interest rates may result from a shift in the demand for money schedule.

---

[4]Changes in interest rates also affect the level of desired holdings of real assets. Therefore individuals may increase their consumption and business firms may increase investment as interest rates decline, and vice versa.

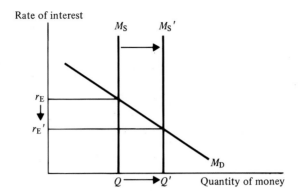

FIGURE 6A.4   Effect of an Increase in the Money Supply on the Rate of Interest

Various limitations of the liquidity preference model stem from the fact that the demand-for-money schedule (M_D) is not constant:

1. It shifts with changes in income (and wealth) of the public. This complicates the analysis considerably because changes in the rate of interest have a significant impact on income via its effect on saving and investment.

2. The demand for money is viewed as a demand for "real" money balances. It is a function of the quantity of goods and services that a given quantity of money will buy. Inflation reduces the purchasing power of money, and deflation increases it. Thus there is actually a different M_D schedule for every price level.

3. Further, expectations about the course of future price level changes, interest rate changes, and other economic events may cause shifts in the M_D schedule.

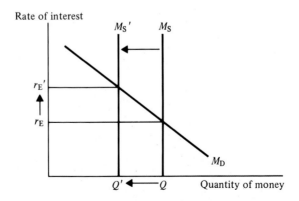

FIGURE 6A.5   Effect of a Decrease in the Money Supply on the Rate of Interest

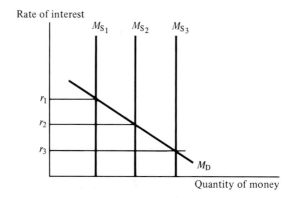

FIGURE 6A.6   **Interest Rate Determination in the Liquidity Preference Model**

Finally, remember that although the monetary effect of interest rates in the discussion above has focused on the demand for money balances, the velocity of money varies inversely with the amount of money holdings. Thus interest elasticity of the demand for money necessarily implies interest elasticity of velocity.

How does the liquidity preference theory of interest rate determination compare with the loanable funds approach? In their general substance the two approaches yield the same results. The principal difference between the two theories is one of methodology. The liquidity preference model is a "stock" theory, focusing on the rate of interest that will result in a given stock of money being held as a desired stock of cash balances. The loanable funds theory, on the other hand, focuses on the flow of funds in the financial system and the equilibrating action of the interest rate in equating the supply and demand of loanable funds. For the purpose of analyzing financial markets and institutions relative to the flow of funds in the financial system the flow orientation and broader focus of the loanable funds approach make it a preferable framework.

Both approaches to interest rate determination are incomplete in the sense that they consider the financial sector without regard to changes in the real sector of the economy. In actuality, of course, events in the real sector are continuously impacting on the financial sector and thus on interest rates.[5]

---

[5]Expectations regarding future changes in the price level and in interest rates also significantly affect the demand for money. In the case of anticipated inflation, of course, wealth holders tend to reduce cash balances (and probably savings as well) in effect to avoid the attendant loss of monetary purchasing power. When interest rates are expected to increase, money holdings may increase. This is a consequence of the incentive to "wait" for higher yields but, more significantly, to avoid capital losses on holdings of debt securities when interest rates rise (and prices of such securities fall).

Finally, we note that a great many empirical studies of "liquidity preference" (the demand for money) have been conducted by economists in recent years. The evidence from these studies indicates that the interest rate affects the demand for money, but not by much. (In technical terms, the demand for money is interest-inelastic.) Income and/or wealth is also a significant variable, but the relationship is less elastic than might be expected. Until recent years the demand for money has been a fairly stable function of income (wealth?) and interest rates. The relative instability of recent years is probably attributable to changes in inflationary expectations and the emergence of new types of deposit accounts (and the resulting definitional problems of what "money" is).

REFERENCES

Ackley, Gardner, "Liquidity Preference and Loanable Funds Theories of Interest: Comment," *American Economic Review* (September 1957), 662–673.

Conard, Joseph, *Introduction to the Theory of Interest* (Berkeley: University of California Press, 1959).

Lerner, Abba P., "Alternative Formulations of the Theory of Interest," in S. Harris (Ed.), *The New Economics* (New York: Knopf, 1950).

Patinkin, Don, "Liquidity Preference and Loanable Funds: Stock and Flow Analysis," *Economica* (November 1958), 300–318.

Tobin, James, "Liquidity Preference as Behavior toward Risk," *Review of Economic Studies* (February 1958), 65–86.

Tsiang, S. C., "Liquidity Preference and Loanable Funds Theories, Multiplier and Velocity Analysis: A Synthesis," *American Economic Review* (September 1956), 539–564.

CHAPTER **7**

The Term Structure
of Interest Rates

Our discussion in Chapter 6 of "the" interest rate was highly simplified and abstract. In reality there are many different interest rates on many different financial contracts. The existence of numerous different interest rates naturally raises questions about what factors account for these variations in rates. The relative level of interest rates on different financial contracts is influenced by a large number of factors, including time to maturity, differences in administrative costs, and the competitive state of the market. However, it is possible to explain most of the differences in rates on financial instruments traded in competitive markets by reference to only a few factors: time to maturity, inflation, credit or default risk, taxability, callability, and marketability (liquidity). In this chapter we deal with the influence of differences in the maturities of financial instruments on yields—the "term structure" of interest rates; and in Chapter 8 we discuss the impact of the various other principal factors on the relative level of interest rates in financial markets.

Keep in mind throughout the discussion in these two chapters that we are focusing on the relationship between the yield on a financial asset and each of the above-named factors while holding all other determining factors constant. In this chapter, for example, we seek to identify the influence of time to maturity on yield while holding constant the influence on yield of inflation, credit risk, taxation, and the other important variables. Similarly, in the next chapter we examine in turn the effect of each of these latter factors on yield while holding time to maturity and all other factors constant. Such a simplification is necessary to an understanding of the impact of each variable. Yet we must keep in mind that day-to-day movements in the relative structure of rates in the financial marketplace reflect the combined influence of all the factors.

MATURITY AND YIELD: YIELD CURVES

Time to maturity appears to be one of the most pervasive influences on the relative structure of interest rates. Usually, though not always, yield to maturity on financial instruments increases as the time to maturity of the instruments increases. In some periods, however—generally when interest rates are extremely high—yields to maturity on financial instruments are lower the longer the maturity of the instruments. In a few rare instances, yields to maturity neither decrease nor increase as the maturity lengthens. Figure 7.1 indicates nominal interest rates in recent years on two corporate securities of differing maturities (1-month commercial paper and AAA corporate bonds). Note that short-term rates and long-term rates often diverged significantly in the 1910–1988 period. These two securities are essentially identical except for time to maturity; thus this difference must account for the yield divergences.

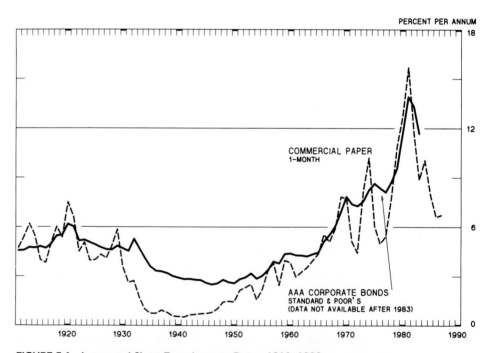

FIGURE 7.1   Long- and Short-Term Interest Rates; 1910–1988

Source: Board of Governors of the Federal Reserve System, Historical Chart Book, *1988.*

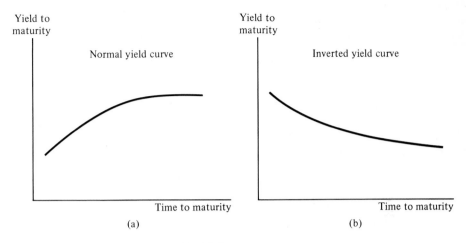

FIGURE 7.2 "Normal" and Inverted Yield Curves

The Yield Curve

The relationship between short- and long-term rates on a particular day on debt instruments that are alike in all characteristics except maturity is referred to as the **term structure of interest rates.** This relationship is usually presented graphically as a yield curve. For example, Fig. 7.2 presents two common types of yield curves. In that figure the yield to maturity (vertical axis) is related to the time to maturity (horizontal axis) for a group of securities that are the same in all respects except their time to maturity. In Fig. 7.2(a) the yield to maturity increases as the time to maturity increases. This positive relationship between yield and maturity is usually referred to as the "normal" yield curve because it is more common.[1] When the yield curve is downward sloping, as in Fig. 7.2(b), this relationship is referred to as an "inverted" yield curve because the "normal" relationship between maturity and time has been turned over or inverted.

The two yield curves in Fig. 7.2 provide a simplified view of the basic relationship between yield and maturity, but it is of course possible to have a yield curve

[1] See John H. Wood, "Do Yield Curves Normally Slope Up? The Term Structure of Interest Rates, 1968–1982," Federal Reserve Bank of Chicago *Economic Perspectives* (July/August 1983), pp. 17–23, for a historical analysis of yield curve structure which suggests that "normal" yield curves are less "normal" than is generally supposed.

that combines elements of each. For example, the yield curve may be upward sloping for one portion of the maturity spectrum but downward sloping for another maturity interval. Indeed, in some periods of increasing rates the yield curve rises through the first year or two, then falls for a few years, and then becomes horizontal. This type of yield curve is referred to as "humped" for obvious reasons.

The Yield Curve and Borrowers and Lenders

The particular yield curve that exists at any time has substantial importance for both lenders and borrowers in financial markets. For example, if the yield curve is upward sloping, those who wish to borrow funds must pay a higher rate to "reach for maturity."[2] Although the borrower reduces liquidity pressures by borrowing long-term rather than short-term, that advantage of long-term borrowing must be balanced against the disadvantage of paying a higher rate to obtain the desired funds (which will be the case with an upward-sloping yield curve). From the perspective of a lender the upward-sloping yield curve indicates that higher yields to maturity may be obtained only by longer-term investing. However, the price variability of longer-term securities is greater than the price variability of shorter-term securities. Thus the investor or lender must balance the higher potential yield from the longer-term securities with the greater price risk (potential capital losses if sold prior to maturity) associated with those securities.

In instances in which the yield curve is downward sloping, the advantages and disadvantages to lenders and borrowers of short- versus long-term investments are altered. From the borrower's perspective a downward-sloping yield curve indicates that the rate required to raise funds in the financial markets is lower for longer-term than for shorter-term securities. It seems then that the borrower would clearly choose longer-term securities in this type of environment, since long maturity and lower rates can be obtained simultaneously. Yet this view ignores the fact that the inverted yield curve generally occurs in a period of high rates (the shape of the yield curve refers to the relationship between short- and

---

[2]By "reaching for maturity" the borrower is seeking to reduce the immediate cash outflows associated with debt. From a financial statement perspective a policy of borrowing long-term rather than short-term improves the various liquidity ratios, such as the current ratio, although it has no impact on the total amount of debt or on leverage ratios such as the ratio of total debt to equity. Short-term borrowing has the advantage of greater flexibility than long-term borrowing but is considered riskier. Long-term borrowing is less risky because short-term interest rates are more volatile than long-term rates and because short-term financing is more likely to necessitate refunding under adverse financial market or operating conditions (since it occurs more frequently).

long-term rates, not the level of rates). It may be preferable, if possible, for the borrower to postpone raising funds or to borrow short-term today (despite the higher rates on short-term relative to long-term borrowing) in the hope of borrowing long-term in the future at lower rates. Moreover, as we will discuss below, the inverted yield curve generally occurs both when rates are high and when they are expected to fall in the future.

The inverted yield curve also has some important implications for the lender. Again it seems that the inverted yield curve represents the ideal situation for the investor—the lender can obtain the higher yield from shorter-term securities, as well as the lower price variability (risk) associated with these shorter-term securities. Yet, again, evaluation of the investment alternatives available is not that simple. Since interest rates are generally high when an inverted yield curve exists, the prices of all interest-bearing securities in the secondary market are low, and the prices of long-term securities are especially low. (Recall that, for any given increase in interest rates, the prices of all fixed-income instruments fall, but the prices of long-term securities fall more than the prices of short-term securities.) Moreover, if rates are high and expected to fall, then the prices of all fixed-income securities are expected to rise, but the prices of long-term securities are expected to rise more than prices of short-term securities. In this type of environment the investor might be better off to purchase long-term securities in order to capture the greater potential price appreciation associated with the securities. In this decision, as in all others, lenders and borrowers must examine the yields and prices on securities today and expectations of the yields and prices tomorrow before making a decision today.

Examples of Yield Curves

A yield curve may be drawn for any group of securities—corporate, government, or municipals—that are identical in all respects except maturity. However, although yield curves for corporate and municipal securities are sometimes constructed for borrowing and lending purposes, the most widely used yield curve is drawn for U.S. government (Treasury) securities. Not only does the U.S. government have an enormous volume of debt outstanding—exceeding $2 trillion—but the debt also offers a number of different maturity ranges, and it is homogeneous in credit risk. In contrast, the volume of debt outstanding from any one corporate or municipal issue is much smaller and usually does not offer a large number of different maturities.[3]

---

[3]Yield curves for corporate and municipal issues are often drawn for a number of different issuers with the same presumed credit quality. However, the usefulness of these yield curves is somewhat limited, since the actual credit quality of the issues often varies.

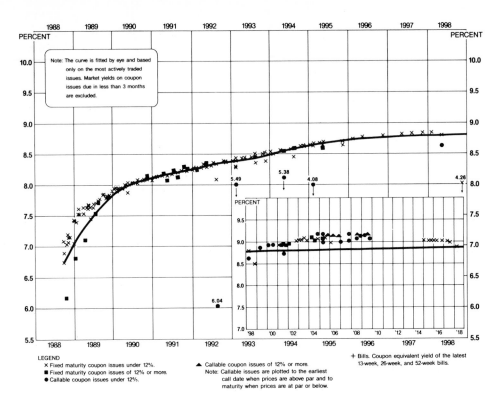

FIGURE 7.3   Yields of Treasury Securities, June 30, 1988 (Based on Closing Bid Quotations)

Source: U.S. Treasury Bulletin.

Normal Yield Curve

An upward-sloping or "normal" yield curve is presented in Fig. 7.3. This yield curve, drawn monthly by the U.S. Treasury, is published in the *Treasury Bulletin*.[4] As is typical for upward-sloping yield curves, the interest rate rises rapidly through the first years of the maturity of the securities and then rises much more slowly thereafter. The yield curve as of June 30, 1988 (Fig. 7.3) reveals a marked increase in rates for maturities from 1988 to 1995 and then flattens for maturities

---

[4]The yield curve as drawn by the Treasury is "fitted by eye" and has a number of securities that do not fall along the curve. Of course, if the yield curve held constant all factors that affect yield except time, then all the securities should fall along the curve. In fact, Treasury securities do differ in a number of respects (marketability and tax factors, for example), and these differences distort the yield curve.

after 1995. Hence from the lender's perspective a significant increase in return (more than 2 percent) could be obtained from extending the maturity of investments from one year to five or six years. Similarly, from the borrower's perspective, relatively small increases in maturities of securities issued resulted in significant increases in required interest rates. Yet beyond six years the increases in rates associated with lengthening maturities are relatively small.

Inverted Yield Curve

A less common yield curve is shown in Figure 7.4. In this yield curve, which is drawn for July 31, 1981, rates are downward sloping, with the exception of a hump for the very short-term maturity issues. This is the case of the inverted yield curve—longer-term rates are lower than shorter-term rates. Note also that the level of interest rates on July 31, 1981 was substantially higher than the level of

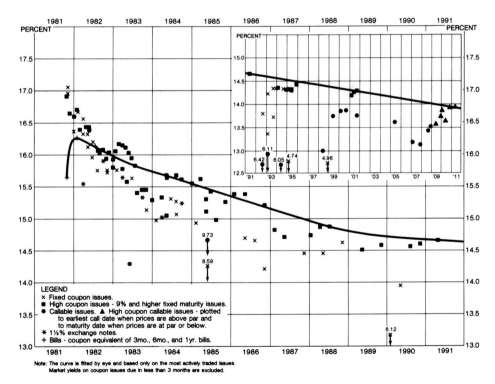

FIGURE 7.4   Yields of Treasury Securities, July 31, 1981 (Based on Closing Bid Quotations)

Source: U.S. Treasury Bulletin.

rates on June 30, 1988. U. S. interest rates in 1981 were extraordinarily high relative to normally prevailing rates in recent decades. Both long-term and short-term interest rates increased sharply in 1979 and 1980, but short-term rates rose the most, resulting in an inverted yield curve that prevailed until rates fell in 1982. When interest rates began to decline, short-term rates decreased more than long-term rates, resulting in the restoration of a "normal," upward-sloping yield curve.

Changes in the shape of the yield curve reflect primarily changes in short-term rates. When all rates are generally increasing, the increase in short-term rates is more pronounced than the increase in long-term rates. As a result, at some point in a rising interest rate cycle, short-term rates may exceed long-term rates, and the yield curve becomes inverted. In contrast, when rates begin to decline, all rates generally fall, but short-term rates fall more than long-term rates, and at some point the yield curve reverts to its "normal" shape.

FACTORS SHAPING THE YIELD CURVE

What factors cause the yield curve to have a particular shape at a particular time and to change shape from period to period? Although there are myriad influences at work, the most significant factors appear to be expectations of market participants, liquidity preference influences, and perhaps some degree of financial market segmentation.

Liquidity Preference

A **liquidity preference** (preference for liquid investments) by lenders underlies the notion that "liquidity premiums" exist in the shape of the yield curve. This view holds that, all else being equal, risk increases for an investor as the time to maturity of an investment security increases. Certainly, the **price risk** of a security—the sensitivity of market price to interest rate changes—increases as time to maturity increases. If interest rates rise, short-term securities sold prior to maturity will result in smaller capital losses than will longer-term securities.[5]

---

[5]Recall, however, that interest rate risk on investment securities includes reinvestment risk as well as price risk. If interest rates rise, the resulting decline in outstanding security prices will result in capital losses on securities sold prior to maturity. But because of higher rates, proceeds of security sales can be reinvested to earn higher yields. Conversely, a decrease in interest rates triggers capital gains but lowers yields on reinvestment. Thus price risk and reinvestment risk affect investor wealth in opposing ways. Liquidity preference term structure theory, in effect, assumes that investor risk aversion causes price risk to be of greater concern to investors than reinvestment risk. Alternatively, proponents of the theory can point to existing empirical evidence of increasing systematic risk of total security returns as maturity increases; security pricing theory thus indicates higher returns as maturities lengthen.

YIELD CURVES, INFLATIONARY EXPECTATIONS, AND RECESSIONS

In the March 10, 1989, Federal Reserve Bank of San Francisco *Weekly Letter,* Frederick T. Furlong offered an analysis of "Yield Curves and Recessions." The yield curve had recently inverted, giving rise to fears of an ensuing recession, given that the prior six recessions had been preceded by an inverted yield curve. (Further, the most severe of these recessions—the 1981–1982 recession, had been preceded by the inverted yield curve of the longest duration.) The only time in the postwar period that an inverted yield curve was not followed by a recession was in the mid-1960s, and even in that case there was a downturn in economic growth.

Inverted yield curves generally occur when interest rates are rising rapidly, Furlong notes. And, he adds,

> "During these periods, it is logical that many observers would come to expect the high and rising level of interest rates to push the economy into a recession, which subsequently would cause interest rates to decline. And because they were expecting interest rates to be lower in the future, the yield curve would flatten or invert at these times, in keeping with the expectations theory of interest rates."

Furlong suggests that the reason that inverted yield curves have occurred in recent decades **only** when economic downturns appeared imminent is that inflation has become such a perennial problem. "Recessions were the only thing that seemed even temporarily to slow the price spiral and the rise in nominal interest rates." Whether or not the early-1989 inversion of the yield curve signaled an impending recession, Furlong speculates, depended largely on the extent to which such inflationary expectations had been squeezed out of the U.S. economy by the shift to a more stringent anti-inflationary monetary policy in the 1980s.

Further, it is axiomatic that general uncertainty mounts as the time horizon lengthens. During periods of real and perceived financial crisis the spread between yields on short-term securities and yields on long-term securities generally increases if the yield curve is upward sloping and narrows if the yield curve is downward sloping. During the Mexican loan crisis of late 1982 (which sparked awareness of the severity of the Third World debt problem), for example, the spread between 3-month Treasury bills and 30-year Treasury bonds stretched to about 5 percent.

In any event, if lenders perceive relatively longer-term lending to be riskier than short-term lending, they will engage in the former only if a higher return is offered. Thus long-term securities must offer a "liquidity premium" if they are to be attractive to investors. Borrowers, on the other hand, are viewed as having a preference for the issuance of longer-term securities; they will borrow on a relatively short-term basis only if sufficiently smaller interest rates are available.

The extent to which lender aversion to long-term securities and borrower aversion to short-term securities influence the term structure of interest rates will likely vary over time, as the degree of such aversion varies. Increased risk aversion on the part of either borrowers or lenders (or both) will result in a more sharply upward-sloping yield curve. Decreased risk aversion will tend to flatten the yield curve. It should be noted that liquidity preference, by itself, cannot account for a downward-sloping (inverted) yield curve. Given that inverted yield curves, while relatively infrequent, do occur, liquidity preference is obviously not the only factor affecting the term structure. And while empirical investigation of liquidity premiums generally confirm their existence, methodological difficulties in disentangling them from other influences on interest rate structure have precluded any definitive measures of their dimensions. (See the appendix to this chapter for a discussion of the relevant empirical evidence.)

Market Segmentation

The term structure of interest rates is determined by the supply of and demand for securities at each maturity. Thus any **institutional** factors—such as operating conventions (an apparent tendency for firms to match maturity of assets and liabilities is one example), regulation, or legal constraints—that affect the supply of and demand for securities of differing maturities will affect the shape of the yield curve. To the extent that this is true, **market segmentation** exists— securities with differing maturities are imperfect substitutes for each other. The segmented markets explanation of the yield curve emphasizes the importance of these elements (with its adherents sometimes also incorporating liquidity preference considerations).

The segmented markets hypothesis emphasizes the behavior characteristics of the major financial institutions that dominate the financial market. By this explanation it is principally the behavior of commercial banks and the Federal Reserve, in conjunction with changes in the demand for funds for inventory accumulation by businesses and changes in other types of demand, that causes increases or decreases in short-term interest rates. And it is changes in the supply of loanable funds by the major financial institutions, such as life insurance companies and pension funds, in connection with changes in the demand for loanable funds by businesses for capital expansion, by households for acquisition of homes, and by others, that cause changes in long-term interest rates. Following the logic of the argument, the financial markets are segmented into subdivisions based on the traditional maturity preferences of market participants. Within each subdivision, changes in the supply of and demand for loanable funds ultimately create a particular term structure. Each participant in the market has a "preferred habitat," securities of different maturities are not perfectly substitutable in investor portfolios, and it would take extraordinarily large changes in the pattern of interest rates to induce investors to shift from one maturity group of securities to another. For example, commercial banks seek relatively short-term securities, given their relatively unstable sources of funds, whereas life insurance companies seek relatively long-term securities, given their relatively stable sources of funds.

According to the segmented markets explanation of the yield curve, interest rate levels for short- and long-term financial markets are determined independently by supply and demand in each market. For example, in Fig. 7.5(a) the short-term rate (r_S) is below the long-term rate (r_L). This upward slope to the yield curve reflects the interaction of the supply and demand for loanable funds such that relative demand pressure in the short-term market is less than in the long-

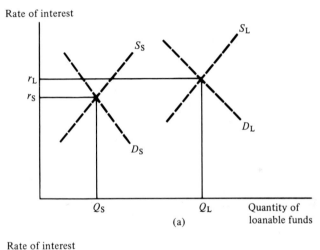

(a)

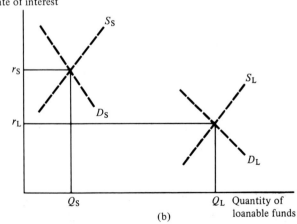

(b)

FIGURE 7.5 Segmented Markets and the Yield Curve

term market. For example, at any given interest rate the demand gap (the difference between the quantity of loanable funds demanded and supplied) is smaller in the short-term market (where S_S is the supply schedule and D_S is the demand schedule) than in the long-term market (where S_L is the supply schedule and D_L is the demand schedule). And according to the segmented markets explanation, these supply and demand schedules are independent and unrelated.

Changes in the yield curve reflect changes in these segmented supply and demand schedules. For example, in Fig. 7.5(b), short-term interest rates are higher than long-term interest rates; that is, the yield curve is inverted, or downward sloping. According to the segmented markets explanation, this inverted yield curve is the result of greater demand pressure in short-term markets than in long-term markets. For example, the Federal Reserve may be following a "tight" money policy by restricting the availability of bank reserves. As a result, the supply of loanable funds from the banking system—which is principally a short-term lender—is constrained. At the same time, if business conditions are strong, business firms may have large inventory accumulation, which is generally financed by short-term borrowing. In contrast, the long-term supply of funds available from life insurance companies and pension funds and the capital spending plans of business firms will probably be much less affected by variations in Federal Reserve monetary policy and in the state of the economy.

Implicit in the segmented markets explanation of the yield curve is an emphasis on changes in the supply and demand for loanable funds in the short-term markets. Although the supply of and demand for loanable funds in the short-term (money) market are viewed as highly volatile, the supply of and demand for funds in the long-term markets are thought to be much more stable. Hence changes in the shape of the yield curve principally reflect shifts in short-term rather than long-term rates. For example, in the upswing of the business cycle, short-term rates rise rapidly (more rapidly than long-term rates), and the yield curve flattens. As the business cycle nears its peak, the supply of short-term funds is restricted by the Federal Reserve, whereas the demand for funds increases as businesses build inventory. As a result, short-term rates rise further, perhaps exceeding long-term rates and creating an inverted yield curve. However, as the economy slows, the Fed relaxes its monetary policy, business demand for inventory financing declines, and short-term rates fall rapidly. At some point the upward-sloping yield curve is restored with short-term rates again lower than long-term rates.

Few (if any) informed observers would regard financial market segmentation as absolute; as maturity-related interest rate differentials increase, there is obviously a heightened economic incentive to set aside institutional preferences and conventions and to circumvent regulatory and legal constraints. The segmented markets theory is best viewed as an application of a potential tendency of securities to become less substitutable for one another as the divergence between their maturities increases. Also, this theory is useful as a framework of analysis that includes other influences on the term structure of rates.

Expectations of Future Interest Rates

Many observers consider the principal influence in determination of the term structure of interest rates to be financial market participants' expectations regarding future interest rates. Indeed, the "pure unbiased expectations theory of the term structure of interest rates" hypothesizes that investor expectations alone shape the yield curve. This theory is described below, but we first offer an intuitive explanation of how both borrower and lender expectations can affect the yield structure.

Suppose there is a widely held expectation among financial market participants that interest rates will increase in the future. Such a consensus forecast may emerge, for example, when the economy commences recovery from a recession, loan demand mounts, and the Fed grows wary of potential development of inflationary forces (and thus is likely to tighten monetary policy). Lenders expecting future interest rates to be higher have an incentive to lend on a relatively short-term basis; this minimizes (or avoids) capital losses when interest rates rise while ensuring timely recapture of their loanable funds to reinvest at the expected higher future rates. Borrowers, on the other hand, have the opposite incentive if they share the expectation of higher future interest rates; they should borrow on a long-term basis to "lock in" today's relatively low interest rates.

At this intuitive level of analysis the approach resembles the segmented markets explanation of the preceding section. Increased availability of short-term loanable funds and decreased availability of long-term loanable funds occur as lenders act on their expectation of higher future rates. Demand for long-term funds (issuance of long-term securities) increases, and demand for short-term funds (issuance of short-term securities) decreases as borrowers act on their expectation of higher future rates. Increased supply of short-term funds and decreased demand for short-term funds result in a decrease in short-term interest rates relative to long-term rates. Decreased supply of long-term funds and increased demand for long-term funds cause long-term rates to mount in relation to short-term rates. The yield curve would become upward sloping (or, if already upward sloping, more pronounced in slope)—forecasting, in effect, higher interest rates in the future.

Consider now the expectation (again, a consensus forecast of borrowers and lenders) that interest rates will *decline* in the future. The reverse set of incentives and likely actions would hold. Lenders will seek to lend on a long-term basis (buy long-term securities) to "lock in" current yields, which are higher than expected future yields. The supply of long-term loanable funds increases, and the supply of short-term loanable funds contracts. Borrowers turn to short-term funding (issue short-term securities) and avoid long-term borrowing as they seek to minimize their interest costs in succeeding periods. The demand for short-term funds thus increases, and the demand for long-term funds decreases. Increased demand for, and decreased supply of, short-term funds drives up short-term interest rates in relation to long-term rates. Decreased demand for, and increased supply of, long-term funds lowers long-term rates in relation to short-term rates. The yield curve would flatten or even invert as short-term rates rose in relation to long-term rates.

The foregoing analysis, while plausible, is somewhat nebulous. Expectations—induced behavior on the part of market participants—is clearly intertwined with liquidity preference and segmented markets considerations. Further, the concept of "short-term" and "long-term" rates is a rather heroic simplification; the actual term structure ranges from days to decades. A much more rigorous and uncluttered treatment of the effect of expectations on the yield curve—one more amenable to empirical testing—is the so-called "pure" unbiased expectations theory.

THE PURE EXPECTATIONS THEORY

In the **pure expectations theory,** investor expectations alone determine the term structure of interest rates. Underlying assumptions of the theory (some of which are obviously counter to reality but are employed to simplify the analysis) include:

1. Homogeneous (uniform) expectations about future short-term interest rates are held by all investors (or at least a sufficiently large number of well-financed investors).

2. No transactions costs exist, so investors can buy and sell securities without reducing their net yields from securities.

3. Investors seek to maximize their yield from securities over their desired holding period. They are risk-neutral, not risk-averse.

4. Securities are perfectly substitutable in investor portfolios without regard to maturities.

The expectations hypothesis thus assumes that investors are indifferent to the maturity of the securities in their portfolios and are concerned only about their return. Hence an investor who had idle funds for three years (a three-year holding period) could invest in a 6-year security and sell the security at the end of three years (the investor has purchased a security whose maturity is longer than the investor's holding period). Or the investor could invest in a 1-year security and reinvest in additional 1-year securities for the full three-year period (the investor has purchased a security whose maturity is shorter than the investor's holding period). And of course, the investor could invest in a security with a three-year maturity, thereby matching precisely the maturity of the security and the holding period of the investor. According to the expectations hypothesis, in making this decision the investor will be guided solely by which security has the highest return over the investor's holding period.

Given the basic assumptions of the expectations hypothesis—that investors are return maximizers, are risk-neutral, and have the same expectations and that all securities are perfectly substitutable in investor portfolios—it may be shown that the structure of the yield curve today reflects expectations about the level of rates in the future. For example, assume that an investor has a two-year holding period. Further assume that the investor has only two investment alternatives: a 1-year credit-risk-free security with a yield of 8 percent or a 2-year credit-risk-free security. Assume also that investors believe that the interest rate one year from now on 1-year securities will be 10 percent.

Given these conditions, what will be the interest rate today on the 2-year security? Of course, once that interest rate is determined, the term structure of interest rates (the yield curve) is established. If investors are indeed expected return maximizers, risk-neutral, and indifferent about the maturity of their portfolios, the yield today on the 2-year security must be 9 percent. Why? First, assume that the yield on the 2-year security was 8 percent. In that situation the investor could get 8 percent by purchasing the 2-year security or 9 percent by purchasing a 1-year security and then reinvesting in another 1-year security at the expected return of 10 percent at the end of one year: $(8 + 10)/2 = 9\%$.[6] Obviously, a return-maximizing investor would not buy the 2-year security. However, the lack of demand for the 2-year security would cause its price to fall and its yield to rise until the yield had increased to 9 percent, at which point the investor would be indifferent between the 1-year security and the two 1-year securities. Now assume that the 2-year security offered a return of 10 percent. In that case the investor would prefer the 10 percent yield on the 2-year security to the 9 percent yield available by purchasing a 1-year security yielding 8 percent today and reinvesting in another 1-year security one year from now at the expected rate of 10 percent on that 1-year security. But the demand for the 2-year security would increase its price, and its yield would fall until the yield equaled that available from purchasing the 1-year security and reinvesting at the end of one year. In equilibrium the holding-period return for an investor must be the same, according to the expectations hypothesis, regardless of the maturity of the securities held. Alternatively stated, the long-term rate of interest will always equal the average of current and expected future short-term rates.

---

[6]This example ignores compounding. It also assumes that investor expectations are realized. However, for the expectations hypothesis to be valid it is not necessary to assume that expectations are realized, only that investors act on their expectations of future rates.

Mathematical Expression

The above example employed the arithmetic average of short-term rates. To be more precise, use of the geometric average (to reflect compounding of interest) is appropriate for stating the expectations theorem in mathematical form. Further, some formal terminology is useful. We employ the prefix t to represent a year (or more generally, **period**) in which a given interest rate exists, and the postscript T to represent the **maturity** (in years or periods) of the security bearing that rate of interest. Also, the capital letter R represents existing rates and the lowercase letter r represents expected future rates. Thus $_1R_2$ represents the prevailing rate in the present year on a 2-year security, and $_2r_1$ represents the expected future 1-year rate in the next year (year 2). Recognizing that $_1R_1$ would indicate the prevailing rate on a 1-year security, the expectations theory dictates that

$$(1 + {_1R_2}) = \sqrt{(1 + {_1R_1})(1 + {_2r_1})}$$

In the above example, $_1R_2$ (the present yield on the two-year security) is 9 percent, $_1R_1$ is 8 percent, and $_2r_1$ is 10 percent. Thus

$$(1 + {_1R_2}) = \sqrt{(1.08)(1 + 0.10)}$$
$$1 + {_1R_2} = 1.08995$$
$${_1R_2} = 0.08995$$
$$\text{or} \quad {_1R_2} = 9 \text{ percent}$$

The general formula for n number of years is

$$(1 + {_tR_n}) = \sqrt[n]{(1 + {_tR_1})(1 + {_{t+1}r_1})(1 + {_{t+2}r_1})...(1 + {_{t+n-1}r_1})}$$

The formula merely expresses the expectations theorem that the prevailing yield on a security of n years to maturity equals the geometric average of the prevailing 1-year rate and the expected future 1-year rates for $n - 1$ years.

However, investor alternatives are wider than a succession of 1-year securities or a security of a maturity that corresponds to the holding period. For example, an investor contemplating a 10-year holding period is not limited to a menu of a 10-year security or ten successive 1-year securities. The investor may instead (and this is a nonexhaustive list of possibilities):

1. Hold successively two 5-year securities;

2. Hold successively a 4-year and a 6-year security;

3. Hold successively five 2-year securities; or

4. Hold successively three 3-year securities and one 1-year security.

According to the pure expectations theory, all these strategies (and all the other myriad possible strategies) would result in the same holding period yield— the yield on the 10-year security, or $_tR10$.

While few, if any, observers believe that the pure expectations theory of the term structure holds exactly in the real world, the importance of expectations in shaping the yield curve is widely accepted. Many knowledgeable financial market observers and participants consider the expectations hypothesis to be the dominant basic explanation of the yield curve. Moreover, considerable empirical evidence supports the importance of expectations in affecting the shape of the term structure of interest rates (as indicated in the appendix to this chapter).

AN ECLECTIC VIEW OF TERM STRUCTURE DETERMINATION

In economic theorizing, the term "eclectic" pertains to taking the apparent best of various theories and assembling a composite doctrine. Such an approach is apt for explaining the term structure of interest rates. Although many observers consider the expectations hypothesis to be the principal (dominant) factor in shaping the yield curve, there is nothing mutually contradictory about any of the explanations. There is no reason why the yield curve may not reflect expectations about future rates modified by a liquidity premium and further modified by institutional rigidities that allow some substitution of securities with different maturities (though not perfect substitutions) in investor portfolios. Indeed, it appears quite likely that each factor does play a role in determining the shape of the yield curve.

For example, recognition of a need for a liquidity premium in order to induce investors to purchase longer-term issues can readily be incorporated into a modified version of the expectations hypothesis. For example, even if expectations are that interest rates in the future will be the same as interest rates today, the yield curve will be upward sloping, as shown in Fig. 7.6. The solid line reflects the yield curve incorporating only expectations factors. But to these factors must be added the liquidity premium, which increases as the time to maturity increases, since risk rises with maturity. Hence the dashed line in Fig. 7.6(a) shows an upward-sloping yield curve, even though expectations are for interest rates in the future to remain unchanged from those today. A similar analysis could be used to incorporate liquidity preference into a yield curve reflecting rising or falling interest rates in the future. If the yield curve were upward sloping because of expectations of rising rates, it would be more upward sloping with the addition of the liquidity premium, as in Fig. 7.6(b). And if the yield curve were downward sloping because of expectations of falling yields in the future, with the addition of the liquidity premium it could actually be upward sloping, as in Fig. 7.6(c).

Financial market imperfections and maturity-related limitations on security substitutability can similarly be incorporated into an eclectic explanation of the processes shaping yield curves. For example, the yield curve for municipal bonds

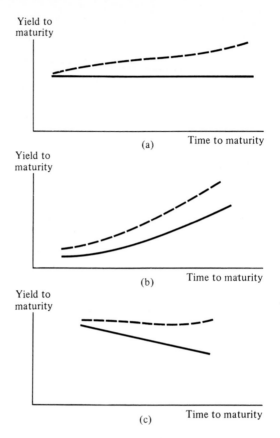

FIGURE 7.6   The Yield Curve Reflecting the Liquidity Premium

is almost always upward sloping because of the limited supply of short-term issues and the tendency of banks—a principal investor in municipals—to limit
their holdings of municipals to issues due in five years or less.

USES OF THE YIELD CURVE

The yield curve is used by a wide variety of analysts for many different purposes. In this section we present a brief discussion of some of the different uses
of the yield curve. The treatment is not exhaustive, but it should provide at least
an introduction to the many ways in which financial analysts and students of the
financial system use the yield curve.

Forecasting Interest Rates

One of the most widely employed applications of the yield curve is in attempts to predict the future course of interest rates. As discussed earlier, changes in interest rates affect the price of fixed-income securities, and decreases in rates are associated with increases in their value. These changes in rates and prices present the opportunity for large profits or risk of large losses to financial market participants. As a result, substantial resources are devoted to forecasting interest rate movements by financial institutions, such as commercial banks, and by others who hold fixed-income securities.

There are a number of approaches to forecasting interest rates. For example, some financial institutions use elaborate forecasts of the various elements of supply and demand for loanable funds in order to anticipate interest rate movements. Forecasts of the supply of loanable funds available from the major providers of funds in the financial marketplace—financial institutions—are prepared and compared with the demand for loanable funds emanating from households, businesses, and governments. As another alternative, elaborate econometric models of the economy, including the financial sector, are constructed by econometric forecasting services, such as Data Resources, Inc., Wharton Econometrics, and others. And of course, the interest rates on financial assets traded in the financial futures markets (such as Treasury bills) may be used to reflect market participants' expectations of future interest rates. For example, in many financial assets, trading occurs for delivery of securities at future periods. (These will be discussed in Chapter 22.)

The yield curve is one among the many approaches to forecasting interest rates. For those who accept the expectations hypothesis, in either its pure or modified form, the shape of the yield curve provides a forecast of future interest rate levels. Implicit in every yield curve is some forward rate of interest. For example, in the illustration of the yield curve provided earlier, if the yield on a 1-year security is 8 percent and the yield on a 2-year security is 9 percent, then the forward rate for a 1-year security one year from now is 10 percent. Since the expectations hypothesis argues that the forward rate and the expected rate are identical, those who follow the expectations hypothesis are provided with a forecasted rate for securities of different maturities at different points in the future.[7] Hence an upward-sloping yield curve would contain implicitly a forecast of higher rates in the future. Indeed, there is frequent reference to the shape of the yield curve in articles in financial publications devoted to a discussion of future interest rate developments. Of course, these predictions might not be (and, in fact, often are not) realized.

---

[7]The forward rate may be calculated from a current yield curve for a 1-year security for any period in the future, a 2-year security for any period in the future, and any other maturity for any period in the future.

Determining Borrowing and Lending Maturities

The yield curve is, of course, useful in forecasting interest rates only to those who are willing to accept some form of the expectations hypothesis. But even though there may be some disagreement about whether the yield curve contains insight into future interest rates, there is no disagreement that the yield curve provides borrowers and lenders with vital information on the impact of alternative maturity choices on either the cost of funds or the potential yield on invested funds. For example, if the yield curve is upward sloping, lenders are able to calculate precisely the impact of extending the maturity of their investment and to compare the extra yield with the higher risk associated with "reaching for yield." In many instances when the yield curve is upward sloping, it tends to flatten out beyond the 10–15-year range. Hence investors have high incentive to lengthen the maturities of their portfolios up to the 10–15-year span but little incentive to increase maturities beyond that.

A similar analysis holds for borrowers facing an upward-sloping yield curve. Assume that borrowers wish to extend the maturity of their debt to reduce the liquidity management problems associated with large amounts of short-term debt. The existing yield curve tells such a borrower approximately what penalty, through higher interest costs, will be associated with lengthening the maturity of the borrowing. If the yield curve rises rapidly through the 10–15-year range but then flattens out, the borrower incurs a substantial penalty for extending maturity through the 10–15-year area but finds it relatively attractive to reach beyond that maturity range as the extra yield per year of extended maturity diminishes.

Selecting Individual Securities

The yield curve can also be used as an investment device in the selection of individual securities for inclusion in a particular portfolio. In viewing the yield curve from this perspective we must keep in mind how the yield curve is constructed—by taking a group of securities that are identical in all respects and examining the influences of varying times to maturity on the yield to maturity. Thus if the yield curve is properly drawn and all factors except time to maturity have been held constant, all the securities should fall along the yield curve. Yet in the actual construction of yield curves, some securities might not fall on the yield curve but might be above or below it. For example, in Fig. 7.7, Security A falls above the yield curve, and Security B falls below it. There are two possible interpretations of this phenomenon, each with quite different implications for investment behavior. One is that the securities are mispriced by the market. For example, for Security A the yield to maturity is Y_A, but for a security with the characteristics of security A and maturity T the yield should be Y. The yield on security A is too high (its price is too low), given its risk and maturity consider-

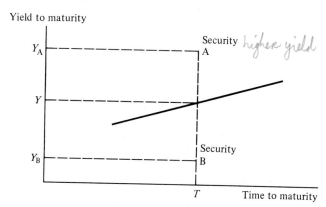

FIGURE 7.7 Individual Securities and the Yield Curve

ations.[8] This interpretation suggests that the investor should purchase those securities that fall above the yield curve. Similarly, for Security B (its price is too high) the yield to maturity is too low for its risk and maturity characteristics. For example, the yield on Security B is Y_B, but it should be Y. This interpretation suggests that the investor should eliminate Security B from the portfolio if it is already included in the existing portfolio and should avoid the security if it is not.[9] But there is a second interpretation for the existence of securities that lie off the yield curve: It might be that the analyst has not been successful in holding all other factors constant in drawing the yield curve. For example, Security A might have some undesirable characteristics (such as greater credit risk) that make its yield higher than the yield curve, and Security B might have some desirable characteristics that make its yield less than that expected from the time to maturity of the security.

Which explanation is correct? Unfortunately, there is no simple and universal answer. However, we note that for the first interpretation to be correct the financial markets must be inefficient—that is, it must be possible to earn higher than "normal" returns without taking higher than "normal" risks. Yet the evidence of numerous studies is that the markets for securities are highly efficient. Moreover, we also know that market professionals—brokerage houses, large commercial banks, and other major purchasers of securities—are consistently en-

---

[8]Again, keep in mind the inverse relationship between price and yield on a fixed-income security.
[9]A more aggressive strategy, which seeks to profit from the mispricing of the security, would be to sell Security B short; that is, borrow the security, sell it when it is overpriced, and buy it back later after its price has fallen in order to return the security to the lender.

gaged in seeking underpriced and overpriced securities. As a result, it seems likely that the opportunities for excess profit to the "nonprofessional" investor in finding securities that lie off the yield curve are probably quite limited.

Pricing New Issues

For existing securities, coupon interest rates are fixed, but prices are variable, being determined by market movements in the general level of interest rates. However, for new securities the price is fixed (usually set by the issuer at or near par), and the coupon interest rate is variable. The issuer—either the issuing firm directly or the investment banking institution working for the issuer—seeks to determine the coupon rate that will make the securities attractive to the market. At or near the par price, too low a coupon rate will make it difficult or impossible to sell the issue, and too high a coupon rate will result in excessive interest costs to the issuing firm. In pricing the new issue—that is, setting the coupon rate— the investment banker may draw up a yield curve for securities of comparable risk. For example, we may imagine that Fig. 7.7 represents such a yield curve and that the issuer wishes to sell securities with a maturity of T. In that case the issuer wants to set the coupon around Y, perhaps a little above Y in order to offer some concession to the market for the purchase of a new issue. In any case the issuer is using the yield curve as a guide in pricing the new issue.

Riding the Yield Curve

One of the most interesting potential uses of the yield curve is what is known as "riding the yield curve." This practice, used by a variety of participants in the money market, consists of seeking to profit from an upward-sloping yield curve by investing in a security whose maturity is longer than the investor's holding period and selling the security prior to maturity. Its usefulness is based on the assumption that one investor's expectations of future interest rates may be more accurate than the average expectations of investors that are embodied in the yield curve. Under some conditions, riding the yield curve may produce "holding period returns" that are greater than those possible through investing in securities whose maturities equal the investor's holding period. Although there is disagreement about the potential gains that are possible through riding the yield curve, we will present the conditions under which doing so may be profitable. First, however, we need to define the holding period return for a fixed-income security:

$$Y_h = Y_o + \frac{T_r(Y_o - Y_m)}{T_h}$$

where

Y_h = the holding period return
Y_o = the original yield
Y_m = the market yield when sold
T_r = the time remaining until maturity when the security is sold
T_h = time held

Referring again to the example used in discussing the expectations hypothesis, suppose that the yield available on a 1-year security was 8 percent and the yield available on a 2-year security was 9 percent and that the investor's holding period was one year. In that case the holding period return involved in purchasing the 1-year security would clearly be 8 percent. What is the holding period return in purchasing the 2-year security and selling it at the end of one year? As is apparent in the equation above for the holding period return, all the information needed to compute the holding period return is known at the time of the decision except the market yield on the security at the time the security is sold. For the moment, let us make the unrealistic assumption that the yield curve remains unchanged, so the 2-year security today is a 1-year security one year from now, and its yield is 8 percent. In that case the holding period yield from purchasing the 2-year security today and selling it after one year is 10 percent:

$$Y_h = 9\% + \frac{1 \text{ year}(9 - 8\%)}{1 \text{ year}} = 10\%$$

The holding period yield is higher than that available from simply holding either the 1-year or the 2-year security until maturity. The high yield results from the higher return obtained from "reaching for yield" by buying the 2-year security plus a capital gain from selling the security at a price higher than its purchase price (since it was purchased to yield 10 percent and sold to yield 8 percent, it must be sold at a price higher than its purchase price). Note, however, that riding the yield curve would not be possible if the expectations hypothesis was entirely correct. In that case the yield on the 2-year security sold one year after purchase would be 8 percent:

$$Y_h = 9\% + \frac{1 \text{ year}(9 - 10\%)}{1 \text{ year}} = 8\%$$

As was explained earlier, if the expectations hypothesis is entirely valid, the holding period return for a given holding period is the same for securities of all maturities. Note also that the example did not include transactions costs. It might be that there are opportunities for higher holding period returns through riding the yield curve but that these extra profits are reduced or eliminated by the transactions costs associated with the strategy.[10]

SUMMARY

The "term structure of interest rates" refers to the relationship between short- and long-term interest rates at a particular time on debt securities that are fundamentally similar in all characteristics except maturity. This relationship is usually presented graphically as a yield curve, generally with the use of U.S. government securities. The yield curve is normally upward sloping—long-term rates higher than short-term rates—but an inverted yield curve—short-term rates higher than long-term rates—also exists from time to time (usually when the level of rates is very high in relation to historical norms). The yield curve has many uses. They include predicting interest rates, determining borrowing and lending maturities, selecting individual securities, pricing new issues, and "riding the yield curve."

The term structure of interest rates is shaped primarily by expectations regarding future interest rate levels, by financial market participants' risk–return behavior (liquidity preference considerations), and institutional characteristics (market segmentation). Expectations appear to be the dominant influence. According to the pure unbiased expectations theory of the term structure, the yield curve is shaped entirely by investor expectations of future interest rates; long-term rates are the average of current and expected future short-term rates. Thus the yield curve will be upward sloping when investors expect rates to rise, downward sloping when rates are expected to fall, and flat (horizontal) when no rate changes are anticipated. An eclectic view of yield curve determination incorporates a modified view of the role of expectations and acknowledges the existence of liquidity premiums and maturity-related imperfections in security substitutability in investor portfolios.

In the next chapter we turn our attention to other factors that influence the yield on financial instruments. Initially, we discuss the influence of inflation on the term structure. Even if the expectations hypothesis is valid in that the relationship between short- and long-term interest rates is a function of expectations of future interest rate levels, the question remains as to why investors may hold expectations of increasing or decreasing rates in the future. One explanation involves inflation. If investors expect rising prices, they expect rising interest rates. As we will explain in Chapter 8, inflation has a profound impact on interest rates.

QUESTIONS

1. What is meant by the term "structure of interest rates"? Why is it often referred to as the "yield curve"?

2. Discuss the meaning of the normal, inverted, and humped yield curves. Under what economic conditions is each likely to exist?

---

[10]The decade of the 1940s (and until 1951) did provide the opportunity for riding the yield curve with very little risk. In that period the Federal Reserve artificially pegged the structure of rates. Not only was the yield curve upward sloping, but it was also unchanging. In that environment, riding the yield curve could be exceptionally profitable.

3. Explain why financial segmentation may exist and how such market imperfections can affect the term structure of interest rates.

4. Explain how changes in the expectations of financial market participants regarding the level of future interest rates may affect the shape of the yield curve.

5. Describe and discuss the pure unbiased expectations theory of the term structure of interest rates.

6. Assume that the rate today on 1-year default-free securities is 11 percent and the rate on 1-year default-free securities one year from now is expected to be 9 percent. What should be the rate on 2-year default-free securities today, according to the expectations hypothesis?

7. Why must investors be offered a premium to purchase long-term default-free securities? What does this assume about investor behavior? How does this assumption differ from that used in the expectations hypothesis?

8. Make a list of major financial institutions, and indicate in which segments of the financial markets each one is active.

9. Explain the various ways in which the yield curve can be used by financial analysts. Which is most relevant to borrowers? Lenders?

REFERENCES

Carleton, W. T., and I. A. Cooper, "Estimation and Uses of the Term Structure of Interest Rates," *Journal of Finance* (September 1976), 1067–1083.

Conard, Joseph, *Introduction to the Theory of Interest* (Berkeley: University of California Press, 1959).

Cox, John, Jonathan E. Ingersoll, Jr., and Stephen A. Ross, "A Reexamination of Traditional Hypotheses about the Term Structure of Interest Rates," *The Journal of Finance* (September 1981), 769–799.

Culbertson, John, "The Term Structure of Interest Rates," *Quarterly Journal of Economics* (November 1957), 485–517.

Elliott, J. W., and M. E. Echols, "Market Segmentation, Speculative Behavior, and the Term Structure of Interest Rates, *Review of Economics and Statistics* (February 1976), 40–49.

Kessel, Reuben, *The Cyclical Behavior of the Term Structure of Interest Rates,* Occasional Paper 91. (National Bureau of Economic Research, 1965).

Latainer, Gary D., "The Term Structure of Interest Rates," in Robert B. Platt (Ed.), *Controlling Interest Rate Risk* (New York: John Wiley & Sons, 1986), 11–27.

Lutz, F. A., "The Structure of Interest Rates," *Quarterly Journal of Economics* (November 1940), 36–63.

Malkiel, Burton, *The Term Structure of Interest Rates* (Princeton, N.J.: Princeton University Press, 1966).

Meiselman, David, *The Term Structure of Interest Rates* (Englewood Cliffs, N.J.: Prentice-Hall, 1962).

Modigliani, Franco, and Richard Sutch, "The Term Structure of Interest Rates: A Reexamination of the Evidence," *Journal of Money, Credit, and Banking,* (February 1965), 37–63.

Nelson, Charles R., *The Term Structure of Interest Rates* (New York: Basic Books, 1972).

Silber, William L., "The Term Structure of Interest Rates," in Murray E. Polokoff (Ed.), *Financial Institutions and Markets* (Boston:Houghton Mifflin, 1970).

Trudgian, William, and R. H. Scott, "A Survey of the Maturity Pattern of Yields," *University of Washington Business Review* (Spring 1971), 65–76.

Van Horne, James, "Interest Rate Expectations, The Shape of the Yield Curve, and Monetary Policy," *The Review of Economics and Statistics* (May 1966), 211–215.

APPENDIX
Empirical Evidence on the Term Structure

As we discussed in Chapter 7, there are a number of differing, though not necessarily contradictory, explanations of the term structure of interest rates. The three most widely discussed explanations are the expectations, liquidity premium, and segmented markets hypotheses. Many analysts accept some form of the expectations hypothesis, but there is considerable disagreement about the relative importance of these three explanations. Fundamentally, of course, the validity of the three explanations is an empirical issue determined by factual evidence rather than by opinion. A substantial volume of empirical literature has attempted to test the validity of these explanations, and a review of a few of these studies is the purpose of this appendix. Unfortunately, however, even though the empirical literature does provide some important information, there are substantial conflicts among the evidence that make definitive conclusions difficult to reach.

One major test of the expectations hypothesis has centered on evaluating the extent to which the forward rate embodied in a yield curve as of a moment of time is an accurate predictor of future interest rates. In these types of studies, sometimes referred to as "perfect-foresight models," the yield on a particular maturity security, such as the 3-month Treasury bill, for some future period (for example, one year from the date on which the prediction is made) is calculated from the existing yield curve. Then, after the fact, the forecasted yield is compared with the yield that actually existed in the particular financial instrument. In general, these studies have not found that forward rates embodied in the yield curve have any great ability to forecast future rates (see the studies of Hamburger and Platt and of Culbertson referenced at the end of this appendix). However, keep in mind also that, at least in recent years, no other procedures have proved especially accurate in forecasting interest rates either.

Although these perfect-foresight models have provided little support for the expectations hypothesis, one must recognize that the hypothesis itself does not require that expectations be realized; it requires only that expectations of future rates be important in determining the structure of rates today.[11] Testing the hypothesis by assuming that the forecasts are realized may impose excessive requirements on the validity of the theory. Recognizing this problem, other investigators (notably David Meiselman) have sought to determine whether reasonable

---

[11]The basic problem, of course, in testing the expectations hypothesis is that the expectations themselves are not directly observable. Rather, indirect observable data must be used to infer those expectations. Some studies (the one by Malkiel and Kane, for example) have attempted to survey expectations directly with mixed results.

models about the formation of expectations of future rates can be used to explain the current term structure.

Meiselman developed an error-learning model in which expectations were assumed to reflect current and past observation of actual events and in which expectations were adjusted in response to this "learning process." In this model, changes in one-year-forward rates were assumed to be related to errors in forecasting the actual one-year rate. Hence the actual one-year rate would be compared with the one-year rate forecasted earlier, and expectations of future one-year rates would be revised to reflect any errors. Meiselman then computed the correlation coefficient between the forecast error and changes in forward rates, using data from the period 1900–1954. His principal finding was that the high correlation found between the forecast error and changes in forward rates provided substantial support for the expectations hypothesis.

Variations of error-learning models have been employed by Van Horne, Kessel, and others. Van Horne found an even higher degree of correlation than Meiselman between forward rate changes and forecast errors. Van Horne's results were consistent with the hypothesis that forward rates reflect a liquidity premium as well as expectations and suggest that liquidity premiums increase at a decreasing rate. Kessel's findings also suggest that liquidity preference plays a role in the term structure. Meiselman found no evidence of liquidity premiums in his study, but Wood, using the same data series, concluded that the data were consistent with the existence of a liquidity premium. (Wood's conclusion was based on his finding that forward rates represented systematically high estimates of future rates.) Evidence from these studies and the studies by Friedman, McCulloch, and others suggest that liquidity premiums do exist in a term structure shaped primarily by expectations, but there is less agreement on how these premiums change as the maturity of a financial instrument increases. Fama investigated term premiums using monthly returns on U.S. Treasury bills (1964–1982) and U.S. bonds (1953–1982) and reported evidence of a liquidity premium for bills but not for bonds. Fama's results also indicated a leveling off of the bill premium at around eight- to nine-month maturities.

Other indirect support for the expectations hypothesis has been provided by studies that have explored the timing of movements in short- and long-term interest rates. If the expectations hypothesis is valid, one would expect that long-term rates would move in advance of short-term rates. Although the evidence of this issue is by no means conclusive, Sargent found that long-term rates did lead rates on 3-month Treasury bills in the period 1951–1960.

Tests of the hypothesis of market segmentation are also difficult to design and evaluate in a meaningful way. If the segmented-markets hypothesis is valid, one would expect that changes in the relative balance of supply and demand in particular segments of the market would produce changes in interest rates in those segments and thereby in the term structure of interest rates. Yet obtaining meaningful measures of supply and demand factors in subsectors of the financial markets is quite difficult. Modigliani and Sutch added supply variables to a model that also included expectations factors in attempting to explain the yield curve. In one study, published in 1966, they attempted to determine whether supply variables associated with "Operation Twist" (the attempt by the Federal Reserve in the early 1960s to alter the shape of the yield curve by changing the amount of short- and long-term government securities in the hands of the public) exerted any influence on the yield curve. They concluded that these supply factors had no more than a minor impact on the term structure. In another article, published in 1967, Modigliani and Sutch attempted to evaluate the segmented markets hypothesis by evaluating the statistical significance of adding supply variables to their basic model. However, measures of the maturity distribution of outstanding debt did not appear to add additional explanatory power to the model. While an extensive study by Dobson, Sutch, and Vanderford is supportive of the Modigliani–Sutch model of term structure behavior, the findings of other researchers (such as Phillips and Pippenger) bring the model into question.

Van Horne tested for evidence of market segmentation via an analysis of changes in long-term bond issue authority of the Treasury in the 1970s. Van Horne found no evidence that the spread between long-term rates and short-term rates was affected by such changes in authority (which would generate expectations of increased supply of long-term securities) and thus no evidence of market segmentation. However, other researchers (Elliott and Echols, Roley, and others) have reported evidence that is consistent with segmented markets.

Taking a different approach to testing the segmented markets hypothesis, Malkiel looked at the portfolio of financial institutions to determine whether these institutions do indeed confine their purchases to a particular maturity. Using data from the period 1955–1965 for such financial institutions as commercial banks and insurance companies, Malkiel could find no evidence that financial institutions appeared to alter the maturities of their portfolios in response to expected return and risk considerations.

Where does this leave us? Just what is the influence of expectations, liquidity premium, and segmented market considerations on the term structure of interest rates? On the basis of the evidence presented here and in recognition of the fact that there are conflicts in the relevant literature it does appear that the yield curve incorporates expectations of future rates to some significant degree. Moreover, there do appear to be liquidity premiums in the yield curve. However, if there are segmented markets supply/demand factors in particular markets affecting the yield curve, these factors appear to be relatively minor and transitory.

REFERENCES

Chambers, D., W. Carleton, and D. Waldman, "A New Approach to Estimation of the Term Structure of Interest Rates," *Journal of Financial and Quantitative Analysis* (September 1984), 233–252.

Culbertson, John, "The Term Structure of Interest Rates," *Quarterly Journal of Economics* (November 1957), 485–517.

Dobson, Steven W., Richard C. Sutch, and David E. Vanderford, "An Evaluation of Alternative Empirical Models of the Term Structure of Interest Rates," *Journal of Finance* (September 1976), 1035–1065.

Elliott, J. W., and M. E. Echols, "Market Segmentation, Speculative Behavior, and the Term Structure of Interest Rates," *Review of Economics and Statistics* (February 1976), 40–49.

Fama, E. F. "Term Premiums in Bond Returns," *Journal of Financial Economics* (December 1984), 529–546.

Friedman, Benjamin M., "Interest Rate Expectations versus Forward Rates: Evidence from an Expectations Survey," *Journal of Finance* (September 1979), 965–973.

Hamburger, Michael J., and Elliott Platt, "The Expectations Hypothesis and the Efficiency of the Treasury Bill Market," *Review of Economics and Statistics* (May 1975), 190–197.

Kessel, Reuben, *The Cyclical Behavior of the Term Structure of Interest Rates* (New York: National Bureau of Economic Research, 1965).

Malkiel, Burton, *The Structure of Interest Rates* (New York: McCalb-Seiler, 1970).

——, and Edward J. Kane, "Expectations and Interest Rates: A Cross-Sectional Test of the Error-Learning Hypothesis," *Journal of Political Economy* (July/August 1968), 453–470.

McCulloch, J. H., "An Estimate of the Liquidity Premium," *Journal of Political Economy* (January/February 1975), 95–119.

Meiselman, David, *The Term Structure of Interest Rates* (Englewood Cliffs, N.J.: Prentice-Hall, 1962.)

Modigliani, Franco, and Richard Sutch, "Innovation in Interest Rate Policy," *American Economic Review* (May 1966), 178–197.

——, "Debt Management and The Term Structure of Interest Rates: An Empirical Analysis," *Journal of Political Economy* (August 1967), 567–589.

Phillips, Llad, and John Pippenger, "The Term Structure of Interest Rates in the MIT-PENN-SSRC Model," *Journal of Money, Credit, and Banking* (May 1979), 151–164.

Roley, Vance, "The Determinants of the Treasury Yield Curve," *Journal of Finance* (December 1981), 1103–1126.

Sargent, Thomas J., "Interest Rates in The 1950's," *Review of Economics and Statistics* (May 1960), 164–172.

Van Horne, James, "Interest-Rate Risk and the Term Structure of Interest Rates," *Journal of Political Economy* (August 1965), 344–351.

Wood, John, "Expectations, Errors, and the Term Structure of Interest Rates," *Journal of Political Economy* (April 1963), 165–166.

CHAPTER 8

Inflation and Other Influences on the Structure of Interest Rates

As we discussed in the previous chapter, the structure, or pattern, of relative interest rates on various financial instruments is heavily influenced by differences in the time to maturity of these financial assets. Yet many other considerations besides maturity affect interest rates. In this chapter we focus on the most significant of these various influences: inflation, default risk, taxes, callability, and marketability. These factors do not include all the influences on the pattern of rates found in financial markets, but they do encompass the major elements. In particular, many of the changes that occurred in interest rates in the past decade can be attributed to changes in the rate of inflation. Given the pervasive influence of inflation on the financial system in recent years, it is important to provide some background information on inflation itself before we discuss its influence on interest rates.

INFLATION

Inflation is commonly defined as an increase in some general index of prices, such as the Consumer Price Index or the broad-based Implicit Gross National Product Deflator.[1] In understanding inflation we should recognize the difference between increases in the prices of particular goods or services, which constitute changes in relative prices and do not necessarily represent inflation, and an increase in a general index of prices, which does represent inflation. In a market-oriented economy, at any time some prices are rising and some prices are falling.

---

[1] The Implicit Gross National Product Deflator is sometimes referred to as the *overall price index*, since it incorporates the prices on all subcomponents of the gross national product: consumption, investment, government spending, and exports.

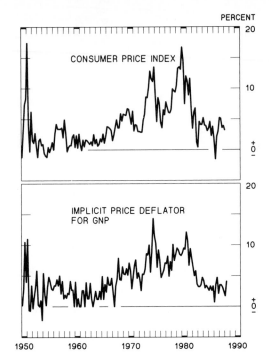

FIGURE 8.1   Comprehensive Price Measures
(Change at annual rates; Seasonally Adjusted, Quarterly)

Source: Board of Governors of the Federal Reserve System, Historical Chart Book, *1988.*

These changes in relative prices are the basic mechanism by which resources are allocated; increases in the price of some particular good or service need have no particular inflationary significance for the overall economy. Yet when an average of all prices—expressed in a price index—rises, the economic problem of inflation becomes a matter of concern. Indeed, the paramount economic problem of the U.S. economy since 1965 has been inflation. As indicated in Fig. 8.1, the purchasing power of the dollar has been greatly eroded in recent years. The entire post–World War II era has been characterized by a rising price level.[2] As measured by the Consumer Price Index (CPI), the price level has declined in only two periods since 1945 (1948–1949 and 1954–1955), and these dips were very

---

[2]The U.S. economy was periodically plagued by inflation before World War II, but such inflationary periods were followed by periods of declining prices. It is estimated that the general price level in 1940 was approximately the same as that in 1800.

slight. Between 1948 and 1965 the CPI rose at an average annual rate of about 1.7 percent, but it increased at an average annual rate of 6.5 percent from 1966 to 1979. "Double-digit inflation" came in 1973 and returned again in 1979 and 1980, receding only after the severe 1981–1982 recession.

Why has inflation been so persistent and often severe in recent decades? There are a great variety of explanations, and it may be of interest to list some of those most commonly cited:

1. *Excessive monetary growth.* A close statistical relationship exists between growth of the money supply and changes in the price level. Though such association does not necessarily mean causation, many economists (so-called monetarists) consider excessive monetary growth to be the salient cause of inflation.

2. *Large and continuous deficit federal spending.* Since 1960 the federal budget has been balanced or in surplus only twice. The deficit spending of the other years has resulted in a huge increase in the national debt. Since increased federal borrowing tends to push up interest rates, it is possible that the Fed will respond by expanding the money supply at an excessive rate, causing inflation. (If the Fed is not thus influenced, there is no necessary reason for deficit spending to cause a large and sustained increase in the rate of inflation, as was made evident in the period of the mid- and late 1980s, when large federal budget deficits and a relatively subdued inflation rate coexisted.)

3. *Externally imposed price "shocks."* The principal example here, of course, is the huge hike in oil prices since 1973. Because of the large and pervasive role of petroleum in the production of goods and services, the OPEC-mandated oil-price increases had to raise the general price level unless there were offsetting declines in other costs. Such price declines, in a modern, industrialized economy, are likely only if employment and output decline sharply—perhaps to an unacceptable degree.[3]

4. *Wages, productivity, and expectations relationships.* Labor costs are the most significant component of the total costs of most goods and services. When wages rise more than productivity (output per hour of work), prices can be expected to rise. Workers have an incentive to press for such inflationary wage increases either to increase their share of the "economic pie" or, if they *expect* inflation, to maintain the size of their current share. Thus inflationary expectations can be self-fulfilling as a "wage–price spiral" develops.

Most of the other possible causes of recent inflation (like the above) are inter-

---

[3]The downward rigidity of many prices in industrialized economies is explained by various legal (i.e., minimum wage laws) and institutional (i.e., labor unions) features of such economies. This phenomenon has been labeled the "ratchet" effect—prices go up but not down. Perhaps the basic reason for the "ratchet" effect is the unwillingness of most modern governments to permit the kind of economic declines that, in previous eras, forced prices (and wages) down.

related. A usual dichotomy of inflation causes is **demand pull** (aggregate demand exceeds aggregate supply because of excessive monetary or fiscal stimulus) and **cost push** (structural imperfections in the economy tend to ratchet up wages and prices). Demand-pull inflation, often characterized as the classic type of inflation, occurs when an excessive demand for goods and services presses on the economy's capacity to meet those demands. Demand-pull inflation is often described as a situation in which "too many dollars are chasing too few goods." Excessive money creation by the central bank is often a cause. Most episodes of so-called runaway inflation, or hyperinflation, in countries around the world have been of the demand-pull type.[4] In the United States the most recent inflationary period began with the acceleration of spending for the Vietnam War in 1966, and the origin of this inflation is an example of demand-pull inflation. In 1966 the economy was near full employment of labor and capital resources following a period of six years of expansion. Nevertheless, tremendous increases in war expenditures were added to the existing private demand; taxes were not increased to "pay for the war." Further, the Fed had pursued generally expansionary monetary policy in the preceding years. The result created a situation in which literally too many dollars did chase too few goods and services, and started one of the most persistent and significant inflationary periods in the history of the United States.

Explanation of the other type of inflation—cost push—emphasizes the importance of the supply side of the supply/demand relationship as the determining factor in producing inflation. In one variant of this view the monopolistic elements of powerful labor unions and large businesses that administratively set prices are crucial in influencing the rate of inflation. Increases in wages negotiated by strong unions cause increases in the costs of producing goods and services. Unless the increased costs are offset by increases in productivity—an uncommon occurrence in recent years—the labor cost per unit of output rises. Business, seeking to restore profit margins, reacts by raising prices. The increase in prices then causes labor to seek higher wages to offset the decline in living standards, and the wage/price spiral has begun. Although this illustration started with the negotiation of higher wages by the unions, it could just as easily have begun with business increasing its prices. In either case, inflation results from an effort by business firms or labor unions to increase their relative share of national income.

Another variant of the cost-push view of inflation's causes stresses the apparent rigidity of some prices in the downward direction; the imperfectly competitive structure of the economy causes prices of many goods and services to rise

---

[4]The German experience in the 1920s provided an excellent illustration of demand-pull inflation fueled by the printing press. By 1923, prices in Germany were 34 billion times as high as in 1921, a phenomenal change in a period of only two years. In this type of environment, in which individual savings accumulated through a period of years become valueless in a period of minutes, there is little incentive for hard work and saving.

readily in response to upward stimulus but to resist downward pressures. According to this view, some producers tend to reduce production rather than lower prices when demand falls. Again, monopolistic elements in the economy are the alleged culprit, along with various market imperfections stemming from government legislation and restrictions. It is argued that such "stickiness" of prices hinders the adjustment of relative prices that is an inherent aspect of a dynamic economy; such adjustment is accomplished not by decreases in some prices but in some prices increasing more than others. An "inflationary bias" thus characterizes the behavior of the general price level. Further, an increase in productive resource costs (such as the large OPEC-engineered increases in the price of oil in 1974 and 1979) causes all prices to rise as producers seek to pass on their higher production costs to their customers.[5]

In reality, demand-pull and cost-push inflation are closely related. Indeed, it is quite difficult to separate existing inflation into the part that is attributable to demand factors and the part that is attributable to the wage/price spiral. Inflation is frequently begun by excess demand. Once inflation starts, however, workers and business management react in such a way that costs rise and prices are increased, setting off a wage/price spiral. Yet the increases in costs and prices can be permanent only if there is sufficient demand to absorb the potential output at the higher price levels.[6] Hence the two types of inflation become intimately connected and frequently indistinguishable.

Consequences of Inflation

Inflation is an economic problem because of its effects on the distribution of income, which pose equity concerns and create social and political tensions, and on the allocation of resources, which pose a threat to economic growth.[7] During inflationary periods, real (inflation-adjusted) income tends to shift from groups that lack the market power, institutional status, legal ability, and/or foresight to keep their money incomes increasing in step with the price level to those groups that do. A powerful union, for example, may impose a cost-of-living adjustment (COLA) labor contract clause (indexing wage rates to the CPI) on man-

---

[5]See Arthur M. Okun, *Prices and Quantities: A Macroeconomic Analysis* (Washington, D.C.: Brookings Institution, 1981) for an interesting exposition of this view.

[6]The U.S. reaction to the increased price of oil established by the Opec countries in 1974 provides an example of the validation of higher prices through the action of the central bank. The Federal Reserve System accommodated the increase in the price of energy by increasing bank reserves and the money supply. As a result, all prices tended to rise. The "losers"—those whose living standard was lowered because of the higher prices—were the individuals and groups who were unable to keep their prices and wages in line with the general price rise.

[7]The point is often made that if all economic units in an economy correctly anticipated the rate of inflation and could adjust their factor receipts accordingly, these various ills of inflation would not result. This is true, but it is hardly descriptive of actual economic behavior.

agement and thus protect its members from inflation. The U.S. Congress may choose to protect certain groups of recipients of government paychecks in a similar fashion, as it has done for Social Security beneficiaries, military retirees, and retired federal employees. On the other hand, such groups as state employees can only hope that state legislators will choose to boost their salaries in keeping with inflation rates in a timely fashion, an action that is not always forthcoming.

Inflation also tends to shift income from taxpayers to government. In the case of progressive-rate income taxes, rising money income (even if it corresponds to falling real income) will move taxpayers into higher tax brackets and may result in a greater proportion of real as well as money income being paid in taxes.[8] In the case of corporations, corporate tax payments increase (even if profits are constant) because cost-based depreciation allowances lag behind real capital consumption.

Inflation is likely to be injurious to both savings and investment. Though it can be argued that efficient financial markets impound expectations about inflation (the risk-return implications) into security prices, inflation will still discourage the flow of savings into financial assets to the extent that savers do not believe in the existence of such efficiency.[9] Certainly, surges of "unexpected" inflation, such as the 1980 price-level spurt (which sent interest rates soaring and bond prices tumbling), persuade many individuals to plow their available funds into personal possessions (and perhaps precious stones and metals), rather than into purchases of financial assets or productive real assets.

Inflation not only jeopardizes the availability of funds for investment but also tends to make most potential investment projects less attractive to business managers. Business firms undertake investment projects according to much the same risk-return decision criteria that characterize the purchase of financial assets. The prospect of continuing inflation (at uncertain rates) has a significant, and often pivotal, impact on the assessment of risk regarding proposed investment projects.

Inflationary expectations thus may tend to distort the flow of funds in the economy so that money capital may be increasingly channeled into nonproductive uses. Efficiency in both the financial markets and the markets for goods and services may diminish as confidence in the future purchasing power of money wanes. Economic growth is inevitably and adversely affected by inflation when its occurrence and pace engender such behavior.

There is a very strong connection both in concept and in practice between

---

[8]The Economic Recovery Tax Act of 1981 included a provision aimed at eliminating the so-called bracket creep caused by inflation after 1984 by "indexing" tax brackets and personal exemptions on the basis of changes in the Consumer Price Index.

[9]Debtors are generally viewed as "gainers" from inflation (and creditors as "losers"), since debts are repaid in depreciated dollars. Whether or not this is true for a particular debt, however, depends on the interest-rate–inflation-rate relationship.

inflation and levels of interest rates. The potential economic consequences of inflation are shaped to a large degree by the nature of the inflation–interest-rate relationship.

INTEREST RATES AND INFLATION

The relationship between changes in overall prices and the level of interest rates has a comparatively simple explanation. Perhaps the best way to provide this explanation is to discuss the impact of changing prices on the financial position of an individual. If interest rates were not related to changing prices, there would be a redistribution of wealth between lenders and borrowers as the result of changing prices. For example, a lender who extended a loan of $1000 would receive only $500 worth of purchasing power in principal repayment if prices had doubled since the time the loan was made. A lending rate of 100 percent (equal to the rate of inflation) for the period of the loan would be necessary for the lender merely to recapture the amount of purchasing power transferred to the borrower when the loan was made; any lesser rate would result in a loss to the lender. The borrower would thus benefit from the inflation if the interest rate was less than the inflation rate. In the example the borrower would acquire $1000 of purchasing power at the time of the loan and would return to the lender only $500 of purchasing power in principal repayment. We would expect, then, that market interest rates would reflect this potential loss to the lender and gain to the borrower such that the rate would adjust upward until there was no loss to the lender and no gain to the borrower from the inflation.[10] Such adjustment in the rate of interest would equate the purchasing power of principal received by the borrower and principal paid to the lender and provide a real return to the lender. At these rate levels, equilibrium would be established, and the inflation would not produce any inflation-induced redistribution of wealth between lenders and borrowers.

The Fisher Effect

This view of the relationship between expected price level changes and interest rate levels may be visualized from the calculations in Fig. 8.2. Usually referred to as the **Fisher effect,** it is named for the economist Irving Fisher.[11] By this expla-

---

[10]There should be a very heavy demand for credit by borrowers in periods when the interest rate does not fully reflect inflation. The experience of the housing industry in the late 1970s provides illustrations of this phenomenon. Individuals were quite willing to borrow to purchase houses, since house prices were rising considerably more rapidly than the cost of money.

[11]Irving Fisher, "Appreciation and Interest," *Publications of the American Economic Association* (August 1896), 1–100.

Nominal rate = Real rate + Expected change in prices.

Examples:
1. Assume that expected increase in prices = 0%, real rate = 3%, and nominal rate
   = 3%.

   Nominal rate = Real rate + Expected change in prices.
         3% =   3%   + 0%

2. Assume that expected increase in prices = 10%, real rate = 3%, and nominal rate
   = 13%.

   Nominal rate = Real rate + Expected change in prices.
       13% =   3%   + 10%.

3. Assume that expected increase in prices = 10%, real rate = 0%, and nominal rate
   = 10%.

   Nominal rate = Real rate + Expected change in prices.
       10% =   0%   + 10%.

FIGURE 8.2   Price Changes and Interest Rates

---

nation there is some basic and underlying *real* rate of interest, independent of expected price level changes, which is determined by the saving habits of the community and the productivity of capital investment.[12] This "real" interest rate is thought to be relatively constant at least in the short run, although the precise level of the real rate is not directly observable. Studies of interest rate levels in periods when inflation was not a problem have led some observers to suggest that the real rate generally ranges from 2 to 3 percent. If this is true, in periods when inflation did not exist, we would expect that the rate lenders charged and borrowers paid—the *nominal* rate—would be 2 to 3 percent, the same as the real rate. But when inflation is anticipated, the nominal rate will increase to add an "inflation premium" to the real rate.

Formally stated, the Fisher effect suggests the *nominal* rate of interest, i, on a financial instrument is determined by a *real* rate of interest, r, and p, the expected rate of change in the general price level over the time to maturity for the instrument:

$$1 + i = (1 + r)(1 + p)$$

or

$$i = r + p + rp$$

---

[12]See Chapter 6 for a more complete description of the determinants of the "real" rate.

If inflation is moderate, the cross-product term rp is the product of two small percentage amounts and is thus negligible. If rp is ignored, then

$$i = r + p$$

But how does this nominal rate change as the price level changes? We must recognize, of course, that the inflation rate that is expected to prevail over the life of the contract is what is important, not the actual or past rate. A lender who contemplates making a loan for one year is concerned with the change in prices that will occur during that one-year period, and the lender is concerned with the current inflation rate only to the extent that it may predict future price change. But how does the nominal rate change as changes occur in the expected rate of inflation?

As discussed above and as illustrated in example 1 of Fig. 8.2, in a period in which the expected rate of inflation is zero, the nominal rate and the real rate should be the same. If the real rate is 3 percent, then the nominal rate should also be 3 percent. But if expectations of inflation increased, we would expect that financial market rates would quickly adjust upward. As illustrated in example 2 in Fig. 8.2, if prices were expected to rise by 10 percent during the duration of the financial contract, we would expect interest rates to adjust upward quickly to 13 percent. At the 13-percent level, neither the borrower nor the lender gains or loses from the expected inflation. For example, assume a one-year loan. The lender provides $1000 of purchasing power and receives back $1130 at the end of the year; if the $130 is the total return to the lender, $100 represents compensation for the loss of purchasing power and leaves the lender's inflation-adjusted financial position unchanged, whereas the $30 represents a "real" return to the lender.

The Fisher effect can be depicted in the loanable funds model as shown in Fig. 8.3.[13] In this figure the initial equilibrium nominal interest rate, i_1, is determined by the intersection of the supply of loanable funds schedule, S_1, and the demand for loanable funds schedule, D_1. At i_1 there is some level of expected inflation, p, and $i_1 = r + p$. Now suppose that p changes (as drawn in Fig. 8.3, p increases by Δp). All borrowers and lenders *now* anticipate an expected inflation rate of $p' = p + \Delta p$. Owing to the higher p, lenders (the suppliers of loanable funds) require a higher i for all levels of lending. The supply of loanable funds schedule shifts from S_1 to S_2, as shown in the figure. Borrowers are willing to pay a higher nominal return for funds, and the demand for loanable funds schedule shifts from D_1 to D_2. A New equilibrium nominal interest rate is established at i_2, with

$$i_2 = i_1 + \Delta p$$

---

[13]For a more detailed treatment and discussion, see Benjamin M. Friedman, "Who Puts the Inflation Premium into Nominal Interest Rates?" *Journal of Finance* (June 1978), 833–845.

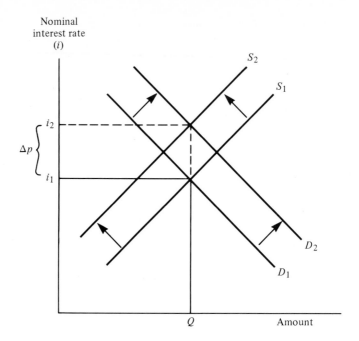

FIGURE 8.3   The Fisher Effect in a Loanable Funds Framework

In this conceptual treatment, r (the real interest rate) and Q (the quantity of funds borrowed and lent) are unchanged. Only i, the nominal interest rate, changes. However, there are a number of reasons to doubt that actual interest rate adjustment to inflation mirrors the outcome of this simple model. The magnitude of inflation premiums impounded into interest rates is affected by a wide variety of factors that are not reflected in this model.

The Magnitude of Inflation Premiums

While the *nature* of the effect of anticipated inflation (and changes in the expected rate of inflation) on financial market behavior is apparent, the *measurement* of the effect is extremely difficult. Inflation premiums cannot be measured by simply relating past or present nominal interest rates to past or present inflation rates. Inflation premiums stem from **expected future inflation rates.** The latter is not directly observable, nor is the real rate of interest. While the real rate of interest is generally believed to be relatively constant in the short term, this has not been conclusively demonstrated. Thus any set of inflation-adjusted interest rates may reflect any combination of the Fisher effect, differences between expected and subsequent actual inflation rates (unanticipated inflation), and possible changes in the real rate of interest. Further, the effects of taxes, risk aversion (inflation forecasts are inherently uncertain), and various other factors are also likely to be impounded into net interest returns after inflation.

The tax base for the application of the federal income tax is the nominal or total interest return, not the inflation-adjusted or real return. Individuals receiving interest income are subject to federal income tax payments on the full amount of interest, not just the "real" return. Even if the financial markets adjusted fully to an expected inflation rate of 10 percent so that the nominal rate rose from 3 percent to 13 percent, the lender would still lose (if actual inflation proved to be 10 percent) because of the extra tax that would be required on the higher interest payments.[14] This implies, of course, that once taxes are considered, an increase in expected inflation from 0 to 10 percent should result in a rise in the nominal rate of *more* than 10 percent. With taxes, nominal rates must always rise by a greater percentage amount than the increase in the expected inflation rate.[15] Mathematically, where r' is the after-tax real rate, i is the nominal rate, and p is the expected rate of inflation:

$$r' = i - it - p$$

or

$$i = \frac{r' + p}{(1 - t)}$$

Thus

$$\Delta i = \frac{\Delta p}{(1 - t)}$$

for some percent increase in expected inflation, Δp. It is apparent that Δi must exceed Δp if r' is unchanged. In the example above, suppose that $\Delta p = 10$ percent. If $t = 40$ percent, then

$$\Delta i = \frac{0.10}{(1 - 0.4)} = 0.1666 = 16.7\%$$

For a *decrease* in the expected rate of inflation, the analysis with taxes suggests a greater percentage reduction in the nominal rate of interest than the percentage decline in anticipated inflation.

Other complicating features of the connection between inflation and interest

[14]From the borrower's perspective, since interest expense is deductible for federal income tax purposes, the impact of higher interest rates on the borrower's position is reduced.
[15]See Martin Feldstein, "Inflation, Income Taxes and the Rate of Inflation: A Theoretical Analysis," *American Economic Review* (December 1976), 809–820.

rates concern the stability of the real rate and the speed with which financial market rates adjust to changes in inflationary expectations. The "pure" Fisher effect basically assumes that the real rate is constant, and the financial markets adjust very quickly to changes in inflationary expectations. Neither of these assumptions may be completely valid. It may be that the real rate is variable, so changes in expected inflation impact partly or completely on the real rate as on the nominal rate. For example, refer again to Fig. 8.3. An increase in the expected rate of inflation from 0 to 10 percent might be associated with a rise in the nominal rate to only 10 percent, in which case the real return to the investor (exclusive of tax considerations) would be 0 percent. Here, of course, the lender would lose as a result of the inflation, whereas the borrower would benefit. Moreover, if the financial markets adjusted slowly to inflation, the real rate of interest could be low or negative during the adjustment period. For example, if expectations of inflation went from 0 percent to 16 percent, the nominal rate might increase this year to 6 percent (implying a real rate of −10 percent), increase further to 10 percent in the second year (implying a real rate of −6 percent), and finally adjust to 19 percent in the third year (implying a real return of 3 percent). During the adjustment period, of course, lenders are harmed by the inflation, while borrowers gain.

Table 8.1 shows "real" long-term (Aaa corporate bond) interest rates for each year from 1960 to 1988, where the "real" rate is *ex post*—an actual inflation measure is subtracted from the nominal return. While the series average is about 4 percent, it is marked by some anomalous movement. The *ex post* real return is low (and negative in 1974) in years in which the inflation rate surged (an unexpected increase in inflation?) and is very high from 1981–1985 (an unexpected decline in the inflation rate?).

In an extensive comparison of nominal interest and inflation rates, Ibbotson and Sinquefield examined Treasury bills, long-term Treasury bonds, long-term corporate bonds, and common stocks for the period 1926–1981.[16] Over this entire period the real return on Treasury bills and bonds, compounded annually, was approximately zero (negative for the tax-paying holder). Corporate bonds yielded an annually compounded real rate of about 0.5 percent, and common stock yielded 5.9 percent. Thus lenders fared poorly over the entire period, although the Ibbotson-Sinquefield analysis indicates that they have generally earned higher real returns in more recent years.

In addition to the historical record of real returns a number of empirical studies have aimed at testing the relationship between nominal interest rates and expected inflation. Given that expected inflation rates can only be inferred (they are not directly observable), and given the other problems of such empirical anal-

---

[16]Roger G. Ibbotson and Rex A. Sinquefield, *Stocks, Bonds, Bills, and Inflation* (Charlottesville, Va.: Financial Analysts Research Foundation, 1982).

TABLE 8.1 "Real" Long-Term Interest Rates, 1960–1988

Year	Inflation Rate[1]	Aaa Corporate Bond Rate	Ex Post Real Interest Rate
1960	1.4	4.4	3.0
1961	1.0	4.3	3.4
1962	2.0	4.3	2.3
1963	1.5	4.3	2.7
1964	1.4	4.4	3.0
1965	2.4	4.5	2.1
1966	3.7	5.1	1.5
1967	3.0	5.5	2.5
1968	4.7	6.2	1.5
1969	5.4	7.0	1.7
1970	4.9	8.0	3.2
1971	4.6	7.4	2.8
1972	4.2	7.2	3.0
1973	6.9	7.4	0.6
1974	9.7	8.6	−1.1
1975	7.4	8.8	1.4
1976	4.5	8.4	3.9
1977	5.9	8.0	2.1
1978	8.1	8.7	0.6
1979	7.8	9.6	1.8
1980	9.7	11.9	2.3
1981	8.3	14.2	5.8
1982	4.3	13.8	9.5
1983	3.9	12.0	8.1
1984	3.7	12.7	9.0
1985	3.2	11.4	8.2
1986	2.6	9.0	6.4
1987	3.3	9.4	6.1
1988	3.4	9.7	6.3

[1]The inflation rate is measured as the average annual percent change in the GNP implicit price deflator.

Source: 1960–1983: William T. Gavin, "Reflections on Money and Inflation," Federal Reserve Bank of Cleveland Economic Review *(Winter 1984), p. 3. 1984–1988: Compiled by authors from* Federal Reserve Bulletin, *and* Survey of Current Business.

ysis, it is not surprising that the results are mixed. (The list of references at the end of this chapter include several of these studies.) In general, both the historical record of real returns and the empirical studies indicate a positive (but less than one-to-one) relationship between changes in nominal interest rates and changes in the rate of inflation. It appears, however, that the Fisher effect has not protected lenders in many periods—perhaps periods of surges in unanticipated inflation.

INFLATION AND THE STRUCTURE OF INTEREST RATES

To this point our discussion of the impact of inflation has been in terms of "the" interest rate rather than the pattern of rates. However, changes in expected inflation should have a variety of effects on the structure of rates. Perhaps the most significant effect should be on the term structure of interest rates. For example, if the inflation rate were expected to increase at an accelerating rate—2 percent next year, 4 percent the year after, 6 percent the third year, and so on—then the term structure should be greater in slope. Longer-term securities would have a higher rate than shorter-term securities. On the other hand, if inflation were quite strong in the current year but were expected to decline over time (for example, an expected rate of inflation of 9 percent in the current year, 6 percent in the second year, and 3 percent in the third year), then the term structure should be downward sloping. Rates on 3-year securities, for example, should be less than rates on 1-year securities.

Changes in the expected rate of inflation might also produce a variety of effects in the structure of rates in more indirect ways. For example, expectations of increases in prices might cause rates on utility bonds to rise more than rates on industrial bonds. The logic behind this argument relates to the differences in pricing flexibility for the two segments of the economy. Utilities, which must obtain regulatory approval of rate increases, may find that inflation is increasing their costs more than their revenues, thereby reducing profitability and increasing the difficulty of repaying principal and interest on bonds outstanding. In contrast, industrial companies often have more flexibility in increasing prices and are thus better able to maintain profit levels and their ability to meet their debt obligations. As another example, since inflation is frequently followed by recession, an increase in inflation may cause rates on lower-quality securities to rise more than rates on higher-quality securities. Lower-quality firms may have an especially difficult time in meeting their debt obligations in recessionary periods, but even a substantial decline in the economy need have no strong impact on the ability of "top-quality" firms to meet their debt obligations. However, since both arguments relate to the association between interest rates and credit risk, we will now explore that topic in some detail.

DEFAULT RISK

When credit is extended by a lender to a borrower, the expectation is—or at least should be—that the terms of the agreement will be fulfilled, interest will be paid as due, and principal will be repaid as scheduled. Unfortunately, it is not uncommon for events to occur during the life of the debt agreement that make it impossible for the borrower to meet the terms of the agreement. For a business, sales might decline because of changes in market taste or a recession in the economy, or costs might increase beyond expectations. For whatever reason the borrower might not have the cash to make timely payment of principal and interest. It is this risk that is described as default or credit risk.

Default Risk Defined

Default risk refers to the probability that the borrower will be unable or unwilling to make the agreed upon payments under a debt contract in a timely fashion. Default occurs whenever the borrower does not make a required payment or whenever the required payment is late. In either case the lender has suffered a loss. If the payment is never made, the lender is unable to invest the funds and earn interest during the period of the delay. As a result, the interest return actually realized by the lender is less, in many cases substantially less, than the rate agreed upon in the loan contract.

Degrees of Default Risk

Default or credit risk exists on virtually all debt instruments. However, the degree of default risk varies widely. It is commonly accepted that U.S. government securities carry little or no default risk, since the U.S. government has the authority to meet its debt obligation by printing money. Indeed, the interest rate on U.S. government securities is often referred to as the "risk-free rate."[17] All other securities carry some degree of default risk. Securities issued by corporations obviously carry default risk. Changes in management, demand for products, costs, and other factors can produce default. We should also recognize that securities issued by state and local governments can carry substantial amounts of default risk as the holders of New York City bonds unfortunately discovered in the mid-1970s. Although many state and local government securities are backed by the taxing power of the issuer, there is no guarantee that this taxing power will be used. Moreover, unlike the federal government, state and local governments do not have the ability to print money to pay their debts.

The Risk Premium

We would expect that financial market rates would adjust to compensate the lender for absorbing default risk. Rates on securities with large amounts of default risk should be higher than rates on securities with low amounts of default risk. There should be a **risk structure** of interest rates. Not only should there be

---

[17]Like all debt securities, U.S. government securities bear "interest-rate" risk—the potential for unexpected changes in price due to changes in prevailing interest rates. For short-term U.S. government securities (such as 3-month Treasury bills) this risk is minimal.

such a pattern, but indeed such relationships do exist and are among the most distinctive aspects of financial markets. The most common description of this relationship is provided by the concept of the risk premium. The **risk premium** is defined as the difference between the market rate on a security (yield to maturity at a point of time) and the risk-free rate for an equal maturity security.

$$\text{Risk premium} = \text{Yield to maturity} - \text{Risk-free rate}$$

The risk premium describes the added return that the market requires over the risk-free rate for the investor to accept the default risk associated with a particular security. For example, if the risk-free rate is 5 percent, and if the market requires a 5-percent premium to accept the default risk on a high-risk security, then the yield to maturity on that security should be 10 percent. On a lower-risk security, for which a 3-percent risk premium might be satisfactory, the yield to maturity would have to be only 8 percent. The entire spectrum of rates on corporate and state and local government securities of a particular maturity can be envisioned as a base "risk-free rate" plus a "risk premium."

Bond Ratings

There are a variety of ways to judge the default risk of various types of securities, but the approach that is most widely used, the one that is incorporated into the legal framework of regulation, is the bond-rating system of Moody's and Standard & Poor's. Both these private organizations will provide, for a fee, a rating of any corporate or state or local government issue. The ratings range from the highest-quality issues through those that have some speculative characteristic and those that are principally speculative to those that are in default.

Figure 8.4 provides a brief explanation of the ratings for the various categories of securities. Note that the rating descriptions are essentially the same for the two agencies, although the symbols vary slightly. Moody's Aaa is "best quality," and Standard & Poor's AAA is "highest quality." When both agencies rate one bond, as they quite commonly do, the ratings are usually identical. As the ratings move from Aaa (AAA) to A and then into the B and C categories, the default risk increases, and we would expect that the risk premium would increase. The first four rating categories (Aaa to Baa or AAA to BBB) are especially significant. These categories collectively are referred to as "investment-grade" securities. They are particularly important, since many financial institutions—including commercial banks—are limited in their security holdings to investment-grade issues.

The risk premium on differently rated corporate issues is graphically represented by Fig. 8.5. Note that, as expected, corporate issues have required higher rates than U.S. government issues. (For the moment, disregard the state and local securities.) Financial markets do demand a higher return for placing funds in

Rating	Description
Moody's	
Aaa	Best quality
Aa	High quality by all standards
A	Upper medium grade
Baa	Medium grade
Ba	Have speculative elements
B	Generally lack characteristics of the desirable investment
Caa	Poor standing; may be in default
Ca	Speculative in a high degree, often in default
C	Lowest grade; extremely poor prospects
Standard & Poor's	
AAA	Highest quality; extremely strong capacity
AA	High quality; very strong capacity
A	Strong capacity
BBB	Adequate capacity
BB	Low speculative
B	Speculative
CCC-CC	High speculation
C	Income bonds on which no interest is being paid
DDD-D	In default

FIGURE 8.4 Bond-Rating Designations

Source: Moody's Bond Record; Standard & Poor's Fixed Income Investor.

corporate securities, which carry default risk, than for investing in the "risk-free" U.S. government issues. Moreover, the risk premium on the lower rate Baa issues is substantially greater than the risk premium on the Aaa issues. In fact, the risk premium on the Aaa issues is often very small, indicating that the financial markets expect a very low probability of default on the securities of the highest quality corporations. Though not shown in Fig. 8.5, the risk premium on B-rated securities would be much larger than that for either Aaa or Baa securities.

One other aspect of the risk structure of rates that is brought out by Fig. 8.5 is the cyclical changes in risk premiums. Risk premiums on corporate issues widen in periods of economic decline and narrow in periods of economic expansion. This relationship is perhaps best illustrated by the difference between the risk premium in the 1930s and those in the 1950s, 1960s, and 1970s. But note also that the risk premiums in the post–World War II period have varied with the business cycle. For example, the risk premium on Baa securities became quite large in the recession of 1974–1975, as well as in the recession of 1969–1970. Declines in business activity associated with recession, especially sharp recession, appear to cause investors to take more seriously the prospect of default on debt securities, so such declines may be associated with greater risk aversion on the part of investors.

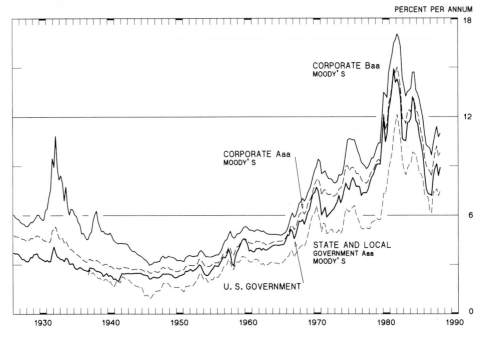

FIGURE 8.5   Long-Term Bond Yields (Quarterly Averages)

Source: Board of Governors of the Federal Reserve System, Historical Chart Book, *1988.*

      Until the 1980s few public issues of bonds were rated below investment grade (i.e., were regarded as bearing speculative elements) by Moody's or Standard & Poor's. In the 1980s, however, a large market in "junk bonds" developed. The investment banking firm of Drexel Burnham Lambert played a major role in the creation of this market by seeking out investors who were willing to take on the higher default risk of low-rated bonds in exchange for a significantly higher yield. The emerging demand for these lower-grade, high-yield bonds was satisfied largely with new issues used to finance successful and unsuccessful corporate takeover attempts. Junk bonds became controversial, partly because of how pro-ceeds from their issue were used and partly because some observers viewed them as bringing a major new risk to the financial system. This perceived new risk stemmed from the alleged high "systematic risk" component of junk bonds; a major downturn in the economy was likely to trigger widespread default by junk bond issuers. Defenders of junk bonds maintained that they were merely a new form of the kind of lending risk that had long been present in the portfolio of such institutional lenders as commercial banks and insurance companies and, moreover, that they constituted an easily diversifiable form of such risk. Whether or not junk bonds are a good deal for investors and the overall economy remains to be seen; a complete business cycle is necessary to make that judgment.

TAXABILITY

Differences in the tax treatment of income from different types of financial instruments are a significant factor influencing the pattern of interest rates in financial markets. Four aspects of the impact of taxation on interest rate structure warrant attention. First, the interest income on certain "municipal" securities issued by state governments and their subdivisions is exempt from federal income taxation. (The Tax Reform Act of 1986 ended such tax exemption for "nonessential" bond issues related to such activities as construction of sporting events arenas, pollution control facilities for private firms, and various industrial inducement expenditures that benefitted private firms.) Further, the interest income on municipal bonds is usually exempt from state and local income taxes in the state of their issue.

Another significant tax factor is the fact that interest income on U.S. treasury securities is exempt from income taxes imposed by state and local governments. A third, minor influence reflects the fact that some U.S. government securities can be used at par prior to maturity to settle estate tax liabilities ("flower bonds"). Finally, before the major revision of the federal income tax law in 1986, a fourth factor—differential treatment of ordinary income and capital gains—had a significant effect on the structure of interest rates. Since it is quite possible that the federal tax laws will change again in regard to the taxation of capital gains, the effect of different tax rates for capital gains and other investment income warrants some discussion.

Exemption of Municipal Interest Income

The exemption of municipal interest income from federal income taxation and the further exemption of municipal interest income from some state and local income taxes has a significant impact on the yield on municipal securities compared with the yield on corporate and U.S. government issues. For example, an investor in the 28 percent tax bracket who could purchase a corporate bond with a yield of 12.5 percent would be better off buying a municipal security, as long as the municipal yield exceeded 9 percent, since the after-tax return on the corporate bond is only 9 percent [12.5% (1 − tax rate)]. The tax advantage of municipal securities should then lead to a large demand for municipals, increasing the price and lowering their return. Indeed, examination of Fig. 8.6 does show that pretax interest rates on municipal securities are substantially below those on corporate and U.S. government securities. It also shows that the differential is larger in the post–World War II period than in the prewar era, reflecting the higher income tax rates in recent years.[18]

A further (though minor) influence on the pattern of rates is the exemption from income taxation of interest income on securities issued in the same state. This consideration is especially relevant in influencing the demand for securities from states with high state and local income taxes. For example, since both New York State and New York City have substantial income taxes, we would expect the residents of New York (both individuals and corporations) to have a special demand for New York securities. As a result, these securities could probably be sold to residents of New York State at a yield lower than those on municipal securities issued by other states and by local governments in states other than New York.

Exemption of U.S. Government Interest Income

The exemption of interest income on municipal securities from the federal income tax stems from the historical concept of the federal and state governments both having sovereignty. Although the Civil War settled the issue of supremacy between federal and state governments, the exemption of interest income on municipal securities from the federal income tax currently serves as a means for the federal government to subsidize (through lower borrowing rates) state and local governments. However, the exemption of interest income on U.S. government securities from state and local income taxes is grounded in the U.S. Constitution and its interpretation by the Supreme Court. Since taxing authority conveys great power, state and local governments cannot tax the interest income from federal government securities.

One should understand that the interest income from U.S. government securities is exempt only from the income tax levies of state and local governments. The interest income from U.S. government securities is fully taxable by the federal government. Since state and local government income taxes are low in comparison with federal income tax, the impact on the relative structure of rates in the financial markets should be minimal. We would expect, however, that the rates on U.S. government securities would be lowered slightly in comparison with corporate and other issues by the exemption of the interest income on these securities from state and local government income taxes.

---

[18]We should note that the differentials in rates on municipals relative to corporate and U.S. government securities also reflect differences in credit risk, as well as differences in taxability. Municipal yields were actually higher than U.S. government yields in the 1920s, when there were considerable problems with defaults on state and local government issues.

Effects of Differential Capital Gains Taxation

When an investor sells a security for an amount greater than its cost, the difference between the net sales price and the cost is called a **capital gain.** When the net proceeds from the sale of the security is less than the total cost, a **capital loss** is sustained. Before the Tax Reform Act of 1986, capital gains from sale of a fixed-income security that had been held for a specified period of time were taxed at only about half the rate of interest income.

Differential tax treatment of ordinary income and capital gains has a significant effect on the yield to maturity of corporate and U.S. government bonds. Bonds that were issued in an earlier, lower-interest-rate period and that carry a lower coupon must sell at a price below par in order to offer a competitive yield to maturity. These so-called discount or deep discount bonds offer the investor a total return (interest return plus capital gains return) that is more heavily weighted toward capital gains than is true of bonds that sell near par. Investors (especially investors in high tax brackets) have a special demand for these issues, bidding up their price and lowering the yield to maturity. As a result, deep discount corporate and U.S. government securities will sell at a lower yield to maturity than comparable bonds that have high coupon rates and sell at a price near par.

One must recognize that this relationship is valid only for taxable securities (corporate and U.S. government issues). For tax-free issues (municipals) the relationship is the reverse. Investors in municipal securities obtain a tax-free return from interest but incur tax liabilities on capital gains from sale of the securities. Hence investors have reason to prefer municipal issues that sell at or near par and that have a return primarily in the form of interest income to those that sell at a discount and return substantial capital gains. As a result, deep discount *municipal* securities should sell at a yield that is *higher* than comparable high-coupon municipal issues.

Flower Bonds

The term **flower bonds** is applied to U.S. Treasury bonds that may be purchased at a discount and used at par value plus accrued interest to satisfy federal estate tax liabilities. The name presumably derives from the connection between funeral flowers and estate tax liabilities; these bonds are also referred to as "tombstone bonds" for equally obvious reasons. However, the provision allowing for the creation of flower bonds was repealed as of March 3, 1971. With no new flower bonds being issued and outstanding flower bonds being used to satisfy estate tax liabilities, the amount of flower bonds has gradually been decreasing.

Flower bonds represent a special group of discount bonds. Issued in an earlier period with coupons that are low in comparison with current interest rate levels, flower bonds must sell at prices below par to attract investors. Yet whereas other discount bonds can provide a capital gain only at maturity, flower bonds can provide a capital gain at the death of the holder and settlement of the estate tax liabilities. A special demand is thereby created for flower bonds from investors seeking to reduce prospective estate tax liabilities. As a result of this special demand, flower bonds offer lower yields than do comparable U.S. government bonds that do not carry the flower bond feature.

CALLABILITY

Callability refers to the ability of the issuer of a security to call it away from the holder (retire it) prior to maturity. Most corporate bonds are callable, some municipal securities are callable, and only a few U.S. government securities are callable. The influence of the call feature on the pattern of yields in financial markets can perhaps best be understood by examining the conditions under which a security might be called and the impact of the call on the positions of the borrower and lender.

The call feature is a characteristic attached to a security that is advantageous to the borrower. This feature allows the borrower to eliminate prior to maturity a security with excessively high interest rates or other undesirable features, such as a restriction on dividend payments. However, if the motive is to reduce interest expense (as it usually is), the bond will be called only if rates have declined since the original issue date. *From the lender's perspective the call feature is undesirable.* A call of the security before maturity is most likely to occur when the opportunities for reinvestment available to the lender are limited and when the potential return available to the lender is low.

Since the call feature is advantageous to the borrower but unfavorable to the lender, callable bonds may be expected to carry a higher interest rate than comparable noncallable bonds. Lenders demand higher interest rates on callable bonds to protect them against the risk of having the bonds called when reinvestment rates are low. Borrowers, in turn, are willing to pay a higher rate for the call feature, since it provides an opportunity to obtain lower-interest financing over the life of the security and to eliminate any undesirable restrictions on management imposed under the terms of the security. As a general rule, in fact, callable bonds do carry higher interest rates than noncallable bonds. However, the interest rate differential appears to be directly related to the level of interest rates. When rates are high, the call feature adds a substantial amount to the required return on the bond. When rates are high in comparison with some past "normal" level of rates, they are usually expected to fall in the future. It is under these circumstances that lenders demand higher returns on callable bonds and borrowers are willing to pay higher rates. When rates are low, callable bonds carry little or no extra return to investors. In periods when interest rates are low in comparison with some past "normal" level of rates there is little expectation that rates will decline further. Lenders are not greatly concerned about the prospect of a call of the securities, nor are borrowers willing to pay a substantial amount to add a call feature to their securities.

MARKETABILITY

One influence on the pattern of interest rates that is difficult to quantify but is nonetheless important is marketability. Although many investors purchase securities with the objective of holding the securities until maturity, their circumstances might change, and they might wish to sell the securities prior to maturity. There are also investors who *expect* to sell their securities prior to maturity. The latter group is especially important in the purchase and sale of relatively short-term securities. Since the ability to liquidate securities prior to maturity without undue price concessions is a favorable characteristic to investors, we would expect that securities with high marketability would carry interest rates that are lower than those of comparable securities with low marketability.

There are various dimensions to the marketability characteristic. First is the simple matter of whether a market exists for the securities in question. Is there trading in the security in which the free interplay of supply and demand determines the price of the security? For many corporate bonds there is no market in which existing bonds are traded. Second, if a market exists, how "good" is that market? Is it possible to buy or sell a large quantity of securities quickly and without substantial influence on price? For example, the market for existing U.S. government securities is broad and deep, and it is possible for the buyer or seller to place large quantities of securities in this market without distorting the market price. One reason for the relatively low rate on U.S. government securities is their high marketability, and one reason for the relatively high rate on corporate bonds is their relatively low marketability. Unfortunately, however, it is very difficult to quantify the precise influence of marketability on relative yield.

SUMMARY

Many factors influence yields on securities. In recent years, inflation has been one of the most pervasive influences on interest rates. According to the Fisher effect, the rate of interest may be viewed as a constant real rate with an inflation premium that reflects expectations of future inflation. Given a constant real rate, the nominal rate will rise and fall in response to changes in inflationary expectations. However, if there are different inflationary expectations for different periods in the future, the maturity or term structure of interest rates will be altered. In addition to being affected by inflation, interest rates on securities are affected by credit or default risk, differences in the taxability of the returns from particular securities, callability, and marketability features. These factors include the major influences affecting interest rate movements, and taken together they explain a substantial portion of the changes that occur in interest rates on different securities.

The financial markets present an intricate network of rates on thousands of financial assets. The general level of interest rates may rise, fall, or remain unchanged on a given day while the pattern of rates within the network is adjusting constantly. Yet disentangling the influences of inflation, credit risk, taxability, callability, and marketability on daily changes in interest rates on financial assets is not easy. However, we hope that the forgoing discussion at least provides a logical framework within which students of financial market developments may organize their analyses. Without an understanding of the underlying forces that are continually influencing the pattern of rates there is no way to see changes in financial markets as anything but a random process.

QUESTIONS

1. Why is it important to distinguish between a change in relative prices and a change in the general level of prices? Can this distinction be applied to the inflationary implications of the oil price increases in 1973 and again in 1979?

2. What has been the rate of inflation in the United States during the last year? Is this inflation caused by demand-pull or cost-push factors? Justify your argument.

3. Identify the major potential economic consequences of inflation. Which of these (if any) would be reduced or eliminated if the Fisher effect were fully operative and there were no unanticipated inflation?

4. Explain how a premium for expected inflation might be impounded into nominal interest rates by financial market forces. How do taxes affect the analysis?

5. How might anticipated inflation affect the *structure* of interest rates? How might increasing uncertainty about future inflation rates affect the level and structure of rates?

6. Assume that prices are expected to increase by the same amount in the next year as in the past year. What is the "real" rate of interest consistent with this forecast? Does the market appear to have fully adjusted to the expected inflation?

7. Is the risk-free rate really risk free? What element of risk might exist in the risk-free rate?

8. Carefully explain the potential impact on the interest rate of bonds issued by large commercial banks of the failure of five major U.S. banks.

9. What should happen to the interest rate on a bond whose rating was changed by Moody's from AAA to Aa? From Baa to Ba?

10. What is the likely effect on the interest rate on deep discount bonds of a return to a differential (and lower) federal income tax rate for capital gains compared to ordinary income? Explain.

11. How would an increase in the income tax rates affect the return on municipal securities? Why?

12. Compare interest rates on corporate, municipal, and U.S. government bonds today

with those one year ago, and see whether the changes in yield from one year to the next and between types of securities can be explained by the factors discussed in the chapter.

13. What are junk bonds? What role do they play in U.S. corporate finance? Why are they controversial?

REFERENCES

Barsky, Robert B., "The Fisher Hypothesis and the Forecastability and Persistence of Inflation," *Journal of Monetary Economics* (January 1987), 3–25.

Choate, G. M., and S. H. Archer, "Irving Fisher, Inflation, and the Nominal Rate of Interest," *Journal of Financial and Quantitative Analysis* (November 1975), 675–685.

Cohan, Avery B., *The Risk Structure of Interest Rates* (Morristown, N.J.: General Learning Press, 1973).

Darst, David M., *The Complete Bond Book* (New York: McGraw-Hill, 1975).

Fisher, Irving, *The Theory of Interest* (New York: Macmillan, 1930).

Fraser, Donald R., and R. Malcolm Richards, "Deep Discount Bonds, the Revenue Act of 1978, and the Efficiency of the Bond Market," *Journal of Economics and Business* (Fall 1984), 323–333.

——, and Jerrold Stern, "Flower Bonds, Tax Changes and the Efficiency of the Bond Market," *Review of Business and Economic Research* (Winter 1983), 13–24.

Friedman, Benjamin M., "Who Puts the Inflation Premium into Nominal Interest Rates," *Journal of Finance* (June 1978), 833–845.

Friedman, Milton, "Factors Affecting the Level of Interest Rates," *Conference on Savings and Residential Financing* (Chicago: U.S. Savings and Loan League, 1968).

Gandolfi, A. E., "Inflation, Taxation, and Interest Rates," *Journal of Finance* (June 1982), 797–807.

Homer, Sidney, and Martin Leibowitz, *Inside the Yield Book* (Englewood Cliffs, N.J.: Prentice-Hall, 1972).

Ibbotson, Roger G., and Rex A. Sinquefield, *Stocks, Bonds, Bills, and Inflation* (Charlottesville, Va.: Financial Analysts Research Foundation, 1982).

Jen, Frank C., and James E. Wert, "Effect of Call Risk on Corporate Bond Yield," *Journal of Finance* (December 1967), 637–651.

Roll, Richard, "Interest Rates on Monetary Assets and Commodity Price Index Changes," *Journal of Finance* (May 1972), 251–278.

Santoni, G. J., and Courtenay C. Stone, "What Really Happened to Interest Rates?: A Longer Run Analysis," Federal Reserve Bank of St. Louis *Review* (November 1981), 3–14.

Sargent, Thomas J., "Interest Rates and Expected Inflation: A Selective Summary of Recent Research," *Explorations in Economic Research* (Summer 1976), 303–325.

Tanzi, Vito, "Inflation Expectations, Economic Activity, Taxes, and Interest Rates," *American Economic Review* (March 1980), 12–21.

Van Horne, James, *Financial Market Rates and Flows,* 2nd ed. (Englewood Cliffs, N.J.: Prentice-Hall, 1984).

PART **III**

FINANCIAL INSTITUTIONS

CHAPTER **9**

The Financial Services Industry: Depository Institutions

The financial services industry in the United States (and indeed throughout the developed world) is a remarkably sophisticated and effective part of the economy. Financial services organizations are able to efficiently move billions of dollars throughout the world at extremely low transactions costs, provide credit and deposit services tailored to the needs of a diverse group of customers, and provide a host of other types of financial services, many relating to investment banking and brokerage services. While the financial services industry has historically been dominated by commercial banks, the market share of the banking industry has been eroding as existing financial service organizations expand their product offering and many nonfinancial firms (such as retailers and manufacturers) enter into the financial services industry. The growth of "securitization," by which borrowers directly access the capital markets for funds and bypass commercial banks, has also contributed to a decline in the market share of commercial banks. In addition, although the financial services industry has been characterized by compartmentalization and specialization of service in past years, the combination of financial deregulation and rapidly changing technology has contributed to a growing overlap of products among different financial service organizations. The structure of financial services is undergoing rapid change, with the result that the future structure of the industry promises to be quite different from that of the past. Some components of the industry and some firms will grow and prosper in the new environments; others will decline and even disappear.

In this and the subsequent chapter we deal with the various types of financial institutions that collectively make up the financial services industry. In this chapter we focus on the institutions that offer deposits—demand, negotiable order of withdrawal deposits (NOW), savings, money market deposits, and other types of time deposits—and hence are known as **depository institutions.** The types of financial services that these institutions provide the public are quite similar (though not identical) and are becoming more alike every year. In addition, these institutions are increasingly dealt with as a group in legislation and regulation, as is illustrated by the Depository Institutions Deregulation and Monetary Control Act (1980) and the Depository Institutions Act (1982).

All financial institutions that are not depository in nature are discussed in the next chapter under the heading of **nondepository financial institutions.** Unlike the depository institutions, which are relatively homogeneous in structure and scope, the nondepository financial institutions include a diverse group that differ widely from each other in terms of the financial services that they offer. Some, such as money market funds, are quite similar to depository institutions in the liquidity characteristics of their liabilities. Others, such as pension funds, are quite distinct from depository institutions in their sources and uses of funds.

THE FUNCTIONS OF FINANCIAL SERVICES ORGANIZATIONS

Although financial service organizations provide a very large number of different products, most financial services can be divided into three areas:

1. transactions services,
2. intermediation services, and
3. insurance, funds management, and securities-related financial services.

Commercial banks have traditionally dominated the first of these functions (transactions services) and have played a major role in the second (intermediation services) but have not, in recent U.S. history at least, played a significant role in providing insurance, funds management, and securities-related financial services.

Transactions services refer to providing means of payment to allow individuals, businesses, and governments to pay their bills. The traditional form of transactions services is the noninterest-earning demand deposit offered by commercial banks. Commercial banks had a monopoly position over the providing of transactions services prior to passage of the Depository Institutions Deregulation and Monetary Control Act (DIDMCA) of 1980. In that year, however, DIDMCA provided for the nationwide offering by all depository institutions (i.e., commercial banks, savings and loans, savings banks, and credit unions) of an interest-bearing transactions account referred to as a negotiable order of withdrawal (NOW) account. Creation of the NOW account and authorization for all depository institutions nationwide to offer this account fundamentally altered the role of commercial banks in providing transactions services. Not only were commercial banks subject to much more competition in one of their principal product lines, but the payment of explicit interest on these accounts tended to place pressure on bank profit margins.

The role of commercial banks in competing for transactions services has also been greatly affected by financial innovations and by changing technology. Many financial service organizations have developed products that are equivalent to the traditional checking account but have other desirable features. The cash management account (CMA) developed by Merrill Lynch, which combines a mutual fund account, a line of credit, and a checking account, is perhaps the most widely publicized though not the only example of this type of financial innovation. Many mutual funds also allow checks to be written against the value of shares in the account. The explosion of the money market fund industry in the late 1970s and early 1980s provided vigorous competition for commercial banks. Even the distinction between transactions and nontransactions deposits at commercial banks (and other depository institutions) was blurred by the passage of the Depository Institution Act (1982), which permitted the money market deposit account, which combines transactions and savings features. The development of new technology with the growth of wire transfer of funds and electronic banking also provides opportunities for new organizations to provide transactions services.

Intermediation services are at the very core of the role of the financial services industry. In providing intermediation services, financial institutions flow funds from savers to investors, thereby contributing to the expansion of saving and investment and more rapid economic growth. They do this by offering deposit vehicles designed to attract funds from savers in competition with other vehicles and using these funds to provide credit to borrowers at acceptable terms. Since the needs of borrowers and depositors differ in terms of maturity, credit risk, and denomination, financial services organizations accept a number of risks in providing intermediation services. They issue deposit and other liabilities that contain limited default risk but make loans carrying considerable risk of default. They also typically provide deposits that are short term and highly liquid, but make longer-term loans that have limited liquidity. Commercial banks and many other financial service organizations earn most of their compensation in the form of an interest spread between their cost of funds and the earnings on their assets by accepting the credit and maturity risks inherit in providing intermediation services.

Insurance, funds management, and securities-related financial services represent a much more diverse set of functions than transactions or intermediation services. Moreover, the type of organization that, historically at least, has provided these services is quite different. Commercial banks have played a very minor role in providing these services, though much of the debate over merging commercial and investment banking centers on which of these services commercial banks should be allowed to offer.

Insurance services fundamentally involve risk management, though the nature of the risk is quite different from those involved in the intermediation function. Funds management, which involves both mutual fund and pension fund asset management, is perhaps more closely related to the intermediation function. The brokerage/securities function, which is an important part of investment banking, has an importance in the financial system that is far beyond the size of its assets.

SIZES AND MARKET SHARES OF FINANCIAL SERVICE FIRMS

Table 9.1 provides information on the total assets of the principal financial service firms of the United States and their market share (their total assets expressed as a fraction of the total assets of all the financial service firms).

The principal financial service firms held total financial assets in 1988 that exceeded $9 trillion. Commercial banks held about 30 percent of the total assets of all financial service organizations, with almost $3 trillion in total assets. Depository institutions together held over $4 trillion, or about half of the total for all financial service organizations. Savings and loans were the second largest individual financial service organization, though private pension funds and life insurance companies were close behind.

The market shares of the different financial service organizations are undergoing significant change. Commercial banks have been losing and continue to

TABLE 9.1   Assets of Principal Depository and Nondepository Institutions, September 30, 1988

Institution	Assets (Billions of Dollars)
Depository	
Commercial banks	2,850.5
Savings and loan associations	1,335.5
Savings banks	275.4
Credit unions	195.0
Total	4,656.4
Nondepository	
Money market funds	326.5
Life insurance companies	1,096.6
Other insurance companies	435.0
Private pension funds	1,085.5
State and local government retirement funds	587.3
Finance companies	476.1
Investment companies	483.9
Security brokers and dealers	129.5
Total	4,620.4
Total depository and nondepository institutions	9,276.8

Source: Board of Governors of the Federal Reserve System, Flow of Funds Accounts, *September 1988.*

lose market share. Savings and loans have also lost market share. Taken together, the depository institutions have lost market share. Life insurance companies have also experienced an erosion of their asset base. In contrast, pension funds (both private and state and local government) have increased the percentage of assets under their control. Mutual funds experienced explosive growth in the early and mid-1980s, reflecting falling interest rates and rising stock prices.

Financial service organizations differ considerably in terms of the level and stability of their profitability. As shown in Table 9.2, commercial banks seem to be among the less profitable of the major financial service organizations in the period from 1975 to 1984. They were particularly less profitable than securities-related firms (especially investment banking organizations). However, on a year-by-year basis the profitability of commercial banks has generally been more stable than the earnings of other major financial service firms.

The number of firms operating in (and the concentration of resources within) each of the subsets of the financial services industry differ considerably.

TABLE 9.2   Profitability in Financial Services[1]
(Average After-Tax Return on Equity)

Industry	1980–1984	1975–1984
Commercial banking	12.2%	12.3%
17 multinational BHCs	13.0[2]	13.1[2,3]
Finance companies[4]	12.6	11.4
Mortgage companies[4]	13.1	13.7[5]
Securities	18.7	16.4
Investment banks	26.0	21.5
Other securities	15.8	14.5
Life insurance	13.4	13.7
Stockholder-owned	15.2	15.6
Mutual	10.5	10.6
Property and casualty insurance	7.4	10.9[6]
Stockholder-owned	7.7	11.2[6]
Mutual	7.4	9.8[6]
Insurance brokerage		
Large firms	18.3	22.5[6]
Small firms	9.2	12.5[6]
Diversified financial firms[7]	13.1	14.0

[1]Returns for commercial banks, securities firms, life insurers, and property and casualty insurers are based on average equity. Because of limited availability of data, returns for finance companies, mortgage companies, and insurance brokers are based on year-end equity. By way of comparison, nonfinancial firms (represented by those included in Standard & Poor's 400 stock index) reported average returns of 13.7 percent over 1980–1984 and 14.0 percent over 1975–1984.
[2]Excludes Crocker and Continental Illinois in 1984.
[3]1976–1984.
[4]Excluding subsidiaries of bank holding companies.
[5]1978–1984.
[6]1976–1984, one complete underwriting cycle.
[7]Aetna Life & Casualty, American Express, Beneficial Corporation, Household International, E.F. Hutton, Merrill Lynch, Transamerica, and Sears Roebuck.

Source: Federal Reserve Bank of New York, Trends in Commercial Bank Profitability, *1987.*

To a substantial extent these differences reflect regulatory factors, though economies of scale and other factors also are undoubtedly important. The commercial banking industry, which is subject to the most severe restrictions on geographical expansion, is composed of almost 15,000 firms. In contrast, the savings and loan industry, which is less constrained by branching regulation, contains fewer than 4000 firms.

Within the nonbank sectors, with no constraints on geographical expansion beyond those contained in the antitrust laws, the number of firms is generally fewer. For example, the life insurance industry consists of about 2000 underwriters, of which 94 percent are stockholder owned and the rest are mutual organizations. The twenty-five largest life insurers accounted for 53 percent of aggregate assets in 1983, while the hundred largest firms accounted for 70 percent. Most life insurance companies not only offer a variety of types of life policies, but are also involved in health insurance and in the sale of annuities (the fastest-growing part of their activities). The other part of the insurance industry—property and casualty companies—contains an even smaller number of firms, fewer than 1000. Of the total, about three quarters are stockholder owned and the remainder are mutual organizations. The twenty-five largest wrote about 60 percent of the total premiums in 1982.

The securities industry is comprised of over 2000 firms that deal with the public and a large number of organizations that deal primarily with other broker/dealers. About 20 percent of these firms dominate the industry, accounting for 95 percent of the assets of all securities firms that deal with the public. A similar degree of concentration exists among finance companies and mortgage companies. The finance company industry is composed of almost 300 firms involved in consumer lending, commercial lending, and lease financing. The hundred largest firms hold approximately 80 percent of the industry's net receivables. Many of these finance companies are subsidiaries of manufacturers (captive finance companies engaged primarily in financing the products of the parent company) and of bank holding companies. In the mortgage company industry (engaged in both mortgage banking and mortgage servicing), ownership by bank holding companies is very common. Subsidiaries of bank holding companies held almost half of the assets of all mortgage servicing firms. The top hundred mortgage servicing firms hold almost 80 percent of the assets of the entire industry.

MAJOR FACTORS AFFECTING THE SIZES AND MARKET SHARES OF FINANCIAL SERVICE FIRMS

Shifts in the market share of commercial banks and other financial service organizations reflect the confluence of a number of economic, technological, and regulatory factors. The principal factors at work, with emphasis on those that have most directly affected depository institutions, are the following.

Inflation and High and Volatile Interest Rates

The inflation rate, and with it interest rates, were relatively low and stable through the 1950s and early 1960s. Beginning in 1966, however, the inflation rate began to rise, interest rates increased, and intense pressure was placed on the financial system. The pressure was most severe at the highly regulated commercial banks, which (along with other depository institutions) were subject to a regulatory structure designed in the 1930s. High inflation and high interest rates encouraged other less regulated financial service firms to develop new products such as money market funds and the cash management account, types of products that the traditional intermediaries could not offer because of regulatory constraints.

Technological Advances

Advances in technology have greatly affected the competitive position of different providers of financial services and the ability of financial institutions to compete directly with the capital market in the intermediation function. Rapid advances in electronic technology have lowered transactions costs for processing financial transactions. The firms that have been most effective in implementing the new financial technology have achieved an edge through lower costs. Perhaps more important, the advances in technology have made the production of diverse financial services within one firm more feasible through increasing the prospects for realizing economies of scope (economies of scope exist when two different products can be produced more cheaply at one firm than two separate firms could produce the products). Also, advanced financial technology has greatly increased the geographical boundaries over which financial services could be produced, thereby substantially intensifying the extent of competition in the industry.

Consumers

More sophisticated consumers have also played a major role in the changing structure of the financial services industry. Greater education in personal money management and high real and nominal returns on financial assets have made funds flow more volatile. Consumers of financial services increasingly move funds around for very small differences in expected returns.

Securitization

Securitization has also had a substantial impact on the structure of the financial services industry. **Securitization** refers to the process of making some or all of the loan portfolio marketable by establishing pools of loans and selling interests (securities) in the pools. Securitization also involves the creation of these pools by investment bankers, thereby bypassing the traditional intermediation process. The phenomenal success of various mortgage pools (most notable the GNMAs) in the 1970s and early 1980s has been the most notable example of securitization. Until early 1986, securitization was limited to the mortgage markets, especially for government insured and guaranteed mortgages related to residential real estate. As a result, the impact of securitization had been most pronounced at thrift institutions rather than at commercial banks. Recently, however, investment bankers have created pools of consumer and commercial loans.

Deregulation

Deregulation has also affected the operations of commercial banks and other depository financial institutions. However, with the exception of the deregulation of commission rates on equity trading in the 1970s, most deregulation has followed changes in market conditions rather than leading the financial system into a new structure. DIDMCA (1980) and DIA (1982) represent the most important recent legislative initiatives to reduce the extent of regulation.

DIDMCA (1980).   The 1980 Depository Institutions Deregulation and Monetary Control Act provided, among other things, for the following:

1. *Uniform reserve requirements.* <u>All</u> depository institutions became subject to the same reserve requirements; only size and type of deposit are relevant in determining reserve requirements.

2. *Fed services.* Services provided by the Federal Reserve such as check clearing and providing vault cash must be offered to all depository institutions and must be priced on the basis of the Fed's production costs plus a "normal" profit margin. Before this legislation was passed, the Fed provided its services only to member banks and then generally without explicit cost.

3. *Regulation Q.* The legislation began the process of <u>eliminating</u> interest rate ceilings on deposit accounts at all depository institutions. It created the Depository Institutions Deregulation Committee with instructions to phase out interest rate ceilings and to eliminate those ceilings completely, no later than March 1986.

4. *Negotiable order of withdrawal (NOW) accounts.* The legislation authorized <u>all</u> depository institutions to offer interest-bearing transactions accounts, generally in the form of NOW accounts. For the first time on a nationwide basis the traditional monopoly by commercial banks of transaction (checking) accounts was broken. Also, for the first time in almost fifty years, explicit interest payments on transactions accounts were allowed.

CARs AND CARDs: THE SECURITIZATION OF PRACTICALLY EVERYTHING

Financial innovation has characterized the financial marketplace in recent years. One of the most significant dimensions of this innovation is the securitization of loans. This process involves the pooling and packaging of loans into securities, which are then sold to investors. Most such securitization has taken place through the packaging of mortgages. Indeed, over $300 billion in mortgage pass-through securities were outstanding in the late 1980s. Recently, assets other than mortgages have been securitized. In particular, loans on automobiles have been pooled, and the securities (known as CARs) have been sold in the capital markets as have been credit card loans (known as CARDs).

CARs are pass-through securities in which the interest and principal on the underlying auto loans are passed through to the security holder. While similar in many respects to the mortgage pass through, the security for the CAR is quite different in being movable and subject to substantial deterioration in value. The collateral for CARDs (certificates of amortizing debts) is even less tangible, since it consists of the advances made to individuals on their credit cards.

The first public offering of CARs took place in March 1985, when $60 million in automobile loans made by Marine Midland Bank were brought to the market by the investment banking firm Salomon Brothers. Salomon Brothers also played a major role in the first issue of CARDs in April 1986, which consisted of $50 million pass-through securities backed by Bank One (Columbus, Ohio) credit card receivables.

CARs and CARDs represent an advanced stage of innovation in the financial marketplace. At the same time they raise questions about whether limits exist to the securitization process. Attempts have been made to securitize bank commercial and industrial loans, for example, as well as other stages of bank credit. To the extent that the limits of the process expand, the role of commercial banks and other traditional lenders changes. The next few years may see further testing of the limits of the securitization process.

While securitization transforms an illiquid asset on the books of a financial institution into a more liquid security, the existence of default or credit risk on the underlying loans presents a serious problem. This problem has been dealt with in a variety of ways. For example, the pass-through securities could be overcollateralized. Or the securities could be insured by a third party. A third possibility is to create a reserve fund made up of the profit on the underlying assets. This was the strategy followed for the CARDs.

For additional information on this topic, see Christine Pavel, "Securitization," Federal Reserve Bank of Chicago *Economic Perspectives* (July/August 1986), 16–31.

5. *Savings and loans.* The lending powers of savings and loans were broadened with passage of the 1980 legislation. In particular, savings and loans were allowed to commit a substantial fraction of their assets to consumer loans. They were also given trust powers. The reforms of the powers of savings and loans contained in this legislation went a long way toward the creation of a "department store of family finance" in the form of savings and loan associations.

Depository Institutions Act (1982). The provisions of this legislation may be viewed in some respects as dealing with the problems that had not been resolved by the 1980 legislation. The DIDMCA of 1980 attempted to deal with the thrift institutions problem and to provide for a gradual elimination of Regulation Q ceilings. By 1982 the thrift institutions problem had become a thrift institutions crisis, and it was reflecting the extraordinarily high interest rate environment of 1981–1982. As a result, the bill provided for the following:

1. *FDIC/FSLIC assistance in merging for floundering and failing institutions.* In past years the regulatory agencies had been constrained in arranging the purchase of a floundering or failing institution by restrictive laws on interstate acquisition of failing institutions according to the following priority schedule: (a) same type of institution, same state; (b) same type of institution, different state; (c) different type of institution, same state; (d) different type of institutions, different state. For example, if the failing institution was a commercial bank in Texas, the first potential acquirer would be another bank in Texas; the second potential acquirer would be a commercial bank located outside Texas; the third potential acquirer would be another type of financial institution in Texas; and the fourth potential group of acquiring institutions would be another type of financial institution located outside Texas.

2. *Net worth certificates.* The 1982 legislation provided for an exchange of debt (called net worth certificates) between depository institutions and the regulatory agencies. While of substantial legal significance in maintaining an adequate capital position for floundering and failing depository institutions, the economic importance of this portion of the 1982 legislation was relatively minor.

3. *Additional thrift institution restructuring.* Savings and loans and other thrifts were given even greater powers to offer deposit-taking and lending services. Savings and loans were permitted to offer demand deposit services to qualified commercial, corporate, and agricultural customers, as well as to expand their consumer lending and to engage in a limited amount of commercial lending.

4. *Money market deposit accounts.* Perhaps the most significant feature of the 1982 legislation was the provision instructing the Deregulation Committee to create (within 60 days) a money market deposit account equivalent to and competitive with money market mutual funds. The Deregulation Committee did create such

[handwritten notes: now Super now-Accts. — reserve require. — Bal $100,000, no # of transactions restricted]

an instrument effective in January 1983. The money market deposit accounts have been phenomenally successful, attracting over $300 billion.

[handwritten notes: 5. Reverse Bank Holding Company Banks given more power to form, share ownership of a service company subsidiary.]

Decompartmentalization

Decompartmentalization of financial institutions has also been an important force in changing the structure of the financial service industry. Rather than individual financial service organizations offering a single service or a limited set of services, the trend has been for financial service organizations to offer a multiplicity of services. Deregulation has made this possible for some of the depository financial institutions. However, more important has been the expansion of financial service offerings by nondepository institutions. This expansion has occurred both for traditional financial service organizations such as Merrill Lynch and American Express (creating financial congeners) and by the expansion of retailers and manufacturers into financial services (creating financial conglomerates).

The financial services that commercial banks offer are quite similar to those offered in earlier years and are generally confined to transactions and intermediation services. Savings and loans have expanded their product offerings from a very narrow base but still remain principally concentrated in transactions and intermediation services. However, there have been dramatic changes in the financial service offerings by insurance companies, retailers, and security dealers. Many of these institutions have become full-service financial firms offering transactions, intermediation, and insurance, funds management, and broker/dealer services.

Globalization

Globalization of the operation of financial service organizations has also affected the operations and structure of these organizations. Funds increasingly flow across national borders both for long-run investment purposes and for short-run liquidity management. Reflecting global funds flows, many financial service organizations have expanded globally. Foreign financial service organizations have entered the U.S. market, and many U.S. financial service firms have expanded abroad. The result of this global integration of financial markets is growing competition among financial service firms.

The impact of entry by foreign banks into the U.S. market has been striking in affecting the market penetration of U.S. banks. As shown in Table 9.3, U.S. banking assets of foreign banks in 1986 exceeded $500 billion. These assets represented 19 percent of the total of all U.S. banking assets. In terms of total assets, the Japanese banks are dominant, though Canadian, British, and Italian banks also play a major role. Foreign banks now account for approximately 20 percent of all commercial and industrial loans outstanding to U.S. addresses.

TABLE 9.3 Banking Operations of Foreign Banks in the United States
Total U.S. Banking Assets [in Billions]¹ of Major Foreign Countries as of December 31, 1986.
Expressed as a Percentage of Total U.S. Banking Assets

Country	1982 $	1982 %	1983 $	1983 %	1984 $	1984 %	1985 $	1985 %	1986 $	1986 %
Japan	113.0	5.0	126.0	5.0	151.3	6.1	181.3	6.1	245.4	8.7
Canada	22.1	1.0	27.8	1.2	38.1	1.5	42.3	1.7	42.4	1.5
United Kingdom	52.2	2.5	53.0	2.3	51.4	2.0	61.2	2.4	40.6	1.5
Italy	14.3	0.7	17.5	0.8	23.9	0.9	29.1	1.1	36.4	1.4
Switzerland	13.0	0.6	13.1	0.6	15.3	0.6	18.3	0.7	24.5	0.9
France	16.6	0.8	16.2	0.7	18.3	0.7	20.7	0.8	22.4	0.8
West Germany	8.9	0.4	7.4	0.3	7.6	0.3	8.8	0.4	11.0	0.4
All other countries	60.5	3.0	70.9	3.1	72.4	2.9	97.2	3.8	103.9	3.8
Total U.S. banking assets of foreign banks	300.6	14	331.9	14	378.3	15	458.9	18	526.6	19
Total assets of domestic banking institutions²	1821.1	86	1986.5	86	2076.8	85	2098.7	82	2285.9	81
Total U.S. banking assets²	2121.7	100	2318.4	100	2455.1	100	2557.6	100	2812.5	100

¹Amounts for each country include the total U.S. banking assets of all banks from that country, namely, the aggregate of the assets of their U.S. branches, agencies, bank subsidiaries, Edge Act and Agreement corporations and New York State–chartered investment companies (called Article XII corporations).

²Includes the total consolidated assets (domestic and international) of all U.S. banks.

Source: Gerald Corrigan, "A Perspective on the Globalization of Financial Markets and Institutions," Federal Reserve Bank of New York Quarterly Review (Spring 1987), 4.

COMMERCIAL BANKS VERSUS OTHER DEPOSITORY INSTITUTIONS

A sharp distinction has traditionally been drawn between the commercial bank and all other depository institutions: savings and loan associations, savings banks, and credit unions. This distinction is usually based on the fact that (in past years, at least) commercial banks created money in the process of lending, whereas other depository institutions did not. Commercial banks add to the money supply by creating demand deposits when they make loans or buy financial assets. In contrast, savings and loan associations and other depository institutions until recently only loaned out the funds left with them, thereby affecting the turnover of money (its velocity) but not the total quantity of money.

THE BANK AS A FIRM: SOURCES AND USES OF FUNDS

Commercial Bank Functions

The sources and uses of funds at commercial banks in the United States reflect the functions banks perform in our economy.[1] For instance, the importance of demand and other transactions deposits as a source of funds reflects the fact that commercial banks remain the dominant financial institution in administering the means of payment. If an individual or a business writes a check, the probability is high that this check will be drawn on an account in a commercial bank and collected through the banking system. However, as the prevailing level of interest rates has increased in recent years, individuals and businesses have economized on their cash balances. Also, the development of new technology, such as electronic funds transfer systems, has further reduced the desired cash balances of economic units. As a result, even though demand and other transactions deposits remain an important source of funds to commercial banks, their growth has been quite slow, and their relative importance as a source of banks' funds has diminished. In addition to offering demand deposit services, commercial banks also offer an outlet for saving by providing a variety of savings accounts and different types of certificates of deposit. Most commercial banks offer passbook savings accounts and small (consumer) certificates of deposit featuring longer maturity and higher rates than savings accounts. The money market deposit account that combines the liquidity of a transactions account with the high yield of a certificate account has become a particularly important source of funds. Moreover, a number of commercial banks (principally the large banks) obtain a

---

[1]Sources and uses of funds at banks also reflect substantial legal constraints. For example, with a few minor exceptions, banks may not invest in equity securities.

substantial quantity of funds from offering large ($100,000 and more) business-type certificates of deposit.

Commercial banks provide essential credit to the economic sectors. Indeed, it can be argued that the provision of credit to the economic sectors is the principal function performed by commercial banks. This credit encompasses loans to individuals, businesses, and governments for a number of different purposes and for a variety of different maturities. Further, some of this credit is extended through lines of credit to businesses and through credit cards in which the credit is activated at the discretion of the borrower. Given the importance of credit creation, it is not surprising to find that the asset portfolio of commercial banks is dominated by loans or that interest payments on loans are the principal source of bank revenue.

In addition to their basic roles of administering the payments mechanism, providing an outlet for individual and business savings, and making credit available to different sectors of the economy, commercial banks also provide a number of services that do not show up directly on their balance sheets. For example, commercial banks offer trust services to individuals and businesses. For a fee, many banks will manage the portfolio of a corporate pension program, manage funds for a minor, and provide other trust services. The assets managed by the bank's trust department, moreover, do not show up on the bank's balance sheet, since they are not owned by the bank. For a fee, banks also provide safekeeping services, the most widely known of which is probably the safe deposit box. Furthermore, commercial banks are increasingly generating income by offering financial advice, also on a fee basis, to their customers. Again, however, this service need not directly influence the asset and liability structure of the bank's balance sheet, though it often does have a substantial impact on the revenue, expenses, and profitability of the banking organization.

Commercial banks have aggressively sought to enter new financial markets and provide new financial services. The entry by commercial banks into the security brokerage industry through the offering of discount broker services is an excellent example of the innovative management approach that has been occurring within the banking industry. To some extent these new services represent efforts by the banking industry to generate increased fee income to offset the decline in income from traditional deposit-taking and lending functions due to increased competition.

Assets and Liabilities

Table 9.4 presents the major assets and liabilities of the commercial banking industry as of January 1989. This table, in conjunction with attention to the various functions performed by commercial banks, will serve as a vehicle for our discussion of the sources and uses of bank funds.

TABLE 9.4   Selected Assets and Liabilities of Commercial Banks, January 1989

Assets	Value (Billions of Dollars)
Loans and Investments	
Loans	2,018.5
Investments	
U.S. government securities	347.7
Other	183.3
Cash Assets	
Currency and coin	27.5
Reserves with Federal Reserve Banks	31.5
Demand balances at U.S. depository institutions	27.8
Cash items in process of collection	76.1
Other cash assets	52.2
Liabilities	
Deposits	
Transactions	585.0
Savings	530.3
Time	976.6
Borrowings Borrowed Funds	492.3
Capital	194.0

Source: *Federal Reserve* Bulletin *(April 1989), A18.*

off B/S acctg. — bankers acceptances

Deposits

As we discussed in the previous section, a principal function of the commercial banking industry is to offer transaction accounts to the public and to administer the payment system. This basic function has been historically reflected in the large amount of demand and other transactions deposits at commercial banks—30 percent of all bank deposits. To offer these services, individual banks must cooperate with other banks on the clearing and processing of checks. This cooperation among banks leads to a large volume of interbank deposits (deposits from one bank held at another bank). In addition, as a part of their vital role in the payments system, commercial banks provide individuals and businesses with currency and coins. This function is reflected on the balance sheet of commercial banks as a $27.5 billion holding of currency and coin.

The role of commercial banks as an outlet for the savings of individuals and businesses is also reflected in the balance sheet of the industry. Time and savings deposits amounted to more than $1 trillion, substantially more than the volume of transactions deposits. These time deposits encompassed the passbook savings account, various types of consumer certificates of deposit, money market deposit accounts, and the large ($100,000 and over) certificate of deposits offered primarily to business firms. Vigorous commercial bank competition has been felt markedly in that market, greatly affecting the balance sheet of the nation's commercial banks. However, the role of passbook savings accounts has diminished sharply in recent years as banks have begun to rely more on money market deposit and certificate accounts.

Assets

The credit-creation function is reflected in the asset side of the balance sheet. By far the greatest part of bank assets is in the loan portfolio. Total loans exceed $2.0 trillion. These loans include credit extensions to households, businesses, and government for a wide variety of purposes. In fact, commercial banks are probably the most diversified lenders among the nation's financial institutions. This diversification is illustrated by Table 9.5, which provides information on the loan portfolio at commercial banks.

Reflecting the traditional orientation of commercial banks toward business lending, a substantial portion of credit extension at these banks is in the form of commercial and industrial loans—loans to businesses for acquiring inventory, carrying accounts receivable, purchasing new equipment, and for the purchase of real estate. Substantial amounts of credit are also extended by commercial banks to other financial institutions, principally to securities firms and to sales and personal finance companies. Indeed, most small sales and personal finance companies obtain the bulk of their funds from commercial banks.

Real estate loans for both the acquisition of single-family homes and the purchase of income-producing property such as apartments and office buildings have grown dramatically. The expansion in real estate lending is in part attributable to the growth in time deposits at commercial banks, which has allowed the acquisition of longer-maturity and less liquid assets and has led to changes in bankers' attitudes about the appropriateness of different kinds of lending. The

TABLE 9.5   Percentage Distribution of Loans at Commercial Banks, January 1989

Type of Loan	Percentage of Total Loans
Real estate loans	36.0
Commercial and industrial loans	32.4
Loans to individuals	19.1
Security loans	2.0
Loans to nonbank financial institutions	1.6
Agricultural loans	1.7
All other loans	7.2
Total	100.0

Source: Federal Reserve Bulletin *April 1989, A16.*

third major type of credit at commercial banks is in the form of loans to individuals—consumer loans for the purchase of consumer durable goods, consolidation of debts, vacations, and other purposes. In recent years, consumer loans have expanded rapidly, particularly in the form of credit extensions under credit card arrangements.

The allocation of loans varies widely among banks of different sizes and locations. Agricultural, consumer, and real estate loans often account for a larger fraction of the total loan portfolio at the smaller banks. In contrast, large banks tend to be more oriented toward business lending.

Commercial banks generally hold substantial amounts of liquid assets. For example, cash and short-term securities usually comprise much larger fractions of total assets at commercial banks than at nonbank financial institutions. Further, a large fraction of the investment portfolio of commercial banks is held in the form of short-term securities, especially the holdings of U.S. Treasury securities. The substantial holdings of liquid assets are attributable to the large volume of volatile transactions deposits as well as to the role played by commercial banks in administering the nation's payments system. In addition, commercial banks play an important role in assisting the U.S. government in financing its own activities. Banks serve as a depository of the U.S. government (tax and loan accounts) as well as for state and local government securities. Tax collections of the U.S. government are deposited at commercial banks.

Nondeposit Liabilities and Capital

To this point, no mention has been made of two important sources of bank funds: nondeposit liabilities and capital. Nondeposit liabilities represent a significant and growing source of funds. They are used for a variety of purposes. For short-term liquidity adjustment, commercial banks frequently borrow from other banks for one day in the federal funds market or sell for a few days with the commitment to buy the federal funds back through repurchase agreements. Eurodollar borrowings that represent the lending of dollar deposits from banks outside the United States are also often used. Longer-term borrowing is also used to allow the bank to expand beyond the size made possible through local deposit funds.

The capital account at commercial banks—common stock, surplus, and retained earnings—plays a quantitatively small but vital role. The owner's equity must provide the original funds for a new bank to acquire its facilities. For an existing bank, capital provides a cushion to protect depositors and other creditors against loss from bad loans, security defaults, theft, and other hazards. Yet the capital account is very small, representing generally no more than 7 or 8 percent of total bank assets. The small capital base limits banks' ability to take risks. For example, assuming that 60 percent of bank assets are invested in loans

OFF BALANCE SHEET BANKING

Off Balance Sheet Banking (OBSB) has greatly expanded in recent years as commercial banking organizations have sought ways to earn income (usually fee income) without producing assets or liabilities on the bank's balance sheet. In a general sense, OBSB refers to the use of contingent claims or contracts whereby the bank agrees to make a loan under certain circumstances. These contingent claims generate fee income but do not affect the bank's balance sheet until and unless the contingency is realized and the loan is actually made.

The most common OBSB activities are loan commitments and standby letters of credit, though operations of commercial banks in interest rate and foreign currency swaps and futures trading are also significant. Johnson and Murphy report that loan commitments exceeded $500 billion at U.S. banks in 1986, while standby letters of credit approximated $200 billion.

Loan commitments are legally binding agreements to lend a borrower a specified amount for a specified purpose, generally at a stipulated rate. In effect, the bank is providing an insurance policy guaranteeing that the potential borrower will have access to funds. The Note Issuance Facility (NIF) is one of the most common types of loan commitments. With a NIF the bank agrees to purchase the short-term commercial paper of a borrower or to provide funds if the borrower cannot sell notes at an interest rate at which the bank would provide credit. For this option the potential borrower pays a fee to the bank.

A standby letter of credit is similar to a loan commitment except that it involves a third party. With a standby letter of credit the bank commits to a third party that if its customer cannot provide funds to meet the terms and conditions of a financial contract, it (the bank) will make the commitment good. Standby letters of credit are used as backup lines of credit to support commercial paper offerings, municipal borrowings, construction lending, and mergers and acquisitions. Banks receive a fee for the standby letter as well as interest if the loan is actually made.

Several factors account for the sharp increase in off balance sheet banking. Regulatory factors (in particular the lack of capital required behind off balance sheet assets and liabilities) have undoubtedly played a role. Reserve requirement and deposit insurance factors also encourage OBSB (recent regulatory changes will, when fully implemented, require capital for OBSB assets and liabilities). The declining profitability at major banks and growing competition from other lenders also seem important. Certainly, the ability to generate fee income through issuing financial guarantees is attractive to many banks. Yet the existence of hundreds of billions of dollars of liabilities for the banking system that do not show up on their balance sheet raise important questions about the future stability of the nation's banks.

Source: Sylvester Johnson and Amelia Murphy, "Going Off the Balance Sheet," Federal Reserve Bank of Atlanta Economic Review *(September/October 1987), 23–30.*

and that capital represents 8 percent of total assets, a bank could afford less than a 15 percent loss experience on loans before it was insolvent (a zero or negative capital position). The ability to absorb losses is even less for many banks (particularly large banks), which operate with much greater loans and much less capital (as a percent of total assets).

OTHER DEPOSITORY FINANCIAL INSTITUTIONS

The other depository financial institutions encompass savings and loan associations, savings banks, and credit unions. They are often grouped together as "thrift" institutions because they all offer an interest-bearing outlet for the savings of individuals and others and because these deposits are highly substitutable in saver's portfolios and therefore highly competitive with one another. Further, these depository financial institutions are becoming more alike and, as a group, are becoming more like commercial banks. For example, they all offer similar savings and checking accounts. However, in size the total assets of all three thrift institutions are considerably smaller than the total assets of the commercial banking industry. Also, even though they are similar in many respects, nonbank depository institutions have substantial differences. Therefore each institution requires a separate discussion.

Savings and Loan Associations

As discussed earlier, savings and loan associations were first formed in the early nineteenth century to provide a source of funds so that individuals could own their own homes. At that time, credit for the purchase of a home was difficult to obtain from a commercial bank, and installment terms were short. The first savings and loans were formed as mutuals, whereby each member or owner placed funds into a pool. The borrowers from the savings and loans would draw funds from the pool when money was needed, and they would gradually pay back the funds so that others could borrow to buy or build a home.

Uses of Funds.   Reflecting this tradition and public policy, the primary use of funds at the more than 3000 savings and loan associations has been the making of loans on single-family dwellings. The result, as indicated in Table 9.6, is that the dominant asset in the portfolio of savings and loans is the mortgage, primarily, though not exclusively, the single-family home mortgage.

The savings and loan association has traditionally been a highly specialized lender. However, with the much wider lending authority permitted by DIDMCA (1980) and DIA (1982), many savings and loans have diversified their loan portfolio to a very significant degree. There has been a sharp increase in multifamily residential and commercial mortgages at the expense of single family mortgages.

TABLE 9.6   Financial Assets and Liabilities of Savings and Loan Associations, 1988 (Billions of Dollars)

Financial Assets	Value	Liabilities	Value
Mortgages	$ 745.2	Deposits	$ 968.7
Consumer credit	60.4	FHLB advances	141.6
Business loans	25.6	Other liabilities	177.1
Time deposits	7.3	Total	1287.4
U.S. Treasury securities	18.7		
Agency securities	208.5		
State and local government securities	1.2		
Other assets	188.6		
Total	1335.5		

Source: Board of Governors of the Federal Reserve System, Flow of Funds Accounts, *September 1988.*

In fact, about one third of the total mortgages held by savings and loans are multifamily residential and commercial mortgages. Relatedly, many savings and loans have chosen to channel their mortgage funds into more liquid mortgage pools rather than hold illiquid local mortgages. In addition, many savings and loans have increased their consumer and business loans substantially, becoming even more like commercial banks.

The diversification of savings and loans into multifamily residential and commercial loans and into direct equity investments in real estate has contributed to severe financial problems for many institutions. Significant overbuilding, disinflation, and the collapse of energy and agriculture contributed to massive loan losses at many savings and loans producing a sharp increase in the failure rate in the industry. The number of savings and loans declined markedly in the mid-1980s as the consolidation trend in the industry accelerated.

Sources of Funds.   Savings and loan associations have three basic sources of funds: deposits, Federal Home Loan Bank (FHLB) advances, and other liabilities. By far the dominant source of funds is the savings accounts of individuals and others. Savings shares include ordinary passbook accounts, as well as many types of certificates of deposit, and the money market deposit account. The composition of these deposits has changed dramatically, with a sharp decline in savings accounts, an increase in the importance of the large certificates of deposit, a large increase in money market deposit accounts after their authorization in late 1982, and entry into transaction accounts with the NOW deposits.

Savings and loan associations borrow funds from their principal supervisory authority, the Federal Home Loan Bank Board. Some of this borrowing occurs for reasons of interest rate differentials (when the advances from the Federal Home Loan Bank are lower-cost funds than savings deposits). FHLB advances

WHAT CAUSED THE THRIFT CRISIS?*

By early 1989 it had become quite evident that the savings and loan industry (the dominant portion of the "thrift industry") was on the verge of collapse. Hundreds of savings and loans were insolvent (i.e., had negative net worth) but continued to operate because the Federal Savings and Loan Insurance Corporation (FSLIC) did not have sufficient funds to close the institutions. Various estimates placed up to 1000 of the remaining savings and loans in the troubled category, operating with large amounts of bad loans and low capital positions. As the Bush Administration began to deal with the problem (one conspicuously ignored by both presidential candidates just a few months earlier), estimates of the cost involved in solving the thrifts crisis ranged upward from $100 billion, much of which would be paid for by the U.S. taxpayer.

The thrift crisis of 1989 was not a surprise. The problems that ultimately culminated in the crisis had been recognized for many years. In fact, the thrift crisis provides an excellent example of the consequences for public policy of ignoring a problem. The thrift crisis is, in a sense, the problem that wouldn't go away.

The thrift crisis reflects the confluence of a number of forces, including unstable economic and financial conditions, the deregulation of an industry that managerially was unready, the existence of a substantial amount of fraud, and the poor quality of regulation precisely at the time when good quality regulation was most needed.

Much of the initial problems for savings and loans stem from the rapid increase in interest rates in the late 1970s and the early 1980s. As traditionally fixed-rate mortgage lenders financed with short-term savings deposits, the industry experienced sharp increases in the cost of funds but a less than comparable increase in revenue in its mortgage portfolio. As a result, many institutions experienced significant losses. Passage of the DIDMCA (1980) and DIA (1982) were partially designed to deal with this interest rate risk problem by allowing savings and loans greater lending and deposit-taking flexibility.

Unfortunately, the interest rate risk problem within the industry in the early 1980s became a credit risk problem in the late 1980s. Many savings and loans took advantage of the broadened powers to make land development loans and commercial real estate loans, to buy junk bonds and equity securities, and to hold a variety of other assets. In many cases the managements of the institutions did not have the expertise to properly appraise the risks involved in these types of assets. As a result, loan losses mounted substantially. The problem was exacerbated by the existence of fraud in some institutions whereby the owners of the institutions had the ability to attract FSLIC-insured deposits to make loans that benefited themselves and their business associates. The collapse of the real estate market in the energy dependent states of the Southwest made the problem even worse. Not insignificant also was the failure of regulation. The regulatory authorities for the savings and loan industry, both at state and federal levels, seemed unwilling and unable to deal with the problem. They were unwilling perhaps because of the historically close associations between the regulators and the regulated and unable because of the lack of available personnel to cope with the explosion in activities at the savings and loans.

The net result of those factors was the thrift crisis of 1989. The ultimate outcome of the crisis of this industry is not totally clear in mid-1989. However, it does seem clear that this will be the costliest collapse ever within the depository institutions sector and one that might result in the transformation of this industry.

*See the **Postscript** at the end of the book.

have been generally large when interest rates are high and when savings and loans find it difficult to obtain funds from savings shares. During these periods of **disintermediation,** when the flow of funds bypasses the financial intermediaries and goes directly to primary securities, savings and loans make heavy use of borrowings from the Federal Home Loan Banks.

As a third source of funds, many savings and loans have tried to develop access to the open capital market as a nontraditional source of funds. One such way, which shows up in the balance sheet as "other liabilities," is for savings and loans to sell bonds backed by the mortgages in their portfolios (so-called mortgage-backed bonds). With increasing competition for funds in recent years there has been a strong trend among savings and loans, especially at the larger institutions, to find such nontraditional sources. And with the authority to offer interest-bearing transactions accounts in the form of negotiable orders of withdrawal (NOW) accounts there will undoubtedly be a substantial change in the mix of sources of funds at savings and loans.

Savings Banks

Savings banks are a type of financial institution that operates in fewer than half the states of the nation. Originating in the northeastern portion of the United States in the early nineteenth century, savings banks were formed to offer an outlet for the saving of the "new" immigrants at a time when other financial institutions did not seek small savings accounts. Authorized by only a few states, fewer than 500 savings banks currently exist. However, since 1980, regulatory restraints on savings banks have been relaxed considerably. The Federal Home Loan Bank Board allows new federal savings banks to be chartered in any state and permits state-chartered savings banks to convert to federal stock associations. These institutions are known as federal savings banks.

As revealed in Table 9.7, sources of funds at savings banks are limited to various kinds of deposits, including passbook savings accounts, money market

TABLE 9.7   Financial Assets and Liabilities of Savings Banks, September 1988 (Billions of Dollars)

Financial Assets	Value	Liabilities	Value
Mortgages	$151.3	Deposits	$212.1
Corporate bonds	13.9	Other	38.5
U.S. Treasury securities	9.8	Total	250.6
U.S. government agency securities	35.1		
State and local obligations	2.0		
Consumer credit	13.7		
Other assets	49.6		
Total	275.4		

Source: Board of Governors of the Federal Reserve System, Flow of Funds Accounts, *September 1988.*

deposit accounts, and a variety of types of certificates of deposit. In attracting funds, savings banks are in direct competition with other depository financial institutions—savings and loan associations and credit unions—as well as with commercial banks. This emphasis on thrift deposits as the basic source of funds is consistent with the history and tradition of the industry. But even though their sources of funds are quite similar to savings and loans and credit unions, their uses of funds are much more diversified than those of either of the other thrift institutions, partly reflecting less regulatory restrictions on portfolio management as well as geographic influences. Given their relatively stable source of funds, savings banks have emphasized long-term investments, principally in mortgages and corporate bonds. Unlike savings and loan associations, however, which hold primarily conventional (noninsured) mortgages, savings banks invest principally in Federal Housing Administration (FHA) and Veterans Administration (VA) insured and guaranteed mortgages. This emphasis on government-guaranteed mortgages reflects the fact that many mortgages acquired by savings banks originate outside the market area of the savings bank.

Beyond the concentration in mortgages, savings banks buy large quantities of high-quality bonds. Indeed, the relative amount of new funds committed to mortgages versus bonds in any one year varies markedly as yields on the two financial instruments change. As with savings and loans, the available sources and uses of funds have been changed markedly by the Depository Institutions Deregulation and Monetary Control Act (1980), which broadened the sources and uses of funds at these institutions.

Credit Unions

The smallest of the nonbank thrift institutions, but one of the most rapidly growing, is the credit union. Established as a cooperative institution, it is one of the newest of the nation's financial institutions. Tracing their roots back only to the 1920s in the United States, credit unions were established to provide consumer credit at reasonable rates to the "laboring classes" at a time when commercial banks viewed such credit extensions as "unproductive." Credit union membership was limited to individuals with a "common bond," either a common employer or membership in a common organization, such as a fraternal club. The growth of credit unions formed by employees of a common employer has been further encouraged by frequent donations of space and other facilities by the employer.

Credit unions have traditionally obtained their funds by offering members one type of account: a share in the credit union. Legally, this share represents an ownership interest in the credit union, but no return is guaranteed. However, this share is functionally equivalent to a deposit and may be insured by the National Credit Union Administration, an agency of the U.S. government. As Table 9.8 shows, of the total $195.0 billion in financial assets held by the roughly 20,000 credit unions in 1988, $180.0 billion was financed with the sale of credit union

TABLE 9.8   Financial Assets and Liabilities of Credit Unions, 1988 (Billions of Dollars)

Financial Assets	Value	Liabilities	Value
Consumer credit	$ 87.5	Credit union shares	180.0
U.S. government securities	23.0	Miscellaneous liabilities	15.0
Time deposits	26.7	Total	195.0
Home mortgage	37.0		
Other	20.8		
Total	195.0		

deposits

Source: Board of Governors of the Federal Reserve System, Flow of Funds Account, *September 1988.*

shares. In recent years, however, there has been some diversification of sources of funds. Many credit unions now offer different returns on different instruments of different maturities. Moreover, a number of credit unions offer share drafts, which are functionally equivalent to demand deposits but pay interest on the account balance and which were authorized nationwide under the Depository Institutions Deregulation and Monetary Control Act of 1980.

The principal use of credit union funds is to make loans to members for nonbusiness purposes. As revealed in Table 9.8, consumer credit is the dominant financial asset held by credit unions. Recently, credit unions have received the authority to offer long-term mortgage loans. However, there are numerous restrictions in the loan portfolio of credit unions, including limitations on rates charged. Maturity of the loan portfolio is also restricted. With the exception of home mortgage loans, credit unions are limited to relatively short-term loans. In addition to these consumer loans, credit unions hold as assets a large amount of investment securities, primarily in the form of U.S. government securities and time deposits. These assets are generally held for liquidity purposes, but they may also be held for income by credit unions when loan demand from members is relatively weak. Since credit unions do not pay any federal income tax, they have no incentive to hold state and local government securities.

SUMMARY

Changes in the economy and in regulations have significantly affected the role of individual institutions. The specialized-role financial system of the United States is changing dramatically. Such technological forces as electronic funds transfer systems and other developments are altering the payments mechanism and other aspects of the financial system. All depository institutions are becoming different from what they were in the past and increasingly like one another. Moreover, in a world of high and unstable interest rates the nature of financial institutions is likely to be altered further. Under the DIDMCA (1980) and the Depository Institutions Act (1982) the area for competition has broadened, and the degree of specialization is further diminishing.

QUESTIONS

1. What are the principal factors affecting the structure of the financial services industry?

2. Discuss the provisions of the Depository Institutions Act of 1982. Compare its purpose with the 1980 legislation.

3. Carefully compare the characteristics of commercial banks with those of other depository institutions. Have their roles become more alike or more different? Why? Explain.

4. Banks perform a number of functions. What are the functions, and how are they reflected in the financial statements of the banking industry.

5. What are the similarities and differences among savings and loan associations, savings banks, and credit unions?

6. Make a list of the areas in which there has been growing competition among depository financial institutions. What are the reasons for the increased competition?

REFERENCES

Benston, George J., *Financial Services: The Changing Institutions and Government Policy* (Englewood Cliffs, N.J.: Prentice-Hall, 1983).

Brumbaugh, Dan, *Thrifts Under Siege* (Cambridge, Mass.: Ballinger Publishing Co., 1988).

Carron, Andrew S., *The Plight of the Thrift Institutions: Studies in the Regulations of Economic Activity* (Washington, D.C.: The Brookings Institution, 1982).

Cooper, S. Kerry, and Donald R. Fraser, *Banking Deregulation and the New Competition in Financial Services* (Cambridge, Mass.: Ballinger Publishing Co., 1986).

Federal Reserve Bank of Atlanta, "Signals from the Future: The Emerging Financial Services Industry," *Economic Review* (September 1983), 20–32.

Fraser, Donald R., and Gene C. Uselton, "The Omnibus Banking Act," *MSU Business Topics* (Fall 1980), 5–14.

Gup, Benton, Donald Fraser, and James Kolari, *Commercial Bank Management* (New York; John Wiley, 1989).

Garcia, Gillian, et al., "The Garn–St Germain Depository Institution Act of 1982," Federal Reserve Bank of Chicago *Economic Perspectives* (March/April 1983), 3–31.

McNeill, Charles, "The Depository Institutions Deregulation and Monetary Control Act of 1980," *Federal Reserve Bulletin* (June 1980), 444–453.

Pearce, Douglas K., "Recent Developments in the Credit Union Industry," Federal Reserve Bank of Kansas City *Economic Review* (June 1984), 3–19.

Polakoff, Murray, *Financial Institutions and Markets,* 2nd ed. (Boston: Houghton Mifflin, 1981).

Rose, Peter S., and Donald R. Fraser, *Financial Institutions,* 3rd ed. (Dallas: Business Publications, Inc., 1988).

Walker, David, "Effects of Deregulation on the Savings and Loan Industry," *The Financial Review* (Spring 1983), 94–110.

CHAPTER 10

The Financial Services Industry: Nondepository Financial Institutions

In the previous chapter we discussed the nature of the nation's depository financial institutions. We pointed out how these depository institutions are becoming more and more similar in function. This "blurring of function" is increasing competition dramatically among the different kinds of depository institutions. In this chapter we provide a further discussion of financial institutions by treating the **nondepository financial institutions.** These include money market funds, insurance companies, pension funds, finance companies, mutual funds, broker/dealers, and mortgage bankers. These nondepository financial institutions are much more diverse among themselves than the depository financial institutions reviewed in the previous chapter. Moreover, major changes are occurring in the functions of some individual nondepository institutions that are sharply altering the degree of competition in the financial system. Nondepository financial institutions are becoming less specialized and are invading the markets of both depository and other nondepository financial institutions. Some nondepository financial institutions are becoming much more like depository institutions. This is especially true for mutual funds and some securities brokerage firms.

As shown in Table 10.1, the services provided by different types of financial institutions have overlapped considerably in recent years. Services offered by commercial banks in 1984 were quite similar to those offered in 1960. In contrast, savings and loans expanded their services substantially during this period and became increasingly competitive with commercial banks. Of particular importance, insurance companies, some retailers (such as Sears) and securities dealers substantially increased their financial services offerings between 1960 and 1984, both by offering services that are not allowed to depository institutions and also by competing directly with commercial banks and savings and loans in offering services that are traditionally only offered by those depository financial institutions.

TABLE 10.1 Financial Services Offered by Depository and Nondepository Institutions, 1960 and 1984

	Banks		Savings and Loans		Insurance Companies		Retailers		Security Dealers	
	1960	1984	1960	1984	1960	1984	1960	1984	1960	1984
Checking	X	X		X		X		X		X
Savings	X	X	X	X		X		X		X
Time deposits	X	X	X	X		X		X		X
Installment loans	X	X		X		X		X		X
Business loans	X	X				X		X		X
Mortgage loans	X	X	X	X		X		X		X
Credit cards		X		X		X	X	X		X
Insurance					X	X		X		X
Stocks, bonds brokerage		X		X		X		X	X	X
Underwriting									X	X
Mutual funds				X		X		X	X	X
Real estate				X		X		X		X
Interstate facilities		X								X

Source: Donald L. Koch, "The Emerging Financial Services Industry: Challenge and Innovation," Federal Reserve Bank of Atlanta, Economic Review, April 1984, 25.

The entry by nondepository institutions into markets traditionally served only by commercial banks and other depository institutions reflects a number of factors. Many nondepository institutions have been attracted to these markets by the perceived high risk-adjusted returns. Entry into new markets allows these nondepository institutions to take advantage of any existing economies of scale in the production of financial services. It also allows them to provide "one-stop" shopping within a financial supermarket. In addition, these nondepository institutions are subject to considerably less government regulation as they innovate new financial services.

Financial services are increasingly offered under the umbrella of one organization. These organizations, such as American Express and Merrill Lynch, are often referred to as **financial supermarkets.** When they combine financial and nonfinancial services, as does Sears, they are often referred to as **financial conglomerates.** These trends represent one more dimension of the revolution in financial services that has affected both depository and nondepository institutions.

MONEY MARKET FUNDS

A money market fund is an investment company that invests in money market instruments: Treasury bills, commercial paper, large CDs, and other types of high-quality, short-term, large-denomination financial instruments. (Their investments are listed in Table 10.2.) These money funds are somewhat similar to depository institutions in that they offer highly liquid and high-yielding accounts. However, legally, money funds offer equity shares rather than deposits, and they are not regulated in the same way as depository institutions. Money market funds are low-cost providers of "deposits," though without deposit insurance.

TABLE 10.2   Assets of Money Market Mutual Funds, September 30, 1988

Assets	Value (Billions of Dollars)
Time deposits	$ 36.4
Security repurchase agreements	41.6
Foreign deposits	22.5
U.S. government securities	31.6
Open-market paper	118.0
Miscellaneous	76.4
Total	$326.5

Source: Board of Governors of the Federal Reserve System, Flow of Funds Accounts, *September 1988.*

These investment companies are a relatively new phenomenon, dating back only to early 1974. Yet in just a few years their assets have grown to over $300 billion. The growth of money market funds has truly revolutionized the financial system, especially the operations of depository financial institutions.

Money market funds developed in response to three factors: (1) interest rates available on financial instruments in the money market during the 1970s and early 1980s reached exceedingly high levels by historical standards; (2) depository financial institutions were prohibited by Regulation Q (during much of this period) from offering these higher (market) interest rates on their deposits; and (3) individuals with small amounts to invest were unable to purchase money market instruments because of their large denominations, frequently $1 million or more. Money market funds moved into this gap with great success, as shown by their remarkable growth. This success reflects the services they are able to offer to the public, services that include interest rates that are higher than those available on many deposit accounts, as well as a number of other convenience features.

Money market funds offer an indirect security (shares in the fund) that has a number of attractive features. In addition to the denomination intermediation mentioned above, money market funds offer **maturity intermediation,** by providing instant liquidity to investors in their shares, and **risk intermediation,** by providing a diversified group of money market instruments managed by professionals. In addition, most money market funds have expedited redemption procedures whereby an investor may contact the fund by toll-free telephone and have funds transferred by wire, or an investor may write checks against the value of the money market fund account. Further, many money market funds are offered by mutual fund management companies that allow transfer of funds between the money market fund and their other funds, thereby giving investors greater flexibility and further enhancing the attractiveness of the money market funds.

The future of money market funds in a period of deregulation and reduced restrictions on interest rates paid by depository institutions is an interesting and important issue. Some observers forecasted that money funds would shrink to almost nothing once depository institutions were free to offer market rates of interest for their funds. That did not happen. Although banks were very aggressive in offering high yields when MMDAs were first authorized, their interest rates on MMDAs frequently fell below those of money market funds. It appears that many funds offer a variety of desired services to their customers (such as the ability to switch funds quickly from money market funds to stock and bond funds) so that they are attractive enough to retain their customers even without interest rate ceilings on depository institution accounts. Barring any serious problems with the credit quality of their assets, money funds should continue to play an important, though quantitatively less significant, role in the U.S. financial system.

CONTRACTUAL FINANCIAL INSTITUTIONS

The **contractual financial institutions** obtain their funds under some form of contract. This group of nondepository financial institutions includes insurance companies (both life insurance and property and casualty companies) and pension funds (both private and public). Their common element—contractually determined sources of funds—is a very important factor in influencing the investment behavior of these institutions. With a relatively assured, predictable, and stable source of funds, each contractual financial institution has great flexibility in investment policy. As a general rule, the contractual financial institutions hold very small quantities of liquid assets and invest in long-maturity assets, which often have very limited liquidity. Moreover, the contractual financial institutions are the major purchasers of equity securities.

Insurance Companies

The insurance industry is divided into two groups—life insurance companies and property and casualty insurance companies—according to the function performed by the individual firm. **Life insurance companies** sell protection against losses from premature death, as well as long-term savings through a buildup of cash value in some policies. Moreover, many life insurance companies actively compete for the management of pension funds for both private and public organizations. In contrast, **property and casualty insurance companies** are more specialized in function, selling protection of property through auto, fire, and other types of insurance. Increasingly, all these services are provided under the umbrella of a financial services holding company. There are over 2000 life insurance companies, of which 94 percent are stockholder owned and the rest are mutual associations. The hundred largest firms account for about three quarters of the assets.

The liabilities of life insurance companies, as presented in Table 10.3, reflect the basic functions of the industry. Life insurance reserves represent the claims on the firms from life insurance policy holders. Similarly, pension fund reserves represent the claims of pension fund beneficiaries. Pension fund reserves have grown much more rapidly than life insurance reserves, reflecting the changing nature of the business of their companies. In fact, while in 1960 life insurance reserves exceeded pension fund reserves by almost five times, by 1988 pension fund reserves were larger. Given their long-term, stable sources of funds from premium payments, life insurance company investments are also long term, as is shown in Table 10.3. The two largest commitments of funds are to corporate bonds ($431.0 billion) and mortgages ($223.1 billion). The corporate bonds are usually medium-to-high-quality issues acquired through private placements by di-

TABLE 10.3   Financial Assets and Liabilities of Life Insurance Companies, September 30, 1988 (Billions of Dollars)

Financial Assets	Value	Liabilities	Value
Demand deposits and currency	$ 4.5	Life insurance reserves	$ 304.0
Corporate equities	108.3	Pension fund reserves	619.3
Corporate bonds	431.0	Other liabilities	117.2
Mortgages	227.1	Total	1040.5
Policy loans	53.5		
Treasury issues	62.6		
Agency issues	74.0		
State and local obligations	11.2		
Open-market paper	33.0		
Miscellaneous assets	91.4		
Total	1096.6		

Source: Board of Governors of the Federal Reserve System, Flow of Funds Accounts, *September 1988.*

rect negotiation with the issuer, and the mortgages are increasingly on income-producing properties such as apartment houses, office buildings, and farm land. Corporate equities represent only about 10 percent of the total financial assets of life insurance companies, though the fraction has been growing as insurance companies penetrate the pension fund market and invest many of these funds in equities. In contrast, since the need for liquidity is minimal, short-term investments held for liquidity purposes represent a very small fraction of total financial assets. Moreover, holdings of state and local government issues are less than 2 percent of total financial assets, reflecting the low tax exposure of the industry.[1]

Growth of total assets at life insurance companies has slowed in recent years. Life insurance companies have found it increasingly difficult to market their products in a period of rapid inflation. The traditional life policies that combine a death benefit with a living benefit in the form of a cash value to the policy (known as whole life) have proven unattractive to households in periods of high interest rates. Moreover, new policies have increasingly been "term" policies as opposed to "whole life." **Term policies,** which contain no savings feature but are pure insurance, result in substantially less assets under management per $1000 of policy coverage.

Most property and casualty insurance is handled by about 900 firms that operate nationally. Automobile insurance accounts for about 40 percent of total premiums, and fire insurance accounts for about 20 percent. The portfolio of

---

[1]A substantial amount of funds (more than $50 billion) of life insurance companies is devoted to policy loans. These are loans to policyholders at fixed rates (often as low as 5 percent) specified in the policy and in amounts based on the cash value of the policy. When interest rates increase, policy loans generally rise as policyholders borrow the relatively cheap money available from this source. (Such policy loans are not available in the case of term insurance policies.)

property and casualty insurance companies is quite different from that of life insurance companies. Property and casualty insurance companies have heavy investments in municipal bonds as well as in corporate equities. The investments in municipals reflect the relatively high tax exposure of these firms, and the equity holdings are intended to offer some hedge against the rising costs of claims in an inflationary environment. As shown in Table 10.4, other insurance companies (primarily property and casualty insurance companies) hold a larger fraction of their assets in liquid investment securities than do life insurance companies. Given their volatility of claims and earnings, however, property and casualty insurance companies alter their portfolio commitment to municipals, as well as to common stocks, rather markedly from year to year.

Pension Funds

Pension funds represent the other type of contractual financial institution. Not only are the assets of pension funds large, but they are growing rapidly as both life expectancy and concern about providing for financial security during retirement years increase. Clearly, a major factor contributing to the growth of pension funds is the aging of the population and the increase in the number of people who are living into their 70s and 80s. Some of the retirement funds—so-called insured plans—are held by life insurance companies and are reflected in Table 10.3. However, most pension plans are not administered by a life insurance company. These pension plans, many of which are administered by the trust department of a commercial bank, are in turn divided into private pension funds (those sponsored by private firms) and state and local government employee retirement funds.[2] This distinction is quite significant, since the investment policies of the two types of funds differ markedly.

As revealed in Table 10.5, a large part (roughly 50 percent) of the assets of private pension funds are invested in equities. The heavy concentration in equities is made possible by the long time-horizon of the pension program, whereby benefits are payable some years in the future.

Over an extended period, the return on equities should exceed the return on debt securities for those investors, such as pension funds, that are able to accept large short-run changes in the value of equity securities. Corporate and government bonds represent the second largest investment holdings of private pension funds. In contrast, highly liquid short-term investments securities do not play a major role in the asset structure of private pension funds. The need for liquidity by pension funds is very limited in comparison with other financial

---

[2]There are, of course, other retirement programs, including the massive Social Security system. However, Social Security payments are made primarily from current Social Security taxes and not from the Social Security trust fund. In addition, the federal government has a variety of retirement programs for employees, but these have few assets set aside to provide future benefits.

TABLE 10.4   Financial Assets and Liabilities of Other Insurance Companies, September 30, 1988 (Billions of Dollars)

Financial Assets	Value	Liabilities	Value
Demand deposits and currency	$ 5.6	Policy payables	$299.2
Corporate equities	77.7	Other liabilities	0.2
Treasury issues	49.8	Total	299.4
Agency issues	27.9		
State and local obligations	145.2		
Corporate bonds	60.5		
Other assets	68.3		
Total	435.0		

Source: Board of Governors of the Federal Reserve System, Flow of Funds Accounts, *September 1988.*

[handwritten margin note: more frequent cash flow required]

institutions. Further, since pension funds are not subject to tax (the tax is paid by the beneficiary at the time benefits are paid), there is no incentive for them to hold tax-free state and local government issues.

The asset portfolios of state and local government pension funds are quite different from the portfolios of private funds. Reflecting the greater restrictions on investment policies that have traditionally been applied to state and local government plans, corporate bonds and other debt securities are the dominant investment. As shown in Table 10.6, U.S. Treasury and corporate bonds totaled $284.0 billion, whereas corporate equities totaled $205.7 billion. However, state and local government pension funds have increased the proportion of their assets devoted to equities in recent years as regulations governing their portfolios have been liberalized.

TABLE 10.5   Financial Assets of Private Pension Funds, September 30, 1988

Financial Assets	Value (Billions of Dollars)
Demand deposits and currency	$ 10.2
Time deposits	84.8
Corporate equities	539.6
Treasury issues	78.4
Agency issues	53.1
Corporate bonds	176.2
Mortgages	5.7
Open-market paper	85.0
Miscellaneous assets	52.6
Total	$1085.6

Source: Board of Governors of the Federal Reserve System, Flow of Funds Accounts, *September 1988.*

TABLE 10.6 Financial Assets of State and Local Government Employee Retirement Funds, September 30, 1988

Financial Assets	Value (Billions of Dollars)
Demand deposits and currency	$ 2.5
Time deposits	20.5
Corporate equities	205.7
Treasury issues	121.0
Agency issues	58.0
Corporate bonds	163.0
Mortgages	15.9
Miscellaneous assets	0.7
Total	587.3

Source: Board of Governors of the Federal Reserve System, Flow of Funds Accounts, September 1988.

OTHER FINANCIAL INSTITUTIONS

Various other financial institutions serve specialized parts of the financial system in addition to the depository and contractual institutions discussed above. We will concentrate on the following: finance companies, investment companies (mutual funds), security brokers and dealers, mortgage bankers, and nonfinancial organizations that are involved in providing financial services (such as retailers). Finance companies provide credit to consumers to purchase consumer durable goods, such as automobiles, and to businesses to buy inventory and other assets. In contrast, investment companies (or mutual funds, as they are more commonly called) pool the funds of many individuals and invest in a variety of financial assets, primarily in equities. Also, while they perform essentially nonintermediary functions, brokers, dealers, and mortgage bankers play a vital role in the securities markets. In addition, some organizations that traditionally did not concentrate on providing financial services have become quite active in recent years in the market for a variety of financial services.

Finance Companies

The finance company industry is composed of about 2800 firms involved in consumer and commercial lending and leasing. The hundred largest firms hold approximately 80 percent of the assets. Many firms are subsidiaries of manufacturing companies (known as capital finance companies) or of bank holding companies.

Finance companies raise funds by short- and long-term borrowing in the money and capital markets. Short-term borrowing is done through banks as well as by selling short-term debt instruments known as commercial paper. Small fi-

TABLE 10.7   Financial Assets and Liabilities of Finance Companies, September 30, 1988 (Billions of Dollars)

Financial Assets	Value	Liabilities	Value
Demand deposits and currency	$ 9.6	Corporate bonds	$159.1
Mortgages	71.6	Open-market paper	252.3
Consumer credit	171.2	Funds from parent	
Other loans (to business)	223.7	companies	112.0
Total	476.1	Other	21.1
		Total	$544.5

Source: *Board of Governors of the Federal Reserve System,* Flow of Funds Accounts, *September 1988.*

nance companies rely mainly on bank credit, whereas the larger finance compan-ies depend almost entirely on open-market paper for their short-term funds. In addition, finance companies sell bonds to raise long-term funds. As shown in Table 10.7, investments are primarly in consumer credit ($171.2 billion) and loans to business ($223.7 billion). At one time, finance companies tended to spe-cialize in either consumer or business credit. However, these firms are becoming increasingly involved in providing both types of credit. Moreover, the relative importance of consumer credit increased markedly in the 1950s and 1960s and then declined in the 1970s, reflecting changes in risk-return characteristics of the alternatives.

Investment Companies

The investment company or mutual fund pools the funds of generally small investors and purchases a diversified portfolio of debt and/or equity securities. As such, it offers to the small investor the opportunity to obtain a diversified portfolio of securities that would be impossible to obtain through direct invest-ments in primary securities. Though investment companies have existed for many decades, the industry as we know it today is principally a post–World War II phenomenon. During the early post–World War II increase in stock prices the investment company industry offered a method for the small investor to obtain high returns. However, with the poor performance of equities in the decade of the 1970s the growth of the mutual fund industry slowed dramatically. As a result, the industry turned to offering funds that specialize in corporate bonds and other fixed income securities (such as municipal bonds), so the proportion of equities in total fund assets has diminished. These changes are reflected in Table 10.8, which lists the financial assets of mutual funds exclusive of money market fund assets.[3] As this table shows, the largest single holding was in the form of

---

[3]This table omits the assets of closed-end investment companies. These organizations are similar to open-end investment companies or mutual funds with the exception that they have a fixed number of shares and the price of these shares is determined by supply and demand in the market where they are traded. However, the total assets of closed-end funds are relatively small.

TABLE 10.8 Financial Assets of Mutual Funds, September 30, 1988 _____

Financial Assets	Value (Billions of Dollars)
Demand deposits and currency	$ 7.3
Corporate equities	190.9
U.S. government securities	128.0
Corporate bonds	59.0
State and local government securities	77.4
Other	21.3
Total	483.9

Note: Assets exclude those of money market funds.

Source: *Board of Governors of the Federal Reserve System,* Flow of Funds Accounts, *September 1988.*

corporate equity, while a smaller proportion was held in the form of state and local government bonds.

Securities Brokers and Dealers

The securities industry is composed of over 2000 firms that deal with the public and a large number of firms that deal primarily with other brokers and dealers. Securities brokers and dealers (also sometimes referred to as **investment bankers**) perform a number of important financial services. As brokers, these firms bring together buyers and sellers of securities—stocks, bonds, mortgages, or other securities—either on a listed securities market such as the New York Stock Exchange or on an over-the-counter (OTC) market. In their capacity as a broker the firms do not assume the price risk of price fluctuation. In contrast, many of these firms act not only as brokers but also as dealers. As a dealer, the firm holds an inventory of securities and is prepared to sell these securities at one price (the asked price), as well as to buy these securities at a lower price (the bid price), thereby making a profit on the transaction. However, this opportunity for profit comes at the risk of loss, since the securities held as inventory by the dealer might decline in price. In their role as dealer these firms play a vital role in the over-the-counter security markets.

The role of security dealers as "market makers," through holding an inventory of securities, is crucial to the efficient functioning of the financial system. By making a market in securities in the secondary market, dealers provide liquidity to the financial markets, which in turn makes it easier to sell new securities in the primary market. It should be kept in mind that most trading of securities in the secondary market is done "over-the-counter" through dealers. Undoubtedly, the efficiency of financial intermediation would be reduced substantially if dealers were unwilling or unable to "make a market" in securities.

Many security brokers and dealers also perform an investment banking function in the primary market because they often work with private organizations, as well as with state and local governments, in their planning for new bond issues. In addition, security brokers and dealers frequently **underwrite** the issue, which means that they buy the securities from the issuer at a specific price, hoping to resell the securities at a higher price. When they underwrite securities, they accept the price risk. In addition, the underwriters use their brokerage offices to find buyers for these securities, which is referred to as the *marketing function.*

The role of securities brokers and dealers as financial intermediaries (in the sense of creating liabilities against themselves and in turn making loans to another party) is minor in comparison to their brokerage and market-making role. As shown in Table 10.9, brokers and dealers finance their assets with security credit consisting primarily of very short-term loans (often for one day) from commercial banks. Their assets consist of holdings of equities, U.S. government obligations, state and local government obligations, and corporate bonds, which is the inventory used in the performance of their market-maker function. In addition, these organizations extend credit to their customers (referred to as **margin credit**) so that their customers can purchase securities. Such extension of credit is an important part of their role as brokers.

Mortgage Bankers

Mortgage bankers are financial institutions that specialize in providing mortgage credit. Similar in some ways to security brokers, mortgage bankers originate mortgages from individuals buying homes (for which the mortgage banker receives a fee) and then sell the loans to a permanent lender, such as a life insurance company or a pension fund. Mortgage banks also deal with businesses in commercial and industrial properties. After the mortgage banker has sold the loan, it is generally serviced by the mortgage banker, for which the mortgage banker receives a servicing fee.[4] Recently, mortgage bankers have originated a large number of mortgage loans and sold them to a government-guaranteed mortgage pool, such as those sponsored by the Government National Mortgage Association (GNMA), or to private pools. Most of the loans originated by mortgage bankers are government guaranteed or insured (VA and FHA), though some mortgage bankers originate nongovernment-guaranteed (conventional) loans.

Mortgage bankers are usually financed through short-term borrowings from banks and others. Financing with bank credit is logical, since many mortgage banking companies are owned by bank holding companies. Uses of funds are principally to finance the inventory of mortgages during the time between the origination of the mortgage loan and its sale to the ultimate lender. Most of these

---

[4]**Servicing** refers to collecting the monthly payments, paying tax and insurance, and any other ordinary services that are required to protect a mortgage lender.

TABLE 10.9 Assets and Liabilities of Security Brokers and Dealers, September 30, 1988

Financial Assets and Liabilities	Value (Billions of Dollars)
Demand deposits and currency	$ 10.3
Corporate equities	13.7
U.S. government securities	29.5
State and local obligations	5.0
Corporate bonds	20.0
Security credit	42.0
Other	9.0
Total assets	129.5
Security credit	$ 61.0
Other	36.5
Total liabilities	97.5

Source: Board of Governors of the Federal Reserve System, Flow of Funds Accounts, September 1988.

mortgages are first mortgages on one- to four-family residential properties, though about 20 percent are construction loans.

Subsidiaries of bank holding companies hold almost 50 percent of the assets of major mortgage banking firms. The remaining mortgage companies are owned by subsidiaries of nonbank firms and savings and loans. A few large mortgage banking firms are independent.

Nonfinancial-Based Financial Service Organizations

One of the most interesting types of firms offering financial services consists of organizations such as retailers, manufacturers, and others whose principal activities have not traditionally involved providing financial services. In some cases, entry into financial services has been motivated by the desire to use the provision of credit to enhance the sales of the principal product of the organization. For example, an automobile-manufacturing firm such as General Motors might establish a finance subsidiary in order to increase the sales of its cars. In many of these cases, however, the finance subsidiary has expanded beyond simply facilitating the sales of the parent and has begun to offer financial services to other customers. In other cases, nonfinancial organizations have established financial service subsidiaries (independent of the parent's activities), attracted only by the desirable risk/return characteristics of those financial service activities. The expansion by Sears into financial services may best be represented by the second of these two illustrations, though financial activities should also contribute to the success of Sears as a retailing organization. Table 10.10 provides a list of financial services offered by major nonbank firms.

TABLE 10.10 Financial Services Offered by Selected Nonfinancial Companies

	General Motors	Ford	ITT	General Electric	Control Data	Gulf & Western	Borg-Warner	Westinghouse	Sears	Marcor	J.C. Penney
Commercial finance											
Commercial lending	1944	1980	1954–1951	1965	1968 1968	1968 1976	*	1961		1966	
Factoring											
A/R and inventory finance	1919	1959		1932	1968	1968	1950	1954			
Venture capital			1971	1970	1971				*		
Consumer finance											
Sales finance	1919	1959	1964	1964	1968	1968	1953	1959	1911 1962	1917	1958
Personal finance		1966	1964	1965	1968	1968	1969			1966	1970
Credit card			1983		1983	1981			*	1957	1958
Real estate											
Mortgage banking			1983	1981	1982		1982		1972	1970	
Residential first mortgages				1981	1982		1982		1961		1981
Residential second mortgages		1972	1965		1979	1966		1969	1961	1966	
Real estate development		1969	1970	1960	1972	1968	1969	1969	1960	1970	1970
Real estate sales and management				1983	1981	1968			1960	1970	1970
Commercial real estate and finance		1960	1980	1963				1969	1961	1966	1970
Insurance											
Credit life insurance	1975	1962	1964	1973	1968	1968	1970	1966	1970		
Regular life insurance			1964	1973	1968	1968	1960		1957	1966	
Property and casualty insurance		1974	1964	1970	1968	1968	1970		1931		1970
Accident and health insurance	1925	1959	1964	1973	1968	1968			1958	1968	1967

Table (rotated 90°). Rows are financial services; year values indicate year of entry recorded in several unlabeled columns.

Service								
Leasing								
Equipment and personal property	1981	1966	1968	1963	1968	1974	1968	1968
Real property leasing	1982	1982					1960 / 1981	1970 / 1970
Investment services								
Lease brokerage								
Investment management	1966						1969	
Mutual fund sales	1982	1966					1969 / 1969	1970 / 1970
Corporate trust and agency								
Custodial services								
Business and personal services								
Travel services	1978					*	1961 / 1981	1971
Cash management services							1981	
Tax preparation services							1966–1970	1969
Financial data processing services	1965				1968			1970
Credit card management services				1965				1969

*Entry data unavailable.

Source: "Financial Darwinism: Nonbanks and Banks Are Surviving," Federal Reserve Bank of Chicago, Staff Paper SM-85-5, p. 2.

SUMMARY

Nondepository financial institutions encompass a diverse group of firms, a much less homogeneous group than is the case for depository financial institutions. Contractual financial institutions, which obtain their funds under some type of contract, include insurance companies and both private and public pension funds. All these organizations are long-term investors, though the securities held in their portfolios differ considerably. Life insurance companies invest primarily in corporate bonds, but a growing proportion of their portfolio is in equities. Property and casualty insurance companies invest principally in state and local government obligations and equities. Private pension funds are heavily invested in equities, but state and local government pension funds are oriented more toward corporate bonds. The portfolios of private and public pension funds, however, are becoming much more alike.

Other financial institutions include finance companies, investment companies (mutual funds), securities brokers and dealers, mortgage bankers, and nonfinancial organizations with financial service operations. Finance companies concentrate on consumer and commercial lending. Mutual funds traditionally have managed equity portfolios, though they have diversified into the management of other financial assets. Securities brokers and dealers are extremely important in the financial system, though more for their brokerage, market-making, and investment banking functions than for their function as borrowers and lenders. Mortgage bankers perform a highly specialized role in the financial system, concentrating primarily on originating and servicing mortgages. Nonfinancial organizations engage in a variety of financial service activities.

All the depository and nondepository financial institutions discussed in this and the preceding chapter perform an important role in the intermediation process. They are involved in that vital link between savers and investors, between surplus and deficit economic units. To a greater or lesser degree, each is an important link in the chain by which saving is channeled to investment. Naturally, their role in the process differs with the nature of the institution; depository institutions play much more of an intermediation role than, for example, property and casualty insurance companies. Moreover, as the needs of savers and investors change and as the nature of government regulation is altered, so do changes occur in the importance of individual types of financial institutions.

The financial system has experienced some turmoil in recent years because of inflation and high interest rates. The nature and functions of different financial institutions have changed and will continue to change. These changes, which reflect (among other factors) both market pressures and government actions, have created a number of current issues that concern the operation and regulation of the nation's financial institutions. We will turn our attention to these current issues in later chapters.

QUESTIONS

1. Why have money market funds experienced such phenomenal growth? What problems and opportunities has this growth created?

2. What is meant by a contractual financial institution? Give some examples of contractual institutions. In what ways are they similar? In what ways are they different?

3. What has happened to the mix of mortgage loans made by life insurance companies? What might account for any changes?

4. Why have pension funds invested so heavily in corporate equities in recent years? What are the potential risks and rewards?

5. What is a finance company? Where do finance companies get their funds? What do they do with these funds? Why are finance companies becoming more similar?

6. Distinguish between the brokerage, market-making, and investment banking functions performed by security brokers and dealers.

7. What is a mortgage banker? What functions do mortgage bankers perform?

8. In what area of financial services have nonfinancial organizations become important? What is the motivation for their entry into financial service?

REFERENCES

Babble, David F., "The Price Elasticity of Demand for Whole Life Insurance," *The Journal of Finance* (March 1985), 225–239.

Cook, T. Q., and J. G. Duffield, "Money Market Funds: A Reaction to Government Regulations or a Lasting Financial Innovation?" Federal Reserve Bank of Richmond *Economic Review* (July/August 1979), 15–31.

Curry, Timothy, and Mark Warschansky, "Life Insurance Companies in a Changing Environment," *Federal Reserve Bulletin* (July 1986), 449–462.

———, and David J. Orge, "The Stochastic Characteristics of Property, Liability Insurance Company Underwriting Profits," *Journal of Risk and Insurance* (September 1981), 390–402.

Dougall, Herbert E., and Jack E. Gaumnitz, *Capital Markets and Institutions,* 5th ed. (Englewood Cliffs, N.J.: Prentice-Hall, 1986).

Fraser, Donald R., "The Money Market Fund as a Financial Intermediary," *MSU Business Topics* (Spring 1977), 5–12.

Malca, Edward, *Pension Funds, and Other Institutional Investors* (Lexington, Mass.: Lexington Books, 1975).

O'Leary, James J., "How Life Insurance Companies Have Shifted Investment Focus," *Banker Monthly Magazine* (June 15, 1982), 2–16.

Pavel, Christine, and Harvey Rosenblum, "Financial Darwinism: Nonbanks—and Banks—Are Surviving," Federal Reserve Bank of Chicago, Staff Study 85-5.

Polakoff, Murray E., et al., *Financial Institutions and Markets,* 2nd ed. (Boston: Houghton Mifflin, 1980).

Rose, Peter S., and Donald R. Fraser, *Financial Institutions,* 3rd ed. (Dallas: Business Publications, Inc., 1988).

Rosenblum, Harvey, and Diane Siegel, "Competition in Financial Services: The Impact of Nonbank Entry," Federal Reserve Bank of Chicago, Staff Study 83-1.

Swift, John R., "Consumer Finance Companies: A Step Back and a Look Forward," *Journal of Commercial Bank Lending* (January 1982), 50–55.

CHAPTER 11

The Role of Government as Lender: Federal Credit Agencies

The role of the federal government in the U.S. financial system—as regulator, borrower, and lender—is of enormous significance. The federal government is by far the largest financial intermediary in the nation's credit markets. Management of the approximately $2.5 trillion national debt by the U.S. Treasury is discussed in Chapter 27. The regulatory role of government in the financial system, the subject of the next chapter, is extremely important. But in addition to being a borrower and regulator on a massive scale, the federal government, through numerous federal credit agencies, is also a major lender.[1]

In this chapter we describe the principal federal credit agencies and their lending programs. Two significant federal agencies—the Federal Reserve System and the Federal Home Loan Bank system—are treated in other chapters because their regulatory role (and, in the case of the Fed, monetary control role) is much more significant than their lending role. Further, while the nature of funding for the federal credit agencies is described briefly, more detailed discussion of the securities issued by these agencies is deferred to Chapter 17, which is concerned with money market instruments. We may note at this point, however, that borrowing by federal credit agencies is fundamentally different from most U.S. Treasury borrowing. The Treasury's financial market activities are primarily devoted to the financing of past federal budget deficits (refunding of maturing debt) and present federal budget deficits (increases in the national debt), although the Treasury also engages in lending operations. (The Treasury's debt management activities and instruments are described and discussed in Chapters 17 and 27.)

---

[1] In 1988 the federal government held more than $250 billion in direct loans, and government-sponsored entities held almost $600 billion of outstanding loans. In addition the Federal government had guaranteed more than $500 billion of other loans.

FEDERAL CREDIT AGENCIES

The federal government's credit activities include not only direct lending but also the guaranteeing of loans made by private lenders. Table 11.1 shows the various direct loan and loan guarantee programs that existed in the 1989 fiscal year. (Some programs conducted by federally sponsored, privately owned agencies are not included in these tables.) The funding for federal credit programs is obtained primarily from borrowing—either directly or indirectly from the Treasury or directly from the public.

Federal credit agencies encompass a diverse group of institutions established to accomplish some public purpose. Included are agencies designed to foster the flow of credit to agriculture and housing, to finance international commerce, and to provide greater availability of credit at lower cost for a number of other purposes. Federal agencies are usually grouped into two basic categories: feder-

TABLE 11.1   Loan Transactions of the Federal Government, 1988 Loans Outstanding (Millions of Dollars)

	Direct Loans	Guaranteed Loans
Funds appropriated to the President	$ 43,285	$ 4,375
Agriculture	117,150	13,032
Commerce	536	438
Defense	1,759	—
Education	11,955	47,610
Health programs	799	2,504
Housing and Urban Development	15,073	306,781
Interior	176	170
Transportation	1,925	4,976
Treasury	685	952
Veterans Administration	1,388	149,705
NASA	899	—
Export-Import Bank	9,905	5,703
Federal Deposit Insurance Corporation	3,649	—
Federal Home Loan Bank Board	1,852	3,077
National Credit Union Administration	123	—
Small Business Administration	7,409	9,974
Tennessee Valley Authority	2,425	1
Other agencies and programs	980	666
Total	$221,973	$549,966

Source: Office of Management and Budget, Special Analyses, Budget of the United States Government, Fiscal Year 1989 (U.S. Government Printing Office, 1989), Table 20.

ally sponsored agencies and federally "owned" agencies. **Federally sponsored agencies** are privately owned, do not receive any direct federal funding, and yet carry an implicit promise of financial support from the federal government because of their particular social function. Their securities, however, do not carry any explicit guarantee by the federal government. The **federally owned agencies** are merely subcomponents of the federal government, from which they receive all or a large portion of their funds. Their securities are generally guaranteed by the federal government. Table 11.2 indicates the amounts of debt outstanding for the various federal and federally sponsored credit agencies in recent periods. Figure 11.1 shows the amount of debt outstanding by major programs of federally sponsored credit agencies.

The major federally sponsored credit agencies and federally owned credit agencies are listed in Table 11.3. The sponsored agencies, which are the major factors in the financial markets, are principally associated with agriculture (the Farm Credit System) and housing (Federal Home Loan Banks, the Federal Home Loan Mortgage Corporation, and the Federal National Mortgage Association). In contrast, the federally owned agencies are involved in a more diverse set of activities. More borrowing has been done by the federally sponsored agencies than by federally owned agencies. Therefore more of our discussion of the characteristics

TABLE 11.2 Federal and Federally Sponsored Credit Agencies, Debt Outstanding (Millions of Dollars, End of Period)

Agency	1984	1985	1986	1987	November 1988
1 **Federal and federally sponsored agencies**	**271,220**	**293,905**	**307,361**	**341,386**	**370,639**
2 Federal agencies	35,145	36,390	36,958	37,981	35,209
3 Defense Department[1]	142	71	33	13	8
4 Export-Import Bank[2,3]	15,882	15,678	14,211	11,978	10,964
5 Federal Housing Administration[4]	133	115	138	183	139
6 Government National Mortgage Association participation certificates[5]	2,165	2,165	2,165	1,615	0
7 Postal Service[6]	1,337	1,940	3,104	6,103	5,842
8 Tennessee Valley Authority	15,435	16,347	17,222	18,089	18,256
9 United States Railway Association[6]	51	74	85	0	0
10 Federally sponsored agencies[7]	237,012	257,515	270,553	303,405	335,430
11 Federal Home Loan Banks	65,085	74,447	88,752	115,725	130,630

(continued)

TABLE 11.2 *(Continued)*

Agency	1984	1985	1986	1987	November 1988
12 Federal Home Loan Mortgage Corporation	10,270	11,926	13,589	17,645	19,500
13 Federal National Mortgage Association	83,720	93,896	93,563	97,057	105,337
14 Farm Credit Banks[8]	72,192	68,851	62,478	55,275	53,420
15 Student Loan Marketing Association[9]	5,745	8,395	12,171	16,503	21,403
16 Financing Corporation[10]	n.a.	n.a.	n.a.	1,200	4,450
17 Farm Credit Financial Assistance Corporation[11]	n.a.	n.a.	n.a.	n.a.	690
MEMO					
18 **Federal Financing Bank debt**[12]	**145,217**	**153,373**	**157,510**	**152,417**	**143,321**
Lending to federal and federally sponsored agencies					
19 Export-Import Bank[3]	15,852	15,670	14,205	11,972	10,958
20 Postal Service[6]	1,087	1,690	2,854	5,853	5,592
21 Student Loan Marketing Association	5,000	5,000	4,970	4,940	4,910
22 Tennessee Valley Authority	13,710	14,622	15,797	16,709	16,876
23 United States Railway Association[6]	51	74	85	0	0
Other Lending[13]					
24 Farmers Home Administration	58,971	64,234	65,374	59,674	58,496
25 Rural Electrification Administration	20,693	20,654	21,680	21,191	19,220
26 Other	29,853	31,429	32,545	32,078	27,269

[1]Consists of mortgages assumed by the Defense Department between 1957 and 1963 under family housing and homeowners assistance programs.

[2]Includes participation certificates reclassified as debt beginning October 1, 1976.

[3]Off budget August 17, 1974, through September 30, 1976; on budget thereafter.

[4]Consists of debentures issued in payment of Federal Housing Administration insurance claims. Once issued, these securities may be sold privately on the securities market.

[5]Certificates of participation issued before fiscal 1969 by the Government National Mortgage Association acting as trustee for the Farmers Home Administration; Department of Health, Education, and Welfare; Department of Housing and Urban Development; Small Business Administration; and the Veterans Administration.

[6]Off budget.

[7]Includes outstanding noncontingent liabilities: notes, bonds, and debentures. Some data are estimated.

[8]Excludes borrowing by the Farm Credit Financial Assistance Corporation, shown in line 17.

[9]Before late 1981 the Association obtained financing through the Federal Financing Bank (FFB). Borrowing excludes that obtained from the FFB, which is shown on line 21.

[10]The Financing Corporation, established in August 1987 to recapitalize the Federal Savings and Loan Insurance Corporation, undertook its first borrowing in October 1987.

[11]The Farm Credit Financial Assistance Corporation (established in January 1988 to provide assistance to the Farm Credit System) undertook its first borrowing in July 1988.

[12]The FFB, which began operations in 1974, is authorized to purchase or sell obligations issued, sold, or guaranteed by other federal agencies. Since FFB incurs debt solely for the purpose of lending to other agencies, its debt is not included in the main portion of the table in order to avoid double counting.

[13]Includes FFB purchases of agency assets and guaranteed loans; the latter contain loans guaranteed by numerous agencies with the guarantees of any particular agency being generally small. The Farmers Home Administration item consists exclusively of agency assets, while the Rural Electrification Administration entry contains both agency assets and guaranteed loans.

Source: Federal Reserve Bulletin, *May 1988.*

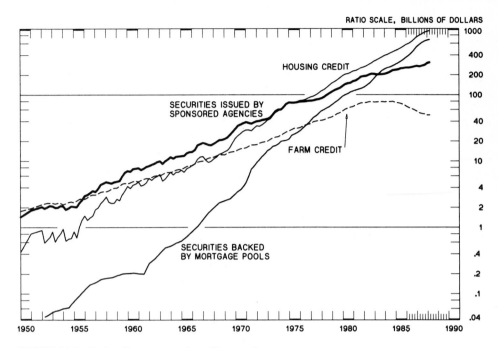

RATIO SCALE, BILLIONS OF DOLLARS

FIGURE 11.1   Federally sponsored credit agencies
(Amount Outstanding; End of Year, 1950–1951; End of Quarter, 1952–)

Source: Board of Governors of the Federal Reserve System. Historical Chart Book, *1988.*

TABLE 11.3   Federal Credit Agencies

Name of Agency	Designation
Federally Sponsored Agencies	
Financing Corporation	FICO
Banks for Cooperatives	BCs or Coops
Federal Home Loan Banks	FHLBs
Federal Home Loan Mortgage Corporation	FHLMC or Freddie MAC
Federal Farm Credit System	FCS
Federal Agricultural Mortgage Corporation	FAMC, or Farmer Mac
Federal National Mortgage Association	FNMA or Fannie Mae
Student Loan Marketing Association	Sallie Mae
Financial Assistance Corporation	FAC
Federal Agencies	
Export-Import Bank	EXIM
Farmers Home Administration	FmHAd
Federal Financing Bank	FFB
Federal Housing Administration	FHA
Government National Mortgage Association	GNMA or Ginnie Mae

of federal agencies as participants in money and capital markets will be concerned with federally sponsored agencies.

Functions of Federal Agencies

Federal lending agencies were created to increase the availability of credit and/or lower its cost for portions of the economy that are assumed to have some special social role. It has been argued, for example, that it is socially desirable for the United States to be a country of "homeowners" rather than renters. Similarly, the concept of the "yeoman farmer" has deep roots in U.S. history. The federally sponsored agricultural agencies contribute to these goals by borrowing funds in the nation's financial markets and lending them to farmers and farm organizations at rates below those available from other credit sources. Since these agencies are able to borrow at rates that are almost the same as those available on direct federal debt, they can provide relatively low-cost funds to their customers.

Like the family farm, home ownership is viewed as having benefits for U.S. society beyond those bestowed directly on homeowners. Thus other major federal credit agencies include housing-related agencies. The Federal Home Loan Banks (FHLBs) borrow in the financial markets and lend these funds to savings and loan associations, which have most of their loans in home mortgages. FHLB lending rises in periods of high interest rates, when the savings and loan industry is having a difficult time raising funds, and falls in periods of low interest rates, when funds flows at the savings and loans are more ample. The Federal Home Loan Mortgage Corporation and the Federal National Mortgage Association exist to purchase mortgages in the secondary market from principal mortgage lenders, such as savings and loan associations, mortgage bankers, and others. By purchasing these mortgages the FHLMC and FNMA not only add to the liquidity of mortgages generally but also provide funds to mortgage lenders to acquire additional mortgages. (The Government National Mortgage Association performs a similar function, as will be explained later.)

Besides encouraging presumably socially beneficial economic activities, it is also argued that federal credit programs ameliorate business cycles and offset alleged financial market imperfections. The former argument, that the goal of economic stabilization is served by federal lending programs, was especially significant during and immediately following the Great Depression of the 1930s, serving as a rationale for creation of agencies offering a source of liquidity and credit that would be immune to private sector economic disturbances. The argument that private financial market imperfections plague agriculture, housing, and small business has been used as a rationale for federal credit programs benefiting these sectors. Another significant source of impetus for certain federal lending programs has been the desire of Congress to provide benefits to groups deemed needy (low-income individuals in need of housing, for example), deserving (such as veterans of military service), or both.

It would take us too far afield to assess in detail either the validity of these various arguments or the degree of success of federal credit programs in attaining their presumed objectives as related to the arguments.[2] However, we may note briefly the likely major financial consequences of government direct loan and guaranteed loan programs.

In the case of direct loans, the federal credit agency acts as a financial intermediary by borrowing and lending funds. The low credit-risk status of the agency allows it to borrow at lower rates than the beneficiary of the agency's lending could borrow. Presuming that the agency passes on this reduction in rate to borrowers, the latter obtain a subsidy that is equal to the rate they would have paid had they obtained a private sector loan less the rate actually paid to the agency. The quantity of funds borrowed by program beneficiaries will increase by the difference between the amount they would have borrowed at the rate charged them by a private sector lender and the amount borrowed at the subsidized rate. (And, of course, some recipients of federal agency loans might not have otherwise been able to obtain credit.)

When a government agency guarantees the loans of borrowers, the default risk for the lender is reduced to zero. Lending to borrowers who can obtain such a guarantee becomes much more attractive. The likely outcome is that a larger quantity of loans will be made at a lower interest rate. Government-guaranteed student loan programs are an example of how loan guarantees can attract loanable funds at relatively low interest rates to a type of loan (and borrower) that would otherwise be confronted with limited lender interest.

While one may or may not agree that particular sectors of the economy benefiting from federal credit programs are "deserving" in terms of their social merits, economic importance, or financial-market-disadvantaged status, several cautionary comments are in order. One is that such programs obviously distort market credit flows. Another is that there is empirical evidence that, while federal credit programs do affect resource allocation, the effect is not nearly so great as the size (and cost) of these programs might suggest. In particular, it is likely that the subsidized credit provided by federal agencies simply replaces, to a significant (though varying) extent, unsubsidized credit that would otherwise have flowed into the favored sector. In any event, however, it is apparent that most of the federal credit programs (and agencies) are firmly entrenched; many have powerful supporting constituencies and are otherwise likely to continue to play a significant role in the financial system for the foreseeable future. We turn now to a description of the most important of these programs and the agencies that

---

[2]For such a discussion, see John H. Hand, "Government Lending Agencies," in M. E. Polakoff and T. A. Durkin (eds.), *Financial Institutions and Markets,* 2nd ed. (Boston: Houghton Mifflin Co., 1981), 216–237. See also Joel Fried, "Government Loan and Guarantee Programs," Federal Reserve Bank of St. Louis *Review* (December 1983), 22–30; and R. G. Penner, and W. L. Silber, "The Interaction Between Federal Credit Programs and the Impact on the Allocation of Credit," *American Economic Review* (December 1973).

administer them. We begin with the principal federal credit agencies and then move to the federally sponsored but privately owned agencies.

FEDERAL LENDING AGENCIES

The major federal lending (and private loan-guaranteeing) agencies are the Federal Financing Bank, the Government National Mortgage Association, the Federal Housing Administration, the Export-Import Bank, the Small Business Administration, the Farmers Home Administration, the Commodity Credit Corporation, the Agency for International Development, the Rural Electrification Administration, and the Veterans' Administration. We are primarily concerned with the first two agencies, but we offer brief descriptions of some of the other agencies.

Federal Financing Bank (FFB)

The Federal Financing Bank (FFB) was established by Congress in 1973 and commenced operations in 1974. The FFB is wholly owned by the federal government. The Secretary of the Treasury serves as chairman of its board of directors and has statutory authority to supervise and direct FFB activities. While the FFB is huge in terms of assets held (more than $140 billion of outstanding loans in 1989), its activities are conducted by a small number of employees.

By creating the FFB, Congress hoped to improve the efficiency of both the borrowing and lending activities of the federal government. The FFB is authorized to purchase or sell obligations issued, sold, or guaranteed by other federal agencies. The FFB is empowered to borrow directly from the public by issuance of its own securities and to borrow from the Treasury. The sole purpose of such debt incurrence is to obtain funds to lend to other federal agencies. The principal intent of Congress in creating an agency with these powers was to consolidate "off-budget" borrowing by federal agencies. Before the establishment of the FFB, many federal agencies had begun to issue securities, separate and apart from U.S. Treasury borrowing. While most of these issues were fully backed by the U.S. government, they lacked a well-developed secondary market and were, of course, less familiar to dealers and investors than their Treasury counterparts. As a result, such issues (75 in 1973) sold at higher required yields than Treasury securities. This problem was corrected by the FFB's establishment, since federal agencies (though not federally sponsored, privately owned agencies) now borrow from the FFB (at the Treasury rate plus 1/8 percent).

The FFB currently limits its funding activities to borrowing from the Treasury. Its first (1974) direct issue sold at almost 20 basis points (0.2 percent) higher yields than Treasury securities of comparable maturities, thus persuading the FFB administration that Treasury borrowing was preferable. (Further, the FFB has unlimited authority for such borrowing from the Treasury, while its authorization for note issuance is statutorily limited to $15 billion.)

The FFB has been the target of criticism for its alleged contribution to the huge expansion in federal lending programs in the past decade. FFB lending is "off-budget"; its funding is outside the Congressional appropriations process and is not treated as part of the official federal deficit. Thus it is argued that the agency induces ballooning of federal credit activity by making it too easy. Further, a 1981 General Accounting Office (GAO) study charged that the FFB had directly contributed to laxness in federal credit agency debt management by not conducting credit analyses or otherwise monitoring agency lending activity. In defense of the agency it can be pointed out that the latter activities are not part of the FFB's charge. Further, while "off-budget" lending has indeed grown enormously in recent years, so has "on-budget" borrowing, which *is* subject to Congressional scrutiny.

The Government National Mortgage Association ("Ginnie Mae")

The Government National Mortgage Association was created in 1968 when the Federal National Mortgage Association was converted into a federally sponsored, privately owned agency. As part of the latter action, the government-subsidized programs of the old FNMA were transferred to the new GNMA, which was (and is) housed in the Department of Housing and Urban Development. GNMA was given responsibility for managing and liquidating certain mortgages transferred to it from FNMA,[3] for providing special assistance (subsidized financing) to segments of the low-income housing market,[4] and for conducting the mortgage-backed securities program—the last function being the most important.

GNMA encourages issuance of mortgage-backed securities by private mortgage lenders by providing the guarantee of the government as to timely payment of principal and interest on these securities. Private mortgage lenders assemble pools of government-insured mortgages and then sell so-called "pass-through" certificates backed by these mortgages to investors. Interest and principal from the pooled mortgages are "passed through" to certificate holders after deduction of fees for the servicing and guaranty functions. In 1987, GNMA guaranteed mortgage-backed "pass-through" securities in the amount of about $115 billion, up from about $82 billion in 1986. At present, "Ginnie Maes" account for about

---

[3]These mortgages (and others acquired since) were formed into pools, and "participation certificates" (PCs) were issued against them to private investors.

[4]One such GNMA program, its "tandem plan" operations in which the agency simultaneously issued commitments to buy certain types of mortgages at an above-market price and sold these mortgages to FNMA or private investors at the market price, absorbing the loss as a subsidy for these types of mortgages, was terminated by 1983 Congressional legislation.

60 percent of outstanding mortgage-backed securities. According to GNMA's FY 1987 annual report, since GNMA's Mortgage-Backed Securities Program was introduced in 1970, the agency has guaranteed over $500 billion in securities collateralized by more than 42,000 mortgage pools. Additional discussion of GNMA's role and significance in the mortgage market is included in Chapter 20.

Other Federal Agencies

Small Business Administration.   The SBA's purpose is to provide (and facilitate private-sector provision) of loans to small businesses. The agency offers both a disaster loan program and a business loan program. The former program features SBA lending (and guaranteeing of private lending) to victims of natural disaster. The latter involves direct lending to small business and SBA support of small business investment companies (SBICs), which provide capital for small firms.

Federal Housing Administration.   Established in 1934, the FHA (which is part of the Department of Housing and Urban Development) is best known for its provision of mortgage insurance. The FHA insures mortgage lenders against loss on loans made in accordance with legal and administrative requirements. Borrowers pay an insurance premium as part of each mortgage payment for FHA mortgage insurance. FHA mortgage insurance has had an enormous and enduring impact on the mortgage markets generally and in the availability of residential housing finance particularly.

A "competitor" for the FHA's mortgage insurance program is the Veterans Administration (VA) mortgage guarantee program established during World War II. No premium is paid by borrowers qualifying for these government-guaranteed mortgage loans. Private sector mortgage insurance companies also provide mortgage insurance, and the aggregate amount of such insurance now rivals that of the FHA program.

Farmers Home Administration (FmHA).   The FmHA offers numerous programs of financial assistance for farms, rural housing, rural community facilities, and rural industrial development. The agency lends to farmers (supposedly unable to otherwise obtain credit on reasonable terms) to acquire, enlarge, or improve a farm. Such loans are secured by mortgages on farm real estate. The FmHA also makes similarly restricted and similarly structured farm operating loans.

The Commodity Credit Corporation (CCC).   The CCC administers government price-support programs for certain crops. The agency "lends" funds to the farmer in an amount determined by crop size and the legislated support price, the crop being pledged as collateral. The farmer can sell the crop and pay the loan or forfeit the crop and retire the loan. (Which action the farmer chooses is obviously determined by the support price–market price relationship.) The CCC also finances construction of farmer-owned storage facilities and provides agriculture export credit and credit guarantees. CCC funds are provided by direct appropriation and by Treasury loans.

The Export-Import Bank (Eximbank).   Established in 1934, the Eximbank has as its purpose the promotion of U.S. exports through its lending activities, its guaranteeing of private export-related loans, and various other activities. In particular, the agency provides, guarantees, and participates in loans to foreign purchasers of U.S. goods and services (or foreign financial institutions making such loans) and insures U.S. exporters against losses from overseas sales. Most of the Eximbank's funding is obtained from loans from the FFB. In 1984 the agency owed the FFB more than $15 billion.

FEDERALLY SPONSORED CREDIT AGENCIES

In 1989 the various federally sponsored credit agencies had outstanding debt of about $375 billion. (In 1965 their debt was less than $14 billion; in 1970, $39 billion; and in 1980, $160 billion.) Since these agencies borrow directly from investors in the financial markets, they are obviously highly significant components of this nation's financial system. As was noted earlier, the most important of these agencies are concerned with agriculture and housing finance. We begin with two housing-related agencies: the FNMA and the FHLMC. (The Federal Home Loan Bank system, which is as much a regulator as a lender, is treated in the next chapter.)

The Federal National Mortgage Association ("Fannie Mae")

The FNMA was created by Congress in 1938 to provide a secondary market in FHA insured mortgages and thus provide liquidity to mortgage lenders. Its functions were altered significantly in the Congressionally mandated reorganization of 1968, which created GNMA. The most important present role of FNMA in the financial marketplace is its considerable contribution to the existence of a strong secondary mortgage market. But since FNMA buys more mortgages than it sells, the agency is also a significant source of funds for the primary mortgage market.

FNMA is a publicly held corporation, all its common stock being held by private shareholders, but five members of its board of directors are appointed by the President of the United States. FNMA's role thus embraces the dual tasks of earning a fair return on its stockholders' investment while pursuing public policy objectives. While the latter aspect of FNMA's role doubtless constrains the former, it is also true that the agency obtains special market advantages from its links to the federal government. In particular, FNMA debt instruments are viewed as only very slightly riskier than U.S. Treasury securities, thus substantially reducing the agency's funding costs. Further, FNMA securities are exempt from registration with the Securities Exchange Commission and from various other regulatory restrictions that apply to private sector securities. FNMA's principal source of revenue is interest earnings on its mortgage portfolio holdings, which exceed $100 billion. (See Table 11.4.) The agency is the largest single private holder of residential mortgages.

As is the case with all federally sponsored credit agencies, FNMA obtains much of its funding by issuing debt securities. The nature of FNMA securities is described in Chapters 17 and 19.

FNMA issues mortgage-backed securities (MBS) under two types of programs. Under one program the agency forms pools of mortgage loans from its own portfolio and issues securities backed by these pools. Under the other program, FNMA swaps (exchanges) mortgage-backed securities for an undivided interest in mortgage pools formed by private lenders. The lenders may hold the securities in their portfolios or sell them. In 1988, the FNMA issued $55 billion of guaranteed MBS, down slightly from $63 billion in 1987.[5]

The Federal Home Loan Mortgage Corporation (FHLMC)

The FHLMC ("Freddie Mac") was established by Congress in 1970 to create a national secondary market in conventional (not FHA-insured or VA-guaranteed) residential mortgages. The FHLMC is "owned" by the Federal Home Loan Bank system, which provided its initial capital and directs its operations. Now that FNMA's mortgage acquisition powers include conventional as well as government-insured mortgages, the two agencies are perhaps somewhat redundant in their public policy purpose. But there are some operational differences in the two agencies. For example, the FHLMC's mortgage-purchase authority is limited to mortgages from financial institutions having their deposits insured by the federal government, whereas FNMA also buys mortgages from mortgage bankers. Further, the FHLMC has been quite innovative in developing new mortgage-backed debt instruments.

The FHLMC issues two types of mortgage-backed securities, participation certificates (PCs) and collateralized mortgage obligations (CMOs). PCs are pass-through certificates that constitute claims on a mortgage pool, with the FHLMC guaranteeing payment. CMOs resemble pass-through securities but offer the features of serial bonds. Interest and principal payments may be semiannual rather than monthly (as on PCs). CMOs are structured into several maturity classes, thus transforming a single mortgage into the equivalent of a short-term, an intermedi-

---

[5]Federal National Mortgage Association, *Annual Report,* 1988.

TABLE 11.4   Federal National Mortgage Association
(Condensed Balance Sheet, in Millions of Dollars) _____

	December 31, 1988
Assets	
Mortgage portfolio, net	$ 99,867
Other assets	12,391
Total assets	112,258
Liabilities	
Bonds, notes and debentures:	
Due within one year	36,599
Due after one year	68,860
Other liabilities	4,539
Total liabilities	109,998
Stockholders' equity	2,260
Total liabilities and stockholders' equity	$118,250

Source: Federal National Mortgage Association, Annual Report, *1988. Reprinted with permission.*

ate-term, and a long-term bond. In 1988 the FHLMC originated about $75 billion of mortgage-related securities.

Further discussion of the FHLMC, FNMA, and GNMA is included in Chapter 20, which is concerned with the mortgage market.

Farm Credit System

The Farm Credit System (FCS) was created by Congress to provide credit to agricultural borrowers throughout the nation. The FCS has indeed been a vital source of credit to the farm sector; by 1980 it held about one third of all farm debt in the United States. The first step in the development of the FCS came in 1916, when legislation established twelve Federal Land Banks, one in each of twelve farm credit districts. These land banks made loans to local Federal Land Bank Associations (of which there came to be more than 400), the latter then supplying mortgage loans and other long-term loans to farmers. In 1923, twelve Federal Intermediate Credit Banks were established to provide short- and intermediate-term credit to farmers and ranchers. The Farm Credit Act of 1933 provided a means for the FICBs to supply their loanable funds to the agricultural sector by the creation of Production Credit Associations (of which there came to be more than 370). Banks for Cooperatives were created in each farm credit district to make short-term loans to production and marketing cooperatives formed by farmers. The FCS is owned by its member borrowers but is regulated, supervised, and examined by the Farm Credit Administration, an independent government agency. The FCS obtains its external funding from issuance of debt securities by its components and also by consolidated FCS issues.

The FCS developed very serious problems in the 1980s as the farm economy plummeted and billions of dollars of FCS loans became uncollectible. The Agricultural Credit Act of 1987 was a much more far-reaching response to the FCS crisis.[6] The 1987 legislation created the Federal Agricultural Mortgage Corporation (dubbed "Farmer Mac") to create a secondary market for agricultural loans, supplied $4 billion of financial assistance to the FCS and called for consolidation and reorganization of the system's sprawling structure, including merger of Land Banks and FICBs.

Student Loan Marketing Association ("Sallie Mae")

The Student Loan Marketing Association was created in 1972 under authority of the Higher Education Act of 1965. Dubbed "Sallie Mae" (in the whimsical tradition of "Fannie Mae" and "Ginnie Mae"), the agency has the purpose of providing liquidity to lenders participating in the Guaranteed Student Loan Program. Sallie Mae does not extend student loans, but rather buys such loans from the financial institutions that do. Further, via so-called "warehousing advances," the agency loans money to lenders for their use in making student loans. Further, for a "commitment fee," Sallie Mae will agree to *future* loan purchases and advances. The loans held by Sallie Mae are guaranteed by the federal government or by state and private sector authorities (and then reguaranteed by the federal government). The loans made by the agency to lenders are fully collateralized by federal securities or guaranteed student loans.

Since 1983, Sallie Mae (like her namesake, Fannie Mae) has been a public company, and equity shares in the association are traded on the New York Stock Exchange. Since late 1981 the agency has borrowed directly in the credit markets; before that time it obtained financing from the Federal Financing Bank. Since becoming privately owned, Sallie Mae has been profitable. Sallie Mae is the principal shareholder in the College Construction Loan Assurance Association, created by Congress in 1987 as a private, for-profit insurance corporation to guarantee and insure loans and bonds issued for college construction and renovation.

The Financing Corporation

The FSLIC Recapitalization Act of 1987 created a new government-sponsored agency, the Financing Corporation (FICO), to provide a financing mechanism for the bankrupt FDIC. FICO was authorized to borrow up to about $10.8 billion via sales of bonds to the general public, and $1.2 billion of bonds were

---

[6]In 1985 Congress created the Farm Credit Capital Corporation in an attempt to assist the weakest banks in the FCS, but legal challenges and other problems prompted Congress to revoke that FCS's charter in the 1987 legislation and replace it with the Farm Credit System Financial Assistance Corporation.

issued in 1987. It soon became evident, however, that this measure was grossly inadequate to deal with the huge problem created by insolvent savings and loan associations. In 1989, the Bush administration proposed the creation of still another government-sponsored agency, the Resolution Funding Corporation, to complete the bailout of the savings and loan industry at an estimated total cost of $157 billion.

SUMMARY

While the principal roles of the federal government in the financial system are as borrower and regulator, the government is also a highly significant lender. In addition to direct lending programs the government's credit activities include lending its guarantee to hundreds of billions of dollars of private sector loans. Federal credit programs are intended to encourage presumably socially beneficial activities (such as home ownership and education), offset alleged financial market imperfections, and contribute to economic stabilization.

Federal credit agencies include federal agencies, which are simply subunits of the federal government, and federally sponsored, privately owned agencies. Federal agencies are funded by direct Congressional appropriations, and direct borrowing from the Treasury via the Federal Financing Bank (which borrows from the Treasury and lends to federal agencies). Federally sponsored credit agencies borrow directly from the public by issuance of their own securities. Since these agency securities are viewed as implicitly backed by the federal government, their interest rates are only very slightly higher than Treasury debt securities. Since both federal agencies and federally sponsored credit agencies enjoy low funding costs (relative to private sector lenders), they can provide below-market lending rates to borrowers.

The largest federal credit programs are in housing and agriculture. Activities of the Federal National Mortgage Association, the Government National Mortgage Association, and the Federal Home Loan Mortgage Corporation have contributed greatly to the establishment of a broad and deep secondary market in mortgages and have channelled large amounts of funds into the primary mortgage markets. The Farm Credit System and other agricultural-lending federal agencies have provided more than one third of the debt capital of the U.S. agricultural sector.

QUESTIONS

1. What is the difference between a "federal agency" and a "federally sponsored agency"? Do the funding costs of these two types of agencies differ significantly? Why or why not?

2. Explain and evaluate the rationale (justification) for federal credit programs. What are the narrow financial effects of these programs? What might be some broader economic and social effects?

3. Describe the Federal Financing Bank in terms of its operations and purpose.

4. Describe and contrast the activities of the Government National Mortgage Associa-
    tion, the Federal National Mortgage Association, and the Federal Home Loan Mort-
    gage Association.

5. Have any of the federal agencies described in this chapter directly benefited you or
    your family? Identify any one of such agencies and describe the nature of the benefi-
    cial activity.

6. What is a mortgage-backed security? How does issuance of these securities facilitate
    the availability of mortgage credit to homebuyers?

7. Describe the structure and role of the Farm Credit System.

8. What is "Sallie Mae"? Explain the purpose of this agency.

REFERENCES

The Budget of the United States Government, 1989, Special Analysis F, Federal Credit Programs (Washington
    D.C.: U.S. Government Printing Office, 1988).

Congressional Budget Office, *Conference on the Economics of Federal Credit Activity* (Washington D.C: U.S.
    Government Printing Office, 1981).

——, *The Federal Financing Bank and the Budgetary Treatment of Federal Credit Activities* (Washington D.C.:
    U.S. Government Printing Office, 1982).

Duncan, Marvin, "Government Lending: Some Insights from Agriculture," Federal Reserve Bank of
    Kansas City *Economic Review* (September/October 1983), 3–6.

Federal Home Loan Bank Board, *Annual Report*, 1988.

Federal National Mortgage Association, *Annual Report*, 1988.

Fried, Joel, "Government Loan and Guarantee Programs," Federal Reserve Bank of St. Louis *Review*
    (December 1983), 22–30.

Hand, John H., "Government Lending Agencies," in Murray E. Polakoff and Thomas A. Durkin (Eds.),
    Financial Institutions and Markets, 2nd ed. (Boston: Houghton Mifflin Co., 1981), 216–237.

PART IV

GOVERNMENT REGULATION AND THE FINANCIAL SYSTEM

CHAPTER **12**

The Role of Government as Financial Regulator

Since their emergence as significant economic entities, banks and other financial institutions have generally been highly regulated (and even directly controlled) by governments. In this chapter we are concerned with the rationale for such regulation and the nature of the present financial regulatory structure in the United States. We begin with a discussion of the economic basis for regulation and then identify certain historical aspects of depository institution regulation in the United States and describe its present structure. The chapter includes a description of the various financial regulatory agencies and their powers and responsibilities. (Note: The terms "bank" and "banking" are used for ease of exposition, but most of the discussion applies to all depository financial institutions.)

THE ECONOMIC BASIS FOR DEPOSITORY INSTITUTION REGULATION

If banking were not regulated to any greater extent than, say, retail grocery stores, our banking system would operate a great deal differently than it does. Banks could be formed and liquidated with minimal limitations on their entry and exit from the banking market. Inefficient and superfluous banks would go out of business. Competition would determine the prices and availability of banking services. Banks would also operate without geographic or portfolio restrictions, free to branch where they pleased and borrow and invest as they pleased. Capital structure would be the prerogative of management. Only the imperatives of the market would operate to direct branching, investment, and funding decisions. Competition would limit branches to the number congruent with public preferences. The cost of a bank's funds would be determined by its business and financial risk profile. And, of course, the penalty for either excessive or inadequate expansion of risk taking would be failure.

But banks (and other depository institutions) are not allowed to operate with such freedom. Both entry (the formation of new institutions) and exit (liquidation of institutions) are controlled and limited, as are geographic expansion and mergers with other institutions. The scope and nature of banking activities are regulated. Bank capital structure is monitored and restricted.

Why is banking—in a market economy—so closely regulated? The principal economic argument for such regulation is that banking, by its very nature, is prone to "market failure" (a tendency toward inherent instability and economic concentration). Further, according to this argument, the costs imposed on society by such market imperfections exceed the direct and indirect costs of regulating the banking system. The aspects of banking that have been alleged to constitute market imperfections relate to "economies of scale" in banking operations and "market failure" problems in bank-depositor relationships.

Competition and Economies of Scale in Banking

Competition is essential for a free market system to operate in optimal fashion. There must be no barriers to entry or operating restrictions of economic origin. The existence of significant economies of scale in banking operations would thus constitute a "natural" competitive constraint. (Other nongovernment barriers to entry—sharply differentiated products and very large capital requirements—clearly do not exist in banking.) When operating economies of scale exist, total costs increase less than proportionately to output: average unit costs decrease as output increases. Substantial economies of scale would lead to a concentration of banking and the withering away of the competitive environment necessary for maintenance of optimal cost–price structure and quality and availability of services. New, small banks could not enter the industry to compete with larger, established banks, and the latter would have a continuing incentive to grow larger through mergers and acquisitions in order to lower further their unit costs and enhance their competitive advantage. Anticompetitive collusion among the shrinking number of banks would likely prove an irresistible temptation. Another possible undesirable aspect of the banking consolidation that economies of scale would precipitate is a concentration of political and financial power in a relatively small number of banks.

Do significant economies of scale exist in banking? There have been numerous empirical studies of this question,[1] and no definitive evidence has emerged

---

[1] For reviews of these studies, see George J. Benston, "Economies of Scale in Banking," *Journal of Money, Credit, and Banking* (May 1972), 312–314; and George J. Benston, Gerald A. Hanweck, and David H. Humphrey, "Operating Costs in Commercial Banks," Federal Reserve Bank of Atlanta, *Economic Review* (November 1982).

that economies of scale exist to such a degree as to justify fears of the inevitability of massive banking concentration in the absence of regulatory restrictions on entry, merger, and branching. Then why is there so much regulation aimed at avoiding excessive concentration of economic and financial power? The answer lies not in theoretical considerations, but rather in the history of our banking system, the attitudes and beliefs of our citizens and their political representatives, and the perceived economic interests of various groups in our society.[2] Further, much of this regulation is really intended to prevent bank failures.

Economies of scale *are* believed to exist in the production and provision of communication, transportation, water, and power services. All these industries are regulated (in varying degrees) for this reason. Much of the regulation of depository institutions is attributable to supposed efforts to prevent the concentration that could result from possible economies of scale in banking, but it is of a different nature than the regulation of transportation, communication, and public utility firms. Regulation of the latter is intended to produce the pricing and quantity-of-production results of a competitive market. Regulation of banking is aimed at creating a competitive environment as well as simulating a competitive outcome, but without the exit aspects (failures) of truly competitive economic sectors. Charter, merger, and branching restrictions and other regulatory provisions are the principal instruments of this policy.

Entry (charter) restrictions regarding the establishment of new banking institutions are justified as preventing "overbanking," which presumably creates a threat to depository institution solvency as well as causing excessive amounts of resources to be devoted to banking activities. Entry into the financial marketplace by new banking competitors is thus controlled by regulators. For example, to obtain a bank charter (a permit to operate commercial banking functions), an applicant must, among other things, establish that (1) there is a need for a new bank, (2) the new bank will be profitable within a reasonable time, and (3) the chartering of the new bank will not cause substantial harm to existing banks in the market areas. The last requirement appears to be rather anomalous in a competitive system. Not only must those who wish to start a new bank show that there is a need for a new firm (for most industries, such need is demonstrated

---

[2]It has been suggested that much of the distrust that surrounds concentration of banking stems from the importance (and nature) of agriculture in the U.S. economy and the special significance of access to credit for farmers. Since the late nineteenth century, U.S. agriculture has been characterized by conditions of growing capital intensity and a chronic scarcity of capital resources. U.S. farmers viewed a decentralized banking system of many small banks as most amenable to their financing needs. The concern was that large banks would drain funds from agricultural areas and use them for industrial financing. Agricultural interests certainly played a large role in the successful effort in the early part of this century to restrict branching by banks and otherwise to limit consolidation of banking structure. They were joined in this effort by the smaller banks, which feared competition from their larger, "big city" counterparts. See Dwight B. Crane, Ralph C. Kimball, and William T. Gregor, *The Effects of Banking Deregulation* (Washington, D.C.: Association of Reserve City Bankers, 1983), 17–20.

after the fact by the market test), but they must also show that no harm will be done to their competitors (in most industries and objective *is* to harm competitors). The purpose of such restrictions on entry is, of course, to limit bank failure stemming from competition, even though the result is likely to reduce the efficiency of the financial system's operations. Although this reduction in number of competing firms does limit the extent and significance of failures, the limitations on entry provide existing firms with the opportunity to earn higher risk-adjusted returns than would be possible with fewer restrictions on entry. In effect, restrictions on entry allow inefficient firms to earn "normal" profits.

Restrictions pertaining to expansion through branching and merger are similarly justified. Although "preservation of competition" is usually the principal argument here, risk of failure (as well as the overall performance of firms) is obviously affected by the number and size distribution of depository institutions ("structure" of the industry). In evaluating requests by existing firms to merge or establish branches, as well as by organizers of new firms to establish additional competitors, the regulatory authorities evaluate the impact of these developments on the safety and stability of other firms in the industry. Limitations on branching and attitudes toward mergers affect the degree of concentration (the share of the market controlled by a few firms) and thereby the stability of individual institutions.

The Market Failure Problem: Bank "Runs"

A potential banking instability problem inherent in the bank-depositor relationship stems from the economic role of depository institutions. These financial intermediaries exist because of the unique characteristics of the assets they afford depositors—demand deposits (money) and highly liquid savings and time deposits. These deposits supply a combination of services and offer an interest return while providing liquidity and minimal risk to the depositor. The contractual relationship between the depositor and the depository institution assumes that funds deposited in demand accounts will indeed be available on demand and that other deposits (at face value) will be available to the depositor according to specified conditions.

Convenient and immediate exit from reliance on a particular agent is not always available to a contracting party, but it is certainly a feature of the depositor–depository institution relationship. A depositor can immediately withdraw demand funds at their face value, and time and saving deposits are also readily available. The cost of such withdrawals is minimal and certainly far less than the cost in time and money of monitoring activities of the institution in which funds are deposited to ensure their safety. The costs to depositors of gathering and analyzing credible information pertinent to the security of their funds exceeds the cost of withdrawing them from institutions.

In this context the "runs on banks" that have marked financial "panics" of past eras can be viewed as economically rational responses by depositors to real, apparent, or merely possible difficulties of banks. During such periods, when some banks experienced difficulty or outright failure, depositors in other institutions lacked access to credible assurances that *their* banks were solvent. Thus they acted to obtain their funds and triggered difficulty and failures for otherwise solvent institutions. This "domino effect" is a type of **external diseconomy,** as economists label such phenomena, stemming from the failure of banks.

To recapitulate, depositors place funds with banks and other depository institutions to secure deposit services and returns. In general, depositors lack convenient access to timely and relevant information about the financing and investing activities of institutions or the willingness and incentive to seek such information or combination thereof. Depositors must rely on the institution's management to maintain a degree of liquidity that ensures the safety of their funds. They have no control over the actions of the management or knowledge of management's plans and intentions. Management has an incentive to pursue institution profitability, perhaps at the risk of maintaining adequate liquidity. In this situation, and in view of the depositors' right to immediate access to their funds, it is both understandable and inevitable that they will exercise that right when they become concerned about the viability of their bank. And the exercise of the withdrawal right by enough depositors will precipitate the bank difficulties or failure that was previously only a possibility.

The Economic Significance of Banking Market Failure

The special aspect of bank deposits that makes banking so susceptible to depositor "runs"—the immediacy of their availability—is also the source of banking's special economic significance. Bank demand deposits are the principal component of the money supply. The transactions accounts offered by banks and other depository institutions offer the liquidity, mobility, and acceptability necessary for our economy's payments system to function with ease and efficiency. Further, banks are the primary source of liquidity for other financial institutions and are the "transmission belt" for the implementation of monetary policy. A safe, sound banking system is thus viewed as essential for a nation's monetary system and financial marketplace.

It has been observed that in many respects a bank's failure is less injurious to affected parties than is failure of other types of business ventures.[3] Bank employee's skills are readily transferable, and customers generally have readily available alternatives. In the absence of government protection of depositors (such as deposit insurance) the households, business firms, and governmental units holding deposits in a failed bank will likely suffer losses, but this is true of creditors

---

[3]See George J. Benston, "Deposit Insurance and Bank Failures," Federal Reserve Bank of Atlanta, *Economic Review* (March 1983), 4–17.

BANK RUNS, BANK PANICS, AND THE ECONOMY

The sharp increase in the number of failing and floundering commercial banks in the 1980s and the thrift crisis of the late 1980s has raised concerns about the stability of the financial system. Questions have been raised about the potential for bank runs and bank panics and for the possibility of a repetition of the Great Depression of the 1930s. In fact, as Ellis Tallman points out, bank runs and bank panics are quite different phenomena (and it is not at all clear that bank runs are undesirable). Moreover, the association between bank panics and economic depression—whether bank panics cause economic depression or whether economic depression causes the panic—is also not completely understood.[1]

Bank runs occur when depositors attempt to liquidate all their deposits at a particular institution. This would most likely occur in response to concern about the stability of that institution. The run, though, is from one institution to another. Since there is no net drain of reserves (the loss of reserves of one institution is completely counterbalanced by the gain of reserves at another institution), there need be no necessary destabilizing effects on the financial system. Bank runs may in fact be useful in that they provide market discipline at individual banks. The positive dimension of this market discipline is without social cost, however, only if the run does not spread to solvent banks and become a bank panic.

Bank panics occur when depositors attempt to convert bank liabilities to currency. Bank panics are a flight from deposits to currency and thus are unlike the flight involved in bank runs from one bank to another. Since a bank panic does reduce bank reserves for the entire banking system, it has the potential of destroying the intermediation process and causing a contraction of economic activity. Bank panics occurred quite frequently in the decades before the formation of the Federal Deposit Insurance Corporation in 1937. Since then, however, while a number of bank runs have occurred, there have been no bank panics.

There are a number of different views about the association between bank panics and economic contractions. The conventional wisdom is that bank panics deepen the steepness of an economic downturn. In this view, associated with the work of Milton Friedman and Ann Schwartz, bank panics reduce the amount of the aggregate money supply, producing a decline in real output, employment, and purchasing power. However, another view (referred to as real business cycle theory) emphasizes the effects of technological and other shocks on the economy that eventually affect the financial services sector. In this view, bank loans and deposits contract because of changed expectations regarding the outlook for the real economy.

Since bank panics are often associated with business cycle contractions, determining which is cause and which is effect is quite difficult. Nevertheless, in either view, bank panics play a role during periods of economic crisis.

---

[1]Ellis Tallman, "Some Unanswered Questions About Bank Panics," Federal Reserve Bank of Atlanta Economic Review (November/December 1988), 2–17.

of any failed firm. What makes bank failure different
There is ample historical evidence that widespread b?
on the entire economy, and in an unregulated bankir
to spread in domino fashion. It is presumed that this ⌐
and indirect costs of regulating bank failure risk.

EMERGENCE OF THE PRESENT REGULATORY FRAMEWORK

Much of the regulatory framework for depository institutions in this country reflects social and political, as well as economic, events and philosophy, but the economic crisis of the 1930s is largely responsible for its present structure.

The Banking Crisis of the 1930s

The number of banks in the United States reached the 30,000 mark in the early 1920s. Bank failures were common during the 1920s; more than 5700 banks failed between 1921 and 1929. Most of these were state banks in rural, agricultural communities. Failures and mergers (many of the latter serving to forestall failure) had winnowed the number of commercial banks to about 25,000 in 1929. The economic collapse known as the Great Depression began in that year.

More than 10,000 banks closed their doors between 1929 and 1933. From June 30, 1929, to June 30, 1933, the number of commercial banks declined from 24,970 to 14,208, and total bank deposits dropped 35 percent (from $49.4 billion to $32.1 billion).[4] The U.S. banking system appeared to be teetering on the verge of collapse. In late 1930 and early 1931, serious banking crises developed. A third "panic" erupted in 1933, after President Roosevelt had taken office. Roosevelt responded with the famous "bank holiday" (a nationwide closing of banks for a brief period), and a wave of bank reform actions was set in motion.

Banking Legislation of the 1930s

The Banking Acts of 1933 and 1935, two banking acts of great importance in U.S. financial history, were passed by Congress. The Banking Act of 1933 (Glass-Steagall Act) separated commercial and investment banking, gave increased regulatory authority to the Federal Reserve System, prohibited payment of interest on demand deposits, and raised the minimum capital of national banks. But most important, the 1933 law established the Federal Deposit Insurance Corporation (FDIC).

---

[4]Board of Governors of the Federal Reserve System. *All Bank Statistics, United States 1896–1955* (Washington, D.C.), 37.

The establishment of federal deposit insurance was intended to protect depositors and, by so doing, reduce the incidence of bank "runs." Insured depositors have no incentive to join in "runs" on institutions in which they have deposits. Insured depositors need concern themselves only with one item of information bearing on the safety of any depository institution—whether or not it is insured. Rightly or wrongly, deposit insurance is frequently credited with having stabilized the U.S. banking system in the wake of crises in the 1930s. An average of only 48 banks per year failed in the first five years after establishment of the FDIC (1934–1939). In 1933, 4000 banks had failed, following 1453 failures in 1932, 2293 in 1931, and 1350 in 1930. Even compared to the generally prosperous period from 1923 to 1929, when an average of 692 banks failed each year, the banking reforms of the 1930s appeared to be working well. During the postwar period, bank failures became relatively rare. From 1960 to 1981 an annual average of fewer than eight banks failed. Then the failure rate rose sharply, reflecting both economic change and deregulation actions. In 1982, 42 FDIC-insured banks failed; in 1983, 48; in 1984, 79; in 1985, 120; in 1986, 138; 1987, 184; and 200 in 1988. While this sharply higher failure rate in recent years is appropriately a matter for concerned attention, bank failures remain a manageable though troublesome phenomenon. In any event, in the U.S. system of a large number of banks (compared to other nations) it is both inevitable and healthy that some banks will fail—or else banks are either being unduly cautious in their lending policies or excessively subsidized by the federal government, or both.

Deposit insurance is funded by the levying of premiums by the insurance agencies on the total deposits of insured institutions. The 1933 Banking Act set FDIC premiums at one twelfth of one percent of the deposits (less certain adjustments) of insured banks. These assessments, to be remitted semiannually, were to provide funds for operating costs as well as maintenance of an insurance fund.

Another highly significant aspect of the Banking Act of 1933 was the section that prohibited commercial banks from underwriting issues of corporate securities and nonguaranteed revenue bonds of state and local governments. At the time, commercial and investment banking were almost totally integrated. The new law thus obliged the numerous institutions performing both functions to choose either commercial or investment banking as their line of business and divest themselves of the other. The author of this legislation (Senator Glass) had sought passage of similar measures before the 1930s, and the banking crisis of the latter period won him enough support to make it part of the 1933 reform package. The separation of commercial and investment banking was regarded as a means of reducing the risk of the former (as were most features of the 1933 act) and thus was intended to help restore public confidence in commercial banks. Further, some legislators were swayed by alleged abuses (of the conflict-of-interest variety) stemming from mixture of the two functions. And, as always, there was concern about the concentration of financial power in institutions exercising commercial banking, investment banking, and trust powers.

The Banking Act of 1935 was primarily intended to strengthen the Federal Reserve System and its monetary management power. The act gave the Federal Reserve Board expanded reserve requirement authority and the power to regulate the rate of interest paid by member banks on time deposits (Regulation Q). To strengthen the board's independence, the Comptroller of the Currency and the Secretary of the Treasury were removed from membership on the board.

The 1935 act also marked the end of easy entry into banking. Congress, seeking to curb the high rate of bank failure that had long characterized the U.S. banking system, gave the Comptroller of the Currency greater authority to exercise discretion in the granting of national bank charters. Applicants for a charter were henceforth to demonstrate the need for the proposed bank and make the case that the new bank would be successful without significantly injuring existing banks. If the applicant's case is not convincing to the Comptroller, or if the Comptroller's own investigation of these issues raises reasons for denial, the charter will not be issued.

Another element of the termination of free banking was the establishment of the FDIC. The FDIC does not charter banks, but it has discretion concerning which banks shall obtain deposit insurance. When a national bank is chartered, the FDIC can be expected to insure deposits of the new national bank. However, state bank applications for deposit insurance are carefully scrutinized and evaluated. To the extent that banks regard deposit insurance as essential for their operations (and the deposits of about 96 percent of U.S. banks are insured), the FDIC has a virtual veto power over the granting of state charters for banks.

The effect of greater restrictions on bank entry is evident in the record of new bank charters (see Fig. 12.1). During the 1920s, new bank charters granted averaged about 360 per year. From 1935 until the U.S. entry into World War II an average of only about 50 new banks were chartered each year. Although this sharp reduction in the rate of new bank chartering largely reflected depressed economic conditions (and thus a decline in requests for charters), it also reflected the fact that charters were more difficult to obtain. In the postwar expansion (1945–1960) the annual average of new bank charters remained below 100. Not until James Saxon became Comptroller of the Currency and relaxed national bank charter restrictions did new bank chartering approach pre-1935 levels. From 1962 to 1965, for example, 514 national banks were chartered.

A New Regulatory Framework

The 1933 and 1935 Banking Acts, in conjunction with previously existing regulation, set in place a regulatory structure that placed the following constraints on banks:

1. Restrictions on pricing of deposits.
2. Restrictions on entry and expansion.

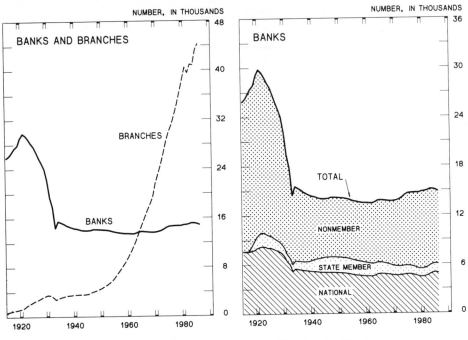

FIGURE 12.1   Commercial Banks in the United States (Number, by Class)

Source: Board of Governors of the Federal Reserve System, Historical Chart Book, *1988.*

3. Restrictions on scope and nature of activities.

4. Restrictions on leverage (minimum capital requirements) and other balance sheet elements.

5. Restrictions on geographic expansion.

Some of these restrictions stem from the traditional U.S. concern over concentration of financial power, with vociferous support in more recent decades from groups that are likely to suffer economic injury from relaxation of these restrictions. Branching and merger restrictions are, of course, the primary example of this aspect of U.S. regulation, but a number of activity restrictions are related to financial power concerns (and fears of competition) as well as failure risk.

The bulk of the restrictions on the formation and operations of U.S. depository institutions relates to curbing failure risk. The purpose of this framework, law, and set of regulations was to limit the degree of risk that a depository institution could take in the assets it acquired and in the securities it offered to the

THE RISE AND FALL OF REGULATION Q

Regulation Q, the Federal Reserve regulation that limited interest paid on deposits at commercial banks, quietly passed away in March 1986. In fact, however, the elimination of Regulation Q had been set into motion by the Depository Institutions Deregulation and Monetary Control Act (DIDMCA) of 1980, which created the Depository Institutions Deregulation Committee (DIDC), the main duty of which was to phase out the regulation over a period of six years.

The origins of Regulation Q go back to the Banking Act of 1933 and 1935, which prohibited the payments of interest on demand deposits and gave the Federal Reserve the power to set interest rate ceilings on time and savings deposits at commercial banks. These restrictions were designed to achieve a variety of purposes, including increasing bank profits by reducing the competition for deposits. The feeling also existed that excessive competition for deposits might cause banks to acquire riskier assets. In fact, however, from 1933 through 1965, Regulation Q interest rate ceilings were of limited significance, since market rates for deposits were generally below the ceiling levels.

The principal purpose of Regulation Q was altered in 1966 at the same time that market rates began to approach and exceed ceiling rates. In that year, interest rate ceilings were imposed for the first time on savings banks and savings and loans. Regulators and other policymakers were concerned about the allocation of credit, especially between business and mortgage lending, and about the effects of the competition between banks and thrifts for deposits on the level of interest rates.

From late 1966 through March 1986, ceiling rates on some categories of deposits were kept below market rates on Treasury securities. However, the goal of affecting the allocation of credit between business and mortgage lending was not achieved. Moreover, the policy had undesirable wealth effects on the small saver. Wealthier investors shifted their deposits to money market securities when market rates exceeded Regulation Q ceilings. Small savers, lacking enough funds to meet the minimum denomination requirements of money market instruments, were forced to earn below-market rates on their bank and thrift deposits. As a result, these small savers—frequently the elderly—lost several billion dollars in potential interest earnings.

The problems caused by the Regulation Q ceilings intensified in the late 1970s as inflation and interest rates rose to higher and higher levels. The regulatory authorities responded in a limited way by increasing the ceilings on some types of time and savings deposits in denominations of $100,000 or less. In addition, the Money Market Certificate, which had a floating rate ceiling, was created in 1978.

However, the persistence of high interest rates and the explosive growth of funds at money market funds in the late 1970s made it evident that Regulation Q could neither restrain competition for deposits nor increase the supply of mortgage credit. Congress finally responded by passing DIDMCA (1980), which provided for the gradual phase-out of Regulation Q over a six-year period. Authority to determine the pattern for the elimination of Regulation Q was placed in the hands of the Deregulation Committee, which was composed of the Secretary of the Treasury and Chairpersons of the

Federal Reserve Board, Federal Deposit Insurance Corporation, Federal Home Loan Bank Board, and National Credit Union Administrator.

Some of the actions of the Deregulation Committee were mandated by Congress, including the establishment of NOW accounts in 1981, and the Money Market Deposit Accounts and super NOWs in 1982 (provided for by the Depository Institutions Act of 1982). Ceilings on the other types of accounts were removed gradually from 1982 through March 1986. By that time the only remaining restriction on the interest rates paid on deposits was (and is) the prohibition of interest payments in demand deposits, which was not affected by DIDMCA.

Source: Adapted from R. Alton Gilbert. "Requiem for Regulation Q: What It Did and Why It Passed Away," Federal Reserve Bank of St. Louis Review (February 1986), 22–37.

public in order to raise funds. These limitations are most severe for the depository financial institutions—commercial banks, savings and loans, mutual savings banks, and credit unions—but they also apply to many nondepository financial institutions. Although there have always been regulatory limitations on the degree of risk that can be assumed by financial institutions, the restrictions became much more severe following the banking legislation of the early 1930s. (In recent decades, some of these limitations on the risk exposure of individual institutions have been relaxed to some extent.)

A few examples might be useful in explaining the limitations on risk produced by the regulation of different financial institutions. Commercial banks may extend credit only through acquiring financial assets that are "nonspeculative" in nature. If municipal securities in the portfolio are rated by one of the rating agencies (such as Moody's or Standard & Poor's), they must be at least of "investment grade." And if financial assets in the portfolio are not rated, then management is responsible for maintaining adequate credit files to demonstrate to the regulatory authorities that their credit extensions represent "sound credit." Not only are there limitations on the quality of individual financial assets held within the portfolio of the financial institutions, but there are also restrictions on the fraction of the portfolio devoted to any borrower. For example, national banks may not lend more than 15 percent (only 10 percent until 1982) of their capital to any one borrower. In addition, national banks may not have real estate loans that exceed their total capital position or 70 percent of their time and savings deposits, whichever is larger.

From a broader perspective the bank regulatory agencies periodically evaluate the liquidity position of the bank, the adequacy of the capital base it has available to offset losses, the quality of its management, and other dimensions of the bank that bear on the risk of default and thereby on the riskiness of the securities offered to the public by these financial institutions. And, of course, a bank or savings and loan association cannot even receive a charter unless it meets minimum capital standards established by the regulatory authorities. Similar types of restrictions on risk bearing and supervisory oversight also apply to other depository institutions.

Still another aspect of risk regulation is the tradition of outside examination. Periodic and unannounced inspections or examinations by officials of the regulatory agencies (examiners) occur at all types of insured depository institutions. The purpose of these examinations is to appraise the "quality of management" of the organization in both its financial and its nonfinancial dimensions. More specifically, the purpose of the examinations is to identify problem areas within the organization and eliminate the problems before they threaten the viability of the organization. The adequacy of internal controls to prevent the theft of assets is evaluated. The extent to which the institution is conforming to the detailed regulations designed to reduce risk and achieve other objectives is examined, and the quality of the asset portfolio is scrutinized. Loans are evaluated as good, substandard, doubtful, or loss. If any asset is of unsatisfactory quality ("loss"), the institution is forced to write off the asset against its capital account. And if the capital account proves inadequate, the institution is forced to raise additional capital through the sale of stock or through other means, such as greater retention of earnings (as opposed to the payment of cash dividends to stockholders).

At the federal level, supervision and examination responsibilities for commercial banks are shared by the Office of the Comptroller of the Currency (OCC), the Federal Reserve system, and the FDIC. The OCC has primary responsibility for national banks, and the FDIC has primary responsibility for insured nonmember state banks. (In the case of state banks, surveillance jurisdiction is shared with state agencies.) The essence of the supervision process is reflected in the bank rating system developed for the Uniform Financial Institutions Rating System. Called CAMEL (for the rating components of capital, asset quality, management, earnings, and liquidity), this rating system results in a composite rating of 1 to 5 for banks. (CAMEL is also used for federally regulated nonbank depository institutions.) An institution with a composite rating of 1 is considered sound in every respect, and at the other end of the rating spectrum a composite rating of 5 applies to institutions considered on the verge of failure. The purpose of the rating system is to help identify institutions that warrant special supervisory attention and concern.

Regulation Since the Bank Reforms of the 1930s

The structure and nature of U.S. banking changed dramatically in the 1930s as a result of the wave of bank failures and the reform legislation it evoked. The reduction in the number of banks proved to be enduring, partly as a result of increased entry restrictions. Figure 12.1 indicates a pattern of declining number (except for a postwar blip of expansion) until recent years. An expanded, tighter net of regulation was cast over depository institutions. Deposit insurance became a salient and, indeed, central characteristic of the U.S. banking system. Bank failures became rare (until the 1980s).

Most of the changes wrought by the banking reforms of the 1930s remain in place today. Some (such as the prohibition of interest-bearing transactions accounts) were undone by the DIDMCA of 1980. Others, such as the separation of commercial and investment banking, are under significant pressure for change. But the increased authority of the Federal Reserve Board, deposit insurance, and other features of the Banking Acts of 1933 and 1935 appear to have become permanent fixtures of our financial system.

After the reforms of the 1930s, banking entered a relatively tranquil period. Banks, like the rest of the U.S. economy, remained generally depressed until World War II. Not until the late 1940s did banking regain its pre-Depression vitality. The ratio of bank loans to assets (only 16 percent in 1945 compared to a 1925 ratio of 63 percent) began to rise steadily throughout the 1950s. This resurgence of banking continued in the vigorous economic expansion of the 1960s, with banks becoming more aggressive, competitive, and less averse to risk. Dramatic expansion of foreign banking activities by U.S. banks occurred, and banks sought new avenues of profitable growth outside traditional banking.

The renewed aggressive and energetic posture of banking inevitably created tensions within the regulatory framework shaped in the 1930s. Banks sought, often successfully, to circumvent regulatory restraints through various organizational and financial innovations. The most important organizational innovation was the formation of holding companies by banks in order to enter service and geographic markets from which banks were barred by state or federal legislation.

Bank Holding Companies.   The Banking Act of 1933 included provisions for Federal Reserve Board supervision and regulation of bank holding companies that held Federal Reserve member banks, but these limited powers did not pertain to formation and expansion of such companies. Not until the Bank Holding Company Act of 1956 was legislation enacted for significant federal regulation over the formation of bank holding companies (BHCs) and their acquisition of additional banks. The act defined a bank holding company as an organization owning 25 percent or more of the stock of two or more banks (thus excluding "one-bank holding companies"). The Fed was given power to supervise bank holding companies, and Fed approval was required for both new acquisitions of banks and the formation of new holding companies. The legislation listed factors to be considered by the Fed in evaluating proposed holding company acquisitions. These factors included the current and prospective financial condition of the holding company and bank in question, needs of the community, and "preservation of banking competition." Further, the 1956 Douglas Amendment to the Bank Holding Company Act prohibits bank holding companies from acquiring an affiliate bank in another state unless the latter's laws permit such entry.

The 1956 legislation was intended to halt interstate banking expansion (existing holdings were "grandfathered"), separate nonbanking activities from bank holding company activities, and avoid concentration of financial resources in holding companies. However, in a classic example of the sometimes perverse consequences of regulatory action, the effect was quite different.

It seems surprising that relatively few bank holding companies were formed before the 1956 legislation, considering their freedom from the geographic and activity restrictions that characterized bank regulation. (In 1954 there were only forty-six bank holding companies.) The reason the device was not used more often lay in the uncertain status of bank holding companies. The pressure for new restrictive legislation from unit banking groups and others and the Fed's stated position on regulation of bank holding companies made it clear that such legislation was likely. Since severe restrictions and even abolition were possible consequences of a new statute, bankers were wary of the holding company form of organization. When the new legislation did emerge in the Bank Holding Act of 1956, it was hardly draconian and mainly clarified the status of BHCs. As a result, it actually *encouraged* their formation and expansion as a means of overcoming geographical and functional barriers.

There was also a major loophole in the 1956 act: bank holding companies controlling only one bank were not included. Since such exclusion of one-bank holding companies (OBHCs) continued their freedom to engage in nonbanking activities, a large increase in the number of OBHCs resulted (more than 1000 existed by 1970). OBHCs could establish loan affiliates across state lines, sell debt instruments not subject to interest rate ceilings, and otherwise engage in activities proscribed to individual banks and (after 1956) multibank holding companies (MBHCs). This loophole was closed with a 1970 amendment of the Bank Holding Company Act of 1956, which brought OBHCs under the purview of the latter act. (Most of the 1973 surge in the number of registered holding companies shown in Table 12.1 stems from inclusion of OHBCs.) The 1970 amendments

TABLE 12.1 Number of Registered Bank Holding Companies, Banks, and Branches Controlled, and Total Deposits (For Selected Years 1957–1987)

End	Number of Registered Holding Companies	Banks Controlled	Total Branches	Deposits (Billions)	Total Deposits as Percent of Total U.S. Commercial Bank Deposits
1957	50	417	851	$ 15.1	7.5%
1970	121	895	3,260	78.1	16.2
1973	1,677	3,097	15,374	446.6	65.4
1979	2,478	4,280	23,765	744.7	67.8
1987	6,503	9,322	41,397	1,787.0	90.2

Source: Board of Governors of the Federal Reserve System, Annual Statistical Digest, *various issues.*

also authorized the Fed to develop a new (somewhat liberalized) list of allowable activities of BHCs.

Today, the bank holding company form of organization is predominant in U.S. commercial banking, with the nation's more than 6,400 BHCs accounting for about 90 percent of all domestic bank deposits (according to the Fed's 1988 *Annual Report*). BHCs have also become a powerful engine of financial innovation and resistance to regulatory restraints.

Consumer Protection Regulation

In the 1960s and early 1970s, a wave of environmental, worker protection, equal opportunity, and consumer protection legislation was enacted by the Congress. Virtually all business firms in the United States were affected, including depository institutions. The principal legislation directed at the financial services industry concerned borrower protection and potential discrimination by lenders. The Truth in Lending Act of 1968 required full disclosure of credit costs and terms on consumer loans. The act also provided for regulation of the content of credit advertising. The Fair Credit Billing Act of 1974 regulated credit card distribution, terms, and cardholder liability. (The Fed's Regulation Z details the features and administrative aspects of these laws.)

Other financial service consumer protection legislation followed. The Fair Credit Reporting Act of 1970 provided for regulation of credit reports furnished to creditors, employers, and insurers. The Real Estate Settlement Procedures Act of 1974 (as amended in 1976) required mortgage lenders to provide borrowers with a detailed statement of lending charges. The Right to Financial Privacy Act of 1978 limited external access to banking records of depositors.

The Fair Housing Act of 1968 forbade mortgage lenders to consider race, color, religion, gender, or national origin in loan decisions. The Equal Credit Opportunity Act of 1974 (as amended in 1976) broadened this antidiscriminatory provision to all credit provisions. The Community Reinvestment Act of 1977 (in effect) forbade discrimination by home lenders on the basis of age or location of buildings and requires regulators to consider the degree to which an institution is satisfying community credit needs when evaluating requests from that institution to branch or merge.

This aspect of the regulatory framework of depository institutions is largely independent of the rest of the structure. These regulations generally stem from political and social (rather than economic) objectives. To the extent that society accepts and endorses pursuit of these goals, the relevant economic issue is how they can most efficiently be achieved.

The Competitive Equality Banking Act of 1987

In 1987 Congress responded to a variety of banking-related issues with legislation entitled the Competitive Equality Banking Act (CEBA). The principal purpose of CEBA was to deny certain types of financial institutions competitive advantages that they had forged out of past regulatory loopholes—particularly so-called "nonbank banks." The Act extended the definition of "bank" under the Bank Holding Company Act to include any institution insured by the FDIC as well as any institution that both accepted transaction accounts and made commercial loans. (Only the latter distinction had previously served as the legal definition of "bank.") CEBA included a variety of miscellaneous provisions, including reaffirmation of Congressional intent to back federally insured deposits with the full faith and credit of the United States, measures to recapitalize the FSLIC, regulations pertaining to the time period in which banks must make deposited funds available to depositors, and an extension of the permissibility of emergency interstate acquisitions of failing banks by out-of-state institutions.

REGULATION OF NONBANK DEPOSITORY INSTITUTIONS

To this point our discussion of the nature and evolving scope and structure of depository institution regulation in this country has focused on commercial banks. By and large, the regulatory system for nonbank depository institutions parallels that for commercial banks and has evolved for much the same reasons and in the same manner. However, there are a number of important differences in regulatory features for the latter group of financial institutions.

The Regulatory Structure

The important nonbank depository institutions are, of course, savings and loan associations, mutual savings banks, and credit unions. A brief discussion of the regulatory structure for each type of institution follows.

Savings and Loan Associations. The dual (both federal and state) system of bank chartering and regulation also exists for savings and loan associations (S & Ls). The proportion of state and federal chartering is roughly half and half. More than 90 percent of all S & Ls are insured by the FSLIC, and these insured institutions account for more than 98 percent of all deposits in savings and loan associations. Federally chartered institutions are regulated and supervised by the Federal Home Loan Bank Board (or FHLBB), which was established in 1932 on the basis of charter. The FHLBB also regulates federally insured, state-chartered institutions (since the FSLIC is part of the FHLBB and also since many state-chartered S & Ls choose to belong to the FHLB system).[5] State-chartered S & Ls are also regulated and supervised by state commissions with various titles.

The regulatory system functions much like the one for commercial banks.

---

[5] As this is written, Congress is considering legislation that would make the FHLBB part of the Treasury Department and bring the FSLIC under the administrative control of the FDIC.

Interstate branching is forbidden, and intrastate mergers and branching are subject to approval. (In general, restrictions on the latter are much less stringent than those on banks.) A similar system for supervision and examination exists, with institutions (like banks) being subject to capital requirements and portfolio restrictions.

Until recent years, S & Ls have been obliged to operate within a framework of severe portfolio restrictions aimed at concentrating lending of these institutions in the form of residential mortgages. Such mortgages, as a result, came to constitute about 80 percent of all S & L assets. (This ratio has declined in recent years.) The FHLBB also required maintenance of prescribed minimum liquidity ratios, loan-loss reserve ratios, and net worth ratios.

Entry restrictions on S & Ls are very similar to those imposed on commercial banks. As noted above, branching regulations for S & Ls are more liberal than those for banks. The FHLBB's policy has been to permit branches for federally chartered S & Ls, unless the state of residence prohibits branches for *all* depository institutions (not just state-chartered S & Ls).

Savings and loan associations have been favored by law and regulation in several respects. Until 1966, S & Ls were not subject to Regulation Q–type ceiling interest rates, and the imposition of these rates (by the Interest Rate Adjustment Act of 1966) was meant to protect the institutions from rate competition. The S & Ls were allowed to pay interest rates that were 0.25 percent higher than commercial banks could offer for deposits. (Deposit rate deregulation after 1980 ended this advantage.) Further, the FHLB has been a significant supplier of funds to S & Ls through what are called **advances.** Unlike Fed discount window lending to banks, which is viewed as temporary, the FHLB funding is quasi-permanent.

The savings and loan industry has also been the recipient of various tax breaks. It was not until 1952 that S & Ls (and mutual savings banks) were made subject to the federal corporate income tax. Even then, these thrift institutions generally avoided federal income taxes until 1962 by means of loan-loss reserve adjustments. However, tax legislation in 1962 and 1969 significantly increased S & L payments of corporate income tax, although a relatively liberal loan-loss deductibility provision remained available to S & Ls having a specified percentage of their total assets in residential mortgages and liquid assets.[6]

The liberalization of depository institution regulation in the 1980s gave sig-

---

[6]The 1969 legislation allowed S & Ls and MSBs to add up to 40 percent of taxable income to loan-loss reserves tax free if 82 percent (for S & Ls) or 72 percent (for MSBs) of assets were held in qualified form, the 40 percent deduction being reduced by 0.75 percent for each percentage point below 82 percent and the 72 percent down to 60 percent (at which point there was no deduction). The Tax Reform Act of 1986 scaled down the qualifying percentage of total assets from 82 percent to 60 percent and set the write-off percentage of taxable income at a flat 8 percent.

BUSH'S BAILOUT PLAN FOR S & Ls*

The first major economic crisis to confront the Bush Administration after the new President took office in 1989 was dealing with the devastated savings and loan industry. On February 6, 1989, President Bush announced his plan for dealing with the shattered S & L industry. The centerpiece of the President's plan was the creation of a new federal agency to raise money to cover the cost of dealing with insolvent S & Ls. The new agency would issue federally guaranteed bonds, the principal being paid by the thrift industry and most of the interest being paid by the U.S. Treasury (i.e., taxpayers). Both banks and thrifts would pay higher deposit insurance premiums. More than 350 insolvent thrifts would be closed or merged. The regulatory structure for thrifts would be overhauled, the FDIC taking administrative control of the FSLIC and the Federal Home Loan Bank Board becoming part of the Treasury Department. The FDIC would assume regulatory responsibility for thrifts and would set capital and accounting standards similar to those of commercial banks.

The idea of a taxpayer bailout for S & Ls generated little enthusiasm on Capitol Hill, but few legislators offered alternatives to the President's proposals. There was, however, considerable skepticism about the projected cost of the plan. Many observers thought that the eventual costs of dealing with the thrift crisis would be much higher than the estimate of the Bush Administration—more than $300 billion in the view of some analysts.

*See the "Postscript" at the end of the book.

nificant new lending powers to S & Ls. Indeed, one reason for these financial deregulatory efforts was to provide an avenue for the thrift industry to return to profitability after the difficulties of the late 1970s. Unfortunately, many S & Ls continued to sustain losses, and a large number of the institutions actually became even less profitable as the result of failures in the use of their new lending powers. The costs of dealing with failed thrifts depleted the coffers of the FSLIC, obliging the agency to ask Congress for new funding in 1987. The issuance of bonds by a newly created federal agency, the Financing Corporation (FICO), provided $10.8 billion. This amount proved to be grossly inadequate. In 1989, newly elected President Bush was obliged to confront the thrift crisis early in his term. As the 1980s drew to a close, the future of the FSLIC, the FHLBB and, indeed, the thrift industry itself remained uncertain.

Mutual Savings Banks. Although chartered and generally supervised by states, most mutual savings banks (MSBs) have availed themselves of FDIC deposit insurance and FHLB system membership. Thus federal regulation and supervision reaches many MSBs through their association with these federal agencies. As in the case of savings and loans, MSBs have been viewed as primarily mortgage lending institutions and regulated accordingly. Entry and branching restrictions, while varying somewhat from state to state, generally parallel those of S & Ls. MSBs also share the tax advantages available to S & Ls.

Mutual savings banks in New England (along with credit unions in that region) had the distinction of serving as subjects of an experiment in interest-bearing transactions in the 1970s. At this time, MSBs in Massachusetts and New Hampshire began offering negotiated order of withdrawal (NOW) accounts and won state court tests of their right to do so. The U.S. Congress then passed legislation limiting NOW accounts and credit union share drafts to New England. In 1980, NOW accounts were permitted nationwide.

Credit Unions.   The National Credit Union Act of 1970 established the National Credit Union Administration (NCUA) for the purpose of insuring, regulating, and supervising credit unions. Credit unions may be either federally chartered (about 13,000 since 1934) or state chartered (about 9000 in 46 states). All federally chartered credit unions must now have NCUA share insurance. Not quite half of the state-chartered credit unions have NCUA insurance, but many are insured through state plans or private insurance companies.

Until recently, the lending and investment powers of credit unions were highly restricted and essentially limited to short-term consumer loans, U.S. Treasury securities, and insured accounts of thrift institutions and commercial banks. In 1977, amendments to the Federal Credit Union Act liberalized lending powers to include residential mortgages, mobile homes, and home improvements. Further liberalization came with the DIDMCA of 1980.

THE REGULATORY STRUCTURE: SUMMARY AND ASSESSMENT

In retrospect, it is clear that three principal policy goals have shaped the regulatory system for depository institutions in the United States:

1. To prevent banking market failure;
2. To prevent concentration of financial power; and
3. To use nonbank depository institutions for limited, specialized purposes—specifically, residential mortgage lending in the case of savings and loan associations and mutual savings banks.

Until the near-collapse of the banking system in the 1930s, government regulation focused primarily on the second goal listed above. Free entry into banking and restrictions on mergers and branching were the principal means to this policy end. The result of these policies has been a very large number of depository institutions and the establishment of vested interests that can always be counted on to oppose measures likely to broaden the geographic (and functional) span of competition.

The banking crisis of the Great Depression led to greater emphasis on bank safety in regulation. The main thrust of the 1930s "reforms" was anticompetitive in nature and (with the exception of the termination of free banking) did little to disturb the system of restrictions already in place. The 1930s legislation simply broadened and tightened the regulatory net and, by instituting deposit insurance, gave the federal government a direct and enduring interest in the risk profile of most banks.

The third objective emerged to become highly significant in the post–World War II period as a response to the public demand for housing. In addition to the shaping of an expanded number of S & Ls to serve this purpose, deposit rate controls were employed as an instrument to this end. It is likely that the regulation-spurred expansion of these institutions came at the expense of commercial banks.

Out of these goals and the means employed to achieve them, and mixed with the U.S. federal system and pluralistic power structure, came a very complex and fragmented regulatory system monitoring and seeking to control a complex and fragmented financial system. We consider next the particular agencies that administer this regulatory structure.

THE FUNCTIONS OF REGULATORY AGENCIES

The substantial amount of detailed regulation of the behavior of individual financial institutions and markets creates a need for appropriate organizations to police and enforce the regulations. In the United States a variety of government regulatory agencies perform these functions. These agencies, frequently specialized along the same lines as the institutions they regulate, exist at both federal and state levels. Moreover, there is considerable overlap among the functions of the regulatory agencies. Indeed, there is overlapping of function not only between federal and state government agencies but also between various federal agencies themselves.

Figure 12.2 indicates both the specialized nature of the regulatory agencies, especially of those that regulate commercial banks, and the degree of overlapping regulation. Note that the degree of regulation is greatest for the depository

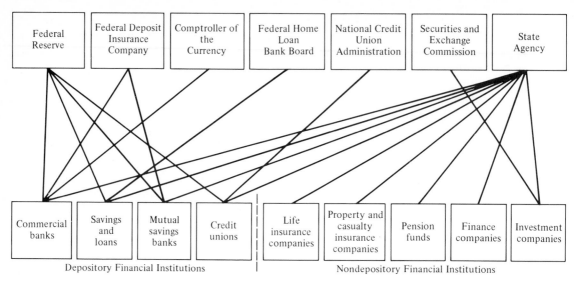

FIGURE 12.2   The Framework of Financial Regulation

financial institutions, reflecting concern for the safety and liquidity of the public's deposits. The overlapping nature of regulation is also most prevalent for the depository financial institutions. However, the amount of regulation is substantial for all financial institutions.

Depository Financial Institutions

Government regulatory agencies that affect the behavior of depository financial institutions exist at both federal and state government levels. At the federal level, three agencies are concerned with regulation of commercial banks: the Federal Reserve System, the Comptroller of the Currency, and the Federal Deposit Insurance Corporation (FDIC). Each state has some agency concerned with bank regulation, usually referred to as the State Banking Commission. As we discussed earlier, the Federal Reserve is the nation's central bank and has sole control over monetary policy. However, the Fed also has substantial supervisory authority over commercial banks (which it shares with other bank regulatory authorities) and sole control over bank holding companies. The Comptroller of the Currency, the oldest of the federal bank regulatory authorities, was established in 1863, when the U.S. Congress passed legislation permitting federal chartering of national banks. The Comptroller has varying supervisory powers with regard to these federally chartered banks. The Federal Deposit Insurance Corporation was established in 1933 to provide deposit insurance for commercial and mutual savings banks. As a part of that function, the FDIC has developed extensive regulations applicable to the activities of banks under its supervision.

The overlapping of supervision at state and federal levels of government reflects the fact that a new bank may be chartered by either the federal or a state government. This procedure—known as the **dual banking system**—immensely complicates the regulation of commercial banking in the United States. If chartered by the federal government, the bank is referred to as a **national bank**, and it must conform to the regulations governing national banks. If the bank is chartered by one of the state governments, it is referred to as a **state bank**, and it must conform to the regulations governing state banks in the state in which the charter was granted. The degree of overlap also reflects the historical evolution of regulation by which three different regulatory agencies were created at different periods of time with different functions: the Comptroller, Federal Reserve, and FDIC.

A state-chartered bank is always subject to regulation and examination by the appropriate state bank-regulating authority. If the state bank is insured (as almost all are), the bank is further subject to the supervision of the Federal Deposit Insurance Corporation. If the state bank is a member of the Federal Reserve (as many are), the bank is also subject to the supervision of the Federal Reserve. The situation can be equally complex for a national bank. The principal supervising agency for a national bank is the Comptroller of the Currency. However, every nationally chartered bank must be insured (hence subject to the supervision of the Federal Deposit Insurance Corporation) and must be a member of the Federal Reserve (hence subject to the supervision of the Federal Reserve System). Standardization of procedures for federal examinations has been attempted by the Federal Financial Institutions Examination Council (FFIEC) established by the Financial Institution and Interest Rate Control Act of 1978.

Similar, though less extensive, overlapping of regulatory authority occurs for the other depository financial institutions. Savings and loan associations are chartered and regulated at both state and federal levels, although there is only one relevant federal regulatory agency, the Federal Home Loan Bank Board and its subsidiary, the Federal Savings and Loan Insurance Corporation. Credit unions are chartered and regulated at both state and federal levels. At the federal level the National Credit Union Administration (NCUA), established in 1970, exercises chartering, regulatory, and supervisory powers for federal credit unions. The National Credit Union Share Insurance Fund (NCUSIF), administered by the NCUA, insures funds in credit union accounts up to a maximum of $100,000. Exhibit 12.1 offers a sketch of the regulatory agencies for financial institutions.

EXHIBIT 12.1 ∎
Regulatory Agencies and Their Scope

Financial institutions are chartered and supervised by various agencies. The following tables give a general explanation of which agency oversees particular areas of regulatory responsibility in financial institutions and provide some background on the agencies themselves. For detailed information on their duties, please contact the regulatory agency directly.

FEDERAL RESERVE SYSTEM

The Federal Reserve System is the central banking system of the United States. It was created by the Federal Reserve Act approved December 23, 1913. The system includes twelve regional Reserve Banks, their twenty-five branches, and the Board of Governors, headquartered in Washington, D.C.

Federal Reserve Banks perform various services for financial institutions, act as fiscal agent for the United States, regulate and supervise member banks and bank holding companies, issue Federal Reserve notes, and hold deposits of and make loans to financial institutions.

COMPTROLLER OF THE CURRENCY

The Office of the Comptroller of the Currency was created by an act of Congress approved February 23, 1863, to be an integral part of the National Banking System.

The most important functions of the Comptroller relate to the organization, operation and liquidation of national banks. The Comptroller's approval is required by law in connection with the organization of new national banks, the conversion of state-chartered banks into national banks, and consolidations or mergers of banks.

FEDERAL DEPOSIT INSURANCE CORPORATION (FDIC)

The FDIC is an independent executive agency established by the Banking Act of 1933 to insure bank deposits. It is headed by a three-member board of directors. The President appoints two members (with approval of the Senate) for terms of six years. The third member is the Comptroller of the Currency.

The FDIC, in addition to insuring funds up to $100,000, has important supervisory and examination powers and acts as receiver for all national banks placed in receivership. The FDIC acts as receiver for state banks if asked to do so by state authorities.

FEDERAL HOME LOAN BANK SYSTEM (FHLB)

The Federal Home Loan Bank System was created in 1932 to provide a central credit system for nonbank mortgage lending institutions. The system is governed by a three-member board. This board, located in Washington, D.C., along with twelve regional Federal Home Loan Banks and member institutions form the system. The system supervises savings and loans, extends loans to them to meet liquidity requirements, provides financial services and administers the FSLIC and the Federal Home Loan Mortgage Corporation.

EXHIBIT 12.1 *(continued)* ▬▬▬▬▬▬▬

FEDERAL SAVINGS AND LOAN INSURANCE CORPORATION (FSLIC)

The FSLIC was established June 27, 1934. The corporation functions under the direction of the Federal Home Loan Bank Board. The FSLIC insures savings accounts up to $100,000 for insured savings and loan associations.

The FSLIC also is authorized to make loans to savings and loans experiencing financial difficulty and, if necessary, act as receiver in cases of liquidation.

NATIONAL CREDIT UNION ADMINISTRATION (NCUA)

The National Credit Union Administration was established as an independent agency within the executive branch of the federal government on March 10, 1970. This agency has primary responsibility for chartering, regulating, and supervising credit unions.

NATIONAL CREDIT UNION SHARE INSURANCE FUND (NCUSIF)

The NCUSIF, created by a law passed on October 19, 1970, was established as a revolving fund in the Treasury of the United States under the management of the NCUA. It insures funds in credit union accounts up to $100,000.

Financial Institutions and Their Regulators

	Chartering and Licensing	Branching		Mergers and Acquisitions		Deposit Insurance	Supervision and Examination
		Intrastate	Interstate	Intrastate	Interstate		
National Banks	Comptroller	Comptroller	[1]	Comptroller	[3]	FDIC	Comptroller
State Member Banks	State Banking Department	Federal Reserve/ State Banking Department	[1]	Federal Reserve/ State Banking Department	[3]	FDIC	Federal Reserve/ State Banking Department
Bank Holding Companies	Federal Reserve			Federal Reserve/ State Banking Department	Federal Reserve/ State Banking Department[4]		Federal Reserve
Savings & Loan Associations (Federal/ State)	FHLB/ State Banking Department	FHLB/FSLIC/ State Banking Department	[2]	FHLB/ State Banking Department	FSLIC[3]	FSLIC/ State Insurance Funds	FHLB/ State Banking Department
Credit Unions (Federal/ State)	NCUA/ State Banking Department	No approval necessary		NCUA/ State Banking Department	NCUA/ State Banking Department[3]	NCUSIF/ State Insurance Funds	NCUA/ State Banking Department

[1] Not applicable.

[2] Generally prohibited for federal thrifts.

[3] The FDIC, FSLIC, and NCUA may arrange interstate acquisitions or mergers of closed or failing federally insured institutions. Details differ across type of institution.

[4] Only if allowed by the state where the bank being acquired is located.

Source: Federal Reserve Bank of New York, *Depository Institutions and Their Regulators,* 1985.

Nondepository Financial Institutions

The various types of nondepository financial institutions are chartered only at the state level, and they are regulated principally by state government, as illustrated in Fig. 12.2. This regulation encompasses specific types of statutory law, such as the "legal list," which limits the types of securities that insurance companies may acquire, and case law, such as the "prudent man" rule, which for decades has influenced the behavior of financial institutions. Since the early 1930s the federally created Securities and Exchange Commission (SEC) has exerted considerable influence on the behavior of financial institutions and markets. The influence on individual institutions is most direct for investment companies (mutual funds), but the SEC affects the behavior of both depository and nondepository financial institutions through affecting their ability to raise funds by offering securities to the public.

The SEC was created to ensure the full disclosure of information to investors prior to the acquisition of securities. In essence, the SEC requires that all securities sold interstate in the United States (with the exception of securities of certain specified types and securities that raise less than a specified amount of funds) be registered with the SEC. In this registration the issuer of the proposed securities must provide relevant financial and nonfinancial data, including potential conflict of interest by insiders and a description of the risk elements involved in the purchase of the securities. Until the registration has become effective (during the period when the SEC staff is reviewing the material), the securities may not be sold. After the registration becomes effective, securities may be sold only after a prospectus containing the relevant information from the registration statement is provided to the purchasers. After the sale, moreover, purchasers may sue the issuers for any misrepresentations contained in the prospectus. The goal of the SEC is not to reduce or eliminate risky securities, however; it is only to see that full disclosure of risk is provided before purchase of the securities.[7]

In addition to its control over the issuance of new securities, the SEC has a variety of controls over the trading of existing securities in the secondary market. For example, the SEC may dictate the rules of trading for regional and national securities markets. To a considerable extent, the SEC has relied on self-policing by the individual exchanges. However, in a number of issues the SEC has dictated important changes in the operations of the security exchanges. For example, before 1975, all members of the New York Stock Exchange were required by exchange policy to charge uniform commissions for trading securities. The SEC then forced the exchange to adopt a negotiated rate structure whereby each

---

[7]One controversial aspect of the disclosure goal of the SEC relates to accounting standards. In some cases the SEC has required the use of accounting procedures for public companies that differ considerably from those generally accepted by the accounting profession.

member would set its own rates in negotiation with its customers.[8] By doing so the SEC hoped to increase the operational efficiency of the financial markets. In addition, the SEC has taken the lead in recent years in integrating the regional securities markets into one national market system.

SUMMARY

The financial system of the United States (and most nations) is characterized by extensive government regulation, particularly of depository institutions. Such regulation is justified on the basis of the macroeconomic significance of banks and other financial institutions and the apparent susceptibility of financial intermediaries to "runs" and other manifestations of "market failure." The present regulatory framework was largely shaped by legislation in the economic crisis of the 1930s, although it has been both modified and extended by subsequent statutes and regulator actions. This regulatory structure for depository institutions consists largely of restrictions on entry and expansion, the scope and nature of activities and leverage, as well as geographic constraints, and is focused on the control of risk taking. Depository institutions are also subject to supervisory oversight and periodic examination by regulatory agencies.

Federal depository institution regulatory agencies include the Federal Reserve System, the Comptroller of the Currency, the Federal Deposit Insurance Corporation (FDIC), the Federal Home Loan Bank system, the Federal Savings and Loan Insurance Corporation (FSLIC), the National Credit Union Administration (NCUA), and the National Credit Union Share Insurance Fund (NCUSIF). In addition, each of the fifty states has an agency concerned with regulation, supervision, and examination (and sometimes chartering) of state-chartered depository institutions.

The various types of nondepository financial institutions are chartered only by state governments and are thus regulated primarily by state agencies. Federal regulatory authority for nondepository financial institutions is exercised principally by the Securities and Exchange Commission (SEC). The SEC administers federal securities laws, which regulate corporate financial disclosure, primary security issues, and secondary securities market trading.

QUESTIONS

1. Why is banking viewed as prone to "market failure"? How is this view related to the extent of banking regulation that exists?

2. What were the principal provisions of the Banking Acts of 1933 and 1935? Which of these provisions have been repealed by more recent legislation?

---

[8]The goal of this action was to reduce commission rates through encouraging price competition. Unfortunately, the goal has been only partly successful. Rates charged on large block transactions with institutions have fallen, but rates on smaller transactions with individiuals have increased.

3. Explain how the possibility of "economies of scale" in banking has been used to justify restrictions on bank mergers and geographic expansion. Evaluate this argument.

4. In what way is control over entry related to the risk of the failure of financial institutions? Should we allow free entry into the financial services industry? What would be the advantages and disadvantages of such a policy?

5. Describe the regulatory framework for banks in terms of the major categories of restrictions, their justification, and recent patterns of change.

6. Why has the holding company form of organization become so important for banks? How are bank holding companies regulated?

7. Describe the rationale and nature of the regulation of nonbank depository institutions, as compared to bank regulation.

8. Why is there overlap among the bank regulatory agencies? What are the advantages and disadvantages of such overlap?

9. Make a list of the major consumer credit laws as they affect financial institutions. What impact might these regulations have on the behavior of financial institutions?

10. What is the Securities and Exchange Commission? What are its functions?

REFERENCES

Altman, Edward I., and Arnold W. Sametz, *Financial Crises: Institutions and Markets in a Fragile Environment* (New York: John Wiley & Sons, 1977).

Benston, George J., "Federal Regulation of Banking: Analysis and Policy Recommendations," *Journal of Bank Research* (Winter 1983), 216–244.

—— (Ed.), *Financial Services: The Changing Institutions and Government Policy* (Englewood Cliffs, N.J.: Prentice-Hall, 1983).

Cooper, S. Kerry, and Donald R. Fraser, *Banking Deregulation and the New Competition in the Financial Services Industry* (Cambridge, Mass.: Ballinger Publishing Company, 1984).

Edwards, Franklin R., *Issues in Financial Regulation* (New York: McGraw-Hill, 1979).

Federal Reserve Bank of Minneapolis, "Are Banks Special?" *Annual Report* (1982), 2–24.

Federal Supervision of State and National Banks, A study by the Comptroller General of the U.S. (Washington, D.C., 1977).

Heggestad, Arnold A. (Ed.), *Regulation of Consumer Financial Services* (Cambridge, Mass.: Abt Books, 1981).

Horvitz, Paul M., "Reorganization of the Federal Regulatory Agencies," *Journal of Bank Research* (Winter 1983), 245–263.

Jessee, M. A., and S. A. Seelig, *Bank Holding Companies and the Public Interest* (Lexington, Mass.: Lexington Books, 1977).

Lapidus, Leonard, et al., *State and Federal Regulation of Commercial Banks*, Vols. 1 and 2. (Washington, D.C.: Task Force on State and Federal Regulation, Federal Deposit Insurance Corporation, 1980).

Maisal, Sherman J., *Risk and Capital Adequacy in Commercial Banks* (National Bureau of Economic Research, University of Chicago Press, 1981).

McCarthy, F. Ward Jr., "The Evolution of the Bank Regulatory Structure: A Reappraisal," Federal Reserve Bank of Richmond, *Economic Review* (March/April 1984), 3–21.

Posner, Richard A. "Theories of Economic Regulation," *Bell Journal of Economics and Management Science* (Autumn 1974), 335–358.

Report of the President's Commission on Financial Structure and Regulation (Hunt Commission) (Washington, D.C.: U.S. Government Printing Office, December 1971).

Report on the Geographical Restriction on Commercial Banking in the United States (Washington, D.C.: U.S. Treasury Department, 1981).

Spong, Kenneth, *Banking Regulation: Its Purposes, Implementation, and Effects* (Federal Reserve Bank of Kansas City, 1985).

CHAPTER **13**

Financial Reform and the Revolution in the Financial Services Industry

The banking and financial services industry of the United States, and indeed of the entire world, has experienced revolutionary changes within the past few decades. The variety of financial services available from traditional financial service organizations such as commercial banks and savings and loans has expanded greatly, while nonfinancial organizations have sought entry into the financial services industry (witness the attempt by Sears to induce consumers to buy their stocks where they buy their socks). The traditional categorization of financial institutions discussed in Chapters 9 and 10 has become increasingly less relevant as financial service organizations become more and more alike.

These revolutionary changes in the financial system reflect a variety of factors including high and volatile inflation rates, rapid changes in technology that have both altered the cost of providing financial services and substantially broadened the geographical area over which these services can be effectively delivered, as well as legislative initiatives that have become characterized as deregulation. The implications of these changes in the financial system are substantial not only for consumers of financial services, but also for managers and employees involved in the production of financial services, as well as the regulators of the nation's financial institutions that are concerned with the efficient operation of the financial system and with the stability of that system.

Three dimensions of this revolution are of special significance: (1) deregulation, (2) the growth of competition from nontraditional financial service organizations, and (3) the growing overlap of services among financial institutions. These developments are, of course, closely interrelated. In fact, the growth of competition from nontraditional financial service organizations and the increasing overlap of functions represent principal causes of the deregulation of depository financial institutions.

In this chapter we concentrate on these dimensions of the revolution and on some of the significant potential implications of the revolution. Since the major legislative initiatives with regard to depository institutions, DIDMCA in 1980 and DIA in 1982, were discussed in Chapter 9 (as well as the causes of this legislative deregulation), these topics will not be treated in any detail in this chapter. Also, some of the major public policy issues that are raised by this revolution, such as the reform of the deposit insurance system, are treated in detail in Chapter 14.

DEREGULATION

Deregulation in banking has three separate though closely related dimensions: *price* (e.g., deposit rate) deregulation, *product* deregulation, and *geographic* deregulation. **Price deregulation** refers to the lifting of legal restrictions on the interest rates that depository institutions may pay to obtain funds (and to a lesser extent, in terms of the importance of the restrictions, on the rates that may be charged for loans, commonly referred to as *usury laws*). **Product deregulation** refers to the removal of the restrictions placed on banks and other depository institutions in the types of services offered, such as investment banking services or insurance underwriting. **Geographic deregulation,** of course, refers to the removal of limitations on the geographic extent over which banks (and other depository institutions) may operate deposit-taking facilities.

Deregulation has focused primarily on price deregulation. (Table 13.1 provides a chronology of deposit rate deregulation.) Virtually all restrictions on the rates that banks and other depository institutions could pay for funds were removed by late 1983, resulting in a proliferation of new deposit instruments (of which the money market deposit account is most notable). In contrast, product deregulation (at least as related to commercial banks) has been relatively limited, although savings and loans have been allowed somewhat to broaden their services to consumers.

Action at the federal level on geographic deregulation has been most notable by its absence, though substantial action has taken place at the state level. Despite the absence of federal action on geographical deregulation, banking organizations have been able to engage in a number of activities interstate without explicitly violating the appropriate statutes. The interstate operation of depository institutions occurs in a variety of forms. For example, a number of bank holding companies already operate banking subsidiaries in more than one state. Most of these organizations had operated interstate before the passage of restrictive legislation and were allowed to continue their operation under "grandfather" clauses in the legislation.

STATES TAKE THE LEAD IN GEOGRAPHICAL AND PRODUCT DEREGULATION

Through late 1988 the U.S. Congress had done remarkably little with regard to expanding the geographical extent over which commercial banking organizations could operate through branches or holding company subsidiaries or with regard to expanding the powers of these organizations to offer a wider variety of products and services. Despite this lack of action at the federal level, individual states have seized the initiative by allowing interstate banking and authorizing expanded powers for their state-chartered banks. Through these actions the states have moved the U.S. banking structure much closer to nationwide banking and have placed great pressure on Congress and the federal regulatory authorities to allow greater product diversification.

States have been especially active in geographic expansion through authorizing, under the provisions of the Douglas Amendment to the Bank Holding Company Act, out-of-state banks to enter their states through holding company acquisitions. The number of such authorizations increased dramatically after the Supreme Court decision in 1985 in *Northeast Bancorp* v. *Board of Governors of the Federal Reserve System,* which affirmed the Board's ruling that interstate compacts were permissible under the Douglas Amendment. At the time of the decision in 1985, twenty-two states had already passed legislation permitting out-of-state entry. By late 1988, virtually all of the fifty states had passed legislation that permitted some form of interstate banking.

The states have been particularly innovative in altering the permissible powers for state-chartered banks that are not members of the Federal Reserve System. Some states allow their state-chartered banks, either directly or through subsidiaries, to engage in full securities activities (national banks and state-chartered banks that are members of the Federal Reserve System may operate discount brokerage firms). In addition, many of these same banks are permitted to engage in unrestricted insurance brokerage and underwriting, direct real estate investment and brokerage, and general equity investments. While most state-chartered nonmember banks are relatively small, more than half of all commercial banks are state-chartered and not members of the Federal Reserve. Moreover, a large bank holding company could engage in these permissible activities through a state-chartered nonmember bank subsidiary.

California has been quite active in expanding bank powers. For example, California law allows real estate investments as well as general equity investment. Moreover, through such equity investments, state banks can enter almost any line of business (except insurance sales or underwriting, which are prohibited). Through late 1988 these banks had been quite active in real estate investments, though most had made little use of their equity investment powers.

The liability of bank holding companies to expand their powers is limited by Section 4 of the Bank Holding Companies Act. That federal law permits bank holding companies to own nonbank subsidiaries only if those subsidiaries are engaged in activities determined by the Federal Board to be "closely related to banking and a proper incident thereto." Most of the expanded powers permitted by California and other states for their state chartered banks are not allowed for BHC nonbank subsidiaries. However, this restriction was reduced in September 1987, when the Federal Reserve Board ruled that Section 4 prohibitions are not applicable to the direct activities of bank subsidiaries of BHCs.

The expanded geographical and product powers permitted by state laws provide an excellent example of the flexibility that exists under a system that provides for charter and regulation of banks at both the state and federal levels (i.e., the dual banking system). That flexibility, though, obviously creates tension between the different levels of regulators and places pressure on the U.S. Congress for changes in federal law.

Source: Gary Zimmerman and Michael Keeley, "States Take the Lead," Federal Reserve Bank of San Francisco Weekly Letter, (September 9, 1988), 1–4.

TABLE 13.1   Chronology of Deposit Rate Deregulation _____

1971	NOW accounts were authorized for thrift institutions in Massachusetts. In the next few years, all New England thrifts were allowed to issue NOWs.
1973	"The wild card experiment": The first use of ceiling-free, small denomination certificates of deposit. The certificate had a minimum maturity of four years; the experiment lasted four months. All depository institutions were allowed to participate.
1978	6-month money market certificates were authorized nationally for all depository institutions.
1980	Authorization of the 2 1/2-year Small Saver Certificate for all depository institutions.
1981	Introduction of nationwide NOW accounts. Introduction of the ceiling-free Individual Retirement Accounts. Introduction of the tax-exempt All Savers certificate of deposit.
1982	Several new accounts paying market-related rates were introduced: 91-day money market certificate. 3 1/2-year ceiling-free deposit. 7- to 31-day time deposit.
1983	Introduction of money market deposit and super NOW accounts. Lowering of minimum deposit on short-term certificates of deposit to $2500. Elimination of ceiling rates on remaining time deposits.
1985	Lowering of minimum deposit on money market deposit and super NOW accounts.
1986	Elimination of remaining deposit rate and balance restrictions.

While many banking organizations have circumvented the barriers to geographical expansion, progress toward actual removal of these barriers has been relatively slow until quite recently. In terms of *intrastate* barriers, several states, including Illinois, Florida, Nebraska, Oklahoma, Texas, and Arkansas, have recently reduced their restraints on geographical expansion of banking organizations. On an interstate basis, many states have recently passed legislation allowing out-of-state banking organizations to enter. The initiatives to allow interstate banking taken by the states since 1985 (the year in which the U.S. Supreme Court explicitly sanctioned state initiatives to allow interstate banking) have been remarkable. Table 13.2 provides a summary of both intrastate and interstate initiatives that have broadened the geographical extent of bank operations.

COMPETITION FROM NONDEPOSITORY ORGANIZATIONS

Many new organizations have begun to offer financial services in direct competition with banks, savings and loans, and other traditional financial service organizations. Perhaps the best example of the competition from nondepository financial institutions is offered by Merrill Lynch, the nation's largest brokerage firm. Table 13.3 presents a list of financial services that Merrill Lynch offers. These include a full range of securities services as well as insurance, real estate lending and brokerage, and employee relocation services. Many of these services are directly competitive with those of depository institutions. For example, Merrill Lynch offers credit for real estate and related purposes and for the purchase of securities. Moreover, with its Cash Management Account (CMA), Merrill Lynch has created a financial instrument that is directly competitive with checking accounts offered by depository financial institutions. Yet Merrill Lynch is able to offer customers investment banking and insurance services that were traditionally prohibited to commercial banks and other depository institutions.

The money market mutual fund provides another example of the growth of new sources of product competition. Money market funds originated in the early 1970s to offer small savers a market rate of interest at a time when the rates available at depository financial institutions were limited by Federal regulations (commonly referred to as Regulation Q). Moreover, many money market funds offered convenient services that have proven attractive to savers, perhaps the most significant of which is the ability to write checks against the value of money market accounts. To a considerable degree the reduction in interest rate ceilings and the widening of the authority to offer checkable deposits allowed depository institutions by DIDMCA and DIA represent a reponse to the financial pressures created by the growth of money market funds.

TABLE 13.2 Broadening the Ability of Banks to Expand Geographically

Intrastate and interstate expansion	*State branching laws*
The following tabulation lists the states that changed laws to permit banks to expand geographically by various methods. It vividly shows the increases in the past two decades in the power of banks to expand.	The listing below shows the current distribution of branching laws by state. As indicated, two of the states that now have only limited branching will allow statewide branching in the 1990s.

Decade	Intrastate expansion		Interstate banking	Statewide branching	Limited branching	Unit banking
	Bank branching	Multibank holding companies				
1970s	Iowa Maine New Jersey New York Ohio Virginia	Georgia Michigan New York	Maine	Alabama[1] Alaska Arizona California Connecticut Delaware Florida[1]	Arkansas[2] Iowa Kentucky Louisiana Minnesota Missouri New Mexico	Colorado Illinois Montana Wyoming
1980	Alabama Connecticut Florida Georgia Indiana Kansas Massachusetts Michigan Minnesota Mississippi Nebraska New Hampshire North Dakota Ohio Oklahoma Oregon Pennsylvania Tennessee Texas Utah Washington West Virginia	Arkansas Illinois Indiana Kansas Kentucky Louisiana Nebraska Oklahoma Pennsylvania Washington West Virginia	All except five states.[3]	Georgia[1] Hawaii Idaho Indiana[1] Kansas[1] Maine Maryland Massachusetts Michigan Mississippi[1,2] Nebraska[1] Nevada New Hampshire New Jersey New York North Carolina North Dakota[1] Ohio Oklahoma[1] Oregon Rhode Island South Carolina South Dakota Utah Vermont Virginia Washington West Virginia	Pennsylvania[2] Tennessee Texas Wisconsin	

[1]Statewide branching by merger.

[2]These states will permit statewide branching in the future: Arkansas in 1999; Mississippi in 1989; and Pennsylvania in 1990.

[3]The five are Hawaii, Iowa, Kansas, Montana, and North Dakota.

Source: D. Amel and M. Jacowski, "Trends in Banking Structure Since the Mid-1970's," Federal Reserve Bulletin, March 1989, p. 121.

TABLE 13.3 Services Offered by Merrill Lynch and Co. _____

Securities Services

Broker and dealer
Commodity futures and options broker
Security underwriting
Investment banking
International merchant banking
Leasing
Dealer in U.S. government and government agency securities
    and in money market instruments
Margin lending
Securities research
Investment counseling
Sale and management of mutual funds.
Cash management account

Insurance Services

Mortgage retirement life insurance
Other life insurance
Annuities
Insurance to real estate lenders against default risk
"Directed" life insurance

Real Estate and Related Services

Real estate financing
Mortgage banking
Real estate management services
Brokerage
Employee relocation

Source: Merrill Lynch and Co.

OVERLAP OF FUNCTIONS

As we noted earlier, the financial services offered by commercial banks are very similar to those provided in 1960; checking accounts (though interest could be paid on some types of checking accounts in 1989 but not in 1960), saving and time accounts, installment loans, business loans, mortgage loans, and credit cards. The powers of savings and loans have been broadened somewhat. For example, savings and loans can offer checking accounts and more diversified types of credit. In terms of credit-granting powers the most significant change at savings and loans has been their ability to offer all types of consumer credit.

Perhaps the most remarkable change is the extraordinary expansion in financial services offered by insurance companies, securities dealers, and retailers. These nondepository institutions now offer virtually every financial service that banks and savings and loans provide. Yet banks and savings and loans cannot offer many of the services provided by these nondepository institutions. Not sur-prisingly, the depository institutions have complained bitterly about inequality of regulation and continue to press the U.S. Congress for legislation that would broaden their powers to offer financial services (product deregulation) and also would allow them to offer these financial services over a broader geographical area (geographical deregulation).

CONSEQUENCES OF THE REVOLUTION IN THE FINANCIAL SERVICES INDUSTRY

Given the legal and regulatory background we have discussed, it is important to examine some of the major consequences of this revolution.

Functions of Depository Institutions

This revolution markedly changed the functions of individual financial insti-tutions. Savings and loan associations have become more like commercial banks. (Britain currently provides an excellent example of this merging of the functions of the thrifts and the commercial banks.) Whether this merging of functions will ever result in total overlap of services is questionable. Savings and loans appear to have some comparative advantage in the origination of mortgages and mort-gage-related credit, and commercial banks seem to possess a corresponding ad-vantage in commercial lending.

At the same time that depository institutions are becoming more alike in their deposit-taking and credit-providing services, the depository institutions are becoming like other nondepository financial service firms. For example, the divi-sion between commercial banking and investment banking (a demarcation that is unusual among major nations to the United States) is rapidly being eroded. Entry by commercial banks into the discount brokerage business provides tangi-ble evidence of this erosion. These functions may continue to converge in the near future. The rapidity with which the gap between commercial and investment banking is being closed provides ample evidence of the validity of the adage that "bankers can innovate faster than regulators can regulate."

Table 13.4 provides one possible scenario for the future banking system. Ac-cording to this view, which is only one of various possibilities, the financial ser-vices firm of the future could consist of three types. One type would be a financial supermarket that would distribute a wide variety of financial services throughout the nation (and even internationally). This group of firms (which might number as few as eight to ten organizations) would include the largest banks like Citicorp as well as other organizations such as Merrill Lynch, American Express, and even Sears. A second group of institutions might be low-cost producers of selected financial services, analogous to the discount brokerage firms. These would likely

TABLE 13.4 Future Banking Structure?

	Type of Organization		
	(1) National Distribution	(2) Low-Cost Producer	(3) Specialty Firm
Money center banks	X		X
Regional banks			X
Local banks			X
New entrants		X	
Nonbank financial institutions	X	X	

be new entrants using the latest electronic technology. Finally, and largest in terms of number, would be various firms concentrating in selected portions of the market (serving particular "niches"). These would include the smaller banks as well as a number of other financial institutions.

Prices and Availability of Financial Services

Certainly, the movement toward financial deregulation affects the price and availability of financial services—to the benefit of most, though not all, consumers. With elimination of Regulation Q ceilings, consumers now receive market rates of interest on their deposits. Similarly, greater competition in the credit market produces a greater availability of credit at lower cost than would otherwise be the case in the absence of deregulation. At the same time, some consumers of financial services who have not been paying full cost for their services are made worse off by deregulation as depository institutions reprice their services. Low-deposit-balance customers who make frequent use of depository financial institutional services lose as a result of the financial revolution.

Geographic Expansion

The remarkable changes taking place in the financial services industry have substantial implications for the geographic expansion of depository institutions, especially for commercial banks that have been particularly affected by legislative restraints on geographic expansion. The restrictive framework that has attempted to confine the operations of depository institutions to a limited geographic area is rapidly eroding. As a result, the geographic area where depository institutions offer their products has expanded and is likely to be extended even more in coming years.

While economic, financial, and technological forces are clearly breaking down the barriers to interstate banking (and also to additional intrastate expansion in those states that continue to restrict such expansion), the movement to full intrastate banking and the complete elimination of the barriers to full interstate banking may require considerable time. Of course, substantial political pressures from some special interest groups are aimed at preventing the reduction or elimination of noncompetitive barriers to geographical expansion by banking organizations. Even if these political pressures are overcome (and it seems certain that they will be at some time), the question remains as to how rapidly banking organizations would actually proceed with interstate expansion. In this regard it should be remembered that (as discussed earlier) many banking organizations already have an interstate presence through nonbanking subsidiaries and through other means. Also, the apparent lack of major economies of scale in banking suggests that interstate consolidation could be slow.

Despite these considerations, however, it seems likely that full interstate banking with some truly national organizations will eventually occur, although the timing is uncertain. The manner in which such expansion will occur is also uncertain. At present it appears that interstate banking will come about through the action of state legislatures. Also, Congress may change the laws allowing bank holding companies to acquire banks anywhere in the United States or to allow branch banking on an interstate basis.

Product Line Expansion

Related to the ability of commercial banking organizations to expand geographically is their ability to increase their product line offerings to the public. Most of the expansion of product lines permitted for depository institutions has focused on thrifts. In the effort to transform the nature of thrifts to make them economically viable, savings and loans and other thrifts were permitted to offer products that traditionally had been limited to commercial banks (in the case of transactions accounts) and products (such as consumer loans) in which banks were prominent lenders but thrifts were not (with the exception of credit unions). Similarly, nondepository financial institutions and certain nonfinancial institutions had entered into direct competition with banks through offering banklike products. The best examples of this new competition are provided by Merrill Lynch, American Express, and Sears, although many others are also important.

The expansion in product line offerings permitted for commercial banks in this revolutionary era has been relatively slight. Probably the most significant new product permitted the commercial banking industry is the money market deposit account, though the reduction in Regulation Q ceilings generally may be viewed as giving banks a greater (or at least more competitive) span of product offerings. Yet the banking industry has increasingly sought to test the limits of its authority to offer new products and at the same time to effect legislative changes that would allow them to offer a wider product mix.

Expansion into discount brokerage provides a good example of banking organizations seeking new product lines. This industry itself was created by the deregulation of exchange commission rates that occurred in May 1974. However, not until the early 1980s did banking organizations begin to offer discount brokerage services to their customers either through the acquisition of existing discount brokerage firms (such as Bank of America's acquisition of Charles Schwab and Chase Manhattan's acquisition of Rose and Co.) or through starting new firms (in which case most transactions were handled through an existing firm).

Entry of banking organizations into discount brokerage represents the first step in the desired entry by these firms into the securities business. Such a step was justified (legally) on the ground that the discount broker offers only execution of transactions, a function that some banks had provided for their customers for many years. Since it does not involve the underwriting or distribution of securities, it is argued, the action did not violate the separation of commercial and investment banking that was provided for in the Glass-Steagall Act. In fact, the banking industry has pressed Congress to modify or eliminate such divisions between investment and commercial banking, giving banks full authority to underwrite and distribute all types of securities.

Considerable differences of opinion exist about the extent of the broadening of bank product lines that will occur in future years. For example, Kaufman, Mote, and Rosenblum, after reviewing all important implications of deregulation, argue that once deregulation is fully in place, banking as a separate industry (distinct from other parts of the financial services industry) will cease to exist.[1] In contrast, industry participants seem to believe that, while the distinctions among providers of financial services will blur, such distinctions will remain important.[2]

Profitability and the Number of Depository Institutions

Greater competition, higher deposit rates, and lower loan rates place substantial pressure on the profitability of depository institutions. While **spreads** (that is, the difference between earnings on assets and the cost of funds) are reduced with growing competition for deposits and loans, it is not at all clear what the ultimate magnitude of the decline in profitability should be. Declining spread may be offset by more efficient operations in other areas of the institutions. Competition associated with less regulation should, to some extent at least, reverse this process. Also, financial institutions might attempt to offset declining spreads by raising fees for services offered (e.g., fees for stopping payment on a check).

---

[1]George Kaufman, Larry Mote, and Harvey Rosenblum, "Implications of Deregulation for Product Lines and Geographical Markets of Financial Institutions," *Journal of Bank Research* (Spring 1983), 8–24.

[2]*New Dimensions in Banking: Managing the Strategic Position* (Rolling Meadow, Illinois; Arthur Andersen and Co. and Bank Administration Institute, 1983).

To the extent that profitability is reduced by growing competition, however, the number of independent depository institutions will shrink as high-cost firms find it impossible to make an acceptable profit. In fact, the number of savings and loans (and to a lesser extent commercial banks) has already declined significantly in the 1980s. The pricing flexibility offered to managers of depository institutions could also contribute to this reduction in the number of institutions. Managers of depository institutions under deregulation have greater flexibility in making decisions, greater opportunity to make correct decisions, and of course greater opportunity to make incorrect decisions. Some of these incorrect decisions will result in failure of the financial institution, thereby reducing the number of independent entities.

Further consolidation among depository financial institutions appears quite likely. However, there remains the question of the extent of such consolidation. For example, the extent of consolidation may be quite different for commercial banks compared with savings and loans. Also, an important question remains as to what the resulting structure of the depository institutions will look like.

A survey done of banking executives by the Bank Administration Institute and the accounting firm of Arthur Andersen and Company projected that the number of banks will decline by almost one third, to 9600. The greatest reduction in the number of banks was projected to occur at small banks (those with total assets of less that $100 million). Medium-sized banks (those with total assets from $100 million to $1 billion) were also expected to experience a shrinkage in their numbers, falling by about 12 percent. In contrast, the number of large banks (those with total assets of over $1 billion) was projected to increase by 26 percent.[3]

This scenario does not imply that small community banks cannot survive a deregulated environment. Given the evidence that economies of scale in providing most financial services are quite limited, any cost disadvantages of community banks (and thrift institutions) are likely to be quite small. As long as financial services remain highly personal in nature, the ability of well-run community organizations to survive and prosper appears not to be threatened. It seems highly unlikely that the financial system of the United States will ever resemble that of England or Canada, in which fewer than ten banks dominate most of the financial market.

Depository Institutions Failure

With diminishing profit margins, growing competition, and increased management discretion permitting managers to make greater mistakes the incidence of failure has increased and is likely to remain high, at least in relation to what it would have been. The incidence of failure will obviously be greatly affected

---

[3]*New Dimensions in Banking: Managing the Strategic Position* (Rolling Meadow, Illinois; Arthur Andersen and Co. and Bank Administration Institute, 1983).

also by the stability of the economy and the level of interest rates. If the failures are limited to small institutions, the effects on the financial system should be small. However, if, as appears likely, large depository institutions fail, the resulting effects on the financial system could be more serious. Indeed, the failure of the First National Bank of Midland (Texas) in 1983 (the third largest bank failure in U.S. history), the rescue in 1984 of the Continental Illinois National Bank of Chicago (the eighth largest bank in the United States), and the failure of First Republic Corporation in 1988 have produced great concern about the stability of the financial system. The tidal wave of failures among savings and loans in the late 1980s placed great pressure on the financial system. Failures of large organizations will undoubtedly continue to place great pressure on the federal deposit insurance system, and these failures appear increasingly likely.

Deposit Insurance

Closely related to the topic of bank failures (and failures by other depository institutions) is the entire subject of deposit insurance. Indeed, the deposit insurance funds of the Federal Deposit Insurance Corporation (FDIC) and the Federal Savings and Loan Insurance Corporation (FSLIC) have been severely strained by the upsurge in the number, and particularly the size, of failing institutions. Whether the rising failure rate is attributable to deregulation and the revolution in the financial services industry is difficult to discern, though it probably has more to do with volatility in the economy than with deregulation.

Deposit insurance, deregulation, and the revolution in financial services are, however, closely and inextricably linked. To deregulate banks and other depository institutions without reforming the present system of deposit insurance might be "putting the cart before the horse."

To a very considerable extent, deposit insurance removes the discipline of the market from bank portfolio behavior. Without deposit insurance, banks that accepted greater risk in their portfolios would find that their costs of funds would rise; potential increases in costs of funds (in a world without deposit insurance) would thus constrain the risk that banks (and other depository institutions) would be willing to take in their portfolios. In contrast, with deposit insurance, more risky portfolios do not necessarily elicit rising funds costs. Traditionally, the deposit insurance agencies have dealt with this problem through constraints on portfolio behavior that limit bank risk: the deposit agencies sell two products, insurance and regulation. Yet with greater bank portfolio management flexibility the ability of the insurance agencies to control bank portfolio risk is sharply reduced.

It thus appears that the revolution in the financial services industry has created a fundamental problem for deposit insurance as this insurance program is currently constituted. This problem will, of course, become more significant if (as appears likely) the financial revolution continues further. These developments make it quite likely that the deposit insurance system will be fundamentally altered. Alternative proposals for reform of the deposit insurance system are discussed in the next chapter.

THE FINANCIAL SERVICES INDUSTRY OF THE FUTURE

The structure of the financial services industry in the recent past has been characterized by change and growing competition. The change stems from environmental factors (such as inflation, high and volatile interest rates, and economic conditions), the development and application of new forms of technology, the demands of more sophisticated customers and the gradual reduction of barriers on depository institutions' pricing, activities, and geographical scope of operations. The net result of this change has been an expansion of competition between individual subsets of the financial services industry (commercial bank versus life insurance company, for example). The beneficiaries of the change and growing competition have been the consumer of financial services, who is now offered a much wider variety of products at prices that more closely approximate the costs of production. The losers, to this point, have been the inefficient producers of financial services with excessive costs and those that are unable to adapt to the shifting competitive environment. There are few reasons to believe that those trends will not continue. If they do, the following scenario appears to be a reasonable outlook.

Regulatory Changes

The regulatory barriers constricting the pricing, activity, and geographical operations of commercial banks (and other depository institutions) will be further reduced, if not eliminated. These constraints limit the ability of depository institutions to offer the financial services demanded by consumers at competitive costs. Without such reductions in regulatory barriers the market share of depository institutions will be further reduced, and their ability to compete effectively will erode. It is ironic that the constraints that were initially imposed to *reduce* the risk of failure of individual financial institutions are now contributing to *increased* failure risk. The ability of commercial banks to diversify credit risk in the loan portfolio is certainly enhanced with broader geographical operations.

The few remaining restrictions on pricing will likely be removed. Interest payments on demand deposits (the lone remaining significant restriction on deposit pricing) will be allowed, and remaining restriction on interest rates charged to borrowers will also be eliminated, a change reflecting the variable rates of interest that depository institutions must pay to obtain funds. Of more significance, bank and other depository institutions will continue to expand their geographical scope of operations through increased electronic services, the expansion of subsidiary activities, and, where permissible, the interstate acquisition of other depository institutions. The move toward nationwide interstate holding company acquisitions (either today or in the near future through a nationwide "trigger" in state legislation) and the geographical expansion of interstate organizations will accelerate over time. At some point it seems likely that the U.S. Congress will change federal law to allow national branching, at which point many of the holding company organizations will be consolidated into branching systems.

Activity or product deregulation represents the most controversial dimension of remaining deregulation. The melding of the characteristics of commercial banks with savings and loans and other thrifts has already occurred with the passage of the DIDMCA in 1980 and the DIA in 1982. As a result, many of the pure legal distinctions among the depository institutions have disappeared. However, the distinction between commercial banks and many other financial service organizations remains constrained by the Glass-Steagall Act. Commercial banks have actively tested the limits of Glass-Steagall through nonbank subsidiaries of bank holding companies, notably in discount brokerage organizations and other securities and investment banking related institutions. However, significant further melding of the financial services firms awaits significant modifications or repeal of Glass-Steagall. Despite political problems caused by the unwillingness of Congress to deal with banking issues when strong lobby groups exist on both sides of an issue, it seems increasingly likely that significant modifications or repeal of Glass-Steagall will occur and that commercial banking and other financial service organizations will be melded even more closely.

A Proposal for Regulatory Reform

There are, of course, a number of different scenarios that encompass the merging of different financial service organizations. One recent proposal was made by Gerald Corrigan, president of the Federal Reserve Bank of New York. An outline of this proposal is contained in Table 13.5. Under this proposal, in addition to financial service firms operating as distinct entities—commercial banks, life insurance companies, etc.—they could also operate as one of three types of holding companies. The three types are as follows.

1. Commercial-financial conglomerates would be allowed to engage in any enterprise desired *and* offer nonbank financial activities. Sears would fall in this category. However, they could not own or control a bank or thrift, they would be barred from any direct access to the payments system, and they could not receive credit from the Federal Reserve's discount window.

2. Financial holding companies could offer the full range of financial services through nonbank affiliates. They could not be owned by a commercial firm. Espe-

TABLE 13.5 The Alternative Structure

	Commercial-Financial Co.	Financial Holding Co.	Bank-Thrift Holding Co.
Owned by commercial firms	Yes	No	No
Offer full range of nonbank financial services	Yes	Yes	Yes
Own and control full range of commercial enterprises	Yes	No	No
Own and control federally insured depositories	No	No[1]	Yes
Issue transaction deposits	No	No	Yes
Issue noninsured transaction accounts	No[2]	Yes	Yes
Pay interest on transaction accounts or deposits	No	Yes	Yes
Subject to required reserves on transaction accounts and deposits	No	Yes	Yes
"Normal" access to payments system	No	No	Yes
"Normal" access to discount window	No	No	Yes
Access to large-dollar final payments system	No	Yes[3]	Yes
Subject to liquidity reserves	No	Yes[3]	Yes
Limited access to discount window	No	Yes[3]	Yes

[1] A financial holding company could, at its option, acquire insured depositories, thereby becoming a bank holding company and in the process obtain access to the payments system and the discount window.

[2] Subject to certain limitations, a financial affiliate of a commercial concern might be authorized to issue certain noninsured transaction accounts.

[3] Within the context of something along the lines of the National Electronic Payments Corporation.

Source: Federal Reserve Bank of New York, 1986 Annual Report, *p. 40.*

cially important, they could not own and control a federally insured depository institution or issue insured transaction deposits (though they could issue noninsured transactions deposits).

3. Bank and thrift holding companies would be fully independent from commercial concerns and would be free to offer a full range of financial services. They could own insured banks and thrifts, which in theory would have full access to both the payments system and the discount window, and they would be subject to regulation by the bank and thrift regulatory agencies.

The Corrigan proposal would allow virtually all financial services to be offered under the umbrella of a single bank holding company. It would also preserve the traditional separation between banking and commerce and would be consistent with the trend of regulation in other developed countries. Further, it would allow the individual financial firm choice as to what pattern it wished to follow.

Although the Corrigan proposal is unlikely to be implemented as initially presented, it does seem reasonable to argue that the principal financial service firms will be allowed to operate within a single organization at some point in the future. The merging and overlap of function that seem almost certain to occur have a number of implications for individual banks and other financial service organizations. First, a significant consolidation in the number of banks, thrifts, and other financial service organizations appears likely. The number of banks and especially savings and loans has already declined. The number is likely to fall substantially more in future years as growing competition makes survival difficult for some firms and as interstate banking broadens the scope of acquisitions. Second, and relatedly, a small number of very large, nationwide financial service organizations will emerge. Some of these will have commercial banks as their lead subsidiaries; others will have different types of financial service firms in the lead. The breakdown of activity and geographical constraints makes the growth of these large firms more likely. The growing globalization of financial markets and the need for U.S. institutions to compete worldwide with very large foreign service organizations also reinforce this trend.

SUMMARY

The revolution in banking and the financial services industry has already dramatically altered the nature of the U.S. financial system. The combination of unstable economic and financial conditions, rapidly changing technology, more sophisticated consumers of financial services, and basic changes in the legislative and regulatory environment have produced a banking and financial services industry that is drastically different from that which existed just a few years earlier. Yet the revolution is not complete. The changes that have taken place in the nature of financial services and the characteristics of institutions that offer these services have not been finished. Further advances in technology are almost certain to occur, as are further changes in the demands for financial services. These economic factors will almost certainly produce additional legislation that extends the reforms embodied in the DIDMCA (1980) and the DIA (1982). As in any radical and rapid change in the nature of an industry, both benefits and costs are involved. There will be winners and losers among the financial institutions themselves and among the consumers of financial services. Some financial institutions will prosper as they meet demands for financial services in a cost efficient way. Similarly, new organizations will enter the financial services industry, offering low-cost financial services with the latest technology. In contrast, some financial institutions that fail to adapt to changing competitive pressures will cease to exist. Many will simply fail, and it appears very likely that a higher (perhaps much higher) failure rate among financial service organizations will be a significant cost of the financial revolution. Other weakened institutions will be absorbed by stronger organizations, contributing to the consolidation of the financial services industry. The pressures placed on the deposit insurance system may be intense, resulting in the likely reform of the deposit insurance system itself.

Consumers should be the principal beneficiaries of the financial revolution, just as consumers are the ultimate beneficiaries of growing competition in any industry. The ability of consumers to obtain market (that is, higher) interest rates on their time and savings accounts since the dismantling of Regulation Q interest rate ceilings in late 1983 is only one example of the benefits that have been produced by financial reform. In addition, the growing competition among financial service organizations should produce the greatest possible quantity of financial services at the least possible cost. In fact, the proliferation of different types of financial services that has accompanied the financial revolution has already provided consumers with a much wider variety of services than existed in earlier years. Unconstrained by regulation, financial service organizations will be able to innovate new products to meet consumer demand.

The benefits to consumers from the financial revolution also come with costs. For some consumers and for those who were not paying the full cost for their services (low-balance depositors, for example), the cost of financial services will rise—and already has risen. Also, the proliferation of financial services with different cost and convenience characteristics will make it more important for consumers to investigate the alternatives available to them, taking more time and research to obtain the necessary information. In addition, to the extent that the deposit insurance system is changed, depositors might have to be more careful about the financial health of the institution in which they leave their funds. Yet these costs seem small in comparison to the potential benefits that flow from the financial revolution.

QUESTIONS

1. Deregulation is usually thought to encompass three dimensions: price, product, and geographic deregulation. Define each, trace their implementation, and discuss the reasons for the different rate of progress toward full implementation.

2. What is meant by "competition from nontraditional organizations"? Discuss the dimensions of this competition and the firms involved. Do these nontraditional organizations have regulatory and/or technological advantages over commercial banks? Explain.

3. Discuss the extent of and motivation for the expansion in financial service activities of insurance companies, retailers, and security dealers.

4. Explain the potential effects of deregulation on the prices and availability of financial services. Will all users of financial services benefit? What are the implications for low-income consumers?

5. Why should deregulation affect the failure rate of depository institutions? Should this be of concern? What if it carries the potential failure of one of the nation's largest banks or savings and loans?

6. Is there a link between deregulation and deposit insurance? Explain.

REFERENCES

Cooper, S. Kerry, and Donald R. Fraser, *Banking Deregulation and the New Competition in Financial Services* (Cambridge, Mass.: Ballinger Publishing Company, 1986).

Corrigan, Gerald, "A Framework for Reform of The Financial System," Federal Reserve Bank of New York *Quarterly Review* (Summer 1987), 1–8.

——, "A Perspective on the Globalization of Financial Markets and Institutions," Federal Reserve Bank of New York *Quarterly Review* (Spring 1983), 1–9.

England, Catherine, and Thomas Huertas, *The Financial Services Revolution* (Boston, Massachusetts: Kluwer, 1988).

Kareken, John H., "Deposit Insurance Reform, or Deregulation Is the Cart, Not the Horse," Federal Reserve Bank of Minneapolis *Quarterly Review* (Spring 1984), 1–9.

Kaufman, George, and Roger Kormendi (Eds). *Deregulating Financial Services: Public Policy in Flux* (Cambridge, Mass: Ballinger Publishing Company, 1986).

——, Lanny R. Mote, and Harvey Rosenblum, "Consequences of Deregulation For Commercial Banking," *The Journal of Finance* (July 1984), 789–805.

Koch, Donald L., "The Emerging Financial Services Industry: Challenge and Innovation," Federal Reserve Bank of Atlanta *Economic Review* (April 1984), 25–30.

Rosenblum, Harvey, and Diane Siegel, "Competition in Financial Services: The Impact of Nonbank Entry," Federal Reserve Bank of Chicago, Staff Study 83–1.

Savage, Donald, "Interstate Banking Developments," Federal Reserve *Bulletin* (February 1987), 79–92.

Short, Eugenie D., and Gerald P. O'Driscoll, Jr., "Deregulation and Deposit Insurance," Federal Reserve Bank of Dallas *Economic Review* (September 1983), 11–22.

Vrabac, Daniel J., "Recent Developments at Banks and Nonbank Depository Institutions," Federal Reserve Bank of Kansas City *Economic Review* (July/August 1983), 33–44.

CHAPTER **14**

Issues in the Regulation and Deregulation of Financial Institutions

As we indicated in the previous chapter, changing economic and financial conditions, rapid advances in technology, and growing consumer sophistication have produced a revolution in banking and the financial services industry. This revolution has raised some issues that involve public policy and proposed legislation and have significantly altered the manner in which depository financial institutions and other financial service organizations are managed. In this chapter we focus on four of these issues:

1. product deregulation;
2. geographical deregulation;
3. reform of deposit insurance; and
4. reform of the regulatory structure.

PRODUCT DEREGULATION

Restrictions on the types of activities in which depository financial organizations may engage (and therefore the types of products that they may offer to their customers) remain substantial, despite the move to deregulate these institutions. Most of the growing overlap in the products offered by the various financial institutions reflects the expansion in activities by other types of financial institutions. Yet depository financial institutions have been prohibited from offering many of the services provided by other financial institutions. These limitations on product activities have been vigorously opposed by many depository financial institutions. Pressure, especially from commercial banks, has built for relaxation of these restrictions. The exact degree and timing of this product deregulation remain among the most significant issues confronting the financial system.

Existing Restrictions on Commercial Banks

The most significant restrictions on the extent of financial services offered by commercial banks relate to the separation of commercial and investment banking that was mandated by the Glass-Steagall Act of 1933. Under this act, banks have not, for more than fifty years, been able to underwrite and deal in corporate debt and equity securities or municipal revenue bonds. Commercial banks also may not manage mutual funds nor sell insurance services.

The principal motivation for these restrictions on commercial bank product activities was apparently to reduce the probability of commercial bank failure. Responding to the enormous number of bank failures in the early 1930s (and indeed throughout the 1920s), bank-related legislation sought to limit commercial bank risk and reduce the number of failures. In addition, separation of commercial and investment banking was motivated by conflict of interest considerations. There was concern that some investment banking subsidiaries of commercial banking firms were acting unethically by using the bank's assets to acquire securities through investment activities that were not suitable for the bank. In addition, there was also concern that loans of some commercial banks were contributing to excessive speculation in the stock market.

Although the argument may be valid that risk reduction at commercial banks requires separation of commercial and investment banking, the large numbers of bank failures in the 1920s and early 1930s were apparently unrelated to this separation. Most of the banks that failed (the overwhelming proportion) were quite small and did not engage in investment banking. In addition, the failure rate at the large banks that did engage in investment banking was quite low.

Product (Service) Deregulation and Risk

The impact of expanding the product (service) limits of commercial banks depends on both the degree of risk currently existing in bank products and the degree of risk that exists in those new product lines that banks might be permitted to enter. Some of these new product lines might have more risk than those traditionally associated with commercial banks, thereby increasing the degree of risk of banking organizations, while others might have less risk, thereby reducing the risk of banking organizations. The concern, of course, is that product deregulation will produce increased risk.

While little is known about the degrees of risk for different types of financial services, the information provided in Table 14.1 provides insight into risk differences for banks, credit agencies other than banks, brokers, real estate–related organizations, investment companies, general merchandise stores, and food stores.[1] Two measures of risk are presented: (1) a measure of the variability of

---

[1] Bank holding companies are treated separately from commercial banks because banks have been allowed some degree of product and geographical flexibility through holding company structure.

TABLE 14.1 Coefficients of Variations and Determination for Selected Banking Activities, 1970–1980

Organization	Coefficient of Variation	Coefficient of Determination
Banking	0.173503	0.622278
Savings banks	0.296098	−0.43451
Banks and trusts except savings banks	0.211527	1
Credit agencies other than banks	0.229455	−0.26771
Savings and loans	0.337307	−0.20784
Personal credit agencies	0.326252	−0.49144
Business credit agencies	0.253581	0.586265
Other credit agencies	0.183474	0.167736
Life insurance	0.100957	−0.163621
Mutual insurance	0.487323	0.095143
Other insurance companies	0.427181	0.202264
Insurance agents, brokers' service	0.118640	0.487375
Real estate	0.216494	0.605346
Real estate operators, lessors of buildings	0.200242	0.645042
Lessors of mining, oil, etc.	0.434163	0.370005
Lessors of railroad property, other property not allocable	0.124316	−0.36543
Condominium management, co-op housing associations	0.542500	0.928662
Subdividers and developers	0.306568	0.560607
Other real estate	0.184351	0.310724
Holding and other investment companies	0.259857	0.792789
Regulated investment companies	0.247479	0.599360
Real estate investment trusts	0.609843	0.421816
Small business investment companies	0.627969	0.808927
Other holding and investment companies except BHCs	0.156598	0.686523
General merchandise stores	0.385963	−0.24442
Food stores	0.106876	0.456074
Bank holding companies	0.198433	0.621591

Note: The coefficient of variation is a measure of risk of the activity by itself. The coefficient of determination is a measure of the correlation of earnings of the firms with banking organizations.

Source: Larry D. Wall and Robert A. Eisenbeis, "Risk Considerations in Deregulating Bank Activities," Federal Reserve Bank of Atlanta Economic Review (May 1984), 6–19.

the profitability of organizations in each activity (naturally, the higher the variability, the higher the risk) and (2) a measure of the association over time of the earnings of each industry with commercial banks (the coefficient of determination). This measure provides an index of risk reduction that might be possible through diversification.

Examination of the data in Table 14.1 suggests that the riskiness of differing financial service activities varies widely. Hence the effects of allowing commercial banks to expand their product offerings on the risk of banking organizations would depend on the specific activities that were permitted. For example, the operations of security brokers and dealers are much more risky (almost twice as much) as commercial banking. In contrast, insurance agency and life insurance company operations appear to be less risky than banking. In evaluating the effects of product deregulation on the risk of commercial banking organizations it is also necessary to evaluate the degree to which different financial service activities are related to banking, as is done with the correlation coefficient. Such an examination suggests that, while security brokers are more risky than banks, they would provide the risk reduction of diversification. Note that the coefficient of determination in Table 14.1 is negative, indicating that the earnings of the security firms would rise (fall) when the earnings of the bank fell (rose), thereby reducing the variability of the earnings of the total organization.

Other Considerations

While risk is certainly an important factor in considering the expansion of the product and service offerings permissible for commercial banks, there are a number of other dimensions to this issue from a public policy perspective. These include the effects on competition and concentration and the potential for conflict of interest. Supporters of extended powers for commercial banks argue not only that it would be equitable (since securities firms have begun to offer bank-type services), but also that it would serve consumers by increasing competition in the securities industry. Small businesses, government units, and residents of smaller communities where competition may not be substantial might obtain particularly large benefits. In contrast, opponents of such expansion argue that commercial banks have such inherent advantages over securities firms that they would quickly dominate the market, producing a great increase in concentration. These opponents argue that consumer welfare would ultimately be harmed. The potential for conflict of interest between commercial and investment banking also exists. However, proponents of increasing bank product flexibility argue that legislative and regulatory developments since enactment of the Glass-Steagall Act (such as the creation of the Securities and Exchange Commission) have made such potential problems much less significant.

Pressure for product deregulation has also come from the growing number of loans that bypass the commercial banking industry and directly access the capital markets, often through various types of loan pools. This process, known as **securitization**, has a number of implications. First, the market for commercial banking services (such as commercial lending) is reduced. Second, the more creditworthy borrowers are more likely to have direct access to the capital markets, leaving the highest-risk borrowers for commercial banks and other similar lenders. Both of these developments make traditional commercial banking less attractive and create heightened pressures from commercial banks to break down the barriers between commercial and investment banking.

Motivation for Product Deregulation

A number of factors would motivate banks to expand their products or activities.[2] These include the following:

1. Profitability or the opportunity to earn "attractive" profits given the risk dimension of the activity.

2. Economies of scale. An important motivating factor in the expansion of financial service offerings is the attempt to utilize effectively the equipment and other resources that are characterized by high fixed costs and low variable costs. The proliferation of electronic technology is particularly relevant in the existence and importance of economies of scale. Banks have extensive investments in electronic equipment that could be used to provide a variety of products.

3. Economies of scope. Closely related to economies of scale, the term "economies of scope" refers to product synergy by which cross-products are offered at less (often substantially less) cost than those two products could be offered by two separate firms.

4. Business similarities. This refers to the existence of management skills, geographic location, or other factors that would make the new activities attractive.

5. Competitive advantage. This refers to the existence of any factor in new activities that will provide competitive advantage to commercial banks.

Banks and Underwriting

Table 14.2 provides a summary of the pros and cons of underwriting securities (one of the principal activities of investment banking), evaluating each of the five factors discussed above. The principal attractive features of underwriting are the high potential profitability (though as Table 14.2 shows, the risk involved in security dealer activities is relatively high), the opportunities for economies of scope, and the competitive advantage of "one-stop financing." The economies of scope might be particularly significant, since customers that banks call on in their lending programs include potential underwriting clients. Yet underwriting has a number of disadvantages also, including the potential conflict of interest in equity underwriting between the bank lending function and the equity underwriting activity, the differences in the "corporate culture" between commercial banking and investment banking, particularly as it relates to compensation

---

[2]For a more complete explanation of these factors, see Bernell Stone, "Business and Bank Reactions to New Securities Powers," Federal Reserve Bank of Atlanta *Economic Review* (May 1984), 41–48.

TABLE 14.2   A Summary of the Pros and Cons Associated with Underwriting _____

Criterion	Strengths	Weakness
Profitability	High sales margin, return on assets	Volatile, business-cycle-dependent and interest-rate-dependent revenue; high systemic risk.
Scope economies	Client base is same as for commercial loans and credit; contacts within business are senior financial officers; "relationship" natures of banking and underwriting are similar and involve similar knowledge and skill sets.	Many companies do not want to obtain long-term underwriting from the same firms that provide them credit and/or short-term financing.
Business similarities	1. Both commercial lending and underwriting are financial services. 2. Knowledge of financing and financial markets is a key to both businesses.	1. Both commercial lending and underwriting involve business-cycle and interest-rate risk. 2. Employee compensation is primarily via direct salary and perquisites in banking rather than bonuses, commission, or profit sharing.
Competitive advantages	There are many organizational, operational, and technical similarities to municipal underwriting. Banks with large calling organizations are often the first source of financing for many companies.	Municipal underwriting is usually won on a competitive bid basis rather than the relationship-service-planning basis on which most corporate underwriters are selected.

(much higher compensation, usually related to performance, in investment banking), and the lack of a retail distribution network in commercial banking. Given these considerations, entry into investment banking could be restricted to a very few large banking organizations.[3]

---

[3] In fact, Stone argues that even with no activity restriction on investment banking, commercial banks would play a very limited role in underwriting. These activities would be limited to debt securities and to some limited role in equity underwriting for regional firms or specialized industries. See Bernell Stone, "Business and Bank Reactions to New Securities Powers," Federal Reserve Bank of Atlanta *Economic Review* (May 1984), 41–48.

TABLE 14.2 *(Continued)*

Criterion	Strengths	Weakness
Competitive disadvantages	Banks are in regular contact with corporate financial officers. Banks could logically place commercial paper, since they have information on companies with investable funds and their balance reporting services are a natural communications link.	Banks lack the brokerage-based retail distribution required for large-scale national underwritings. Current bank market making is limited to municipals and government securities rather than corporate debt and equity. Most banks lack the syndication and distribution structures of the investment banks and brokers firms. Only the most senior officers in commercial banks receive compensation commensurate with that provided to professionals in major investment banking firms; top salaries in most banks are for management rather than professional skills, although some banks are now using commissions and other incentive structures in security trading, leasing, and consulting, but this usually occurs in holding company units outside of the commercial lending area.

Geographical Deregulation

The issue of geographical deregulation encompasses the expansion of intra-state and interstate banking, though our emphasis here is on interstate activities of banking organizations. As discussed in the previous chapter, banking organizations have found numerous ways to circumvent the legislative restrictions that prohibit or severely restrict interstate banking. Yet the two relevant federal statutes that provide for these restrictions on interstate banking have remained in place. The McFadden Act and the Douglas Amendment to the Bank Holding Company

JOINT VENTURES IN BANKING

Commercial banks and other financial service organizations have sought out new organizational forms and strategies in order to deal with an increasingly uncertain and competitive environment. One approach that some banks have developed is that of forming joint ventures with other banks or with nonbanking firms. Calem reports that 36 joint subsidiaries were formed in 1983 and that bank holding companies have become quite active in recent years in forming joint subsidiaries. In addition, in some cases, such as when banking organizations offer mutual funds jointly in cooperation with mutual fund companies, there may not be a formal venture created.[1]

Joint ventures are used by banking organizations to expand into various types of activities that are legally permissible. Joint ventures with insurance companies and mutual fund management companies are particularly common. For example, in 1986, Wilbur National Bank (a small New York bank) leased space in its main branch to John Hancock Mutual Life Insurance Company so that the insurance company could sell life and disability insurance at that location. Similarly, Chase Manhattan Bank in 1985 arranged with the Dreyfus Corporation (a large manager of a variety of mutual funds) for Chase to act as the organizer and manager of the "Park Avenue Funds" with Dreyfus as the sponsor and distributor of the funds. As a third example, in 1984, Bankers Trust New York Corporation, Xerox Credit Corporation, Phibro-Salomon Inc., and American International Group Inc. formed a joint venture specializing in municipal bond insurance.

Joint ventures offer a number of potential advantages. In some cases they may be the only legal route by which the bank may offer the service. This is the case with insurance and mutual fund products. In other cases in which the joint venture is only one among a number of alternative structures (acquisition or internal expansion, for example) the joint venture has a number of positive features. Both parties in a joint venture share the risk, while internal expansion forces a firm to absorb the risks alone. Joint ventures also often offer easier access to capital, a factor that is especially relevant for small banks, and joint ventures offer economies of scale. Compared to mergers and acquisitions, joint ventures offer the advantage of speed; they are easier to establish and also to dissolve if the project is unsuccessful.

[1] See Paul Calem, "Joint Ventures: Meeting the Competition in Banking," *Federal Reserve Bank of Philadelphia* Business Review *(May/June 1988), 13–21.*

Act prohibit interstate banking through branching or holding company acquisitions unless expressly permitted by individual states. (Savings and loans may operate interstate with the permission of the Federal Home Loan Bank Board.)

While full interstate banking involving interstate deposit-taking facilities remains prohibited, the pressures for change are growing intense. The development of an integrated economic and financial system and the increased mobility of population make the continued restrictions on bank locations less desirable. At the same time the rapid expansion of electronic banking reduces the cost of servicing accounts over wide areas and thereby makes interstate banking more possible from a technological perspective. Also of substantial relevance is the fact that nonbank organizations that offer financial services in direct competition with commercial banks are able to operate without geographic restrictions.

As is the case with any economic change, there are potential benefits and costs involved in the move to interstate banking. The issues that are raised by interstate banking have three principal dimensions: (1) the effects of interstate banking on concentration, competition, and the efficiency of the banking system, (2) the effects of interstate banking on the flow of credit and savings, and (3) the effects of interstate banking on risk in banking and the "safety and soundness" of the banking system.

Concentration, Competition, and Efficiency

Substantial concern exists about the effects of interstate banking on the concentration of financial resources. This concern focuses on the potential domination of the financial system by a few banks, a situation that exists in both Canada and Great Britain.[4] This potential domination by a few institutions could have a number of undesirable effects. First, competition may decline in the banking and financial services industry, thereby producing higher prices charged to consumers of banking services. Second, the concentration of banking resources in a few banks creates the potential for severe repercussions in the financial system if any one of these large banks were to fail. The effect of the failure of one bank would be quite different in a financial system of ten banks than in a financial system of more than 14,000 banks, as currently exists in the United States. Third, concentration of financial resources might lead to political power in the hands of large banks, thereby possibly affecting banking legislation and the regulation of banking organizations. The political influence of large banking organizations would exist at both federal and state government levels, though the effects might be especially significant at the state level.

While all these concerns reflect serious potential disadvantages associated with interstate banking, other considerations reduce their significance. First, it appears highly unlikely that the concentration of financial resources in the hands of a few banks would ever (or at least anytime in the near future) approach that of Canada or Great Britain. There appear to be at least two reasons for this, one economic and the other political.

First, domination of the banking system by larger banking organizations would require significant economies of scale in the banking industry; that is, if

---

[4]The five largest banks in Canada in 1982 controlled 75 percent of bank deposits. In contrast, the five largest banks in the United States controlled only 19 percent of domestic deposits. See Richard F. Syron, "The New England Experiment in Interstate Banking," Federal Reserve Bank of Boston, New England *Economic Review* (March/April 1984).

scale economies were substantial, the larger banking organizations could produce banking services at lower costs and thereby sell these services at lower prices. Smaller banks would not be able to compete in this environment and would exit the industry either by failure or by being absorbed by the larger banks. However, the evidence on economies of scale and the relationship of bank costs to bank size is quite consistent and indicates that large banks have few cost advantages over smaller banks. In addition, holding company subsidiaries seem to have no cost advantage over independent banks. Those economies of scale that appear to exist in banking seem to be exhausted quickly, perhaps with total assets of less than $100 million, while diseconomies may exist for very large banking organizations.

The U.S. antitrust laws are the second reason for the expectation that banking concentration will not approach that of Canada or Great Britain. Every bank merger and holding company acquisition must be approved by at least one of the bank regulatory authorities and by the Antitrust Division of the U.S. Department of Justice. In their review of proposed mergers and holding company acquisitions, appropriate consideration must be given to the effects of the consolidation on concentration and competition.

The effects of interstate banking on concentration must be considered within national, regional, and local markets. Within this perspective it is not at all clear that the removal of geographical restraints on bank operations would produce, at least in the short run, any important increase or decrease in concentration. Interstate banking could result in either an increase or a decrease in concentration, depending on the expansion plans of banking organizations. Certainly, if the largest banking organization expanded by establishing new banks (referred to as *de novo* banks), then the level of concentration would be essentially unchanged. Also, if the consolidation occurs principally through regional banks affiliating with each other to form national banking organizations, the number of major banking organizations would actually increase with interstate banking. Similar arguments can be made for regional and local markets, though the potential for interstate banking producing an actual reduction in concentration in regional and local markets appears greater, given that interstate banking will often result in new entrants by out-of-market banking organizations.

A related question that arises is whether interstate banking and the potential consolidation that may accompany it will substantially reduce competition and harm the performance of banking organizations in meeting the financial needs of their customers at reasonable costs. While any opinions about the competitive effects of interstate banking are speculative, fortunately a large amount of empirical evidence is available on the effects of expansion by banking organizations through holding companies and branching. Though this evidence principally relates to intrastate expansion, it seems reasonable to expect that the conclusions of the studies would be relevant to interstate expansion, also. There is virtually no evidence in any of this literature that the consolidation associated with interstate banking would harm the performance of the commercial banking industry.

Much of the interstate expansion by banking organizations would likely occur through holding company acquisitions. Previous research on the effects of holding company acquisitions on the performance of their acquired banks is reasonably consistent in its findings.[5] As a general rule, banks acquired by holding companies appear to make a number of changes in their portfolios, service charges, operating revenues, and expenses, including the following: higher service charges and loan rates, higher rates paid on time and savings and deposits, more loans, more municipal securities, less cash, and fewer U.S. government securities. Both revenue and expenses increase, with the result that profit appears to change very little. Although some of these changes might produce improved bank performance and others might reduce bank performance, there is little evidence from this literature that holding company expansion sharply reduces bank competition and performance. One of the reasons for this finding appears to be that holding company affiliates do not appear to be operated with any greater economies of scale than comparable independent banks.

A number of studies have also examined the effects of expansion by banking organizations through branching. Studies have examined the relationship of branching to the rates charged on various types of loans as well as the relationship of branching to interest rates paid on time deposits and to bank service charges on demand deposits. The evidence of these studies is less consistent than that of the studies of holding company expansion. Some studies have found that branching leads to reduced loan rates, and others have found that branching is associated with higher loan rates. Similar conflicting evidence has been found with regard to the relationship between branching and other dimensions of bank performance, but virtually all studies have found that branch banks had higher loan/deposit ratios than unit banks. However, the prices and quantities of financial services offered do not appear to be substantially affected by branch bank expansion.[6]

The evidence on the effects of interstate banking on concentration and competition thus suggests that interstate banking appears likely to produce some increase in concentration, though not a massive one. However, the increase in concentration is not likely to have any significant negative effects on competi-

---

[5]This literature is reviewed in Larry A. Frieder and Vincent P. Apilado, "Bank Holding Company Research: Classification, Synthesis, and New Directions," *Journal of Bank Research* (Summer 1982), 80–95.

[6]Two relevant studies by Horvitz and by Kohn. See Paul M. Horvitz, "Concentration and Competition in New England Banking," Research Report No. 2, Federal Reserve Bank of Boston, 1958; Ernest Kohn, "Branch Banking, Bank Mergers, and the Public Interest, New York State Banking Department, 1964. Also see Donald R. Fraser, "Does Branching Matter?" *Journal of Financial Research* (Winter 1978), 61–69.

tion. In fact, competition may actually increase with interstate banking, producing benefits to consumers of banking services. While the concern about the potential political power associated with interstate banking remains a serious one, the likelihood that the U.S. banking system will remain relatively fragmented reduces the significance of this potential problem.

Effects of Interstate Banking on the Flow of Credit and Savings

Concern also exists over the possibility that interstate banking will draw savings away from rural areas into urban areas and more generally that a large nationwide branch banking system will channel funds in a socially undesirable way. In contrast, proponents of interstate banking argue that the entry of banks into new geographical markets will increase the flow of credit to these markets.

Existing evidence about the efficiency of financial markets would suggest that neither of these arguments has substantial merit. Financial markets appear already to be highly efficient in allocating funds to their best risk-adjusted return. Existing local banks are certainly not limited to local investments, but place large amounts of funds in money and capital markets. Similarly, local sources can place their funds locally with a bank or other depository institutions or invest those funds nationally or internationally. As a result, interstate banking is unlikely to have any major effect, either positive or negative, on funds flow.

Interstate Banking and Risk

The third major issue relating to interstate banking is the potential effects on the probability of failure of individual banking organizations (as contrasted to the effects of a bank failure on the economic and financial system). Since interstate banking is likely to lead to some consolidation, producing fewer but larger banks, this issue is to a considerable extent a question of whether small or large banks are likely to experience a greater failure rate. It is sometimes argued that small banks have greater failure risk because they are unable to diversify their loan portfolio geographically and by industry as effectively as large banks. In addition, it is also argued that the management of many small banks have neither sufficient expertise nor sufficient depth to deal with the increasingly complicated competitive environment. On the other hand, the experience of large banks with loan losses in their international and energy loan portfolios might suggest greater risk for large banks. Also, large banks make more extensive use of liability management and thus are more exposed to liquidity and other types of risk if their depositors should lose confidence in the organization.

While the evidence on the relationship between bank size and risk is rather limited, that evidence suggests that large banks are neither more nor less likely to fail than small banks.[7] In addition, the deregulation of deposit rates that occurred in the late 1970s and early 1980s does not appear to have affected the risk dimension of small versus large banks.

DEPOSIT INSURANCE

There are two important questions about the deposit insurance system that apply to banks and other depository institutions.[8] First, does the existing fixed-rate system of deposit insurance encourage the insured institutions to take on an appropriate amount of risk? Second, does the existing system of deposit insurance result in the deposit insurance agencies assuring an appropriate amount of risk? The answer to both these questions appears to be "no." The deposit insurance system encourages the insured institutions to take *excessive risk,* and, as a result, it results in the deposit insurance agencies taking on excessive risk. Further, these problems have become more significant with deregulation, particularly with deposit rate deregulation and the increase in 1980 in the amount of insured deposits to $100,000, actions that for the first time allowed deposit institutions to market large, rate-ceiling-free deposits without credit risk.

Deposit Insurance and Risk

Fixed-rate deposit insurance encourages depository institutions to take excessive risk in a variety of ways. Under the fixed-rate deposit insurance system the institutions are encouraged to choose a portfolio of assets that carries excessive risk and to support that portfolio with less capital. With deposit insurance the cost of deposits to the insured depository institutions does not increase with its greater portfolio risk, though the returns do. (Firms that lack government guarantees of their debt will experience rising borrowing costs as the risk of future bankruptcy increases.)

Asset Risk.   The effect of the fixed-rate deposit insurance system on asset risk may be explained with the use of Fig. 14.1. The horizontal axis shows the level of asset risk as represented by the variability of total return on the assets. The vertical axis measures the expected return on the bank's assets and the cost of

---

[7]See David D. Whitehead and Robert L. Schweitzer, "Bank Risk and Bank Size: A Note on the Evidence," Federal Reserve Bank of Atlanta *Economic Review* (November 1983).

[8]These questions and possible answers to the questions are developed by Timothy Campbell and David Glenn in "Deposit Insurance in a Deregulated Environment," *Journal of Finance* (July 1984), 775–785.

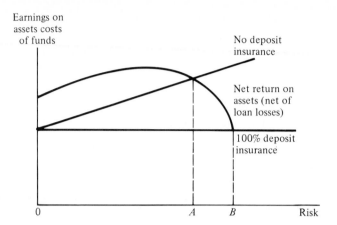

FIGURE 14.1   **Deposit Insurance and Bank Risk**

funds with no deposit insurance and with 100% deposit insurance. Since the cost of funds will remain unchanged with higher risk if deposits are fully insured, the bank will be encouraged to take higher risk—*OB,* as compared to *OA* with no deposit insurance. In fact, the net returns on assets is shown to turn down with excessive portfolio risk, but if it does not, bank management would be encouraged to take on unlimited amounts of risk.

Risk at Credit Unions.   A recent study by Clair attempted to quantify the effect of deposit insurance on risk taking at credit unions (and also by implication the effects on other depository institutions).[9] The credit union industry provides an excellent case study vehicle, since federal deposit insurance became available to credit unions only in 1971. Analyzing the portfolio behavior of credit unions, Clair found increased credit risk following the availability of deposit insurance, reflecting reduced capital ratios and rising delinquency rates on the loan portfolio. In fact, the evidence was very strong that the implementation of deposit insurance at credit unions produced portfolio adjustments toward greater risk.

To a certain degree this moral hazard problem can be reduced through restraints placed on banks by legislation and regulation. For example, bank risk taking is constrained by the general prohibition of banks holding equity securities and by severe limitation on the types of debt securities that banks may hold. Also, the regulatory authorities establish minimum levels for equity capital and assess the risk level of the bank through regular on-site examination. Yet the ef-

---

[9]Robert T. Clair, "Deposit Insurance, Moral Hazard and Credit Unions," Federal Reserve Bank of Dallas *Economic Review* (July 1984), 1–10.

fects of this regulation are only partially successful, particularly because of deregulation.

Deposit Insurance and Treatment of Failed Insured Institutions

When an insured depository institution fails, its deposit insurer (FDIC for
banks, FSLIC for savings and loan associations, NCUA for credit unions) is responsible for the orderly disposition of its assets and liabilities. The primary responsibility of the insurance agencies, of course, is ensuring that insured depositors have ready access to their funds. However, in discharging the latter
responsibility, deposit-insuring agencies usually act as receiver for failed institutions (declared insolvent by the chartering agency).

Deposit insurance agencies can carry out their mission of protecting depositors of failed or failing insured institutions by any of the following approaches.
In the case of an FDIC- or FSLIC-insured institution failure the agencies may
choose to:

1. liquidate the closed institution and pay depositors the full value of their insured deposits up to the maximum amount (sharing any losses due to an excess
of the amount of insured deposits over the proceeds of liquidated assets with
uninsured depositors and creditors); or

2. instead of paying insured depositors directly, transfer their deposits to
another institution (a method first used by the FDIC in 1983); or

3. assist in the process of the failed institution being absorbed by another (new
or existing) institution (called a **purchase-and-assumption transaction**); or

4. reorganize the troubled institution (which would ordinarily require nondeposit creditor cooperation and concessions); or

5. take over operations of the failed institution as a rechartered "Deposit Insurance National bank."

The agencies generally employ either the liquidation or purchase-and-
assumption method, the FSLIC being much more apt to attempt to keep failing
S & Ls viable (via FHLB advances and other efforts) than the FDIC in the case of
its insured institutions that flounder.[10] While both the FDIC and FSLIC employ
the purchase-and-assumption approach in the great majority of insured institution failures, the FDIC has been much more willing to liquidate failed institutions

---

[10]However, the FDIC has occasionally used direct infusions of funds into troubled banks to avert
their failure. Examples include First Pennsylvania Bank (1980), Continental Illinois National Bank
(1984), and First City of Texas (1987), the latter two being very large banks. Also the Federal Home
Loan Bank Board has used a management consignment program on a number of occasions,
whereby a failed savings and loan is turned over to another management group.

than has the FSLIC, and for the FDIC, prior to the 1982 Penn Square Bank fail-ure, all deposit payoffs since 1960 involved banks having average deposits of $8 million. From 1934 to 1984 the FDIC handled 344 payoff cases (including four-teen deposit transfers) and 403 assumption cases.

The 1933 legislation that created the deposit insurance system for commer-cial banks provided only for liquidation and deposit payoffs. A 1935 amendment provided that the FDIC could use its funds to arrange a purchase-and-assumption transaction (rather than proceed with liquidation) if the agency regards this mea-sure as serving to "reduce the risk or avert a threatened loss to the corporation." A purchase-and-assumption transaction is often less costly to the FDIC than a deposit payoff, and the larger the failed bank, the more likely that this will be the case. Further, finding a merger partner for larger banks tends to be easier than for smaller banks. Another reason for the FDIC and FSLIC desire to avoid deposit payoffs, particularly for larger institutions, is concern for the effect that liquidations have on public confidence in depository institutions generally and their effects on uninsured depositors specifically. When insured institutions are liquidated and deposit payoff proceeds, uninsured depositors are likely to expe-rience losses and, in any event, must await sale of assets and settling of claims before receiving even partial restitution.

Until recently, in purchase-and-assumption cases, all depositors and general creditors were fully protected against loss irrespective of the size of their deposit accounts (although stockholders and any subordinated creditors were likely to sustain losses). Thus uninsured depositors had an incentive to place funds in larger institutions, since such institutions are less likely to be liquidated in the event of failure. It was also clear that the greater the likelihood that failure of an institution would be handled via a purchase-and-assumption, the less motivation uninsured depositors had to scrutinize and monitor the failure risk of institu-tions in which they hold deposits. Concern about these behavioral effects of the use of the purchase-and-assumption technique prompted the FDIC to modify the method, beginning with eleven cases in 1984. In these cases, uninsured deposi-tors received only a specified percentage (ranging from 35 to 75 percent) of their deposit claims instead of the entire amount.

In purchase-and-assumption transactions a portion of the failed institution's assets and all its deposits and nonsubordinated liabilities are assumed by the merger partner. The FDIC, as receiver, retains dubious (or clearly worthless) assets of the failed bank. (Recently, the FDIC has also provided financial assis-tance to facilitate "open-bank mergers" of failing savings banks.) The financial assistance provided to the acquiring institution by the FDIC is intended to cover, in whole or in part, the shortfall between the amount of liabilities assumed by the latter firm and the value of assets being obtained. Such agency assistance may be cash or, in recent years, promissory notes on which the magnitude of interest payments is linked to performance of transferred assets. Further, the FDIC often indemnifies takeover banks against potential liabilities of the acquired institu-tion that may surface in the future.

The Competitive Equality Banking Act of 1987 gave the FDIC authority to take over failing banks and operate them as "bridge banks" for up to three years. The FDIC used this authority in 1988 when the First Republic organization in Texas became insolvent.

The collapse of the savings and loan industry in Texas (and in some other states) in the late 1980s created a severe problem for the Federal Savings and Loan Insurance Corporation. This insuring agency was unable to close insolvent savings and loans because of inadequate balances in the insurance fund. Yet the extent of the insolvencies at the savings and loans grew day by day, as did the potential liabilities of the insurance fund. In late 1988 the Federal Home Loan Bank Board moved more forcefully under its "Southwest Plan" to merge insolvent institutions with the assistance of private investors.

Proposed Changes in the Deposit Insurance System

A number of proposed changes in the deposit insurance system have received serious attention. The most important proposals include changes in the coverage of deposit insurance, replacing the present flat-rate premium for deposit insurance with variable-rate premiums (based on risk), and altering purchase-and-assumption transactions in a way that would expose uninsured depositors to more risk. Provision of deposit insurance by the private insurance industry is another suggestion.

One Hundred Percent Deposit Insurance.   Full deposit coverage is urged on the grounds of greater efficiency and equity. The efficiency argument is based on the generally accepted concept of failure in that segment of the financial information market bearing on the financial condition of depository institutions and stemming from the liquidity of deposit claims. But limited deposit insurance leaves depository institutions unprotected against runs by uninsured depositors. And the greater the degree of public disclosure of the problems of distressed banks, the more likely such runs are. First Republic Bank of Texas experienced massive deposit withdrawals (in 1987) due to concern about the credit quality of its loans.

Some Arguments for and against 100 Percent Deposit Insurance.   The equity argument for 100 percent deposit insurance is based on the evident preference of the deposit insurance agencies to employ the purchase-and-assumption method, rather than deposit payoff, whenever possible in the case of failures of large institutions. Only very unlucky uninsured depositors (such as those in the Penn Square Bank case) or the relatively few uninsured depositors in small banks ever sustain deposit losses as the result of institution failures. The impact of this alleged inequity is heightened in the competition among depository institutions for large deposits. Since the likelihood of a deposit payoff (and losses for unin-

PROPERTY HELD
BY THE DEPOSIT INSURANCE AGENCIES:
THE DISPOSABLE AND THE NONDISPOSABLE

With the large increase in the number of failed banks and savings and loan associations in the late 1980s the two principal federal deposit insurance agencies (the FDIC and the FSLIC) became the owners of literally billions of dollars in assets. Most of these assets consist of the property pledged to secure defaulted business, real estate, and consumer loans. As a result, the insurance agencies are among the largest owners of commercial and residential real estate in Texas (and elsewhere) as well as business capital goods, and inventories.

Disposition of these assets is a major task and involves the attention of a large number of employees. At the FDIC the liquidation division handles these assets while the Federal Asset Disposition Agency (FADA) was established to manage the property acquired through savings and loan failures. The task facing these managers is to liquidate the assets in a way to maximize their value to the deposit insurance agencies. While disposition of real estate in the depressed markets of Texas is complicated by the potential of further reducing property values through "dumping" additional real estate into the market, in most instances the process involves relatively straightforward analysis of business alternatives.

In some cases, however, the assets acquired prove rather difficult to dispose of. For example, the *Wall Street Journal*[1] reports that FDIC liquidators have had to "dispose of" a sunken tugboat, an X-rated movie, and a thoroughbred stud with venereal disease. However, recently, while liquidating a bank in Booker, Texas, they faced perhaps their most difficult task. During the liquidation process of counting the cash, checking the records, and otherwise proceeding through the normal routine the FDIC discovered a rather unusual asset in a styrofoam cooler located in one part of the bank: a human skull and other human bones. The FDIC was finally able to get the county sheriff to take the bones but declared that "we won't take them back without a court order." Apparently, these assets are not only difficult to value but also have a poor secondary market.

[1]John E. Yang, "*Here's a Cooler You Don't Want to Bring to the Company Picnic,*" Wall Street Journal *(January 23, 1987),* p. 25, column 1.

sured depositors) is inversely related to institution size, larger institutions have an unfair advantage in competing for uninsured deposits.

The principal argument against 100 percent deposit insurance is its negation of whatever degree of constraint on depository institution risk taking is exercised by uninsured depositors (so-called "market discipline"). In effect, it accentuates the moral hazard problem. Since depositors do not fear losses in the event of institution failure, their criteria for selection of an institution in which to deposit funds need not include the safety and soundness of the institution. Selection based purely on the drive toward greater yields would provide depository institutions with yet another incentive to undertake larger risks. Another argument against 100 percent deposit insurance centers on the increase in risk to insurance funds (since almost 30 percent of U.S. domestic deposits are uninsured). But what such expanded coverage would most likely mean is virtual termination of deposit payoffs in favor of other approaches (and such necessary legislation as to protect the agencies from unknown, contingent liabilities of failed institutions). More important, expanded coverage may have the effect of retarding (if not reversing) the pace of deregulation because of the increased risk to the deposit insurance agencies.

Other Proposed Changes in Coverage.   Other proposals include 100 percent insurance on demand deposits but limited (or no) insurance on time deposits. The argument here is that public policy required compulsory insurance only for transaction accounts, that is, money. Runs on other accounts can be avoided by proper maturity management of time deposits and sufficiently stringent early withdrawal provisions (including prohibition thereof). The argument has considerable appeal. Uninsured demand deposits currently amount to about $125 billion, but the bulk of these funds are in business accounts (much of the balances being of the compensating balance variety), and about three fourths of this amount is offset by loans. Thus the increase in exposure to the FDIC insurance funds would be only about $50 billion, while eliminating the risk of runs from the type of account most subject to run-type withdrawals.

The major flaw in any proposal hinging on a distinction between transactions and nontransactions accounts is the increasing difficulty of doing so. Such differentiation is now limited to a designated number of permissible monthly withdrawals—hardly a sturdy peg on which to hang eligibility for deposit insurance.

Introducing an element of voluntarism in the amount of deposit insurance obtained has also been proposed. For example, one way to provide depositors with an avenue of obtaining additional insurance protection is to provide depository institutions with the option of securing such protection for their deposits. A more radical variation is to shift all premium payments for deposit insurance to depositors and allow them to purchase whatever the amount of protection they select. But all these proposals are fraught with practical difficulties. The basic problem is the nature of deposit insurance as a "public good" and the "free rider" problem inherent in such cases. All depository institutions and depositors benefit from the existence of deposit insurance because it reduces the risk of system failure. But because this risk is low, no individual institution or depositor has a strong incentive to purchase deposit insurance.

As a practical matter, 100 percent deposit insurance has been virtually already in effect, mainly because of the dominance of the purchase-and-assumption approach to handling bank failures and to the precedent set by the regulatory response to the difficulties at Continental Illinois in 1984 and First Republic in 1987. The elevation of the deposit insurance ceiling to $100,000 in 1980 has also played a significant role. This latter development had repercussions beyond simply expanding the proportion of total deposits covered by insurance. By bringing large certificates of deposit into the protected fold, various means of obtaining insurance protection for large sums came into being, the emergence of deposit brokering perhaps being the most significant. The present problem is thus not one of inadequate deposit protection, but rather one of reconciling such protection with an increasingly deregulated and risky banking environment.

Risk-Related Deposit Insurance Premiums

The FDIC has proposed a change in the pricing of deposit insurance, albeit a rather modest one. Although a system of risk-related insurance premiums is consistent with the FDIC's focus on market discipline, the agency supported the change primarily on the basis of equity.

Past resistance to variable insurance rates by the deposit insurance agencies and other regulators has been justified primarily on the basis of practical difficulties of implementation. It is also argued that since differences in deposit insurance premium rates would become public knowledge, high-premium (riskier) banks could suffer unduly from withdrawals by concerned, uninsured depositors. Given the level of disclosure that now exists, this concern is perhaps superfluous. The operational problems of risk-based deposit insurance pricing remain.

In concept, risk-related deposit insurance pricing is difficult to fault. Each insured bank would pay a total premium equivalent to the product of probability of its failure and the cost to the insurance fund of such failure. If premiums thus fully reflected risk (the ideal), and if there were no other constraints on depository institution use of deposit funds, each institution could then accept risk until the corresponding increment in the insurance premium was just equal to incremental returns. In this "ideal" case, marginal costs and marginal benefits of risk would be equal, and the optimum degree of risk taking would result. In addition to being economically efficient the system would be equitable in the sense that each insured institution would pay a premium commensurate with its potential cost to the insurance fund. Much of the administrative and compliance costs of regulation and capital and capital adequacy standards could be eliminated, although the cost of deposit insurance agencies monitoring and examining insured depository institutions would continue and almost certainly increase. (The examining function would be necessary as part of the rate-setting process.)

What the FDIC plan would accomplish is far from this "ideal" outcome but it would achieve partial alleviation of the clear inequity in which low-risk institutions subsidize high-risk institutions. It may serve also as a further means of imposing market discipline on the risk-taking propensities of institutions if (as is likely) the inclusion of institutions in the "high" and "very high" risk classification is made public. This is particularly true if measures were undertaken to increase the risk of loss to uninsured depositors (and general creditors). And, of course, while the proposed additional premium charges for riskier banks might be modest, they may be sufficient in some instances to deter banks from undertaking excessive risk. Further, the proposed new system would provide both an incentive and an approach for the deposit insurance agencies to develop an improved system of risk measurement.

It is important that development of a credible, generally acceptable, and reasonably "accurate" system of risk measurement precede adoption of a more rigorous (compared to the modest FDIC initiative) approach to risk-related deposit insurance pricing. Improper pricing of premiums may result in unintended and injurious behavior on the part of depository financial institutions. Premiums that are too high may encourage undue conservatism, and premiums that are too low may motivate excess risk taking on the part of banks. In either event, neither equity nor efficiency in resource allocation is well served. Although it must be recognized that flat-rate insurance premiums are necessarily too high or too low for most institutions, it is also true that their risk behavior cannot currently alter their deposit insurance costs.

Private Insurance

One other proposal is to substitute private insurance entirely for government (FDIC) insurance. Proponents of this proposal argue that private insurers would be more skillful in properly measuring and pricing risk than the FDIC (because they have a profit incentive to do so). However, concern exists about the potential for banking panics and runs under private deposit insurance, especially in the wake of failures of such systems (for a number of thrift institutions in Ohio and Maryland in 1985). Depositors at a privately insured bank would be concerned about the ability of the insurance company to meet its obligations in the event of bank failure. In addition, even ignoring this problem, the potential difficulty exists of insurance companies being unwilling to insure deposits on a large scale, since bank failures are not independent. For example, since an economic contraction increases the failure risk for all banks simultaneously, the insurance companies cannot depend on diversification of risk to make their overall risk acceptable.

REFORM OF THE REGULATORY STRUCTURE

The United States has an extremely complex structure of government agencies concerned with the regulation of commercial banks and other depository institutions. At the federal level the Federal Reserve System, the Comptroller of the Currency, and the Federal Deposit Insurance Corporation are involved with bank regulation.[11] The Federal Home Loan Bank Board regulates savings and loans, and the National Credit Union Administration regulates credit unions. Similar organizations exist at the state level to regulate the various types of depository institutions. The functions of these organizations often overlap, with the result that an individual depository institution may be and usually is subjected to regulation by more than one regulatory agency. Such overlap of regulation is often cumbersome and frequently produces inequity in the regulation of different institutions.

Pros and Cons of the Current System

As Horvitz points out, there are three reasons to be concerned about this multiplicity of regulation of depository institutions.[12] First, the large number of government agencies performing the same function increases the cost of supervision. Second, the overlapping of jurisdictions by the regulatory authorities could potentially create gaps in regulation that would perhaps lead to safety and soundness problems in the depository financial institution system. Third, the regulatory agencies may promulgate conflicting and contradictory regulations.

While these concerns are certainly important, they are not all of equal importance. The first problem—that of cost effiency—may be of minor significance, since it appears that consolidation of the regulatory authorities would produce only small reductions in examination costs. The savings would be minor, since the regulatory authorities through their own cooperation (specifically via the Financial Institutions Examination Council) have reduced the extent of overlapping examinations to a very significant extent. The third concern—that of conflicting regulatory rulings—appears to be of more significance. In some instances the conflicts in interpretation of rulings is a technical matter, though sometimes of considerable significance to individual banks. In others the different regulatory interpretations reflect matters of policy, one agency being more "liberal" than another with regard to a particular regulatory policy. For example, in the early 1960s the then Comptroller of the Currency, James Saxon, substantially broadened the operating powers of national banks through interpretive rulings.

The second problem—that of gaps in regulatory powers—is perhaps the major problem that arises from the multiplicity of regulatory authorities. One of the most significant examples of these gaps is the regulation of bank holding companies and their subsidiary banks. The Federal Reserve Board has legal responsibility for regulation and supervision of all holding companies. However, the banks that are subsidiaries of a holding company may not be regulated by the

---

[11]The FDIC also regulates insured savings banks.
[12]Paul Horvitz, "Reorganization of the Financial Regulatory Agencies," *Journal of Bank Research* (Winter 1983), 245–261.

Fed. If the subsidiary bank is a nationally chartered bank, for example, the principal regulatory agency is the Comptroller of the Currency. Effective supervision of this banking organization would require full continuing coordination between the Fed and the Comptroller, a degree of coordination that may or may not exist in practice.

Although each of the above concerns would lead to a recommendation for consolidation of the regulatory agencies, there is also a strong case for not changing dramatically the present regulatory structure. This argument emphasizes the benefits of competition and diversification. By this argument the present multiplicity of regulatory agencies leads to innovation by financial institutions in the offering of new financial services. The lack of concentration of regulatory power allows for competition among the regulatory authorities in fulfilling their functions effectively and at minimum cost (the opponents of this view would argue that the competition is "competition in laxity"). When individual banks have the option of switching regulators from the FDIC to the Comptroller of the Currency (by switching from a state to a national charter), it is frequently argued that this option may affect the operations of the regulatory authorities (in a favorable way).

Proposals for Regulatory Agency Reform

There have been numerous proposals for reforming the regulatory agencies. For example, the Commission on Money and Credit in 1961 argued that regulatory authority should be consolidated into the Federal Reserve. However, while in 1971 the Hunt Commission recommended consolidation of the regulatory agencies, it proposed taking away most of the regulatory powers of the Federal Reserve. In fact, the proper role of the Federal Reserve in the regulation of banks and other depository institutions has been a focal point of controversy in all proposals for reform of the regulatory structure.

The Federal Reserve is the only regulatory authority that also has macroeconomic stabilization objectives. While the Fed combines monetary policy and bank supervision, its principal function is the formulation and implementation of monetary policy. The Fed's direct bank supervision is limited to a relatively small number of banks, though its supervisory powers over all bank holding companies is a burdensome activity.

Many proposals for regulatory reform have argued that combining monetary policy and bank supervision may involve an inherent conflict of functions. Such a combination can cause problems in that the supervisory function draws attention of Fed policymakers away from their monetary policy activities. The Fed's exercise of its regulatory power also may cause political controversy that may make the operation of monetary policy more difficult. In contrast to this view, however, some observers have argued that the Fed needs examination data and other data in bank operation in order to properly execute monetary policy.[13] Not surprisingly, the Federal Reserve has strongly opposed the reduction or elimination of its supervisory functions. In fact, the Fed has argued that "The Federal Reserve as the nation's central bank must remain substantially involved in the regulation and supervision of the financial and banking system because those functions impinge upon its general responsibilities."[14]

The most recent proposal for reform was made in spring 1984 by the Task Group on Regulation of Financial Services, more commonly referred to as the Bush Task Group.

This task group made recommendations that included the following.

1. A new federal banking agency would be created. This agency would take over the regulation of federally chartered banks and the regulation of all bank holding companies except the bank holding company parent of the fifty largest banks. The new federal banking agency would also have the power (taken from the Fed) to establish the permissible activities for bank holding companies (the Fed would have veto power over any such activities that it perceived as being detrimental to the safety and soundness of the banking system). The Office of the Comptroller of the Currency would be absorbed by the new federal banking agency, which would be part of the Treasury department.

2. The Federal Reserve would take over the examination and supervisory role of the FDIC for state-chartered and insured banks. The Fed could delegate this power to the individual state by certifying that the individual state banking departments were competent to assume such responsibilities. The standard for such delegation would be set by the new Federal Banking Agency, the Federal Reserve Board, and the FDIC, though decisions on individual applications would be set by the Federal Reserve Board. The regulatory jurisdiction of the Federal Reserve would, in fact, be increased substantially by these recommendations. If the proposal were implemented, the number of banks subject to Fed jurisdiction would rise from about 1000 to almost 10,000 (representing about two thirds of all commercial banks). In addition, the Fed would retain jurisdiction of about 70 percent of the domestic assets of bank holding companies.

3. The FDIC would have no day-to-day regulatory activities and would focus on its insurance functions. It would set insurance premiums on the basis of the riskiness of a bank's activities and would have the ability to examine any banks that were experiencing financial distress. The only banks that the FDIC would exam-

---

[13]Peterson explored this issue and could find no evidence that the Fed has used examination data in the conduct of monetary policy. See Manfred Peterson, "Conflicts Between Monetary Policy and Bank Supervision," *Issues in Bank Regulation* (Autumn 1977).

[14]The Federal Reserve Position and Restructuring of Financial Regulation Responsibilities," Federal Reserve *Bulletin* (July 1984), 547.

ine would be troubled institutions—those with a CAMEL (capital, asset quality, management, earnings, and liquidity) rating of 3, 4, or 5.[15]

The task group also recommended that depository thrift institutions be allowed to remain under the regulation of the Federal Home Loan Bank Board only if they maintained a minimum percentage of their assets in mortgage loans, that all securities regulations applicable to banks and thrifts be placed in the Securities and Exchange Commission, and that all antitrust activities be centralized in the Department of Justice. In fact, under these recommendations a bank that had a large portfolio of mortgage loans would be insured by the FSLIC and regulated by the Federal Home Loan Bank Board, just as a savings and loan that had diversified out of mortgages would be treated as a bank for insurance and regulation purposes.

The recommendations of the Bush task group were very much a political compromise. While they would achieve some degree of consolidation, the amount of that consolidation is quite limited. Moreover, the amount of the consolidation of the regulatory agencies that the task force finally recommended was reduced from its original recommendations after opposition from the Federal Reserve. Cost savings produced by the implementation of these recommendations would be quite modest. Reform of the regulatory structure appears to remain an important though unresolved issue.

SUMMARY

The revolution in the financial services industry has raised a number of issues that are significant to public policymakers as well as to others. Additional deregulation beyond the elimination of deposit rate ceilings, to encompass product and geographical deregulation, remains an important public policy issue. The separation of commercial and investment banking as mandated by the Glass-Steagall Act is one of the most controversial issues confronting the financial system. Elimination of the barriers between commercial and investment banking would affect both the profitability and risk dimensions of banking organizations, though some nonbank activities carry more risk than commercial banking, while others carry less risk. In addition, full entry by commercial bank organizations into underwriting all types of securities has substantial advantages and disadvantages to banking organizations, such that some banks might choose not to enter investment banking even if they were permitted to do so.

The third dimension of deregulation—geographic deregulation—principally in-

---

[15]The CAMEL rating system was adopted by the three bank regulatory agencies on November 21, 1979. Bank examiners assign a numerical value to each of the dimensions of bank performance ranging from 1 to 5, where 1 is the best rating. See Barron H. Putnam, "Early Warning Systems and Financial Analysis in Bank Monitoring," Federal Reserve Bank of Atlanta *Economic Review* (November 1982), 6–14.

volves the issue of interstate banking. Despite concern that removal of barriers to interstate banking would lead to massive consolidation, substantial increases in concentration, and reduced performance of the banking industry, the existing literature suggests that these concerns might not be valid. Given the existence of relatively limited economies of scale and the fact that geographical expansion through acquisitions requires approval by the regulatory authorities, any modest consolidation that seems likely to occur might actually increase rather than reduce competition in many of the markets for financial services.

Closely related to product and geographical deregulation is the issue of deposit insurance. While deposit insurance has worked reasonably well for over fifty years, the deregulation movement has created substantial problems for the existing system of fixed rate premiums. The freedom that has come to managers of depository institutions with deregulation has allowed many to take on excess risk and thereby to put excessive risk on the deposit insurance agencies. A number of proposals have been put forth to solve this problem, including risk-based premium rates and increased "market discipline" to curb risk taking.

Deregulation has also raised the issue of reforming the regulatory structure for depository institutions; the current uncoordinated structure reflects the traditional separation of functions of different depository institutions. It is argued that the existence of separate regulatory agencies creates problems of cost efficiencies and coordination and could lead to potential problems in handling distressed financial institutions. Further, as depository institutions become more alike, the need for one regulatory agency for all depository institutions becomes more evident. Yet others argue that the existence of a number of regulatory agencies provides the opportunity for innovation in regulation. The Bush task group report in 1984 recommended partial though not complete consolidation of the regulatory agencies.

QUESTIONS

1. What reasons may be given to justify the separation of commercial and investment banking? How does the Glass-Steagall Act do this? What securities activities are permitted to commercial banks?

2. Compare the risk of commercial banking with that of other related activities as shown in Table 14.1. Explain the significance of the coefficient of variation and the coefficient of determination.

3. Would a large number of banks be expected to enter the underwriting business if such an activity were not prohibited?

4. If all barriers to geographical expansion by banks were eliminated, would we expect massive consolidation? Explain.

5. Explain the effect of fixed-rate premium deposit insurance on the risk-taking behavior of depository institutions. Would variable rate insurance premiums affect risk taking?

6. What are the advantages and disadvantages of allowing market discipline to work in banking?

7. Explain the costs and benefits of the proposed consolidated regulatory structure.

REFERENCES

Benston, George, "Why Continue to Regulate Banks?" *Midland Corporate Finance Journal* (Fall 1987), 67–82.

Campbell, Tim S., and David Glenn, "Deposit Insurance in a Deregulated Environment," *Journal of Finance* (July 1984), 775–784.

Clair, Robert R., "Deposit Insurance, Moral Hazard, and Credit Unions," Federal Reserve Bank of Dallas *Economic Review* (July 1984), 1–12.

Cooper, K., and D. Fraser, "The Rising Cost of Bank Futures: A Proposed Solution," *Journal of Retail Banking* (Fall 1988), 5–12.

Dunham, Constance, and Richard F. Syron, "Interstate Banking: The Drive to Consolidate," Federal Reserve Bank of Boston, New England *Economic Review* (May/June 1984), 11–28.

Felgran, Steven D., "Shared ATM Networks: Market Structure and Public Policy," Federal Reserve Bank of Boston, New England *Economic Review* (January/February 1984), 23–38.

Fraser, Donald R., "Structural and Competitive Implications of Interstate Banking," *Journal of Corporation Law* (August 1984), 643–654.

Furlong, Frederick, "Changes in Bank Risk-Taking," Federal Reserve Bank of San Francisco *Economic Review* (Spring 1988), 45–56.

Gilbert, Gary G., "An Analysis of the Bush Task Group Recommendation, for Bank Regulatory Reform," *Issues in Bank Regulation* (Spring 1984), 11–16.

Kane, Edward, "No Room for Weak Links in the Chain of Deposit Insurance Reform," *Journal of Financial Services Research* (September 1987), 77–111.

Keeton, William R., "Deposit Insurance and the Deregulation of Deposit Rates," Federal Reserve Bank of Kansas City *Economic Review* (April 1984), 28–46.

King, B. Frank, "Interstate Banking: Issues and Evidence," Federal Reserve Bank of Atlanta *Economic Review* (April 1984), 32–45.

———, "Interstate Expansion and Bank Costs," Federal Reserve Bank of Atlanta *Economic Review* (May 1983), 40–45.

Pyle, David H., "Deregulation and Deposit Insurance Reform," Federal Reserve Bank of San Francisco *Economic Review* (Spring 1984), 5–15.

Whitehead, David D., and Jan Luyties, "Can Interstate Banking Increase Competitive Market Performance? An Empirical Test," Federal Reserve Bank of Atlanta *Economic Review* (January 1984), 4–10.

PART V

FINANCIAL MARKETS

CHAPTER **15**

Risk, Return, and the Efficiency of Financial Markets

This chapter is the first of nine chapters that focus on the nature and role of financial markets in the financial system. The principal objective of these chapters is description and analysis of the instruments and operations of the financial marketplace, but they also fill another important need by providing an integrated view of the U.S. financial system. The latter objective is best achieved in this part of the book, for it is in financial markets that deficit and surplus economic units and financial intermediaries "come together" to exchange financial instruments. The financial marketplace is the "engine" of the financial system, the arena in which interest rates and security prices are established and huge sums of funds flow among market agents.

Previous chapters of this book introduced various important aspects of financial markets and provided a description of the role they play in the financial system. This chapter offers a more detailed treatment of certain of these topics. It is followed by chapters that focus on the principal types of financial markets, the financial instruments traded in them, and the ways in which the operations of financial institutions are influenced by events in the financial marketplace.

This chapter first offers an analysis of the asset-pricing function of financial markets (Section A) and then provides an overview of the various types of financial markets (Section B).

SECTION **A**

ASSET PRICING
IN FINANCIAL MARKETS

The role of the financial system in the saving–investment process was described in preceding chapters. Chapter 2 indicated the essential role of saving in economic growth, and it described how financial markets (and the other components of the financial system) facilitate this expansion of an economy's productive capacity by providing a mechanism for external financing to economic units seeking funds to invest. Succeeding chapters described interest rate determination, the significance of the level and structure of interest rates, various financial intermediaries, and the role of government in the financial system.

The previous chapters focused primarily on **aggregate** saving and investment and the various factors that affect their magnitudes. The discussion in those chapters was concerned with the quantity of saving by surplus economic units and with the reasons for such saving, not with what (or why) particular financial assets might be chosen as a repository for savings. Similarly, discussion of which financial instruments might be used by borrowers or of what decision criteria would be employed to select among alternative instruments was also deferred to the present chapter.

Underlying aggregate saving and investment, of course, are innumerable individual economic decisions made by participants in the financial marketplace, and the principal factors bearing on these decisions warrant additional discussion. Specifically, the determination of prices and yields of financial instruments traded in financial markets and thus the allocation of the funds of surplus economic units among deficit economic units hinge on the supply of and demand for these instruments. The nature of the process underlying the pricing of securities is thus of considerable significance to an understanding of financial markets. In turn, an understanding of this process requires some attention to certain aspects of financial behavior, particularly those relating to **portfolio selection**— how surplus economic units allocate saved funds among the various financial instruments created by deficit units and intermediaries.

PORTFOLIO SELECTION AND DIVERSIFICATION
Risk, Return, and Expected Utility

Chapter 2 included an introductory discussion of the process by which prices of financial assets are determined. We indicated there that the price of a financial asset is a function of its **expected return** and the degree of **risk** associated with that expected return. The expected return is simply the weighted average of all possible returns, where the weights are the probabilities of each possible return. A common measure of the risk associated with the expected return is the variance (or the standard deviation, which is the square root of the variance) of the probability distribution of possible returns. Table 15.1 shows a sample calculation of expected returns for two hypothetical securities, with possible returns and corresponding probabilities as shown. Table 15.2 indicates how the variance (and standard deviation) of the return of each hypothetical security is calculated.

As indicated in Tables 15.1 and 15.2, Security A and Security B offer expected returns of 12.2 percent and 7.7 percent, respectively. That "expected return" is a statistical artifact is evidenced by the fact that the calculated expected return for the two securities does not correspond to any of their particular possible returns. Nonetheless, to the extent that the identification of possible returns and their associated probabilities of occurrence reflects full and proper use of all available relevant information, the expected return calculation does offer an intuitively satisfying assessment of the likely profitability of a financial asset. The variance (and thus the standard deviation) measures the "spread" between the various possible rates of return and the expected return. The smaller the

TABLE 15.1 Calculation of Expected Return

Security A				
Possible Rate of Return		Probability of Possible Rate of Return		
0%	×	.3	=	0.0%
10%	×	.2	=	2.0%
18%	×	.4	=	7.2%
30%	×	.1	=	3.0%
		Expected rate of return	=	12.2%

Security B				
Possible Rate of Return		Probability of Possible Rate of Return		
5%	×	.3	=	1.5%
8%	×	.4	=	3.2%
10%	×	.3	=	3.0%
		Expected rate of return	=	7.7%

TABLE 15.2   Calculation of Variance of Security Returns _____

Security A

Possible Rate of Return	−	Expected Rate of Return	=	Variation of Possible from Expected Rates of Return	Variation Squared	×	Probability of Possible Rates of Return	=	
0%	−	12.2%	=	− 12.2%	148.84	×	.3	=	44.65%
10%	−	12.2%	=	− 2.2%	4.84%	×	.2	=	.97%
18%	−	12.2%	=	5.8%	33.64%	×	.4	=	13.46%
30%	−	12.2%	=	17.8%	316.84%	×	.1	=	31.68%

Variance of returns = 90.76%

Standard deviation of returns = $\sqrt{90.76\%}$ = 9.5%

Security B

Possible Rate of Return	−	Expected Rate of Return	=	Variation of Possible from Expected Rates	Variation Squared	×	Probability of Possible Rates of Return	=	
5%	−	7.7%	=	− 2.7%	7.29%	×	.3	=	2.187%
8%	−	7.7%	=	.3%	.09%	×	.4	=	.036%
10%	−	7.7%	=	2.3%	5.29%	×	.3	=	1.587%

Variance of returns = 3.81%

Standard deviation of returns = $\sqrt{3.81\%}$ = 1.95%

"spread," the greater the confidence one can attach to an expected return measure—the smaller the variance (standard deviation), the smaller is the degree of risk associated with realization of the expected return.

Although expected return and variance calculations are useful in security selection, they cannot alone necessarily resolve a choice among alternative securities. Consider, for example, a choice between Security A and Security B of the example above. Security A offers a 12.2 percent expected return versus a 7.7 percent expected return for Security B, but Security A's returns are subject to greater risk (a standard deviation of about 9.5 percent versus Security B's approximately 2 percent).[1] Does the higher expected return of Security A offset its greater variability in returns relative to Security B? The answer to this question depends on preferences regarding risk and return. Attitudes and behavior

---

[1] In effect, the standard deviation, as a risk measure, incorporates the degree to which possible returns differ from the expected return and the associated probability of such deviations. Thus positive deviations (possible returns *exceeding* the expected return), as well as negative deviations (possible returns *less than* expected returns), are reflected in the standard deviation calculation. Since investors are likely to be troubled by the latter possibility and not the former, it is important to remember that standard deviation measures reflect not only undesired variability in returns but also total variability.

toward risk differ among individuals, and since risk is generally associated with security returns, risk–return preferences must be taken into account in security choices.

The concept of **expected utility** combines expected return, risk, and risk–return preferences.[2] Thus we will assume that investors (for the sake of brevity we will now use the popular term for surplus economic units seeking to acquire financial assets with saved funds) are averse to risk and seek to maximize **expected utility** from their investments. (As the reader probably already knows, "utility" is the economist's label for happiness.) In other words, investors will select securities that offer the mix of expected return and associated risk that, given their risk–return preferences, makes them the most content.

To illustrate, suppose that Mr. Wary and Ms. Bold are two investors evaluating our Security A, with its expected return of 12.2 percent and standard deviation of 9.5 percent, and Security B, with expected return of 7.7 percent and standard deviation of 2 percent. Mr. Wary, who is very risk averse, will maximize expected utility by investing in Security B; in his utility function the lower risk (as measured by the standard deviation) compensates for the lower return, as compared with security A. Ms. Bold, who is less risk averse than Mr. Wary, will maximize expected utility by investing in Security A, with its higher expected return (and higher risk).

We have to know the degree of risk aversion that characterizes the risk–return preferences of an investor in order to predict the choice between securities (such as those in the example above), one of which offers a higher expected return than the other but also higher risk. We can confidently predict the (rational) choice, however, when the decision involves two securities with the same expected return but differing risk or with the same risk but differing expected returns. In such cases, one investment possibility "dominates" the other. The risk-averse investor should select the security with the highest expected return for a given degree of risk or the security with the lowest degree of risk for a given expected return. This "dominance" principle holds also for **portfolios**—collections of securities. An **efficient portfolio** is a collection of securities that offers the highest possible expected return for the level of portfolio risk or the lowest level of risk for a given expected portfolio return. We look now at some aspects of efficient portfolios that have considerable significance for security pricing.

Security Selection for Efficient Portfolios

It should be recalled that the purpose of the present discussion is to consider how investor selection of financial assets affects security pricing in financial markets. To this point we have considered only individual securities and have as-

---

[2]The concept of expected utility, together with its relation to portfolio selection, is developed much more rigorously in several of the references cited at the end of this chapter. We choose to develop only an intuitive appreciation of the concept in this book.

serted that investors will select financial investments on the basis of securities' expected returns and risk according to each investor's own risk–return preferences. To the extent that investors are risk averse, they will purchase riskier securities only if such securities offer expected returns commensurate with their additional risk. We can expect, then, that financial markets will "price" securities so that their expected returns and risk are commensurate.

The story does not end here, however, because investment in a single security, though not unheard of, is not representative of aggregate financial market behavior. Most security selection decisions are made in the context of adding (or not adding) a particular security to an existing portfolio of securities. Since an investor is concerned with the return and risk characteristics of the total **portfolio,** the relevant aspects of a potential addition to the portfolio are the change (if any) in the portfolio's expected return and risk resulting from acquisition of the security.

The expected rate of return for a portfolio is simply the weighted average of each constituent security's expected rate of return. The weights are the proportions of each security's invested value relative to total portfolio value. Thus the effect of a potential new investment on portfolio expected return can be readily determined. The effect on portfolio risk (as measured by portfolio standard deviation), however, is much more complex. Except in the highly unlikely case that the possible returns of the security under consideration are "perfectly positively correlated" (they move in the same direction and in the same magnitude) with the possible returns of the portfolio as currently constituted, the standard deviation of the reconstituted portfolio will not be the weighted average of its constituent securities' standard deviation of returns. Indeed, a portfolio will never have a standard deviation of possible returns equal to the weighted average of the standard deviation of returns of its component securities unless returns of all these securities are perfectly positively correlated. This phenomenon is what makes possible the risk-reducing effects of diversification. It also causes the relevant risk measure of an individual security (the risk level reflected in the security's price) to be not the standard deviation of its returns but the *incremental risk* to a portfolio of the inclusion of the security in that portfolio.

Covariance

In mathematical terms the returns of the various assets in a portfolio may be viewed as random variables. The **covariance** is the measure of the extent to which these random variables vary in the same way and to the same degree.[3] The mathematics of covariance calculation is rather complex, and we need not employ it

---

[3]Covariance and correlation are obviously closely related concepts. The covariance measure for two securities is equal to the coefficient of correlation between the two securities multiplied by the standard deviations of the two securities.

here.[4] For our purposes, all that is necessary is an intuitive appreciation of how the covariance relationship among security returns may have the effect of lowering portfolio variance (and thus standard deviation) when securities are combined in portfolios. This effect is essentially due to the fact that, to the degree that the behavior of the returns of the various securities is independent (the returns are not perfectly positively correlated), unusually low returns on some securities are not likely to occur in the same periods when unusually low returns occur on other assets in the portfolio. The effect is a "balancing out" of returns among the various assets in the portfolio.

Suppose now that an investor holding a portfolio with equal amounts of investment in Security X and Security Y is considering adding another financial asset, Security Z, to the portfolio. What are the relevant decision variables? One key variable is the expected return of Security Z, since the new portfolio's expected return would be the weighted average of the expected returns of Securities X, Y, and Z. The variance (or standard deviation) of Security Z *alone*, however, is *not* relevant to the investor's decision except as it affects the portfolio's variance. The relevant measure of risk for Security Z is the *change* in the risk of the portfolio as the result of adding Security Z (in whatever amount) to the portfolio. The degree of change in the portfolio's variance that will result is a function of the covariance of Security Z's returns with those of Security X and Security Y, as well as Security Z's "own variance."

As more and more assets are added to a portfolio, the contribution of the incremental assets' "own variance" to portfolio variance becomes less and less. In a well-diversified portfolio the incremental asset's "own variance" term is insignificant, and only the covariance of its returns with those of the other assets in the portfolio will have an impact on portfolio risk. Such a degree of diversification can be achieved with as few as eight to twelve stocks (if they are selected from unrelated industries). Indeed, diversification becomes superfluous at some relatively small number of securities because it becomes more and more difficult to identify securities that offer a pattern of possible returns that are *not* highly correlated with returns of securities already included in the portfolio. This is true whether the investor diversifies "naively" (by selecting cross-industry stocks at random) or "efficiently" (by assessing covariance relationships).

The covariance-calculation approach, unfortunately, requires such a huge number of inputs and computations that it is not practical to apply it to portfolio selection in the form outlined above. This approach requires an assessment of expected return, expected variance, and covariance of returns for each security

---

[4]Many investment and business finance textbooks offer a mathematical and graphical exposition of the risk-reducing effects of diversification in portfolio selection. See, for example, R. A. Haugen, *Introductory Investment Theory* (Englewood Cliffs, N.J.: Prentice-Hall, 1987, 39–102) for an excellent development and discussion. The architect of modern portfolio theory is H. M. Markowitz, whose seminal work is cited in the references at the end of this chapter.

being considered for inclusion in a portfolio with all other securities currently or potentially included in the portfolio. For n securities there are $n(n-1)/2$ covariances, so an analysis of only twenty-five securities would require twenty-five expected returns, twenty-five variances, and 300 covariances.

The key to a more operational approach to efficient portfolio selection lies in the distinction between two kinds of risk relating to security returns: systematic and unsystematic.

Systematic Versus Unsystematic Risk

Recall that the returns of most securities are positively correlated (tending to move in the same direction) but are not perfectly positively correlated (magnitudes and direction of movement not exactly equal). Why is this so often true? The answer is twofold. First, virtually all business enterprises are affected by economywide events, but not to the same degree. A recession, for example, will have a much more serious impact on a firm in the recreation field than on one in the retail grocery business. An economic upswing, on the other hand, will be much more stimulating to recreation-related business firms than to food-related firms. Such broad economic developments affect returns on securities of virtually all firms in all industries, but they affect some much more than others.

The variability in returns of securities that is attributable to economywide trends and events is termed **systematic risk.** Because, by definition, this type of risk pertains to all firms (and thus returns of securities of all firms), it cannot be diversified out of a portfolio. Systematic risk is embodied in the positive covariance that exists among most security returns (in varying degrees).

Unsystematic risk is firm specific and not the result of economywide developments. Successful new products or services, crippling strikes, filing of product liability suits, cost-cutting new processes—these are examples of events in an enterprise's existence that are independent of those affecting other firms and that give rise to positive or negative variability in returns. Such unsystematic variability in the returns of the securities of a given firm is unrelated to the variability in returns of other firms and thus can be eliminated from an efficiently diversified portfolio.

It is this distinction between systematic (undiversified) and unsystematic (diversifiable) risk that underlies an operational approach to portfolio selection and provides an important conceptual framework for understanding financial market behavior—the capital-asset pricing model.[5]

---

[5]For purposes of exposition this description of the capital asset pricing model is highly simplified and skirts various conceptual difficulties involved with the model. For a more rigorous development of the model and discussion of some of its shortcomings as a positive theory of security market behavior, see J. D. Martin, S. H. Cox, and R. D. MacMinn, *The Theory of Finance* (Hinsdale, Illinois: Dryden Press, 1987), 237–251.

THE CAPITAL-ASSET PRICING MODEL

Suppose that an individual investor holds an efficient portfolio of financial assets. To qualify as "efficient," the portfolio must be characterized by the following factors:

1. No other collection of financial assets could offer a greater expected return at the same level of risk or could offer a lower level of risk without some decrease in expected return.

2. All unsystematic risk has been eliminated by diversification. (This second aspect of the portfolio is actually implicit in the first.)

The risk-return tradeoff is now a **systematic risk** versus expected return tradeoff, and it will be determined by the investor's risk–return preferences. The more risk averse the investor, the lower the level of systematic risk(s) he or she will be willing to assume and thus the lower the level of expected return(s) the investor can anticipate. How may systematic risk be measured to allow investors to efficiently construct portfolios to satisfy their preferences?

The basis for development of a measure of systematic risk is a **market index**—an available measure of returns for a collection of financial assets. For the stock market, for example, the Standard & Poor's 500 Stock Composite Index offers a measure of average returns for a broad sample of equity securities. The returns for a given security can then be compared with this index of returns to develop a measure of variability in this security's returns relative to "market" returns. This measure can be developed from the covariance of the individual security's returns with market returns, and it serves as an index of a security's systematic risk.

The **beta coefficient** (which statistically is the covariance between a security's returns and market returns, divided by the variance of market returns) provides an index of systematic risk. If a security has a beta of one, its degree of systematic variability in returns corresponds to that of overall market returns. A beta greater than one indicates a degree of systematic variability exceeding that of the "market portfolio," and a beta less than one indicates a less systematically variable pattern of returns than that of the overall market. A beta of zero indicates an absence of systematic variation in returns relative to the market—a (systematic) risk-free security.

Given the prevalance of risk aversion, one would expect securities with high betas to be priced to offer higher expected rates of return than low-beta securities offer. In Fig. 15.1, the "security market line" shows this expected relationship. (Note that at a beta equal to one, the expected return is that of the overall market portfolio, R_M.) The beta of a portfolio is the weighted average of the betas of the various securities in the portfolio. An investor can thus tailor a portfolio with the degree of systematic risk (and expected return) consistent with his or her preferences.

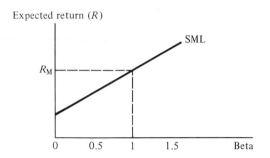

FIGURE 15.1   The Security Market Line (SML)

The body of portfolio theory underlying the "market model" suggests that there is a single portfolio of risky securities that is optimal for all investors—the market portfolio itself. This optimal combination, in theory, consists of all risky securities in existence in the proportions in which they are outstanding in the securities markets.

If a particular security was not included in this optional portfolio or was held in less than its proportionate value relative to all securities, its price would fall, and its expected return would increase. The rise in the expected return of the security would prompt its purchase by investors, which would result in its inclusion in the optimal portfolio in the proportion of its relative value in the securities market. On the other hand, holdings of a security in excess of its proportionate value would trigger its sale by investors, driving down its price and lowering its aggregate value. Security prices are thus the "adjustment variable" for optimal portfolio composition. As was previously indicated, the market portfolio has a beta of one. Does this imply that a beta of one is optimal for all investors? The answer is no because a very risk-averse investor can mix risky security holdings with riskless securities (beta of zero) in whatever proportions fit that investor's risk–return preferences (a weighted average beta perhaps somewhere between zero and one). A less risk-averse investor, on the other hand, can borrow (in theory, though not in practice, at the risk-free rate of interest) and invest the proceeds in the market portfolio of risky assets. This **leveraging,** as the use of low-interest borrowed funds to acquire high-interest assets is called, allows the investor to increase the expected rate of return, but only with a commensurate increase in risk.

Figure 15.2 shows the foregoing relationship, the "capital market line." All points along the line RM represent combinations of expected rates of return and standard deviation of return corresponding to mixtures of investments in riskless securities and the market portfolio of risky securities. (At R the investor holds only riskless securities, and at M only risky securities.) Combinations of expected return and risk on the line to the right of M correspond to investments in the

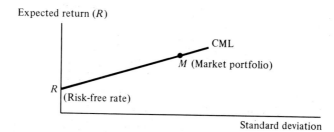

FIGURE 15.2   The Capital Market Line (CML)

market portfolio that include the use of borrowed funds. (As the capital market line, CML, is drawn here, borrowing at the risk-free rate is assumed to be possible. Differential borrowing and lending rates simply change the intercept and slope of the CML.)

In practice, of course, one can only approximate the requirements of this theoretical construct, but close approximation is possible. In terms of market-related variability of returns, U.S. Treasury bills are a reasonable proxy as a "riskless" asset. And although one can hardly include holdings of all risky securities in a portfolio, a market-index mutual fund offers a readily available investment medium that will exhibit much the same behavior as would characterize such a portfolio.

To the extent that investors do construct portfolios in the foregoing manner the implications for the behavior of financial markets is profound and to some extent startling.

Financial Asset Pricing in an Efficient Market

The portfolio theory sketched in this chapter is a normative theory: It does not necessarily describe what investors do; rather, it describes what they should do to achieve certain presumed objectives in the context of an investment environment that is assumed to exhibit certain key characteristics. Whether or not and to what extent investors do behave in accordance with the theory of portfolio selection is an empirical question, and the evidence in this regard is somewhat mixed. Before assessing the results of these empirical studies, however, let us consider the implications of portfolio theory for financial asset pricing in the financial markets.

The theory suggests that investors will seek to hold diversified portfolios in which unsystematic risk is minimal or nonexistent. These portfolios should be **efficient**—no other possible portfolio can offer a greater expected return without some increase in risk or a lower level of risk without some decrease in return. Further, to the extent that these efficient portfolios include holdings of risky assets, this collection of risky assets should be a microcosm of all market securities, in both type and proportions held.

Now suppose that all investors do behave this way. Securities are priced according to their expected returns and relevant risk. The revelant risk to our diversified investors is not total risk but only systematic risk. Unsystematic risk does not matter because it will not affect portfolio risk. *Thus unsystematic risk plays no role in the pricing of financial assets.* Indeed, securities are priced according to investor demand on the basis of their existence as part of the universe of securities (the market portfolio). If the total market value of Security X, for example, were 1 percent of the market value of all securities, each investor would seek to buy the amount of Security X that would make its proportion of the total market value of that investor's portfolio equal to 1 percent. Demand and supply would equilibrate to maintain a price for Security X that would maintain that same proportion (1 percent) of total (and individual portfolio) market value. Variations from that equilibrium price would result in market actions to restore it, since such price variations would alter Security X's proportion of total market value. An increase in price, for example, would cause that proportion to become greater than 1 percent. Investors would consequently reduce (sell) their holdings of Security X in an effort to restore the original proportion. As a result of this increased selling of Security X, the price of Security X would fall until the equilibrium price was reached. The reverse process would hold if, in the opposite kind of disturbance to equilibrium, the price of Security X fell below the equilibrium price. Similar equilibrating forces keep the risk-free rate of interest at (or moving toward) an equilibrium level.

Arbitrage Pricing Model

The capital-asset pricing model (CAPM) has a number of serious problems as a positive theory of security market behavior. The model has been criticized for its unrealistic assumptions, some empirical research results are counter to the model's predicted outcomes, and even the empirical testability of the CAPM has been persuasively challenged.[6] Questions about the CAPM have stimulated interest in an alternative model of security pricing called the **arbitrage pricing model** (APM). The APM's underlying assumptions are less restrictive than the CAPM, and the APM's empirical testability (at least in principle) is less suspect (albeit

---

[6]In 1977 an important paper regarding the testability of the CAPM was published by Richard Roll ("A Critique of the Asset Pricing Theory's Tests. Part I: On the Past and Potential Testability of the Theory," *Journal of Financial Economics,* March 1977). Roll asserted that past tests of the CAPM were tautological, meaning that the outcome of the tests was determined by the nature of the tests, not by the nature of the stock return behavior that served as input for the tests. Second, Roll argued that the CAPM could never be tested because the true market portfolio contains every asset in the economic system and it is not possible to determine the efficiency of such a portfolio in an expected return–standard deviation framework.

not universally accepted). The APM possesses the same intuitive core as the CAPM, namely, that security risk is made up of systematic (nondiversifiable) and unsystematic (diversifiable) risk components and that only the former is significant for equilibrium expected security returns.

The APM takes its name from its equilibrium condition—financial market arbitrage will serve to equilibrate risk and return by generating changes in security prices until there no longer exists any opportunity for arbitrage profits. As to how equilibrium expected returns are determined, the APM allows for multiple economic influences ("factors") but leaves identification of these factors to empirical investigation. As for the expected return for any particular security, the sensitivity of that security to each of the underlying factors is also part of the return-generating process, such sensitivity also being an empirical question. To date, empirical research (see the end-of-chapter references) suggests that <u>at least three or four significant factors exist</u>, including unanticipated changes in the rate of inflation, industrial production, the term structure of interest rates, and the default risk premium on bonds. (The relevance of all these economic phenomena for stock prices would scarcely surprise an economist, even if he or she had never heard of the APM.) However, the nature of the APM causes its empirical testing to be complex and the results of such investigations to be rather tenuous. Thus no definitive empirical conclusion about the APM can yet be drawn.

FINANCIAL MARKET EFFICIENCY

Chapter 1 introduced the notion of the relationship of risk, returns, information, and the efficiency of financial markets. Financial markets maximize their contribution to the efficient allocation of resources in an economy when financial assets are priced to reflect their levels of expected return and risk. The first part of this chapter has sketched the process by which an individual investor may select a portfolio that offers maximum expected return for a given level of risk or minimum risk for a given expected rate of return. To the extent that holdings of such efficient portfolios characterize investor choice, the aggregate economic effect will be a set of security prices that properly channel invested funds to the most productive uses. To better grasp this concept, visualize the saving–investment process for the entire economy as an aggregate portfolio selection process in which countless individual portfolios are combined to direct the flow of saved funds into investment uses. If all these individual portfolios are efficient, this "aggregate" portfolio is efficient, and the funds are made available to finance the most promising investments, the related risk of which is consistent with societal preferences.

Although the reach of the foregoing concept may, in practice, exceed our grasp, the considerable degree to which such resource-allocative efficiency is possible is due to the existence of financial markets. Efficient investor choice among financial assets is made possible by the wide array of available instruments and by the various institutions and mechanisms that exist to facilitate portfolio selection. Efficient investor assessment of expected returns and risk is made possible by the vast information-gathering, analysis, and dissemination network that financial markets provide. Empirical studies indicate that publicly available information items relating to security returns and risk are impounded into security prices virtually concurrently with their generation—an attestation to the remarkable efficiency of this nation's financial markets.

Paradoxical though it may seem, efficiency in security market behavior necessarily implies randomness in security price behavior. Information arrives to the markets in random fashion, and if information is immediately impounded into security prices, then such prices will fluctuate randomly. The term **random walk** is thus applied to the behavior of security prices. Randomness in security price behavior (independence of successive price changes) is an empirical question to which much research has been devoted. Most empirical evidence supports the random walk hypothesis.

Evidence that successive price changes in securities are independent has no necessary implication for the relationship of price changes to other forms of financial information. The random walk simply indicates that all information embodied in previous prices is reflected in current prices. While this is a necessary condition for an efficient market in regard to all financial information, it is not a sufficient condition. Thus the random walk hypothesis is called the **weak form** of market efficiency.

So-called **semistrong** market efficiency asserts that security prices continuously reflect all publicly available financial information. One implication of this hypothesis is that analysis of publicly available information cannot be used to earn superior returns in security market trading. This conclusion has generated a great deal of rather pointless controversy by putting financial analysts and other participants in the huge financial information industry on the defensive. But the fact is that the collection, analysis, and dissemination of financial information are necessary for semistrong market efficiency to exist. Information does not affect security prices by some magic process. Rather, information is brought to the financial marketplace so swiftly because the rewards for timely, relevant information are so great. But the information market is sufficiently competitive to allow for only a "normal" return on the resources committed to the analysis of financial information. Publicly available information is "always" already reflected in security prices; only a normal expected return is available to the investor acting on such information. At the semistrong level of market efficiency, however, superior returns are possible for the holder of new, private information that is not available to the public.

At the strong-form level of efficiency, even private (or "insider") information is so swiftly impounded into stock prices that the search for such information is unlikely to result in a net positive payoff. Unlike the weak and semistrong forms of market efficiency, there is little empirical evidence in support of the strong-form hypothesis of market efficiency (and many academic observers, including the present authors, as well as practitioners view its underlying theoretical premise as dubious).

There is a great deal of empirical research that supports the weak-form market efficiency hypothesis, and the evidence in favor of semistrong efficiency is almost as great. But there also exist a number of anomalies in security price behavior that are counter to a presumption of market efficiency. Some of these anomalous patterns perhaps reflect statistical, not financial market, quirks, but it is likely that pockets of inefficiency do indeed exist in the financial markets. The ultimate proof of their existence, however, may be their disappearance as they are discovered and exploited, for such exploitation will put an end to them. A more serious challenge to the notion of prevailing efficiency in markets is posed by those who point to such phenomena as the 25 percent plunge in stock market values on October 19, 1987 (when the Dow-Jones Industrial Average fell 508 points). What new information accounted for this debacle? While there are those who contend that market efficiency is holding sway during such events, it is not necessary to be so purist to view financial market efficiency as the ordinary (and ultimately prevailing) order of things. Security markets essentially reflect human striving for economic gain, and security market behavior generally reflects rational economic calculation. But human behavior is shaped by much more than economic considerations, and such other dimensions of human behavior sometimes spill over into the economic arena. But the existence of such anomalies does not change the fact that financial market efficiency is the normal state of affairs—the best way for investors to bet.

We turn to an overview of financial markets in Section B of this chapter, followed by a more detailed examination of their nature in the eight succeeding chapters.

SECTION B

TYPES OF FINANCIAL MARKETS

A "market" is simply a place where sales and purchases of some items are made. Financial markets are the markets in which financial instruments are traded. The prices of the traded financial instruments are determined in the financial markets by supply and demand. Certain characteristics of financial markets result in a highly competitive marketplace. These include a large number of participants and an extensive communications network capable of rapid gathering and dissemination of information. (As was noted earlier, the principal anticompetitive influence in the financial system is the prevalence of government regulation.)

As was indicated in Chapter 1, financial markets can be categorized in a number of ways. Perhaps the most useful distinctions are money versus capital markets and primary versus secondary markets. The trading of financial instruments having a maturity of one year or less constitutes the **money markets;** the trading of securities having a term to maturity exceeding one year makes up the **capital markets.** New issues of securities are sold (and purchased) in **primary markets;** previously issued securities are bought and sold in **secondary markets.** These categories obviously overlap. There are primary and secondary money markets and primary and secondary capital markets. Further categorizing is possible in term of the origin (bank versus nonbank) of the financial instrument in the money market and the type of obligation (debt versus equity) in the capital market.

THE MONEY MARKETS

Money markets provide the means for short-term lending and borrowing and thus play a key role in the management of liquidity by business, governmental, and household economic units. Money market instruments are generally characterized by high degrees of marketability and capital certainty (predictability of expected market value at future dates), and they are thus highly liquid. The purchase of such instruments is a convenient means of temporary employment of excess cash, and their issue is a convenient means of financing a temporary excess of cash outflow over cash inflow.

The reader perhaps has noted that both singular (money market) and plural (money markets) terms are employed in this book for this particular component of the financial system. Both uses are correct in that the money market is a single system for the short-term exchange of funds for a financial asset, but it is also composed of numerous segments that differ both in the nature of instruments used and in the types of participants. One of the most useful distinctions among these various components of the money market is between the direct, or customers' ("retail"), money market and the central, or "open," money market.

The customers' money market is encountered everywhere, since it involves the transactions between local financial institutions and their customers. The central market is geographically centered in this country in New York City, and it typically involves "wholesale" transactions of very large amounts (frequently millions of dollars). The central money market, however, is connected to the rest of the country by an extensive communications network (telephone, teletype, and computer facilities) that permits widespread participation.

As might be expected, large money center and regional commercial banks are very active participants in central money market transactions. As net suppliers of money market instruments, commercial banks are surpassed only by the federal government. But the money market banks (the large banks located in New York City and other major financial centers) also supply funds to the central market as liquidity management actions and, in the case of the largest New York banks, as dealers in money market instruments. (The role of commercial banks in the money markets will be described in much greater detail in the next chapter.)

The federal government is one of the most active participants and a principal borrower of funds in the money market. This is evidenced, for example, by the fact that the dollar magnitude of U.S. Treasury bills outstanding at the end of 1988 exceeded that of all other money market instruments combined. In the course of conducting its open-market operations the Federal Reserve System deals continuously in money market instruments, mostly Treasury bills. (As described in Chapter 4, Fed purchases of Treasury bills supply reserves to the banking system, and sales withdraw reserves—with corresponding impact on the money supply.)

Foreign governments and institutions are major net suppliers of funds to U.S. money markets, mostly as a result of U.S. trade deficits in its balance of payments. These deficits mean that more dollars are supplied to the rest of the world than are used to buy U.S. goods and sevices, and many of these "excess" dollars are used to buy money market instruments. The governments of oil-exporting (OPEC) nations are often important foreign participants in the money market.

Other important lenders in the money markets are state and local governments and nonbank financial intermediaries. Cash flows for state and local governments typically follow a "lumpy" pattern: Large inflows tend to occur at periodic intervals, but outflows are generally continuous. This results in holdings of temporarily idle cash, which these governmental units often use to purchase money market assets. The emphasis of nonbank financial institutions on long-term lending results in temporary holdings of idle funds when demand for long-term credit slows, and these funds may be placed in the money market.

Perhaps no component of the money market more clearly illustrates its liquidity-management function than the market for federal funds. Federal funds are reserve balances at Federal Reserve banks, and the market for them is primarily their purchase (borrowing) and sale (lending) among financial institutions in order to adjust liquidity or reserve positions. Trading in federal funds is generally accomplished by telephone. Transactions in federal funds are typically single-day loans, the sale being effective on the contract day and payment due the following day.

Treatment of the various instruments of the money market and further description of the participants and workings of the domestic money market are offered in Chapters 17 and 18. The international money market is the subject of Chapter 25.

THE CAPITAL MARKET

The framework for the borrowing and lending of funds for periods longer than a year is called the capital market. Some observers view the capital market as composed of markets for intermediate (not more than ten years to maturity) and long-term (more than ten years to maturity) funds. And of course, the capital market has both a primary and a secondary component. A further categorization of the capital market is possible in terms of the market for equity instruments and the market for debt instruments.

Types of capital market instruments include federal government notes and bonds, state and local government securities, mortgages, corporate bonds, and corporate equities. Federal government borrowing, though quite large in amount, does not dominate the capital market to nearly the same degree that it dominates the money market. Corporations are the principal demanders of capital market funds (suppliers of capital market instruments). Equity instruments (common and preferred stock) constitute the largest portion of corporate obligations in the capital market, but corporate bond and mortgate debts are also very large amounts. Residential (as opposed to commercial) mortgages, however, dominate the mortgage market. State and local government securities, which offer the lure of nontaxable interest, are also a major factor in the capital market.

Individuals, both as lenders and borrowers, play a much more significant role in the capital market than in the money market. More than half of household investment in debt and equity capital market instruments is channeled through intermediaries, and the remainder is invested directly. The total amount of direct and intermediated investment in the capital market by the household sector greatly exceeds that of the government and business sectors. In terms of the total amount of capital market borrowing, the household sector ranks second to the business sector, the government sector placing a close third.

Commercial banks play a very significant role in the capital market, though not to the same extent as in the money market. The capital market activities of commercial banks include mortgage lending, considerable equity and bond investment (through trust departments), intermediate-term lending to business and consumers, and the financing of other capital market institutions and agents. These agents and institutions include brokers, dealers, and investment banks.

The underwriting role of investment banks in primary security issues is examined in Chapters 19 and 21, and Chapter 25 describes the international dimensions of investment banking. In addition to underwriting security issues, investment banks are involved in real estate mortgage financing, project financing, and various other capital market activities.

Brokers and dealers perform an essential "middleman" function in the capital market. Brokers, of course, facilitate the buying and selling of financial instruments by others, and they are compensated by a fee or commission for their efforts. Dealers, on the other hand, assume risk by buying and selling securities for their own account, and their compensation must come in the form of the "spread" between the prices at which they sell (the "ask" price) and buy (the "bid" price) securities. More than 5000 firms in this country are registered with the Securities and Exchange Commission as brokers and dealers in securities.

The organized securities exchange and the "over-the-counter" (OTC) securities market, the arenas in which dealers and brokers ply their trade, are institutions of considerable importance in the capital markets. (The OTC also plays a significant role in the money market, a huge amount of trading in short-term debt instruments taking place through its facilities.) The organized exchanges are essentially secondary markets for outstanding long-term debt and equity instruments. Primary issues of these securities, even if subsequently listed on organized exchanges, are generally channeled through the OTC market, although new issues that constitute additions to outstanding issues are sometimes distributed through organized exchanges.

With this overview of the money and capital markets—characteristics and participants—now complete, we can briefly consider some interrelationships between these two types of financial markets.

LINKAGES BETWEEN THE MONEY AND CAPITAL MARKETS

The money and capital markets are highly interrelated. Many suppliers and demanders of funds use both markets, their degree of activity in either market shifting over time as their own situations and financial conditions change. A firm may tap the money market for temporary funding of long-term capital needs while waiting for more favorable capital market conditions. As has already been noted, a number of types of financial intermediaries and "middlemen" (commercial banks, brokers, and dealers) operate in both markets. Funds are constantly being "rolled over" from one market to the other; collections of long-term obligations may be plowed into short-term ones or vice versa. Further, a borrower may pay a short-term obligation while concurrently borrowing long-term or vice versa.

As was discussed in Chapter 7, the term structure of interest rates is closely linked, although money market interest rates tend to be more sensitive (and variable) and capital market instrument prices (particularly equity securities) to be more volatile. In general, these two components of financial markets are so interrelated as to really amount to one market, but a market in which time to maturity and various other factors result in differing characteristics among the instruments traded.

FUTURES MARKETS

separate from capital & mkt.

To this point we have discussed only "spot" markets for financial assets, which are characterized by the purchase or sale of financial instruments for immediate delivery. Of growing importance in the financial system are **financial futures markets,** which are concerned with the purchase or sale of financial assets for future delivery. A futures market is essentially an organized market in which forward (or futures) contracts are traded. A forward contract provides for delivery of a prescribed amount of a particular asset at a certain date.

The economic value of futures markets is in their provision of a means of risk avoidance to individuals or business firms. By entering into a futures contract the transacting party "locks in" a certain price for an item, the market price of which may fluctuate in random fashion. Sale of an asset through the vehicle of a futures contract allows the seller to avoid the potential loss that would result from a price decrease, but it also obliges the seller to forgo the potential gain that would result from a price increase. In effect, such a seller is willing to forgo the possibility of the gain in order to avoid the possibility of a loss.

The use of the futures market to avoid the risk of price changes is called **hedging.** Farmers, for example, often sell futures contracts to ensure a certain price for the sale of crops or livestock, and food processors often buy such futures contracts to "lock in" a purchase price. This particular type of forward contracting is carried on in the **commodity futures market.** The financial futures markets serve a similar function by providing participants the means of ensuring a given security price (yield on a future investment or borrowing rate).

In addition to **hedgers,** who use futures markets to avoid risk, participants in these markets include **speculators,** who take positions in an attempt to turn profits on price changes. Though often maligned, speculators help to "make the market" and, by their willingness to accept risk, perform a legitimate and necessary economic function.

Chapter 22 explores futures markets in detail, describing their modes of operation, and the ways in which they can be used to avoid risk and seek profits, and analyzes their economic significance.

SUMMARY

The primary function of financial markets is the efficient allocation of the saved funds of surplus economic units for the use of deficit economic units. Transfers of saved funds from savers to their ultimate users is accomplished by the exchange of these funds for financial instruments issued either by the ultimate users or by intermediaries (which also purchase the financial instruments issued by ultimate users). The supply of and demand for these various types of financial assets determine their prices (and yields).

The demand for a particular financial asset is a function of market perceptions regarding its likely returns and the degree of risk associated with those returns. Thus financial assets are priced in financial markets according to expectations regarding their future returns and risk. Over time, the extent to which these market expectations correspond to subsequent realities is a function of the quality and quantity of information provided to the marketplace and of the speed with which relevant information relating to risk and returns of securities is impounded in security prices.

Resources made available by saving will be allocated to their most productive possible uses (consistent with society's preferences) only if the securities that serve as a vehicle for their transfer to ultimate users are priced according to their expected returns and risk. In turn, such expectations must reflect prompt and proper analysis of all available information pertaining to future security returns and associated risk. The financial markets are said to be efficient when these conditions are met.

Financial markets can be efficient in the aggregate only to the extent that the countless decisions of market participants relating to portfolio choice constitute efficient selection of financial assets. Aggregate market efficiency will prevail to the degree that the markets are dominated by holders of efficient portfolios—no other possible portfolio offers a higher expected return for a given degree of risk or a lower degree of risk for a given level of expected return. In theory, such an efficient portfolio can be constructed for any investor for a combination of risk-free assets and the risky market portfolio of assets that satisfies the risk–return preferences of the investor. Thus to the extent that such an approach to portfolio selection characterizes financial market behavior, securities will be priced according to their expected return and their systematic risk—the degree of the security's variability in returns relative to the market portfolio's variability in returns. The operational measure of systematic risk (beta) can be estimated empirically.

The financial markets can be divided, somewhat arbitrarily, into the money market and the capital market. Financial instruments having a year or less to maturity are traded in the money markets. All other securities are traded in the capital markets. Both money and capital markets have a primary component (for new issues of securities) and a secondary component (for the trading of previously issued securities). Both debt and equity (ownership claims) instruments are traded in the capital market, but only debt securities are traded in the money market. The two markets are closely linked by funds flows and by yield structure.

QUESTIONS

1. What is an "efficient portfolio"? Is holding a *single* direct security likely to be efficient? Indirect security holdings?

2. Explain the relationship among expected return, risk, and expected utility. Will maximization of expected return necessarily maximize an investor's expected utility?

3. Why is diversification of security holdings likely to reduce risk more than expected return?

4. Define systematic and unsystematic risk, and explain their significance for efficient portfolio selection.

5. Explain and compare the "security market line" and the "capital market line."

6. What is meant by the "efficiency" of financial markets? What conditions are necessary for financial market efficiency?

7. What is the difference between "weak-form" market efficiency and "semistrong" market efficiency?

8. Describe the various ways in which financial markets can be categorized.

9. What are some major differences in the characteristics of the money market and the capital market? Similarities? Linkages?

10. What are futures markets? What economic function do they perform?

REFERENCES

Bellemore, D., H. Phillips, and J. Ritchie, *Investment Analysis and Portfolio Selection: An Integrated Approach* (Cincinnati, Ohio: Southwestern, 1979).

Fama, E. F., "Efficient Capital Markets: A Review of Theory and Empirical Work," *Journal of Finance* (May 1970) 383–417.

——, *Foundations of Finance* (New York: Basic Books, 1976).

——, and A. Laffer, "Information and Capital Markets," *Journal of Business* (July 1971) 289–298.

Jensen, M., "The Foundations and Current State of Capital Market Theory," in Jensen, M. (Ed.), *Studies in the Theory of Capital Markets* (New York: Praeger, 1972).

——, "Capital Markets: Theory and Evidence," *The Bell Journal of Economics and Management Science* (Autumn 1972), 357–398.

Lorie, James H., Peter Dodd, and Mary H. Kimpton, *The Stock Market: Theories and Evidence,* 2nd ed. (Homewood, Ill.: Richard D. Irwin, 1985).

Markowitz, H., *Portfolio Selection* (New Haven: Yale University Press, 1959).

Martin, John D., Samuel H. Cox, and Richard D. MacMinn, *The Theory of Finance: Evidence and Applications* (Hinsdale, Illinois: Dryden Press, 1987), 237–287.

Roll, Richard, "A Critique of the Asset Pricing Theory's Tests," *Journal of Financial Economics* (March 1977) 129–176.

——, and Stephen A. Ross, "An Empirical Investigation of the Arbitrage Pricing Theory," *Journal of Finance* (December 1980).

Ross, Stephen A. "The Arbitrage Theory of Capital Asset Pricing," *Journal of Economic Theory* (December 1976), 343–362.

Shanken, Jay, "The Arbitrage Pricing Theory: Is It Testable," *Journal of Finance* (December 1982), 1129–1140.

Sharpe, W., *Portfolio Theory and Capital Markets* (New York: McGraw-Hill, 1970).

Stiglitz, Joseph E., "Information and Capital Markets," in William F. Sharpe and Cathryn M. Cootner (Eds.), *Financial Economics: Essays in Honor of Paul Cootner* (Englewood Cliffs, N.J.: Prentice-Hall, 1982).

CHAPTER 16

Operations of Financial Institutions in the Financial Markets

Understanding the financial markets—changes in interest rate levels, relative patterns of interest rates, and the flow of funds within financial markets—requires an understanding of the operations of financial institutions. As discussed earlier, financial institutions dominate most financial markets in the United States and other developed countries. Moreover, pressures on financial markets are usually transmitted through financial institutions. For example, monetary policy initially operates on the reserve and liquidity positions of commercial banks and other depository institutions and then affects the real sector of the economy largely through the portfolio adjustments depository institutions make in their financial asset positions in response to changing risk–return opportunities. Similarly, pressures on the mortgage markets produced by monetary policy and other economic and financial developments are usually transmitted through portfolio adjustments made by savings and loan associations. Knowing why some markets are highly volatile while others are quite stable requires an understanding of the behavior and roles of different financial institutions.

In this chapter we illustrate some characteristics of the operations of financial institutions in financial markets. Chapters 9 and 10 provided some insights into the sources and uses of funds at major financial institutions. There are substantial differences in the operations of different financial institutions. Nonetheless, some basic similarities should be highlighted if we are to fit the pieces of the financial-markets system together. We present initially an overview of the role of financial institutions and then concentrate on how different financial institutions use financial markets in controlling both interest rate (or term structure) risk and credit risk, two principal determinants of their successful operations.

THE BASIC ROLE OF FINANCIAL INSTITUTIONS

Financial institutions sell financial services (or products) for which they receive payment. This payment usually results in financial institutions having funds to manage and invest, as well as obligations or liabilities to its customers. Moreover, the sale of services frequently involves the creation of financial instruments of considerable importance to financial markets. The motivation for the financial institutions is usually profit, as it is for nonfinancial profit-seeking enterprises, but the motivation is more complex for financial institutions than for most nonfinancial organizations. For example, the fact that some financial institutions are mutual rather than stock associations raises important questions about the motivation of management.[1] Further, many financial institutions—especially commercial banks and other depository institutions—are involved with the public interest and are thus subject to intensive regulatory pressures (as discussed in Chapter 12). As a result, although predictions of the portfolio behavior of financial institutions using the risk-return framework developed in Chapter 15 are useful, other factors must also be considered. A few examples may help to explain the role of financial institutions in financial markets.

Commercial Banks

The commercial bank may be viewed as marketing both deposit and lending services.[2] In exchange for funds credited to demand deposit accounts the bank offers convenient transfer of funds to third parties. In exchange for funds placed in a savings and/or time deposit account the bank offers interest payments. As discussed earlier, banks also offer nondeposit liabilities, such as federal funds purchased, repurchase agreements, and Eurodollar liabilities, for which interest is paid. Many of these types of deposit and nondeposit liabilities are money market instruments. For example, the large negotiable certificate of deposit (CD) is one of the major instruments of the money market.

Once the funds have been credited to customer accounts, the management of a bank faces the problem of obtaining a sufficient return to pay for the services

---

[1]Mutual organizations are owned by their customers—depositors, borrowers, policyholders—rather than by shareholders. The mutual form of organization (along with traditional stock ownership) exists in the savings and loan industry, saving banks, and the insurance industry. All credit unions are "owned" by member depositors and borrowers.

[2]Banks do, of course, offer other services that are not related to either deposit taking or credit creation. For example, banks offer trust services, cash management, and data processing services, to name only a few. However, the essence of commercial banking involves taking deposits and extending credit.

provided (the costs are labor and equipment costs for demand deposits and interest for time and savings deposits) and to earn a "satisfactory" return on invested capital.

The invested funds may be committed either to loans, in which a personal relationship exists between the lender and the borrower, or to securities, in which the commitment is impersonal in nature.[3] In the former case the bank provides loanable funds but does not become directly involved in the money or capital markets. This **customer's market,** though extremely important in providing loanable funds, is not generally viewed as a part of the money and capital markets. In the latter case the bank both provides loanable funds and acquires a money market instrument, such as a Treasury security (bill, note, or bond) or a municipal security.

In its credit extension—either through making loans in the customer's market or purchasing securities in the money or capital market—the management of the bank must make basic portfolio management decisions. These decisions, which encompass both asset management and liability management, are referred to collectively as **funds management.** For example, decisions must be made about the maturity structure of assets compared with the maturity structure of liabilities. Management may match closely the maturities of assets and liabilities. Management may concentrate in the customer's market with short- or long-term fixed-rate loans or may make only variable-rate loans. In terms of credit risk, management may accept large amounts of credit risk in the portfolio or may pursue a very cautious posture and make only extremely high-quality loans and purchase only highest-quality securities in the money and capital markets. In both decisions, management will presumably be guided by the desire to increase the risk-adjusted profits of the organization—subject, of course, to legal and regulatory constraints on portfolio management.

Bank management has considerable flexibility in making the interest-rate-risk and credit-risk decisions. Moreover, the flexiblity has increased in recent years.[4] At one time, bank management was essentially constrained to adjusting the interest-rate risk of its total portfolio by altering assets alone (that is, asset management). But with the development of the markets for large CDs, federal funds, repurchase agreements, and Eurodollars, bank management can buy and sell financial instruments in the money and capital markets to obtain the desired portfolio maturity. Moreover, through credit extensions in the customer's market and to a lesser extent through security purchases, management can alter the credit-risk dimensions of the portfolio to achieve a desired position.

---

[3]Banks, of course, must keep reserve requirements set by the regulatory authorities and must also meet minimum liquidity needs established by management.

[4]Yet there remain considerable limitations on bank portfolio management. For example, commercial banks may not generally hold equity securities in their portfolios.

Other Depository Institutions

The role of the other depository institutions—savings and loans, savings banks, and credit unions—may be analyzed in a similar fashion. Each offers deposit and credit services. Traditionally, these deposit services have consisted primarily of passbook savings accounts, but in recent years, each type of institution has achieved considerable portfolio flexibility by offering a large variety of certificate accounts. In addition, under the Depository Institutions Deregulation and Monetary Control Act (DIDMCA) of 1980, each has now achieved the legal authority to offer third-party payment devices to individuals through NOW accounts for savings and loan associations and savings banks and share drafts for credit unions. These institutions now also offer money market deposit accounts, which have no regulatory deposit interest-rate ceiling. From the asset side of the balance sheet, each institution offers credit accommodation through its loan portfolio in the customer's market, and each participates in the money and capital markets through the purchase of such securities as U.S. government bills, notes, and bonds, corporate issues, and to a minor extent, municipal bonds. Indeed, the asset portfolio flexibility of savings and loans and other nonbank depository institutions was increased substantially by DIDMCA (1980) and DIA (1982).

These other depository financial institutions must also arrange the maturity and credit-risk dimensions of their portfolio to meet their desired positions. Most assets held by savings and loans are mortgages, and most assets held by credit unions are consumer installment loans. Savings deposits, money market deposit accounts, and certificates of deposit (mostly under $100,000) represent the principal sources of funds of these institutions. As a general rule, they have less flexibility in adjusting their portfolios than commercial banks have. Access to the money and capital markets through the issuance of new securities is more restricted for savings and loans, savings banks, and credit unions than it is for commercial banks. However, these institutions have been innovative in gaining access to the money market through the sale of large CDs and to the capital market (at least for savings and loans) through the sale of mortgage-backed bonds.

On the asset as well as the liability side of the balance sheet these various nonbank depository institutions have less flexibility. Tradition and legal constraints are more significant in determining the average maturity of the portfolios of savings and loans, savings banks, and credit unions than for the more diversified commercial banks (though there is considerable flexibility in altering the risk structure of the assets of these institutions). Furthermore, analyzing the goals of these institutions is complicated, since most are mutual organizations.

Contractual Institutions

When we turn to the contractual institutions—life and property and casualty insurance companies and private and public pension funds—the analysis of function and motivation becomes even more complex. These institutions do not sell deposit services. The service offered by insurance companies is protection, and the service offered by pension funds is a change in the time distribution of cash inflows to individuals who sacrifice current consumption for greater future consumption. These institutions obtain funds to manage as a result of the difference between the time that cash is received through premiums (insurance companies) and contributions (pension funds) and the time that cash is paid out in the form of benefits. Consequently, although these types of financial institutions do have some flexibility in altering the maturity structure of their liabilities through borrowing in the money and capital markets, the flexibility stems principally from borrowing not associated with their basic services. These basic services give rise to a maturity structure of liabilities that is quite inflexible and is determined essentially by the nature of the service itself.

On the asset side of the balance sheet the flexibility of contractual financial institutions in performing their credit-accommodation function is much greater. Moreover, contractual-type financial institutions provide a much larger portion of their credit through the money and capital markets (compared with the customer's market) than do the depository financial institutions.[5] Although insurance companies are subject to state regulation of the types of securities placed in their portfolios, the maturity and credit characteristics of the mortgages and bonds acquired are determined to a very considerable degree by management judgment. Similarly, pension funds (especially private pension funds) are able to acquire equity and debt securities of different credit and maturity characteristics subject only to the "prudent man" rule.[6]

The form of organization of these contractual type institutions, however, presents additional complications. While most life insurance companies are stock associations, most of the aggregate assets held by life insurance companies are held by the larger mutual organizations. Similarly, a substantial proportion of the assets of property and casualty insurance companies is held by mutual organizations. For pension funds the motivation of management (the trustees of the fund) is even more complex. Not only do the beneficiaries of the pension plan usually have no influence on the portfolio management policies of the fund, there are pressures from the sponsoring companies in private pension programs because, to these companies, contributions to the fund represent expenses of doing business.

---

[5]This implies that on the asset side of the balance sheet the relationship between the contractual financial institution and its customers is less personal than is the relationship of commercial banks and its customers.

[6]The "prudent man" rule, which has long been embodied in case or common law, states that an individual who manages the funds of others in a fiduciary capacity should make investment decisions as a prudent man would do. The investment manager can then be held liable for loss only if he or she behaves in an imprudent manner.

FINANCIAL INSTITUTIONS AND RISK MANAGEMENT

All financial institutions provide financial services as they seek to achieve their goals of profitability, market shares, and other related objectives. These services result in financial institutions managing funds and having obligations or liabilities to customers. To a considerable extent the management of a financial institution has the flexibility to alter the maturity and credit-risk dimensions of its portfolio as it draws funds from the money and capital markets and as it invests funds in different markets. The decisions made by the managements of individual financial institutions with regard to the interest-rate and credit-risk dimensions of the institutions' portfolios have enormous implications for the structure of yields in the money and capital markets. Financial institutions make portfolio adjustments in response to changes in relative yields in the financial markets, but these portfolio adjustments in turn produce additional changes in relative yields. We now turn to a discussion of each of these considerations and evaluate in more detail how financial institutions may vary the maturity and credit-risk dimensions of their portfolios in the attempt to achieve their objectives.

MATURITY MANAGEMENT

Most financial institutions are involved in maturity intermediation, whereby the average maturity of their liabilities is less than the average maturity of their assets. Indeed, most financial institutions purchase assets whose maturity is longer than the maturity of their liabilities. In addition, most credit extensions by financial institutions have traditionally involved the acquisition of fixed-rate financial assets, either in the customer's market or in the money and capital markets. Yet in a world in which both the level of interest rates and the relationship between short- and long-term rates (the term structure) change dramatically over time, the profitability and indeed the viability of financial institutions may be substantially affected by maturity management.

BUSINESS FLUCTUATIONS AND THE INTEREST-RATE CYCLE

Interest Rates and the Business Cycle

Both the level of interest rates and the relationship between short- and long-term rates are closely related to the various levels of business activity. Table 16.1 provides a simplified view of these relationships. The business cycle is often di-

TABLE 16.1 The Business Cycle and the Interest Rate Cycle _____

Stage of the Business Cycle	Level of Interest Rates	Term Structure
Expansion	Rising	Moderately upward-sloping
Peak	High	Flat or downward-sloping
Contraction	Falling	Slightly upward-sloping
Trough	Low	Strongly upward-sloping

vided into four periods: the **expansion** phase, when real income, production, and employment are rising; the **peak,** when the economy reaches its productive capacity; the **contraction,** when real income, production, and employment are falling; and the **trough,** at which point the decline ceases, and the economy is poised for another expansion. Although no two business cycles exactly repeat themselves and there are distinctive elements to each phase of the cycle, sufficient similarities permit the cycle to be divided into recurring patterns.

In the expansion phase of the cycle, interest rates are generally rising. The demand for loanable funds by businesses, households, and governments strengthens, and the supply of loanable funds is restrained by Federal Reserve monetary policy. Reflecting segmented-market and/or expectations factors, the yield curve is moderately upward-sloping with long-term rates higher than short-term rates. However, the yield curve is shifting, since short-term rates generally rise more than long-term rates, producing a flattening of the yield curve, so the difference between long- and short-term rates narrows. As the economy approaches its peak, interest rates continue to rise, peaking at about the same time as general business conditions do.[7] At or near the peak in general business conditions the term structure of interest rates may change dramatically. Market participants may expect a fall in rates in the future, and the Federal Reserve may induce exceptional pressures in the money market. As short-term rates continue to increase more than long-term rates, the yield curve continues to flatten until at some point, short-term rates exceed long-term rates. At this point the yield curve becomes downward-sloping or inverted. This shift in the yield curve is shown in Fig. 16.1 as a move from the yield curve in stage 1 to the yield curve in stage 2.

As the economy passes its peak and moves from stage 2 into stage 3 (declining general business conditions), interest rates begin to fall. The demand for loanable funds declines as businesses reduce inventory levels and curtail plant and

---

[7]Interest rates may be viewed as a "coincident" indicator in that movements in open-market rates coincide with movements in the general economy. However, in earlier periods in U.S. financial history, interest rates were viewed as a lagging indicator, moving behind changes in general business conditions.

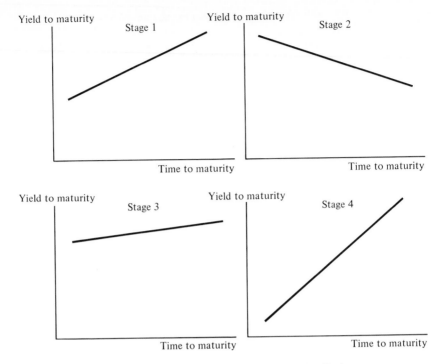

FIGURE 16.1   The Yield Curve at Different Stages of the Business Cycle

equipment expenditures, consumers reduce their purchases, and state and local governments retrench. The supply of loanable funds is stimulated by an easing of monetary policy, and perhaps the anticipated rate of inflation declines. Short-term rates usually fall more rapidly than long-term rates, reflecting both expectations and segmented-market considerations. As a result, the yield curve begins to return to its "normal" shape, indicating that short-term rates are lower than long-term rates. Finally, as the economy approaches bottom at the depths of the recession, the yield curve becomes sharply upward-sloping, as shown in stage 4 of Fig. 16.1.

Interest Rates and Risk at Financial Institutions

Interest-Sensitivity Measurement.   The effects of changing interest rates on the profitability of a financial institution depends on the difference between its interest-rate-sensitive assets (ISAs) and its interest-rate-sensitive liabilities (ISLs). This difference is commonly referred to as the "gap" and may be expressed in dollar terms in Eq. (16.1) as

$$\text{Gap \$} = \text{ISA\$} - \text{ISL\$} \tag{16.1}$$

The effects of changing interest rates on the profitability of a financial institution may also be expressed in relative terms; either as the *relative gap ratio* (RGR) as in Eq. (16.2) or as the *interest-sensitivity ratio* as in Eq. (16.3):

$$\text{Relative gap ratio} = \frac{\text{Gap\$}}{\text{Total assets}} \tag{16.2}$$

$$\text{Interest sensitivity ratio} = \frac{\text{Interest-sensitive assets}}{\text{Interest-sensitive liabilities}} \tag{16.3}$$

Interest-sensitive assets are those whose interest returns are subject to changes during the planning horizon. These would include all variable or adjustable rate assets whose returns are adjusted during the planning horizon to reflect changes in market interest rates. Interest-sensitive assets would also include all assets whose maturity is equal to or shorter than the planning horizon. For example, if the planning horizon were six months, all those assets whose maturity were six months or less would be defined as rate-sensitive assets within a six-month planning horizon. In short, all assets that are repriced during the planning horizon are defined as interest-sensitive. *Interest-sensitive liabilities* are defined in a manner similar to interest-sensitive assets and include all variable-rate liabilities whose costs adjust automatically to changes in market interest rates within the planning horizon and also all those liabilities whose maturity is equal to or less than the planning horizon.

The establishment of a planning horizon is crucial to understanding the effects of changing interest rates on the profitability of a financial institution. (Conceptually, of course, over a sufficiently long planning horizon, *all* assets and liabilities are interest rate sensitive.) Most financial institutions measure their interest sensitivity over a one-year period and for a number of shorter periods during the year (a procedure known as establishing **maturity buckets**). For example, as shown in Table 16.2, ABC Financial Company has measured its interest sensitivity over a one-year period and over three maturity buckets: 0–90 days, 91–180 days, and 181–365 days. Over the entire one-year period the ABC Financial Corporation has a *negative* gap of $74 million; that is, interest-sensitive liabilities exceed interest-sensitive assets by $74 million. Its interest-sensitivity ratio for the one-year planning horizon is 0.838. The ABC Financial Company would be referred to as having a liability-sensitive portfolio over a one-year planning horizon. Note, however, that the interest-sensitivity position of the firm varies substantially for the three maturity buckets: over the 0–90 day period it is only slightly liability sensitive, and over the 181–365 days it is asset sensitive (rate-sensitive assets exceeded rate-sensitive liabilities).

TABLE 16.2 Interest Rate Sensitivity Analysis (ABC Financial Company, December 31, 19XX)

Asset/Liability (in millions)	0–90 Days	91–180 Days	181–365 Days	Total Within 1 Year	Over 1 Year	Total
Selected Assets						
Due from banks and federal funds sold	64	1	—	65	2	67
Investment securities	19	24	40	83	185	268
Loans	178	24	34	236	175	411
Total selected assets	261	49	74	384	362	746
Selected Liabilities						
Demand deposits	—	—	—	—	158	158
Savings deposits	155	—	—	155	70	225
Time deposits	130	55	28	213	79	292
Other liabilities	89	—	1	90	6	96
Total selected liabilities	374	55	29	458	313	771
Interest-sensitivity gap	(113)	(6)	45	(74)	49	(25)
Gap ratio	(.146)	(.008)	.058	.096		
Interest-sensitivity ratio	.697	.891	2.552	.838		

if interest rates ↑, profits ↓

The effect of changing interest rates on the profitability of a financial institution may be calculated with the use of Eq. (16.4):

$$E(\Delta NII) = \text{ISA\$ } E(\Delta\pi) - \text{ISL\$ } E(\Delta\pi) = \text{GAP\$ } E(\Delta\pi) \qquad (16.4)$$

where

$$E(\Delta NII) = \text{GAP\$ } E(\Delta\pi)$$

Δ = change in

$E(\Delta NII)$ = expected change in net interest income (where net interest income is total interest income minus total interest expense)

$E(\Delta\pi)$ = the expected change in interest rates

From Eq. (16.4) it is clear that the change in profit of a financial institution (where change in profit is defined as change in net interest income) is equal to the gap times the expected change in interest rates. Hence for an asset-sensitive organization (that is, one with a positive gap and an interest-sensitivity ratio greater than one), rising interest rates will produce an increase in profits and falling interest rates will result in a decline in profits. Conversely, for a liability-sensitive financial institution, increasing interest rates produce declining profits, while falling interest rates produce an increase in profitability. For a zero gap financial institution (with rate-sensitive assets equal to rate-sensitive liabilities) the profitability of the institution is isolated from changes in interest rates (though not completely, as will be explained below). These relationships are summarized in Table 16.3.

Interest-Sensitivity Management.   Financial institutions may seek to manage their exposure to interest-rate risk in a variety of ways. These various approaches may be classified as defensive and aggressive. Under a **defensive** strategy the financial institution would seek to keep its gap at or near zero and its interest-sensitivity ratio at or near one. With this policy (if the policy were successfully implemented), profitability would be largely unaffected by changes in interest rates. In fact, after the extremely wide fluctuations in interest rates that occurred in the late 1970s and early 1980s (and the substantial effects of those interest rate fluctuations on the profitability of financial institutions, particularly savings and loans), many financial institutions have followed such a defensive policy. Note, however, that such a policy does not ensure an adequate level of profitability but only that the profits will be relatively stable. In contrast, with an **aggressive** policy the financial institution would seek to profit from expected interest-rate movements by altering its portfolio. For example, if interest rates were expected to increase, the institution could shift to an asset-sensitive position. This could be done, for example, by increasing the amount of rate-sensitive assets and/or reducing the amount of rate-sensitive liabilities. Rate-sensitive assets could be increased by making more variable-rate and fewer fixed-rate loans or by reducing the maturity of new fixed-rate loans. The amount of rate-sensitive liabilities could be reduced, for example, by selling longer-term certificates of deposit. In contrast, if

TABLE 16.3   **Relationship Between Interest Rate Changes and Profitability**

	Portfolio Sensitivity	Profitability Relationship with Interest Rate Changes
$Gap	Interest Sensitivity Ratio	*Profit vs. interest rate*
Positive	>1	Direct
Negative	<1	Inverse
Zero	=1	No effect

interest rates were expected to fall, an opposite strategy would be appropriate: shift to a liability-sensitive portfolio by reducing the amount of rate-sensitive assets and increasing the amount of rate-sensitive liabilities.

The effects of varying interest rates on profitability vary considerably from commercial banks to savings and loans. Commercial banks have been quite successful in blunting the impact of fluctuating interest rates on their operating profits through maintaining a relatively small gap position. In contrast, savings and loans have had considerable exposure to interest-rate fluctuations due to a large (and negative) gap.

Problems with Interest-Sensitivity Management.   While the management decision rules discussed above for defensive and aggressive policies seem quite simple, in fact a number of problems make the implementation of such policies quite difficult. Some of these problems are the following.

1. The need to define the planning horizon or horizons. Initially, interest-sensitivity management was done with only one planning horizon. However, such a policy ignores the timing of the repricing of assets and liabilities and may cause substantial difficulties if the planning horizon is relatively long. For example, suppose that a financial organization follows a defensive interest-sensitivity management policy and sets the gap equal to zero. Suppose that all the rate-sensitive assets are repriced on the first day of the year, while the rate-sensitive liabilities are repriced on the last day of the year. Even if the institution were to set the gap at zero (ISA = ISL), it would not insulate its profits from interest-rate fluctuations. This problem is reduced by using a maturity bucket approach (as discussed above) in which the planning horizon includes several subintervals (maturity buckets). Yet using maturity buckets does not totally resolve the problem, and it creates additional complexities of its own in understanding the interest-sensitivity position of the organization. With maturity buckets it is not possible to determine the interest-sensitivity position of the organization but only to specify its gap over different maturity buckets; that is, with maturity buckets there is no single index number of the interest-rate risk of the organization.

2. The implicit assumption of the model that rate changes for assets and liabilities move in proportion to open-market rates. For example, if open-market rates rise by 10 percent, then the returns on rate-sensitive assets will increase by 10 percent, and the cost of rate-sensitive liabilities will increase by 10 percent. However, it is quite possible (and indeed probable) that the return on rate-sensitive assets will increase by a percentage different from 10 percent (perhaps 5 percent) and that the cost of rate-sensitive liabilities will increase by a percentage different from 10 percent (perhaps 8 percent). In this case, again, maintaining rate-sensitive assets equal to rate-sensitive liabilities will not stabilize profits.

3. The model assumes that management can adjust the portfolio of assets and liabilities to achieve a desired gap position. In fact, management may be constrained substantially by its customers' desires, especially in the near term. Although a financial institution may wish to sell longer-term certificates of deposit in order to reduce its liability sensitivity, it might find that its customers do not want these longer-term CDs. Similarly, a financial institution might want to make variable-rate rather than fixed-rate loans but might find that its customers resist variable-rate loans.

4. The predictability of interest rates. Using interest-rate-sensitivity management from an aggressive perspective requires that the direction, magnitude, and timing of interest rate movements be forecasted. Unfortunately, the ability of financial market participants to forecast interest-rate movements during recent years has been very poor. Hence an aggressive interest-sensitivity management policy may result in lower rather than higher profitability.

5. The model focuses exclusively on the profitability effects of interest-rate movements to the exclusion of the effects of interest-rate changes on the market values of assets and liabilities. Profitability is, of course, important and should be one of the principal goals of the management of a financial institution. Yet shareholders are interested in the market value of their stock, and share value is affected not only by the profitability of an organization but also by changes in the market value of assets and liabilities. Changes in the market value of the assets and liabilities of a financial institution are ignored in the gap model.

Duration Gap Model.   One potential solution to the problem produced by the narrow focus of the gap model on profitability is use of the duration gap model. As discussed in Chapter 2, duration (the weighted average time over which *all* payments are made on a financial instrument) may be used to measure the effect of interest-rate changes on the value of financial investments. The **duration gap model** takes into account the overall interest-rate exposure of the financial institution, including the effects both on profitability and on the market value of the assets and liabilities of the institution. **Duration gap analysis** focuses on the effect of interest-rate changes on the value of the equity of the institution. It may be explained by the use of the following example.[8]

Assume the following balance sheet for a financial institution:

1. Cash reserves (C)

2. 2½-year business loans, amortized monthly (BL)

3. 30-year mortgage loans, amortized monthly (ML)

4. 1-year single payment certificates of deposit (CD)

5. 5-year single payment certificate of deposits (CDs)

6. Net worth or capital (K)

---

[8]This example is drawn from George Kaufman, "Measuring and Managing Interest Rate Risk: A Primer," Federal Reserve Bank of Chicago, *Economic Perspective* (January/February 1984), 16–29.

Interest on the deposits is assumed to be paid at maturity, and the deposits may not be redeemed prior to maturity. The interest rate on loans is assumed to be 13 percent, that on deposits is assumed to be 11 percent, and cash assets are assumed to earn no explicit interest. Income is defined to include not only interest income but also the immediate recognition of asset value gains and losses. Hence income is defined as economic income.[9] All assets and liabilities are carried on the bank's books at market value.

The initial condition of the financial institution is provided in Table 16.4. The dollar amount of each asset and liability item is provided, as is the given duration of each asset. The projected annual income statement is also given, and the return on capital is 18 percent.

What is the effect of an increase in interest rates of two percentage points (200 basis points)? As shown in Table 16.5, the increase in interest rates reduces the value of the organization (note that net worth or K is 66 after the increase in interest rates compared to 100 before). The market values of both assets and liabilities decline, but the value of the assets declines more than the value of the liabilities, reflecting the longer duration of the assets. Projected annual net income also falls, since interest costs rise more than interest revenue. (Note that cash is assumed to earn a small return at the higher interest rate.)[10]

What would the financial institution do if it wished to eliminate the effects of rising (falling) interest rates on the market value of its equity? Such an immunization would occur if it were to follow Eq. (16.5):

$$\text{DGAP} = D_A - wD_p = 0 \qquad (16.5)$$

where

$$D_A = \text{average duration of assets}$$
$$D_p = \text{average duration of deposits}$$

$$w = \frac{P}{P + K} \quad \text{or} \quad P/A, \quad \text{where } P \text{ is the total amount of deposits}$$

For example, in the example discussed above, $D_p = 2.3$ years and $P/A = 0.9$. This yields a duration gap of $4 - 0.9(2.3) = 1.9$ years. An increase in interest rates produced a decline in the market value of equity. If the bank wished to immunize the market value of its equity against interest-rate changes, it could reduce the

---

[9]In practice, financial institutions usually recognize gains and losses on assets only when they are realized.

[10]It might also be noted that while the market value of equity and the return on assets both declined, the return on equity actually increased (from 18 to 21 percent). The increased rate of return on equity reflected the sharp decline in the market value of equity. Presumably, shareholders are more concerned with the value of their investment than with the return on equity.

TABLE 16.4 Initial Conditions

Balance sheet

Assets	Dollars*	D (yrs.)†	Liabilities	Dollars*	D (yrs.)†
Cash	100	0	CD (1 yr.)	600	1.0
BL (2 ½ yr.)	400	1.25	CD (5 yr.)	300	5.0
ML (30 yr.)	500	7.0	Net worth (K)	100	5.5
Total	1000	4.0	Total	1000	2.65

wgt. avg. ←   → *wgt. avg.*

Deposit duration

$$D_p = \frac{600(1) + 300(5)}{900} = 2.33 \text{ years}$$

Projected annual income statement for year

	Interest yield	Market value ÷ total assets	Interest ÷ total assets (percent)	
Revenues				
Cash	0	.1	0	
Loans	13	.9	11.7	11.7
Expenses				
Deposit	11	.9	9.9	9.9
Net income				1.8

Summary accounts

$$K = \$100$$
$$K/A = 10\%$$
$$NI = 1.8\%$$

*All accounts are valued at market (present) value.
†Approximate.

Source: George G. Kaufman, "Measuring and Managing Interest Rate Risk: A Primer," Federal Reserve Bank of Chicago Economic Perspectives (January/February 1984), 17.

aggressive — + DGAP when expect interest rate ↑

duration gap to zero either by shortening the duration of its assets by 2.1 years to 1.9 years, by lengthening the duration of its deposits to 4.4 years so that 0.9 (4.4) = 4 years, or by some combination of the two. The relationship between interest rates, duration, and the market value of equity is illustrated in Table 16.6.

Limitations of Duration Analysis.   Despite the desirable focus on the market value of equity as the principal goal of interest-rate-risk management, duration gap analysis is not widely used by financial institutions. In fact, duration gap analysis is much less frequently used than dollar gap analysis. There appear to be two basic reasons for the infrequent use of duration gap analysis in managing interest-rate risk.

review

TABLE 16.5   Assume Interest Rate Increase of 200 Basis Points

Balance sheet

Assets	Dollars*	Liabilities	Dollars*
Cash	100	CD (1 yr.)	589
BL (2 ½ yr.)	390	CD (5 yr.)	272
ML (30 yr.)	437	Net worth (K)	66
Total	927	Total	927

Projected annual income statement for year

	Interest yield	Market value ÷ total assets	Interest ÷ total assets (percent)	
Revenues				
Cash	2	.11	0.2	
Loans	15	.89	13.4	13.6
Expenses				
Deposits	13	.93	12.1	12.1
Net income				1.5

Summary accounts

K = $66
K/A = 7.1%
NI = 1.5%

*All accounts are valued at market (present value).

Source: George G. Kaufman, "Measuring and Managing Interest Rate Risk: A Primer," Federal Reserve Bank of Chicago Economic Perspectives (January/February 1984), 18.

First, duration gap analysis is complex both conceptually and in its calculations. For example, estimating the effects of interest-rate changes on the market values of assets and liabilities, and hence on equity, makes the implicit assumption that parallel shifts occur in the yield curve when interest-rate levels change. Yet as was discussed earlier in this chapter, parallel shifts in the yield curve seldom occur; in fact, there appear to be historical patterns in the relationship between the shape of the yield curve and the level of interest rates. In addition,

TABLE 16.6   Relationship Between Interest-Rate Changes and Market Value of Equity

Duration Gap	Relationship with Interest-Rate Changes
Positive	Inverse
Zero	No effect
Negative	Direct

TABLE 16.7   The Credit-Risk Management Process _____

Step 1.	Determination of desired level of credit risk
Step 2.	Evaluation of credit risk of alternative financial assets
Step 3.	Variation of credit risk over various level of business activity

duration calculations require substantial information on the cash flows associated with each asset, information that is often difficult to obtain and also costly.

Second, not only are duration calculations difficult to make, but the duration of assets and liabilities must be recalculated frequently. Since duration changes with interest-rate levels, every time there is a significant change in the level of interest rates, the duration of the portfolio must be recalculated. Such recalculations may require additional information on the assets in the portfolio before duration can be estimated.

Credit-Risk Management.   The operations of financial institutions in the money and capital markets may also be viewed in terms of management control over the credit risk embodied in the asset side of the portfolio.[11]

The credit-risk management process for banks is analogous to the default-risk rating process for corporate and municipal bonds. Bank credit analysts must grade the quality of loan applications just as bond ratings analysts grade the quality of bond issues and establish a rating based on the perceived risk of default. With bank credit, of course, the credit grading process leads to a positive or negative decision on the credit request, though the grading may also be useful in establishing an interest rate to be charged on the loan. The credit risk management process may be subdivided into three components: First, determine the desired level of credit risk; second, evaluate the credit risk of alternative financial assets; and third, vary the degree of credit risk over various levels of business activity. Taken together, these three steps, which are shown in Table 16.7, constitute the credit policy of a financial institution.

Thus the first step in formulating a credit policy is to determine the desired level of credit risk in the portfolio. To some extent the regulatory authorities have already done this for many financial institutions. For example, banks (with

---

[11]Proper management of credit risk is crucial to the survival of the institution. For example, the Federal Deposit Insurance Corporation has estimated that credit quality was the major reason for more than 80 percent of the failures of commercial banks in the 1980–1982 period. In contrast, interest-rate risk caused by the mismatching of the volume of rate-sensitive assets and rate-sensitive liabilities was a minor factor in the failure of commercial banks during this period. It might be expected, of course, that the relative importance of interest-rate risk and credit risk would be the opposite for savings and loans, interest-rate risk being the principal cause of failure in those years. For bank data in recent years, see Federal Deposit Insurance Corporation, *Deposit Insurance in a Changing Environment,* 1983.

few exceptions) are prohibited from acquiring equity securities and may purchase only debt securities that are nonspeculative in nature. Many other financial institutions may acquire only securities that are on a "legal list," which usually means securities that contain relatively low risk.

Despite these legal restrictions, the management of financial institutions still have some discretion in determining the degree of credit risk. This discretion is usually greater for contractual financial institutions than for depository institutions, which are more intimately involved in the payments system. In lending operations, management may restrict lending to loans of very high quality or may make loans of lower quality. It can also purchase Aaa or lower-rated bonds. Naturally, different degrees of risk should be associated with different degrees of return. In making this decision, management should examine its risk preferences as well as the desires of shareholders.

Once the desired degree of credit risk is specified, the financial institution must select securities and structure its portfolio in such a way as to meet its objectives. In the customer's market, in which there is a personal relationship between the lender and the borrower, the financial institution must perform a credit analysis. This analysis evaluates the probability of default by looking at the character of the borrower, the capacity of the borrower to generate income to repay the loan, and the collateral that can be pledged to reduce the risk exposure of the lender. The importance of these factors—known as the "Cs of credit"—varies widely from lender to lender and with different types of loans. Yet they form the basis of the credit-risk evaluation process for most institutions.

Capacity
Collateral
Character
Conditions
Capital

Character refers to the honesty and integrity of the borrower. Although direct measurement of this characteristic is difficult, indirect evidence is provided by the borrower's history of credit relationships. Such a history is provided by checking with customers of the borrower, local credit bureau records, past banking relationships, and other similar sources. The **capacity** of the borrower to generate means to repay the loan relates to the use of the funds from the loan and focuses on the ability of the borrower to generate cash flows from that use to service the debt. The principal distinction with regard to use of funds is whether the loan is for working capital or for the purchase of plant and equipment. Working capital loans may be repaid from the liquidation of the assets during the normal cash cycle, at least if the working capital expansion is seasonal rather than permanent (permanent additions to working capital should be analyzed in a fashion similar to that of plant and equipment loans). In contrast, loans for the purchase of fixed assets usually would be repaid over a more extended period from the income and cash flow produced by the asset. Loans for this purpose are usually lengthy in maturity and are referred to as **term loans.** While cash flow from the proceeds of the loan is the principal source of repayment, collateral represents the secondary source of repayment. **Collateral** refers to those assets such as securities, inventory, accounts receivable, and plant and equipment that the lender may obtain and liquidate in the event that the borrower is unwilling or unable to fulfill the terms of the loan contract.

In purchasing money- and capital-market instruments the financial institution often has the option of using credit evaluation by the credit-rating agencies—Moody's and Standard & Poor's—either as substitutes for or supplements to its own credit analysis. These agencies have already analyzed the financial position of a given borrower and have issued a rating that summarizes the credit risk involved in the issue. Although these ratings are certainly not infallible, considerable evidence indicates that they are reasonably accurate guides to differences in credit risk among securities.

Finally, the financial institution may wish to adjust the credit-risk posture of its assets over the business cycle as the risk–return relationship among different securities changes. For example, risk premiums between high- and lower-rated corporate bonds tend to widen in periods of recession and to narrow in periods of economic expansion. A similar though less pronounced movement exists in the municipal market. This tendency might suggest a strategy of investing in lower-quality securities in recession and switching to higher-quality securities later in the expansion. Of course, such a policy would imply that the markets are inefficiently pricing risk over the business cycle, and that may not continue in the future. Moreover, a financial institution can achieve a desired credit-risk position for its entire portfolio by taking large risks in the loan portfolio and low risk in the securities portfolio or by effecting some other mixture of risk in the two segments of the asset portfolios.

MATURITY MANAGEMENT, CREDIT-RISK MANAGEMENT, AND THE BASIC FUNCTIONS OF FINANCIAL INSTITUTIONS: A SYNTHESIS

The total risk of a financial institution, especially a depository institution, may be viewed conceptually as a combination or sum of its interest rate risk and credit risk.[12] Thus as shown in Eq. (16.6),

$$R_t = IRR_t + CR_t \qquad (16.6)$$

where

$$
\begin{aligned}
R_t &= \text{the total risk for the } t^{\text{th}} \text{ firm} \\
IRR_t &= \text{interest rate risk for the } t^{\text{th}} \text{ firm} \\
CR_t &= \text{credit risk for the } t^{\text{th}} \text{ firm}
\end{aligned}
$$

One organization may have high interest-rate risk but low credit risk, producing a moderate degree of total risk. For example, savings and loans in the early 1980s had high interest-rate risk but quite low credit risk. Another organization may

---

[12]A number of other dimensions of risk exist, including the risk of not having sufficient cash to meet the needs of depositors, and are usually referred to as **liquidity risk.** However, the example concentrates on those dimensions of risk that are generally considered to be the most significant.

have high credit risk but relatively low interest-rate risk. Many commercial banks fell into this category in the early 1980s. While it is certainly difficult to quantify exactly the degree of interest-rate and credit risk assumed by financial institutions, Eq. (16.6) at least provides a framework for analysis of these risks.

As was discussed earlier, the present functions of the major financial institutions are heavily influenced by the historical evolution of the institutions. Custom and tradition, partly incorporated into law and regulation, among other factors, have shaped the services offered by individual financial institutions and thereby their sources and uses of funds. Yet within these limits the managements of financial institutions have considerable discretion in their participations in the money and capital markets and in the risks that they assume. They alter the interest-rate and credit-risk dimensions of their portfolios in response to changes in the level and term structure of interest rates and to changes in credit-risk premiums among different types of financial market instruments and as they attempt to achieve a desired total risk position.[13] Through their reaction they in turn produce additional changes in the patterns of yields in financial markets.

Savings and loans, for example, are by tradition and regulation primarily long-term lenders on single-family properties. Yet in periods of high interest rates, some savings and loans may become heavy investors in money market instruments, as an inverted yield curve makes long-term fixed-rate mortgages unattractive. Savings banks, which have more discretionary power in asset selection, may shift their asset structure toward corporate bonds and away from mortgages if relative returns on corporate bonds are particularly attractive. Commercial banks may seek to sell large amounts of longer-term CDs in anticipation of rising interest rates, and they may seek to place these funds in variable-rate commercial loans.

Numerous additional examples could be presented of the behavior of financial institutions and the implications of their behavior for the money and capital markets. For our purposes it is sufficient to recognize that portfolio adjustments by financial institutions with the use of money- and capital-market instruments are profoundly important. Financial institutions acquire most of the instruments of the money and capital markets; indeed, many of the instruments of the financial markets, particularly the money market, are the liabilities of financial institutions. Their purchases and sales of Treasury bills, federal funds, CDs, and bonds and mortgages are so important to the financial markets that it is impossible

---

[13]While the discussion in this chapter has focused on interest-rate and credit risk, some analysts also include management risk in their discussion of the risk dimensions of a financial institution. Management risk refers to exceptional or spectacular failures resulting from management misuse of its portfolio management powers, especially the new asset/liability powers that have come with deregulation. Management risk reflects the potential that an inexperienced manager may become involved in activities that require far more expertise and sophistication than that manager possesses. Beyond the part of management risk that is embedded in interest-rate risk and credit risk, the exact dimensions of this risk are difficult to quantify.

to understand how financial markets operate without also understanding how financial institutions operate. In fact, the determination of equilibrium in financial market rates and in the portfolios of financial institutions should be viewed as a simultaneous or joint solution.

SUMMARY

Financial institutions play a key role in the financial system, simultaneously issuing and acquiring financial instruments, the "raw material" of the financial markets. An understanding of the financial markets—both the money market and the capital market—is impossible without an understanding of the way financial institutions behave.

A financial institution faces both asset- and liability-management problems in the financial management of its entire portfolio. In short, it faces numerous funds-management decisions. These decisions include the maturity-management decision, which is concerned with the average maturity or duration of assets and liabilities. In making this decision the financial institution must recognize the relationship between the business fluctuations and the interest-rate movements and must also adopt either an aggressive or a defensive strategy. Management decisions also encompass credit-risk considerations, in which the management of the financial institution must determine a desired level of credit risk, evaluate the credit risk of alternative financial assets (both loans and securities), and decide whether the level of default risk should be varied with business fluctuations.

We have attempted to explain financial institutions' behavior within a context of the management of maturity and credit risk and to explain briefly how these concepts relate to the strategies of some specific institutions. It is impossible to convey the full scope and complexities of the behavior of financial institutions within such a brief space, but we have tried to fit the financial institution into a financial markets framework.

QUESTIONS

1. In what sense are all financial institutions alike? In what sense are all financial institutions different?

2. What is the customer's market? How does it differ from the money and capital markets?

3. Compare the flexibility in credit and maturity management of depository and nondepository financial institutions.

4. What are the four stages of the interest-rate cycle? How do the levels of interest rates and the term structure of interest rates change in these four stages?

5. Distinguish between rate-sensitive and nonrate-sensitive assets.

6. Compare an aggressive and a defensive strategy.

7. Assume a period of rising interest rates. How would a defensive portfolio be adjusted? An aggressively managed maturity portfolio?

8. What is meant by duration gap management? What policy should be followed to immunize against interest-rate changes?

9. Explain the process involved in managing the credit risk exposure of a financial institution.

REFERENCES

Baker, James V., *Asset/Liability Management* (Washington: American Bankers Association, 1981).

Bender, Barret, and Thomas W. F. Lindquist, *Asset/Liability and Funds Management at U.S. Commercial Banks* (Rolling Meadows, Ill.: Bank Administration Institute, 1982).

Bierwag, G., and G. Kaufman, "Duration Gaps for Financial Institutions," *Financial Analysts Journal* (March/April 1985), 68–71.

Buck, Walter H., "Risk-Management Approach to Pricing Loans and Leases," *Journal of Commercial Bank Lending* (April 1979), 2–5.

Greenbaum, Stuart, and George Kantas, "Interest Rate Uncertainty and the Financial Intermediary's Choice of Exposure," *Journal of Finance* (March 1983), 141–147.

Hess, Alan C., "Duration Analysis for Savings and Loan Associations," *Federal Home Loan Bank Board Journal* (October 1982), 12–14.

Kaufman, George, "Measuring and Managing Interest Rate Risk: A Primer," Federal Reserve Bank of Chicago *Economic Perspectives* (January/February 1984), 16–29.

Rosenberg, Joel L., "The Joys of Duration," *Bankers Magazine* (March/April 1986), 62–67.

Sexton, Donald F., "Determining Good and Bad Credit Risks Among High and Low Income Families," *Journal of Business* (April 1977), 236–239.

Simonson, Donald G., and George H. Hempel, "Improving Gap Management for Controlling Interest Rate Risk," *Journal of Bank Research* (Summer 1982), 109–115.

Toeves, Alden L., "Gap Management: Managing Interest Rate Risks in Banks and Thrifts," Federal Reserve Bank of San Francisco *Economic Review* (Spring 1983), 20–35.

CHAPTER 17

The Money Market: U.S. Treasury and Federal Agency Securities, Federal Funds, and Repurchase Agreements

In this chapter we begin an extensive discussion of the various instruments of the money market and the different characteristics of the money market. We initially concentrate on two vitally important institutions in the market: the Federal Reserve and government security dealers. This leads us to a discussion of four money market instruments that are closely related to these institutions: U.S. Treasury securities, agency securities, federal funds, and repurchase agreements. Other principal money market instruments—domestic and Eurodollar negotiable certificates of deposit, bankers acceptances, and commercial paper—are treated in Chapter 18. In each case we present the characteristics of the instruments and the markets, discuss the major participants in the markets, and evaluate the significance of the markets for the participants and for the financial system. Before looking at the details of the markets, however, we provide an overview of the money market and of the role of security dealers in that market.

THE MONEY MARKET: AN OVERVIEW

Nature of the Market

The money market provides a facility in which financial market participants may adjust their liquidity positions. Participants with a temporary liquidity surplus may dispose of their excess funds by purchasing money market instruments. Those with temporary liquidity deficiencies may eliminate them by selling money market instruments held in their portfolios (asset management) or by borrowing—that is, by issuing new money market instruments (liability management). Therefore the money market is often analyzed as an indicator of the degree of financial pressure in the economy and of the current posture of monetary policy.

As such, the money market, like all financial markets, provides important information to market participants. It mirrors the liquidity pressures on financial institutions. In addition, the Federal Reserve injects reserves into the banking system and withdraws reserves through its operations in the money market.

Money Market Instruments

There are a number of differences among the financial instruments of the money market, but there are certain basic characteristics that all money market instruments share. These similarities reflect the basic liquidity-adjustment function of all the instruments of the market. For example, all money market instruments must be, by definition, short-term, and they are characterized by relatively little credit risk. These two features promote substantial price stability to the purchaser. In addition, as a means of liquidity management, a money market instrument should have a high degree of marketability in the event that the holder wishes to dispose of the asset prior to its maturity.

Money market instruments are relatively homogeneous, substitution among the different instruments of the market occurring in the portfolios of market participants based on risk–return considerations. In fact, interest rates on most money market instruments are related. It is indeed meaningful to discuss increases or decreases in interest rates in the money market generally apart from changes in rates on individual money market instruments.

This similarity in rates is reflected in Table 17.1, which presents interest rates over time on a number of money market instruments.[1] These instruments are **federal funds** (short-term loans between commercial banks), **Eurodollar deposits** (dollar-denominated deposits at foreign banks), **domestic certificates of deposit** (large, business-oriented certificates issued by major commercial banks), **bankers acceptances** (time drafts drawn on major banks in which the bank has guaranteed payment), **Treasury bills** (short-term U.S. Treasury securities), and **commercial paper** (short-term unsecured promissory notes issued by large businesses). Two important generalizations can be made on the basis of this information.

1. At any one time there is a fairly low spread among the rates on these instruments. For example, in early 1989 the spread was only 99 basis points (0.99%).

2. The rates on these instruments tend to move up or down by similar amounts. For example, between 1986 and 1989 the 3-month CD rate increased by 269 basis points, and the commercial paper rate increased 257 basis points.

Both relationships reflect the similarity among the money market instruments and the homogeneity of the market.

Although there are important similarities among money market instruments,

---

[1]The rates in Table 17.1 are not fully comparable because some rates (those of Treasury bills, for example) are calculated on a bank discount basis.

TABLE 17.1 Money Market Rates (In Percent)

	1976	1980	1982	1984	1986	1989 (Jan.)
Federal funds	4.65	18.90	12.26	10.23	6.80	9.12
3-month CD	4.66	18.65	12.27	10.37	6.51	9.20
3-month Eurodollar deposit	5.01	19.47	13.12	10.73	6.71	9.28
90-day bankers acceptance	4.62	17.96	11.89	10.14	6.38	8.93
3-month Treasury bill	4.35	15.49	10.61	9.52	5.98	8.29
90–119-day commercial paper	4.66	18.07	11.89	10.10	6.49	9.06

Sources: Board of Governors of the Federal Reserve System, Annual Statistical Digest, 1974–1989, pp. 85–89; Federal Reserve Bulletin, various issues.

there are also important differences. These differences reflect the various factors, discussed in Chapter 8, that produce differences in yields on financial instruments. For example, the yield on Treasury bills is generally the lowest of all money market rates, reflecting the bills' freedom from default risk. In fact, yields on Treasury bills are frequently used as proxies for the "risk-free" rate. In addition, the interest rate on Treasury bills is reduced in relation to other money market rates by the existence of an excellent resale or secondary market and by the fact that the interest income on Treasury securities is exempt from state and local government income taxes. Reflecting these factors, the 3-month Treasury bill rate is the lowest of all the money market rates given in Table 17.1 for each period for which information is provided.

The whole structure of relative rates in the money market may be explained by reference to credit risk, liquidity, tax, and other factors. Throughout these two chapters, as we discuss the nature of the various money market instruments, we will also point out the relevant characteristics that influence their relative interest rates in the market. Table 17.2 provides the size dimensions of the various instruments.

THE ROLE OF THE FEDERAL RESERVE

The central bank of the United States—the Federal Reserve System—plays a vital role in the money market. The Federal Reserve's role in the money market is so important that it is not an exaggeration to state that an understanding of the working of the money market requires an understanding of the role of the Fed. Indeed, Stigum refers to the Fed as the most watched player in the money market.[2]

[2]See Marcia Stigum, The Money Market (Homewood, Ill.: Dow-Jones/Irwin, 1983), Chapter 8.

TABLE 17.2 Volume Outstanding of Selected Money Market Instruments (Billions of Dollars)

	1980	1988
U.S. Treasury bills	216.1	398.5
Federal funds borrowings and repurchase agreements	103.9	368.6
Certificates of deposit ($100,000 or more)	225.0	579.4
Bankers acceptances	54.7	58.3
Commercial paper	124.8	425.1

Source: Board of Governors of the Federal Reserve System, Federal Reserve Bulletin and Flow of Funds Accounts.

The significance of the Fed in the money market reflects the predominance of open-market operations in the implementation of monetary policy. With open-market operations the Fed buys and sells securities, principally U.S. Treasury bills, in the money market as deemed appropriate. The trading desk of the New York Federal Reserve Bank implements the policy directives of the Federal Open-Market Committee by buying and selling securities in the money market from U.S. government security dealers. When the Fed purchases securities, reserves at depository institutions increase, and downward pressure is placed on money market rates. In contrast, when the Fed sells government securities to the dealers, the reserves of depository institutions are reduced, and upward pressure is placed on money market rates.

The Federal Reserve, through the trading desk of the New York Fed, operates in the money market almost on a continuous basis, acting as a seller or as a buyer. Unlike those of other market participants, the Fed's transactions are not governed by profit considerations; the Fed buys or sells to achieve its monetary policy objectives. In addition, the Fed often buys or sells securities in the money market as an agent for the accounts of foreign official institutions such as foreign central banks and for the U.S. Treasury.

The volume of Fed transactions in the money market is truly massive. For example, in 1988 the Fed's gross purchases of U.S. Treasury bills amounted to around $20 billion, and its gross sales of bills totaled over $8 billion. While the Fed also buys longer-term government securities, the volume of such transactions is much less than that of bills.

The Fed influences the money market not only through open-market operations but also through the lending that it does to banks through its discount window. The Fed provides reserves to depository institutions that have a temporary reserve shortfall, thereby relieving pressure on the money market. In contrast, when reserves are ample, depository institutions repay their borrowings from the Fed. In any case, Federal Reserve discount window operations have a considerable influence on interest rates in the money market.

GOVERNMENT SECURITY DEALERS

Inside mkt trade among dealers themselves.

Role of Dealers

The money market is not limited to any one place (though activity in New York City is very important). Rather, the money market is an **over-the-counter** (or over-the-telephone) market, whereby trading for securities is carried on by private business firms that hold inventories of securities and stand ready to buy and sell securities at posted rates. These businesses are security dealers[3] (commonly called "government security dealers" because of the importance of government securities to their operation), and their function is of crucial importance to the effective operation of the financial markets. These security dealers also play an important role in the operation of monetary policy, since some of them (the accredited U.S. government security dealers) engage in purchases and sales of securities with the Federal Reserve Bank of New York trading desk for the Federal Open-Market Account. As of the late 1980s, thirty-five dealers reported their activities daily to the Federal Reserve Bank of New York.

Dealer Activities

The principal function of government security dealers is to make a market in U.S. government and other securities. They **make the market** by holding an inventory of securities and offering to buy and sell these securities at announced bid (buy) and ask (sell) prices. They do not generally charge a commission on their transactions, but rather seek to profit from the spreads between the bid (buy) and ask (sell) prices. These spreads are, however, quite narrow, so dealer profits from their trading activity require a large volume of transactions. For example, spreads on Treasury bills are often as low as 8 basis points. While spreads are higher on longer-term securities, they remain quite narrow for all such securities, necessitating a large volume of transactions in order for the dealer to earn a reasonable return.

---

[3]These dealers are those that conduct a significant amount of trading with retail customers as well as with other dealers, operate in size in the major maturity areas of the money market, and are adequately capitalized and managed by responsible personnel. They may conduct business with the trading desk of the New York Federal Reserve Bank but in return must report their transactions, financing, and inventories daily to the New York Fed.

Dealers hold positions in most money market instruments, though the size of the position varies with the individual dealer and with the nature of the instrument. The Treasury bills are usually the largest single security held in dealer portfolios, though major positions are maintained in other U.S. Treasury securities, federal agency issues (particularly the mortgage-backed securities issued by the Government National Mortgage Association), and other money market instruments such as certificates of deposit.

Dealer trading activity may be divided into two groups: trades among the dealers themselves, sometimes referred to as the **inside market,** and trades between dealers and their nondealer customers, sometimes referred to as the **outside** or **retail market.** Trading among dealers in the inside market often takes place with the assistance of interdealer brokers, who themselves do not make markets or hold securities for their own account. These brokers operate on a commission basis. It has been estimated that more than 80 percent of the interdealer transactions are accomplished through brokers.[4] Brokers provide anonymity to dealers and allow dealers to protect information about their positions from other dealers. Brokers also facilitate transactions by reducing the need to survey a large number of dealers for market prices.

Virtually all trading in the dealer market is done over the telephone. The dealer market for U.S. government securities and for other money market instruments is truly an over-the-counter market. Each dealer organization quotes prices over the telephone to nondealer customers or to bankers in the retail market. Potential buyers survey the various dealers and negotiate price before consummating a transaction.

Dealer Financing

Dealers are extremely highly leveraged institutions; that is, their equity capital base is very small, and they operate almost entirely with borrowed funds. In fact, in some cases the securities held by a dealer may total 500 to 600 times the dealer's equity capital base. The borrowed funds used to finance the dealer's position are very short-term in maturity, often overnight. The transactions themselves are often in the form of repurchase agreements, whereby the dealer sells a security to the lender with the obligation to repurchase the security at a specified time (usually the next day) at an agreed price. The funds are provided by a variety of lenders. At one time, commercial banks were the dominant source of dealer funds. However, bank credit has declined as a funds source as dealers have broadened their funding options to include large corporations, insurance companies, savings institutions, federal agencies, and state and local governments.

---

[4]Timothy Q. Cook and Bruce J. Simmons, *Instrument of the Money Market,* 7th ed. (Federal Reserve Bank of Richmond, 1986), p. 36.

Profit Sources

Security dealers seek to make a profit in three ways.

1. They attempt to profit by selling their inventory of securities for a higher price than the price at which the securities were purchased. Like any business firm with an inventory, the dealer seeks to mark up the inventory over cost in order to earn a return on invested capital. A dealer that holds an inventory of Treasury bills, CDs, bankers acceptances, or other money market instruments will offer to sell each of the securities (ask) at a price higher than the price the dealer is willing to buy that security (bid). This potential profit is known as the **spread.**

2. Dealers seek to earn a return from the **carry,** from earning more on their securities portfolios than they pay to obtain the funds to support the purchase of their security holdings. This can be done if the maturity of their securities portfolios exceeds the maturity of their liabilities and if the yield curve is upward sloping.

3. Dealers may seek to increase their profit by varying the size and average maturity of their portfolios with changes in expectations of future interest rate levels. For example, expectations of falling interest rates would lead dealers to expand the size and lengthen the maturity of their portfolios, whereas expectations of increasing interest rates would lead dealers to reduce the size and shorten the maturity of their portfolios.

The important role that dealers play in the financial system was made evident in an unfortunate way in the early 1980s. The financial collapse of several dealers resulted in severe financial strains for depository institutions doing business with these dealers (and even a few failures). As a result, congressional pressure developed for greater regulatory scrutiny of dealers and their activities.

U.S. GOVERNMENT SECURITIES

The debt of the U.S. government is enormous—more than $2.7 trillion. Moreover, this debt, the cumulative result of all deficits during past years, is very short-term in average maturity. Therefore Treasury securities have played (and continue to play) a vital role in the financial markets, especially in the money market.

Types of U.S. Government Securities

Government securities (or **governments,** as they are frequently called) are usually divided into three separate groups: bills, notes, and bonds.[5] The differ-

---

[5]Our discussion deals only with marketable government securities. A substantial part (about one third) of the U.S. debt consists of nonmarketable savings bonds, debt sold to U.S. government trust funds, debt sold to foreign central banks, and other types of nonmarketable issues. These nonmarketable securities play no direct role in the financial markets.

ences among these types of securities include maturity, minimum denomination, and method of payment of interest. Bills are issued with an original maturity of one year or less in a minimum denomination of $10,000, and they are discount instruments (the original purchase price is less than par value). Notes are issued with an original maturity of one to ten years, usually in a minimum denomination of $1000, and they are generally sold at par and carry a specific coupon rate. Bonds, by far the smallest portion of the U.S. government debt, are usually sold in maturities of more than 10 years, are generally sold in minimum denominations of $1000, and, like notes, are coupon instruments.[6]

Composition of the U.S. Treasury debt is shown in Table 17.3. Roughly two thirds of the U.S. debt consists of marketable securities, and of these marketable debt instruments, notes are the largest category and bills are by far the second largest group. This particular mix of bills, notes, and bonds suggests that the maturity of the federal debt is fairly short. Indeed, in recent years the average maturity of the U.S. debt has generally ranged between two and three years. Information on the ownership of the federal debt is also presented in Table 17.3, which gives the ownership of all (marketable and nonmarketable) U.S. government debt. The U.S. government itself—through its agencies, trust funds, and the Federal Reserve—is a major investor in federal securities. U.S. government agencies and trust funds held $550.4 billion (most of which were nonmarketable issues), and the Federal Reserve held $229.2 billion (entirely in marketable issues). Commercial banks were also major investors in U.S. government securities, holding over $200 billion. And individuals, principally through nonmarketable savings bonds, held large amounts of federal government securities.

Yield Calculations

Calculation of the yield to the investor on coupon issues (notes and bonds) is relatively straightforward. The yield may be expressed as either the **current yield** or the **yield to maturity,** where

$$\text{Current yield (CY)} = \text{Interest/Price} \tag{17.1}$$

and yield to maturity is defined as the discount rate that makes the present value of the cash flow from a bond equal to its current market price:

$$p = I_1/(1 + r)^1 + I_2/(1 + r)^2 + \cdots + I_n/(1 + r)^n + P'_n(1 + r)^n \tag{17.2}$$

where P = price of bond, I = interest payments, P'_n = par or principal payments, n = number of periods until maturity, and r = yield to maturity.

---

[6]See Chapter 27 for further discussion of government securities within a perspective of fiscal policy and debt management.

TABLE 17.3 Interest-Bearing Government Debt by Type and Ownership, September 30, 1988 _____

	Amount (billions of dollars)
By type	
Marketable	$1,802.9
Bills	398.5
Notes	1,089.6
Bonds	299.9
Nonmarketable	797.0
By holder	
U.S. government agencies and trust fund	550.4
Federal Reserve banks	229.2
Private investors	1,819.0
Commercial banks	203.0
Money market funds	10.8
Insurance companies	135.0
Other companies	86.0
State and local governments	N.A.
Individuals	179.8
Foreign and international	334.3
Other	N.A.

Source: *Federal Reserve* Bulletin *(June 1989), A30.*

The yield to maturity is a more accurate measure of the return on a coupon instrument, since it takes into account the periodic interest payments, the price of the bond, and the gain or loss to the investor at the maturity of the bond. It is called the yield to maturity because it assumes that the purchased bond is held until maturity.

Unlike bonds, however, Treasury bills and most other money market instruments carry no explicit coupon payment. Rather, the holder of the instrument earns a discount return, and the instruments themselves are referred to as discount instruments. The returns on these instruments are usually quoted on a discount basis, using a 360-day year (commonly referred to as a bank discount basis yield). In these quotations the price of the bill is deducted from par, producing the discount. This discount is then divided by par and expressed as a percentage at an annual rate using a 360-day year.

For example, suppose that the price of a 91-day bill as established in the secondary market was $96.295 per $100 face amount (for a $10,000 face amount

bill the price would be $9629.50). The discount basis return would then be calcu-
lated as in Eq. (17.3):

$$\frac{100 - 96.295}{100} \times \frac{360}{91} = 14.657 \tag{17.3}$$

This bank discount yield understates the "true" yield on the bill and thus is
not comparable with the yield to maturity on a coupon issue. The extent to which
the discount yield understates the true yield on the bill varies with the maturity
of the instrument and the level of interest rates. The longer the term to maturity,
the greater the understatement. Similarly, the higher the yield, the greater the
understatement.

The **coupon equivalent yield** on a Treasury bill or other discount instrument
may be calculated by dividing the discount by price (rather than par) and using
a 365-day year (rather than a 360-day year). In the above example the yield that
is comparable with yields on coupon instruments (that is, the coupon equivalent
yield) is

$$\frac{100 - 96.295}{96.295} \times \frac{365}{91} = 15.432 \tag{17.4}$$

It is also possible to convert the discount yield directly to a coupon equivalent yield with the use of Eq. (17.5)[7]:

$$\text{Coupon equivalent yield} = \frac{365 \times \text{Discount basis yield}}{360 - (\text{Discount basis yield} \times \text{Days to maturity})} \tag{17.5}$$

In the example given above, the coupon equivalent yield is

$$\text{Coupon equivalent yield} = \frac{365 \times .14657}{360 - (.14657 \times 91)}$$

$$= \frac{53.498}{360 - 13.337}$$

$$= \frac{53.498}{346.663}$$

$$= 15.43 \text{ percent}$$

Primary Market

The market for government securities, like the market for other financial
instruments, may be conveniently divided into the market for new issues (the

---

[7]For a more complete discussion, see *Securities of the United States Government and Federal Agencies,*
32nd ed. (First Boston Corporation, 1986).

primary market) and the market for existing issues (the secondary market). Although there is considerable overlap among the major participants in these two parts of the government security market, the Federal Reserve plays an especially important role in the primary market, and security dealers play a vital role in the secondary market.

The Federal Reserve acts as an agent for the Treasury in the sale of new U.S. government securities. Since new U.S. government securities with a maximum maturity of one year (which qualify as money market securities) consist of Treasury bills only, our discussion in this chapter of the primary market for government securities will be limited to bills.

All bills are sold through an auction technique. Each week, 91-day and 182-day bills are auctioned. In addition, 52-week bills are auctioned monthly. Bids may be submitted to any Federal Reserve Bank and to any branch of a Federal Reserve Bank. These bids may be **competitive** (both a price and a quantity are specified by the bidder) or **noncompetitive** (only a quantity is specified). The competitive bidder may receive the entire amount desired, part, or none at the average price established by the competitive "tenders." Anyone may offer a competitive tender, but most such tenders are made by professionals—security dealers and major banks. Noncompetitive tenders are generally made by smaller investors, often individuals. The maximum noncompetitive tender is $500,000 for bills and $1,000,000 for notes and bonds. The amount of noncompetitive tenders is usually small in relation to the amount of competitive tenders, although the volume of noncompetitive tenders usually increases sharply in periods of high and rising interest rates.

The usual auction pattern for the weekly issues is as follows:

1. The offering is announced on Tuesday.

2. The bills are auctioned the following Monday.

3. The bills are issued on the Thursday after the auction.

For 52-week maturity bills the following schedule is typical:

1. The offering is announced every fourth Friday.

2. The bills are auctioned the following Thursday.

3. The bills are issued on the following Thursday.

In a tender form used for 26-week bills the tenderer must indicate whether the bid is noncompetitive or competitive (in which case the price must be specified to three decimal places). The tender is for a minimum of $10,000 and must be in multiples of $5,000. Also, it is important to note that the bills are issued in book-entry form; that is, the purchaser of the bills does not receive physical possession of the securities. Instead, the purchaser obtains a statement of account from the U.S. Treasury that provides relevant information about the transaction such as the amount of securities, interest earnings, date of isue, and date of maturity.

Secondary Market

As was discussed earlier in this chapter, security dealers play an important—indeed, a crucial—role in the money market.[8] This is especially true in the secondary market for government securities. Government security dealers, operating in the OTC market, play a vital role in establishing and maintaining the "depth, breadth, and resiliency" of the government securities market.[9] Dealers hold an inventory of government securities and stand ready to buy and sell these securities at posted prices. Treasury bills also dominate dealer trading activities. In most weeks, well over half of all dealer transactions in government securities occurs with bills.

Participants in the Short-Term Government Security Market

Treasury bills and other short-term government securities are bought and sold for liquidity-adjustment purposes by a wide range of financial market participants. These investors, who value high liquidity and low risk, are especially attracted to Treasury bills. Major investors in Treasury bills include the Federal Reserve and commercial banks.

The Fed uses bills for most of its open-market operations, since it can buy and sell large amounts of securities in the bill market with minimal disruption of the market. At one time the Fed's open-market operations were characterized as "bills only," although now the term "bills preferably" would be more accurate. Commercial banks use bills for liquidity adjustment, as well as for collateral (public deposits at banks must be secured by "pledging" specific assets, such as government securities). In addition, other financial institutions, nonfinancial corporations, state and local governments, and a diverse group of other investors hold Treasury bills.

Interest Rates on Treasury Bills

As we saw in Table 17.1, interest rates on Treasury bills are the lowest of the rates on money market instruments. This pattern reflects three important factors.

1. The Treasury bill is assumed to have no credit risk; in fact, the risk-free rate is often proxied with the Treasury bill rate.

---

[8]For an excellent discussion of the role of dealers in the U.S. government securities market, see the article by McCurdy listed in the references at the end of the chapter.
[9]A market that has "depth, breadth, and resiliency" is one that can absorb a large volume of securities or purchase orders with minimal impact on existing market prices.

2. The marketability of Treasury bills is very high. Since bills are short-term, they have little interest-rate or market risk, as well as being free of credit risk. And as has already been noted, there is an exceptionally good secondary market for bills, reflecting the position of dealers in the market.

3. The interest return on Treasury bills (as on all Treasury securities) is exempt from taxation by state and local governments.

FEDERAL AGENCY SECURITIES

The U.S. government not only affects the credit markets through its direct borrowing but also has a substantial effect through the borrowing of its agencies. In fact, in recent years, borrowings by federal agencies have grown quite rapidly. As discussed in Chapter 11, Federal agencies encompass a diverse group of institutions established to accomplish some public purpose. Included are agencies designed to foster the flow of credit to agriculture and housing and to provide greater availability of credit at lower cost for a number of other purposes. Not only do the functions of the different agencies vary, but the methods of financing the agencies also differ. Most agency securities are sold with original maturities of one to ten years, but there are also agency securities with extremely short and extremely long maturities. In this chapter we concentrate on those agencies whose financing is essentially short-term. Additional discussion of the market for longer-term agency issues is offered in Chapter 19.

Characteristics of Agency Securities and the Agency Market

Agency securities come in a variety of shapes, sizes, and forms, reflecting the existence of different agencies with different purposes. Short-term agency securities, which fall within the money market, are usually sold in denominations of $50,000 or more, whereas intermediate- and longer-term agency securities are generally sold in much smaller denominations. The maturity of agency securities is often quite short. For example, the Federal National Mortgage Association relies heavily on the sale of discount notes whose maturities range from 30 to 270 days. Taken together, roughly 20 percent of agency issues are short-term; however, the maturity distribution varies widely among the agencies.

New agency securities are generally sold through fiscal agents on a subscription basis. The fiscal agent establishes a syndicate of dealers that brings securities to market. Similar to U.S. Treasury securities, the issues of government-sponsored agencies are exempt from registration with the Securities and Exchange Commission. Secondary markets in agency securities, maintained by security dealers, are quite good, but they are much less well-developed than markets for direct Treasury debt, a situation reflecting the smaller positions of dealers in these securities, as well as the smaller volume of transactions.

Federally sponsored credit agencies sell two types of securities: (1) coupon-bearing bonds and (2) discount notes. Discount notes have become more common in recent years, particularly for short-term securities issued by the agencies.

Purchasers of Agency Securities

Agency securities are purchased by a number of different investors. The largest single investor group comprises commercial banks, which hold about 20 percent of agency issues. Banks find agency issues attractive because they have many of the same desirable characteristics as Treasuries but carry slightly higher yields. Other investors include U.S. government accounts and Federal Reserve Banks, with about 10 percent of the market, and a diverse group of individuals, nonfinancial businesses, and other investors.

Investors in agency securities are attracted by a combination of yield, liquidity, and risk. Agency issues normally trade at a yield premium to U.S. Treasury issues of the same maturity. They have very good liquidity, better than most money market instruments, though not as good as Treasury bills. They also have very low credit risk. Some agency securities are backed directly by the federal government, and others are perceived to have the implicit guarantee of the U.S. government. In addition, as with U.S. Treasury notes, interest income from some types of agency securities is exempt from state and local taxation.

Interest Rates on Agency Issues

Interest rates on agency issues are generally very close to those offered on comparable maturity Treasury securities. The small premium reflects market perceptions that the issues of these agencies carry the implied guarantee of the United States government.

There is some evidence that the yield spread between agency and Treasury issues has widened in recent years. This increase appears to reflect the extraordinarily rapid rate of growth in agency debt. In addition, the yield spread is highly variable over the business cycle, apparently reflecting changing risk perceptions, as well as relative supply factors.

FEDERAL FUNDS

Definition of Federal Funds

The term **federal funds** refers to short-term loans in immediately available (that is, collected) funds, and the **federal funds market** refers to the buying (borrowing) and selling (lending) of these immediately available funds. Traditionally, federal funds transactions have involved bank reserves; however, the term **immediately available** is really the crucial one in defining a federal funds transaction.

In contrast with the settlement of a transaction by check, in which the borrower does not have use of the funds for at least one business day and in which the lender does not surrender use of the funds for at least one business day, a federal fund transaction provides immediately usable funds to the borrower and takes immediately usable funds from the lender at the time of the transaction.[10] Large institutions—both financial and nonfinancial—endeavoring to maximize income manage their cash positions carefully, particularly in periods of high interest rates, and prefer to avoid the delays associated with the normal check-clearing mechanism. They prefer trading in these immediately available (federal) funds to using delayed-availability checking or "clearinghouse" funds.[11]

Role in Financial System

The federal funds market plays an important role in the financial system. It has become the principal device whereby major commercial banks and large nonfinancial corporations adjust their liquidity positions. In seeking to dispose of temporarily idle funds, market participants compare the yield available on federal funds with the yields offered on other highly liquid money market instruments. In covering a temporary shortfall in liquidity, market participants compare the cost of borrowing federal funds with the cost of other types of short-term funds. Further, the federal funds market is closely related to Federal Reserve monetary policy. As the most liquid of all the various parts of the money market, the federal funds market is quickly affected by Federal Reserve actions to expand or contract the volume of bank reserves. Therefore the federal funds rate has been closely observed by market participants as an indicator of monetary policy.[12]

Federal Funds Transactions

The federal funds market began in the 1920s as an interbank market in which one bank with excess reserves and another bank with deficient reserves would trade reserve balances. For example, as illustrated in Table 17.4, Bank A has ex-

---

[10]The Federal Reserve System, through its wire transfer network, plays an important role in the immediate transfer of federal funds. The selling bank will instruct its Federal Reserve Bank to immediately transfer funds to the buying bank. If the buying bank is located in a different district than the selling bank, the Fed will transfer funds immediately through an interdistrict transfer.

[11]The term "clearinghouse" comes from the fact that traditionally checks are settled among banks in clearinghouses, at which representatives of the banks physically exchange checks drawn on each bank.

[12]The degree of usefulness of the funds rate as a guide to Fed policy is a function of the Fed's operating procedures. As will be discussed later in this chapter and in Chapter 26, during the 1970s the Fed used the funds rate as a target variable, but the apparent October 1979 shift to a reserves-based operating procedure reduced the usefulness of the funds rate as an indicator of Fed actions. However, during the 1980s the Fed, following an eclectic monetary policy, again emphasized the Federal funds rate as an important monetary variable.

TABLE 17.4 Federal Funds Transactions

I

Bank A			
Reserves	$ 15	Deposits	$100
Other assets	95	Capital	10
Total assets	$110	Total liabilities and capital	$110

Bank B			
Reserves	$ 5	Deposits	$100
Other assets	105	Capital	10
Total assets	$110	Total liabilities and capital	$110

II

Bank A			
Reserves	$ 10	Deposits	$100
Federal funds sold	5	Capital	10
Other assets	95		
Total assets	$110	Total liabilities and capital	$110

Bank B			
Reserves	$ 10	Deposits	$100
Other assets	105	Federal funds borrowed	5
		Capital	10
Total assets	$115	Total liabilities and capital	$115

cess reserves, and Bank B has deficient reserves (we assume a 10 percent reserve requirement). If Bank B were to end the contemporaneous reserve computation period with this deficiency, it would be assessed a penalty, and if Bank A were to end with a reserve surplus, it would incur an opportunity cost through the loss of income from the funds it could have invested in earning assets. In this type of situation the needs of both banks could be satisfied through the sale of federal funds by Bank A to Bank B.[13]

As illustrated in Table 17.4 (II), if Bank A sells 5 dollars to Bank B, the reserve needs of both banks are satisfied. Bank A gets rid of an excess of cash (a nonearning asset) and has an interest-earning asset—loans to domestic commercial banks or federal funds sold. Bank B has eliminated its reserve deficiency by purchasing 5 dollars in the federal funds market and thus has incurred a 5-dollar liability—federal funds borrowed—which it must repay at the termination of the borrowing agreement (generally one day). Although there are a number of ways in which the transaction can be handled, a federal funds purchase and sale of this nature is traditionally consummated through the Federal Reserve System, and the ownership of reserves at the Fed changes as the result of the transaction.

Important Aspects

Certain aspects of federal funds transactions should be highlighted. From a monetary policy perspective it is important to note that federal funds transactions do not create any new bank reserves, but they do result in more effective use of existing reserves. One can easily see, by looking at Table 17.4 (I and II), that the total amount of bank reserves before and after the federal funds transaction is $20. Thus federal funds transactions do not create any new reserves. Their significance for monetary policy is that a banking system with an effective federal funds market can support a larger volume of bank credit on a given reserve base than can one that does not have a well-developed federal funds market.

From the perspective of the lending and borrowing banks the federal funds transaction represents a short-term, generally unsecured loan. The federal funds sale appears on the books of the lender as a loan to a bank, and it appears on the books of the borrower as a nondeposit liability. As a nondeposit liability it is not subject to reserve requirements or to FDIC assessment.[14] If the borrowing bank fails, however, the nondeposit liability (federal funds purchased) is subordinated to the claims of depositors. Therefore access to the federal funds market

---

[13]The two banks could be brought together through federal funds brokers that are quite active in this market. As another possibility, the intricate network of correspondent banks that exists in the United States could be the vehicle for bringing the two banks together. For example, the selling bank might be a small bank that uses a larger bank as its "upstream" correspondent.

[14]The absence of reserve requirements on federal funds borrowings must be qualified, since occasionally (as in the fall of 1979) the Fed attaches reserve requirements on federal funds borrowings that exceed some base level.

may be eliminated quickly for banks that are perceived as having financial difficulties.

Some Recent Developments

The federal funds market has undergone enormous changes and phenomenal growth in recent years. These developments include a substantial change in the purpose for which participating institutions use the federal fund market, a broadening in the types of institutions that use it, and a lengthening in the maturity of many federal funds transactions. Reflecting these developments, the volume of federal funds transactions has soared.

One of the most significant changes in the federal funds market has been the more aggressive use of the market as a source of funds, primarily by the larger banks of the nation. Whereas the federal funds market was originally used as a temporary device to cover reserve shortfalls or excesses, the market has increasingly been used as a more permanent source or use of reserves. For larger commercial banks the federal funds market has become a major part of their liability-management program. Instead of maintaining large amounts of funds in short-term, highly liquid assets, such as Treasury bills, many commercial banks have minimized holdings of liquid assets and purchased federal funds in the open market when they needed additional liquidity. In addition, many commercial banks have used the federal funds market as a means of expanding their earning-asset portfolios beyond the size made possible through ordinary deposit sources of funds. For example, consider a bank that has demand, savings, and time deposits of $800 million. It may buy another $400 million in the federal funds market and thereby expand its lending ability well beyond the level that is possible with its $800 million deposit base. (Note that funding assets with federal funds borrowings increases bank exposure to interest-rate risk because these funds are short-term and must continuously be "rolled over.")

These uses of the federal funds market give rise to the buying of funds, but there is also a more permanent use of the federal funds market that gives rise to the selling of funds. Many small banks now use the federal funds market as a means of placing otherwise idle funds rather than buying Treasury securities or other money market instruments. (Indeed, many small banks continually supply their large correspondent banks with federal funds as part of their overall correspondent relationship.) Such a use of the federal funds market is quite different from the traditional use of the one-day reserve adjustment discussed above.

An important part of the changing nature of the federal funds market involves the development of repurchase agreements (discussed later in the chapter) and the increasing participation by other depository financial institutions. Savings and loans, in particular, have become active suppliers of federal funds. This development has allowed the banking system to draw funds from a new source and has contributed to a more fully integrated financial system.

Monetary Policy, the Federal Reserve, and the Federal Funds Market

The federal funds market has played an important role in the monetary policy process. During many periods the Fed has implemented monetary policy by establishing a narrow target range for the federal funds rate. If the Fed wished to ease monetary conditions (supply new reserves at a faster rate), it would reduce the target federal funds rate (with the expectation that this move would be consistent with a faster growth rate in the money supply). To tighten monetary conditions, the Fed would raise the target federal funds rate (with the expectation that this move would be consistent with a slower growth rate in the money supply). Reflecting this action by the Fed, the federal funds rate is watched intently by outsiders for indirect evidence on the posture of monetary policy.

Interest Rates on Federal Funds

Prevailing interest rates on federal funds are highly volatile. Since the federal funds market is intimately related to bank reserve adjustments, the rate on federal funds on any given day will fluctuate widely, up and down, as bank reserve conditions shift. Moreover, Federal Reserve action to change bank reserve positions will frequently produce large but short-term movements in the federal funds rate. Indeed, on a daily basis the federal funds rate is by far the most volatile of all money market rates. And even over a longer term the volatility of the federal funds rate in comparison with other money market rates is noticeable. When rates are generally falling, the funds rate will often fall more than other money market rates do. When rates are rising, the funds rate will often rise more than other money market rates.

REPURCHASE AGREEMENTS

Repurchase agreements (repos, or RPs) represent one of the most rapidly growing segments of the money market. A repo represents a transaction by which one party (the seller) acquires funds by selling a security (commonly a U.S. government security) and simultaneously agrees to buy the security back at a later date at an agreed price. Most repos are overnight, payment being in immediately available funds. As such, the repo is quite similar to a federal funds transaction that carries with it the pledge of a security as collateral.

Table 17.5 illustrates a typical repo between a bank and a corporate customer. From the corporate customer's perspective the repo transfers funds from a noninterest-earning demand deposit to an interest-earning, secured loan to the bank. The corporate customer gives up the deposit insurance coverage that existed on the first $100,000 of the deposit but receives a security pledged against

TABLE 17.5   Effects of Repurchase Agreement

	Bank	Corporate Customer
Before RP	$1 million demand deposit	$1 million demand deposit
Creation of RP	−$1 million demand deposit +$1 million RP borrowing	−$1 million demand deposit +$1 million collateralized RP loan
Completion of RP agreement	+$1 million demand deposit −$1 million RP borrowing	+$1 million demand deposit −$1 million RP loan

the loan. The bank, as borrower, achieves a flexible source of funds (especially valuable prior to the elimination of Regulation Q on most time and savings deposits) that is not subject to reserve requirements and that has a relatively low cost (usually under the federal funds rate).

Characteristics

The repo market, like most other portions of the money market, is a wholesale market in which major institutional buyers and sellers deal in large denomination transactions. Most RP transactions are for amounts of at least $1 million. The interest rate on the repo is determined by negotiation between the lender and borrower and is unrelated to the interest rate on the security underlying the transaction. RP transactions are arranged by telephone contact between the market participants (hence it is an over-the-counter market) that may be located throughout the United States and indeed throughout the entire world.

RP transactions are quite similar to federal funds in many ways, including settlement in immediately available funds. Market rates on repos and federal funds tend to be very similar, though repo rates are usually slightly lower than federal funds rates (owing to the collateralized aspect of repos). As a result of these similarities, repurchase agreements and federal funds are often discussed as one subject.

The "reverse repurchase agreement" forms an important dimension of the repo market and is merely a repo viewed from the perspective of the lender. For example, in an RP the borrower (or seller of the security) receives the funds and then uses those funds to repurchase the security at the maturity of the agreement. With a reverse RP, however, the lender (or buyer of the security) advances the funds, which are then repaid at the termination of the agreement.

Participants

The major participants in the repo market are commercial banks, government security dealers, business corporations, and state and local governments. The Federal Reserve also engages in repo transactions in implementing monetary policy.

Large commercial banks use the RP market principally as a source of funds. In that role, repos are a substitute (often a less costly substitute) for federal funds borrowings. Government security dealers are another major demander of funds in the repo market, often using overnight repos to finance their large inventory. The major suppliers of funds are large business corporations and state and local governments that use the repo market as a vehicle for the temporary investment of idle funds. In this capacity, repos offer relatively high yields, great liquidity, and little risk.

SUMMARY

The money market plays a vital role in the efficient functioning of the financial system by providing facilities for liquidity adjustment. A financial market participant with a temporary liquidity surplus may dispose of that surplus by purchasing money market instruments, and one with a temporary liquidity deficiency may eliminate that shortfall by selling money market instruments in its asset portfolio or (where possible) issuing new money market instruments. The major participants in the money market include the Federal Reserve through its open-market and discount window operations, government security dealers that make a market in major money market instruments, major commercial banks, and a variety of financial and nonfinancial businesses. Purchases and sales of money market instruments are based on risk–return considerations, and market participants engage in frequent substitution of one instrument for another. This substitution tends to create a relative similarity (though not equality) among rates on different money market instruments.

Treasury securities, especially Treasury bills, federal agency securities, federal funds, and repurchase agreements (repos) are major instruments of the money market. Treasury bills offer market participants a discount instrument that has no default risk and high liquidity. Federal agency securities have many characteristics similar to U.S. Treasury securities, though without the explicit Treasury guarantee their credit risk is higher. Federal funds also offer extremely high liquidity and represent a major adjustment vehicle for commercial banking organizations. Repos are quite similar to federal fund transactions but are secured.

QUESTIONS

1. The money market is sometimes viewed as a homogeneous entity. What evidence would you give to support this view? What are the reasons behind this argument?
2. What is the role of the Federal Reserve in the money market?

3. What function do security dealers play in the money market? How do they seek to make a profit?

4. Compare the characteristics of Treasury bills, notes, and bonds.

5. A 90-day Treasury bill is selling at a price of $96.45 percent of par. What is the discount basis yield? What is the coupon equivalent yield?

6. A 120-day Treasury bill is selling to provide a discount basis yield of 8.85 percent. What is the coupon equivalent yield?

7. Compare the characteristics of Federal agency securities with U.S. Treasury securities in terms of credit risk, liquidity, taxability, and other relevant characteristics.

8. Discuss the use of the federal funds market by large commercial banks.

9. What is a repurchase agreement? Compare the use of a repurchase agreement with that of federal funds.

10. Why should the interest rate on repurchase agreements be near but often below that on federal funds?

REFERENCES

Banks, Lois, "The Market for Agency Securities," Federal Reserve Bank of New York *Quarterly Review* (Spring 1979), 7–21.

Bolten, Steven, "Treasury Bill Auction Procedures: An Empirical Investigation," *Journal of Finance* (June 1973), 577–585.

Bowsher, Norman, "Repurchase Agreements," Federal Reserve Bank of St. Louis *Review* (September 1979), 17–22.

Federal Reserve Bank of Richmond, *Instruments of the Money Market,* 7th ed., 1986.

The First Boston Corporation, *Handbook of Securities of the United States Government and Federal Agencies,* 32nd ed., 1986.

Fraser, Donald R., and Peter S. Rose (Eds.), *Financial Institutions and Markets in a Changing World,* 3rd ed. (Dallas: Business Publications, Inc., 1987).

Lucas, Charles, Marcus Jones, and Thom Thurston, "Federal Funds and Repurchase Agreements," Federal Reserve Bank of New York *Quarterly Review* (Summer 1977), 33–48.

Lumpkin, Stephen A., *Repurchase and Reverse Repurchase Agreement* (Federal Reserve Bank of Richmond, January 1987), 15–23.

McCurdy, Christopher J., "The Dealer Market for United States Government Securities," Federal Reserve Bank of New York *Quarterly Review* (Winter 1977–78), 35–47.

Sivesind, Charles M., "Noncompetitive Tenders in Treasury Auctions: How Much Do They Affect Savings Flow?" Federal Reserve Bank of New York *Quarterly Review* (Autumn 1978), 24–28.

Stigum, Marcia, *The Money Market: Myth, Reality, and Practice* (Homewood, Ill.: Dow-Jones-Irwin, 1983).

Tucker, James F., *Buying Treasury Securities at Federal Reserve Banks* (Federal Reserve Bank of Richmond, 1982).

Willis, Parker B., *The Financial Funds Market: Its Origin and Development* (Federal Reserve Bank of Boston, 1970).

CHAPTER **18**

The Money Market: Domestic and Eurodollar Certificates of Deposit, Bankers Acceptances, and Commercial Paper

In the previous chapter we discussed the basic functions of the money market, the roles played by the Federal Reserve and by security dealers, and the characteristics of the markets for Treasury securities, federal agency securities, federal funds, and repurchase agreements. In this chapter we continue our discussion of money market instruments by examining the role of certificates of deposit, both domestic and Eurodollar, bankers acceptances, and commercial paper. It is important to keep in mind that all of the various money market rates are highly interrelated. Changes in the interest rates on one money market instrument, for example, produce portfolio adjustments on the part of market participants that are likely to bring about changes in the prices and yields on other money market instruments.

CERTIFICATES OF DEPOSIT

Certificates of deposit may be divided into domestic and Eurodollar varieties.[1] We discuss each of these separately, though of course they are very closely related financial instruments in terms of credit risk and interest rate features.

Domestic CDs

A **certificate of deposit** (CD) is a receipt indicating that a depositor has placed a particular amount of funds at a bank for a particular period of time,

---

[1] Another type of CD is known as a "Yankee CD." This is a CD issued and payable in dollars by the branch office of major foreign banks located in the United States. They are also known as foreign domestic CDs.

and in return the bank has agreed to pay a certain rate of interest over the life of the deposit or at maturity. A domestic CD is issued by a U.S. bank located within the United States. There are numerous types of certificates of deposit of different sizes, and CDs are issued by different kinds of depository financial institutions, but the certificate that is considered to be a money market instrument is one issued by a major bank in large denominations ($100,000 is considered the minimum amount, but units of $1,000,000 or more are common), is negotiable, and is traded in a secondary market. The CD as a money market instrument is a relatively recent development, dating back to the early 1960s. Yet the CD has become one of the major money market instruments (in terms of volume outstanding) in a very short time. The existence and growth of CDs represent an important example of the innovative characteristics of our financial markets.

Origin of the CD

The large, negotiable, business-oriented CD was the product of a changing financial environment and the response of large banks to that changing environment. Interest rates increased in the post–World War II era. The response was the action by First National City Bank of New York (now Citibank) and other large banks to maintain their share of the flow of credit.

Large New York banks have traditionally been wholesale financial institutions, obtaining deposits from businesses and lending to businesses. In obtaining deposit funds these banks (like all banks) were prohibited from paying interest on demand deposits. Moreover, they were generally unwilling to pay competitive interest rates on time deposits. Consequently, as interest rates increased in the post–World War II period, corporate treasurers began to look for ways to earn interest on their temporarily idle funds and began to reduce their balances at commercial banks in order to commit funds to Treasury bills and other money market instruments. Responding to this reduction in their sources of funds, Citibank designed the large CD with characteristics similar to other money market instruments and arranged with a securities dealer to create a secondary market in these financial instruments. Not only did the creation of the CD allow the major banks to offer their customers a financial instrument that was fully competitive with existing money market instruments, but it also allowed the major banks for the first time to manage their liabilities beyond one-day adjustments through the federal funds market. With CDs the major banks could meet unexpected loan demand by buying funds rather than by turning down loan requests or by liquidating assets. To a considerable extent the creation of the large CD was the beginning of extensive use of modern liability management by the nation's major banks.

The introduction of the CD proved a great success with corporate treasurers and other investors. The volume of the large CDs outstanding moved upward sharply to more than $50 billion in the mid-1960s, to more than $90 billion by 1974, and to well over $200 billion by the early 1980s. Around this trend line of rapid growth, however, there were periods of substantial retrenchment. In 1966 and again in 1969 the magnitude of CDs shrank as Regulation Q rate ceilings made the CDs unattractive in relation to other money market instruments. However, in the early 1970s, Regulation Q ceilings were removed from the large CDs. As a result, fluctuations in the amount of CDs outstanding in recent years have principally reflected the demand for funds by large banks, which in turn is a function of the strength of loan demand at these banks.

Characteristics of CDs

The average maturity of most CDs is very short. There is no maximum maturity, but most CDs are issued for periods of under one year. The average maturity of the large CDs issued by the major banks in the United States generally varies between two and four months. Most CDs are issued for large denominations, and a round lot in the secondary market is usually $1,000,000. Interest on CDs is computed on the basis of par (a nondiscount instrument) and on the basis of a 360-day rather than a 365-day year. Payment is normally made in immediately available (federal) funds.

Buyers and Sellers

Most CD buyers are nonfinancial corporations, though there are a variety of other buyers, including money market funds. About two thirds of all CDs sold by the larger banks (and about 90 percent of all CDs issued are sold by the larger banks) are sold to individuals, partnerships, and corporations (IPCs). Most of the sales to IPCs are to business, but it also appears that smaller banks sell a larger percentage of their CDs to individuals than larger banks do—a not-unexpected finding.

Most CDs are issued by the nation's largest banks. The major banks of the nation use the CD market both as a means of liquidity adjustment and as a means of raising additional funds to meet loan demand. With an active CD market the bank has the alternative of either liquidating short-term assets or issuing CDs to meet liquidity needs. Presumably, the bank makes that choice in light of the relative cost of funds from asset versus liability management. In addition, the bank may use the CDs to provide funds to support a loan portfolio larger than would be possible through its other deposit sources.

Roughly one quarter of domestic CDs are issued by a small number of very large commercial banks, frequently referred to as **money center banks.** The remainder of the CDs sold (about three quarters of the total volume) are brought to market by about 200 large regional banks. However, most of the CDs sold to large national and multinational buyers are placed by the money center banks.

Regional banks tend to place their CDs with regional investors that are more familiar with the bank.

CDs are sold directly to investors and also through dealers. Direct sales allow the bank to raise funds at lower cost than through dealers and to avoid the possibility that existing CDs will be placed back on the market and compete with new CDs that the bank is using to raise funds. However, sale through dealers may offer the advantage of speed in placing an issue and also may allow the bank to place a larger amount of CDs.

There is a well-developed secondary market for CDs. Indeed, the existence of a strong secondary market has been one of the major reasons for the growth of the CD market. Dealer trading in large negotiable CDs frequently exceeds $1 billion per day. Though large both in absolute magnitude and as a fraction of the volume of CDs outstanding, this amount of trading is still much smaller than that in federal funds or Treasury bills. Moreover, the CD market is not homogeneous, since the CDs of different banks carry different degrees of credit risk.

Interest Rates on CDs

Interest rates on the large CDs are higher than those on Treasury bills of comparable maturity. This differential reflects the greater degree of credit risk on CDs, the thinner secondary market for them, and the greater tax exposure for holders of CDs (interest on CDs is taxable at all levels, but interest on T-bills is not taxable at the state and local level). There are now also differences in rates that reflect the banks of issue. In the early years of CD market development there was relatively little differentiation of CDs, one from another, by credit risk (except for the very crude distinction between prime and nonprime banks). Increasingly, however, purchasers of CDs are now making important distinctions among different banks. These distinctions have become built into the relative yield structure on CDs, a process known as *tiering*.

Eurodollar CDs

A **Eurodollar CD** is similar in many repects to a domestic CD: It is a dollar-denominated time deposit at a bank with a specified rate of interest and a stated maturity. However, the Eurodollar CD is issued by a bank outside the United States, either by a foreign branch of a U.S. bank or a foreign bank. While a Eurodollar CD may be issued anywhere outside the United States, most Eurodollar CDs are sold by banks in London, the center of the Eurodollar market.

Eurodollar CDs were originated by the London branch of Citibank in 1966. The principal motive was to avoid Regulation Q deposit-rate ceilings then in effect on domestic CDs. However, since the early 1970s, when deposit rate ceilings were removed on large negotiable domestic CDs, Eurodollar CDs have been used to fund Eurodollar lending and to do so at rates lower than other Eurodollar time deposits.

Like domestic CDs, Eurodollar CDs are offered in a variety of maturities, though maturities between one month and one year are most common. The buyers are similar to those of domestic CDs—generally large corporations— though in recent years, money market mutual funds have become major purchasers of Eurodollar CDs. Similar to domestic CDs, Eurodollar CDs are sold directly to retail customers and also to dealers, many of which are the same dealers as for domestic CDs.

Eurodollar CDs are part of a much larger market for Eurodollar time deposits.[2] These **Eurodollar time deposits** (of which Eurodollar CDs are only a part) represent dollar-dominated fixed-rate deposits with foreign banks having maturities from overnight to several years, most maturities being in the one-week to six-month range. While the total size of the entire Eurodollar market is unknown, it has been estimated that the Eurodollar market exceeds $1 trillion.[3]

Eurodollar CD rates are higher than those of domestic CD rates. This difference reflects a number of factors, but principally liquidity and credit risk considerations. Although an active secondary market exists for Eurodollar CDs, the liquidity of these instruments is substantially less than that of domestic CDs. The higher perceived credit risk appears to reflect concern over the loan portfolio of Eurodollar banks as well as the potential of sovereign risk. The latter risk is the potential that the British government would interfere with payment on the Eurodollar CD at maturity by a bank located in London. Also, Eurodollar CDs do not carry FDIC insurance.

BANKERS ACCEPTANCES

One of the oldest and yet one of the least common of all money market instruments is the bankers acceptance. Its long history reflects its use in financing international commerce, whereas the relatively small quantity of acceptances outstanding stems from the specialized nature of this financial instrument. Yet in recent years the volume of acceptances outstanding has increased substantially.

A **bankers acceptance** is a time draft drawn on a commercial bank ordering the bank to pay a particular amount to the holder of the draft at the time of its maturity. This draft becomes an acceptance when the bank accepts responsibility for making payment on it and stamps "accepted" on the face of the draft. Once

---

[2]Eurodollar CDs are sometimes called "tap CDs," since they were created in order to tap the Eurodollar market.

[3]Timothy Q. Cook and Bruce J. Summers, *Instruments of the Money Market*, 7th ed. (Federal Reserve Bank of Richmond, 1986).

the bank—generally a money center or well known regional bank—has guaranteed payment at maturity, the draft (now a bankers acceptance) becomes a money market instrument. With the backing of the bank, investors are willing to buy and sell the acceptance in the secondary market for liquidity-adjustment purposes.

Creation of a Bankers Acceptance

While there are a number of ways by which a bankers acceptance may be created, many bankers acceptances arise in the process of financing international trade. A simple example will illustrate the process by which acceptances are created. This process is illustrated in Fig. 18.1. Assume that a U.S. wholesaler wishes to import computers from a West German manufacturer. Domestically, this type of transaction would generally be financed with the use of open-book trade credit. But the German exporter—lacking knowledge of the U.S. importer and/or the existence of different laws between the two countries and perhaps for other reasons—will probably be unwilling to ship the goods on open account. But the U.S. importer might not have adequate funds to pay cash for the merchandise. With the creation of a bankers acceptance, however, this problem can be solved, particularly if its creation is part of a letter of credit arrangement.

This financing arrangement requires the U.S. importer to obtain from a U.S. bank a letter of credit in favor of the exporter. This letter of credit allows the exporter to draw a time draft (order for payment at a specified future date) against the U.S. bank, payment of which is guaranteed by the bank if all required documents are presented and the other terms of the letter of credit are met. (In effect, the bank's credit standing is interposed between the importer and the exporter.) Confident of payment for the goods, the exporter can ship the merchandise and turn the letter of credit over to its bank in West Germany. The exporter's bank then draws a draft on the U.S. bank and sends the draft to the importer's bank in the United States. The U.S. bank, after making sure that all supporting documents are in order, stamps "accepted" on the face of the draft, converting the time draft into a bankers acceptance.[4]

Financing in the Bankers Acceptance Transaction

Note that the U.S. bank is only guaranteeing payment of the time draft at maturity. It is not necessarily financing the transactions. The transaction is financed by whichever party holds the acceptance. For example, Table 18.1 presents three different versions of the financing of the transaction. In alternative 1 we first note that the German exporter has exchanged its inventory for money

---

[4]**Sight drafts** are sometimes employed in settlement of international obligations, in which cash payment (rather than "acceptance") is immediate, once the process of document verification and approval is complete. Obviously, bankers acceptances cannot be created from sight drafts.

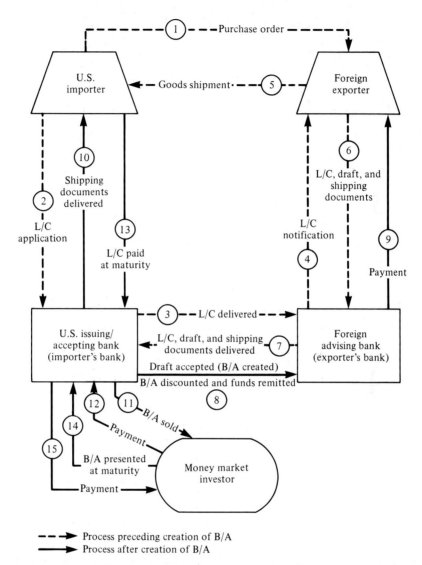

FIGURE 18.1   Example of Bankers Acceptance Financing of U.S. Imports: A Bankers Acceptance is Created, Discounted, Sold, and Paid at Maturity

Source: Timothy Q. Cook and Bruce Summers, Instruments of the Money Market, *5th ed. (Federal Reserve Bank of Richmond, 1981), 115.*

TABLE 18.1   Financing Alternatives in Creation of a Bankers Acceptance _____

Alternative 1

U.S. BANK		U.S. IMPORTER		SECURITY DEALER
+Customer's liability on acceptance (due to bank)	+Bankers acceptance	+Inventory	+Liability on bankers acceptance	

GERMAN BANK		GERMAN EXPORTER	
+Bankers acceptance	+Demand deposit (of exporter)	+Demand deposit −Inventory	

Alternative 2

U.S. BANK		U.S. IMPORTER		SECURITY DEALER
−Customer's liability on acceptance (due to bank)	+Bankers acceptance	+Inventory	+Liability on bankers acceptance	+Bankers acceptance −Demand deposit of U.S. Bank
	−Demand deposit of security dealer +Demand deposit of German bank			

GERMAN BANK		GERMAN EXPORTER	
+Demand deposit at U.S. bank	+Demand deposit of German exporter	+Demand deposit −Inventory	

TABLE 18.1 *(Continued)* _____

Alternative 3

U.S. BANK		U.S. IMPORTER		SECURITY DEALER	
−Customer's liability on acceptance	+Bankers acceptance	+Inventory	+Liability on bankers acceptance		
−Bankers acceptance (own bill)	+Demand deposit of German bank				

GERMAN BANK		GERMAN EXPORTER	
+Demand deposit at U.S. bank	+Demand deposit of German exporter	+Demand deposit	
		−Inventory	

(a demand deposit at a West German bank). The U.S. importer has obtained the inventory and has a short-term liability in favor of the bank. And the U.S. bank has both a new asset (customer's liability on acceptance) and a new liability (bankers acceptance), and the items are of identical magnitude. But who has financed the transaction? In this case the financing has been done by the West German bank that holds the acceptance and that has made payment to its customer, the exporter. Indeed, whoever holds the acceptance is financing the transaction. In alternative 2 the West German bank has sold the acceptance to a security dealer and received payment in the form of a check drawn on a U.S. bank. In this case the security dealer holds the acceptance and is doing the financing. In alternative 3 the West German bank has sold the acceptance to the U.S. bank. The U.S. bank in this case is doing the financing, and the bankers acceptance is referred to as an "own bill" (since the bank has purchased its own acceptance).

Uses of Acceptances

Acceptances are used principally to finance the international movement of goods. This includes imports to and exports from the United States as well as the movement of goods among other countries of the world. As shown in Table 18.2

TABLE 18.2   Acceptances Outstanding, December 1988 (Millions of Dollars)

Holder		
Accepting banks		$ 9,082
Own bills	8,018	
Bills bought	1,064	
Federal Reserve banks		1,493
Own account	0	
Foreign correspondents	1,493	
Others		56,103
Basis		
Imports into United States		14,991
Exports from United States		15,622
All other		36,065
Total		$66,678

Source: Federal Reserve Bulletin April 1989, A23.

$15 billion of the $67 billion of acceptances outstanding as of December 1988 were associated with imports into the United States, and $15 billion of acceptances outstanding were associated with the financing of exports from the United States. The "others" category includes acceptances used to finance the transfer of goods between countries outside the United States (called third-country bills), the shipment of goods within the United States, and for a variety of other purposes.

Characteristics of Acceptances

Acceptances are money market instruments that have exceptionally low credit risk for a private instrument. The credit risk is low because the acceptance is guaranteed by both the drawer and a major commercial bank (**two-name paper**). The acceptance is also secured by the goods that are being financed. In addition, the secondary market for acceptances is relatively good. However, the denomination of an acceptance is established by the amount of goods financed, and its maturity is frequently established by the amount of time involved in the shipment of the goods. Either of these—or both—might be inconvenient to the investor. Most acceptances have maturities of 90 days or less. In addition, the market for acceptances is composed of a fairly narrow set of buyers. As a result of the interaction of all these factors, acceptances tend to sell at a rate premium relative to Treasury bills, although the premium over Treasury bills is quite small.

Participants in the Acceptance Market

Acceptances are attractive to a variety of businesses. From the importer's perspective, the process of arranging a letter of credit and creating a bankers acceptance is a relatively inexpensive way to finance a purchase. The acceptance rate is generally well under the prime rate, although the borrower must usually pay a fee of 1.0 to 1.5 percentage points to the accepting bank. From the perspective of the accepting bank it can serve the needs of its customers and earn a fee without committing any of its own funds. Furthermore, if it wishes, the bank can invest in its own acceptances ("own bills") as part of its liquidity management. Indeed, as Table 18.2 shows, most acceptances held by banks are "own bills." There are a number of investors who find the risk–return characteristics of acceptances attractive, notably foreign banks and nonbank firms.

The low cost of acceptances relative to bank loans is illustrated in Table 18.3. It is assumed that the borrower is able to get bank credit at the prime rate and that the bank requires 20 percent to be held at the bank in the form of a demand deposit (known as a compensating balance). With a 13 percent prime, then, the total cost to the borrower is 15.6 percent. For the bankers acceptance the market rate on the acceptance was 11.35 percent. Assuming that the acceptance commission is 1.50 percentage points, the total cost to the borrower on a discount basis is 12.85 percent. Converting this to a nondiscount rate (for 90-day credit) yields a cost of 13.4 percent, substantially below the cost of bank credit.

Interest Rates on Acceptances

Given the quite low credit risk on acceptances, the yield premium required in the market for acceptances relative to Treasury securities is relatively slight. The yield spread for 90-day bankers acceptances over 90-day Treasury bills has generally been less than 200 basis points and in some periods has been near zero.

COMMERCIAL PAPER

Commercial paper is one of the most rapidly growing segments of the financial markets. Commercial paper consists of the short-term note issues of very large "blue-chip" quality business firms. Maturity is always 270 days or less (to

TABLE 18.3   A Comparison of the Cost of a Bank Loan and Bankers Acceptance Financing

Bank Loan		Bankers Acceptance	
Prime rate	13%	Discount rate for acceptance	11.35
Implicit cost of 20 percent compensating balance	2.6%	Acceptance commission	1.50
Total cost to borrower	15.6%	Total cost to borrow on a discount basis	12.85
		Total cost to borrower	13.40

avoid registration requirements of the Securities and Exchange Commission). Denominations range widely, although most commercial paper is sold at a discount without an explicit coupon rate, and interest is figured on a bank discount basis in the same manner as for Treasury bills.

Amount Outstanding

As shown in Table 18.4, commercial paper outstanding exceeds $400 billion; thus commercial paper is one of the largest of all the money market instruments. Moreover, the volume of commercial paper outstanding has grown at an exceptional rate, especially since the late 1960s. For example, commercial paper outstanding amounted to less than $20 billion until 1966, but it expanded to more than $30 billion by 1970 and to more than $50 billion by 1975. In fact, the rapid growth of commercial paper has caused concern among commercial banks that a large portion of the business sector—very large and high-quality businesses—are bypassing the banking system and engaging in self-financing. However, although the growth of commercial paper has been explosive, it has also been unstable. In particular, the volume of commercial paper tends to fall during periods when risk premiums on corporate debt issues rise. For example, the volume of commercial paper declined in 1970 following the bankruptcy of the Penn Central Corporation with a substantial volume of commercial paper outstanding. And the volume of commercial paper declined again in 1980–1982 as the severe recession produced concern on the part of buyers of commercial paper about the creditworthiness of some of the issues in the market.

The cost of commercial paper is frequently—indeed, usually—below the cost of short-term borrowing from banks, particularly when the cost of bank borrowing is adjusted to include the cost involved in compensating balance requirements. (However, the "true" cost of commercial paper must include issuing costs and the cost associated with maintaining a backup line of credit at a commercial bank.) In fact, although there has been a substantial upward trend in the volume of commercial paper outstanding, there has also been a marked change in the growth rate of commercial paper, reflecting differences in the commercial paper rate and the prime rate.

Nature of Issues

Commercial paper is usually divided into groups on the basis of the nature of the issues and method of sale. By nature of issuer, commercial paper may be classified as **financial-company paper** and as **nonfinancial-company paper.** By this distinction, as shown in Table 18.4, most commercial paper is issued by finance-related firms, such as General Motors Acceptance Corporation. In fact, about 70 percent of all commercial paper is issued by finance-related businesses. By method of sale, commercial paper may be classified as **dealer-placed** or **directly**

TABLE 18.4 Volume of Commercial Paper Outstanding December 1988 (Millions of Dollars)

All issuers	455,017
Financial companies	
Dealer-placed paper	
Total	159,947
Bank-related	1,248
Directly placed paper	
Total	192,442
Bank-related	43,155
Nonfinancial	
companies	102,628

Source: Federal Reserve Bulletin April 1989, A23.

placed. In the former group are those firms that sell their paper with the aid of security dealers, generally paying one eighth to one fourth of 1 percent commission to dealers. In the latter group are the businesses that sell their paper directly to the ultimate investors.[5]

As shown in Table 18.4, most financial-company paper is sold directly to ultimate buyers. This type of paper is usually sold by very large financial firms, such as General Motors Acceptance Corporation, and major bank holding companies, such as Citicorp. These firms regularly issue commercial paper (in fact, Citicorp has a regular auction of commercial paper) and find it cost efficient to maintain their own staffs in order to market their notes. Moreover, the firms usually rely on commercial paper for the bulk of their short-term funds and use commercial banks more heavily. These smaller financial companies find it unattractive to market their securities directly and instead use dealers to find buyers. Although Table 18.4 does not classify the issues of nonfinancial companies by method of sale, most of these issues are placed through dealers. In fact, dealer-placed paper has grown more rapidly than directly placed paper in recent years, primarily because of entry into the commercial paper market of nonfinancial issuers.

Nature of Investors

Major buyers of commercial paper include large commercial banks (which frequently purchase commercial paper for their trust departments or for their customers), nonfinancial corporations, insurance companies, and private pension funds. Although complete data are not available, it appears that about 20 percent of all commercial paper is held by corporations engaged in manufacturing, mining, and wholesale or retail trade. Another 10 percent is held by life

---

[5]There are actually only a small number of issuers of commercial paper, around 700 to 800. Most commercial paper is issued by fewer than 100 business firms.

insurance companies. Commercial banks themselves appear to hold very little commercial paper for their own accounts. Households, which have traditionally held only small amounts of commercial paper, have become somewhat more active in investing in this financial instrument as the minimum denominations have been reduced in recent years.

Nature of the Market

The market for commercial paper is essentially a primary market. A well-established secondary market does not exist for commercial paper, principally reflecting the large number of issues and the resultant fragmentation of the market. However, the impact of the lack of an established secondary market on the liquidity of commercial paper is reduced by two considerations. First, the maturity of most commercial paper is very short. The average maturity of most directly placed paper is usually 20 to 40 days, and the average maturity of dealer-placed paper is usually 30 to 45 days. Second, many issuers—particularly dealers—are willing to buy back the paper before maturity in the event of severe liquidity pressure on the investor.

not really a dealer, though.

Commercial Paper Ratings

Although the default rate on commercial paper has been low, investors remain concerned about the credit quality of the commercial paper that they place in their portfolios. As a result, in seeking to find buyers for their issues, commercial paper businesses usually pay the rating agencies in order to obtain a rating for their commercial paper. Standard & Poor, Fitch's, and Moody's provide ratings for commercial paper. For example, Standard & Poor rates commercial paper issues from A (highest quality) to D (lowest quality). The A-rated companies are further divided into three groups; A-1, in which credit quality is extremely high; A-2, in which credit quality is very good and essentially without weakness; and A-3, in which credit quality is good though with at least one weakness. Similar ratings are provided by Moody's, which classifies commercial paper on a P (Prime 1) system.

Interest Rates on Commercial Paper

As was shown in Chapter 17, interest rates on commercial paper generally exceed rates on Treasury bills by a substantial margin. The difference reflects the interaction of credit risk, liquidity, and tax considerations. Commercial paper clearly carries greater risk than Treasury bills, and this higher credit risk is reflected in a risk premium in the interest rate structure. Interest rates on different issues of commercial paper also vary. Commercial paper sold by the very largest financial companies (generally directly) usually carries a lower rate than directly placed paper sold by less well-known companies.

Interest rate differences between commercial paper and T-bills also reflect liquidity and tax considerations. There is no established secondary market for commercial paper, but there is an excellent secondary market for Treasury bills. In addition, the return on commercial paper is taxable at all levels of government, whereas the return on T-bills is taxable only at the federal level. Both considerations tend to increase the yield on commercial paper compared with Treasury bills.

The commercial paper rate also has an important association with the bank prime rate. For large, well-established, high-quality firms, short-term funds are available either through bank borrowings at or below the prime rate or through the issuance of commercial paper. If the commercial paper rate falls in relation to the prime, borrowers will substitute commercial paper as a source of funds for short-term bank borrowings, and that action will tend to raise the commercial paper rate and lower the bank prime rate until the normal relationship between these two sources of funds is restored. Conversely, if the commercial paper rate rises in relation to the bank prime rate, borrowers will substitute bank borrowing for the issuance of commercial paper, and that will tend to raise bank lending and lower the commercial paper rates until the normal rate relationship is restored.

There is one fundamental and important difference between the commercial paper rate and the prime rate. Although the commercial paper rate (and indeed all rates on money market instruments) is determined by the free interplay of supply and demand in a competitive market, the prime rate is an administered rate set by commercial bank management. The bank prime rate has traditionally been viewed as a base rate, other rates being established as an upward or downward adjustment from prime. However, the prime rate has diminished in importance in recent years as banks have devised innovative lending devices to compete more effectively with open-market rates. As a result, banks have frequently been able to provide funds to their customers at rates below prime.

SUMMARY

Certificates of deposit are a relatively new (though very important) instrument of the money market, encompassing both domestic bank certificates and Eurodollar CDs issued by banks outside the United States. The growth of these large ($100,000 and over) negotiable CDs reflects their ability to simultaneously meet the needs of banks and investors. Banks use the CD market to raise funds as part of their asset/liability management, while investors, principally large businesses, have found in the CD a vehicle that offers attractive yields and good liquidity.

Bankers acceptances represent a time draft drawn on a bank where the bank has accepted liability for payment of the draft at maturity. Although bankers acceptances are historically a very old instrument, their volume is small in relation to other money market instruments, reflecting the specialized function of the instrument in financing international commerce.

Commercial paper consists of short-term unsecured notes issued by large and high-quality business firms with a maturity of 270 days or less. The volume of commercial paper outstanding is large and has grown very rapidly, reflecting the low cost of this source of funds. Rates on commercial paper are generally higher than those on the large CDs or on bankers acceptances, reflecting the reduced liquidity of commercial paper and the absence of a developed secondary market as well as the higher perceived credit risk for commercial paper.

Interest rates on all the money market instruments are closely interrelated, reflecting the similar role that they play in investor portfolios and the similar characteristics of the instruments themselves. However, while similar in terms of credit risk, liquidity, and other characteristics that affect their yields, money market rates do differ among the various instruments. Treasury bill rates are usually the lowest of all money market rates, reflecting their low credit risk and high liquidity. Interest rates on other money market instruments usually move up from the Treasury bill rate "anchor," reflecting the different characteristics of the instruments, though the pattern of rates is often affected by short-run changes in relative supply and demand factors.

QUESTIONS

1. It is sometimes argued that the CD market has matured and that growth will be slower, though more steady, in the future. What factors have produced the rapid growth in the CD market? Why might growth be slower in the future?

2. Compare the credit-risk characteristics of domestic and Eurodollar CDs. Of what importance is sovereign risk in this comparison?

3. In a bankers acceptance transaction the holder of the acceptance is financing the transaction. Do you agree? Explain.

4. Compare the cost of bankers acceptance financing with that of financing through bank credit. What adjustment must be made for bank discount basis calculations? Would this same adjustment be necessary for commercial paper?

5. What is commercial paper? Why do businesses sell commercial paper? If cost is a principal reason, why don't all businesses sell commercial paper?

6. What are the principal factors that result in changing yield spreads between CDs (and other money market instruments) and Treasury bills?

REFERENCES

Cook, Timothy Q., and Bruce J. Summers, *Instruments of the Money Market,* 7th ed. (Federal Reserve Bank of Richmond, 1986).

Dufey, Gunter, and Ian H. Giddy, "Eurocurrency Deposit Risk," *Journal of Banking and Finance* (Vol. 8, 1984), 567–589.

Fraser, Donald R., and Peter S. Rose (Eds.), *Financial Institutions and Markets in a Changing World,* 3rd ed. (Dallas: Business Publications Inc., 1987).

Goodfriend, Marvin, "Eurodollars," Federal Reserve Bank of Richmond *Economic Review* (May/June 1981), 12–18.

Harvey, Jack L., "Bankers Acceptances Revisited," Federal Reserve Bank of Chicago *Economic Perspectives* (May/June 1983), 21–31.

Hurley, Evelyn, "The Commercial Paper Market Since Mid-September," Federal Reserve *Bulletin* (June 1982), 327–334.

Melton, William C., "The Market for Large Negotiable CDs," Federal Reserve Bank of New York *Quarterly Review* (Winter 1977–78), 22–34.

Shadrack, Fred, "Demand and Supply in the Commercial Paper Market," *Journal of Finance* (September 1970), 837–872.

Slovin, Myron B., and Marie-Elizabeth Sushka, "An Econometric Model of the Market for Negotiable Certificates of Deposit," *Journal of Monetary Economics* (October 1979), 551–568.

Stigum, Marcia, *The Money Market* (Homewood, Ill.: Dow-Jones-Irwin, 1983).

CHAPTER 19

The Capital Market: Bonds

The previous two chapters concentrated on financial instruments that are short-term, are highly liquid, and carry minimal risk. These market instruments are very homogeneous, serving market participants—individuals, businesses, and governments—as liquidity-adjustment vehicles.

The long-term financial instruments of the capital market are much less homogeneous. This heterogeneity reflects the different role of the capital market in the financial system. While the money market exists to provide liquidity-adjustment vehicles, the capital market provides an efficient means for channeling savings into investment. The capital market is composed of a number of different subcomponents (separate capital markets) loosely integrated through substitution by market participants of one type of instrument for another through portfolio adjustments. In this chapter and the next two we will discuss financial instruments that are "long-term" in nature. These capital market instruments vary widely in terms of credit risk, market or interest-rate risk, liquidity, and other characteristics. And they are used by market participants for a variety of purposes. They include bonds issued by corporations, state, and local governments, and the federal government, mortgages issued by individuals, businesses, and governments, and common and preferred stocks.

This chapter concentrates on bonds; mortgages and equity securities are discussed in the next two chapters. A discussion of the general characteristics of the capital market is presented initially, followed by a discussion of the market for corporate, municipal, and U.S. government debt. In each instance the discussion not only provides the basic details of the market, but also focuses attention on the enormous changes that have been occurring in these markets in recent years. The rapid inflation of the late 1970s and early 1980s placed great strain on the functioning of the capital market generally and the debt portion of the capital market in particular. In fact, the question of whether the bond market was dead was a subject of serious discussion following the extremely high interest rates in 1981 and 1982. After the stock market crash of October 1987, additional questions were raised about the future of the capital markets, though this time the concern was more with equity than with debt markets.

DIMENSIONS OF THE CAPITAL MARKET

The capital market is massive, exceeding $8 trillion. Mortgages—home, multifamily, commercial, and farm—exceed $3 trillion. In addition, the total volume of equities outstanding exceeds $3 trillion, while the bond issues of corporations and state, local, and federal governments approximate $2 trillion.[1] Yet the growth of the major components of the capital market has been quite different in recent years. Total mortgage credit outstanding exploded in the inflation of the late 1970s and early 1980s after more than doubling in the short period from 1971 to 1978. The bond market has also experienced rapid growth, particularly in the corporate and municipal segments (U.S. government debt has grown rapidly with the large government deficits, but most of the new federal debt has been financed short-term.) In contrast, new sales of equity securities by the nation's corporations have generally been relatively limited.[2]

Not only is the capital market large, but it is also quite diverse. Characteristics of the major instruments of the capital market differ widely in terms of credit risk, interest rate risk, marketability, taxability, and the other factors that influence relative yields. This diversity is reflected in the wide range of yields shown in Table 19.1. For example, as of January 1989, yields on state and local government securities (municipals) were substantially below yields on U.S. Treasury and corporate issues, primarily reflecting the tax-free status of the interest income on these securities. Yields on Treasury securities were below yields on corporate bonds in response to the higher credit risk associated with corporates compared with governments. Moreover, Baa-rated corporate or state and local issues carried higher rates than Aaa-rated securities because of the higher credit risk. It is also interesting to note that, as of January 1989, the yield curve was slightly downward sloping, since longer-term governments offered slightly lower yields than shorter-term issues.

---

[1]Equities are valued at market price.

[2]There are also a number of bonds issued by foreign organizations in the U.S. capital market. These include issues of foreign corporations and foreign governments and their agencies. They are generally compared with and competitive with domestic corporate bonds. The volume sold in the United States principally reflects interest rates in the United States as compared with other capital markets of the world.

TABLE 19.1 Yields on Capital Market Instruments, January 1989 (Percentages)

Instrument	Yield, %
U.S. Treasury notes and bonds	
5-year	9.15
10-year	9.09
30-year	8.93
State and local notes and bonds	
Aaa	7.23
Baa	7.67
Corporate bonds	
Aaa	9.62
Baa	10.10
Dividend/price ratio	
Preferred stocks	9.31
Common stocks	3.64
Mortgages	10.55

Source: Federal Reserve Bulletin *(April 1989).*

CORPORATE BONDS[3]

Characteristics of Corporate Bonds

A corporate bond represents a *contract* whereby the issuer (the corporation) agrees to pay interest at specified times and to repay principal, usually $1000, at the maturity date of the bond.[4] The bond itself may have a number of different characteristics. Some bonds have claims on specific assets of the issuer (usually land and buildings, in which case the bonds are referred to as **mortgage bonds**).[5] Other bonds have claims not on specific assets of the company but only on the general creditworthiness of the issuer (in which case the bond is referred to as a **debenture bond**). Increasingly, bond issues are debenture rather than mortgage bonds. The security for the bond, as well as other aspects of the issue, is specified

---

[3]For an excellent review of the corporate bond market, see the article by Zwick listed in the references at the end of this chapter.

[4]Corporate bonds vary substantially in maturity, but maturities have been reduced in recent years as investors have become more reluctant to commit funds for long periods in a world of high inflation and unstable conditions.

[5]There are a variety of different types of security for bonds in addition to real estate. For example, collateral trust bonds have the securities of other companies pledged to secure the bonds. In addition, guaranteed bonds have as their security the guarantee of their principal and interest payments by another corporation, often the parent corporation of the one that issued the bonds.

in the **indenture.** This agreement states the rights of the lenders and the obligations of the borrower. Enforcement of the indenture is under the control of a **trustee** (generally the trust department of a commercial bank) acting under the general guidelines of the Trust Indenture Act of 1939.

Corporate bonds differ in a number of ways other than security. Some bond issues have their claim on assets or income subordinated to other issues. These **junior** or **subordinated bonds** obviously carry greater risk to the purchaser than do the senior bond issues of the same corporation. Some indentures require that the issuer establish a **sinking fund** to retire the bond issue. Sinking fund specifications usually require that the issuer provide a trustee with funds sufficient to retire a portion of the issue at specified times prior to maturity. For example, assume a $1 million bond issue with a 10-year maturity. The sinking fund may require that the issuer provide the trustee with funds sufficient to retire $100,000 (face value) of bonds each year. Hence at the end of the ninth year there will be only $100,000 (face value) of bonds outstanding. The trustee may retire the bonds either by purchasing them in the open market (if the bonds have a secondary market) or by calling the bonds by a random call process.[6]

Many—indeed most—corporate bond issues also have **call provisions** under which the issuer may choose to retire the entire bond issue prior to maturity. It is important to distinguish this call feature from the sinking-fund provision. With the sinking fund the issuer must retire a portion of the bonds prior to maturity, but only a portion is retired during the life of the issue. With the call provision the issuer may or may not retire the issue prior to maturity; the decision is usually determined by whether rates have fallen since the bond was originally sold. But if and when the bonds are called, all of the issue must be retired at one time.[7]

The influence of the call provision on the yield on a corporate bond was discussed in Chapter 8. As was pointed out there, the call feature is viewed as undesirable by purchasers of bonds. No only do these long-term investors generally not want to get their cash back before they had planned, but the call usually occurs in periods of relatively low interest rates, when reinvestment opportunities are limited. As a result, corporate bonds that are callable generally must carry a higher yield than comparable bonds that are not callable, especially in periods when interest rates are high and are expected to fall.

Some bonds are also sold with a conversion feature. These **convertible bonds** allow the holder, at his or her option, to convert the bond into another financial instrument, generally common stock. The conversion terms—the number of shares of common stock into which one bond may be converted—are specified

---

[6]Some sinking funds retire only a portion of the bond prior to maturity. The remainder that must be retired at maturity is referred to as a balloon maturity.

[7]Most corporate bond indentures specify that the right to call may not be exercised for a specific period after the issuance of the bond, in which case the bond is said to have a deferred call privilege. Such "call protection" has the effect of reducing somewhat the higher interest rate callable issues must offer relative to noncallable issues.

in the indenture, and they usually remain fixed during the life of the bonds. Convertible bonds are frequently sold by industrial corporations, often by relatively lower-quality industrial firms. Treasurers of many corporations attach the conversion feature to their bond issues to reduce the amount of cash payments. (Because the conversion feature is attractive to investors, convertible bonds can be sold at a lower coupon interest rate than nonconvertible bonds.) Moreover, issuers hope that if the price of their stock rises, the bonds will be converted to common stock at a price that is higher than the current common stock price. By this logic the convertible bond allows the issuer to sell common stock indirectly at a price higher than the current price. From the buyer's perspective the convertible bond is attractive because it offers the opportunity to obtain the potentially large return associated with stock but with the safety of a bond.

Supply of Corporate Bonds

The corporate decision to issue bonds depends on the rate of expansion of assets, particularly fixed assets, and the availability and cost of alternative sources of funds. The rate of expansion of assets determines the need for funds. In periods when dollar amounts of assets are growing rapidly, either because of a rapid expansion of assets measured on a constant dollar basis or because of rapid price inflation, corporations need large amounts of funds. Although some of the needed funds may be available internally through the retention of earnings, the growth of assets usually requires the injection of external funds, either debt or equity. Corporate treasurers must determine the proportion of funds to be provided by short-term debt, long-term debt, and equity.

In recent years, most of the external funds raised by corporations have taken the form of debt. There are many reasons for this reliance on debt as an external financing source, but two in particular stand out. First, interest payments on corporate debt are tax deductible, whereas dividend payments on equity (either preferred stock or common stock) are not. This difference sharply reduces the effective cost of debt as compared with the cost of equity. For example, assume that both debt and equity have a pretax cost of 10 percent and that the corporation's marginal tax rate (t) is 0.34 percent. The after-tax cost of debt is then only 6.6 percent $(10\% - 0.34\,[10\%])$, whereas the after-tax cost of equity is 10 percent.[8] The second reason for the dominance of debt financing relates to inflation. With debt, corporations take on the commitments to repay a fixed amount of dollars. These fixed nominal dollar payments become a smaller quantity of real dollars with inflation. (Dividend payments, on the other hand, generally tend to be set at a roughly constant proportion of total earnings.)

Although there has been a strong upward trend in the ratio of debt to total

---

[8]Actually, since investors view equity instruments as riskier than debt instruments, the pretax cost of equity should exceed the pretax cost of debt, making the comparison even more striking.

assets on corporate balance sheets, the mix of short- versus long-term debt has been less stable and predictable. The mix of short- versus long-term financing is very much dependent on the business cycle and the availability and cost of short-term versus long-term funds. Larger firms with access to the commercial paper market and to other short-term sources are likely to have greater flexibility in their financing mix than small firms that are totally dependent on commercial bank and trade credit.

Leasing also provides a major alternative to bond financing for many corporations. Instead of borrowing to obtain the funds to purchase a capital asset, such as a building or some new equipment, a corporation may sign a long-term noncancelable lease to obtain the use of the capital asset for its economic life. Although such alternatives are available only for assets that are inherently "leasable," there has been an expansion in the volume of such "finance" leases in recent years. Comparisons of the relative advantages of leasing versus bond financing are complex, involving tax considerations and the impact of the decision on the financial statements of the borrower.

Buyers of Corporate Bonds

As shown in Table 19.2 the principal buyers of corporate bonds are contractual-type financial institutions. Life insurance companies and private and public pension funds account for almost 60 percent of the total volume outstanding of these types of bonds. However, households, savings banks, and property and casualty insurance companies (shown as other insurance companies in Table 19.2) are also major buyers of corporate bonds. Foreign investors also are major investors in corporate bonds, holding roughly 13 percent of all such bonds. Perhaps the most significant change in the relative importance of different buyers of corporate bonds is the increase in purchases by foreigners. For example, in 1973, foreign buyers held only $17 billion of these bonds, representing only 6.5 percent of the total bonds outstanding. Yet by late 1988, foreign buyers held 171.2 billion or 13 percent of the total outstanding. The rapid growth of foreign buyers reflects the accumulation of dollars in the hands of foreign individuals, businesses, and governments, reflecting persistent deficits in the U.S. balance of payments. It also reflects the attractive returns available on U.S. securities and the perceived political stability in the United States.

As was discussed in Chapter 10, life insurance companies seek stability of cash flow and invest primarily in corporate bonds and mortgages. However, their investments in corporate bonds are concentrated in issues that are noncallable or that have limited prospect of call. Although life insurance companies are the principal investors in corporate bonds, their relative share of the corporate bond market has diminished in recent years. This trend principally reflects the relatively slow growth in total assets of life insurance companies.

Pension funds have increased dramatically as important buyers of corporate

TABLE 19.2   Holdings of Corporate and Foreign Bonds Classified by Investors, September 1988 (Billions of Dollars)

	Amount Outstanding	Percentage of Total
Household	88.4	6.7
Foreign	171.2	13.0
Commercial banking	86.1	6.5
Savings banks	54.9	4.6
Life insurance companies	431.0	32.8
Private pension funds	176.0	13.4
State and local government retirement funds	163.0	12.4
Other insurance companies	60.5	4.6
Open-end investment companies	59.0	4.5
Brokers and dealers	20.1	1.5
Total	1310.2	100.0

Note: The data include a small amount of dollar-denominated bonds issued by foreign corporations.

Source: Andrew Silver, "Original Issue Deep Discount Bonds," Federal Reserve Bank of New York Quarterly Review *(Winter 1981–82), 22.*

bonds. For private pension funds this increase reflects their explosive growth in total assets (the share of total portfolio devoted to corporate bonds has actually diminished as they have purchased more equity securities). In the case of public pension funds, not only have they had a rapid growth in total assets, but the share of the total portfolio devoted to corporate bonds has increased. The importance of households as holders of corporate bonds has also increased, not only directly but also indirectly through their ownership of shares in open-end investment companies (mutual funds).

The Market for Corporate Bonds

The Primary Market.   The primary market for corporate bonds—the market for newly issued corporates—may be divided into two components: private placements and public offerings. With a **private placement** the seller of the issue places the entire bond offering with an institutional investor, such as a life insurance company or a pension fund. The terms of the issue are determined through negotiation between the seller and the buyer. Most private placements are made by industrial firms. Sellers of bond issues frequently find a private offering attractive because of the speed with which the offering can be consummated (the time-consuming process of registration with the Securities and Exchange Commission is not required). Further, buyers like being able to tailor the terms of the issue specifically to their needs and often obtain higher interest rates on private placements. The share of total new bond issues that are made through private offerings has decreased to well under 50 percent, although there are great cyclical fluctuations in the ratio of private to public offerings, principally reflecting the availability of funds at life insurance companies, the major buyers of bonds through private placements.

Public issues of bonds are generally made through an underwriter, and the bonds are sold to a large number of investors, individual as well as institutional. The underwriters—investment banking companies—purchase the bonds from the corporate issuer and then resell them to investors at a higher price. This purchase may either be done through open competitive bidding (the laws of most states require that public utility issues be sold through competitive bidding) or through negotiation between the issuer and the underwriter. The underwriter assumes the market risk that bonds may not be salable at the expected price. The underwriter also has the responsibility of finding buyers for the issue. Many underwriters have large regional and national sales representatives, who make placement of the issue easier.

A significant development in the primary market for corporate bonds (and also for equities) in recent years has been the advent of **shelf registration** (SEC Rule 415). The Securities and Exchange Commission allowed shelf registration on an experimental basis in February 1982 and made the rule permanent in early 1984. Under shelf registration, large companies may file a single registration statement for all their financing for up to two years. Permission to sell securities through shelf offerings was a boon for large corporations that employ frequent external financing; more than $20 billion was raised through this means in the first year that it was allowed. While shelf registration may be used for either bonds or stocks, most have been bond sales. In a shelf registration of securities with the SEC the issuing corporation need not proceed immediately with sale of the securities following SEC approval. The issue can rather be put "on the shelf" for future sale. Further, the securities amount approved for issue need not be issued all at one time. Firms can market these "preregistered" new issues when the funds are needed (and in the amounts needed) and when market conditions are most favorable. Thus shelf registration provides greater timing flexibility in selling securities and reduces the frequency of securities registrations (thus reducing cumulative issue costs). Further, in a shelf registration the issuer need not specify a managing investment banking underwriter in the registration process but can rather employ the lowest-cost method of marketing the issue when it is actually sold—perhaps seeking bids from investment bankers. (This spur to competition among investment bankers is not applauded by the securities industry, which has generally opposed shelf registration.)

Secondary Market.   Corporate issues have traditionally been purchased by long-term investors with the expectation of holding the securities until maturity. Consequently, there has been relatively little need for a well-developed secondary market. In recent years, however, institutional investors have emphasized improving the performance of their portfolios by more frequent trading of their bond holdings. As a result, the secondary market for corporate bonds has expanded. However, even though many corporate bonds are traded on the New York Exchange, most trading in existing corporate bonds takes place in the over-the-counter market. As was discussed earlier, investment banking firms hold an inventory of bonds and post bid (buy) and ask (sell) quotes for selected issues. Through this process these security dealers make the secondary market in corporate bonds.

The difference in trading activity in the secondary market for corporate bonds between over-the-counter and listed (auction) markets partly reflects the historical development of U.S. financial markets. It also reflects the needs of the institutions that dominate the corporate bond market. Activity in the listed markets has historically been dominated by equities, reflecting the broad public appeal of equities to the individual investor. As a result, bond trading developed principally in the over-the-counter market, in which well-capitalized dealers could trade large quantities of bonds with institutions. This market is dominated by fewer than 25 dealers who constitute the wholesale market and who also trade with retail brokers.

Yield on Corporate Bonds

Corporate bond yields vary widely, reflecting the credit-risk characteristics of the issuer, the maturity of the issue, and other relevant characteristics of the issue, such as the call feature. Yields on corporate securities usually exceed yields on comparable maturity U.S. Treasury issues. The yield spread may be attributable to the higher credit risk on corporate issues, as well as to the fact that interest income on corporate bonds is subject to income tax at both the federal and local levels of government, whereas interest income on U.S. Treasury securities is exempt from state and local income taxes. Another factor is that most corporate issues are callable, but most U.S. Treasury issues are not. The difference between yields on corporate issues and yields on municipals (state and local government bonds) is also affected by these factors, but especially by the tax exemption of interest income on municipals at the federal level.

There are also striking differences in the yields on different-quality corporate bonds, reflecting risk considerations as well as other factors. As shown in Table 19.1, yields on Baa corporate issues (the lowest group of investment-grade issues) exceeded yields on Aaa corporate issues by 48 basis points as of January 1989, indicating the higher credit risk of the Baa issues. Lower-quality corporate issues would of course carry even higher-risk premiums. Also of considerable significance, the risk premium between the high- and low-grade corporate issues tends to vary over the business cycle, increasing during recession and narrowing during expansion, as both the actual riskiness of the securities and the market's reaction to risk changes over the cycle.

Original-Issue Deep-Discount Bonds

One of the most significant innovations in the corporate bond market in the early 1980s was the development of original-issue deep-discount bonds. These are bonds that, when issued in the primary market, carry coupons that are well below the required return prevailing in the market and hence must be sold at substantial discounts from par. At the extreme the bond could have no coupon (the so-called zero coupon bond, or "zeros") in which case all the return to the investor would be in the form of appreciation from the discounted value to par. The first publicly issued deep-discount bond came to the market in March 1981 (a Martin Marietta Corporation bond). Following the successful placement of that issue, a number of additional deep-discount bonds were sold. In fact, in 1981, almost 14 percent of all publicly placed corporate bonds were discount bonds.

There are a number of advantages and disadvantages of original-issue discount bonds from the perspective of the borrower and the investor. A comparison of these advantages and disadvantages relative to current coupon bonds is given in Table 19.3. From a tax perspective, original-issue deep-discount bonds offer an advantage to the borrower, since the issuer may, for tax purposes, deduct interest expense at the yield (effective) rate of interest on the bonds, even though no cash is paid out until the maturity of the instrument. While an advantage to the issuer, the tax feature is a disadvantage to the investor, since taxes must be paid each year on an interest income amount (computed on the basis of the actual yield) that exceeds cash actually received (until the maturity of the issue). The disadvantage of this feature for taxable investors is so great as to lead to the purchase of most original-issue deep-discount bonds by nontaxable investors such as pension funds.[9] Original-issue deep-discount bonds also differ substantially from current coupon bonds in the probability of call. Given that these bonds will sell at market prices well below par, it is very unlikely that the bonds will be called. This is obviously a disadvantage to the issuer, though it is an advantage to the investor.

Original-issue deep-discount bonds also differ from current coupon bonds in terms of reinvestment rate risk. **Reinvestment rate risk** refers to the possibility that the intermediate cash flows from a bond may be reinvested at rates different from the yield to maturity (the yield to maturity calculation discussed in Chapter 2 implicitly assumes that intermediate cash flows are invested at the calculated yield to maturity). The original-issue deep-discount bond has less reinvestment rate risk than the current coupon bond, since a smaller fraction of the return occurs prior to maturity. (For zero coupon bonds there is no reinvestment rate risk.) For other issues the importance of reinvestment rate risk depends on the timing of their cash flows.

---

[9]Discount created at the original issue of the bond (referred to as original issue discount) in the primary market is taxed as ordinary income. Discount created in the secondary or aftermarket by, for example, an increase in interest rates may be taxed as capital gains.

TABLE 19.3 Summary of Advantages and Disadvantages of Original-Issue Deep-Discount Bonds Relative to Current Coupon Bonds _____

Feature	Impact on Borrower	Impact on Investor
Tax treatment	Advantage	Disadvantage for taxable investor; of no consequence to nontaxable investor
Call protection	Disadvantage	Advantage
Reinvestment risk protection	Can be advantage, disadvantage, or of no consequence, depending on cash flows	Advantage
Intermediate holding period yield volatility	Of no consequence	Can be advantage or disadvantage, depending on investor's expectations of future interest rate movements and views on rate volatility
Credit risk	Of no consequence	Disadvantage

Source: Andrew Silver, "Original Issue Deep Discount Bonds," Federal Reserve Bank of New York Quarterly Review *(Winter 1981–82), 22.*

Price-volatility and credit-risk considerations also distinguish these two types of bonds. Price volatility (price risk) is higher for original-issue deep-discount bonds than for comparable maturity coupon bonds, since the duration of the deep-discount bonds is longer.[10] This price volatility is of no direct consequence to the issuer of the bonds, though it may be a disadvantage to the purchaser, depending on interest rate changes. With regard to credit risk this dimension of risk is greater for discount bonds because the return of cash is slower for these bonds. Credit risk, then, is clearly a disadvantage to the investor for discount bonds.

The market yield on discount bonds (compared to current coupon bonds) reflects the net effects of these advantages and disadvantages. Discount bonds were brought to market at yields below current coupon issues in the first few years of their existence, thereby producing benefits to the issuers in terms of the

---

[10]As discussed in Chapter 2, price volatility for a given interest rate change is a function of duration rather than maturity. Duration is longer for deep-discount bonds (all else being equal) because a larger portion of total cash flows to holders of these bonds (all cash flows in the case of zero coupon bonds) is deferred until the bond maturity date.

cost of funds. Investors also have appeared to have gained in that they have greater alternative investment opportunities.

Junk Bonds

One significant change in the corporate bond market in the 1980s was the explosive growth in the volume of newly issued low-quality bonds. These "junk bonds" (sometimes called "high-yield bonds") are frequently issued in the process of corporate takeovers, often as a part of the financing package in leveraged buyouts (LBOs). Their common characteristic, however, is that at the time of original issue, the bonds were rated less than investment grade (that is, less than Baa for Moody's or BBB for Standard & Poor). Since they carry a higher risk of default, they offer to the market a potentially higher return. Through the late 1980s the returns to investors were sufficiently high to offset the losses produced by a greater incidence of defaults. However, serious concerns have been raised about the potential for a substantial increase in corporate bankruptcies because of the sharp increase in financial leverage associated with the LBOs and the rise of junk bond financing.

STATE AND LOCAL GOVERNMENT BONDS

State and local government bonds comprise all issues of state governments and their political subdivisions, including cities, counties, school districts, and a variety of special-purpose governmental units. The volume of state and local government bonds outstanding is smaller than the volume outstanding of other major securities traded in the capital market. Yet the amount of municipals outstanding has grown very rapidly in recent years as a result of intense pressure on state and local governments to provide new services (and higher levels of existing services) to their constituents, joined with a reluctance on the part of these constituents to pay higher taxes to pay for the services and the demand for tax-free income by investors in high tax brackets.

Characteristics of Municipal Bonds

Municipal bonds differ markedly in their characteristics. Perhaps the most important distinction is between **general obligation** (GO) bonds and **revenue** bonds. The governmental unit that issues general obligation bonds pledges the taxing power of the government to pay interest and repay principal at maturity. These "full faith and credit" bonds, as they are called, are generally used to provide such basic government services as education and police and fire protection, for which either explicit fees are not charged or the fees that are charged provide only a small portion of the total cost of the service. General obligation bonds

THE EXPLOSION OF JUNK

The volume of low-rated (or junk) bonds has literally exploded, exceeding $100 billion by the late 1980s. The development of these types of bonds—rated below the investment grades of Baa for Moody's or BBB for Standard & Poor— has sharply altered both the available funding sources for U.S. corporations and the set of portfolio choices facing bond investors. It has also raised important public policy concerns about the potential effects of junk bonds on the stability of U.S. corporations.

Over 20 percent of all bonds publicly offered by U.S. corporations in 1985 were either nonrated or rated below investment grade. In contrast, there were almost no speculative-grade bonds sold publicly in the 1970s. Concerns raised by this explosion of junk includes the following:

1. The growth of junk bonds has contributed to an excessive amount of corporate debt and in turn to downgrading of ratings of corporate debt by Moody's and Standard & Poor. In fact, downgradings consistently led upgradings in the 1980s. Of course, these downgradings further add to the volume of junk bonds. (Bonds that were investment grade but are downgraded to speculative grade are referred to as "fallen angels.")

2. The growth of junk bonds has contributed to an undesirable restructuring of U.S. industry through leveraged buyouts (LBOs). With an LBO, control of a corporation changes with the funds provided by junk bond financing, resulting in a sharp increase in the volume of debt relative to equity on the corporation's balance sheet.

3. The growth of debt (fostered by junk bonds) threatens to increase sharply the number of corporate bankruptcies in future economic declines.

Where there are obviously risks associated with the growth of junk bonds, there are also some positive factors:

1. Junk bonds allow access to the capital markets to many corporations that earlier had not been able to obtain such financing. This easier access to bond financing may result in a greater availability of funds and lower-cost funds than were previously available from other credit suppliers (such as commercial banks).

2. Junk bonds have offered investors returns sufficiently high to offset their greater risk of default. In fact, the default rate (about 0.12 percent per year on the average) has been well under the yield differential between low- and high-quality bonds. Whether this pattern will continue in the future, however, is less certain, given the greater use of debt by U.S. corporations.

After reviewing the pros and cons of junk bonds, Fons argues, "In spite of their recent notoriety, however, low-rated bonds do have a legitimate role in the marketplace and in the financial structure of firms that make use of them."[1]

---

[1] Jerome S. Fons, "Junk Bonds and Public Policy," Federal Reserve Bank of Cleveland Economic Commentary (February 1, 1986), 4.

have been the slowest-growing portion of the total debt issues of state and local governments in the post–World War II period.

Most of the growth in municipals has been among the revenue bonds. These bonds are sold to finance some specific revenue-raising service, such as a toll highway, a sewer treatment and delivery system, or a university dormitory.[11] As a general rule, the governmental unit that originates the bond issue does not guarantee payment of principal and interest; such payment is strictly dependent on the revenue generated by the project being financed. However, there is frequently an implied promise that the governmental unit will bail out a revenue bond project if it experiences financial difficulties. Thus the riskiness of revenue bonds varies widely. Yet many revenue bonds have extremely low credit risk. For example, a revenue bond issued by a municipal utility district to provide electric-generating facilities for a community experiencing rapid and stable growth would generally be viewed as relatively low risk. An example of such a low-risk issue would be pollution control revenue bonds in which the funds are used to install pollution control equipment on an Exxon oil refinery, with bond payments based on receipts from a long-term lease signed by Exxon.

Whether they are general obligation or revenue bonds, however, municipal securities have a number of characteristics that are quite different from those of corporate bonds. Two in particular should be mentioned: **denomination** and **maturity.** Most municipal bonds are sold with minimum denominations of $5000, whereas most corporate bonds carry $1000 minimum denominations. This higher minimum for municipals partly reflects the attraction of the tax-free municipals to wealthier investors. However, the second characteristic—maturity—is at present of more significance. Corporate bonds are usually sold with a single maturity—so-called **term bonds**—but municipal securities usually carry multiple maturities, and they are referred to as **serial bonds.** These bonds, which mature in series, will have a portion maturing at the end of one year from the date of issue, another portion maturing at the end of the second year, and so on, through the last maturity date of the issue.[12] The serial nature of the municipal bond issue makes the sale of the security more complex. Since some investors want short-term securities, others want intermediate-term securities, and still others want long-term securities, it is usually not possible to place an entire municipal issue with one investor. Moreover, the serial nature of municipal securities makes their sale slower and thereby increases the price risk exposure of underwriters.[13]

---

[11]Among the important type of revenue bonds are airport revenue bonds, college revenue bonds, hospital revenue bonds, housing revenue bonds, industrial development bonds, public power revenue bonds, student loan revenue bonds, and toll road revenue bonds.

[12]In a sense a serial bond is similar to a term bond with a sinking fund. However, the investor in a serial bond knows exactly when the bond held will be retired, whereas the investor in the term bond with a sinking fund does not know whether his or her portion of the issue will be retired prior to maturity.

[13]Serial bonds became common in municipal finance after it was found that term bonds with sinking-fund provisions were frequently associated with fraudulent manipulation of the sinking fund.

The supply of municipal bonds was significantly affected by the 1986 tax act. One of the purposes of that act was to reduce the use of municipal bonds for the financing of nongovernmental functions (such as financing sporting facilities) and for interest arbitrage purposes (selling municipal bonds at one interest rate and investing the proceeds at a higher rate). These were viewed as inappropriate use of the indirect federal government subsidies provided by the exemption from federal income taxation of the interest income earned on municipal securities. The 1986 Tax Act affected the supply of municipal government securities by placing a limit on the amount of certain types of municipal securities that can be sold with the tax-free status and by making interest income on certain other types of municipal securities fully taxable. Specifically, the 1986 Tax Act established four classes of state and local government securities.

Class 1: Public-Purpose Bonds. These are securities issued to meet essential government services. Interest income on these bonds remains fully tax exempt. There is no ceiling on the amount of these bonds that may be sold with the interest exemption feature.

Class 2: Nongovernmental Bonds. These are bonds sold by state and local governments for quasi-governmental purposes such as to provide low-interest-rate loans for the purchase of residential buildings. A ceiling was placed on the amount of these bonds. In addition, while the interest income on these bonds remains tax exempt, it is treated as a tax preference item, which may indirectly raise the holder's tax payments through the alternative minimum tax.

Class 3: Nonessential Municipals. These are state and local government issues that were issued for what Congress considered nonessential functions such as building a sport stadium. Interest income on these issues is fully taxable.

Class 4: Previously Issued Municipals. All municipals sold before August 7, 1986, continue to be exempt from the federal income tax.

Demand for Municipals

Municipal bonds have historically been preferred by investors in relatively high tax brackets in order to take advantage of the tax-free status of the interest on the securities of state and local governments. At one time, commercial banks were the dominant buyers of municipals. However, declining bank profits throughout much of the 1980s reduced their need to hold municipals for tax shelter purposes. In addition, the 1986 tax act eliminated the ability of commercial banks to deduct the interest expense associated with the purchase of municipal securities acquired after August 7, 1986, except for small-issue public-purpose bonds. The elimination of this interest arbitrage activity at commercial banks should significantly reduce the long-run role of commercial banks in the municipal markets.

The demand for municipals is now quite different than it was before the 1986 Tax Act. High-income individuals and other entities exposed to relatively high tax rates continue to be attracted to municipals for their tax exemption.[14] The reduction in the maximum marginal rate provided by the 1986 tax act does reduce the demand for municipals somewhat, but this is countered by the elimination of other tax shelter vehicles (especially real estate). A separate category of investors are attracted to the taxable municipals. These investors compare the returns established on municipals with those offered on corporate issues (and to a lesser extent on U.S. government securities) in making their portfolio decisions. The ownership structure of municipal securities is shown in Table 19.4.

The Market for Municipals

Primary Market.   The primary market (the market for new issues of state and local governments) is subject to more regulation than is the primary market for corporate issues. New municipal securities are usually sold on a competitive basis (almost always so for general obligation bonds) and with a great deal of publicity. The issuer must provide advance notice of the issue and of the terms of the offering. Bids must be made by potential buyers according to a specified format, and there is a specified method for selecting the lowest bidder. Until recently, the low bid was determined by the **net interest cost method** (which does not adjust for

TABLE 19.4   Ownership of Municipal Securities, September 1988 (Billions of Dollars)

	Percentage of Total
Held by:	
Commercial banks	20.6
Households	35.7
Life insurance companies	1.5
Other insurance companies	19.4
Mutual funds	19.0
Other investors	3.8
Total outstanding	100.0

Source: Board of Governors of the Federal Reserve System, Flow of Funds Accounts, *Assets and Liabilities Outstanding, 1988.*

---

[14]The tax rate at which the investor would be indifferent between municipal and corporate bonds may be calculated as
$$R_m = R_c(1 - t)$$
where R_m = rate on municipal bonds, R_c = rate on corporate bonds, and t = tax rate.

the time value of money), but awards are now increasingly made on the basis of "true" or time-adjusted interest. Commercial banks play a major role in the primary market for general obligation bonds. However, commercial banks are proscribed by law from underwriting revenue bonds—a restriction that the banking industry has for many years sought to eliminate.[15]

Secondary Market.   The secondary market for municipal securities is quite similar to the secondary market for corporate bonds.[16] The market is primarily over-the-counter. Most investors purchase the securities to hold for some time rather than to trade. However, there is some evidence that the market is more active in relation to its size than is true for corporate bonds. As was discussed earlier, banks view municipals as a residual use of funds and are not reluctant to sell municipals from their portfolios when loan demand increases. Moreover, property and casualty insurance companies liquidate their municipals during unprofitable years.

Yields on Municipals

As we saw in Table 19.1, yields on municipals are lower than yields on corporate or government issues of comparable quality. A principal reason is the tax-exemption feature of interest income on the issues of state and local governments. However, this differential varies widely as interest rates change. In periods of high and rising rates the differential tends to narrow, and it usually widens in periods of falling rates. In addition, there is a risk-premium differential between high-grade and low-grade municipals. This differential is quite high, larger than for corporate issues, though it appears to be less cyclically sensitive than the risk premium for corporate issues.

U.S. GOVERNMENT AND GOVERNMENT AGENCY SECURITIES

Since most of the characteristics of direct U.S. government debt and of the debt of government agencies have already been discussed, we will comment only briefly here on a few important dimensions of the role of governments in the

---

[15]An interesting and important aspect of the municipal market is the existence of insurance for many new issues. Municipal bond insurance represents an unconditional promise to pay the bondholder any principal and/or interest due but unpaid. In return for this guarantee the insurance company receives a one-time fee. Most such insurance is written by American Municipal Bond Assurance Corporation and Municipal Bond Insurance Association.

[16]The serial nature of municipal bond issues reduces the liquidity of the secondary market.

capital market. Though once the dominant instrument of the capital market (with the exception of mortgages), U.S. government securities have become less significant in recent years. One reason is the increasingly short maturity of the debt. Another reason is the growing efficiency of the market for corporate and state and local government bonds. At one time, liquidity in the capital market was reserved for U.S. government securities. However, the liquidity of corporate and state and local government bonds has so improved that this role of U.S. Treasury obligations has increasingly diminished.

It is Treasury coupon issues—notes and bonds—that play a role in the capital market. These securities are widely held. Besides being held by the U.S. government and the Federal Reserve, Treasury notes and bonds are held by commercial banks, life insurance companies, fire, casualty, and marine insurance companies, savings banks, state and local governments, nonfinancial corporations, individuals, and other investors. With its absence of credit risk and relatively good secondary market the intermediate- and long-term Treasury issue appeals to a number of investors. However, the ownership of governments tends to vary with the maturity of the security. Commercial banks invest more in coupon issues with maturities of less than ten years. State and local governments are heavy investors in long-term government securities of twenty years or more to maturity, principally through their retirement funds, although they are also heavily invested in securities with 1- to 5-year maturities.

The primary and secondary markets for coupon issues are very similar to those for bills. New issues are often offered to the public in exchange for existing issues that are about to mature (a refunding offer) or in exchange for issues that will mature at some future date (an advance refunding offer). The investor may submit either a competitive or a noncompetitive tender, as in the bill auctions. Existing U.S. government coupon issues of all available denominations and maturities may also be purchased in the secondary market through U.S. government security dealers.

As shown in Table 19.1, the yield on U.S. government security issues is lower than that on corporate bonds, although the yield varies with the maturity of the issue, reflecting the shape of the yield curve. This reduced yield stems from the lower credit risk on governments than on corporates, the greater liquidity due to a deeper secondary market, and the freedom from federal income tax on the interest income from U.S. government securities.

Although many agency securities—with the exception of mortgage-related issues—are short-term in nature and more properly considered as part of the money market, some agencies offer longer-term securities. For example, as of December 31, 1984, the Federal National Mortgage Association had outstanding about $50 billion in debenture bonds with a maturity exceeding one year. At the same time the FNMA had outstanding almost $400 million of mortgage-backed bonds with a maturity of more than one year and about $1.5 billion in capital debentures with a maturity of more than one year.[17] The Farm Credit System also had large amounts of long-term debt securities outstanding.

CATS AND TIGRs AND STRIPS — *should know)*

An important innovation occurred in the government securities market in the early 1980s with the development of Certificates of Accrual on Treasury Securities (CATS) by Salomon Brothers, Treasury Investment Growth Receipts (TIGRs) by Merrill Lynch, and certain other similar securities such as the LIONs created by Lehman Brothers. These securities were designed to offer an assured yield to a tax-exempt investor (such as an IRA account) with a relatively low-denomination financial instrument. With these securities a portfolio of government securities is acquired by the underwriter (thereby reducing the volume of Treasury debt "floating" in the market) and certificates are sold that represent interests in the portfolio. The financial returns were structured such that the investor obtained a specified return at the maturity of the instrument. Since most were zero coupon instruments, there was no reinvestment rate risk. Also, since the portfolio of assets consisted of U.S. Treasury securities, the credit risk on the certificates was minimal. As a result, the securities proved very attractive for retirement accounts. The U.S. Treasury in 1985 began to offer to the market its own zero coupon bonds, referred to as Separately Traded Registered Interest and Principal Securities (STRIPS). Since the Treasury began to offer these bonds, the demand for the CATS and TIGRs has diminished.

SUMMARY

The capital market encompasses a diverse group of securities—bonds, mortgages, and equities—issued by economic units. In contrast to the money market, which is very homogeneous in nature, the capital market is quite fragmented. Its securities have considerable differences in credit risk, interest-rate risk, marketability, and other characteristics. The substantial differences in relative yields on capital market instruments reflect these underlying differences in the characteristics of the instruments themselves.

One of the most important subcomponents of the capital market is the bond market. The bond market comprises corporate, municipal, and U.S. government debt. The volume of new corporate bonds is principally determined by the growth rate of corporate assets, as well as by the relative cost of bonds versus other sources of funds. Most corporate bonds are purchased by contractual financial institutions that pay little or no taxes, such as pension funds. The primary market for corporate bonds includes large numbers of both private and public placements. The secondary market for corporate bonds has not

---

[17]Federal National Mortgage Association, *Guide to FNMA Debt Securities*, March 7, 1985.

been well developed, although the volume of trading in recent years has expanded as institutional investors have sought to improve the performance of their portfolios.

The volume of new municipal bonds reflects the demands of population growth, as well as the expansion of municipal financing into nontraditional areas. Municipal bonds include both general obligation and revenue bonds, but recently the most rapid growth has occurred in revenue bond issues. The principal distinguishing feature of municipal bonds is the exemption of their interest income from the federal income tax. This tax feature means that municipals are attractive to investors who are exposed to a potentially high federal income tax rate. The 1986 Tax Act substantially affected both the supply of and demand for municipals.

Increasingly, the market for U.S. government securities (as well as the market for government agency securities) is developing characteristics that are more like those of the money market than of the capital market. In particular, the maturity of government debt has become very short. U.S. government debt in the capital market includes both notes and bonds. The supply of new U.S. government debt in the capital market principally reflects the size of the government deficit and Treasury maturity management decisions. Purchasers of government debt include most major economic and financial institutions.

The bond portion of the capital market, as well as the mortgage and equity markets, is constantly in the process of evolution. Bond characteristics are modified to make them more relevant to changing market conditions, and the relative importance of different purchasers of bonds alters over time. The development of original-issue discount bonds in the corporate market and TIGRs, CATS, and STRIPS in the Treasury market are examples of such innovations in the bond market. Moreover, recent periods of high inflation and unstable conditions, as well as high and unstable interest rates, have caused major problems for the bond market and for the markets for all fixed-income instruments. Therefore we must recognize that this "snapshot" of the bond market as of the late 1980s may become increasingly unrepresentative over time.

QUESTIONS

1. What are the major instruments of the capital market? Which are the most important? Compare their characteristics.

2. Referring to Table 19.1, explain the differences in yield among the capital market instruments.

3. Describe the different characteristics of corporate bonds and the impact of these characteristics on the yields on the bonds.

4. Why have corporations used debt rather than equity as their principal source of funds?

5. Who are the principal buyers of corporate bonds? Explain their motivation.

6. Discuss the advantages and disadvantages of original-issue deep-discount bonds. Which seem to be most significant in affecting the buyers of these bonds?

7. Who are the principal buyers of state and local government bonds? Explain their motivation. Why have commerical banks reduced their purchase of municipals? Why have individuals increased their purchases?

8. Explain how you might determine—from the perspective of after-tax yield—whether you would find it desirable to buy municipal bonds.

9. Distinguish between a revenue bond and a general obligation bond. Would you expect the yield on a revenue bond to exceed the yield on a general obligation bond? Explain.

REFERENCES

Becketti, Sean, "The Role of Stripped Securities in Portfolio Management," Federal Reserve Bank of Kansas City *Economic Review* (May 1985), 20–31.

Bee, David C., "Rethinking Tax-Exempt Financing For State and Local Governments," Federal Reserve Bank of New York *Quarterly Review* (Autumn 1982), 20–40.

Fabozzi, Frank, and Irving M. Pollack (Eds.). *The Handbook of Fixed Income Securities* (Homewood, Ill.: Dow-Jones-Irwin, 1983).

Homer, Sidney, and Martin Leibowitz, *Inside the Yield Book* (Englewood Cliffs. N.J.: Prentice-Hall. 1972).

Jensen, Frederick H., "Recent Developments in Corporate Finance," Federal Reserve *Bulletin* (November 1986), 747–756.

Leibowitz, Martin L., "An Analytical Approach to the Bond Market," in Summer N. Levine (Ed.), *Financial Analysts Handbook I: Methods, Theory and Portfolio Management* (Homewood, Ill.: Dow-Jones-Irwin, 1975).

———, "The Municipal Rolling Yield: A New Approach to the Analysis of Tax Exempt Yield Curves," in Frank J. Fabozzi, Sylvan Fedstein, Irving M. Pollack, and Frank G. Zorb (Eds.), *The Handbook of Municipal Bonds* (Homewood, Ill.: Dow-Jones-Irwin, 1983).

Loey, S., "Low-Grade Bonds: A Growing Source of Corporate Funding," Federal Reserve Bank of Philadelphia *Business Review* (November/December 1986), 3–12.

Proctor, Allen J., and Kathleen K. Donahoo, "Commercial Bank Investment in Municipal Securities," Federal Reserve Bank of New York *Quarterly Review* (Winter 1983/1984), 26–37.

Sherwood, H. C., *How Corporate and Municipal Debt Is Rated* (New York: Wiley, 1976).

Silver, Andrew, "Original Issue Deep Discount Bonds," Federal Reserve Bank of New York *Quarterly Review* (Winter 1981–82), 18–28.

Zwick, Burton, "The Market for Corporate Bonds," Federal Reserve Bank of New York *Quarterly Review* (Autumn 1977), 27–36.

CHAPTER **20**

The Capital Market: Mortgage Instruments

In the preceding chapter we discussed the nature of the financial instruments traded in the bond market and the characteristics of the bond market itself. Discussion focused on the nature of corporate, municipal, and U.S. Treasury and government agency securities. In this chapter we analyze the nature of another capital market security—the mortgage—and the characteristics of the mortgage market. Although this analysis could have been incorporated into the discussion of the bond market (in fact, mortgage bonds are generally included in a treatment of the bond market), we have chosen to treat the mortgage market separately. Such treatment is warranted by the specialized nature of mortgage instruments, the traditional social concern afforded to mortgages, and the enormous size of the mortgage market itself. Moreover, the mortgage market has changed markedly in recent years.

Mortgage debt represents the largest component of the capital market, exceeding $3 trillion at the end of 1988. Furthermore, mortgage debt outstanding has grown very rapidly in recent years. For example, total mortgage debt amounted to only $207 billion in 1960 and less than $500 billion in 1970. To a considerable extent, the rise in mortgage debt outstanding reflects the increase in construction costs in an inflationary environment. However, a substantial part of the recent increase in mortgage debt is attributable to the increase in prices for single-family housing in recent years.

A mortgage is a debt instrument secured by real property—land and/or buildings.[1] Mortgages are subdivided into four categories: **home** (one- to four-family

---

[1] There are also **chattel mortgages,** which use other types of property—inventories, autos, etc.—as collateral and which are frequently used in short-term lending. The discussion of the mortgage market in this chapter does not include chattel mortgages.

dwellings), **multifamily residential** (apartment houses), **commercial** (office buildings and industrial buildings), and **farm**. Of this group, home mortgages represent the largest component, accounting for about two thirds of all mortgages outstanding as of the end of 1988. Commercial mortgages were a distant second, accounting for about 18 percent of the total. The amount of mortgages and the composition of total mortgages outstanding for selected years since 1960 are shown in Table 20.1.

The mortgage market is important not only because it is large, but also because there is great public interest in the flow of funds to mortgages, especially to mortgages on single-family dwellings. The idea that each American family should have the opportunity to own its own home has deep roots in public policy discussion. There is intense interest in the availability of mortgage credit for single-family housing, and there is great concern whenever the availability is restricted. Moreover, the mortgage market has been one of the most dynamic portions of the capital market. Innovations in the mortgage market have become commonplace in recent years as revolutionary developments have occurred in housing finance.

CHARACTERISTICS OF MORTGAGES

A mortgage is a debt contract in which real property—land and/or buildings—serves as security for the contract. The traditional mortgage has been long-term—20 to 30 years—for residential properties and somewhat shorter-term for commercial properties. The traditional mortgage has had a fixed rate; that is, the lender and borrower have agreed on a rate that remains fixed during the entire life of the contract. But the high and volatile interest rates of recent years have resulted in the emergence of adjustable-rate mortgages (ARMs) as a significant

TABLE 20.1   Mortgage Debt Outstanding at Year End, 1960–1987
(In Billions of Dollars)

	1960	1965	1970	1975	1987
Farm	$ 12.8	$ 21.2	$ 31.2	$ 50.9	$ 88.9
Residential					
One- to four-family	141.3	212.9	280.2	491.7	$1,925.2
Multifamily	20.3	37.2	58.0	100.3	273.8
	$161.6	$250.1	$338.2	$592.0	$2,199.0
Commercial	32.4	54.5	82.3	158.6	655.3
Total	$206.8	$325.8	$451.7	$801.5	$2,854.3

Source: Board of Governors of the Federal Reserve System, Federal Reserve Bulletin, various issues.

and viable alternative to the traditional fixed-rate mortgage. ARMs' share of the conventional mortgage market grew from 5 percent in 1981 to about 50 percent in 1983, and has since fluctuated from about 25 percent to 55 percent, depending on mortgage market conditions. Both fixed-rate and adjustable-rate mortgages, particularly single-family home mortgages, have had relatively small penalties for prepayments.

Types of Mortgages

Claims of the mortgagor on the real property involved in the debt contract vary widely. The **first-mortgage contract** is by far the most common for both residential and commercial properties. With this contract the lender has first claim on the real property pledged to secure the contract. Many properties—both residential and commercial—are further financed with mortgages whose interests are subordinate to those of the first-mortgage holder. Since these "junior" or **second mortgages** carry a greater amount of risk to the lender, they are usually made at a higher interest rate and for shorter terms. Junior mortgages have become increasingly common in recent years as rapid escalation of property values has made it difficult for buyers to make the cash down payments associated with the purchase of real property. As a result, sellers have been forced to accept a second or junior mortgage to be able to complete the sale.

Increases in interest rates in recent years and the periodic episodes of diminished credit availability have produced a number of innovations in mortgage contracts in addition to the advent of adjustable-rate mortgages. Increasingly, lenders on income-producing properties have sought to obtain a share of the inflation-induced increases in the value of property being financed. Life insurance companies and other traditional lenders on apartment houses and office buildings have frequently required various types of **equity kickers** (or **shared appreciation**) in order to justify the loan. These arrangements provide the lender with, in addition to the interest return, a share in any increases in gross rentals from the property that presumably may occur with rising prices. The **wraparound** feature has also become common in both residential and commercial mortgages. By this arrangement the lender (the seller of the property) gives the borrower (the buyer of the property) a mortgage for the full amount of the property (less a standard down payment), but the lender retains liability for the existing mortgage. The new mortgage, in effect, is wrapped around the old mortgage. From the buyer's perspective the wraparound provides complete financing for the purchase of the property without resort to a junior mortgage. From the seller's perspective, since the wraparound is usually at a higher rate than that of the original mortgage, there is the prospect of a gain equal to the spread between interest expense on the old mortgage and interest income on the new mortgage.

Insured Versus Conventional Residential Mortgages

The U.S. government has played a major role in the residential mortgage market since the 1930s. One of the most visible aspects of the attempts to improve the flow of credit to home mortgages stems from the government mortgage insurance and guarantee program. Begun in 1934, the mortgage insurance program of the Federal Housing Administration (FHA) has had an enormous impact on the availability of housing. Financed by a mortgage insurance fee, the FHA program has reduced the risk exposure of lenders. Moreover, it has encouraged the growth of amortized loans and has contributed to the maintenance of quality in the construction of residential units. A Veterans Administration guarantee program currently exists that performs functions similar to those of the FHA insurance program. The growth and acceptance of these types of federally sponsored programs have resulted in the split of the mortgage market into two subcomponents: **insured** (FHA or VA) and **conventional** (not FHA or VA). (However, this dichotomy has become less meaningful in recent years as private insurance of conventional mortgages has become common.) In 1988, of total residential mortgage debt outstanding of about $2.4 trillion, the FHA-insured and VA-guaranteed component was about $450 billion, and the remainder was conventional mortgages. (See Figure 20.1.)

Residential mortgage debt outstanding is much greater than the amount of commercial mortgage debt (about $900 billion in 1988) and farm mortgage debt (about $85 billion in 1988). (See Figure 20.2.) There is no provision for government insurance or guarantee for commercial mortgages, but (as we discussed in Chapter 11) the government is a prominent lender and loan guarantor in the farm mortgage market.

THE PRIMARY MORTGAGE MARKET

Mortgage credit is provided through both the primary and secondary mortgage markets. The primary market provides mortgage funds, and the loans or securities backed by them are sold in the secondary market. It is useful to discuss separately the primary and secondary market for mortgages in order to describe fully the dramatic developments in the secondary mortgage market in recent years. We begin with the primary market, noting briefly the economic influences underlying the demand for mortgage credit and then treating in more detail the supply of mortgage funds.

The Demand for Mortgage Funds

The demand for mortgage funds stems from underlying economic factors associated with the growth and mobility of population. Increases in population and rapid geographic shifts in population result in expanded demand for hous-

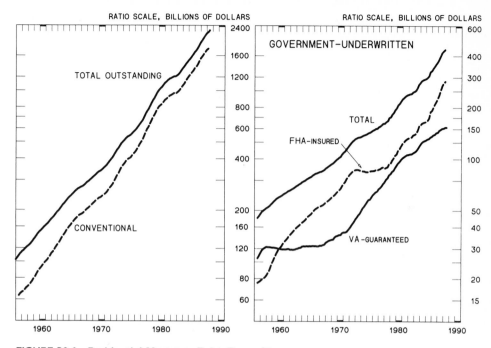

FIGURE 20.1   Residential Mortgage Debt, Type of Loan
(Amount Outstanding, End of Quarter)

Source: Board of Governors of the Federal Reserve System, Historical Chart Book, *1988.*

ing, office buildings, commercial structures, and other types of properties. Since real-property acquisition is usually accomplished with borrowed funds, any in-creases in the demand for real property lead to increases in the demand for mortgage funds. In addition, inflation in construction costs or the belief that real property (either residential or commercial) is an effective inflation hedge also contributes to an increase in the demand for mortgage funds.

In understanding the demand for mortgages it is useful to distinguish the various segments of demand by different types of mortgages. Expansion of the population in an area, of course, will increase the demand for mortgages. So will increases in the mobility of a given population. In addition, the demand for mortgages to finance office buildings and apartment houses may be explained within an investment decision–making framework that is similar to the analysis made for a new project or a new piece of business equipment. The demand for the office space or rental units must be estimated, vacancy rates and operating costs must be forecast, and a rate of return on the investment must be calculated. This investment rate of return can then be compared with the cost of funds in determining the demand for funds. But the demand for farm mortgages, particu-

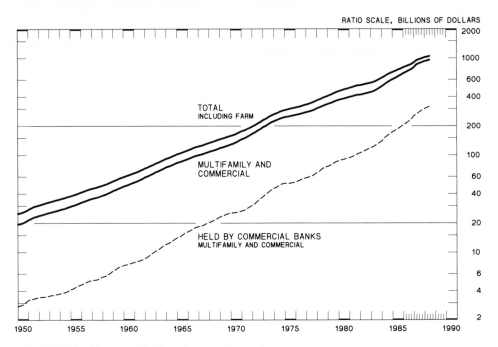

FIGURE 20.2   **Mortgage Debt on Income Properties**
(Amount Outstanding, End of Quarter)

Source: Board of Governors of the Federal Reserve System, Historical Chart Book, *1988.*

larly mortgages on farm and ranch land, is more complex—perhaps the most complex portion of the total demand for mortgage funds. Although a portion of this segment of mortgage demand may be explained by rate-of-return consider-ations, it must also be recognized that farming and ranching in many areas retain individual family ownership characteristics that make the demand for farm mort-gage funds more complex to understand and project.

The largest component by far of the aggregate demand for mortgage credit is for financing residential housing. Both demographic and economic factors un-derlie the demand for residential mortgage funds. These include the price of housing services compared to the prices of other goods and services, the level and distributions of income, age distribution of the population, family size, the rate of household formation, tastes and preferences, and a variety of other fac-tors. And, of course, the quantity of demand for mortgage credit is directly linked to the cost and availability of mortgage funds. As shown in Figure 20.3, which indicates the annual rate of change in residential construction and mortgage debt since 1950, there has been considerable volatility in both new residential mortgage lending and construction in recent years.

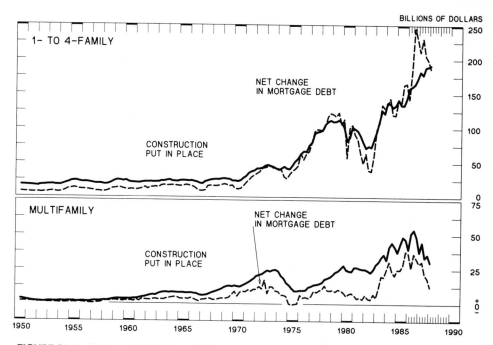

FIGURE 20.3   Residential Mortgage Debt and Construction
(Annually, 1950–1951; Seasonally Adjusted Annual Rates, Quarterly, 1952–)

Source: Board of Governors of the Federal Reserve System, Historical Chart Book, 1988.

The Supply of Mortgage Funds

The primary market for mortgages (the market for newly created mortgages) has traditionally been a very local one involving local financial institutions, particularly savings and loan associations. The initial lender is known as the **originator** of the mortgage. The originator may either retain the mortgage for its own portfolio or dispose of the mortgage in the secondary market. In a variant of this pattern the mortgage bank, which has traditionally served as agent for such permanent lenders as pension funds and insurance companies, originates a mortgage loan and for a fee provides the necessary services during the life of the loan, such as maintaining records, accepting payments, and paying tax and insurance on the property. Although most mortgage lenders other than mortgage banks have held the mortgages they originated, there has been a growing tendency to originate and then dispose of mortgages in the secondary market.

Increasingly, the primary market for mortgages has broadened with the development of mortgage-backed securities. Indeed, these mortgage-backed securities have changed the mortgage market so greatly that in many respects it is now similar to the corporate bond market. These securities include the Government National Mortgage Association (GNMA) pass-through certificates and the mortgage-backed securities of the Federal National Mortgage Association (FNMA) and the Federal Home Loan Mortgage Corporation (FHLMC), as well as private pass-through certificates and various types of mortgage-backed bonds. (More will be said about these securities in the discussion of the secondary markets in mortgages.)

Figures 20.3, 20.4, and 20.5 indicate trends in mortgage lending over the past three decades for both residential and income properties. Information on the ownership of single-family homes, multifamily residential, commercial, and farm mortgages is provided in Tables 20.2 through 20.5. Examination of these data suggests a number of important generalizations about the supply of mortgage funds. First, as is true for most financial instruments, the supply stems principally from financial institutions. Second, most mortgages are held by thrift institutions and contractual-type financial institutions. Savings and loans dominate the home mortgage market, and they are also the most important lenders on multifamily

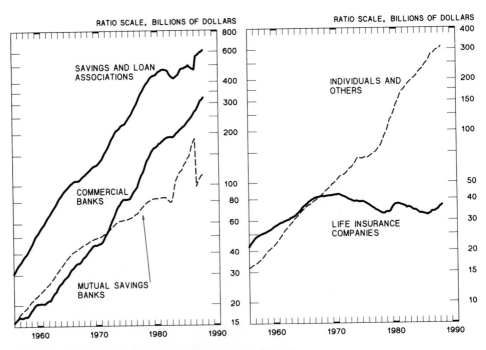

FIGURE 20.4   Residential Mortgage Debt, Type of Lender (Amount Outstanding, End of Quarter)

Source: Board of Governors of the Federal Reserve System, Historical Chart Book, 1988.

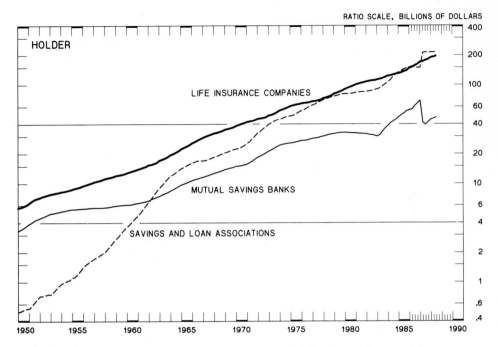

RATIO SCALE, BILLIONS OF DOLLARS

HOLDER

LIFE INSURANCE COMPANIES

MUTUAL SAVINGS BANKS

SAVINGS AND LOAN ASSOCIATIONS

1950 1955 1960 1965 1970 1975 1980 1985 1990

FIGURE 20.5 Mortgage Debt on Income Properties, Multifamily and Commercial (Amount Outstanding, End of Quarter)

Source: Board of Governors of the Federal Reserve System, Historical Chart Book, *1988.*

residential properties. Savings and loans, life insurance companies, and commercial banks are the principal suppliers of commercial mortgage funds.[2] Households and government-sponsored agencies are the principal investors in farm mortgages. The importance of government activity in the mortgage market is evident in these tables. Mortgage pools and government-sponsored agencies account for almost 20 percent of total home mortgages, over 10 percent of multifamily residential mortgages, and over 30 percent of farm mortgages.

In the early 1970s, Real Estate Investment Trusts (REITs) were significant suppliers of mortgage funds, especially from income-producing property, such as office buildings and apartment houses. These REITs included short-term lenders, long-term lenders, and equity investors. Many were sponsored by large commercial banks. However, many REITs experienced massive loan losses on their investments during the 1974–1976 period.

---

[2]The large amount of commercial mortgages held by commercial banks is somewhat misleading because a substantial fraction of these mortgages represents property in the stage of construction. Upon completion the permanent lending will generally be done by a life insurance company or savings and loan association.

TABLE 20.2   Ownership of Home Mortgages, 1987 (Billions of Dollars)

Amount outstanding	$1,925.2
Held by	
Households	171.3
U.S. government and government-sponsored credit agencies	123.9
Mortgage pools	653.9
Commercial banking	275.8
Savings institutions	598.9
Life insurance companies	13.2

Source: Federal Reserve Bulletin, June 1989.

A REIT is a trust or a corporation (with publicly traded shares) that participates in the financing and/or ownership of real estate properties. By pooling shareholders' funds and investing them in either mortgages or income-producing properties or both, REITs provide investors with professional management, a relatively small capital requirement, a high payout of earnings, and a degree of liquidity and diversification not available in most other real estate investments.

The Tax Reform Act of 1986 stimulated interest in REITs (which were already undergoing a modest revival). The income tax changes of 1986 did not give any tax benefits to REITs but rather took tax advantages away from alternative real estate investments. Thus the REIT, which never had any particular tax benefit, is now more competitive with other real estate investments. For example, real estate limited partnerships (RELPs) were hit hard by tax reform. RELPs are organized not as corporations but rather with a general partner and a group of investors who are limited partners. The general partner buys and manages the real estate properties and sells participation units to the investors, who share in the income from operation and sale of the properties. The attractiveness of RELPs has been greatly diminished by the loss of their ability to serve as a tax shelter.

TABLE 20.3   Ownership of Multifamily Residential Mortgages, 1987 (Billions of Dollars)

Amount outstanding	$273.8
Held by	
Households	75.4
U.S. government and government-sponsored credit agencies	19.9
Mortgage pools	16.4
Commercial banking	33.3
Savings institutions	106.4
Life insurance companies	22.5

Source: Federal Reserve Bulletin, June 1989.

TABLE 20.4 Ownership of Commercial Mortgages, 1987 (Billions of Dollars)

Amount outstanding	$655.3
Held by	
Households	63.3
Commercial banking	267.7
Savings institutions	150.9
Life insurance companies	166.7
Farmers Home Administration	6.7

Source: Federal Reserve Bulletin, June 1989.

Financial Deregulation and the Home Mortgage Market

A current public policy concern regarding the supply of mortgage funds is what role the traditional mortgage lenders—the thrift institutions—will play in future residential mortgage lending. Until the late 1970s the thrifts (savings and loan associations and mutual savings banks) generally accounted for more than half of new residential mortgage lending each year. But in the 1980s the share of new residential mortgage financing provided by thrifts began to decline. However, the thrifts increased their indirect mortgage lending by increasing their holdings of mortgage-backed securities.

The reasons for the relative decline in the importance of thrifts as direct mortgage lenders during the 1980s were the related phenomena of economic and regulatory change. The most important economic development was the prolonged and largely unanticipated rise in interest rates that began in the late 1960s. Higher interest rates increased the cost of funds to thrifts, and as market interest rates rose above the Regulation Q deposit rate ceilings that were imposed on thrifts in 1966, disintermediation (the withdrawal of funds from depository institutions by savers in favor of nonregulated instruments) began to drain thrift deposits (their principal source of funds). Since thrifts held more than three fourths of their earning assets in long-term, fixed-rate mortgages, they were badly squeezed between interest revenue levels reflecting older, lower interest rates

TABLE 20.5 Ownership of Farm Mortgages, 1987 (Billions of Dollars)

Amount outstanding	$88.9
Held by	
Households	21.4
U.S. government and government-sponsored credit agencies	42.4
Commercial banking	14.4
Life insurance companies	9.9

Source: Federal Reserve Bulletin, June 1989.

and interest expense levels reflecting new, higher interest rate levels. The increases in deposit rate ceilings permitted by regulators in the 1970s were of no help in the latter regard, although they did stem the tide of disintermediation somewhat.

The problems of the thrift institutions played a large role in the financial deregulatory legislation of 1980 and 1982 (the Depository Institutions Deregulation and Monetary Control Act and the Garn–St. Germain Depository Institutions Act). These acts removed deposit rate ceilings and gave thrifts broadened lending authority. In 1980 the Federal Home Loan Bank Board authorized adjustable-rate mortgages for federally chartered associations, an action soon emulated by most state regulatory authorities. Thrifts now had the powers and freedom to deal with both the disintermediation problem and the problem of asset/liability mismatch. They could both compete for funds and use those funds to develop a more diversified and earnings-rate-flexible asset portfolio. However, some observers feared that higher funding costs for thrifts would result in higher mortgage lending rates and that thrift portfolio diversification would result in reduced mortgage lending by these institutions.

There are good reasons, however, to believe that the thrift deregulation that occurred in the early 1980s will not result in a long-run "shortage" of mortgage credit. The financial marketplace is highly flexible and adaptive, and the fungibility of funds has been amply demonstrated. To the extent that (and if) thrifts reduce their long-run role in housing finance, it is likely that new home mortgage lenders will enter the market, and long-run equilibrium mortgage rates will thus be little affected. What economic and regulatory change have rather accomplished is not a shrinkage in mortgage credit but a transformation in the nature and structure of the mortgage market and its instruments. The most notable aspects of this remarkable transformation are the dramatic development of the secondary mortgage market and the development of new mortgage instruments.

Thrift institutions and other lenders originating mortgages in the primary market can sell them to investors in the secondary market either as mortgages or as securities backed by pools of mortgages. It is through this market that such financial institutions as pension funds invest in mortgages, thus indirectly becoming a source of mortgage funds. Increasingly, mortgages are originated in the primary market solely for placement in the secondary market. Thus the secondary mortgage market is more than a source of liquidity for the primary market— it also serves as a supply channel for new mortgage credit. Before we examine the structure and significance of the secondary mortgage market, however, the various types of primary mortgage instruments warrant attention.

Types of Mortgage Contracts

Table 20.6 summarizes a variety of types of mortgage instruments used in residential financing. The conventional, long-term, fixed-rate home mortgage remains the most popular with borrowers, the various type of variable-rate mortgages having become common only in the 1980s. The adjustable-rate mortgage

TABLE 20.6   **Varieties of Home Financing**

Mortgage Type	Interest Rate	Maturity	Payments
Conventional	Fixed.	Fixed, often 30 years.	Fixed over term of the loan.
	May be scarce when interest rates are climbing because lenders do not want to risk being locked into lower income.		
Adjustable Rate (ARM) or Variable Rate (VRM)	Indexed to a market rate (for example 6-month Treasury bill rate). Starting rate may be lower than on conventional because borrowers share risk of rising rates with lender.	Fixed, but sometimes can be extended in lieu of increase in monthly payment when interest rate rises.	May change when interest rate changes or only at specified intervals, such as annually or every 3 to 5 years. If payments do not increase with interest rates, result may be negative amortization (see GPM below).
	These mortgages take many forms. To protect yourself, shop around for favorable terms, including limits on the increase in rate permitted in any one year and over the whole term and limits on payment increases and negative amortization.		
Graduated Payment (GPM)	Fixed.	Fixed.	Low at start. Increase gradually as predetermined during first 5 or 10 years, then level out.
	Because of lower starting payments, may appeal to young borrowers who anticipate increased income in future years. CAUTION: Early payments might not cover interest due. Unpaid interest is added to outstanding principal, increasing the debt. This is called NEGATIVE AMORTIZATION, and borrowers may get a shock if they decide to sell in a few years and discover reduced equity in the property. However, some GPMs may include arrangements to prevent negative amortization.		
Graduated Payment Adjustable	Adjustable as in ARM or VRM.	Fixed, up to 40 years.	Similar to GPM. During first 10 years, may be less than required to fully amortize loan. Adjusted within that period and every 5 years thereafter to ensure full payment.
	Federal savings and loans and mutual savings banks were authorized in July 1981 to offer this mortgage, which combines graduated payments with adjustable interest rates. Payment adjustments may be quite large because of these two areas of change.		

(continued)

TABLE 20.6 *(Continued)* _____

Mortgage Type	Interest Rate	Maturity	Payments
Renegotiable Rate (RRM)	Fixed for 3 to 5 years, then renegotiated.	Short-term loan (3 to 5 years) but amortized over longer term, usually up to 30 years.	Payments will change as interest rate changes.
	Short-term loan is automatically renewable; but if new interest rate is not acceptable, the borrower must either refinance or sell the property. The interest rate increases permitted each year and over the life of the loan may be limited.		
Shared Appreciation (SAM)	Fixed.	Fixed.	Fixed.
	In return for lower interest rate the borrower agrees to share with the lender a percentage of any increase in the value of the home—at specified future dates or when it is sold, whichever occurs first. This plan may appeal to first-home buyer as a way to make the purchase affordable. But remember that an increase in value must be shared with the lender; sharing a *decrease* in value may or may not be part of the agreement.		
Wraparound (WRAP)	Fixed.	Fixed.	Fixed.
	The lender combines an existing mortgage on the property (bearing a lower rate) with a new mortgage for the balance needed (at a higher rate) to provide a lower overall cost to the borrower. This is possible only if the existing mortgage is assumable by the buyer. (All FHA and VA mortgages are assumable.) *not sure anymore*		
Balloon Payment	Fixed or adjustable.	Fixed. Traditionally 5 years but may be shorter or longer.	Fixed, usually based on 20 to 30-year amortization, but at end of term, debt will not be fully paid. Borrower must pay off remaining "balloon" balance or refinance at prevailing rates.
	Because of short-term and balloon payment, the down payment may be as little as 5 percent.		
Reverse Annuity (RAM)	May be adjustable.	May be fixed with refinancing option.	Loan due when home is sold or on death of borrower.
	This plan calls for periodic payments to homeowners based on a loan against their equity in a home. It is designed to appeal to older people who may be having difficulty living on reduced incomes.		
"Take-Back"	Usually fixed.	Usually short term.	Usually a high down payment. May call

TABLE 20.6 *(Continued)*

Mortgage Type	Interest Rate	Maturity	Payments
			for balloon payment at maturity.
	This is a loan by the seller of the property who agrees to take the mortgage in order to facilitate the sale.		
Federal Housing Administration (FHA) insured	Set by FHA. Usually more favorable because of the protection afforded lender. Seller may have to pay "points," an amount to raise lender's return to market levels.	Fixed.	Fixed or graduated, depending on FHA options.
	Available from lenders approved by FHA. Properties to be mortgaged must meet FHA requirements.		
Veterans Administration (VA) guaranteed	Fixed. Lower than others but seller may have to pay points.	Fixed. Usually 25–30 years.	Fixed or graduated, depending on VA options.
	Terms are eased because of VA guarantee. No or low down payment. Veterans should check with VA for eligibility requirements and for other assistance related to housing.		
Buy-Down	Below market rate, for a specified period or for the life of the loan.	Fixed.	Fixed for term of the buy-down; usually increase thereafter.
	A seller or home builder pays an amount to a lender "up front" who then gives to buyers below-market rate loans. The borrower should realize this arrangement may increase the purchase price of the home.		

Source: Department of Consumer Affairs, Federal Reserve Bank of Philadelphia.

(ARM) maintains the traditional long-term nature of the mortgage contract but allows the rate and/or the maturity of the instrument to vary with changes in open-market rates in the capital market. For example, an increase in interest rates in the capital market would lead to an increase in the interest rate on the loan or to a lengthening of the maturity of the loan or to some combination of the two. On the other hand, a reduction in interest rates in the capital markets would lead to a decrease in the interest rate on the loan or to a reduction in its maturity or some combination of the two.

Mortgages with provisions for periodic adjustment of the contract interest rate have become common in the United States only in the past decade. Not until 1979 did the Federal Home Loan Bank Board (FHLBB) grant variable-rate mortgage authority to thrift institutions under its regulatory purview, and these "VRMs" were tightly regulated and restricted. In 1981 the FHLBB and other regulators significantly liberalized ARM regulations. Regulatory limitations on the frequency and size of periodic rate adjustments were removed; such limits ("caps") are now in the realm of the market-determined and borrower/lender-negotiated. Lenders can employ any index for interest-rate adjustment that is readily verifiable by the borrower and not under the control of the lender. (A commonly used index for ARMs is the U.S. Treasury's "constant maturity index," an index determined by the Treasury through a survey of U.S. government security dealers.) Rate changes (optional for increases but mandatory for decreases) can be reflected in any combination of changes in monthly payment, loan term, or principal balance.[3] The only significant remaining regulatory restrictions pertained to disclosure requirements (at the time of loan application) and notification requirements to the borrower when a rate adjustment is scheduled.

The ARM market has grown dramatically since the 1981 regulatory liberalization; the conventional mortgage market share held in ARMs grew from less than 5 percent in early 1981 to more than 50 percent by 1984. As interest rates declined in 1985 and 1986, so did ARMs' share of the market, but rising rates led to a 40–50 percent market share in 1987–88. ARMs have significantly altered the nature of residential housing finance in this country. Borrowers are now confronted with a wide array of mortgage programs that they must evaluate. Further, borrowers choosing ARMs (instead of a fixed-rate mortgage) must adjust financially and psychologically to periodic changes in their mortgage payments. Given that all borrowers will not successfully adapt, it is very likely that default risk for ARMs will be greater, on the average, than for fixed-rate mortgages.

Compared to fixed-rate mortgages, ARMs sharply change the division of interest-rate risk between borrower and lender. With the traditional fixed-rate mortgage (particularly with small prepayment penalties) the interest-rate risk was held by the lender. If rates increased, the lender was locked into a low-yielding asset. Yet if rates fell, the borrower could prepay the mortgage, and the lender would then be able to reinvest only at lower rates. With adjustable-rate mortgages and to a lesser extent with **renegotiated-rate mortgages** (which feature less frequent adjustments), much of the interest-rate risk has shifted to the borrower. What the borrower gains in return is a lower *initial* interest rate—which may often enable potential home buyers who were "priced out" of the fixed rate mortgage market to qualify for ARMs and thus purchase houses. The aggregate effect of ARMs may thus be to make the housing industry (noted for its boom-or-bust nature) less sensitive to economywide changes in interest rates and credit availability. For lenders, ARMs effectively shorten asset maturities, cause

---

[3]When interest rate increases are totally reflected in changes in the principal balance, the unchanged monthly payment may be (in the early years of an ARM term) less than total interest charges, resulting in "negative amortization" as the unpaid interest is added to the principal balance.

asset values to be less sensitive to interest rate fluctuations, and otherwise alleviate interest-rate risk and facilitate asset/liability management. Thus mortgage lenders, too, may gain from ARMs some degree of insulation from the effects of interest-rate fluctuations.

In addition to the ARM there are a number of other alternatives to the fixed-rate mortgage (FRM). These include the **renegotiated-rate mortgage** (RRM), the **graduated payment mortgage** (GPM), and the **growing equity mortgage** (GEM). The RRM, which has been generally available since 1981, is essentially a three-to-five year "rollover" mortgage, the mortgage rate being subject to renegotiation at the end of that term. The GPM features an escalating schedule of loan amortization payments, the lower monthly payments in early years making it easier for applicants to qualify for a loan. (The hope is that borrower income will rise at least as fast as scheduled payment levels.) The **graduated payment adjustable mortgage** (GPAM) combines the adjustable interest rate feature of the ARM with the reduced initial interest payments of the GPM. This complex instrument generally incorporates changes in monthly payments, loan term, and principal balance to reflect interest rate adjustments.

The GEM is a variant of the traditional fixed-rate mortgage; the interest rate is fixed for the term of the mortgage. Like the GPM, the GEM features an escalated payment schedule, but unlike the GPM, all the payment increases are applied to the principal balance. The escalated principal payment accelerates loan maturity and home equity accumulation. GEMs are typically paid off in 12 to 15 years. The reduction in loan term that the GEM features allows borrowers to obtain them at a lower interest rate than is available for a comparable standard fixed-rate mortgage.

THE SECONDARY MORTGAGE MARKET

The secondary market for mortgages, especially home mortgages, involves both individual mortgages and mortgage pools. The mortgage pools may be either federally insured or conventional. Each passes through to the holder of the security both interest and principal payments, whether regularly scheduled principal payments or repayments. Mortgage bankers have been very active in the creation of mortgage pools. In contrast, with a mortgage-backed bond, only interest payments are made to the holder of the security prior to the maturity of that security. Savings and loan associations have been active in the sale of mortgage-backed bonds as a means of obtaining additional sources of funds. (Technically, mortgage-backed bonds are not pools, since the securities holder does not have a joint interest in the mortgage and the issuer continues to record the mortgages on its balance sheet.)

The secondary market for mortgages serves the same role as the secondary market for any security by providing liquidity to the primary market. Primary market lenders thus are likely to extend more mortgage loans (and at lower rates), given the existence of a secondary market. But the secondary mortgage market's significance extends beyond this provision of liquidity to primary lenders. Its development has served virtually to eradicate the view of the mortgage market as localized and mortgages as highly illiquid. The secondary mortgage market has become an important link between the home buyer and a wide range of investors—pension funds, insurance companies, investment companies, and individuals in the United States and abroad—that have little or no interest in primary mortgage origination. Further, many primary mortgage originators sell most of their mortgage loans, earning the bulk of their revenues in the form of loan origination and servicing fees rather than interest income. In the early to mid-1970s, only about one third of new residential mortgages were sold in the secondary market. In 1980 the proportion had climbed to almost 50 percent, and it has continued to mount in more recent years.

The dramatic expansion of the secondary mortgage market has almost certainly smoothed the flow of funds into mortgage lending by attracting a wider spectrum of investors. It is also likely that the total volume of mortgage lending has been greater as a result. The fixed-rate, long-term mortgage—which has been threatened as volatile interest rates created maturity gap problems for the traditional mortgage lenders, thrift institutions, that rely on liquid deposits as their principal source of funds—has been bolstered by its attraction for pension funds and life insurance companies, which traditionally seek long-term investments. In general, the growth of the secondary market has expanded the sources of mortgage credit and more fully integrated the housing finance sector with the aggregate capital market. While thrift institutions still originate more residential mortgages than any other single source (about one third), their share of net additions to mortgage credit has declined. Home loan funding through the secondary mortgage market has become a viable alternative to the traditional funding by deposits in thrift institutions.

Much (and perhaps most) of the surge in secondary mortgage market development stems from federal government policy. We now seek to identify the major elements of government activity in the secondary market for mortgages.

The Role of FNMA, GNMA, and the FHLMC

Intervention by the federal government in this nation's housing finance market began in the 1930s as a "New Deal" response to the widespread mortgage defaults and foreclosures of the Great Depression. Since that time, a web of federal housing policies has evolved that includes regulation, taxation, and direct market intervention. We are concerned here with the government's intervention in the secondary mortgage market.

Chapter 11 includes a description of the principal federal and federally sponsored agencies that are concerned with housing finance. Recall that the Federal Housing Administration (FHA) and the Veterans Administration (VA) insure and guarantee, respectively, qualified mortgage loans. Recall also that the Federal National Mortgage Association (FNMA, or "Fannie Mae") was created to purchase FHA-insured (and later, VA-guaranteed) mortgage loans from lenders—the government's first venture into the secondary mortgage market.

In the late 1960s and early 1970s the federal government significantly expanded its role in the secondary mortgage market. The primary purpose was to help mortgage lenders, buffeted by disintermediation arising from the gap between market interest rates and Regulation Q deposit ceilings, replenish their loanable funds. In 1968, FNMA was partitioned into a federally chartered, privately owned agency and a new federal agency, the Government National Mortgage Association (GNMA). GNMA's principal function was to lend its payment guarantee to privately issued securities backed by pools of FHA-insured and VA-guaranteed mortgages (GNMA "pass-through" certificates), thus encouraging development of this vital secondary market instrument. FNMA, unburdened of its nonsecondary market responsibilities, significantly expanded its role in mortgage purchase and issue of mortgage-backed securities (MBS). (See Chapter 11 for a description of FNMA programs.) Then, in 1970 the Federal Home Loan Mortgage Corporation (FHLMC) was established. The FHLMC—a publicly managed corporation capitalized initially by the sale of stock to the Federal Home Loan Banks (and under the aegis of the Federal Home Loan Bank Board)—was intended to be "a FNMA" for the savings and loan industry. The FHLMC was empowered to buy conventional residential mortgages (FNMA was then limited to purchase of FHA-insured and VA-guaranteed mortgage loans) made by FHLBB member institutions. Both FNMA and the FHLMC issue large amounts of mortgage-backed securities.

FNMA has expanded both the types of mortgages it purchases and its MBS programs. As described in Chapter 11, its "swap" program—in which it trades its securities for mortgages held by primary market lenders—has been a boon to the latter. FNMA, like GNMA, has also incorporated the new types of mortgage instruments into its purchase and MBS programs. The FHLMC has similarly broadened and expanded its operations. In particular, the FHLMC's introduction of **collateralized mortgage obligations** (CMOs) is notable. CMOs are mortgage-backed bonds that resemble pass-through securities but are structured into different maturity classes in the fashion of serial bonds. For example, the FHLMC's first issues of CMOs in 1983 divided the cash flow from the underlying mortgage pool into a short-term group of securities (which received all principal payments on the mortgage until the total principal payments for this security group was paid), an intermediate-term security group (next in line for principal payments), and a long-term group (last to receive principal payments). The latter feature reduces, for holdings of the longer-maturity CMOs, the relatively high reinvestment risk (from mortgage prepayment) that generally characterizes mortgage pass-through certificates.

The Tax Reform Act of 1986 created a new mortgage-backed securities vehicle that allows the attractive features of the CMO to be combined with certain accounting and taxation treatments that are highly desirable for issuers. The Real

Estate Mortgage Investment Conduit (REMIC) is essentially a tax code classification that is intended to facilitate the issue of multiple-class mortgage-backed securities. While almost any mortgage security is eligible for issuance as a REMIC, multiple-class mortgage-backed securities have been the most popular instrument to be issued as REMICs.

MORTGAGE YIELDS

Calculation of the yield on mortgages, including the yield on the various types of mortgage pools, is complicated by a number of factors. Initially, many home mortgages are written with the requirement that the borrower pay the lender "points" (a point is 1 percent of the value of the loan) as a means of increasing the yield to the lender. These points raise the true yield above the contract rate. Moreover, the true yield to maturity on a mortgage is not known to the investor at the time of purchase because the extent of prepayment is not known and can only be estimated. For example, estimates of yields on GNMA pass-through securities are based on the assumption of a 12-year average life. However, individual GNMA pass-throughs may be prepaid more quickly or slowly than this assumed term, in which case the yield would differ from that initially calculated.

Since the credit characteristics of individual mortgages vary widely, it is not surprising that the yields on mortgage instruments also vary widely. However, some generalizations can be made. Yields on insured mortgages tend to move with general capital market rates, though with a lag. In the period from 1950 to 1965, yields on FHA mortgages averaged about 150 basis points above the yield on Aaa corporate bonds. In the early and mid-1970s the yield spread narrowed, but it widened again in the 1978–1982 period, when mortgage rates rose to record levels. It is likely that mortgage rates will move more in line with corporate bond rates as the bond market and the mortgage market become more interrelated. The yield on conventional mortgages generally exceeds the yield on FHA mortgages, generally by 1/4 to 1/2 a percentage point.

Market yields on FHA-insured and VA-guaranteed mortgages are fairly uniform across the country, but yields on conventional mortgages reflect local variations in risk, demand, and supply. The latter phenomenon is likely to fade slowly as the mortgage market becomes more integrated with the national capital market.

SUMMARY

Mortgages are fixed-income instruments secured by real property. Taken as a group, mortgages are the largest component of the capital market, and home mortgages are the largest component of the mortgage market. Mortgages vary in their claims on the pledged prop-

STRIPPED SECURITIES IN THE MORTGAGE MARKET

The development of stripped securities represents one of the most significant innovations in the financial marketplace in recent years. Stripped securities are created by separating or stripping the principal and interest payments from an underlying debt security and selling the claims to the payment streams as a separate set of securities. By creating securities with different cash flow properties than the underlying debt instruments, the stripped securities offer portfolio managers additional opportunities to structure the risk–return mixture of their balance sheets. Stripped securities exist for both Treasury- and mortgage-backed securities.

Treasury-backed stripped securities are perhaps the simplest to understand. The cash flow from a Treasury bond, for example, is separated into a claim on the principal portion of the underlying security (called a principal-only or PO) and a claim on each of the interest payments (called an interest-only or IO). In effect, each of the POs and IOs is a zero coupon bond. As such, there is no reinvestment rate risk, since there are no intermediate cash flows. With the absence of reinvestment rate risk and no credit risk an investor can lock in a fixed return on the security. In addition, by picking different mixtures of IOs and POs the investor can perhaps better match the maturity of the securities with his or her holding period.

Stripped Treasury securities were originated in the early 1980s by investment banking firms attempting to meet the demand for zero coupon Treasury securities. In 1985 the Treasury created its own STRIPS (Separate Trading of Registered Interest and Principal of Securities). By 1988, Treasury STRIPS approximated $50 billion.

Mortgage-backed stripped securities are created from mortgage pass-through securities. Like Treasury STRIPS, mortgage-backed STRIPS take the cash flow from an underlying securities pool and divide it into IOs and POs. However, while Treasury securities are usually stripped into a considerable number of separate securities, the mortgage securities are usually stripped into only two parts: a PO STRIP representing all principal payments and an IO STRIP representing all interest payments. Hence mortgage STRIPS are *not* zero coupon instruments. Reflecting the different features of the mortgage STRIPS from the Treasury STRIPS, the mortgage STRIPS do not serve the purposes of reinvestment rate risk reduction and maturity matching.

Mortgage STRIPS behave differently than Treasury STRIPS principally because of the prepayment possibilities on the underlying mortgages. Prepayment rates depend primarily on the level of interest rates; falling rates produce higher prepayments, while rising rates lead to reduced prepayments. Prepayment rates make the price of the mortgage stripped POs extremely sensitive to interest-rate changes. With falling rates the cash flow is accelerated through prepayments, the result being that the price increases not only because of the lower discount rate but also because of the more rapid receipt of cash. Of course, the decline in price of the POs is also substantial because of both the higher discount rate and the reduced prepayments. The price behavior of the IOs is even more interesting. Since falling rates increase prepayments, which reduce the total amount of interest paid on the IOs, the price of the IO may actually fall with declining rates. Conversely, since rising rates reduce prepayments and thereby increase the total amount of interest paid, the price of an IO may actually rise with rising interest rates. This unusual price behavior of the IOs makes them attractive vehicles to hedge the interest-rate risk of a portfolio.

The organized market for mortgage-backed stripped securities began in 1986 when the Federal National Mortgage Association issued $200 million of securities backed by FHA/VA mortgages. Since then, the volume of mortgage-backed STRIPS has grown substantially, exceeding $20 billion in 1988.

Adapted from Sean Beckett, "The Role of Stripped Securities in Portfolio Management," Federal Reserve Bank of Kansas City Economic Review *(May 1988), pp. 20–31.*

erty; they include first mortgages and various types of junior mortgages. The mortgage has traditionally had a fixed rate, though various types of mortgages have increasingly been devised that carry variable rates. The adjustable-rate mortgage (ARM) market has grown dramatically since 1981. Mortgages may also be characterized as insured (or guaranteed) if protected by the FHA or VA or as conventional if not.

The demand for mortgages reflects the demand for real property, since most purchases of real property are financed with borrowed funds. Recent inflation, which has increased the price of real property, particularly residential property, has substantially increased the demand for mortgage funds. The supply of mortgage funds stems primarily from financial institutions, such as savings and loan associations, mutual savings banks, pension funds, and life insurance companies. Government agencies play a major role in the mortgage market.

Both the primary and secondary mortgage markets have grown in recent years, but the secondary market has experienced tremendous expansion, particularly because of the growth of mortgage pools, such as those represented by GNMA pass-through certificates and the mortgage-backed securities of FNMA and the FHLMC. A large number of private financial institutions, such as mortgage banks and savings and loan associations, are active in buying and selling individual mortgages in the secondary market. The remarkable development of the secondary mortgage market has attracted new lenders to mortgage instruments and has probably better integrated the mortgage market with the aggregate capital market. The financial innovation and structural adjustments that have characterized the mortgage market in recent years are a consequence of broader changes in the economic and financial environment.

QUESTIONS

1. Describe the basic characteristics of a mortgage as a debt instrument, contrasting it with a bond.
2. Explain the following terms:
   a. Junior mortgage
   b. ARM
   c. "Equity kicker"
   d. "Wraparound" mortgage.
3. Residential mortgages are often dichotomized as "insured" or "conventional." Explain the significance of these terms.

4. What are the principal economic, demographic, and financial factors determining the demand for mortgage funds?

5. Identify the most significant suppliers of mortgage funds. Explain why thrift institutions became relatively less significant mortgage lenders in the early 1980s.

6. Describe the principal features of the following types of mortgages:
   a. Standard fixed-rate mortgage
   b. Adjustable-rate mortgage
   c. Graduated payment mortgage
   d. Growing equity mortgage.

7. What is a mortgage pool? What is the difference between a "pass-through" mortgage security and a mortgage-backed bond?

8. Why is the distinction between the primary and secondary markets for mortgages less clear than for other securities? How does the secondary mortgage market broaden and deepen the primary mortgage market?

9. Describe and compare the roles of FNMA, the FHLMC, and GNMA in the mortgage market.

10. What is a REMIC?

REFERENCES

Barth, James, Joseph Cordes, and Anthony Yezer, "Federal Government Attempts to Influence the Allocation of Mortgage Credit: FHA Mortgage Insurance and Government Regulations," in *Conference on the Economics of Federal Credit Activity, Part II—Papers* (Washington, DC: Congressional Budget Office, 1981), 159–232.

Brockschmidt, Peggy, "The Secondary Market for Home Mortgages," Federal Reserve Bank of Kansas City *Monthly Review* (September/October 1977), 11–20.

Brueggem, W. B., and L. A. Stone, *Real Estate Finance* (Homewood, Ill.: Richard D. Irwin, 1981).

Dougall, Herbert E., and Jack E. Gaumnitz, *Capital Markets and Institutions,* 4th ed. (Englewood Cliffs, N.J.: Prentice-Hall, 1980).

Guttentag, J. M., *Mortgage Passthroughs: Structure and Policy* (Washington, D.C.: Mortgage Insurance Companies of America, 1982).

The Housing Finance System and Federal Policy: Recent Changes and Options for the Future (Washington, D.C.: Congressional Budget Office, 1983).

Jones, Marcos T., "Mortgage Designs, Inflation, and Real Interest Rates," Federal Reserve Bank of New York *Quarterly Review* (Spring 1982), 20–27.

Kaufman, George G., *The Role of Traditional Mortgage Lenders in Future Mortgage Lending: Problems and Prospects,* Federal Reserve Bank of Chicago Staff Memoranda, 1984.

Lasko, Warren, "The Ginnie Mae Mortgage-Backed Securities Program," *Housing Finance Review* (Winter 1987), 293–301.

Melton, William C., "Graduated Payment Mortgages," Federal Reserve Bank of New York *Quarterly Review* (Spring 1980), 21–29.

———, and Diane L. Heidt, "Variable Rate Mortgages," Federal Reserve Bank of New York *Quarterly Review* (Summer 1979), 22–32.

Mortgage-Backed Bond and Pass-Through Symposium (Charlottesville, Va: Financial Analysts Research Foundation, 1980).

Panos, Konstas, "REMICS: Their Role in Mortgage Finance and the Securities Market," *FDIC Banking and Economic Review* (May/June 1987), 11–18.

The Secondary Market in Residential Mortgages (Washington, D.C.: Federal Home Loan Mortgage Corporation, 1982).

Severind, Charles M., "Mortgage Backed Securities," Federal Reserve Bank of New York *Quarterly Review* (Autumn 1979), 1–10.

Susswein, Donald B., "What Do REMICs Mean to You? Understanding the Building Blocks," *Mortgage Banking* (March 1987), 24–29.

Timms, R. H., *Mortgage-Backed Securities* (Chicago: U.S. League of Savings Institutions, 1977).

Villani, Kevin E., "The Secondary Mortgage Markets: What They Are, What They Do, and How to Measure Them," *Secondary Mortgage Markets* (February 1984), 24–44.

Waldemand, Michael, and S. P. Baum, *The Historical Performance of Mortgage Securities, 1972–1980* (New York: Salomon Brothers, 1980).

Winger, A. R., and M. R. Thomas, *Secondary Markets in Mortgages* (Federal Home Loan Bank of Cincinnati, 1978).

Wyman, Stephen B., "The Metamorphosis of Real Estate Lending," *Journal of Commercial Bank Lending* (March 1988), 44–54.

CHAPTER **21**

The Capital Market:
Equity Securities

Equity means an ownership claim, and equity securities evidence ownership in incorporated enterprises. Equity securities are thus an institutional aspect of a private enterprise economy, a means of holding wealth, and a source of new capital funds for corporations.

Equity securities are of great significance to the saving–investment process in a market economy for two reasons. One is that new issues of stock are often an important source of external capital funds. The second basic role of equity securities in the financing flows of corporations is less obvious. It concerns the institutional role of corporate stock as a means of ownership and the financing role played by corporate retained earnings. Corporate retained earnings (or "undistributed profits") are the major single source of funds for corporations (when depreciation and other noncash revenue deductions are included). And although retained earnings represent "corporate saving," the corporation is only an organizational framework—retained earnings are really shareholder saving. In this sense, corporate stock is a saving–investment instrument of much greater significance than is indicated by the magnitude of the proceeds of new stock issues. Indeed, internal financing—mostly retained earnings plus "capital consumption allowances" (depreciation)—accounts for most of corporate equity funding. To understand better the relationship between equity securities, internal financing, and external funding, it is useful to review the sources and uses of corporate funds.

BUSINESS CORPORATION EQUITY FINANCING

The nature of the flow of funds for a nonfinancial business corporation can be readily assessed by considering the structure of a representative balance sheet for such a firm. In the table below, the various groups of assets, liabilities, and equity items are listed in the conventional format, where "current" means an asset or liability of maturity of one year or less.

Assets	Liabilities and Stockholder Equity
Current Assets	*Current Liabilities*
Cash and short-term financial assets	Trade payables
Trade receivables (credit extended	Other short-term debt
to customers)	*Noncurrent Liabilities*
Inventories	Bonds payable
Noncurrent Assets	Other long-term debt
Plant and equipment	*Stockholder Equity*
Buildings	Equity shares outstanding
Land	Retained earnings

Business assets are "financed" with liabilities and stockholder equity. Such financing needs are often characterized as a need for "working capital"—current assets minus current liabilities—and "plant" (all noncurrent assets). Such a framework focuses on the firm's long-term financing structure. In equation form:

$$WC \; + \; NCA \; = \; NCL \; + \; SE$$

where WC = working capital, NCA = noncurrent assets, NCL = noncurrent liabilities, and SE = stockholder equity.

The firm's financing needs and sources can now be seen in terms of changes (Δ) in these various balance sheet components:

$$\Delta WC \; + \; \Delta NCA \; = \; \Delta NCL \; + \; \Delta SE$$

Thus a business corporation has only two means of financing its working capital needs (essentially inventories plus any excess of short-term trade credit extended over trade credit utilized) and plant and equipment expansion and replacement: an increase in long-term debt or an increase in stockholder equity. In this context, short-term funds are part of working capital and thus do not finance it. (Indeed, many firms generally limit their use of short-term financing to working capital needs.) An increase in long-term (and short-term) debt is solely *external* financing. An increase in stockholder equity may result from an increase in retained earnings, which is part of *internal* financing,[1] and from the issuance of new equity shares, which is *external* financing.

---

[1]Internally generated funds of business firms also include the amount of depreciation and various other items of operating expenses that do not involve an actual cash outlay. (These expenses are subtracted from corporate revenues in computing earnings but do not reduce corporate cash.) In the absence of price changes, the amounts of such items (in cost-based accounting) would provide for "capital maintenance"—the replacement of depreciating items as they are consumed in operations. With increasing prices the funds needed to replace buildings and equipment have to be financed, just as do expansions in plant.

Internal Financing

Business corporations generate their own financing to the extent that their cash inflows for a period exceed the sum of all cash outflows for that period, including taxes and dividends. A convenient measure of this amount is obtained by adding depreciation for a period to the amount of after-tax earnings not distributed to shareholders in dividend payments (retained earnings).

Fluctuations in both the absolute amount of internally generated funds and its proportion of total business funding can be attributed largely to cyclical swings in business activity. The amount of internal funds generated is of course a direct function of earnings, rising markedly during upswings in business activity and dipping in periods of business recession.[2] Because of the sluggishness of the U.S. economy in the late 1960s and early 1970s, for example, the percentage of total business financing accounted for by internally generated funds dipped from more than 75 percent to less than 60 percent. Much of the increase in external funding is new debt. In recent years (notably in the 1981–1982 recession), corporations have, in general, reacted to disappointing amounts of internally generated funds by reducing their holdings of short-term liquid assets and substantially increasing the degree of leverage (ratio of debt to equity financing) in their financial structure.

External Financing

A firm's decision to issue new equity securities is determined by both financial and nonfinancial factors. The fact that control of the corporation may be altered by the sale of such securities is the principal nonfinancial factor for nonregulated firms. Financial factors include (for given financing requirements) the following:

1. The degree of availability of internal financing relative to total financing needs.

2. Cost of alternative external financing sources, specifically the interest rate.

3. Current market price of the firm's stock (which governs the cost of equity financing).

Thus the use of external equity financing is likely to be significant only during periods of relatively high stock prices, especially if interest rates are concurrently high and total business financing needs are great. The U.S. tax structure

---

[2]Retained earnings constitute the portion of total earnings not paid to stockholders as dividends. Thus changes in the amount of retained earnings can result from changes in dividend policy of corporations (increases or decreases in dividend payout as a percentage of earnings), as well as from changes in overall earnings. As a practical matter, corporations are generally very reluctant to reduce dividends, and they increase dividends only when it appears quite likely that the higher dividend can be easily sustained.

is biased against external equity financing relative to debt financing, since unlike interest payments, dividend payments are not deductible expenses for income-tax purposes. Further, new issues of equity shares dilute earnings per share, although the projects financed from the funds provided should generate sufficient future earnings to make such dilution temporary. Finally, external equity financing is unfavorable in relation to internal financing because the former necessitates a costly and time-consuming registration process with the Securities and Exchange Commission. Also, shareholders view internal financing as making capital gains more likely (at the cost of forgoing dividends).

Reflecting the relatively low after-tax cost of debt and the relatively high after-tax cost of equity, U.S. corporations have increasingly relied upon debt financing for their external funds. In fact, with large numbers of stock repurchases and with substantial amounts of equity being retired as the result of debt-financial mergers, the amount of equity outstanding has declined substantially.

As shown in Table 21.1, the amount of net/new equity (new equity sold less existing equity retained) has been negative in seven of the ten years from 1979 to 1988. In fact, net/new equity was negative in each of the five years ending in 1988, and exceeded $100 billion in 1988. U.S. corporations have dramatically altered the debt/equity mix of their balance sheets, a change which obviously increases the risk of default in economic contractions.

CHARACTERISTICS OF EQUITY SECURITIES

For the investor, equity securities are riskier than debt securities but offer the possibility of higher returns. For the issuing firm, equity securities are a less risky means of financing than debt because there is no fixed commitment for payments to the holder of the stock. There are two types of equity securities: preferred stock and common stock.

Preferred Stock

Preferred stock offers a prescribed dividend per share, which must be paid to preferred stockholders before any dividends can be paid to common stockholders. Preferred stock usually carries a **cumulative** feature, which means that preferred dividends that are not paid in a given period or periods "accumulate" and must be paid in total before any common stock dividends are paid. The other major "preference" of this class of stock is a priority claim (relative to common shareholders) against corporate assets in the event of corporate liquidation.

Use of preferred stock issues is relatively infrequent in this country. Pre-

TABLE 21.1 Net Funds Raised in Credit Markets for Nonfinancial Corporate Business 1979–1988
(Dollars in Billions)

Sources of Funds	1979	1980	1981	1982	1983	1984	1985	1986	1987	1988
Total	$60.1	$70.7	$90.7	$49.8	$77.9	$95.8	$50.9	$121.3	$68.9	$62.4
Debt	68.0	57.8	102.1	43.4	54.4	170.3	132.4	202.1	145.4	192.9
Equity	−7.8	12.9	−11.5	6.4	23.5	−74.5	−81.5	−80.8	−76.5	−120.5
Percent										
Debt	113.1	81.8	112.6	87.1	69.8	177.8	260.1	116.6	211.0	309.1
Equity	−13.1	18.2	−12.6	12.9	30.2	−77.8	−160.1	−66.6	−111.0	−209.1

Source: Federal Reserve Flow of Funds Accounts, March 10, 1989.

ferred stock is similar to bonds but with one very significant difference—unlike interest, preferred stock dividends are not a tax-deductible expense. As a result, preferred stock is a relatively expensive means of raising funds. To the issuing corporation the only significant advantage of preferred stock, relative to bonds, is that preferred dividends may be "passed" (not paid) without the threat of bankruptcy that nonpayment of the bond interest would invoke. However, there is a significant advantage to a corporation investing in the preferred (and common) stock of another corporation—80 percent of dividends received by corporations are not subject to federal income tax. This aspect (partial tax exemption of dividends) of preferred stock makes the instrument attractive for inclusion in the portfolio of marketable securities held by most corporations. Corporate demand for preferred stock stemming from this tax advantage has the effect of lowering before-tax required yields on preferred stock, partly off-setting its unfavorable after-tax cost disadvantage (relative to debt).

In recent years a number of corporations (particularly banking organizations) have issued adjustable-rate preferred stock. This adjustable-rate feature has advantages for both the issuer and purchaser of preferred stock. In the case of the issuer a fixed financing charge is avoided, which is particularly significant when the level of interest rates and required yields are high. For the investor the adjustable rate feature results in the preferred stock trading at or near its par value irrespective of interest rate fluctuations. This reduction in interest-rate risk is particularly important for temporary investments, which is a common characteristic of corporate preferred stock holdings. Adjustable-rate preferred stock generally offers a yield that is tied to the prevailing interest rate on various U.S. Treasury securities.[3]

Common Stock

Unlike ownership of bonds or preferred stock, common stock ownership carries no corporate commitment to a fixed periodic return or payment of principal. Ultimate ownership rights to corporate assets are held by common stockholders, and the right to vote for members of the corporation's board of directors is inherent in common stock (although some corporations, generally those that are family controlled, have nonvoting classes of common stock). Though occasionally important (as in so-called "takeovers"), this right to participate in corporate control is usually of minor significance to investors. They tend to value instead the right to unlimited participation in the fruits of company growth and profitability—dividends and capital gains—that common stock ownership brings.

---

[3]For a description of the introduction and early use of adjustable-rate preferred stock by banking organizations, see Kerry Cooper and Donald R. Fraser, "The Boom in Preferred Stock Issues," *The Bankers Magazine* (November/December, 1983), 73–77.

Other Features of Equity Securities

Many preferred stocks have **convertible** provisions that enable their holders to convert them into common stock at a stated ratio of common shares for each preferred share presented for conversion. Issuers often sell convertible preferred stock because this feature's attractiveness to investors results in a lower cost relative to straight preferred stock. In addition, preferred stock is sometimes issued without a conversion feature but with attached purchase option warrants that can be used to acquire common stock at a privileged subscription price. The effect of such warrants on the preferred stock price, of course, is determined by the value of the warrants. The value of the warrants, in turn, is a function of the stated subscription price relative to the market price of the common stock.

Most preferred stock is **callable,** which means that the issuer has the right to redeem the preferred shares at a stated call price. Although the call price will ordinarily exceed the investor's purchase price for the preferred stock and thus result in an investor gain if exercised, the callable feature is still a disadvantage for the investor. The reason is that the issuing firm is likely to exercise the callable provision only when market yields have fallen (and security prices have risen) to the point at which refunding the preferred stock issue is attractive. Thus investors who are obliged to sell back their preferred stock will have relatively less attractive investment opportunities in which to place the proceeds.

OWNERSHIP OF EQUITY SECURITIES

The distribution of ownership of outstanding equity securities for 1975–1988 is shown in Table 21.2. Households constitute the largest holders of equity securities. Holdings by institutions, particularly by pension funds, have become much more important in recent years. Private pension funds are the largest institutional holders of common stocks, followed by insurance companies (all types) and mutual funds. Increased holdings by both life and property insurance companies are largely the result of relaxation of restrictions on the scope of their investments that began in the 1960s.

Foreign ownership of stocks of U.S. corporations has, in aggregate market value of shares held, increased dramatically. Increased foreign equity investment in this country coincided with the general increase in foreign direct and portfolio investment in the United States during this period.

THE PRIMARY MARKET FOR EQUITY SECURITIES

In a **public offering** of equity securities, new issues of corporate stock may be sold directly to investors by the issuing firm or indirectly through investment banking institutions and dealers. Such public offerings of new issues dominate

TABLE 21.2   Market Value of Total Holdings of Corporate Equity Securities by Sector and Selected Institutions, 1975–1988 (End of Calendar Year; Billions of Dollars)

	1975	1980	1984	1988
Households	$660	$1222	$1492	$1806
Foreign	35	65	94	193
Savings banks	4	4	4	8
Life insurance companies	28	47	64	95
Other insurance companies	14	32	50	76
Private pension funds	89	176	294	500
State and local government retirement funds	24	44	98	206
Mutual funds	34	42	80	191
Brokers and dealers	3	3	6	14

Source: Board of Governors of the Federal Reserve System, Flow of Funds Accounts, Assets and Liabilities Outstanding, 1975–1988.

the primary market for equity securities. Most public offerings of new equity issues are distributed to investors through investment bankers via underwriting or agency selling arrangements. The role of investment bankers in the issue of new equity securities parallels their role in the issue of new corporate bonds, as described in Chapter 19. New public issues of equity securities are subject to the regulations and disclosure requirements of the Securities Act of 1933, as administered by the Securities and Exchange Commission (SEC).

The other (relatively minor) segment of the primary equity market is the **private placement.** In the case of private placements, firms sell securities directly to a single investor or a small group of investors (ordinarily institutional investors). New stock issues are rarely privately placed. Private placement is generally limited to issues of high-grade preferred stocks of public utility firms and to issues of small, financially sound firms for whom use of an investment banker is either infeasible or unattractive because of the relatively small size of the new issue. Overall, direct issue by all these various means accounts for less than 15 percent of new common stock issues and less than 5 percent of new preferred stock issues.

In the usual public offering of equities the investment banking syndicate buys the securities from the issuing firm (the **underwriting** function) and then sells them to investors. Again, these investment banking arrangements parallel those for bond issues. However, equities are also sold via certain arrangements that are not employed for debt securities. While these selling arrangements do not account for a particularly large proportion of total external financing, they warrant mention:

1. Sale of a new issue of common stock to current stockholders at a "privileged subscription price";

2. Sale of new shares of stock to current stockholders as part of a "dividend reinvestment" plan; and

3. Sale of new shares to employees via some company savings or incentive plan of stock purchase.

The initial offering of new common shares of stock to current stockholders (the **preemptive right** of shareholders to maintain their proportionate share of ownership) may be required by the law of the state of incorporation or by the corporate charter. Even if not required, such a **rights offering** may offer an issue cost advantage to a corporation. The term "rights offering" stems from the issuance to present shareholders of rights that entitle them to buy new shares of common stock (or sometimes convertible bonds or convertible preferred stock) at a discount from current market price. Each shareholder is entitled to purchase the proportion of the new issue that corresponds to the proportion of his or her holdings of stock already outstanding. For example, suppose a corporation with 1,000,000 shares of outstanding common stock issues a rights offering of 100,000 shares. Each shareholder will receive one right for each share held, but 10 rights must be exercised for each new share purchased at the subscription price.[4] These rights have a value corresponding to the difference between the market price of the stock and the privileged subscription price, adjusted for the increase in the number of shares that the issue entails. To ensure complete distribution of new securities in a rights offering, the issuing firm may engage an investment banker (or bankers) in a standby arrangement that obligates the latter to acquire any shares not purchased by stockholders.

Dividend reinvestment plans, as a means of issuing new equity shares, are of relatively recent vintage. These plans simply require agreement by a current stockholder that the dividends declared by the firm will be applied to the purchase of new securities instead of being distributed in cash. The advantage to the shareholder of such plans is the avoidance of the reinvestment costs that might otherwise be incurred.

To make a public offering of securities in the United States, a company must first file a detailed registration statement with the SEC. The SEC reviews the statement and generally issues comments or asks for further information before declaring the registration statement effective, after which the securities can be sold to the public. The preparation and approval of the registration statement can be very time consuming. An initial securities registration can involve several

---

[4]For the reader who is curious as to how shareholdings that are not a multiple of 10 are handled, the answer is simple. The issuing firm may act as a clearinghouse for exchange of rights (or a market for the rights will otherwise emerge), facilitating the sale of rights by shareholders to other shareholders. Thus in the example above, a shareholder currently holding 12 shares might buy one new share and sell two "rights" to another shareholder, who holds 18 shares, enabling the other shareholder to acquire two new shares.

months of joint effort of company personnel, independent accountants, legal counsel, and underwriters and their counsel. Review by the SEC may take four to six weeks for an initial offering. Once securities are registered with the SEC, a listing for trading on a national securities exchange may usually be achieved without undue difficulty.

As we noted in Chapter 19, since 1983, firms can avail themselves of "shelf registration" procedures to "preregister" a debt or equity securities issue. Shelf registration allows the issuing firm flexibility in regard to both the amount and the timing of the securities offering. Also, under the shelf registration procedure the issuing firm need not specify a managing investment banking underwriter, thus creating greater competition among investment bankers.

THE SECONDARY MARKET FOR EQUITY SECURITIES

Secondary markets exist for many financial instruments, but the secondary market for corporate stocks is the largest in dollar volume and number of trades. Trading in the organized exchanges is dominated by equities in both dollar volume and number of trades. In the over-the-counter market the total dollar volume of bond trading exceeds that of equities, but more trades involve equities than bonds. Such secondary market dominance is not surprising in view of the fact that the estimated market value of outstanding equities exceeds $1 trillion.

The SEC regulates the secondary markets for securities under the statutory authority of the Securities Act of 1934. In addition to imposing disclosure requirements on publicly owned corporations, this statute charges the SEC with regulatory purview over the organized security exchanges, the over-the-counter market, investment banking firms, brokers, dealers, and investment companies. Security trading is also subject to state regulation and to "private sector regulation" by the organized security exchanges and the National Association of Security Dealers (NASD).

The Security Exchanges

There are two national organized security exchanges, the New York Stock Exchange (NYSE) and the American Stock Exchange (AMEX), accounting for about 80 percent and 10 percent, respectively, of all organized exchange trading (in terms of number of shares traded). The other 10 percent is accounted for by the eleven regional organized exchanges, the bulk of trading occurring on the Midwest, Pacific, and Philadelphia exchanges.

To have its securities listed on an organized exchange, a firm must meet the trading volume and disclosure requirements of that particular exchange. The most stringent requirements are those of the NYSE, followed by the AMEX. The largest corporations are listed on the "Big Board" (the NYSE), and smaller (but national) firms are generally listed on the AMEX. The regional exchanges list securities of mostly regional firms, but they also list some NYSE and AMEX stocks ("multiple listing" cases), and trading volume in the latter category generally exceeds that in the former. More than 2000 stocks are listed on the NYSE.

Particular securities are traded at a designated **post**, a location on the floor of the exchange. At each post, all trades are orally voiced (loudly) and recorded. Exchange members trade in a variety of capacities. Some act as **specialists** in a particular security or securities. (The specialist is charged with the responsibility for "making a market" in security—selling when others will not sell and buying when others will not buy.) Some members trade for their own accounts, and some trade for accounts of other members. Most members, however, trade for commission brokerage firms and thus perform a pure broker function.

The OTC Market

The trading of securities not listed on organized exchanges is conducted in the over-the-counter market (which is really mostly an "over-the-telephone" market). The OTC market is essentially a network of dealers who "make the market" in the various OTC securities. Dealers stand ready to buy any reasonable quantity of the security (or securities) in which they deal at the bid price and sell at the asked price. The dealer's gross profit margin stems from the spread between the bid and asked prices.

It is estimated that more than 14,000 various stock issues are actively traded in the OTC market. Such broad activity is made possible by an extensive and sophisticated communications network. Telephone and teletype facilities connect dealer trading rooms throughout the country. The National Association of Security Dealers Automatic Quotation (NASDAQ) system provides current bid and asked prices on a continuous basis for more than 4700 stocks (compared to about 1500 on the NYSE and fewer than 800 on the AMEX). These quotations are made possible by having dealers in regularly quoted securities input any change in bid and asked prices into a central computer. Dealers seeking current quotations on these stocks are readily able to access the computer memory, and all bids and offers (and names of dealers) for a given stock can be instantly displayed on a video device. In 1982 the NASDAQ National Market System—offering a number of advances in information and order processing—was launched.

The principal equity securities traded in the OTC market include bank stocks, insurance company stocks, and stocks of small, regional, and closely held corporations. There is also a great deal of OTC trading in stocks listed on organized exchanges. The trading of stocks listed on exchanges is referred to as the "third market" (organized exchange and OTC trading being the other two), and indeed, the dollar volume of such trading is about 10 percent of NYSE volume. There is also a "fourth market," in which institutions exchange securities directly without involving brokers or dealers, but it is of minor importance at present.

Trading in equity securities in the secondary market is dominated by contractual financial institutions, especially on the NYSE. It is estimated that institutions currently account for about two thirds of total trading (in dollar volume) on the NYSE. The growth in institutional dominance of the equities secondary market is a consequence of increased institutional ownership of equities, more frequent trading, and the fact that trades generally involve large blocks of stock. It is likely that the ability of the institutions to employ considerable analytical and information resources for purposes of security analysis has contributed to secondary market efficiency—the pricing of securities in accordance with informed perceptions of risk and expected return.

VALUATION OF EQUITY SECURITIES

The nature of returns on investment in equity securities differs in a number of respects from an investment in debt securities, including the following:

1. Equities have no fixed date of maturity; rather, they constitute perpetual-life investments.

2. Returns are more variable, since there is no contractual commitment to pay dividends each period as there is for the payment of interest.

3. The potential for capital gains and losses is generally much greater in comparison with debt security investments.

The periodic percentage return (r_t) on an equity investment is the algebraic sum of the dividend paid for the period (D_t) and the difference between the price at the end of the period (P_t) and the price at the beginning of the period (P_0), divided by the beginning price, or

$$\frac{D_t + (P_t - P_0)}{P_0}$$

Since there is no "payment of principal at the maturity date," the basis of equity security value is expected dividends. Although capital gains (and losses) affect periodic returns on equity securities, these price changes can be attributed to changes in market expectations regarding the magnitude of future dividends and to changes in market perceptions of the riskiness of the security or other factors affecting the market rate of discount applied to the expected future dividends to be paid. The price of an equity security can thus be viewed as the present value of all expected future dividends, discounted at an appropriate market rate of interest. The market rate of discount is largely determined by the market's assessment of the variability of future dividend payments; the greater that perceived variability is, the greater the discount rate will be. The discount rate represents the required market rate of return—what the security must yield to investors. An equity security will be priced (in equilibrium) to yield the required rate of return to investors.

The risk–return framework described in Chapter 15 indicates that equity securities, like all financial assets, will be priced according to expected return and their degree of "systematic" risk. (Recall that systematic risk is the incremental risk that a security poses for a portfolio—the portion of total risk that cannot be diversified away.) Thus for a given stream of expected future returns, the greater the variability of this stream relative to expected overall market returns, the lower will be a stock's price, and vice versa. In practice, this measure of market-related variability in returns is calculated as the stock's beta, as indicated in Chapter 15. A beta of 1 implies that a stock's systematic variability in returns will correspond to overall market returns. A beta greater than 1 indicates that the systematic variability of a stock's returns exceeds the degree of variability in market returns, and vice versa for a beta less than 1.

Capital market theory thus suggests that the greater the magnitude of a stock's beta, the greater will be its expected return (the lower will be a stock price for a given pattern and amount of expected future receipts). The theory also suggests that a stock's diversifiable, unsystematic risk is unrelated to its price (and expected returns).

Considerable empirical research has been conducted to test these postulated risk–return relationships for equity securities. Of course, empirical tests cannot include actual measures of investor expectations; rather, they focus on average returns over long time periods. It is supposed that such long-run average returns will approximate expected returns. These various studies indicate that, indeed, higher returns have generally resulted from holdings of higher-beta portfolios, but not to the degree predicted by capital market theory. Similarly, lower-beta portfolios are associated with returns that are somewhat higher than would be expected from the theoretical framework but smaller than returns of higher-beta portfolios. Thus the statistical evidence is somewhat clouded, although it offers general support for the theory.

Stock Market Efficiency

How quickly security prices adjust to reflect the "proper" risk–return relationship is a function of **capital market efficiency.** As indicated in Chapter 15, a financial market is characterized as efficient when financial asset prices continuously reflect all available information relevant to security values, as analyzed and assessed by knowledgeable individuals who buy and sell securities according to this analysis and assessment. Efficient markets are important to the economy because they allocate scarce economic resources in such a way that the economic utility of society is maximized. Three forms of stock market efficiency are postulated: weak, semistrong, and strong.

In its **weak** form, market efficiency exists when all information pertaining to future security price behavior that can be gleaned from past price movements is continuously reflected in current stock prices. (An implication of this is that "abnormal" profits—profits exceeding those commensurate with a security's risk—cannot be earned by "charting" past patterns of stock prices.) In its **semi-strong** form, stock market efficiency exists when all publicly available information is impounded in stock prices at all times. Much information relevant to security prices is, of course, not publicly available but is known only to "insiders." The **strong** form of stock market efficiency suggests that all relevant information, including "inside information," is immediately impounded into stock prices.[5]

There have been numerous attempts to empirically test the implications that flow from the various forms of the efficient markets hypothesis. In general, these studies find that stock prices are established in the capital market according to investor expectations regarding future returns from the stock and the volatility (risk) associated with these returns. It further appears that the information underlying the formation of investor expectations is impounded very quickly into security prices. This apparent high level of security market efficiency augurs well for the process of resource allocation in the economy.

Although the preponderance of the evidence supports the efficiency of the equity markets, there are a number of anomalies in security market returns that have appeared that do raise questions about market efficiency.[6] For example, the weak form of the efficient markets hypothesis implies that there should be no pattern to stock market returns. Yet there does appear to be a *weekend effect* in stock prices, whereby stock returns are consistently lower on Mondays and higher on Fridays than on other days of the week. In addition, there appears to be both a *January effect* and an *October effect,* whereby the returns from holding stocks are higher than expected in January and lower than expected in October.

Empirical regularities that are inconsistent with the semistrong version of the efficient markets hypothesis have also been found. For example, a number of studies have found that small firms have earned higher returns than large firms. Moreover this *small-firm effect* is concentrated in January. Further, there is evidence of a *low price–earnings effect,* low price–earnings ratio stocks obtaining higher returns than high price–earnings ratio stocks. If the small firm effect and

---

[5]Stock market behavior has been characterized as a "random walk" and postulations regarding its efficiency as "random walk theory." The term stems from the fact that information flows occur in random fashion, and if security prices continuously reflect all information (changing as new information becomes available), the path of stock prices will be a "random walk." For an excellent (and highly readable) account of random walk theory and related empirical studies, see Richard Brealey, *An Introduction to Risk and Return from Common Stocks* (Cambridge, Mass.: MIT Press, 1969). A rather entertaining treatment of this subject can be found in Burton G. Malkiel, *A Random Walk Down Wall Street* (New York: Norton, 1975).

[6]This literature is summarized in Douglas K. Pearce, "Challenges to the Concept of Stock Market Efficiency," Federal Reserve Bank of Kansas City *Economic Review* (September/October 1987), 16–33.

the low price–earnings ratio effect were related to the risk of those types of stocks, then this evidence would not be inconsistent with the efficient markets hypothesis. However, the observation that small firms have higher stock returns than large firms and that low price–earnings ratio stocks have higher returns than high price–earnings ratio stocks does not seem to be fully explainable by differences in risk.

Not surprisingly, the evidence on market efficiency is most mixed in the strong-form version of the efficient markets hypothesis. Research hypothesis on the use of insider information does not support the efficient markets hypothesis. Studies that have evaluated the stock market performance of legal insider trading have found evidence of abnormally high returns. In addition, trading strategies based on publicly available information on insider trading activity do appear to earn unusually high returns.

In short, while markets do, in general, behave in a manner consistent with the efficient markets hypothesis (especially in the weak and semistrong forms), there appear to be exceptions to the generalizations that markets are efficient. These exceptions are troubling to students of financial markets. More research is obviously required to determine whether these exceptions are statistical illusions and also whether they are large enough to have economic significance.

The 1987 Crash and Market Efficiency

The precipitous decline in the stock market on October 19, 1987, also has raised questions about market efficiency. On that day the Dow-Jones Industrial Average of thirty "blue-chip" stocks fell 508 points, or 22.61 percent, the largest one-day decline in its history. (It is interesting and perhaps significant to note that the decline occurred on a Monday in October.) A number of reasonable suggestions have been made regarding the cause of that decline. For example, interest rates had increased substantially in the few weeks preceding the crash. Moreover, there was growing concern about the "twin" (budget and trade) deficits and the international value of the dollar. Further, some observers have stressed the importance of computer-guided trading of stocks and of the growing use of financial futures in managing the riskiness of equity portfolios. (See the box on pages 503–504 for some other explanations.) It is significant to note that (as shown in Table 21.3) the market decline was worldwide and that the fall in stock prices in New York was considerably less than that in many other markets.

The October 1987 stock market crash may also be explained in terms of the efficient markets hypothesis. In an efficient market the current price of a financial instrument such as a share of stock depends on the stream of dividends that investors expect to receive in the future from holding the security and the required discount rate on the security (reflecting its risk). Increases in stock price result from increases in expected dividends or from decreases in the required

TABLE 21.3 October 1987 Changes in World Stock Prices*

Country	Percent Stock Price Change
Australia	−58.3
Hong Kong	−56.3
Singapore/Malaysia	−40.1
Mexico	−38.7
Norway	−29.8
United Kingdom	−26.1
Spain	−25.5
Switzerland	−23.4
Belgium	−23.2
West Germany	−22.9
Netherlands	−22.6
France	−22.0
Canada	−21.8
United States	**−21.5**
Sweden	−20.7
Italy	−15.5
Austria	−14.9
Japan	−12.6
Denmark	−12.6

*Percent changes between September 30 and October 31, 1987, local currency indexes.

Source: Paul Bennett and Jeanette Kelleher, "The International Transmission of Stock Price Disruption in October 1987," Federal Reserve Bank of New York Quarterly Review *(Summer 1988). 18. Data from Morgan Stanley Capital International. Reprinted with permission.*

rate of return. Conversely, decreases in price result from decreases in expected dividends or increases in the required rate of return.

This efficient market explanation of the level of stock prices (generally discussed in terms of the entire stock market rather than the prices of individual stocks) has been challenged with the argument that stock prices are too volatile to reflect changes in expectations of future dividends. In this excess volatility or rational bubble argument (frequently associated with research done by Robert Shiller[7]), fads and mass psychology play a significant role in affecting the level of stock prices. As a result, according to this argument, there may be lengthy

---

[7]Robert J. Shiller, "Do Stock Prices Move Too Much to Be Justified by Subsequent Changes in Dividends"? *American Economic Review* (June 1981), 421–436.

SOME POPULAR NOTIONS REGARDING THE CRASH OF '87

"Wall Street has supplanted Las Vegas, Monte Carlo and Disneyland as the place where dreams are made, where castles appear in the clouds. It was Pinocchio's Pleasure Island where children (and the adults whose bodies they inhabited) could do and have whatever they wanted, whenever they wanted it.

But now it's morning and the binge seems to be over. Many have hangovers. Many have worse. The jackasses are clearly identifiable. And the rest of us, who pretended not to notice, are left with the job of cleaning up the mess."

Robert B. Reich, *New York Times* (October 22, 1987)

"People are beginning to see that the five-year bull market of the Eighties was a new Gatsby age, complete with the materialism and euphoric excesses of all speculative eras. Like the Jazz Age of F. Scott Fitzgerald's . . . , the years combined the romance of wealth and youth with the slightly sinister aura of secret understandings."

William Glaberson, *New York Times* (December 13, 1987)

"We've been through quite a few years in which we felt we had reached the millennium, which was high rewards and no risk. We are now understanding that is not the case."

Peter G. Peterson, *New York Times* (December 13, 1987)

"Ultimately, we will view this period as one in which we made a very important mistake. What we did was divorce our financial system from reality."

Martin Lipton, *New York Times* (December 13, 1987)

"On Monday, October 19, Wall Street's legendary herd instincts, now embedded in digital code and amplified by hundreds of computers, helped turn a sell-off into a panic."

David E. Sanger, *New York Times* (December 15, 1987)

"Futures and options are like barnacles on a ship. They take their life from the pricing of stocks and bonds. When the barnacles start steering the ship, you get into trouble, as we saw last week."

Marshall Front, *Christian Science Monitor* (October 30, 1987)

"One trader's gain is another's loss, and the costs of feeding computers and brokers are a social waste."

Louis Lowenstein, *New York Times* (May 11, 1988)

"We probably would have had only a 100- to 150-point drop if it hadn't been for computers."

Frederick Ruopp, *Christian Science Monitor* (October 30, 1987)

"This (restrictions on programmed trading) will make it a market where the individual investor can tread without fear of the computers."

Edward A. Greene, *New York Times* (November 3, 1987)

> "Investors knew that stocks were overpriced by any traditional valuation measure such as price/earnings ratios and price to book value. They also knew that the combination of program trading and portfolio insurance could send prices plummeting."
> Anise C. Wallace, *New York Times* (November 3, 1987)
>
> "In my mind, we should start by banning index option arbitrage and then proceed with other reforms which will restore public confidence in the financial markets. The public has every reason to believe that the present game is rigged. It is. Many would be better off in a casino since there people expect to lose but have a good meal and a good time while they're doing it."
> Donald Regan, U.S. Senate Hearings, Committee on Banking, Housing and Urban Affairs (May 24, 1988, pp. 76–77).
>
> *Source: G. J. Santoni, "The October Crash: Some Evidence on the Cascade Theory," Federal Reserve Bank of St. Louis Review (May/June 1988), 18–33.*

periods when stock prices deviate from the prices that are consistent with the fundamentals. The October 1987 stock market crash is certainly consistent with the excessive volatility hypothesis, though it obviously does not prove the validity of that argument. There seems to be little question that the crash has intensified the debate about the efficiency of the stock market.

SUMMARY

The market for equity securities is primarily a secondary market. Although equity issues thus account for only a relatively small part of the flow of capital funds from surplus economic units to deficit economic units, the equity market is an important component of the financial system of any predominantly private enterprise economy. In such an economic system, ultimate ownership of corporate business is held by common stockholders—an aspect of considerable economic significance in a variety of ways. In terms of business financing, the very significant role played by internally generated funds (depreciation and retained earnings) can be viewed as possible only by acquiescence of shareholders (who forgo dividends to the extent of earnings retention). A capital base of equity ownership is also necessary for business borrowing.

The decision to use new issues of equity securities to raise capital funds is governed by a number of factors. One is the availability of internally generated funds relative to total financing needs. Such availability, in turn, is a function of a firm's profitability and dividend policy. Another key factor is the current market price of the firm's stock, which determines the cost of equity financing. Further, the cost of alternative external sources of funds (that is, interest rates) is of critical importance. The cost of borrowed funds, relative to equity funds, is significantly lowered by the deductibility of interest payments (but not of dividends) for federal income-tax purposes.

Both theory and most empirical evidence suggest that the equities market is a highly efficient market in which expectations relating to stock returns and associated risk determine stock prices and in which information relevant to such expectations is quickly used by investors. Certain anomalies have surfaced in recent years, however, including the 1987 stock market crash, which have raised questions about market efficiency.

QUESTIONS

1. In view of the relatively small proportion of the economy's flow of funds that is accounted for by new equity issues, why is the equities market considered to be such an important component of the financial system? Why are new equity issues relatively infrequent?

2. Define and compare "internal" and "external" equity financing. Is the existence of a well-developed equities market significant for the internal financing of business firms? Why?

3. Explain the following terms:
    a. Preferences of preferred stock
    b. Convertibility features of securities
    c. Callable securities
    d. Stock options

4. Discuss the nature of the various alternative procedures relating to a new issue of equity stock.

5. Describe the process by which an equity security price is determined in the stock market.

6. What is "stock market efficiency"? Why is it important to the economy?

7. Describe the nature and structure of the secondary market in equities.

REFERENCES

Brealey, Richard A., *An Introduction to Risk and Return from Common Stocks* (Cambridge, Mass.: MIT Press, 1969).

Garner, C. Alan, "Has the Stock Market Crash Reduced Consumer Spending?" Federal Reserve Bank of Kansas City *Economic Review* (April 1988), 3–16.

Lorie, James H., and L. Fisher, "Rates of Return on Investment in Common Stock," *Journal of Business* (July 1968), 291–316.

———, and M. Hamilton. *The Stock Market: Theory and Evidence* (Homewood, Ill.: Richard D. Irwin, 1973).

Malkiel, Burton G., *A Random Walk Down Wall Street* (New York: Norton, 1975).

Modigliani, Franco, and Richard A. Cohn, "Inflation, Rational Valuation, and the Market," *Financial Analysts' Journal* (March/April 1979), 3–23.

New York Stock Exchange, *Fact Book* (annual).

Pearce, Douglas K., "The Impact of Inflation on Stock Prices," Federal Reserve Bank of Kansas City *Economic Review* (March 1982), 3–18.

———, "Challenges to the Concept of Stock Market Efficiency," Federal Reserve Bank of Kansas City *Economic Review* (September/October 1987), 16–33.

Report of the Presidential Task Force on Market Mechanisms (Washington, D.C.: U.S. Government Printing Office, January 1988).

Robbins, Sidney, *The Securities Markets: Operations and Issues* (New York: The Free Press, 1966).

Santoni, G. J., "The Great Bull Markets 1924–1929 and 1982–1987: Speculative Bubbles or Economic Fundamentals?" Federal Reserve Bank of St. Louis *Review* (November 1987), 16–29.

Shiller, Robert J., "Do Stock Prices Move Too Much to Be Justified by Subsequent Changes in Dividends?" *American Economic Review* (June 1981), 421–436.

Teweles, R. J., and Edward S. Bradley, *The Stock Market Exchange,* 5th ed. (New York: John Wiley and Sons, 1982).

CHAPTER 22

Futures, Options, and Swaps

This chapter discusses three relatively recent types of financial instruments and the markets in which they trade. The three instruments—futures, options, and swaps—are important vehicles in the hedging of the risk inherent in financial transactions and are used by some market participants as a means to increase returns through speculation about the future prices of financial instruments. They are used most frequently to hedge against interest rate and currency fluctuation risk, though their use in hedging risk in equity markets has recently received wide publicity. This chapter initially provides an overview of each of these instruments and markets and then compares and contrasts their characteristics and their uses for hedging and speculation.

THE NATURE OF FINANCIAL FUTURES MARKETS

Futures markets involve transactions calling for delayed delivery; that is, the price is determined today, but delivery of the product occurs at some specified date in the future. More specifically, a futures transaction is one in which the purchase or sale of a standardized contract (a **futures contract**) on an organized market is accomplished now while delivery of the product purchased or sold takes place at some future date.[1] For example, an investor who contracts through the Chicago Board of Trade in August to purchase (or take delivery of) a futures contract in U.S. Government bonds for delivery in December is participating in

---

[1]For an excellent review of the financial futures markets, see Marcelle Arak and Christopher J. McCurdy, "Interest Rate Futures," Federal Reserve Bank of New York *Quarterly Review* (Winter 1979–1980), 33–46.

the futures market. Similarly, an investor who contracts in August to sell (or make delivery on) such a contract in December has entered into a futures contract. Note that the price (and the number of contracts) at which the item is traded is set at the time of the purchase and the sale (August), not at the time of delivery (December). As another example, through the International Monetary Market, an investor might purchase or sell a contract for British pounds for delivery at some future date.[2]

Development of Futures Trading

Futures markets have existed in agricultural commodities for decades. At present, trading takes place on organized commodities futures markets for a wide variety of agricultural products. For example, trading of corn, oats, soybean, soybean meal, soybean oil, wheat, barley, flaxseed, and rapeseed occurs among the grain products. In livestock and meat products, trading occurs in feeder cattle, live cattle, hogs, and pork bellies. In the food and fiber group, cocoa, coffee, cotton, orange juice, and citrus fruits are traded.[3] Reflecting increased investor interest, as well as greater price variability in commodities generally, the number and volume of commodity futures traded have increased substantially in recent years.

The development of organized trading in financial futures is quite a recent phenomenon. Trading in major foreign currency futures was started by the International Monetary Market in the early 1970s. Today, organized foreign currency futures markets exist for the British pound, West German mark, Japanese yen, and a variety of other currencies. The first organized market for interest-bearing financial assets was established by the Chicago Board of Trade in 1975 for the purchase and sale of futures contracts in Government National Mortgage Association (GNMA) pass-through certificates. Shortly thereafter, the International Monetary Market originated trading in 3-month Treasury bills. In addition to these financial instruments, trading of futures contracts now occurs in Treasury bonds, Treasury bills, Treasury notes, large-denomination domestic certificates of deposit, Eurodollar deposits, the Standard & Poor's 500 Index, New York Stock Exchange Composite Index, and a number of other financial assets. In terms of volume, these financial futures markets have been a great success. Participation now includes major financial institutions, as well as a number of nonfinancial

---

[2]The size of a contract, of course, varies among instruments. For example, the contract for 90-day Treasury bills on the International Monetary Market is for $1,000,000 of bills. The U.S. Government bond contract is for $100,000 of bonds, and the contract size for the French franc is 250,000 francs.

[3]Futures trading also occurs in both precious and nonprecious metals, including copper, gold, platinum, and silver, as well as in lumber and plywood. A recent and important addition to the commodities list is trading in oil futures. In addition, a large variety of other commodities are traded on a less active basis than those listed in the text.

institutions, and the volume of trading has been substantial. As shown in Table 22.1, trading in foreign currency futures markets exceeded 19 million contracts in 1986 while financial instrument trading exceeded 95 million contracts.

Participants in Futures Markets

Any individual or institution that is exposed to risk associated with fluctuating interest rates of financial assets or changes in the value of foreign currencies is a potential hedger in the market. Since many (perhaps most) individuals and institutions are exposed to such risk, the potential number of participants is quite broad. Certainly, the nation's major financial institutions offer a potentially fertile source of hedgers. And with the increasing importance of international commerce and the growth of the multinational corporation, the exposure to foreign currency risk has increased. Since many more people are familiar with interest rates and foreign currencies than with pork bellies, it seems that the potential group of speculators in the financial futures market, compared with the commodities market, should also be large. Given the wide spectrum of individuals and institutions with a potential interest in financial futures markets, it is not surprising that these financial instruments have expanded rapidly and have received considerable publicity in the financial press.

Futures Versus Forward Contracts

It is important to distinguish between the futures markets and the forward markets. In purpose these markets are quite similar in that they are used both by hedgers to reduce risk and by speculators to take risk in order to obtain large potential return. However, there are two very important differences between the futures and forward markets. One difference relates to the nature of the contract traded, and the other relates to the valuation of the investor's contract.

TABLE 22.1   Volume of Trading in Financial Futures, 1976–1984 (Number of Contracts)

Year	Financial Instrument	Currencies
1976	108,550	201,804
1977	604,622	393,234
1978	1,595,363	1,345,527
1979	4,570,694	2,003,746
1980	10,212,968	3,718,635
1982	31,251,497	8,264,391
1984	51,003,284	16,660,892
1986	96,886,878	19,061,077

Source: Commodity Futures Trading Commission, Various Annual Reports.

The **futures markets** are organized markets in which trading in a standardized contract takes place under rules prescribed by the futures exchange. Since trading is actually done with the "clearinghouse" of the exchange, there is no risk to market participants that the other party to the contract will default. Moreover, most participants in the futures markets do not plan to take delivery of the item purchased (or make delivery in the case of a sale); the purpose of the transaction is to shift risk, not to obtain (or transfer) possession of an asset. Instead of making or taking delivery on futures contracts, most participants "close out" their sale or purchase positions by entering into an offsetting position with the clearinghouse.

In contrast, **forward market** trading involves a much less formal set of rules and does not take place on an organized exchange. A forward contract is tailored to the needs of the participants and is an agreement between the participants directly. It is quite likely that buyers and sellers will take and make delivery on the contract. Before the development of the organized financial futures markets there was little forward trading in interest-bearing financial assets. However, there was (and still is) a great deal of forward trading of foreign currencies among the participants on the foreign exchange market to hedge their foreign currency risks.

The second important difference between the futures and forward markets relates to valuation and payment for the contract. In the forward market the gain or loss on the contract is realized at the maturity of the contract. For example, an individual who sold a contract in the forward market would realize a gain at the maturity of the contract if the value on the asset had fallen and a loss if the value of the contract had increased. In contrast, in the futures contract the contract value is "marked to market" each day. The daily gain or loss (based on the "settlement price" for the day) is transferred at the end of the day. As a result, at the time of maturity of the contract the only funds that are transferred are those from the last trading day of the contract. Although the total amount gained or lost from a forward and a futures contract is thus the same, the timing of that gain or loss is quite different in the two markets.

Futures Contracts: An Illustration

Tables 22.2 and 22.3 present information on selected futures markets. For example, Table 22.2 presents market prices for trading in the British pound, Canadian dollar, and Deutsche mark in the foreign currency futures markets on January 13, 1989. On that day an individual or business firm could have purchased or sold a contract for delivery of the British pound in March or June 1989. The price per pound established by the free interplay of supply and demand was $1.7568 for March delivery and $1.7418 for June delivery, indicating the expectation by market participants that the pound would decline in relation to the dollar during that period. Similar interpretations can be placed on the prices in the futures markets for the Canadian dollar, though the West German mark was expected to appreciate slightly.

TABLE 22.2   Prices of Foreign Currency Futures, January 13, 1989

Delivery Date	Price
British Pound	
March	$1.7568
June	1.7418
Canadian Dollar	
March	0.8331
June	0.8290
September	0.8249
Deutsche Mark	
March	0.5462
June	0.5515

TABLE 22.3   Prices and Yields of Selected Financial Futures Contracts, January 13, 1989

	Treasury Bonds (Chicago Board of Trade)	
Settlement Date	Price ($100,000 Principal)	Yield, %
March	$90-13	9.046
June	90-05	9.076
September	90-00	9.094
December	89-28	9.109
March 1990	89-25	9.120
June	89-22	9.131
September	89-19	9.143
December	89-16	9.154
March 1991	89-14	9.161
June	89-12	9.169
	Three-Month Treasury Bills (International Monetary Market)	
Settlement Date	Price ($1 Million Principal)	Yield, %
March	$91-85	8.15
June	91-81	8.19
September	91-79	8.21
December	91-70	8.30

Note: Prices are per $100. U.S. Government bonds are expressed as 32nds.

In contrast to the foreign currency futures market, in which only prices are quoted, the futures market for interest-bearing financial assets quotes both price and yield, although trading usually takes place in terms of price. For example, in Table 22.3 the price of the U.S. Government bond for future delivery up to June 1991 is specified as of January 1989. A contract for delivery in September 1989 could have been purchased or sold for 90 and 00/32 per $100 value as of that date; that is, a contract with a principal value of $100,000 could have been bought or sold for $90,000 (ignoring commission costs). The yield on these bonds for September 1989 delivery was 9.094 percent. Note that the prices established in the futures markets indicate that market participants in January 1989 were expecting an increase in interest rates. A similar explanation holds for the futures markets in 3-month Treasury bills, but the price quotation is in terms of hundredths rather than in thirty-seconds.

Buying and Selling Financial Futures Contracts

Participants in the financial futures markets place either a buy or a sell order for a standardized contract. The dimensions of the contract vary with the nature of the financial instrument traded. An International Monetary Market contract for 3-month Treasury bills for example, consists of $1 million par value of Treasury bills. The Chicago Board of Trade contract for the U.S. Treasury bond (the most widely traded futures contract) consists of $100,000 principal balance of bonds. Delivery dates also vary with the type of financial instrument.

Purchases or sales of contracts in financial markets are made on the floor of the relevant exchange through a futures commission merchant who is registered with the Commodity Futures Trading Commission.[4] The actual transaction is accomplished by members of the exchange at the "trading pit" through an **open outcry** system, in which potential buyers and sellers shout their offers. The seller's contract is not with the buyer, nor is the buyer's contract with the seller; rather, both contracts are with the exchange clearinghouse. To maintain the financial viability of the clearinghouse and thereby to allow buyers and sellers to participate in the market without fear of loss, the members of the clearinghouse must provide a margin (in effect a performance bond) for each contract, and their customers must in turn provide a margin. The size of these margins varies with the nature of the contract and the specific exchange, generally ranging between 3 and 10 percent of the futures contracts' face value.[5]

Most futures contracts are not settled before the delivery date of the contract.[6] Indeed, most participants in the markets do not intend either to take deliv-

---

[4]The Commodity Futures Trading Commission has regular authority over trading in both commodity futures and financial futures.

[5]The ability to obtain future delivery of $1 million par value of Treasury bills with such a low "investment" provides enormous leverage and potential for gain or loss to those speculating in financial futures markets. Traders in futures contracts are also required to post "maintenance margins" as the value of their contracts fluctuate.

ery or to make delivery at maturity. Rather, the market participants—either buyer or seller—terminate the contract when their speculative or hedging objective has been met (or when it is clear that the objective will not be met) by taking an offsetting position. For example, an individual who had bought a contract in January in 3-month Treasury bills for delivery in March could eliminate the obligation to accept delivery of the bills by selling a contract for delivery of the March 3-month Treasury bill contract.

Uses of the Financial Futures Markets: Interest-Bearing Securities

As we discussed above, the financial futures markets are used by two different groups for two different reasons. Hedgers use the financial futures markets to shift risk, and speculators use them to accept risk in their search for high returns. The ways in which each group uses the markets are discussed in this section. Since hedging in these markets is a more complex process than speculating, our treatment of hedging is necessarily much more detailed.[7]

Hedging

There are two basic types of hedges, the short (sell) hedge and the long (buy) hedge. The **short hedge** involves the sale of a futures contract and provides protection against interest rate increases (and thus lower security prices). A short hedge is used to protect against losses that would otherwise result from a rise in interest rates, as is the case, for example, when financial assets are held that are to be sold at some future date and when future borrowing is scheduled. The **long hedge** involves the purchase of a futures contract and provides protection against falling interest rates (and thus higher security prices). The long hedge is used to protect against potential losses that would otherwise result from a decrease in interest rates, such as planned future purchases of financial assets (and reinvestment risk generally). Both the short hedge and the long hedge are generally conducted in the financial instrument held by the investor and giving rise to the risk being hedged.[8] For example, if the investor held 3-month Treasury bills (the cash

---

[6]Usually fewer than 1 percent of all contracts are settled by delivery. Indeed, it is not unusual for some instruments to have no contracts settled by delivery in some years.

[7]Our discussion omits transactions costs. Naturally, any gains would be reduced by the amount of the transactions costs, and any losses would be increased. However, transactions costs represent a minor consideration for most activity in the financial futures market. Moreover, our purpose in this chapter is only to illustrate the uses of the market, not to calculate the exact gains and losses involved in individual transactions.

[8]A cross hedge also exists. This type of hedge occurs when the hedger purchases or sells in the futures market a security that is different from the cash asset held. For example, an investor may hold bankers acceptances for which there is no futures market. To hedge against rising interest rates, the investor may execute a short cross hedge in the Treasury bill market and rely on the usual high correlation among money market rates to reduce risk. Naturally, a cross hedge may be either short or long.

or spot market position), the short hedge would be conducted in the 3-month Treasury bill futures market.

The Short Hedge.   Assume that a savings and loan wants to sell its portfolio of U.S. Treasury bonds during the next few weeks but is concerned that interest rates may rise over that period and the price of the bonds may fall. The savings and loan protects itself from the effects of an interest-rate rise by selling T-bond contracts for future delivery (twelve in the example in Table 22.4). Later, after interest rates have increased, the savings and loan will have a loss in the cash market but a gain in the futures market. The savings and loan takes a position in the futures market (short) that is the opposite of its cash or spot market position (long). As a result, fluctuations in interest rates will cancel their effects on the value of the savings and loan's position; a gain in the futures market will (roughly) offset a loss in the spot market (and vice versa).

The Long Hedge.   The long hedge is generally used to reduce the risk of falling interest rates and thereby to "lock in" the currently high rates. For example, assume that a savings and loan, savings bank, commercial bank, or other institutional lender anticipates a large inflow of funds in the near future but that it also anticipates that when those funds become available, rates will be below current levels. The investor can lock in the currently high rates on securities by executing a long hedge. The mechanics of this long hedge are illustrated in Table 22.5.

Assume that the investor wishes to commit $1 million to U.S. Government bonds in the future. To lock in the current yield, the investor can buy ten June bonds futures contracts at 96-00. When the funds become available, the investor uses the $1 million to purchase the bonds at the price of 97-00. Note that the investor's expectations have been realized; rates have fallen from their January

TABLE 22.4 The Short Hedge

Cash Market	Futures Market
Now	Now
Holds $1 million Treasury bonds prices at 101-00 or $1,010,000 total	Sells 12 June T-bond contracts at 95-16 or $1.146 million total
Later	Later
Bond prices at 99-00 or $990,000	Buys 12 June T-bond contracts at 97-16 or $1,170,000
Net change: ($20,000)	Net change: $24,000

TABLE 22.5 The Long Hedge ———————————————————————————————

Cash Market	Futures Market
Now	Now
Decision to lock in high yield on $1 million principal bonds at 94-00	Purchase of 10 June bond futures contracts at 96-00
Later	Later
Purchase of $1 million principal balance bonds at 97-00 Opportunity Loss: $30,000	Sale of 10 June bond futures contracts at 99-00 Gain: $30,000

levels. At the same time the investor sells the futures contracts at 99-00. As a result, the investor has a gain of $30,000 on the futures transaction (the futures contract was purchased at 96-00 and sold at 99-00). This gain offsets the opportunity loss of 30,000 (the difference between the price of 97-00 paid for the bonds earlier and the price that would have been paid if the investor had bought the bonds at a price of 94-00). As a result, the investor has locked in the higher yield available at the time the decision was made to purchase the bonds instead of having to accept the lower yields available at the time the funds become available.

Speculation

For the financial futures markets to work effectively, market participants must include both hedgers and speculators. If the hedgers are to use the financial futures markets to shift risk, that risk must be assumed by someone. From this perspective the existence and active participation of speculators is quite essential for the workings of these markets. And in the financial futures markets (as in all futures markets) there is ample opportunity for gain (or loss). Speculators may gain through trading in the financial futures markets "by knowing better than the market what the future will be." Market expectations of future interest rates are embodied in the prices and yields established in the financial futures markets. If the speculator believes that the actual prices and yields will be different from market expectations, then an opportunity for gain exists if the speculator is correct and the market wrong. This opportunity for gain exists regardless of whether the speculator believes that prices will be above or below what the market expects. It is necessary only that prices vary from expectations, not that they rise, to create the opportunity for gain for the speculator.

Suppose that the speculator believed that interest rates would fall substantially in the future, whereas the market believed that rates would increase. In this situation the speculator could purchase a futures contract in the hope that the

---

INTEREST RATE FORECASTS: FUTURES MARKETS VERSUS ECONOMISTS

Futures markets prices may be used to obtain forecasts of interest rates in the future for a variety of types of financial contracts, including Treasury bills, notes, and bonds. How accurate are these forecasts? How does their accuracy compare to those of professional economists? The forecasts implied in futures markets prices are, of course, "free," while forecasts made by professional economists are costly, at least to their employer. A recent study provides evidence on these questions.

Michael Belongia observed on June 30 the 3-month Treasury bill rate implied by the December T-bill futures contract and on December 31 the rate implied by the June contract. (Additional information was provided from observations on the March futures contract from the previous September 30 and on the September contract from March 31.)[1] These data were then compared with actual T-bill rates on the day the relevant contract ceased trading. A separate set of six-month-ahead forecasts of the 3-month T-bill rate was generated from the nine economists regularly interviewed by the *Wall Street Journal* over the period December 1981 through June 1986. Comparisons of the futures market forecasts with those of the economists indicated that the futures market forecasts were no less accurate. This of course would seem to raise the question of how economists justify their large salaries. It might be that economists principally serve a public relations role, relating their firms to the external public, or it might also be that interest-rate forecasting is really not a significant part of their jobs. Economists may do many things that are of value, but one thing that they didn't seem to do is to forecast interest rates more accurately than could be done by anyone with access to the financial press and quotes on futures market prices.

[1] *Michael T. Belongia, "Predicting Interest Rates: A Comparison of Professional and Market Based Forecasts," Federal Reserve Bank of St. Louis Review (March 1987), 9–15.*

---

market expectation was incorrect. If rates did fall substantially and prices did rise substantially, the speculator would of course have a gain. But the real possibility for gain (as well as loss) would occur from the leverage that is possible in the financial futures market due to the low margin requirement.

Assume that after one day the market had revised downward its expectations of interest rates and thereby revised upward its expectation of the prices of securities. The decrease in expected rates could result from a more expansive Federal Reserve monetary policy, a decline in the economy, or a variety of other factors. In this situation the speculator could sell the contract at a higher price. However, the speculator could incur large losses if rates moved up rather than down.

As was mentioned earlier, the speculator can profit from the expectation of falling prices and rising rates, as well as of rising prices and falling rates. In the former instance the speculator would sell the futures contract (take a short position) rather than buy the contract (take a long position). The speculator would do so on the expectation that prices would fall and rates would rise. However, speculating in the financial futures market is not for the timid.

Uses of the Financial Futures Markets: Foreign Currencies Hedging

Hedging in the foreign currency futures market serves the same purpose as hedging in the interest-rate futures market—the reduction of risk. In the interest-rate futures market the investor hedges to protect against the risk associated with fluctuations in interest rates. In the foreign currency futures market, one hedges to protect against the risk associated with fluctuations in the value of currencies. Naturally, hedging in the foreign currency futures market is most necessary for businesses—financial and nonfinancial—that operate internationally. Such hedging may take the form of a short (selling) hedge or a long (buying) hedge.

Short Hedge. Suppose that a bank in New York has excess funds to invest in short-term securities. Suppose further that the interest rates on 90-day British government securities are attractive in relation to the interest rates on 90-day U.S. government securities—19 percent versus 6 percent, for example. There is no interest-rate risk if the investor buys 90-day British government securities and holds them for 90 days. However, the interest is paid in British pounds, not U.S. dollars, so the investor is taking the risk that the value of the pound might fall during the 90-day holding period (exchange-rate risk). Such a reduction in the value of the pound could reduce or eliminate the interest-rate advantage from the purchase of the British security. To reduce such foreign exchange risk exposure, the investor may engage in a short or (sell) hedge.

Details of the short hedge are illustrated in Table 22.6. The investor, the New York bank, bought 62,500 British pounds in June (cash or spot market) in order to purchase 90-day British government securities. At the same time the investor sold 62,500 British pounds for September delivery. Note that the futures price of the British pound was below the current price ($1.95 per pound for September delivery versus $2 per pound, an annualized discount of 10 percent), indicating that the market was expecting the pound to depreciate against the dollar.[9] If the bank had not hedged against the decline in the value of the pound, it would have incurred a loss in September at the time the British securities matured and the pounds were converted into dollars. This loss of $6250 would have more than offset the interest-rate advantage of purchasing the British securities. With the hedge, however, the investor makes an offsetting gain of $6250 on the futures

---

[9]In practice, the interest-rate difference between similar U.S. and British securities and the percentage difference between the cash or spot rate of exchange and the forward rate of exchange should be quite similar. (See Chapter 24 for an explanation of why this is true.)

TABLE 22.6 Short Hedge in Foreign Currencies Futures Market

Cash Market	Futures Market
June 1	
Buy 62,500 British pounds at $2 per pound = $125,000	Sell 62,500 British pounds for September delivery at $1.95 per pound = $121,875
September 1	
Sell 62,500 British pounds at $1.90 per pound = $118,750; loss = $6250	Buy 62,500 British pounds (September delivery) at $1.85 per pound = $115,625; gain = $6,250

transactions, so the currency risk was eliminated. Note again that the hedge reduced the potential return on the investment as well as reducing risk. For example, if the bank had not hedged its position and the pound had appreciated rather than depreciated as expected, the bank would have had the higher interest return plus the gain on the currency transaction. However, with the hedge that possible gain was eliminated.

Long Hedge.   A long (or buying) hedge occurs when the currency is bought in the futures market and sold in the cash market. Table 22.7 provides an illustration of a situation that would be appropriate for a long hedge. In this case we assume a multinational firm with a manufacturing facility in the United States and one in Britain. We further assume that the British firm has excess funds for a period of three months and that the U.S. plant has a deficiency of cash for operating expenses. Management would like to transfer funds from the British to the U.S. plant but is concerned about the foreign currency risk. In this instance the currency risk could be reduced by a long hedge—the British pound would be sold in the cash or spot market in order to make the transfer, and the British pound would be bought in the futures market.

TABLE 22.7 Long Hedge

Cash Market	Futures Market
June 1	
Sell 62,500 pounds at $2 per pound = $125,000	Buy 62,500 pounds for October delivery at $2.05 per pound = $128,125
September 1	
Buy 62,500 pounds at $2.05 per pound = $128,125; loss = $3125	Sell 62,500 pounds for October delivery at $2.10 per pound = $131,250; gain = $3125

As illustrated in Table 22.7, the multinational firm would sell 62,500 pounds at $2 per pound, obtaining $125,000 to transfer from its British to its U.S. manufacturing subsidiary. At the same time it would execute the purchase of 62,500 pounds for October delivery at $2.05 per pound. In September, when it was necessary to transfer the funds back to the British subsidiary, the multinational firm would buy 62,500 pounds in the cash or spot market at the now higher price of $2.05. It would thus have a loss of $3125 on its cash transaction. However, it would sell 62,500 pounds for the futures market for $2.10 and would have a gain of $3125. The gain and the loss would offset each other, and the firm would have accomplished its operating purpose without gain or loss from the currency transaction.

Speculation

As in the interest futures markets, the efficient operation of the foreign exchange futures markets depends on the participation of both speculators and hedgers. Speculators accept risk to reap large gains from betting that the market expectations will be incorrect. For example, suppose that the speculator observed that the price for delivery of the British pound three months hence was $2.10 per pound, and further suppose that the speculator believed that the pound would be worth more than $2.10 at that time. The speculator could purchase a contract for delivery of pounds three months hence. Since the contract size on the International Monetary Market is 62,500 pounds, the investor would pay $131,250 for the contract. However, the initial margin for the contract—the amount the investor must commit at the time of the purchase—would be only $2800. If the 3-month pound futures contract rose to $2.15 on the day after the transaction, the speculator would have a gain of $3125 ($134,375 selling price less $131,250 buying price), or more than 100 percent in a one-day period. Conversely, if the price of the contract fell to $2.05, the speculator would lose $3125, or almost 100 percent of the original investment.

If the expectation were for a decline in the value of the pound, the speculator could execute a sell order on the futures contract. In this instance, if the price declined to $2.05, the investor would gain $3125. Conversely, if the price advanced to $2.15, the investor would lose $3125. Again, as in the illustration with the interest rate futures, the speculator can make a profit whether exchange rates rise or fall.

Stock Index Futures

One of the most recent developments in the financial futures markets has been the establishment of contracts for trading stock indexes. The first such contract was established in early 1982 by the Kansas City Board of Trade for trading in the Value Line Average. Since that time, contracts have been created by other exchanges for trading in a number of different stock market indexes. For example, the Standard & Poor 500 Stock Index futures contract is traded on the Chicago Mercantile Exchange, the New York Stock Exchange futures contract is traded on the New York Futures Exchange, and a number of other stock indexes are traded on other exchanges.[10]

The stock index futures proved very successful after their introduction in 1982, with a substantial number of contracts traded. In fact, trading in the Standard & Poor Stock Index futures contract, the most widely traded stock index contract, totaled almost 1.5 million contracts in 1982. In addition, the Value line Index futures contract volume exceeded 350,000 contracts in 1982. By mid-1984, trading in all the various stock index contracts exceeded 10 percent of the trading volume for all futures contracts traded on all the futures exchanges in the country.

The stock index futures are quite similar in their operation to futures contracts in interest-bearing financial assets and foreign currencies. However, there is one notable and significant difference. For interest-bearing financial instruments and foreign currencies the contract specifies a deliverable grade asset suitable for making delivery at the termination of the contract. Hence the buyer of a T-bill contract agrees to take delivery of a 13-week Treasury bill with $1,000,000 face value, and the seller of the contract agrees to make delivery of that bill. In contrast, for stock index futures, no delivery is possible (while theoretically it might be possible to deliver the constituent parts of the Standard & Poor 500 Index, such an activity is not practical). The stock index futures contracts specify that settlement at maturity of the contract is made in cash. For the Standard & Poor 500 Stock Index, settlement is $500 times the value of the index at the maturity of the contract. If the S&P were 165, the value of the contract would be $500 × 165 or $82,500. For this contract the initial margin was only $2000 for a hedger (and $6000 for a speculator).

Stock index futures are also similar to other contracts in their functions: hedging and speculating. For hedgers who wish to shift risk, stock index futures would be useful to any investor who had a diversified portfolio whose returns moved together with market returns.[11] For speculators who wish to accept risk to obtain potential profits, stock index futures offer the potential to achieve substantial gains due to the great leverage that exists (as with other futures contracts).

A simple example may be useful in illustrating the use of stock index futures contracts for hedging. Suppose, for example, that an institutional investor is managing a diversified portfolio of stocks with a total market value of $100,000,000. Suppose also that the portfolio manager was satisfied with the qual-

---

[10]Financial futures based on indexes are not limited to stock indexes. For example, in 1985 the New York Coffee, Sugar, and Cocoa Exchange began offering futures contracts on the monthly consumer price index.

[11]The ability to use stock index futures to hedge against stock market movements is greater for institutions with diversified portfolios than for individuals with less diversified portfolios. The success of the hedge depends on the correlation between the returns on the portfolio and those on the market. An individual investor with only four or five stocks, for example, would likely have a portfolio that was not highly correlated with the entire market.

ity of stocks in the portfolio but was concerned about the impact of a general market decline on the value of the portfolio. In that case the manager could execute a short hedge in a stock index futures contract, such as the Standard & Poor 500 Index contract. The number of contracts sold can be illustrated with the use of Eq. (22.1):

$$\frac{\text{\$ Value of portfolio}}{\text{\$ Value of contract}} \times \text{Weighted beta of portfolio} \tag{22.1}$$
$$= \text{Number of contracts}$$

If the weighted beta of the portfolio (that is, the beta value of the stocks in the portfolio weighted by their relative importance in the portfolio) is equal to 1 (in which case the portfolio moves exactly with market movements), then the number of contracts is simply the ratio of the value of the portfolio to the value of the contract. If the value of the contract is $82,500, for example, then for this case the portfolio manager would sell approximately 121 contracts. However, if the portfolio were more risky than the market (with beta of more than 1), then the manager would have to sell more than 121 contracts. On the other hand, a defensive portfolio with a beta of less than 1 would require the sale of a smaller number of contracts.

OPTIONS

Nature of Options

Options represent contracts that provide their holders with the right (but not the obligation) to buy or sell a particular financial instrument at a specified price (referred to as a **striking price**) on or before a specified date (referred to as the **expiration date**). In contrast, futures contracts convey both the right *and* the obligation to buy a financial instrument at a specified price on or before a specified date.

A **call** option gives the buyer the right (but not the obligation) to buy an underlying instrument at a specified price (called the **exercise** or **strike price**) and the seller the right (and also the obligation) to sell the underlying instrument at the same price. For this right the buyer pays a fee to the seller determined by supply and demand conditions in the options market, referred to as a **premium.**

A **put** option gives the buyer the right (though not the obligation) to sell a specified underlying security at the price stipulated in the contract and the seller the obligation to buy the underlying security as with call. The premium is determined by the interplay of supply and demand in the options market.[12]

Like futures markets, options contracts are standardized contracts that trade on organized exchanges. Fulfillment of the contract is guaranteed by the market clearing corporation. Unlike futures contracts, however, buyers are not required

---

[12]Both U.S. and European options exist. U.S. options allow the holder to exercise the option at any time prior to its expiration date. European options allow exercise only at the expiration date.

to put forward a margin (since their loss is limited to the premium paid for the option), though sellers of put and call options must maintain margin positions.

Options are traded on a wide variety of financial and nonfinancial assets, including individual stocks, general stock market indices, foreign currencies, and Treasury securities of various maturities. In addition, options are traded on futures contracts. The Chicago Board Options Exchange trades options on individual stocks, stock indexes, and bonds. Options on stocks and indexes are also traded on the American Stock Exchange, the Pacific Stock Exchange, the Philadelphia Stock Exchange, and the New York Stock Exchange. The International Monetary market of the Chicago Mercantile Exchange trades options on foreign currency futures, while options on foreign currency themselves are traded on the Philadelphia Stock Exchange. Given the large variety of different types of options contracts, the discussion in this chapter will focus on the general nature of options, and on their various uses.

Option Payoffs

As was discussed above, a call option gives the holder the right (but not the obligation) to buy the asset at a prespecified price at any time before the expiration of the option. The buyer of the option is said to have a **long** position in the option and will benefit if the price of the underlying asset increases. On the other side of the transaction is the seller of the call option, referred to as the **writer** of the option. The writer of the option agrees to sell to the buyer of the call option a specified quantity of an asset (stock, bond, etc.) at the prespecified price (the striking price) at the option of the holder at any time until expiration. While the buyer of the call has the right but not the obligation to buy the asset, the seller has the obligation to sell the asset if the holder exercises the option. For accepting this risk the writer of the option obtains a fee (determined by the interplay of supply and demand in the market). The buyer of the option pays the fee.

The payoff on a call option is shown in Fig. 22.1. As shown in Panel A, the gross payoff from holding a call option increases as the price of the security rises. Up to P^1, however (which is the striking price), the holder of the option would not exercise it and would allow it to expire. (Up to that price the holder of the option has a loss equal to the amount paid to purchase the option and shown by the difference between the gross payoff and the net payoff.) It is important to note that the payoff for an option is a zero-sum game; that is, the gain (loss) to the holder of the option is the same as the loss (gain) to the writer.

The payoff for a put option may be analyzed in a similar fashion, as shown in Fig. 22.2. As the price of the security underlying the option falls (as shown in Panel A), the value of the put increases (after the price falls to P_1). Again, the difference between the gross and net payoffs reflects the price of the option paid by the buyer and received by the seller. While the buyer of the put gains from a fall in price, the seller (or writer) loses (if the price of the underlying asset falls below P_1).

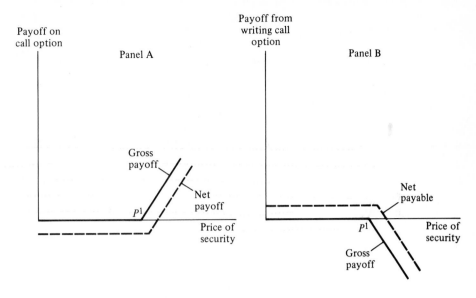

FIGURE 22.1   Payoff on Call Option

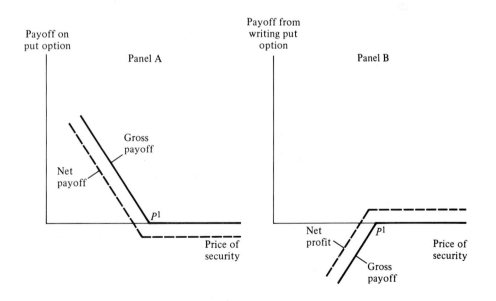

FIGURE 22.2   Payoff on Put Option

524   CHAPTER 22   FUTURES, OPTIONS, AND SWAPS

Options and Futures

Options and futures are similar in a number of characteristics and can be used (where both exist) as alternative strategies to achieve the same objective. If an investor wishes to gain from the anticipated increase in the price of an asset, he or she could buy a futures contract or buy a call option. Conversely, if the investor wanted to gain from the anticipated decline in the value of an asset, he or she may buy a put or sell a futures contract.

There is one very significant difference between the option transaction and the futures transaction that influences the desirability of using one or the other. With the options contract the holder cannot lose more than the initial price of the option—that is, the payoff to the holder is not symmetrical (as shown in Figs. 22.1 and 22.2). However, with the futures transaction the holder may lose substantially more than the initial investment—the payoff for a futures transaction is symmetrical. This difference is more significant for a speculator than for a hedger, though it is important for both.

Hedging with Options

Options may be used to hedge against the volatility of prices in financial markets in a variety of ways. For example, suppose that a large commercial bank had a portfolio of U.S. Government bonds and was concerned about a decline in their prices if interest rates increase. The bank could, as discussed earlier, sell a futures contract. If interest rates increased, the cash market value of the bank's bond portfolio would fall, but this loss would be partially or completely offset by the gain on the short position on the futures market or on a long position in a put option. A similar analysis could be done for hedging foreign currency risk or the market risk involved in a stock market portfolio.

SWAPS

Swaps are one of the most recent techniques devised to manage interest rate risk (and also for other purposes). First developed in Europe in 1981, swaps have exploded in volume since then and now total over $200 billion. In an interest rate **swap,** two firms that want to change their interest rate exposure in different directions get together (usually with the help of some financial intermediary) and exchange or swap their obligations to pay interest (just the interest payment obligations are swapped, not the principal).

Assume that one firm has long-term fixed-rate assets financed with short-term variable-rate liabilities. Further assume that another firm has short-term variable-rate assets financed with long-term fixed-rate liabilities. Both firms are exposed to interest-rate risk, but their exposures are quite different. The first firm gains

HOW A SWAP WORKS

This example is based on an actual transaction that was arranged by an investment bank between a large thrift institution and a large international bank; it is representative of many swaps that have been arranged since 1982. "Thrift" has a large portfolio of fixed-rate mortgages. "Bank" has most of its dollar-denominated assets yielding a floating-rate return based on LIBOR (the London Interbank Offered Rate).

On May 10, 1983, "Intermediary," a large investment bank, arranged a $100 million, 7-year interest-rate swap between Thrift and Bank. In the swap, Thrift agreed to pay Bank a fixed rate of 11 percent per year on a $100 million bond it issued in the Eurodollar market. Thrift also agreed to pay Bank the 2 percent underwriting spread that Bank itself paid to issue this bond. In exchange, Bank agreed to make floating-rate payments to Thrift at 35 basis points (0.35 percent) below LIBOR. Intermediary received a broker's fee of $500,000.

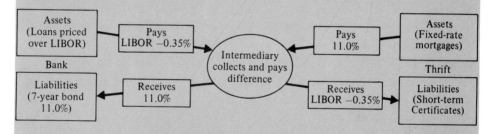

Twice a year, Intermediary (for a fee) calculates Bank's floating-rate payment by taking the average level of LIBOR for that month (Column 2), deducting 35 basis points, dividing by 2 (because it is for half a year), and multiplying by $100 million (Column 3). If this amount is larger than Thrift's fixed-rate payment (Column 4), Bank pays Thrift the difference (Column 5). Otherwise, Thrift pays Bank the difference (Column 6).

1	2	3	4	5	6
				Net Payment from	Net Payment from
		Floating-Rate Payment 1/2	Fixed-Rate Payment 1/2	Bank to	Thrift to
Date	LIBOR	(LIBOR − 0.35%)	(11%)	Thrift	Bank
May 1983	8.98%	—	—	—	—
Nov 1983	8.43%	$4,040,000	$5,500,000	0	$1,460,000
May 1984	11.54%	5,595,000	5,500,000	$95,000	0
Nov 1984	9.92%	4,785,000	5,500,000	0	715,000
May 1985	8.44%	4,045,000	5,500,000	0	1,455,000

The swap allows both Bank and Thrift to reduce their exposure to interest risk. Bank can now match its floating-rate assets priced off LIBOR, while the fixed-rate interest payments on its bond issue are covered by Thrift. At the same time, Thrift can hedge part of its mortgage portfolio, from which it receives fixed interest earnings, with the fixed-rate payment it makes to Bank. However, the floating-rate payment Thrift receives is linked to LIBOR, while its cost of borrowing is more closely linked to the T-bill rate. Since LIBOR and the T-bill rate do not always move in tandem, Thrift is still exposed to fluctuations in the relation between LIBOR and the T-bill.

Source: Jan G. Loeys, "Interest Rate Swaps: A New Tool for Managing Risks," Federal Reserve Bank of Philadelphia Review (May/June 1985), 19.

if interest rates fall, whereas the second firm loses if interest rates decline. Of course, if interest rates increase, the first firm loses, and the second firm gains.

For firms having this type of interest-rate exposure (for example, a bank and a savings and loan) the swap of interest payments allows each firm to benefit. The first firm substitutes fixed-rate liabilities for its variable-rate liabilities and thereby reduces its interest-rate risk. The second firm substitutes variable-rate liabilities for fixed-rate liabilities and also reduces its interest-rate risk.

The box above provides more detailed information on the mechanics of a swap. It deals with a swap between a thrift institution with a large portfolio of fixed-rate mortgages and a bank with a portfolio consisting primarily of variable-rate loans tied to London Interbank Offered Rate (LIBOR). On May 10, 1983, the thrift and the bank arrange, through a large investment bank, a swap transaction for $100 million at 7 percent. The thrift agrees to pay the bank a fixed rate of 11 percent per year, payable semiannually. This covers the 11 percent rate the bank is committed to pay on a 7-year bond. The thrift also pays the 2 percent spread incurred by the bank at the time it issued the bond. In return, the bank agrees to make floating rate payments to the thrift at 35 basis points below LIBOR. The investment bank earns a fee of $500,000 for bringing the thrift and the bank together.

The swap of the interest payment obligations reduces interest rate risk for both the bank and the thrift. Although interest rate risk is reduced, it is not eliminated. The floating rate payment that the thrift received is linked to LIBOR, where its cost of borrowing is tied more closely to the T-bill rate. Because the correlation between movements in T-bill and LIBOR rate is less than perfect, interest rate risk is not fully eliminated.

There are a variety of participants in the interest-rate swap market. Commercial banks and other financial and nonfinancial organizations use the swap market to reduce their interest-rate exposure. In addition, commercial and investment bankers, brokers, and dealers in the swap markets arrange swap transactions for others and earn income from creating a market for swaps. Major commercial banks in the United States play a particularly active role in the swap market, as shown in Table 22.8. In recent years an active secondary market has developed for swaps.

TABLE 22.8 Top 25 U.S. Banks by Notional Value of Swaps Outstanding (In Thousands)

June 1987 Rank by Asset Size	Notional Value	Bank	Notional Value June 1987	Notional Value Dec. 1986	Notional Value Dec. 1985
1	1	Citibank	$90,838,000	$66,071,000	$33,380,000
2	5	Chemical Bank	67,253,000	35,531,000	16,051,133
3	7	Bankers Trust	66,828,183	51,565,862	23,541,000
4	6	Manufacturers Hanover Trust	52,550,000	37,956,000	22,413,601
5	4	Morgan Guaranty Trust	50,780,600	40,193,800	21,450,700
6	3	Chase Manhattan Bank	40,051,644	21,948,194	9,994,300
7	8	Security Pacific National Bank	28,457,392	14,739,495	1,328,598
8	9	First National Bank of Chicago	19,381,043	17,722,840	8,458,000
9	2	Bank of America	14,472,000	11,489,000	7,367,000
10	15	First Interstate Bank	13,882,489	11,343,601	7,176,760
11	13	Marine Midland Bank	10,139,480	4,242,480	3,154,600
12	11	Mellon Bank	6,629,518	5,956,720	2,440,046
13	14	Irving Trust	4,898,851	2,437,141	502,400
14	10	Continental Illinois	4,615,319	4,923,875	3,322,362
15	16	Bank of New York	4,534,529	3,573,540	1,216,076
16	19	Bank of New England	2,319,680	1,412,192	312,333
17	22	Philadelphia National Bank	2,281,844	1,210,426	684,000
18	23	Harris Trust	2,117,715	2,109,170	1,603,700
19	20	Citibank South Dakota	2,100,000	945,000	0
20	21	Seattle–First National Bank	1,825,362	1,799,569	754,300
21	12	Bank of Boston	1,819,239	1,931,948	1,482,270
22	24	Comerica Bank–Detroit	1,540,716	1,565,716	1,168,000
23	26	Bank One Columbus	1,524,790	1,362,790	1,607,280
24	25	National City Bank	1,344,218	1,229,218	658,400
25	18	NCNB–North Carolina	1,228,709	689,942	10,000

Source: Steven D. Felgren, "Interest Rate Swaps: Use, Risk, and Prices," Federal Reserve Bank of Boston New England Economic Review (November/December 1987), 29.

SUMMARY

Innovation and change have characterized the financial markets in recent years. Reflecting substantial volatility in interest rates and stock prices, as well as in the performance of the economy itself, the financial marketplace has innovated a number of new financial instruments and markets that allow portfolio managers to adjust their risk position. The three financial instruments covered in this chapter—futures, options, and swaps—all provide market participants with ways to hedge against price volatility in different financial assets, notably fixed income instruments such as bonds, stocks, and foreign currencies. They also allow other participants to accept risk by playing a speculative role in the market. While they are similar in this regard, there are also important differences in their characteristics that make one more suitable than another in particular circumstances.

QUESTIONS

1. What is a futures market? How does a futures market differ from a forward market?

2. Does hedging in the futures market eliminate risk? Explain.

3. If the Federal Reserve "pegged" interest rate levels as it did in the 1940s, and if the world returned to fixed exchange rates, what would be the implications of these developments for the financial futures markets?

4. Imagine that you are an exporter of shoes to England and have sold shoes today on a 90-day open account. How would you use the financial futures market to hedge your currency risk?

5. What costs (both explicit and implicit) are associated with hedging?

6. Imagine that you are the manager of a pension fund with a diversified portfolio of stocks. How would you use the stock index futures contracts to hedge against the possibility of a decline in the value of your portfolio? What determines the number of contracts traded? If you traded this number, could you be certain of eliminating that risk? Explain.

7. What is a put option? What is a call option? How do options differ from futures in characteristics and uses?

8. What is an interest rate swap? How is it used?

REFERENCES

Arak, Marcelle, and Christopher J. McCurdy, "Interest Rate Futures," Federal Reserve Bank of New York *Quarterly Review* (Winter 1979–1980), 33–46.

Bacon, Peter W., and Richard E. Williams, "Interest Rate Futures: New Tools for the Financial Manager," *Financial Management* (Spring 1976), 32–38.

Booth, James R., Richard L. Smith, and Richard W. Stolz, "Use of Interest Rate Futures by Financial Institutions," *Journal of Bank Research* (Spring 1980), 15–20.

Burger, Albert E., Richard W. Long, and Robert H. Rasche, "The Treasury Bill Futures Market and Market Expectations of Interest Rates," Federal Reserve of St. Louis *Monthly Review* (June 1977), 209.

Chance, Donald, *An Introduction to Options and Futures* (Chicago: Dryden Press, 1989).

Chicago Board of Trade, *Options on Treasury Bond Futures,* 1983.

——, *An Introduction to Financial Futures,* 1983.

Corgel, John B., and Gerald D. Gay, "The Impact of GNMA Futures Trading on Cash Market Volatility," *AREUEA Journal* (Vol. 12, No. 2, 1984), 176–190.

Cornell, Bradford, and Marc R. Reinganum, "Forward and Future Prices: Evidence from the Foreign Exchange Markets," *Journal of Finance* (December 1981), 35–45.

Nix, William E., and Susan W. Nix, *The Dow Jones–Irwin Guide to Stock Index Futures and Options* (Homewood, Ill.: Dow-Jones-Irwin, 1984).

Poole, William, "Using T-Bill Futures to Gauge Interest-Rate Expectations," Federal Reserve Bank of San Francisco *Economic Review* (Spring 1978), 7–19.

Rothstein, Nancy H., *The Handbook of Financial Futures* (New York: McGraw-Hill, 1984).

Stevens, Neil A., "A Mortgage Futures Market: Its Development, Uses, Benefits Costs," Federal Reserve Bank of St. Louis *Monthly Review* (April 1976), 12–19.

CHAPTER 23

The Flow of Funds Accounts in the U.S. Economy

One of the most useful techniques for the analysis of financial markets is the flow of funds accounts. These accounts, published quarterly by the Federal Reserve System, are to a considerable extent a companion to the National Income Accounts published by the U.S. Department of Commerce. But whereas the National Income Accounts focus on the "real" or nonfinancial side of the economy by providing information on the Gross National Product and other measures of production, the flow of funds accounts focus on the financial side of the economy by providing information on lending and borrowing and other such financial transactions. Data from the flow of funds accounts allow the financial analyst to understand financial market developments more completely. The flow of funds framework may also be used to forecast future developments in the financial markets.

In this chapter we begin with a discussion of the concept of the flow of funds accounts, with emphasis on the use of the flow of funds accounts in understanding sources and uses of funds for different sectors. We then explore the types of information contained in the Federal Reserve's flow of funds data that assists in our understanding of the sources and uses of funds for the financial system and for particular financial markets within the financial system.

CONCEPT OF THE FLOW OF FUNDS

The flow of funds accounts in concept are quite simple: The economy is divided into a number of sectors that are thought to be homogeneous in terms of basic economic behavior; statements of sources and uses of funds for each sector are created; and an interlocking matrix of the sectors for the entire economy is constructed. The basic sectors encompass business, household, and government components of the economy. In addition, a sector statement for financial institutions is prepared. For each sector a balance sheet of assets, liabilities, and net worth at a point in time is constructed, as in Table 23.1.

Assets

The assets are divided into two categories: real assets and financial assets. These distinctions are of substantial importance in our understanding of the role of financial markets. **Real assets** appear on the balance sheet of only one economic unit. Examples are inventory, land, and plant and equipment. In contrast, financial assets—since they are obligations of their issuers—appear on the balance sheet of more than one economic unit. For example, the accounts receivable held by one business as an asset appear on the books of another business as a liability—accounts payable. Similarly, a corporate bond held by an individual as an asset also appears on the balance sheet of the issuing corporation as a liability. Real assets represent the fundamental production capacity of the economy, while financial assets represent an essential lubricant that contributes to the effective functioning of the economy. An economy's wealth may be measured by adding up its real assets (as expressed in the balance sheets of its participants) but not its financial assets (since financial assets and liabilities cancel out).[1]

Financial assets include corporate bonds, U.S. government bonds, municipal bonds, mortgages, common stock, preferred stock, and other types of financial instruments. These assets could be money market or capital market instruments, debt or equity, primary (direct) or indirect securities, and intermediated or non-intermediated instruments and could be acquired in either primary or secondary markets.

Liabilities and Net Worth

On the right-hand side of the balance sheet the two basic components are liabilities and net worth (both of which are financial in nature). The liabilities represent the funds that this economic unit or sector owes to other economic units. It is conventional to divide these debts into short-term (or current) and long-term liabilities. The liabilities of this sector, of course, are the financial assets of some other sector. The net worth account represents the difference between the value of the assets and the value of the liabilities. For a business firm, net worth is usually referred to as "book value."

---

[1]The most basic financial asset, *money*, for example, is an asset to the holder but a liability to the issuer. If the money is checkbook money—demand deposits, NOW or super-NOW accounts— it is a liability of the issuing bank. If it is government money—currency and coin—it is a liability of the government. In either case it appears on the books of two economic units, the holder and the issuer.

TABLE 23.1   Sector Balance Sheet, December 31, 1989

Real assets	10	Short-term liabilities	5
Financial assets	20	Long-term liabilities	5
		Net worth	20
Total assets	30	Total liabilities and net worth	30

Fundamental Equalities

The balance sheet for a sector or for an individual economic unit must balance. The sum of the assets must equal the sum of the liabilities and net worth. In Table 23.1 the assets (30) do indeed equal the liabilities (10) plus the net worth (20). However, for a sector (or for an individual economic unit) the amount of net worth need not equal the amount of real assets, and the amount of liabilities need not equal the amount of financial assets. In the example in Table 23.1, net worth (20) exceeds real assets (10), and liabilities (10) are less than financial assets (20). The balance of net worth compared with real assets and the amount of financial assets compared with real assets are very important magnitudes. Algebraically, the fundamental equalities for a sector are as follows:

[Real assets (A_R) + Financial assets (A_F) = Liabilities (L) + Net worth (NW)]

or

$$A_R + A_F = L + NW$$

However, for a particular *sector*,

$$A_R \neq NW \quad \text{and} \quad A_F \neq L$$

Of course, for the *entire economy*,

$$A_R = NW \quad \text{and} \quad A_F = L$$

More will be said of the significance of these relationships below.

To this point, we have a sector balance sheet at a moment of time, not a flow of funds statement. The balance sheet is static in concept, whereas the flow of funds statement is dynamic in concept. The flow of funds statement measures the sources and uses of funds for a sector over some time period. The transition from the static to the dynamic is accomplished by constructing a second balance sheet for the same sector at a different moment of time (see Table 23.2). The determination of the sources and uses of funds from the first to the second point in time is accomplished by comparing the two balance sheets (Table 23.3).

In measuring the sources and uses of funds as they appear in Table 23.3 we must stay within the fundamental accounting identity, in which sources of funds are

TABLE 23.2   Sector Balance Sheet, December 31, 1990

Real assets	20	Short-term liabilities	5
Financial assets	40	Long-term liabilities	15
		Net worth	40
Total assets	60	Total liabilities and net worth	60

TABLE 23.3   Sector Balance Sheet, December 31, 1989, to December 31, 1990

Uses of Funds		Sources of Funds		
Real assets (investments)	+10	Liabilities (borrowing)		+10
		Short-term	0	
		Long-term	+10	
Financial assets (lending)	+20	Net worth (saving)		+20
Total uses	+30	Total sources		+30

1. increases in liabilities,

2. increases in net worth,

3. decreases in assets,

and uses of funds are

1. decreases in liabilities,

2. decreased in net worth,

3. increases in assets.

In comparing Tables 23.1 and 23.2 we note that real assets rose by 10 and financial assets rose by 20, both increases representing a use of funds. These uses of funds were financed by an increase in liabilities of 10 and an increase in net worth of 20, both representing a source of funds. It should be noted, of course, that since the two balance sheets (Table 23.1 and 23.2) must balance, the "Changes in Sector Balance Sheet" (Table 23.3) must also balance. Total sources of funds must equal total uses of funds.

Activities

Each of the sources and uses of funds presented in Table 23.3 has been labeled to represent the nature of the activity. Hence the increase in real assets is termed *investment,* and the increase in financial assets is called *lending.* On the sources side of the statement an increase in liabilities is referred to as *borrowing,* and an increase in net worth is termed *saving.* If desired, the last account—saving—can be broken down further into income and consumption for an individual or profit after taxes less cash dividends for a business.

To both construct a more meaningful flow of funds statement and explain more completely the role of financial markets, we can divide the sources and uses of funds into real and financial accounts, as in Table 23.4. By this division, saving represents a "real" source, and investment represents a "real" use. In contrast, borrowing represents a financial source, and lending represents a financial use. For example, in Table 23.4 the sector we have been discussing has saving of 20 and investment of 10. Any sector such as this one with more saving than investment, $S > I$, is referred to as a **surplus** unit. If saving were less than investment, $S < I$, the sector would be called a **deficit** unit. Looking now at financial transactions, we see that total financial sources are 10 and total financial uses are 20. This sector is described as a **net creditor.** In contrast, if total financial sources were more than total financial uses, the sector would be described as a net borrower or **net debtor.**

We are now in a position to explain more fully the fundamental relationships that are applicable to the flow of funds accounts. As we do so, we must carefully distinguish what must be true for a sector from what must be true for the entire economy. From the perspective of a sector, saving need not equal investment. Indeed, it is the fact that *saving and investment are not equal for individual sectors that creates the role of financial markets.* Some sectors, such as households, are surplus sectors; others, such as businesses, are deficit sectors. Similarly, from the perspective of the sector, financial sources and financial uses need not be equal; the sector may be a net debtor or a net creditor. Yet since total sources must equal total uses, there is a fundamental relationship between real sources and uses and financial sources and uses:

1. A surplus sector (with saving greater than investment) must dispose of that surplus by lending, or repaying debt. The surplus sector must be a net creditor in the same amount as the surplus. In Table 23.4 the sector has a surplus of 10 (saving of 20 and investment of 10). It also has a net creditor position of 10 (lending of 20 and borrowing of 10). Hence the surplus sector is a supplier of funds to financial markets.

TABLE 23.4   Real and Financial Sources and Uses of Funds December 31, 1989, to December 31, 1990

Real Uses		Real Sources	
Investment	**+10**	**Saving**	**+20**
Financial Uses		*Financial Sources*	
Lending	+20	Borrowing	+10
Total uses	+30	Total sources	+30

2. A deficit sector (with saving less than investment) must finance that deficit by selling financial assets, or borrowing, where selling financial assets (calling in loans) is a reduction in these assets, and borrowing represents an increase in liabilities. (The reader may wish to change the numbers in Table 23.4 to prove the truth of this statement.) Hence the deficit sector is a demander of funds in financial markets.

From the perspective of the entire economy the relationships are quite different: Investment must equal saving (the fundamental identity of realized saving and investment). Furthermore, from the perspective of the entire economy, financial sources must equal financial uses. Yet it is not these equalities that are of interest to the student of financial markets. It is the basic inequalities at the sector level that are of interest, since it is these inequalities that create the need for intermediation and thus a role for financial markets.

The Household Sector as the Principal Supplier of Funds

Table 23.5 presents the sources and uses of funds for the household sector—actually, the sector is composed of households, personal trusts, and nonprofit organizations—for the first quarter of 1989.[2] Gross saving (prior to considering the depreciation of real capital assets held by the sector) amounted to $863.5 billion. Borrowing, which is represented by the net increase in liabilities (total borrowing minus repayment of existing debt), amounted to $278.1 billion, so total sources of funds for the sector amounted to $1,141.6 billion. On the uses side of the balance sheet, capital investment—principally homes and household durable goods—was $712.4 billion, and the acquisition of financial assets on a net basis

TABLE 23.5   Flow of Funds Account for Household Sector, 1989I (Billions of Dollars)

Capital investment	$ 712.4	Net increase in liabilities	$278.1
Residential construction	233.8	Gross saving	863.5
Consumer durable goods	459.4		
Other	19.2		
Net acquisition of financial assets	436.9		
Statistical discrepancy	−7.7		
Total uses	$1141.6	Total sources	$1141.6

Note: Data are for the first quarter, seasonally adjusted annual rates.

Source: Board of Governors of the Federal Reserve System, Flow of Funds Accounts, *June 2, 1989.*

---

[2]It is important to note that the flow of funds provides no data on subsections of each sector (types of businesses, for example) or on the gross changes in assets and liabilities. For example, borrowing is the net increase in liabilities between two time periods, which is the amount of new borrowing minus the volume of debt repayments.

was $436.9 billion. Since the sources and uses of funds for the sector must balance by definition, and since the data in Table 23.5, which are gathered by the Federal Reserve from a variety of sources, do not balance, it is necessary to add a separate item, called "Statistical Discrepancy," which is always a use of funds and which takes a magnitude and sign that are just sufficient to balance the sources and uses.

As revealed by Table 23.5, the household sector as usual was a net surplus sector in 1989; that is, its gross saving exceeded its gross investment in real assets by around $150 billion. Necessarily, then, the household sector had to dispose of this surplus as a net creditor in financial markets and did so by lending (acquisition of financial assets). Lending was $436.9 billion. Furthermore, as shown in Table 23.6, the household sector's lending was principally concentrated in the acquisition of intermediated or indirect securities. For example, the largest categories of lending—the building of pension fund reserves—involved the acquisition of indirect securities. In contrast, the acquisition of primary securities directly from the issuer was concentrated in debt securities (principally U.S. government securities), while holding of equities declined substantially.

Business and the U.S. Government as Principal Deficit Sectors

In most years the two principal deficit sectors (and thereby principal demanders of funds in the financial marketplace) are the business sector and the U.S. government. However, the relative importance of these two sectors as deficit units and thereby as demanders of funds varies substantially over time.

TABLE 23.6 Distribution of Net Acquisition of Financial Assets by the Household Sector, 1989I (Billions of Dollars)

Total net acquisition of financial assets	$428.9
Checkable deposits and currency	−41.8
Time and savings accounts at commercial banks and savings institutions	91.8
U.S. government securities	188.0
State and local obligations	10.8
Corporate and foreign bonds	−0.2
Mortgages	−8.7
Open market paper	−2.9
Money market fund shares	63.4
Mutual fund shares	3.6
Other corporate equities	−157.1
Life insurance reserves	4.3
Pension fund reserves	284.2
Other	−6.5

Note: Data are for the first quarter, seasonally adjusted annual rates.

Source: Board of Governors of the Federal Reserve System, Flow of Funds Accounts, *June 2, 1989.*

TABLE 23.7 Flow of Funds Accounts for the Business Sector, 1988 _____

Capital expenditures	$395.7	Net increase in liabilities	$100.6
Net acquisition of financial assets	52.6	Gross saving	366.8
Statistical discrepancy	19.1		
Total uses	$467.4	Total sources	$467.4

Source: Board of Governors of the Federal Reserve System, Flow of Funds Accounts, *June 2, 1989.*

Business. Table 23.7 provides data for 1988. In 1988 the business sector was a deficit sector (as it has been in most years) with capital expenditures ($395.7 billion) exceeding gross saving ($366.8 billion) by $28.9 billion. As a result, the sector was a large net demander of funds from the financial markets, with borrowing of $100.6 billion and lending of $52.8 billion.

Even in the few years when the business sector has been a surplus sector it has been a major demander of funds from financial markets. For example, in 1983 the business sector obtained over $150 billion from the financial markets. Most of these funds are borrowed, with very little new funds raised with equity. Table 23.8 provides the distribution by type of security of the net increase in liabilities for the business sector (note that equity issues are treated as liabilities).

U.S. Government. The U.S. government emerged in the 1980s as the major deficit sector, making enormous demands on the financial markets. This deficit position of the federal government is partly attributable to tax and expenditure policies that were implemented in 1981 and 1982, including a large reduction in personal and corporate income taxes. (Chapters 27 and 28 examine the macroeconomic implications of the policies.) Table 23.9 provides information on the financial market consequences of these policies.

Since the U.S. government expenses all expenditures as incurred (rather than distinguishing between fixed investment or capital expenditures and current ex-

TABLE 23.8 Distribution of the Net Increase in Liabilities for the Business Sector, 1988 (Billions of Dollars) _____

Net increase in liabilities	$100.7
Corporate equities	−130.5
Bonds	97.2
Mortgages	15.1
Bank loans	55.7
Other loans	26.5
Trade debt	−4.0
Foreign direct investment	41.6
Other liabilities	−0.9

Source: Board of Governors of the Federal Reserve System, Flow of Funds Accounts, *1988.*

**TABLE 23.9 Flow of Funds Account for the U.S. Government Sector, 1988
(Billions of Dollars)**

Net acquisition of financial assets	$−54.0	Net increase in liabilities	$ 137.9
Discrepancy	6.3	Surplus	−185.6
Total uses	$−47.7	Total sources	$− 47.7

Note: Data are for the fourth quarter, seasonally adjusted annual rates.

Source: Board of Governors of the Federal Reserve System, Flow of Funds Accounts, March 10, 1989.

penditures), the flow of funds accounts show only deficit or surplus and the financial consequences of the deficit or surplus. In 1988, as shown in Table 23.9, the U.S. government had a deficit of $185.6 billion (this deficit or negative surplus is the difference between its total receipts and its total expenditures). This, of course, required the U.S. Treasury to make large demands on the financial markets, with borrowing exceeding $135 billion. The treasury also reduced its financial investments by over $50 billion in order to pay its bills.

SOURCES AND USES OF FUNDS IN FINANCIAL MARKETS

As discussed previously in Chapter 19, the corporate bond market is one of the major financial markets in the United States. The supply of corporate bonds is dominated by nonfinancial corporate business. However, both finance companies and foreign issues account for a substantial part of the supply of new corporate bonds. Viewing the corporate bond market from a demand perspective (see Table 23.10), one can see that most corporate bonds in 1988 were sold pri-

**TABLE 23.10 Sources and Uses of Funds in the Corporate Bonds Market, 1988
(Billions of Dollars)**

Net issues	$144.1	Net purchases	$144.1
Nonfinancial corporate business	97.4	Life insurance companies	49.7
Finance companies	37.3	Private pension funds	26.5
Foreign	9.4	State and local government retirement funds	16.9
		Other insurance companies	7.7
		Household	−18.7
		Commercial banks	15.7
		Mutual savings banks	−2.3
		Foreign	19.7
		Other	28.9

Source: Board of Governors of the Federal Reserve System, Flow of Funds Accounts, 1988.

marily to insurance companies, pension funds, and foreign investors. The insurance companies and pension funds, in turn, obtained their funds by selling securities to the saving surplus sectors, while foreign purchases reflected high U.S. interest rates.

As discussed in Chapter 20, the mortgage market is an especially large component of the domestic financial market. Spurred by rising prices for homes and other real property, as well as the traditional heavy use of borrowed funds to purchase these types of assets, the increase in mortgages has developed at a very rapid rate. Total mortgages increased by $267.0 billion (see Table 23.11), which is almost double the increase in corporate bonds outstanding. Most ($196.4) of the mortgages were for the purchase of homes, and most ($195.7) were originated by households. In terms of the acquirers or purchasers of mortgages an examination of Table 23.11 reveals that, as with most financial instruments, most purchasers are financial institutions. In fact, more than one half of the mortgages were purchased by savings institutions and commercial banks. Saving institutions generally concentrate in home mortgages, whereas commercial banks are more active in the acquisition of commercial mortgages. Very few mortgages, as a percentage of the total increase in mortgages, are acquired directly by households or other basic nonfinancial sectors of the economy, with the exception of govern-

TABLE 23.11   Sources and Uses of Funds in the Mortgage Market, 1988 (Billions of Dollars) _____

Net change in mortgages	
Home mortgages	$196.4
Multifamily residential	15.0
Commercial	57.9
Farm	−2.3
Total	267.0
Borrowed by	
Households	195.7
Nonprofit institutions	2.3
Nonfinancial business	69.1
Other	−0.1
Total	$267.0
Acquired by	
Households	−11.0
Savings institutions	76.4
Commercial banking	74.3
Insurance	21.5
Agricultural credit agencies	6.8
Mortgage pools	91.2
Other	7.8
Total	$267.0

Source: Board of Governors of the Federal Reserve System, Flow of Funds Accounts, _1988._

ment-sponsored mortgage pools, which by 1988 had become the largest single buyer of mortgages.

USING THE FLOW OF FUNDS TO FORECAST FINANCIAL MARKET PRESSURES

The flow of funds accounts are historical in nature; that is, they record what has happened in the financial system during some specified past period. Although this information is useful in providing perspective and understanding of trends in financial markets, there are limits to the practical usefulness of historical data. Reflecting these limitations is the fact that a number of financial market participants have developed models that forecast future flows of funds in the financial markets. These forecasts of future flows of funds are then used to identify potential pressures in financial markets, such as a shortage of funds in the mortgage market or a particularly large supply of municipal securities relative to the anticipated demand for municipals. In addition, these forecasts of future flows of funds can be used to explain changes in the general level of interest rates, as well as changes in interest rate levels in one market (municipals, for example) compared with changes in interest rate levels in another market (corporate bonds as another example).

Most forecasts of future flow of funds movements begin with forecasts for the entire economy, including the strength of expenditures in the business sector for plant expansion and inventory building, as well as consumer purchases of houses and such durable goods as automobiles. Further, the strength of the economy is one of the major determinants of budget balance in the government sector, especially the federal government. Once expenditure patterns are anticipated, these expenditures are translated into predicted borrowing behavior. For example, a prediction of a large expansion in business plant and equipment expenditures would imply a large demand for business borrowing, especially for long-term funds in the bond market. A prediction of a large increase in household demand for home ownership would imply a large demand for single-family mortgage credit. Increasingly, financial analysts have also had to contend with the impact of inflation on credit demands. For example, if household demand for homes remains the same but the price of houses rises by 15 percent, then household demand for credit to finance house purchases would increase by roughly 15 percent.

Forecasts of the demand for credit must then be combined with forecasts of the supply of credit in order to anticipate financial market pressures. The supply of credit ultimately reflects the volume of saving of the household, business, and government sectors. However, since most saving is done by individuals, analysis frequently focuses on the saving behavior of the household sector. These saving-pattern forecasts are then turned into supply-of-funds estimates by making assumptions about the disposition of saving. For example, the financial markets would be affected differently if households chose to use their saving by acquiring savings deposits at savings and loan associations rather than increasing their contribution to pension funds, given the different investment patterns of these institutions. In addition, since most saving is used to acquire securities issued by financial institutions (an intermediated flow of funds) rather than to acquire primary securities directly, it is important to forecast the portfolio management practices of the major financial institutions. Finally, and particularly important in explaining the supply of funds available from commercial banks and other depository financial institutions, one should include some expectation regarding the posture of Federal Reserve monetary policy. For example, the anticipation of a stimulative monetary policy would imply a large supply of funds available from financial institutions, especially commercial banks. In contrast, the anticipation of a restrictive monetary policy would imply a smaller supply of funds available from commercial banks and other financial institutions. Once these forecasts of supply of and demand for funds in financial markets are prepared, it is then necessary to put them together to predict financial market pressures. Of course, after the fact, supply and demand must balance. However, the financial analyst can use these individual estimates to predict financial market pressures in individual markets and the changes in the flows of funds and in interest rates that will be necessary to make the total supply of and demand for funds balance.

A number of businesses, mostly financial institutions, prepare forecasts of the flow of funds. They include the investment banking firm of Salomon Brothers, the large commercial bank, Bankers Trust Company, and the Life Insurance Association of America.

SUMMARY

Flow of funds analysis provides useful information on the suppliers and demanders of funds in financial markets and on interest rates in those markets. In concept, the flow of funds accounts are quite simple. The economy is divided into sectors that are relatively similar in terms of economic behavior. Balance sheets are constructed for each sector at particular points of time. Changes in these balance sheets between different times are then calculated. These balance sheet changes then become the raw material for a statement of sources of funds for a sector and a statement of uses of funds for a sector. These statements must conform to certain basic identities for a sector, such as that investment need not equal saving nor lending equal borrowing, but total sources must equal total uses. Yet although the basic concept of the flow of funds is relatively simple, the flow of funds data, as published by the Federal Reserve, are both complex and exceedingly useful.

Because the economy is divided into basic and similar sectors and sources and uses of funds are constructed, it becomes possible to determine the surplus or deficit nature of the sectors, their principal financial liabilities as additional sources of funds, and their principal financial assets as other uses of funds. Moreover, by placing the sectors side by side and examining the interlocking nature of the flow of funds accounts, one can determine the role played in financial markets by different participants. Using the concept of sources and uses of funds also allows the forecast of future financial conditions. It is not surprising that many analysts of financial market developments view the flow of funds data provided by the Federal Reserve as indispensable to their work.

QUESTIONS

1. Under what conditions might the business sector not be a deficit sector? What would be the implications for interest-rate movements if business was a surplus sector?

2. If buying and selling of existing bonds and stock is not investment from a social perspective, of what importance is it?

3. What are the basic factors that account for the domination of financial institutions in the total flow of funds? Under what economic conditions may the share of funds that flows through financial institutions diminish?

4. Make a list of "real" assets, and compare that list with another list of financial assets. Why is it that society's wealth is the sum of its real assets, not of its financial assets?

5. If you were an analyst of financial markets, what information in addition to that provided by the Federal Reserve would you want?

6. Comment on the validity of each of the following:
   a. Saving must equal investment both for a sector and for the economy.
   b. Lending plus investment must equal borrowing plus saving for the sector but not for the economy.

REFERENCES

Board of Governors of the Federal Reserve System, *Flow of Funds Accounts: 1946–1975; Annual Total Flows* and *Year-End Assets and Liabilities* (December 1976).

Board of Governors of the Federal Reserve System, *Introduction to Flow of Funds* (February 1975).

Copeland, M. A., *A Study of Moneyflows in the United States* (New York: National Bureau of Economic Research, 1952).

The Flow of Funds Approach to Social Accounting (New York: National Bureau of Economic Research, 1962).

Freund, William C., and Edward D. Zinbarg, "Application of Flow of Funds to Interest Rate Forecasting," *Journal of Finance* (May 1963), 231–248.

Polakoff, Murray, et al., *Financial Institutions and Markets,* 2nd ed. (Boston: Houghton Mifflin Co., 1981), ch. 2, 25.

Ritter, Lawrence S., *The Flow of Funds Accounts: A Framework for Financial Analysts* (New York: Institute of Finance, New York University, 1968).

Taylor, Stephen, "Uses of Flow-of-Funds Accounts in the Federal Reserve System," *Journal of Finance* (May 1963), 249–258.

PART VI

THE INTERNATIONAL FINANCIAL SYSTEM

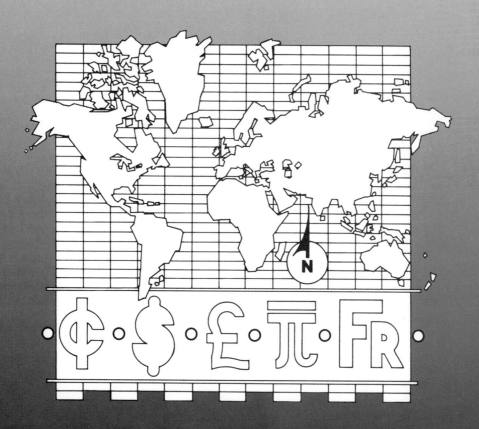

CHAPTER **24**

The International Monetary System

The scope and volume of international financial transactions have grown at a remarkable rate in recent decades, paralleling the huge increase in international trade and investment that has occurred since World War II. Such international financial transactions include payments for goods and services sold to and bought from foreign buyers and financial investing and borrowing across national borders. International financial intermediation has become a phenomenon of considerable significance to the world economy, and the international money and capital markets in which such external intermediation is accomplished have grown enormously in the postwar period.[1] During this period of vast expansion in international trade and investment the United States has joined the ranks of many other nations for whom international commerce is an integral and essential part of economic activity. Figure 24.1 depicts the huge expansion in U.S. international trade since 1950.

In this chapter we offer a survey of the international monetary-financial system. Considered initially are the essentials of the international payments system and the foreign exchange market. The principal elements of the process of exchange rate determination among the currencies of the world's nations are identified and discussed. Balance of payments measures, problems, and adjustments are treated in the context of their implications for exchange rates.

---

[1]International financial intermediation differs from domestic financial intermediation only in the fact that the economic entities having "surplus" funds (savers) and the economic entities in a "deficit" position (borrowers) are residents of different nations. (And, of course, different currencies are generally involved.)

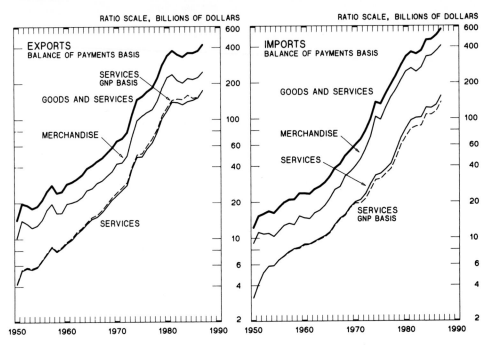

FIGURE 24.1   U.S. International Transactions, Goods and Services (Annually)

Source: Board of Governors of the Federal Reserve System. Historical Chart Book, *1988.*

FUNDAMENTALS OF THE INTERNATIONAL MONETARY SYSTEM

The fact that different nations have different currencies is the basic distinction between domestic payments systems and the international payments system. International trade and international borrowing and lending thus generally involve an exchange of currencies, as well as an exchange of goods, services, or financial instruments.[2] For example, if a Japanese firm exports goods to the United States, either the U.S. buyer must convert dollars to (sell dollars for) Japanese yen in order to make payment or the Japanese seller must accept dollars and subsequently convert them to yen. Similarly, purchasers of foreign securities must generally make payment in the currency of their denomination, and travelers abroad must exchange their home currency for the currencies of the coun-

---

[2]Currency conversion is not always necessary for transactions among residents of different countries. The U.S. dollar, for example, has "vehicle currency" status; in effect, it is an international currency that is often used for international trade and investment transactions without currency exchange taking place.

tries they visit. The **exchange rate** is the price of one currency in terms of another currency and is determined in the **foreign exchange market.**

The Foreign Exchange Market

International markets for foreign exchange exist for the purpose of buying and selling various national currencies. The buying and selling of foreign exchange (that is, foreign currencies) by governments, individuals, and firms is done for various reasons, including international trading, overseas travel by tourists, foreign investments, and speculation. The foreign exchange market is conducted by banks, foreign exchange brokers, and foreign exchange dealers through an extensive international telephone and cable communications network. Virtually every nation in the world has some type of foreign exchange market, but the bulk of the world's foreign exchange trading takes place in the large cities that are major financial centers: New York, London, Paris, Zurich, Amsterdam, and Rome. The most significant participants (in terms of trading volume) are the large multinational commercial banks of the United States, Western Europe, and Japan.

There are two basic types of foreign exchange transactions (and rates)—"spot" and "forward." (The foreign exchange market, in turn, can be viewed as consisting of a "spot market" and a "forward market.") A **spot transaction** involves immediate delivery (within one or two days) of the currencies being traded, and the rate of exchange is the "spot rate." A **forward transaction** involves a forward exchange contract calling for delivery of the currencies being exchanged at a fixed future date at a specified exchange rate. The latter is the "forward rate" of exchange. Forward contracts generally involve periods of one, three, or six months, but contracts in major currencies for other periods are available. There is an active forward market for only the world's major currencies, such as the U.S. dollar, British pound, French franc, Swiss franc, Japanese yen, and West German mark. (Foreign currency futures trading is discussed in Chapter 22.)

Exchange rates are generally quoted in a given country as the amount of the nation's currency (referred to as **local** or **home currency**) required to buy *one* unit of another nation's currency. An exchange rate is the price of currency expressed in terms of another currency. The exchange rate between the U.S. dollar and the French franc, for example, may be expressed as $0.125/FF in the United States and 8FF/US$ in France. When the French franc *depreciates* in relation to the U.S. dollar, it becomes cheaper in U.S. dollars; for example, it might depreciate from $0.125/FF to $0.10/FF over some time period. When the franc *appreciates,* it becomes more expensive in relation to the dollar, for example, an increase in the exchange rate from $0.10/FF to $0.125/FF. Note that the opposite holds for the other currency; the value of the U.S. dollar relative to the French franc appreciates when the franc depreciates and vice versa.

The fact that spot exchange rates fluctuate is the basic reason for the existence of the forward market in foreign exchange. The sale and purchase of foreign currencies for future delivery are accomplished by forward contracts (generally provided by banks) in which the exchange rate is contractually fixed. The size and economic significance of the forward market for foreign exchange stem primarily from the existence of foreign exchange risk, and the efforts of participants in international commerce and investment to reduce or eliminate such risk. **Foreign exchange risk** pertains to potential losses or gains from changes in exchange rates and results from unhedged **foreign exchange exposure**—principally the holding of foreign currencies or receivables denominated in foreign currencies and the owing of debt dominated in foreign currencies. Such foreign currency receivables and payables arise in the ordinary course of business for multinational corporations and international traders. Home currency values of foreign currency assets or liabilities change when the value of the foreign currency changes. When the foreign currency increases in value in relation to home currency, the home currency value of foreign-currency-denominated assets increases (a **gain** to the holder), and the home currency cost of foreign-currency debt increases (a **loss** to the debtor); the reverse holds for a decline in the value of the foreign currency.

The forward market can be used to hedge foreign exchange risk by, for example, selling forward the proceeds of foreign currency receivables and buying forward the amount of foreign currency needed to pay debts denominated in the foreign currency. Since the forward exchange rate is established at the time the forward sale or purchase is made, future changes in the exchange rate will not alter the amount of home currency to be received (from collection of a foreign currency receivable) or paid (for payment of a foreign currency debt).

An example may be useful. Suppose a U.S. importer buys goods from a British exporter, with payment of £100,000 to be made in 60 days. Assume that the current spot rate is £1 = $1.50; the home currency (U.S. dollar) equivalent of the debt is $150,000. If the pound were to appreciate against the dollar over the succeeding 60 days, the U.S. dollar equivalent of the £100,000 debt would increase (vice versa for depreciation of the pound). The importer can hedge this foreign exchange risk by entering into a forward contract with a bank to buy £100,000 at the forward rate of, say, £1 = $1.52. The forward purchase of £100,000 for $152,000 "locks in" the amount of the importer's obligation. When the debt to the British exporter is due, the U.S. importer delivers $152,000 to the contracting bank, collects £100,000, and makes payment as scheduled. The U.S. importer need not be concerned with the U.S. dollar value of the pound on that date or during the intervening 60 days.

Forward exchange rates for a given currency frequently differ from that currency's spot rate of exchange. If the forward rate exceeds the spot rate, the difference is a **premium.** If the forward rate is less than the spot rate, the difference is called a **discount** on the currency. For example, if the spot rate of the French franc is $0.12/FF and the forward rate for French francs to be delivered in three months is $0.125, then a forward premium of $0.005/FF (approximately 4 per-cent) exists for 3-month francs in the forward market. Why might francs be trad-ing at a premium in the forward market? The answer is that although forward rates (like spot rates) are determined by supply and demand, the "market" appar-ently expects the spot rate of exchange of the franc relative to the dollar to appre-ciate.[3] If the market's expectation was that the franc was likely to depreciate in relation to the dollar, forward francs would trade at a discount. Such expectations are impounded into forward exchange rates by the activities of hedgers seeking to avoid losses from exchange rate changes and by speculators seeking to obtain gains from such changes. (Chapter 22 offers additional discussion of forward and futures trading in foreign currencies.)

Exchange Rate Determination

What causes exchange rates of currencies to depreciate or appreciate in rela-tion to other currencies? The answer to this question is implicit in the fact that an exchange rate is a price. Like the price of any item (in a free market), the ex-change rate for a currency is determined by supply of and demand for that cur-rency. With supply unchanged, an increase in demand will push the price higher, and a decrease in demand will lower the price.

Figure 24.2 depicts determination of the "price" of British pounds (£) in terms of dollars. Note the effect on the exchange rate of shifts in the S and D curves. Note further that the *supply of pounds* to the foreign exchange markets is the *demand of dollars,* and the *supply of dollars* is equivalent to the *demand for pounds.* This is true because British pounds are supplied to the foreign ex-change market in order to obtain U.S. dollars and vice versa. Thus the demand for one currency is equivalent to the supply of the other currency.

Understanding exchange rate determination thus amounts to recognition of the various transactions that give rise to the supply of (and demand for) a given currency in the foreign exchange market. International trade is of paramount importance in exchange rate determination. When a country exports goods and services, this gives rise to demand for the nation's currency. U.S. exporters, for example, want to be paid ultimately in dollars, and foreign importers must ex-change their own currencies for dollars. (Note again that the demand for dollars is the supply of foreign currencies in exchange for dollars.) When a country imports goods and services, the foreign exporters wish to be paid in their own currencies. Thus U.S. importers must supply dollars to the foreign exchange market (their contribution to the demand for the particular foreign currency). When a coun-try's exports of goods and services are not equal to its imports, this aspect of

---

[3]Future spot rates, like stock prices, can only be predicted; they cannot be "known." Thus the forward rate is only a predictor of future spot rates, but it is likely to incorporate all publicly available information pertinent to a currency's value as analyzed and assessed by knowledgeable individuals. Forward rates are generally believed to be unbiased estimates of future spot rates.

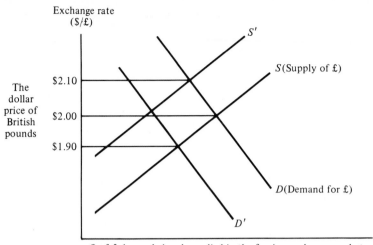

FIGURE 24.2   Quantity Q of British Pounds Demanded and Supplied in the Foreign Exchange Market.

international currency flows will tend either to raise (if exports are greater than imports) or lower (if exports are less than imports) the exchange rate of its currency relative to the currencies of its trading partners.

However, transactions other than foreign trade also give rise to supply of and demand for a nation's currency. These include expenditures of tourists, military expenditures abroad, gifts and grants to foreign governments or residents, payments of interest and dividends to foreign investors, and international investment (called "capital flows"). Investment in a country by foreign investors has the same effect as an export of the nation's merchandise; the demand for the country's currency is increased.[4] On the other hand, investment in a foreign country increases the supply of the investors' home currency in the foreign exchange market, just as does a home import of merchandise. The effect is the same for **foreign direct investment** (the extent of foreign ownership amounts to control of a productive facility) or **foreign portfolio investment** (purchase of domestic securities by a foreign national or purchase of foreign securities by a resident). Demand and time deposits held abroad by residents have the same effect as do direct and portfolio investments held abroad by residents. Demand and time deposits held in a country by foreign residents constitute demand for that country's currency, just as does foreign investment in that country.

Table 24.1 summarizes the items giving rise to the supply and demand for a

---

[4]The remarkable appreciation of the value of the U.S. dollar in the early 1980s was attributable primarily to large inflows of foreign investment to the United States; the U.S. had large trade deficits during this period.

TABLE 24.1   Home Currency Supply/Demand Effects of International Transactions _____

Supply of home currency to foreign exchange markets (uses of foreign exchange) is increased (decreased) by increases (decreases) in:	Demand for home currency in the foreign exchange market (sources of foreign exchange) is increased (decreased) by increases (decreases) in:
Imports of goods and services	Exports of goods and services
Purchases of residents traveling abroad	Purchases of foreign tourists
Investment abroad	Investment in home country by foreign residents
Remittances of interest and dividends to foreign investors	Receipts of interest and dividends from foreign investments
Gifts and grants to foreign governments and residents	Gifts and grants received from foreign residents

nation's currency in the foreign exchange market. Table 24.2 shows a summary of U.S. international transactions for recent years.

In addition to the items listed in Table 24.1, the supply of and demand for a nation's currency (and thus its exchange rate) are also affected by speculators' transactions in that currency and by "hedging" transactions by business firms and banks.[5] The magnitude of these amounts (and thus their influence on exchange rates) have increased substantially in recent years. The net of supply and demand from these many and varied transactions constitutes a nation's balance of payments, measures of which are considered to be very useful in analyzing the path of past, present, and expected exchange rates, and the next section of this chapter describes such measures. Before moving to that topic, however, we should note the principal economic forces underlying exchange rate (and balance of payments) determination.

Government Intervention.   Government intervention—usually by action of the central bank—in the foreign exchange market can and does affect exchange rates. All nations' central banks hold amounts of the currencies of other countries as part of their "official reserve assets." Such foreign currency holdings can be used to buy home currency in the foreign exchange market, thus boosting demand for home currency and (for a time) its value. Alternatively, central banks can buy foreign currencies with home currency, thus increasing the supply of home currency in the foreign exchange market and decreasing (for a time) its value. (Exhibit 24.1 describes the mechanics of such intervention in terms of a hypothetical Federal Reserve operation.)

However, the ability of a nation's central bank to affect the value of its currency is limited. The volume of trading in major currencies is huge—billions of dollars a day. Thus a very large volume of foreign exchange transactions must be

---

[5]Hedging techniques involve various means of balancing potential exchange losses with potential foreign exchange gains and usually incorporate both spot and forward market transactions.

TABLE 24.2 U.S. International Transactions, Summary (Millions of Dollars; Quarterly Data Are Seasonally Adjusted Except as Noted.[1])

Item Credits or Debits	1986	1987	1988
1 Balance on current account	−138,827	−153,964	−135,332
2 Not seasonally adjusted	—	—	—
3 Merchandise trade balance[2]	−144,547	−160,280	−126,525
4 Merchandise exports	223,969	249,570	319,905
5 Merchandise imports	−368,516	−409,850	−446,430
6 Military transactions, net	−4,372	−2,369	−4,229
7 Investment income, net	23,143	20,374	2,602
8 Other service transactions, net	2,257	1,755	6,404
9 Remittances, pensions, and other transfers	−3,571	−3,434	−3,531
10 U.S. government grants (excluding military)	−11,738	−10,011	−10,052
11 Change in U.S. government assets, other than official reserve assets, net (increase, −)	−2,000	−1,162	3,641
12 Change in U.S. official reserve assets (increase, −)	312	9,149	3,566
13 Gold	0	0	0
14 Special drawing rights (SDRs)	−246	−509	474
15 Reserve position in International Monetary Fund	1,500	2,070	1,025
16 Foreign currencies	−942	7,588	−5,064
17 Change in U.S. private assets abroad (increase, −)	−96,303	−86,297	−92,029
18 Bank-reported claims[3]	−59,975	−40,531	−57,493
19 Nonbank-reported claims	−4,220	3,145	−6,627
20 U.S. purchase of foreign securities, net	−4,297	−4,456	−7,474
21 U.S. direct investments abroad, net	−27,811	−44,455	−20,435
22 Change in foreign official assets in the United States (increase, +)	35,507	44,968	39,012
23 U.S. Treasury securities	34,364	43,361	41,703
24 Other U.S. government obligations	−1,214	1,570	1,351
25 Other U.S. government liabilities[4]	2,054	−2,824	−1,278
26 Other U.S. liabilities reported by U.S. banks[3]	1,187	3,901	−269
27 Other foreign official assets[5]	−884	−1,040	−2,495
28 Change in foreign private assets in the United States (increase, +)	185,746	166,522	171,726
29 U.S. bank-reported liabilities[3]	79,783	87,778	78,877
30 U.S. nonbank-reported liabilities	−2,906	2,150	3,778
31 Foreign private purchase of U.S. Treasury securities, net	3,809	−7,596	19,886
32 Foreign purchases of other U.S. securities, net	70,969	42,213	26,961
33 Foreign direct investments in the United States, net[3]	34,091	41,977	42,224
34 Allocation of SDRs	0	0	0
35 Discrepancy	15,566	18,461	16,548
36 Owing to seasonal adjustments	—	—	—
37 Statistical discrepancy in recorded data before seasonal adjustment	15,566	18,461	16,548

TABLE 24.2 *(Continued)*

Item Credits or Debits	1986	1987	1988
Memo			
Changes in official assets			
38 U.S. official reserve assets (increase, −)	312	9,149	−3,566
39 Foreign official assets in the United States			
(increase, +)	33,453	47,792	40,290
40 Change in Organization of Petroleum Exporting Countries official assets in the United States (part of line 22 above)	−9,327	−9,956	−2,909
41 Transfers under military grant programs (excluded from lines 4, 6, and 10 above)	101	58	86

[1]Seasonal factors are no longer calculated for lines 6, 10, 12–16, 18–20, 22–34, and 38–41.
[2]Data are on an international accounts (IA) basis. Differs from the Census basis data for reasons of coverage and timing; military exports are excluded from merchandise data and are included in line 6.
[3]Includes all kinds of depository institutions besides commercial banks, as well as some brokers and dealers.
[4]Primarily associated with military sales contracts and other transactions arranged with or through foreign official agencies.
[5]Consists of investments in U.S. corporate stocks and in debt securities of private corporations and state and local governments.

Source: Data are from Bureau of Economic Analysis, Survey of Current Business *(Department of Commerce).*

conducted by a central bank to affect foreign exchange rates. The amount of home currency purchases that can be effected by a central bank is limited to the amount of foreign currency it holds or can borrow. The central bank can theoretically create and sell all the home currency it wishes, but only at the risk of creating inflationary pressures as a result of such new money creation.

Nonetheless, government intervention is a very significant element in exchange rate determination. Indeed, for 25 years after World War II, such intervention was the central element in the world monetary system. While this exchange rate system (the Bretton Woods system, described later in this chapter) is now defunct, government intervention in the foreign exchange markets remains a key element in exchange rate determination.

Comparative Inflation and Interest Rates. Table 24.1 lists the *transactions* giving rise to a nation's sources and uses of foreign exchange. Numerous economic forces give rise to such transactions, but for our present purposes we need to note that the effects of *relative price levels* on international trade flows and *relative interest rates* on international capital flows are of special significance. Obviously, the demand for imported goods and services is greater (all else equal) when their prices (in home currency) are lower than domestic goods. It is equally obvious that demand for foreign financial assets is greater when they offer real, risk-adjusted returns that exceed real returns on domestic financial assets of equivalent risk. But it is also apparent that if trade and capital flows are unimpeded and the foreign exchange market is similarly free of government intervention, supply/demand forces will eventually eliminate such price and interest rate advantages of the foreign goods and financial assets. The increased demand for the foreign

EXHIBIT 24.1 ▪▪▪▪▪▪
The Mechanics of Foreign Exchange Market Intervention

Suppose that the Federal Reserve purchases dollars (in other words, sells foreign currency—most often Deutsche marks) in foreign exchange markets in an attempt to prevent (or slow) the dollar from depreciating.[1] To do this, the Fed must have some Deutsche marks, which it typically acquires either by selling some of its nonnegotiable DM-denominated securities to the Bundesbank or by borrowing DM from the Bundesbank in exchange for a DM-denominated account. Since both of these transactions are between central banks only, they have no impact on the size of either country's money stock.

The Fed then buys dollar-denominated demand deposits of foreign commercial banks held at U.S. commercial banks and pays for them from its DM deposits at the Bundesbank. This produces an increase in foreign commercial banks' reserve accounts at the Bundesbank and a decrease in their demand deposits held at U.S. commercial banks. On the other hand, for U.S. commercial banks, both their reserve accounts at the Fed and their demand deposit liabilities to foreign commercial banks have declined. Since U.S. commercial banks' reserves have fallen while West German commercial banks' reserves have risen, the U.S. money stock will decrease and West Germany's money supply will increase as a result of this foreign exchange market operation.

As this example of unsterilized intervention shows, the U.S. money supply has not been insulated from the foreign exchange market transaction. If, however, central banks do not want their foreign exchange intervention to affect their domestic money supply, they may sterilize its impact with an offsetting sale or purchase of domestic assets. Continuing the previous example, if the Fed does not want U.S. commercial banks to lose reserves as a result of its foreign exchange intervention to support the dollar, it can purchase U.S. government securities equal to the amount of reserves that banks lose, thereby maintaining the level of reserve accounts of the U.S. commercial banks. In this manner the negative impact of intervention on the reserves of U.S. commercial banks is exactly offset with no subsequent change in the U.S. money stock.

In a similar fashion the Bundesbank could neutralize the impact of the U.S. intervention on the West German money supply by draining the newly created reserves from the West German commercial banking system.[2] If completely sterilized, the foreign exchange operation affects neither country's money supply. Private portfolios contain fewer dollar-denominated securities and more DM-denominated securities, while the Fed's portfolio contains more dollar-denominated securities and fewer DM-denominated securities.

---

[1] Although the Federal Reserve is portrayed here as the initiator of exchange market intervention, the analysis would not differ significantly in the case of intervention by foreign authorities.

[2] The institutional arrangements for accomplishing this may differ across the countries; the exact means used are not important here. Moreover, if the Fed acquired DM (used to purchase dollars) by selling DM-denominated securities in private capital markets, the West German money supply would not be affected by the intervention activity, and the Bundesbank would not have to sterilize the operation.

Source: D.S. Batten and J. E. Kamphoefner, "The Strong U.S. Dollar: A Dilemma for Foreign Monetary Authorities," Federal Reserve Bank of St. Louis *Review* (August/September 1982), 7.

goods by home country residents corresponds to increased demand for the foreign currency and thus an increase in its value relative to home currency. Thus home currency prices of the foreign goods will rise as it takes more home currency to acquire the same purchasing power in the foreign currency. The elimination of the real interest rate differential for foreign financial assets is a somewhat more complex process but would also come about as the result of relative nominal interest rate and exchange rate adjustment.

According to conventional economic theory, two equilibrium conditions exist in free international goods and capital markets toward which economic forces drive exchange rates. According to **purchasing power parity** (*PPP*), the same collection of goods purchased with different currencies should have the same cost as measured in any one of the currencies. According to **interest rate parity** (*IRP*), in free international capital markets, real interest rates will be identical across all currencies.

The direct *short-run* implication for exchange rates of PPP is that a nation's currency will tend to depreciate in the foreign exchange market when its rate of price level inflation exceeds that of other nations and appreciate when its inflation rate is less than that of other nations. Over a longer term, exchange rate movements would thus tend to equal inflation differentials between countries. Also, in the short run, *IRP* suggests that relatively high nominal rates of interest attract capital inflows (and discourage capital outflows), thus boosting a high-interest-rate currency's foreign exchange value. The reverse holds for low-interest-rate currencies. In the *long run,* in a freely functioning market, relative interest rate levels are likely to be fully reflected in relative exchange rates and thus to exert little influence on the magnitude of capital flows. The relationship between exchange rates and interest rates is extremely important and is discussed in more detail later in this chapter.

Other Factors Influencing Exchange Rates.   In addition to relative inflation and interest rates, other influences on the supply and demand for foreign exchange include relative rates of growth in national income, expectations, and tastes and preferences. When national income rises, the level of spending for foreign goods, services, and travel is likely to rise also. Further, domestic producers have less incentive to pursue export sales when their home markets are growing. Thus the effect of a booming economy (when the prospering nation's trade partners are less fortunate) may be to weaken its currency!

Expectations also affect the demand for and supply of foreign currencies, sometimes in "self-fulfilling" prophecy fashion. A currency that is expected to increase in value is clearly more desirable to hold than a weak currency. Demand for the former "strong" currency by foreign exchange speculators, multinational corporations, governments, financial institutions, and other foreign exchange market participants will increase and demand will decrease (supply will increase) for the latter "weak" currency. Expectations are thus of great significance in international capital flows. Political factors also influence the direction and magnitude of capital flows (as they influence expectations regarding future currency values and safety).

Tastes and preferences for imported versus domestic goods and services are also important as an underlying factor in the demand function for foreign currencies. And, of course, government policies and restrictions play a highly significant role in most nations.

Measures of Balance of Payments Deficit and Surplus. In technical terms a country's balance of payments always "balances" because it is accounted for with the conventional double-entry bookkeeping model in which the sum of the debits (uses of foreign exchange) always equals the sum of the credits (sources of foreign exchange). This accounting equality corresponds to the economic identity of realized demand and supply (what is bought is identical to what is sold). However, these accounting and economic identities are not useful for evaluating demand and supply conditions for a currency, nor therefore are they useful for forecasting increases or decreases in the exchange rate for a currency.

Useful measures of a country's balance of payments can be developed by separating transactions that reflect fundamental economic uses and sources of foreign exchange (so-called autonomous items) and those currency flows that merely finance (or otherwise facilitate) autonomous transaction items (so-called accommodating or compensating transactions). Although there is disagreement about whether certain items are accommodating or autonomous, many foreign exchange transactions fall clearly into one category or the other. A "balance" in the balance of payments is computed as the receipts and payments of foreign exchange among some group of accounts that is considered to be autonomous in nature.

Exhibit 24.2 shows how certain widely used measures of the balance of payments are calculated. The **balance of trade** is simply the difference between exports and imports of merchandise. There is certainly no argument that these transactions are autonomous, since they reflect both a nation's appetite for foreign goods and its capacity to earn foreign exchange by selling merchandise to other nations. A **deficit** in the trade balance reflects an excess of merchandise imports over exports, and a **surplus** reflects an excess of exports over imports.

The **balance of goods and services** adds to the trade balance the net amount of payments of interest and dividends to foreign investors and receipts of interest and dividends from foreign investment, receipts and payments relating to international tourism, certain military-related transactions, and various other "services." When government and private gifts and grants ("unilateral transfers") are included, the **balance on current account** is determined. Figure 24.3 shows the trade and current account balances for the United States since 1950.

To this point, there is general agreement that these current account items are "autonomous" (rather than "accommodating"). However, there is a degree of ambiguity in the **capital account** category, which includes changes in items relat-

EXHIBIT 24.2 ▮▮▮▮▮▮▮
The Balance of Payments

Just like an individual or a corporation, a country produces a deficit when it spends more than it takes in. The nation (or individual or corporation) unavoidably must run down its wealth or borrow to finance that deficit. When a deficit occurs between countries, resulting from their trade and capital flows with one another, it is called a *balance of payments deficit*. In the balance of payments terminology, wealth is called *international reserves*. It is composed of gold, strong currencies that other nations are willing to accept, and special drawing rights at the IMF. The table below lists the main types of transactions involved in a nation's balance of payments accounting.

Economists distinguish between the balance of trade and the balance of payments, and they use several different but related measures of both of these concepts (see the table below). The official settlements balance is the one meant when references are made to the balance of payments. It measures changes in official reserve assets and short-term capital among governments.

A Nation's RECEIPTS	less	Its PAYMENTS	equal	The Nation's BALANCE OF PAYMENTS[1]
EXPORTS of Merchandise		IMPORTS of Merchandise		
Services		Services		Balance of Trade
Private and government aid		Private and government aid		Balance of Goods and Services
CAPITAL INFLOWS From Investment Government borrowing Long-term private borrowing		CAPITAL OUTFLOWS From Investment Government lending Long-term private lending		Balance on Current Account
Short-term private borrowing Liquid Nonliquid		Short-term private lending Liquid Nonliquid		Basic Balance[2]
SALES of Reserves		PURCHASES of Reserves		Official Settlements Balance

[1]Each balance in this table is a cumulative measure of all the items above it.
[2]The basic balance is also known as the balance on current and long-term capital account.

Source: John H. Boyd, David S. Dahl, and Carolyn P. Line, "A Primer on the International Monetary Fund," Federal Reserve Bank of Minneapolis *Quarterly Review* (Summer 1983), 7.

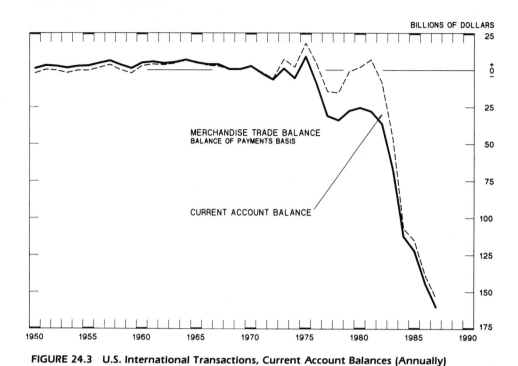

FIGURE 24.3   U.S. International Transactions, Current Account Balances (Annually)

Source: Board of Governors of the Federal Reserve System, Historical Chart Book, *1988.*

ing to foreign ownership of domestic assets and domestic ownership of foreign assets (capital movements). The **balance on capital account** does not include current account items but only short-term and long-term capital movements. The **basic balance,** which adds net changes in long-term (but not short-term) capital movements to the current account balance, is one view of a nation's fundamental balance of payments. The basic balance excludes private short-term capital movements (a large portion of which are changes in ownership of demand and time deposits) on the grounds that these transactions largely constitute financing of autonomous flows. For example, an oil-exporting nation may deposit dollars received from a sale to a U.S. importer in a time deposit in a New York bank. The "autonomous" transaction is the U.S. oil import, and the increase in foreign ownership of U.S. bank deposits is accommodating. Some short-term capital movements, however, are not accommodating but may be autonomous investment resulting from current or expected economic developments (interest rate or exchange rate changes). To the extent that the latter types of short-term capital transactions exist in significant magnitude, the basic balance is suspect as a fundamental measure of a country's balance of payments position.

    Capital movements can significantly affect a nation's balance of payments and thus the exchange rate for its currency. From World War I until recent years

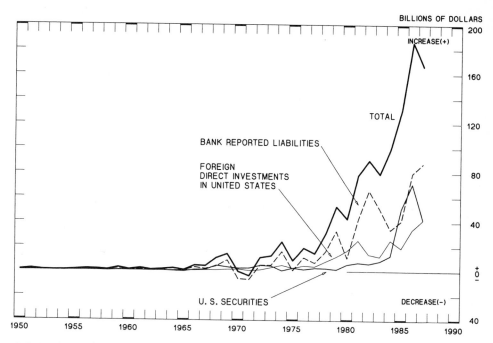

FIGURE 24.4   U.S. International Transactions, Changes in Foreign Private Assets in United States (Annually)

Source: Board of Governors of the Federal Reserve System, Historical Chart Book, 1988.

the United States was a "capital exporter"—investing more abroad than was invested in this country by foreign residents. However, foreign investment in the United States has increased dramatically in recent years (see Fig. 24.4) as this country has moved from creditor to debtor status as a nation. Such capital inflows served to "finance" (to a large degree) the huge current account deficits of the United States in the period since 1975. (Net capital inflows exceeded $110 billion in 1983–1984 alone.)

What is called the "official settlements balance" in Fig. 24.2 is the algebraic sum of the basic balance and net private short-term capital movements (inflows less outflows). The official settlements balance, or "overall balance," of a nation corresponds to the amount (ignoring statistical discrepancies) of the change in official reserve assets of that nation for the given period. **Official reserve assets** (also called "foreign exchange reserves") are composed primarily of the national government's holdings of convertible foreign currencies (currencies that can be readily exchanged for other currencies) and gold. (Private sector holdings are not included in official reserves.) The fact that the algebraic sum of the current and capital accounts equals the change in reserve assets stems from the relationship between the various balance of payments accounts and the supply and demand for foreign exchange.

When a nation experiences a **surplus on current account,** it is earning more foreign exchange from the transactions included in these accounts (mostly international trade in goods and services) than it is using for these transactions. Alternatively stated, the quantity of the nation's home currency demanded in the foreign exchange market for current account transactions exceeds the quantity of home currency supplied (in exchange for foreign currencies) for these transactions. Thus a current account surplus (by itself) necessarily results in a net increase in foreign exchange holdings for the surplus country. If this nation also has a **surplus on capital account** (resulting in an overall balance of payments surplus), its holdings of foreign exchange are further increased. This overall increase in foreign exchange holdings (a surplus on the official settlements balance) is reflected in a corresponding increase in foreign exchange reserves. The reverse would hold for an overall balance of payments *deficit;* official reserves will decrease (the deficit must be "financed"). By definition the net change in a nation's foreign exchange reserves must equal its overall balance.

There are two "lines of defense" for a nation that is experiencing a deficit in its current account transactions: capital account transactions and official reserves. In effect, a country can, for a time, finance a current account deficit by increasing its liabilities to foreigners, decreasing financial claims on foreigners, decreasing foreign investment, or decreasing official reserves. A nation enjoying a current account surplus may "use" the surplus to lend to other countries (run a capital account deficit), add to its foreign exchange reserves, or some combination thereof. In both cases, however, economic forces impose limits on the duration of such cases. A current account deficit nation will eventually exhaust its official reserve holdings and encounter limits to its borrowing capacity. A current account surplus nation is unlikely to retain indefinitely the capacity or appetite to hoard foreign exchange reserves and accumulate financial claims against other nations. Prolonged imbalance in a nation's balance of payments results in appreciation or depreciation of that nation's currency in the foreign exchange market. Such change in currency values alters trade and capital flows in ways that eventually restore balance of payments equilibrium.

Analysis of the balance of payments position of a nation varies according to its exchange rate system. This is true because the nature of the adjustment process for imbalances in the balance of payments differs depending on whether the affected nation is on a fixed or flexible exchange-rate regime. Thus a discussion of the difference between fixed and flexible exchange-rate systems is now appropriate, and the following section offers such a description in a historical context.

MODERN EXCHANGE RATE SYSTEMS

A **fixed-exchange-rate system** exists when nations seek to keep exchange rates for currencies approximately constant. During the era of the international gold standard (approximately 1870–1914), currencies were convertible into gold, and gold flowed freely across international boundaries. The effect was a system in which exchange rates were kept fixed (within boundaries termed the "gold export" point and the "gold import" point) because each currency unit was defined in terms of gold, and international gold flows kept exchange rates among currencies in line with relative gold equivalents. Balance of payments "equilibrium" was supposed to prevail under the international gold standard because of the following scenario. Nations having trade surpluses gained gold, and their money supply increased. The increase in the money supply resulted in higher prices for the nation's goods and services, thus reducing exports and increasing imports until the surplus was eliminated. Nations having trade deficits experienced a gold outflow, a decline in the money supply and in prices, which spurred exports and discouraged imports to the point of eliminating the trade deficit. This "equilibrating specie flow price mechanism" obviously presumes totally flexible prices or else a high tolerance for unemployment (the consequence of a declining money stock if prices *don't* fall) on the part of deficit nations.

World War I destroyed the international gold standard, and the Great Depression of the 1930s aborted attempts to restore it. The scope of this book does not warrant an analysis of this turbulent period in international finance, but the effect was to make the world's nations eager for an orderly system of international exchange rates after World War II. A structure aimed at achieving such a system was developed in an international conference held at Bretton Woods, New Hampshire, in 1944. The **Bretton Woods system** was a gold exchange standard in which currency values were defined in terms of gold (at par, or "parity," value), but gold flows were limited to official (central bank) transactions. The U.S. dollar played a central role in the Bretton Woods system. It was a "reserve currency"—dollars became the most important part of official reserves—and the values of the currencies of International Monetary Fund member nations were defined in dollars as well as in gold. The Bretton Woods agreement was intended to develop a system of "stable but adjustable exchange rates" that would facilitate the recovery of international trade and investment after the war.

The Bretton Woods System

Under the fixed-exchange-rate regime established at Bretton Woods a nation's central bank held amounts of monetary gold and currencies of other nations (especially U.S. dollars) as "official reserves" in order to be able to defend the parity value of its own currency. The Bretton Woods agreement allowed for a "parity band" of ±1 percent in which a currency's value could fluctuate. When the home currency's value in the foreign exchange market dropped below the parity value by more than 1 percent, a nation's monetary authority was expected to exchange reserve assets for its home currency in the foreign exchange market. The increased demand for home currency raises its "price" relative to other currencies. Similarly, when the value of a nation's currency rose above parity by more than 1 percent, its central bank was expected to lower the exchange rate by selling its currency for foreign currencies.[6] This increase in supply of the home currency would lower its value in the foreign exchange market. In addition to such foreign exchange market intervention, nations could seek to protect the parity value of their currency by pursuing economic policies aimed at achieving balance of payments equilibrium.

The International Monetary Fund.   The most important institution established by the Bretton Woods charter was the **International Monetary Fund** (IMF). The IMF began operations in 1947. Its original funding was provided by contributions of member nations in gold and their own currencies. Each member was assessed a contribution quota (and voting power) according to its relative significance in world trade. Insofar as "enforcement power" to monitor the compliance of the nations signatory to the Bretton Woods agreement (often referred to as the "IMF countries") to its terms can be said to exist, the IMF held such power. The primary purpose of the IMF was to assist nations in their efforts to maintain the parity value of their currencies and to provide for an "orderly" approach to devaluation or upvaluation of currencies when parity values could not be maintained. The principal activity of the IMF in pursuit of this objective was the provision of convertible currency loans to nations experiencing "temporary" balance of payments problems. Such lending provided deficit nations with funds to intervene in the foreign exchange market to protect the value of their currencies.

In addition to its lending role the IMF serves as a consultative agency to member nations and is a principal source of international economic information. Nations that are forced to devalue their currencies have often found the IMF a source of (sometimes unwelcome) advice as well as resources when grappling with various problems posed by devaluation.[7]

Special Drawing Rights.   Central bank holdings of official reserves—primarily gold and holdings of foreign currencies—were necessary for the maintenance of stable exchange rates under the Bretton Woods system. As international trade expanded in the 1950s and 1960s, IMF officials and the world's monetary authorities became concerned that growth in official reserves was not keeping pace. Gold and the U.S. dollar were the two principal official reserve assets. The supply of monetary gold grew very slowly year by year (if at all), and it was not until the 1960s, as a result of the development of large deficits in the U.S. balance of payments, that U.S. dollars became abundant abroad.

---

[6]A nation gains official reserves by operations to keep its currency value from rising above parity.
[7]Devaluation, which reduces the "price" of a nation's currency in terms of other currencies (and increase the price of other currencies), can narrow or eliminate a trade deficit because cheapened exports and more expensive imports tend to increase the former and decrease the latter. Such adjustment, however, occurs only after a lag. For a time after devaluation the trade deficit will generally worsen because prices (in foreign currencies) change immediately, but quantities of exports and imports change slowly. (This adjustment pattern is called the "*J*-curve effect" for obvious reasons.)

To provide additional international reserves, the IMF's members agreed (in the late 1960s) to create and distribute (as allocated according to quotas) a new type of international reserve asset: **special drawing rights (SDRs)**. SDRs were termed "paper gold" because they were then backed by IMF gold holdings, but they are essentially bookkeeping entries. The value of SDRs stems from their mandated acceptability among the central banks of the IMF nations in exchange for convertible currencies. The conditions governing the exchange and holding of SDRs are tightly detailed in the IMF articles of agreement and include provisions for interest payments to nations holding an amount of SDRs in excess of their past allocation. International reserve assets have grown by the amount of SDR creation and distribution (now totaling more than $22 billion), although it should be recalled that SDRs cannot be used as a means of payment except to settle central bank transactions.

The SDR also serves as a "common denominator" of currency values. Its value is a weighted average of the values of the U.S. dollar, the German mark, the British pound, the French franc, and the Japanese yen—the currencies of the world's principal trading nations. Thus the SDR is a means of denominating international obligations that minimizes the risk of losses due to unexpected exchange rate changes. For example, a U.S. investor purchasing foreign bonds denominated in, say, British pounds will sustain losses (when pounds are converted to U.S. dollars) if the pound depreciates in relation to the dollar. An SDR-denominated bond reduces the risk substantially, since the SDR's value relative to the dollar is determined by four other currencies.

The End of the Bretton Woods System.   The U.S. dollar played a key role in the Bretton Woods system of exchange rates. The dollar accounted for more than three fourths of official reserves and was the principal "intervention currency" employed by central banks to maintain their currencies' parity value in the foreign exchange market. The values of the currencies of the IMF member nations were defined in dollars as well as in gold. The U.S. dollar itself was valued at $35 an ounce of gold, and central banks of other IMF nations could present dollars to the Federal Reserve for conversion to gold.

The paramount position of the U.S. dollar in the Bretton Woods system put the U.S. currency (and thus the system) under persistent and precarious pressure. U.S. balance of payments deficits provided other nations with reserve assets (in the form of dollars) and generally increased world liquidity. However, as holdings of dollars abroad mounted, the will and ability of the United States to maintain convertibility of dollars into gold became increasingly suspect. Diminished confidence in the dollar resulted in the presentation of dollars for gold at a pace that eroded U.S. gold reserves to less than $10 billion (at $35 an ounce) by 1970, compared to almost $25 billion in 1949.

A more fundamental problem was the overvaluation of the dollar relative to the currencies of its trading partners. Although the recovery of the economies of Western Europe and Japan after World War II was complete by the 1960s, exchange rates still generally reflected the economic conditions of 1949. Further, other governments were reluctant to upvalue their currencies (for fear of endangering *their* balance of payments), and the United States could not devalue the dollar in the absence of the cooperation of these governments.

By 1970 the situation for the dollar was critical. The U.S. balance of payments deficit reached $10 billion in that year, and it became evident that the next year would bring an even larger basic balance deficit (it turned out to be $23 billion) and the first balance of trade deficit for the United States in this century. Finally, in August 1971 the U.S. government ended convertibility of the dollar into gold, and the dollar was allowed to "float" in the foreign exchange market. The latter step meant that the dollar's exchange rate would be set by supply and demand, without central bank intervention. The floating dollar promptly fell substantially in value relative to most major currencies.

It was not the intent of the U.S. government to destroy the Bretton Woods system but only to force a realignment of currency values that would properly "price" the dollar in relation to other currencies. Such a realignment occurred in December 1971 (the Smithsonian Agreement), and the dollar was formally devalued by raising the dollar price of gold. This IMF agreement also called for a widening of parity bands from ±1 percent to ±2¼ percent.

The Smithsonian Agreement soon began to fall apart as more and more major currencies were allowed to float. In February 1973 the United States was obliged to devalue the dollar again. By mid-1973 the fixed-exchange-rate system established by the Bretton Woods agreement had been supplanted. The new exchange-rate system was one in which most major nations allowed their currencies to float in the foreign exchange market, and other nations fixed their currency's value in relation to one of these floating major currencies.

A great deal of government intervention continued in the foreign exchange markets despite the collapse of the Bretton Woods system. Most of the nations that belonged to the European Economic Community (EEC) wished to maintain fixed exchange rates among themselves. The European Monetary System (EMS) was created to allow EMS member countries to fix the value of their currencies in relation to one another but allow exchange rates relative to the currencies outside the EMS to float. For example, the French franc and the West German mark have a fixed exchange rate (although they are subject to occasional devaluation and upvaluation), but both currencies float in value relative to the U.S. dollar. (As of this writing, eight of the twelve EEC nations belong to the EMS, the United Kingdom, Greece, Portugal, and Spain having not yet joined the system.) Maintenance of the EMS exchange rates necessarily requires central bank intervention by the EMS member nations.

Many nations, particularly less developed countries, maintain the values of their currencies relative to the U.S. dollar, some other major currency, or some composite currency such as the SDR. Again, their central banks must intervene in the foreign exchange market to maintain the value of the home currency rela-

EUROPE '92: EUROPEAN ECONOMIC INTEGRATION

Six nations—France, West Germany, Italy, the Netherlands, Belgium, and Luxembourg—were the original signers of the 1957 Treaty of Rome, which laid the foundations for the European Economic Community (EEC). The Treaty had four principal provisions:

1. *Free trade:* The elimination of tariffs, quotas, and other trade barriers between the EEC nations.

2. A *customs union:* A uniform tariff schedule among EEC members for the imports of non-EEC nations.

3. A *common market:* The elimination of all barriers to movement of labor, capital, goods, and services among EEC nations.

4. Adoption of a *common agricultural policy* among the EEC nations.

The United Kingdom, Ireland, and Denmark joined the EEC in 1960. More recently, Spain, Greece, and Portugal have joined the EEC, raising its membership to a dozen nations.

In the first three decades of its existence the EEC had a great deal of success in efforts to achieve free trade among member nations, establish a customs union, and adopt a common agricultural policy. Achievement of a truly common market proved to be more difficult. In 1985, however, the European Commission (the EEC's executive branch) issued a "white paper" calling for the implementation of measures to dismantle all barriers to flows of goods, services, capital, and labor among EEC nations by 1992. The Commission set forth about 300 directives that, if and when fully implemented, would harmonize taxes on goods and services, establish uniform standards for product safety and performance, eliminate border controls, create open competition throughout the EEC for public works and supplies contracts, provide mutual recognition for university degrees and for various professional certificates, and wipe out all barriers to cross-border marketing and banking, insurance, and other financial services. The EEC parliament subsequently endorsed the "white paper" in the Single European Act of 1985. This remarkable act endorsed the principle of "mutual recognition" among ECC nations—firms or products approved and regulated in one EEC nation should be free to operate or to be sold in all EEC nations.

Successful implementation of the Single European Act (popularly termed "Europe '92") would create an economic "United States of Europe," with products and services flowing as easily among the EEC nations as among America's 50 states. An economically unified and integrated EEC would create a common market of more than 320 million people with a GNP about equal to that of the United States and with exports equal in magnitude to the combined total of U.S. and Japanese exports.

tive to the reference currency or currency composite. For example, if some nation sets the unit value of its currency as SDR 2, its central bank will sell home currency when its foreign exchange rate rises significantly above SDR 2 and buy home currency (with foreign currency reserves) when the rate falls significantly below SDR 2.

A few nations, notably the United States and the United Kingdom in the 1980–1985 period, have experimented with freely floating exchange rates—letting the foreign exchange market determine home currency value without government intervention. However, the behavior of the U.S. dollar in the 1980s led to successive agreements among the world's major economic powers (the Plaza agreement in 1985 and the Louvre accord in 1987) that reinstituted coordinated central bank intervention to maintain exchange rate stability. However, the success of the new attempt to manage the international monetary system clearly depended on the ability of the participating nations to maintain low inflation rates and otherwise keep their economic profiles in some degree of harmony.

Balance of Payments Adjustment: Fixed Versus Flexible Exchange Rates

A balance of payments problem (imbalance) emerges when a nation is using more foreign exchange to acquire goods, services, and financial assets of other nations than it is earning by the sale of its goods, services, and financial assets to other nations. As we discussed previously, a nation has a **deficit on current account** when imports of goods and services exceed exports of goods and services. A nation has a **deficit on capital account** when capital outflows (purchase of foreign financial assets and payment of foreign financial obligations) exceed capital inflows (sale of financial assets to foreigners and reduction in net receivables from foreigners). Surpluses exist when the reverse conditions hold, but a balance of payments surplus is seldom considered a problem.

The balance of trade (merchandise exports–merchandise imports) is often cited as an indicator of a country's balance of payments position, but in fact it is only one component, though a very important one. The trade balance is the major component of the current account balance, but a deficit balance of trade may be offset by a surplus on service accounts. Further, a deficit on current account can be "financed" indefinitely by a surplus on capital account. The balance of payments position for this country in the late nineteenth century is a case in point.

When the sum of the current and capital accounts (the "overall balance") represents a balance of payments deficit, the nation in question has a problem. Figure 24.5 depicts such "fundamental disequilibrium" when there is excess demand for foreign exchange, where D_0 is the original demand schedule, D_1 is the new demand schedule, and S is the supply of foreign exchange schedule. An overall deficit in the balance of payments must be financed either by using foreign currency reserves held by the government or by government borrowing

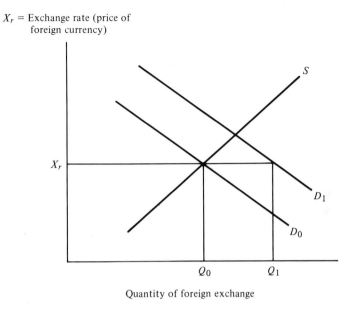

X_r = Exchange rate (price of foreign currency)

X_r

S

D_1

D_0

Q_0 Q_1

Quantity of foreign exchange

FIGURE 24.5 Balance of Payments Disequilibrium

from foreigners. There are practical limits to such financing for any nation. A continuing deficit in the overall balance of payments must eventually be corrected. Aside from drawing down its foreign currency reserves and/or international borrowing to finance the excess demand for foreign exchange depicted in Fig. 24.5, a deficit nation must take one or more of the following actions:

1. Increase the price of foreign exchange in home currency (change the exchange rate—devaluation).
2. Use restrictive monetary/fiscal policy indirectly to induce lower import demand and increase exports, or
3. Employ direct controls to bring the demand for foreign exchange in line with supply.

Devaluation of the Currency. Excess demand for foreign exchange can be eliminated by reducing the home currency's value in the foreign exchange market, as shown by the change in the exchange rate to X_{r2} in Fig. 24.6. This new exchange rate reflects a higher price (in home currency) for foreign exchange and thus for foreign goods, services, and financial assets. It also reflects a lower price (in foreign currency) to foreigners for the nation's goods, services, and financial assets.

In Fig. 24.6 the new exchange rate (X_{r2}) results in a decline in the quantity demanded of foreign exchange equal to ($Q_1 - Q_2$)—the result of higher prices for foreign goods, services, and financial assets. Since home goods, services, and

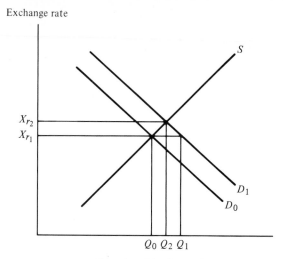

FIGURE 24.6   **Effects of an Exchange Rate Change**

financial assets are now cheaper to foreigners, more home currency is demanded in the foreign exchange market (which means that more foreign currency is supplied in exchange), so the supply of foreign exchange increases by $Q_2 - Q_0$. And, of course, supply of and demand for foreign exchange are now equal at Q_2 (and X_{r2}).

Allowing the exchange rate to change in this fashion is termed **devaluation** of the home currency under a fixed-exchange-rate system and **depreciation** if the nation in question is under a flexible-exchange-rate regime. The difference is much more political than economic. Devaluation is a deliberate, government-initiated (and announced), and relatively infrequent change in the exchange rate. Depreciation, in its pure form (as with freely floating exchange rates) is a market phenomenon; smaller changes occur more often as demand and supply fluctuate.[8] There are various gradations of exchange-rate changes in between, such as "crawling pegs," which are systematic periodic devaluations occurring at roughly

---

[8]The reverse of devaluation and depreciation is, of course, **upvaluation** and **appreciation** of the currency. Unlike devaluation, upvaluation is never a necessary course of action imposed on a government. Probably the main reason that upvaluation was such a rare occurrence under the Bretton Woods system was the economic effects of upvaluation (such as reduced exports), which were unpopular in many quarters. The gradual and "market" nature of currency appreciation makes it much more acceptable than upvaluation, which is perhaps a significant advantage of flexible rates.

regular time intervals. (The "crawling peg" approach is employed by some nations that have very high inflation rates.)

Devaluation (or substantial depreciation) of a currency is not without cost to the devaluing nation. A devaluation results in immediate relative price changes, but the quantity of exports and imports responds more slowly. It takes time for purchasing and production patterns to respond to price changes. During this adjustment period, foreign currency reserves must further decrease, or external borrowing (perhaps from the IMF) must increase. There are other costs of adjustment during the economic disturbance created by a devaluation. Resources must be reallocated, decisions made, and information communicated as a direct result of devaluation. The domestic price level is likely to rise as imports become more expensive, perhaps exacerbating inflationary pressures that gave rise to the devaluation. Social and political disturbance may result from the differential impact of the devaluation across producers, consumers, and other wealth holders in the economy.[9]

Thus although a devaluation will almost invariably correct a deficit in the balance of payments, the process is not as smooth as the shifting of curves in a diagrammatic model may suggest. Indeed, a country has good reason to use its international reserve assets and external borrowing to defer (and perhaps avoid) changes in its exchange rate. Further, nations may (and often do) seek alternative approaches to balance of payments adjustment when these alternatives (rightly or wrongly) are perceived to be less costly in economic, social, and political terms than devaluation.

Monetary and Fiscal Policy Measures.   A government may choose to employ macroeconomic policy measures to correct a balance of payments deficit, either as an alternative to devaluation (or to prevent depreciation) of its currency or to reinforce the effects of a decline in the foreign exchange rate for its currency. The appropriate policy measures are, of course, those that will encourage exports and capital inflows and discourage imports and capital outflows.

The quantity of imports is largely determined by the level of a nation's income and the relationship between the prices of imported and domestic products. When national income rises, the level of spending on imported goods and services increases along with increases in spending for domestic goods and services. The appropriate economic policy response, then, is as apparent as it is regrettable: curtail growth in national income. To the extent that such deflationary policy curbs the nation's inflation rate relative to that of its trading partners, a further reduction in imports may be gained via a reduction in the marginal and average propensities to import as a result of the ensuing shift in relative prices. Successful macroeconomic policy efforts to reduce income growth and

---

[9]Economic disturbance occurs also in the case of upvaluation and is one reason for the reluctance of nations to upvalue their currencies.

the rate of inflation not only will curtail imports but also will spur exports. In the face of declining (or static) domestic demand for their products, home producers will turn to export markets to increase their sales. Such export expansion will be facilitated by the relatively lower prices of home producers in world markets.

Deflationary monetary and fiscal policies aimed at slowing economic expansion and inflation thus can be expected to "improve" the current account balance by spurring exports and restraining imports. How about the capital account balance? International capital flows, insofar as economic variables are concerned, are a function primarily of relative interest rates.[10] Both direct and portfolio long-term and short-term investments abroad are, of course, directed to earn the highest expected real rate changes as well as nominal yields—commensurate with the risk assumed. In general, higher interest rates will attract capital inflows and discourage capital outflows, though it must be recognized that nominal interest rates will be adjusted for anticipated inflation and exchange rate changes.[11] Economic policy measures to increase interest rates can thus be expected to "improve" capital account balance. The policy prescription, then, is tighter monetary policy. Restrictive monetary policy acts to "improve" the balance of payments on both current and capital accounts.

Foreign Exchange and Other Direct Controls.   As we noted in the foregoing discussion, both devaluation and price–income–interest-rate adjustments to correct a balance of payments deficit impose costs on a nation. To avoid these costs, some nations use direct controls on international commercial and financial flows to correct a balance of payments imbalance. However, this approach (which is particularly prevalent among less-developed nations) has its own set of costs and related shortcomings.

In the context of the supply/demand framework of exchange-rate determination the effect of controls is to force the supply of and demand for foreign exchange into equality at some fixed exchange rate. Various types of governmental control mechanisms accomplish this. Except for problems of avoidance and evasion, which inevitably accompany such control systems, the quantity of imports and capital flows can be adjusted to a considerable degree. Further, such controls can be used in conjunction with (as well as instead of) devaluation or deflationary economic policy in order to hasten the adjustment process. **Tariffs,** the imposition of a required payment on goods traded across national borders by the gov-

---

[10]Political factors are important to both the direction and magnitude of capital flows among the world's nations. For example, election of leftist governments in Europe or angry growls from the Soviet Union invariably spur increases in European and OPEC nation investments in the presumably safer and more politically stable United States.

[11]Relative inflation rates among nations, interest rates, and exchange rates among currencies move together over time, but with a lag. It is the lag effects that inject additional economic uncertainty (along with additional political risk) into international investment.

ernment of the importing nation, have a long history. The effect of a tariff is to raise the price of imports. The presumed result is to reduce domestic demand for imported goods. Tariffs may be used to protect domestic producers from foreign competition as well as for reasons concerning balance of payments, and it is not always possible to distinguish between these motivations.

The precise effect of tariffs on quantities of imports is seldom easy to project. **Quotas** avoid this forecasting problem by simply limiting the category of imports to some desired amount, which can further be applied to amounts per country of origin.[12] Aside from the incentive that quotas provide smugglers, an allocation problem is created by this type of import control—the determination of who will get what amount of the limited supply of the imports to which quotas apply. Since this problem is generally handled by government agencies that grant import licenses to chosen applicants, opportunities for bribery and other misconduct are created.

Tariffs and quotas reduce demand for imports and thus the demand for foreign exchange. **Subsidies** to exporters are intended to increase exports and thus increase the supply of foreign exchange. Such export subsidies exist in varying degrees in nearly all nations and take a variety of forms. Special tax treatment and low-interest-rate financing for exporters are the most popular devices in industrialized nations, whereas developing countries combine these approaches with more direct preferential treatment for their export industries.

Exchange Controls. Foreign exchange controls, frequently in conjunction with import licensing requirements, are common in developing nations. In fact, most countries employ foreign exchange restrictions of some sort. In economically advanced nations, such restrictions are generally limited to capital account (financial) uses of foreign exchange, but developing nations frequently have control systems that embrace both current and capital account transactions.

A system of complete foreign exchange control involves mandatory conversion of residents' foreign currency receipts into home currency within some designated time period. The government thus "takes possession" of all foreign exchange receipts and allocates these receipts to would-be users. Since foreign exchange must be obtained for the government agency responsible for such allocation, the licensing of imports is a requisite component of the system. In effect, every (legal) use of foreign exchange becomes subject to government approval.

Multiple exchange rates may also be employed. For example, in addition to receiving prompt licensing approval, the importation of essential foodstuffs or

---

[12]So-called voluntary quotas emerge when a foreign government, by request of the importing nations, agrees to limit its exports of a particular commodity or commodities to the requesting country. A recent example is the Japanese agreement to limit automobile exports to the United States. Such agreements, needless to say, are won by explicit or implicit threats to impose other, more drastic, restrictions.

raw materials, rather than the import of "luxury" items, may warrant a preferential exchange rate (more foreign currency for a given amount of home currency). At the extreme a wide range of exchange rates may apply to various uses of foreign exchange with necessities and items relating to economic development being favored.

The effect of an exchange control system is depicted in Fig. 24.7 for a single, fixed exchange rate. The official exchange rate is R_0, and q_0 is the quantity of foreign exchange being supplied to residents from government holdings. The dashed line labeled D is the demand curve that would hold in the absence of exchange controls, but the effective demand curve is the horizontal line with its origin at R_0 on the vertical axis. At R_0, q_0 of foreign exchange is supplied and "demanded," excess demand of $q_1 - q_0$ existing at R_0.

It is the excess demand for foreign exchange that leads to the problems of evasion and bribery that often characterize exchange control systems. Importers and others desiring foreign currency have a strong incentive to circumvent the controls by bribing officials and other means. Such problems, along with the administrative costs of maintaining the control bureaucracy and the compliance costs imposed on users of foreign exchange, are significant disadvantages of exchange control systems. The more comprehensive these systems are, the greater will be the costs.

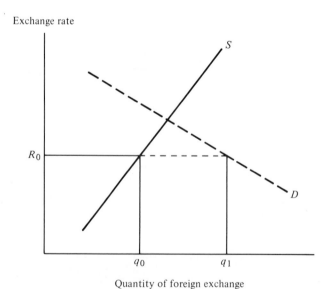

FIGURE 24.7   A Directly Controlled Exchange Rate

Balance of Payments Surplus.   The foregoing discussion focused on the case of a deficit in the balance of payments. Finance ministers are much less likely to lose sleep over a surplus in the balance of payments than they are over a deficit. A surplus can be used to build up a nation's reserve assets, to reduce external debt, for international lending, or for economic assistance grants. None of these options pose any particular short-term problems for a country maintaining a fixed exchange rate. Moreover, in the case of a flexible exchange rate, an appreciating currency (because it results in cheaper imports) can dampen any inflationary pressures existing in an economy for which international trade is a large component. However, since an appreciating home currency means higher foreign currency prices for exports, sales of exports may suffer.

Policy alternatives for elimination of a payment surplus are the exact opposite of those we have reviewed for the deficit case:

1. *Upvaluation* of currency (for fixed exchange rates) allowing the currency to *appreciate* (in the case of flexible exchange rates),
2. *Stimulating* aggregate demand via monetary and fiscal policy, or
3. Using direct controls to *discourage* capital inflows and withdrawing any export-stimulation programs.

It is not necessary to discuss these actions, both because we wish to avoid redundant treatments and because of the comparative infrequency (other than appreciation) of the use of these policy measures.

INTEREST-RATE AND EXCHANGE-RATE RELATIONSHIPS

As we noted previously, an important aspect of the international financial system is the relationship among interest rates, exchange rates, and the rate of inflation. Extension of the so-called Fisher effect, the view that the observed interest rate is the sum of a "real" rate and the expected rate of inflation, to the international realm ("Fisher open") holds that interest rates in different nations reflect differences in their relative rates of inflation. If real rates of interest are approximately equal among nations, nominal interest rates will differ only by differences in expected rates of inflation. As with "Fisher closed," observed reality will not adhere exactly to this theory because of market "imperfections," but the concept is nonetheless a useful one.

"Fisher open" ties in rather nicely with a similar concept regarding the behavior of relative exchange rates. The so-called purchasing-power parity theorem postulates that, like relative interest rates, exchange rates will change to adjust for differential inflation rates among nations. For example, if the inflation rate in France for the next year was expected to exceed that of the United States by 5 percent, one would expect per annum interest rates in France to exceed those of the United States by 5 percent, and one would also expect the French franc to depreciate by 5 percent in relation to the U.S. dollar over that time period.

When interest rate differentials are equal to rates of change in exchange rates, an investor gains nothing by borrowing in a low-interest currency and investing in a high-interest currency; the decline in exchange-rate value offsets the additional interest earnings. Opportunities for gain arise when a significant difference develops between the interest-rate differential and the expected percentage change in the exchange rate. Suppose, for example, that the difference in French and U.S. interest rates in the instance cited above was 6 percent instead of 5 percent. The investor could then gain approximately 1 percent (interest-rate differential less the expected exchange-rate change) by investing in French francs instead of dollars. It would also be cheaper to borrow in U.S. dollars than in French francs; indeed, one could perhaps turn a profit by borrowing dollars and investing in francs. As more and more investors exploited these opportunities for "interest-rate arbitrage," the difference between the expected rate of change in the exchange rate and the interest differential would shrink for the following reasons.

1. Increased borrowing of U.S. dollars would tend to raise U.S. interest rates.

2. Increased investment in francs would tend to lower French interest rates.

3. Increased demand for francs in the foreign exchange market would tend to raise the value of the franc relative to the dollar in the spot market, thus increasing the expected future decline in the franc's exchange rate relative to the dollar.

The eventual result of these developments would be approximate equality of the U.S.–French interest-rate differential and the expected rate of depreciation of the franc relative to the dollar, and thus there would be an end to the profit incentive for interest rate arbitrage.

The existence of the forward market for foreign exchange facilitates interest-rate arbitrage. An investor can "cover" the investment by selling the invested currency forward, thus protecting the potential profit from unexpected changes in the exchange rate. An example of covered interest arbitrage follows.

Assume the following data for pounds sterling (£) and U.S. dollars ($):

> Spot rate: $2.00/£
> One-year forward rate: $1.98/£
> Interest rates:
> United Kingdom (£)   10%
> United States ($)   8%

The forward discount on the pound is

$$\frac{\$1.98 - \$2.00}{\$2.00} = -1 \text{ percent}$$

An arbitrageur could profit by the following sequence of actions.

1. Borrow $200,000 for one year at 8 percent and convert loan proceeds to £100,000 at spot rate of $2.00.

2. Invest £100,000 at 10 percent for one year.

3. Execute a one-year forward contract for delivery of £110,000 (principal of £100,000 and interest of £10,000 on the above investment) at the forward rate of $1.98/£, or $217,800.

4. One year later, collect principal and interest totaling £110,000, deliver the £110,000, and collect $217,800 on the forward contract.

5. Pay the principal ($200,000) and interest ($16,000) on the loan, realizing a net profit of $1800.

The use of the forward market for "covering" interest-rate arbitrage introduces an additional factor that helps bring interest-rate differentials into approximate equality with discounts and premiums on currencies. The forward selling of pounds, which increases the supply of forward pounds, tends to lower the forward rate for the pound, thus increasing its discount. In the foreign exchange market this decrease in the forward rate, in conjunction with the increase in the spot rate that results from an increased demand for spot pounds, tends to increase the discount on the pound above the initial 1 percent. In the money market, increased borrowing of dollars is tending to raise U.S. interest rates, and increased lending in pounds sterling is tending to lower U.K. interest rates; the net effect is a reduction in the interest differential between the two nations. As the interest differential narrows and the discount on the pound (premium on the dollar relative to the pound) rises, the profit to be gained by covered interest-rate arbitrage approaches zero. In a relatively free market, interest-rate parity (equivalence of the interest rate differential with the forward/spot exchange-rate differential) will be attained by this scenario.

The international money market for major currencies is a relatively free market, and interest-rate parity generally holds for these currencies. Thus when considering alternative currencies for borrowing or investment purposes, one must adjust the stated interest rate for any premium or discount on the currency. *A premium should be added to the interest rate and a discount subtracted from it.* Thus nominal rates can be misleading in terms of the ultimate cost of debt or the return on an investment in a foreign currency. Many corporate financial managers, attracted by low interest rates, borrowed heavily in Swiss francs in the 1960s. When the value of the Swiss franc soared in the 1970s, these same managers discovered that it took far more of their home country currencies to pay the Swiss franc debt than had been anticipated; for many the effective rate of interest was five or six times the nominal rate.

The foreign exchange market offers fertile ground for speculators. As described in Chapter 22, one means of speculating on the future value of a currency is offered by the foreign currency futures market. Trading in currency futures is similar to forward market transactions in foreign exchange.

The international money and capital markets and the foreign exchange market are closely intertwined. Interest rates in the money and capital markets and forward exchange rates are jointly determined by the interaction of transactions in these markets.

SUMMARY

International funds flows, whether for the exchange of real or financial assets, are complicated by the existence of different currencies in different countries. The trading of currencies in foreign exchange markets is a derivative of the trading of real and financial assets among residents of different nations. When a trader, investor, or traveler must make payments in a currency other than his or her home currency, the foreign currency must be obtained in the foreign exchange market in exchange for home currency. Similarly, foreign currencies received by international traders and investors will generally be converted into home currency in the foreign exchange market. Foreign currency exchange may be accomplished for "immediate" delivery in the spot market (at the "spot rate") or by means of a forward contract specifying delivery at a future date at a specified exchange rate (the "forward rate").

International commercial and financial transactions thus result in the purchase and sale of currencies in the foreign exchange market. When governments do not intervene, as in a system of flexible (or "floating") exchange rates, the supply of and demand for a currency determine its "price" (rate of exchange) in other currencies. Thus when a country develops a trade deficit (its imports exceed its exports) that is not offset by other currency flows, the supply of its currency to the foreign exchange market will exceed demand, and the currency's exchange rate will fall (depreciate). Such depreciation results in the country's exports being cheaper (in terms of foreign currency prices) and its imports being more expensive (in home currency prices). These relative price shifts should serve to boost exports, curb imports and thus correct the deficit. (The reverse will hold for a balance of payments surplus.)

When a government attempts to maintain a fixed rate for its currency, it is obligated (through its central bank) to intervene in the foreign exchange markets when the exchange rate threatens to move above or below some percentage of the pegged rate. Government intervention involves buying home currency in the foreign exchange market when its exchange rate weakens, thus buoying it up with increased demand. Such purchases of home currency are accomplished with "official reserves"—currencies of other nations held by the central bank. When the exchange rate moves excessively upward, the central bank will sell home currency in the foreign exchange market for other currencies, adding them to official reserves. In this case the increased supply of home currency lowers its exchange rate.

Since the 1971–1973 collapse of the world fixed-exchange-rate system established by the 1944 Bretton Woods agreement, the United States, Japan, and most of the major Western nations have allowed their currencies to float in foreign exchange markets, although central bank intervention has become frequent since 1985. Most "Third World" nations, however, still have fixed exchange rates for their currencies, although they are fixed in relation to floating currencies. The nations belonging to the European Monetary System maintain a fixed-rate regime among themselves but let their currencies float against those of nations outside the EMS.

Interest rates and exchange rates are closely related (which is to say, the money and capital markets and the foreign exchange market are closely linked). In free markets, interest-rate differentials among nations can be expected to reflect anticipated exchange-rate changes. In the case of the major currencies for which a well-developed forward market exists, covered-interest arbitrage will generally maintain interest-rate parity—the approximate equivalence of interest-rate differentials and forward premiums/discounts on currencies.

QUESTIONS

1. What is meant by "spot" exchange rates versus "forward" exchange rates? What market forecast is implied by a difference in these rates for a given currency at a given point in time? What implication is there for a nation's interest-rate structure when the spot and forward exchange rates for its currency diverge?

2. Define foreign exchange risk. Explain the relationship between foreign exchange risk and the existence of the forward market in foreign exchange.

3. Exchange rates of currencies in the foreign exchange market are determined by supply and demand. What are the principal determinants of quantities demanded and supplied?

4. Explain how a nation's central bank can intervene in the foreign exchange market to increase or decrease the value of its currency.

5. Name and define four "balances" of the balance of payments. How does each compare to the overall balance of payments?

6. How does a nation attempt to maintain the par value of its currency under a fixed exchange rate system? When is devaluation necessary and when should revaluation be accomplished?

7. How is devaluation (with fixed exchange rates) or depreciation (with flexible exchange rates) likely to correct a deficit in the balance of payments?

8. What is "interest-rate parity"? What is the implication of interest-rate parity for the effective rate of interest in cross-currency borrowing and lending?

REFERENCES

Bame, Jack J., "Analyzing U.S. International Transactions," *Columbia Journal of World Business* (Fall 1976), 72–84.

Batten, Dallas S., and James E. Kamphoefner, "The Strong U.S. Dollar: A Dilemma for Foreign Monetary Authorities," Federal Reserve Bank of St. Louis *Review* (August/September 1982), 3–12.

———, and Mark Ott, "Five Common Myths About Floating Exchange Rates," Federal Reserve Bank of St. Louis *Review* (November 1983), 5–15.

Chrystal, K. Alec, "A Guide to Foreign Exchange Markets," Federal Reserve Bank of St. Louis *Review* (March 1984), 5–18.

Coombs, Charles A., *The Arena of International Finance* (New York: Wiley, 1976).

Cornell, Bradford, and Alan C. Shapiro, "Interest Rates and Exchange Rates: Some Empirical Results," *Journal of International Money and Finance* (December 1985), 431–442.

Eiteman, David K., and Arthur I. Stonehill, *Multinational Business Finance,* 4th ed. (Reading, Mass.: Addison-Wesley, 1988), Ch. 1–2.

Fieleke, Norman S., *The International Economy Under Stress* (Cambridge, Mass.: Ballinger, 1988), Ch. 5.

Grabbe, J. Orlin, *International Financial Markets* (New York: Elsevier, 1986).

International Monetary Fund, *Annual Report,* 1988.

Kubarych, Roger M., *Foreign Exchange Markets in the United States* (Federal Reserve Bank of New York, 1983).

Melvin, Michael, *International Money and Finance,* 2nd ed. (New York: Harper & Row, 1989).

Shapiro, Alan C., *Multinational Financial Management* (Boston: Allyn and Bacon, 1989), Ch. 2–7.

Solomon, Robert, *The International Monetary System, 1945–81* (New York: Harper & Row, 1982).

Williamson, John, "The Case for Managed Exchange Rates," in John Adams (Ed.), *The Contemporary International Economy: A Reader,* 2nd ed. (New York: St. Martin's Press, 1985), 307–330.

CHAPTER 25

International Banking and Financial Markets

Multinational firms—both financial and nonfinancial—and international financial markets are of enormous significance in the world economy. They link together international commerce and investment with domestic economic activity. In this chapter we describe and discuss the role of international banking and financial markets, particularly the Eurodollar and Eurobond markets.

THE NATURE AND SIGNIFICANCE OF INTERNATIONAL FINANCIAL MARKETS

International financial centers have existed for many years. The city of London, for example, was the focus of international trade financing in the nineteenth century. But only after World War II did international financial markets (markets for financial assets external to the countries in whose currency the assets are denominated) develop to any significant extent. Reflecting the U.S. dollar's dominant role in the world after World War II, the first international money market was in dollars. It became known as the **Eurodollar market** because European banks began the practice of accepting deposits and making loans in U.S. dollars in the early 1950s. As other currencies (particularly the West German mark) became more significant in the "offshore" money market, the more general term "Eurocurrency market" came into use. This period was also characterized by rapid development of international capital markets, particularly the **Eurobond market** (bonds denominated in a currency other than that of the country in which they are sold).

A further significant development in capital market lending was **Euro-credit** syndicated loans, which are large medium-term international loans provided by

TABLE 25.1   The Eurocurrency Market Size, Selected Years (Based on Foreign Liabilities of Banks in Major European Countries, the Bahamas, Bahrain, Cayman Islands, Panama, Canada, Japan, Hong Kong, and Singapore. Billions of Dollars, Rounded to the Nearest $Billion, at End of Period)

	1980	1982	1984	1986	1987
Gross liabilities to:					
Nonbanks	$ 278	$ 432	$ 497	$ 699	$ 814
Central banks	128	91	96	105	151
Other banks	1,172	1,645	1,793	2,879	3,544
Total	$1,578	$2,168	$2,386	$3,683	$4,509
Eurodollars as % of total gross liabilities in all Eurocurrencies	76%	80%	82%	71%	66%
Dollar liabilities of foreign branches of U.S. banks as % of total gross liabilities in all Eurocurrencies	20%	18%	15%	9%	8%

Source: International Economic Conditions, *Federal Reserve Bank of St. Louis (April 1989).*

a group of banks from various nations. Since Eurodollars have been the principal currency for both Eurobonds and Eurocredit lending, our discussion focuses initially on them.

The Eurodollar Market

A **Eurodollar** is simply a dollar-denominated time deposit in a bank outside the United States.[1] The **Eurodollar market** is the intermediation of these offshore dollars. It is a huge market, amounting to an estimated $4.5 trillion in 1988 (a very large part of this amount is interbank deposits), and it is primarily a market for short-term funds. Eurodollar deposits are accepted and lent by **Eurobanks,** which are simply banks that perform this function. Many Eurobanks are branches of U.S. banks. The Eurodollar market is roughly 70 percent of the **Eurocurrency market** (see Table 25.1) for currencies on deposit outside their home countries.

Eurodollars have existed for many decades, but only since the late 1950s has the Eurodollar market been of sufficient size to play a significant role in the international financial system. The stage was set for the Eurodollar market by the dominance of the U.S. dollar in the postwar period. The dollar's central role stemmed from the fact that the United States accounted for such a large share of

---

[1]The amount of offshore dollar demand deposits is minimal; Eurodollar deposits are essentially time deposits for a specified period (sometimes as short as a single day) and at a specified rate of interest. Thus Eurodollar deposits cannot be used as a means of payment but rather must first be converted into a demand deposit of a U.S. bank.

world trade and the fact that the dollar was convertible into most other currencies in the late 1940s and 1950s. As the various Western European economies recovered during the 1950s, dollar deposits began to accumulate in banks in these nations, particularly in Britain and France. Some of these dollar deposits were Russian. The Soviets feared that their deposits would be confiscated or "frozen" if their holdings were in U.S. banks. British banks, proscribed in 1957 from financing nonresident trade transactions with domestic currency, were eager to obtain dollar deposits for this purpose. British banks and other Eurobanks were able and willing to offer attractive deposit rates for Eurodollars, and this attracted dollars from U.S. residents (confronted with Regulation Q interest rate ceilings in the United States), as well as European holdings of dollars. The United States experienced balance of payments deficits in much of the 1960s (buying more from abroad than the United States sold abroad). Though not a necessary condition for the Eurodollar market's existence, such deficits surely contributed to its growth.

The existence and rapid growth of the Eurodollar market are primarily due to past and present differences in regulatory constraints between the United States and other countries, particularly interest-rate restrictions and reserve requirements. Domestic banking regulation, in conjunction with the freedom allowed foreign-currency banking activities by most European nations, is the principal reason why Eurobanks can successfully compete with their U.S. counterparts for dollar deposits and loans. The absence of reserve requirements on Eurodollar deposits makes them a cheaper source of funds for Eurobanks than their domestic deposits, on which reserve requirements are generally imposed.[2] Competition for these deposits results in most of their cost advantage being passed on to depositors in the form of higher deposit yields. The cost advantage could also be reflected in lower interest rates on Eurodollar loans, but borrowers tend to be much more responsive to rate differentials than depositors, and domestic and offshore lending rate differences (except for those reflecting differential risk) tend to be quickly "arbitraged" away. (A comparison of domestic and offshore rate structures is offered in a subsequent section of this chapter, including a discussion of the significant role of the risk associated with offshore depositing and lending.)

The "spread" between dollar deposit interest rates and dollar loan interest rates is smaller in the Eurodollar market than in the United States, a feature that attracts both depositors and borrowers. The absence abroad of such deposit costs as Federal Deposit Insurance Corporation assessments, as well as the absence of reserve requirements, makes Eurobank dollar deposit rates higher than U.S. bank

---

[2]Reserve requirement ratios differ considerably among nations, and the central banks of some countries (such as the United Kingdom and the Netherlands) pay interest on reserves. Few major countries, however, have higher average reserve requirements than the United States, and interest is not now paid on reserves of U.S. depository institutions.

deposit rates. Further, various economies exist in the Eurodollar market that allow Eurobanks to offer both more attractive yields to depositors and more attractive lending rates to borrowers. The Eurodollar market is largely an "interbank" market, more than 85 percent of Eurodollar liabilities being owed to other banks. Ultimate borrowers tend to be large corporations or governmental entities with very low credit risk. Both deposits and loans tend to be in very large denominations. These features, characteristics of a "wholesale" market, result in significant operating cost reductions to banks participating in the Eurodollar market.

Eurodollar lending rates are usually based on the London Interbank Offered Rate (LIBOR), which, as the name suggests, is the prevailing interbank deposit rate. A borrower of Eurodollars will pay the current LIBOR plus a premium based on the term of the loan and the lending bank's assessment of the borrower's credit standing. A frequent arrangement is the Eurocredit floating rate, by which interest is paid every six months as the loan "rolls over" and a new, current interest rate is assessed. (For example, such a loan arrangement might involve a rate of LIBOR plus 1 percent established at six-month intervals until maturity.)

The extensiveness of interbank transactions involving offshore U.S. dollar deposits is due to several factors. In Europe the Eurodollar market serves much the same function as does the market for federal funds in the United States. Very large banks that are perceived to be very strong financially can attract offshore dollar deposits at relatively low interest rates and lend them (at some small but attractive "spread") to banks that do not enjoy such status. Further, interbank lending reflects attempts by offshore banks to diversify their assets by countries and currencies as well as maturities. Finally, many interbank transactions are among affiliates, so tax considerations and certain regulatory requirements are also factors contributing to their high volume. Offshore dollars are generally not subject to reserve requirements, and Eurobanks typically hold only nominal reserves against Eurodollar deposits. Interbank transactions do not reflect a final extension of credit, however, and thus have little or no monetary impact.

A useful concept for assessing the size and growth rate of the Eurodollar market is to view it as a segment of an overall market for dollar intermediation—a market segment that has certain differentiating characteristics relating to risk and returns. In this view the growth of the Eurodollar market relative to the domestic dollar market becomes a function of the relative risks and returns of these two competing markets. This concept also suggests that growth in the offshore market comes at the expense of (and not in addition to) growth in the domestic market.[3]

An assessment of the nature of the Eurodollar market is facilitated by an understanding of the process by which Eurodollars come into existence.

---

[3]See Jurg Niehans and John Hewson, "The Eurodollar Market and Monetary Theory," *Journal of Money, Credit, and Banking* (February 1976), 1–27, for a rigorous statement of this concept. For a very readable variant of this argument, see Ian Giddy, "Why Eurodollars Grow," *Columbia Journal of World Business* (Fall 1979), 54–60.

Creation of Eurodollars.   A Eurodollar comes into existence when a deposit in a U.S. bank is transferred to a Eurobank. For example, suppose that to earn a slightly higher yield, a firm holding a dollar time deposit in a New York bank elects to shift the deposit to a bank in London. The firm can obtain a demand deposit from the New York bank at maturity of the time deposit and then transfer ownership of the demand deposit to the London bank in exchange for a time deposit there. At this point a Eurodollar deposit has been created.

The London bank, which now holds a demand deposit in the New York bank, is unlikely to leave these funds idle. Instead, the bank will lend the acquired funds to a commercial firm or governmental entity, or it will "place" them in the Eurodollar interbank market. In the former transaction the borrower obtains ownership of the demand deposit in the New York bank, and credit extension has occurred. In the latter transaction, another bank (assume a Paris bank) acquires the funds in the U.S. bank, and there is no final extension of credit. Such interbank lending of the funds may involve many banks before credit is extended to an ultimate borrower. In turn, this borrower's expending of the funds sets the stage for another potential iteration of revolving ownership of the demand deposit in the New York bank. At some point, however, a non-U.S. recipient of the deposit will wish to convert the funds to his or her own currency. Such currency conversion transfers ownership of the deposit to the supplier of the local currency. In general, Eurodollar deposits have the potential to generate any (or all) of the following:

1. An increase in world lending as the credit-granting capacity of Eurobanks is increased by Eurodollar deposits but the lending capacity of the U.S. bank that holds the original deposit is not decreased.

2. An increase in the world volume of U.S. dollar deposits.

3. A multiple increase in credit to the extent that loaned Eurodollars are redeposited in the Eurodollar market.

4. A shift in the location of credit granting from U.S. banks to Eurobanks.

Although these potential effects are of consequence, it is also important to recognize what Eurodollar creation does not do. It does not change the U.S. money supply because only the ownership, not the quantity, of U.S. bank deposits is involved. And even though a multiple expansion of world credit due to Eurodollar creation is possible, such a multiplier effect requires at least the passive assent of European central banks—allowing Eurodollars exchanged for their currencies to be redeposited in the Eurodollar market. Note further that the extension of credit that occurs because of Eurodollar creation is no different than if the demand deposits in the U.S. bank had never been exchanged for a Eurodollar deposit but had been loaned by the U.S. bank to the borrower (who instead acquired the funds in the Eurodollar market). Note also that the time deposit in the London bank plays a passive role; it is not "money" in the strict sense of a means of payment.

In sum, economists generally agree that the Eurodollar market does not significantly increase the capacity of the financial system to create money and credit.[4] European banks cannot create Eurodollars in the process of making loans (as is possible in their own currencies); they can instead only lend U.S. bank deposits that they own as a result of Eurodollar creation by a previous owner of those deposits. As was noted above, a shift of U.S. demand deposit ownership from a U.S. resident to a foreign resident does not change the U.S. money supply.

U.S. and Eurodollar Money Market Interest Rates.   As was previously indicated, interest rates on Eurodollar deposits are higher than U.S. interest rates on deposits, and Eurodollar lending rates tend to be somewhat lower than U.S. lending rates. This spread advantage allows Eurobanks to compete effectively with domestic U.S. banks for deposits and loans. Eurobanks can operate profitably on this leaner margin because, unlike the deposits of U.S. banks, their dollar deposits do not have the costs associated with statutory reserve requirements, deposit insurance fees, and other regulatory constraints.

Although Eurodollar deposit rates are generally somewhat higher and loan rates consistently slightly lower than U.S. rates, the magnitude of the difference between domestic and external rates often varies. What may be some reasons for this variation?

In the formative years of the Eurodollar market, difference in the degree of liquidity between it and the domestic market might have been properly viewed as a significant factor in the size of differentials between the markets. Given the present size of the Eurodollar market and its apparent efficiency, however, it is difficult to ascribe much significance to this factor.

The most important factor explaining the size of interest-rate differentials and changes in the differentials is relative risk in the two markets.[5] Market imperfections, particularly those relating to differences in the institutional and regulatory structure of domestic and external markets, also play a significant role. In the external–domestic market rate comparison there is no foreign exchange risk; a Eurodollar differs from a U.S. dollar only in its location, not in its value relative to other currencies. However, greater risk is attached to Eurodollars in the strict sense of the degree of assurance that an obligation will be honored on the basis of agreed terms—**credit risk.** This risk is not associated only with potential developments in the country in which external borrowing occurs, since the possibility always exists that the home country will take actions that restrict or impair obligations in the external money market. Finally, since the perceived degree of the

---

[4]See Gunter Dufey and Ian H. Giddy, *The International Money Market* (Englewood Cliffs, N.J.: Prentice-Hall, 1978), 107–154, for a complete conceptual discussion of this issue and a description of empirical research regarding the "Eurodollar multiplier."

[5]Various controls employed by the United States during the 1963–1974 period to control capital outflows almost certainly had a significant effect on external–domestic money market rate differentials. However, no such controls exist at the time this book is being written.

risk attached to Eurodollars varies over time, interest-rate differentials also vary over time.

Other Offshore Currency Markets

Offshore currency markets have evolved not only in Europe but also in Asia, the Caribbean area, and the Middle East in recent years. Though still quite small in relation to the Eurocurrency market, these markets are likely to increase in significance in the future if Third World economic development accelerates.

The Asian currency market is centered in the city-state of Singapore. It originated in 1968, when Singapore eliminated withholding tax on interest payments on foreign currency deposits in Singapore banks. Largely as a result, the Singapore Asian dollar market expanded from less than $31 million in 1968 to $112 billion by 1983.[6] Like the much larger Eurocurrency market, the Singapore market is primarily an interbank market, and the bulk of deposits are U.S. dollars. Most ultimate borrowers are located in Asia, but U.S. and European banks account for about 70 percent of all loans. Banks outside Singapore supply about three fourths of Asian currency deposits. As might be expected, interest rates are generally quite close to those prevailing in the Eurocurrency market. Hong Kong is a strong competitor of Singapore as Asia's principal offshore currency market. It is a premier banking and financial center, although its dollar market is only about half the size of Singapore's. Hong Kong will become part of the People's Republic of China in 1997, and this prospect clouds its future as a financial center. Another Asian financial center of great importance is Tokyo, the significance of which will increase as Japan relaxes its capital controls. Japan's financial influence has grown enormously in recent years as Japan's consistently large export surpluses have made it the world's largest creditor nation. Tokyo has thus joined the ranks of the world's great financial marketplaces despite past and present relatively stringent capital market regulation and restrictions on the activities of domestic and foreign financial services firms (and limitations on market entry of the latter).

The likely beginnings of a significant offshore currency market exist in the Middle East, particularly in Bahrain and Kuwait. The billions of dollars of oil revenues that are generated in this part of the world offer the potential for considerable financial development of the region. At present, however, most of these funds are placed outside the region.

A large offshore currency market, which is really an offshoot of the Eurocurrency market, is centered in the Caribbean. The Bahamas, the Cayman Islands, and the Netherlands Antilles have attracted financial operations because of their

---

[6]The origins and nature of the Asian dollar market are described and assessed in Kenneth Bernauer, "The Asian Dollar Market," Federal Reserve Bank of San Francisco *Economic Review* (Winter 1983), 47–63.

favorable tax climate. Many U.S. banks have Caribbean branches, which serve as a center for their offshore operations. However, almost all of the U.S. branches in the Caribbean are "shell" branches, that is, places where sets of accounting records are maintained rather than sites where business is transacted.

Major Participants in International Money Markets

Given the diversity of borrowers and lenders in the external financial intermediation process, one of the more remarkable features of international money markets is the uniformity of treatment of these participants. Operating in a framework that is relatively free of government regulation, these markets have not developed the kind of segmentation that characterizes many domestic money markets. The only significant distinctions among borrowers and lenders are standard economic criteria relating to risk and volume.

Banks from around the world participate in the Eurocurrency and other international money markets as both suppliers and users of funds, and they are the nucleus of the external financial intermediation process. External and domestic financial market linkage is largely accomplished by the continual flow of bank funds between domestic markets and international markets. (International banking is discussed in more detail later.)

Large multinational corporations, which also play an important role in international money markets, are the principal group of ultimate borrowers. The international money market offers two major related advantages to corporate borrowers: availability of funds, even when domestic credit is tight, and a minimum of restrictions on the use of the funds. Further, external credit is often less expensive than domestic credit. For the multinationals the fluidity, breadth, and relative freedom of international money markets make them an ideal medium for moving funds around the world. These characteristics, along with generally higher deposit yields, also result in corporations being principal suppliers of funds to the Eurocurrency and other external money markets, as well as users of those funds.

Governments and governmental entities are becoming increasingly important participants in international money markets. As suppliers of funds to these markets, the OPEC states are notable, accounting for deposits of many billions of dollars per year. For political as well as economic reasons the OPEC states find these markets attractive depositories for surplus funds generated by their sales of oil. In addition to yield and liquidity advantages, international markets offer anonymity and a separation of jurisdiction over funds from the country in whose currency the funds are denominated.

Governmental entities of considerable importance in the Euromarkets are various central banks. Central banks supply funds directly to the Eurocurrency market via deposits of dollars in Eurobanks and holdings of dollars and other

JAPANESE FINANCIAL POWER

As the 1980s came to an end, the death of Japan's emperor focused worldwide attention on a nation that had become an economic superpower in an incredibly short time. The possibility loomed that Japan might become a major force in world politics as well as in world markets. Certainly no nation with such economic power had ever before failed to reach for geopolitical power as well. Japanese financial and economic eminence was indeed remarkable, as the following facts (circa 1989 and in terms of U.S. dollar measures) make clear.

The Tokyo Stock Exchange (TSE) was the world's largest stock market on the basis of market capitalization. Not only had the TSE displaced the New York Stock Exchange as the world's largest stock exchange, but the Osaka Stock Exchange displaced the London exchange as the third largest!

In terms of total deposits and assets, nine of the world's largest banks were Japanese.

A single Japanese securities firm, Nomura Securities, possessed more capital than all the leading U.S. securities firms combined.

The Japanese postal savings system held assets of about $1 trillion, more than those of the twelve largest U.S. banks combined.

Japan was the world's largest creditor nation as the result of many years of bulging export surpluses in the nation's foreign trade. Japan holds more than $1 trillion in foreign assets. Foreign direct investment exceeded $35 billion in 1988. Japanese ownership of real assets (real estate and companies) in the United States exceeds $25 billion.

Since 1960, total Japanese net new investment has averaged about 15 percent of GNP, compared to about 5 percent of GNP in the United States.

What would Japan do with its economic superpower status? One observer recalled the remark of Dean Acheson (President Truman's Secretary of State) about Britain's post–World War II status: "Britain has lost an empire but has not yet found a role." Japan, it appeared, had gained an empire—at least a commercial one—but had not yet found a role.

currencies with commercial banks in their countries, which subsequently deposit the funds in Eurobanks. Central banks are also borrowers in international money markets, along with various other governmental entities.

Eurodollar borrowers include U.S. banks, especially during periods of monetary stringency in the United States. Branches of U.S. banks located abroad may lend dollar deposits to the parent bank.[7]

---

[7]Such borrowing by the U.S. home office from a foreign branch is subject to a 3 percent reserve requirement. This reserve requirement on Eurocurrency liabilities was imposed by the Depository Institution Deregulation and Monetary Control Act of 1980.

INSTRUMENTS OF THE EUROCURRENCY MARKET

Most Eurocurrency funding is in the form of fixed-rate, fixed-term time deposits in maturities ranging from overnight to six months (although multiyear maturities are not unusual). Interbank liabilities account for the bulk of Eurocurrency time deposits. The rate of interest paid on these deposits is market-determined and is highly competitive. The remainder of Eurocurrency deposits are in negotiable certificates of deposit (CDs), either fixed-rate or floating-rate (FRCDs). Banks also issue floating-rate notes (FRNs) to obtain Eurocurrency funding and are joined in this avenue of financing by nondepository firms. FRCDs and FRNs are traded in secondary markets.

As was noted earlier, most loans in the Eurocurrency market are made on a floating-rate basis. While LIBOR has become less dominant as the bench mark for Eurocurrency lending in recent years, it remains the usual base rate for floating rate loans. Terms of Eurocurrency lending range widely, as borrowers' needs span such a wide spectrum: overnight requirements, working capital sourcing, export–import financing, and long-term capital project funding. Intermediate- and long-term lending in large amounts (called "Eurocredits") is often syndicated among a number of Eurobanks.

The banking syndicates that usually provide Eurocredit loans are not permanently affiliated; rather, they are formed by banks willing to participate in a particular loan. The borrower engages a **managing bank** (or banks) to put together a syndicate of participating banks and draw up a loan agreement. The managing bank receives a management fee (a percentage of the loan) for its effort. **Lead banks** in the syndicate (those providing most of the funds) will receive from the managing bank a **participation fee** (a share of the management fee). A relatively small number of banks—the largest Japanese, European, and U.S. banks—dominate syndicated Eurocredit lending. The volume of such lending contracted significantly after the emergence of the so-called "Third World debt problem" in the early 1980s.

Consortium banks also play a significant role in syndicated Eurocredit lending. These multinational banking consortia are joint ventures of two or more banks of different nations, and unlike the banking syndicates, they are permanently affiliated. These consortia both channel business to their parent banks and undertake their own projects. Projects conducive to consortium handling, in addition to syndicated loans, include Eurobond issues, multicurrency loans, and merger or acquisition efforts across international borders.

A variation of Eurocurrency financing that has become a significant instrument in the Euromarkets in recent years is the note issuance facility (NIF). NIFs, provided by banks to their prime customers on a fee basis, commit the banks to stand ready to purchase customer notes (in amounts within prescribed limits and during a designated time period) at a price that results in the agreed spread over

LIBOR. The borrower will choose to sell notes under the NIF only if a better rate cannot be obtained from other lenders. The increasing use of NIFs has had the effect of greatly increasing the volume of "Euronotes" (or "Euro–commercial paper") issued.

THE INTERNATIONAL DEBT PROBLEM

The volume of international lending to developing nations, whether by individual financial institutions or by international banking syndicates, grew enormously in the 1970s. A major buildup of debt to developing nations began after the first round of huge OPEC-engineered increases in the price of oil in 1973–1974. Many oil-importing developing nations borrowed heavily to finance their oil import costs, which grew from $4 billion in 1973 to $20 billion in 1978 to (after the second "oil-price shock" of 1979) more than $50 billion in 1980. In what was hailed as the "recycling of petrodollars," international banks used deposits of oil-exporting nations to lend to oil-importing nations. But large borrowing by developing nations was not limited to oil-importing deficit nations; oil-exporting nations such as Mexico and Venezuela also borrowed heavily in the 1970s. According to data of the Organization for Economic Cooperation and Development (OECD), the medium- and long-term indebtedness of 158 developing nations exceeded $800 billion by 1988. Of this amount, about $500 billion was owed to commercial banks and other financial institutions.[8] U.S. commercial banks held loans to developing nations amounting to more than $100 billion in 1988, about two thirds of which were claims of the nine largest U.S. banks. And, reflecting its Eurodollar market funds sourcing, about three fourths of developing nations' external debt is in U.S. dollars. (The growth in developing nations' debt in recent years is shown in Table 25.2.)

International lending to developing nations suddenly became a serious problem in the early 1980s as a series of economic events caused the debtor nations to be unable to service their foreign debts on schedule. The sharp rise in market interest rates in the late 1970s and early 1980s resulted in much higher debt-servicing costs for these nations. In addition, the worldwide economic malaise of 1980–1982 greatly reduced export earnings of the developing nations via both export quantity and price declines. Since export earnings are necessary for payment of foreign debts (as the principal source of foreign exchange), the ability of developing nations to repay their escalating debt costs was diminished. By late

---

[8] For description and analysis of developing nation debt, see Norman S. Fieleke, "International Lending on Trial," Federal Reserve Bank of Boston *New England Economic Review* (May/June 1983), 5–13, and Norman S. Fieleke, *The International Economy Under Stress* (Cambridge, Mass.: Ballinger Publishing Co., 1988), 67–112.

TABLE 25.2   Developing Countries—by Alternative Analytical Categories: External Debt, by Class of Creditor, End of Year, 1981–89[1], Selected Years (In billions of U.S. dollars) _____

	1981	1983	1985	1987	1989
Oil exporting countries					
Total debt	$126.5	$149.0	$164.2	$192.2	$208.4
Short-term	53.4	57.4	46.9	48.7	54.4
Long-term	73.2	91.6	117.3	143.5	154.0
To official creditors	23.6	28.9	40.8	58.9	65.1
To financial institutions[2]	33.2	39.2	50.8	57.3	60.9
To other private creditors[3]	16.4	23.5	25.7	27.2	27.9
Non-oil developing countries					
Total debt	$617.3	$745.1	$853.2	$1,025.8	$1,071.5
Short-term	103.5	117.5	113.2	134.7	130.9
Long-term	513.8	627.6	740.0	891.2	940.6
To official creditors	194.3	240.6	300.7	405.7	464.4
To financial institutions[2]	159.4	218.6	268.3	313.0	309.1
To other private creditors[3]	160.1	168.4	171.0	172.5	167.1
Net oil exporters					
Total debt	$137.8	$173.3	$188.0	$217.9	$233.2
Short-term	9.1	11.4	14.1	15.6	16.5
Long-term	128.7	161.9	173.9	202.2	216.6
To official creditors	33.1	42.9	50.6	69.1	87.0
To financial institutions[2]	43.5	68.9	74.7	85.9	85.1
To other private creditors[3]	52.2	50.1	48.6	47.2	44.5
Net oil importers					
Total debt	$479.5	$571.8	$665.2	$807.9	$838.4
Short-term	94.4	106.1	99.1	119.0	114.4
Long-term	385.1	465.7	566.0	688.9	724.0
To official creditors	161.2	197.7	250.1	336.6	377.4
To financial institutions[2]	115.9	149.7	193.6	227.0	224.0
To other private creditors[3]	107.9	118.3	122.4	125.3	122.6

[1]Excludes debt owed to the Fund.
[2]Covers only public and publicly guaranteed debt to banks.
[3]Includes all unguaranteed debt on the presumption that this is owed mainly to private creditors, some of which may be banks but cannot be separately identified.

Source: International Monetary Fund, World Economic Outlook, *(October 1988), Washington, D.C.*

1982 the possibility of widespread default on foreign debts was a major policy concern, given the potential of such default to trigger an international banking crisis. While a crisis was avoided by the restructuring (rescheduling) of major loans,[9] by the easing of interest-rate pressures, and by a measure of economic recovery around the world, it appeared that the dangers to the world financial system posed by the international debt problem would not quickly be eliminated.

_____

[9]According to the International Monetary Fund, by 1983 about thirty developing nations (with aggregate foreign debt exceeding $400 billion) had completed or were attempting debt refinancing.

It is equally apparent that Eurocredit lending to developing nations has been dramatically affected. In particular, the willingness of smaller banks to join in syndicated sovereign lending has been dampened considerably.

At the present time the ability of the developing nations to pay the interest and principal on their debt to U.S. and European banks is very much in doubt. Widespread default by LDCs could seriously endanger the viability of these banks, almost certainly necessitating government financial support. A series of restructuring of loan repayments, "bridge" loans, and an increase in International Monetary Fund lending served to avert outright default in the early 1980s. Beginning in 1983, interest rate declines and a quickening of import demand in the developed nations (particularly the United States) also served to ease the crisis. Nonetheless, the problem remained acute. The world's financial system remained at risk. Further, a tragic paradox of some of the world's poorest nations transferring capital to some of the richest came to pass as debtor nations sought to achieve an export surplus to earn foreign exchange for interest payments.

In late 1985, U.S. Treasury Secretary James Baker offered what came to be known as the "Baker Plan" for dealing with the debt problem. Baker's proposals amounted essentially to economic structural reforms in the debtor nations combined with continued, slightly expanded lending from creditor banks and international lending agencies and commitments from the industrialized nations to maintain open markets for the exports of developing nations. The Baker Plan focused on the fact that the economic progress of the debtor nations was a necessary condition for servicing the debt.

The success of the Baker Plan was modest at best. In 1987, U.S. and European creditor banks, led by Citibank, began formal recognition of the high probability that a large portion of their outstanding loans to developing nations was uncollectible by greatly increasing their loan loss reserves. (Citibank alone added $3 billion to its reserve account, and the banks collectively increased reserves by more than $25 billion.) The action, along with the announcements of many banks that, by one means or another, they planned to dispose of some of their questionable international loans, signaled a tougher policy in dealing with debtor nation governments. These actions were followed by new proposals from individual U.S. lawmakers, the Japanese finance ministry, and others for a new approach to the debt problem.

The fundamental problem of the nations that cannot service their external debt is one of capital outflows. Nations that have experienced strong economic expansion in recent years, such as South Korea, have had no difficulty in generating and retaining adequate capital to pay interest and principal on debt. But nations with stagnant economies and hyperinflation cannot even retain the investment capital of their own people, let alone attract foreign capital. Unless there is widespread fundamental economic change and progress among these debtor nations in the next decade, it is unlikely that the debt problem will have a happy resolution.

THE BRADY PLAN FOR THIRD WORLD DEBT

On March 10, 1989, Nicholas Brady, the U.S. Secretary of the Treasury, announced a new approach to the Third World debt problem—a "Brady plan" to replace the "Baker Plan" of his predecessor, James Baker (who had been boosted to the office of Secretary of State by his friend, George Bush). The Brady Plan, like the Baker Plan, emphasized the need to restore vigorous economic growth to the debtor nations. Unlike Secretary Baker, however, Secretary Brady called for a significant measure of debt reduction by the creditor banks.

In the address that launched the Brady Plan the Secretary suggested three ways to achieve significant, mutually beneficial debt reduction. One way was for the World Bank and the IMF to guarantee interest payments of bonds issued by the debtor nations in exchange for bank debt (at a hefty discount). These "exit bonds" would carry a lower rate of interest than the original debt but, because of their much higher probability of payment, would be worth approximately as much as the real value of the debt that they replaced. A second path proposed by Brady was action to eliminate the regulatory, tax, and accounting rules that acted as disincentives for banks to debt reduction. Brady also called for changes in bank negotiating practices with debtor nations that would make it difficult for creditor banks to receive interest payments made possible by new loans to these nations unless these banks participated in the new lending.

Secretary Brady used the term "voluntary debt reduction"—not "debt forgiveness." But many observers (not just the government officials of the debtor nations) called for exactly that—and in massive amounts. The Brady Plan was rather limited in detailing how far "voluntary debt reduction" was to go. Meanwhile, the upward surge in interest rates of 1987 and early 1988 was further pinching the debtor nations. Whether or not the Brady Plan was to be more successful than the Baker Plan in dealing with the Third World debt crisis thus remained to be seen.

THE INTERNATIONAL BOND MARKET

In addition to the active market in intermediate-term financing via the various Eurocurrencies (and Eurobanks), large amounts of international capital market funds flows are accomplished by note and bond issues. There are two types of international bonds: foreign bonds and Eurobonds. The Eurobond market is a relatively recent phenomenon, but foreign bonds have existed for many years.

Foreign bonds are sold to investors in a foreign capital market; the bonds are denominated in the currency of the country in which they are issued. A foreign bond issue differs essentially from a domestic bond issue only in the fact that the issuer is not a resident of the country in which the bonds are sold. For example, a U.S. firm may issue bonds in the London capital market, but the securities are underwritten by British banks and denominated in pounds sterling. A frequent disadvantage of foreign bonds is that banks and governments often subject such issues to close scrutiny and tight control. Long-term borrowers in international markets may avoid such controls by the issuance of **Eurobonds,** securities denominated in a currency other than that of the country of issue. Table 25.3 indicates the magnitudes of new international bond issues in recent years.

Eurobonds are truly international bond issues. They are typically underwritten and marketed by a multinational group of financial institutions, and they are sold to investors in a number of countries. Eurobonds may be denominated in any of one or several major currencies, although the U.S. dollar is the most common denomination, as shown in Table 25.3. This table also identifies major Eurobond issuer categories. Governments and their various entities account for a large portion of total Eurobond volume, but non-U.S. companies are also major issuers. U.S. companies' participation increased sharply in the early 1980s as the value of the U.S. dollar surged on foreign exchange markets. After the U.S. dollar began its long decline in value in 1985, demand for dollar-denominated Eurosecurities waned, and U.S. company issuance of Eurodollar bonds decreased. The effect of dollar weakness on Eurodollar bond demand was compounded by the 1984 repeal of the U.S. withholding tax on interest paid to foreign bondholders, an action that made such domestic U.S. securities as U.S. Treasury bills and notes much more attractive to foreign investors. (The advent of shelf registration for securities issuance in the United States also increased the relative attractiveness of domestic markets to U.S. corporate borrowers.)

In recent years, **floating-rate notes** (FRNs) have become a major instrument in the international capital market. The so-called Euro-FRN (also called floating-rate Eurobonds) is generally priced at LIBOR plus some spread, the margin of which reflects issuer credit risk. The increased popularity of FRNs reflects, in part, the market's desire for both protection against interest-rate risk and shorter maturities for capital market instruments. (In the early 1980s, FRN growth also stemmed from a switch by many banks from direct Eurocredit lending to FRN purchase.) FRNs generally feature 5- to 10-year maturities, interest rate adjustments occurring every three or six months. Governments have been major issuers of FRNs.

Why the Eurobond Market Exists

As with the Eurocurrency market, a major reason for the emergence of the Eurobond market is its freedom relative to most domestic securities markets. Whereas most governments tightly regulate bond and note issues denominated in their own currencies, Eurobond issues are allowed a great deal more flexibility. Costs of issuance thus tend to be smaller and disclosure requirements much less stringent than for domestic and foreign bond issues. Eurobonds also offer tax advantages to the investor. Eurobond interest is generally not subject to a withholding tax, and the fact that Eurobonds are usually in bearer form means that neither owner's identity nor country of residence need be a matter of public

TABLE 25.3 Principal Features of International Bond Markets (Billions of Dollars)

| | 1986 | 1987 | 1988 | | | | |
	Year	Year	Year	Q1	Q2	Q3	Q4
Total Issues	$227.1	$180.8	$224.9	$55.0	$63.7	$53.2	$52.9
of which: Eurobonds	187.7	140.5	177.2	40.5	53.4	41.8	41.5
Foreign bonds	39.4	40.3	47.7	14.4	10.3	11.5	11.4
By Currency							
US dollar	$124.9	$65.5	$85.1	$17.5	$21.9	$26.5	$19.2
Deutsche mark	17.1	15.0	23.7	7.4	4.2	5.9	6.2
Swiss franc	23.2	24.3	26.6	9.1	7.0	5.5	5.1
Japanese yen	23.7	26.7	22.2	4.5	8.4	3.7	5.6
Pound sterling	11.0	15.1	21.8	6.4	8.9	3.1	3.4
Canadian dollar	5.1	6.0	12.9	3.2	4.3	2.2	3.1
ECU	7.1	7.4	11.3	1.9	3.2	2.0	4.2
Major Borrowers							
Japan	$34.3	$44.4	$50.9	$8.8	$14.6	$17.5	$10.0
United States	43.1	21.5	17.8	3.3	6.5	4.0	3.9
United Kingdom	19.5	12.7	24.5	7.0	6.8	4.8	5.9
Canada	16.8	9.0	13.2	2.9	3.7	3.1	3.5
France	13.6	8.9	16.2	4.1	5.0	4.9	2.2
Germany	11.8	10.0	12.4	3.1	1.6	3.5	4.3

Source: Barclay's Review, *February 1989.*

record. It is estimated that roughly half of all Eurobonds are held by individuals, and it is assumed that tax avoidance is a prime motive for this distribution of ownership.[10]

If there were no government controls and restrictions or other market imperfections in the flow of international capital funds, the Eurobond market would not exist. Capital movements among nations would be effected by foreign bond issues in national markets. Further, if such unrestricted capital flows across national borders existed, interest-rate differentials would shrink to magnitudes reflecting only present and anticipated premiums and discounts on currencies.

Most restrictions on international capital flows reflect differences in the institutional and economic structure of nations—in both kind and degree of development—and in efforts of governments to control capital inflows and outflows for economic policy reasons. A striking example of the nature and impact of the latter type of restriction is the 1963–1974 program of the United States to control capital outflows.

Until 1963 the New York foreign bond market was the principal source of foreign capital for the world's nations, although the West German, Swiss, and London markets were significant. New York offered a broad, deep, and efficient market characterized by relatively low interest rates and issuance costs. However, U.S. government concern over this country's balance of payments deficits prompted a series of actions, beginning in 1963, that were intended to reduce sharply the outflow of U.S. dollars to borrowers in other nations. (In the 1960–1964 period, private outflows of long-term and short-term capital increased from about $4 billion to almost $6.5 billion.)

In mid-1963 the United States imposed an **interest equalization tax** [IET] on the value of foreign securities purchased by U.S. residents. Except for the various exempted securities (those of Canada, developing nations, and international financial institutions), the IET had the effect of sharply curtailing the U.S. market for new foreign bonds. Predictably, foreign borrowers turned next to U.S. banks for direct loans. In 1965, such bank lending was brought under the purview of the capital-outflow controls program, and steps were also taken to curb direct foreign investment by U.S. business firms.

The U.S. capital-outflow controls program was an enormous stimulus for the Eurocredit and Eurobond markets (and to a lesser extent the Eurodollar market). Foreign borrowers who were shut out of the New York foreign bond market turned to Eurobond issues, as did many U.S. firms seeking long-term funds for

---

[10]Until 1984, U.S. dollar-denominated Eurobonds were preferred by some non-U.S. residents to domestic issues of U.S. securities because the latter was subject to a 30 percent withholding tax on interest paid to investors from countries lacking tax treaty exemption. Repeal of the withholding tax in June 1984 removed this barrier to foreign ownership of U.S. securities, largely at the expense of the Eurobond market. (Repeal also ended the incentive for U.S. companies to issue bonds through offshore subsidiaries in order to provide exemption from withholding tax for foreign investors.)

their foreign operations. Dollar-denominated Eurobonds served as a means of tapping the large pool of offshore deposits in Europe and elsewhere, since access to the domestic U.S. capital market was impeded by the IET and related measures. The volume of Eurobond issues rose from only $150 million in 1963 to $557 million in 1964, to more than $1 billion by 1966, and to more than $2 billion in 1967. Eurocredit lending also increased greatly in this period.

Interest Rates on International Bonds

Interest rates on foreign bonds and Eurobonds generally approximate those of domestic bonds of the country in whose currency they are denominated. Exceptions to this general paralleling of domestic and international bond rates occur when a country imposes capital controls for balance of payments or other reasons. For example, the interest equalization tax included in the 1963–1974 U.S. program to curtail capital outflows significantly increased the effective interest cost of foreign bond issues in this country. On the other hand, Switzerland, when it has had persistent surpluses in its balance of payments (and thus a strong currency), has often encouraged international borrowers to borrow Swiss francs.

In addition to home country interest rates and the effects of home government policies, international bond rates are directly related to bond rates in other currencies and prevailing Eurocurrency money market rates. As in the case of the Eurocurrency loans previously discussed, effective interest rates on Eurobonds are directly related to anticipated exchange rate changes. If the currency in which a Eurobond is denominated appreciates, the percentage increase in exchange-rate value relative to an investor's home currency is an addition to the investor's investment yield rate and vice versa for depreciation.

The market for dollar-denominated Eurobonds and the Eurodollar market are closely linked. Eurobond holders frequently shift into short-term holdings of Eurobonds when current or expected rate differentials make such a move attractive. Central banks in countries of Eurobond issue may prefer (and thus encourage) the purchases of dollar-denominated Eurobonds with Eurodollars, since this reduces use of domestic currency and thus minimizes exchange rate pressures. As Eurodollars are shifted into Eurobonds, rates on the former tend to rise, and the rate differential between Eurodollar loans and Eurobond yields narrows until such substitution ceases to be attractive to investors.

Swaps in the Eurobond Market

The rapid development of the large market for interest-rate and currency swaps has even more closely linked the Eurobond and Eurocurrency markets, while giving a major boost to the former. **Swaps** are simply financial transactions in which contracting parties agree to exchange streams of payments over an agreed time period. Swaps allow a borrower to obtain funds in the market in which the best rate and terms can be obtained while securing the terms for interest payment (fixed or floating rate) and currency of payment of interest and principal that the borrower prefers.

A simple example of a "plain vanilla" **interest-rate swap** emerges from a case in which Firm A can obtain a lower interest rate on a $1 million fixed-rate loan but seeks to avoid interest-rate risk by making floating-rate interest payments, while Firm B has the opposite situation. An interest-rate swap involves these steps:

1. Firm A borrows $1 million on a 10 percent fixed-rate basis, incurring the obligation to make semiannual fixed-interest-rate payments of $50,000.

2. Firm B borrows $1 million on a floating rate basis, incurring the obligation to make semiannual interest payments on the basis of LIBOR plus 25 basis points.

3. Firm A agrees to pay Firm B semiannual payments equal to the product of LIBOR plus 50 basis points times the "notional principal" (no actual principal changes hands) of $1 million.

4. Firm B agrees to pay Firm A semiannual payments of $51,250 (equivalent to 10.25 percent on $1 million of "notional principal").

The effect is thus to give both Firm A and Firm B the debt payment terms they want while sharing with each other their comparative advantage in fixed-rate versus floating-rate borrowing. Actual interest-rate swaps are generally more complex than this simple example and are used not only to transform debt cash flows from fixed to floating rate, but also for asset-related cash flows.

A **currency swap** usually involves an exchange of principal as well as interest payments and, as the name implies, involves payments in different currencies. Currency swaps protect against foreign exchange risk just as interest-rate swaps protect against interest-rate risk and frequently involve an effort to exploit a comparative advantage in obtaining funding in a particular currency. Currency swaps are often combined with interest rate swaps.

It has been estimated that more than three fourths of international bond and note issues in recent years have been swap-related. In addition to serving as a catalyst for international securities issuance, swaps have become a major international market in their own right, amounting to more than $400 billion.

The multinational nature of Eurobond issues epitomizes the internationalization of finance in recent decades. To a remarkable degree the financial systems of the world nations have become linked together in recent decades by the emergence of huge, efficient international financial markets and by the corresponding development of multinational financial institutions. We turn now to the latter aspects of the international financial system, focusing primarily on the international operations of this country's commercial banks.

THE ROLE OF COMMERCIAL BANKS IN THE INTERNATIONAL FINANCIAL SYSTEM

Commercial banks play a key role in the international financial system. The importance of banks for international trade is apparent when one recognizes that payment for internationally traded goods is accomplished essentially by changes in the ownership of bank deposits. Banks also dominate the foreign exchange market, and they are primarily responsible for the worldwide efficiency of that market. Many banks are multinational organizations, and through their global operations they facilitate international investment as well as world trade.

Financing International Trade

The Payments Mechanism.   A nation's banking system contributes to the operation of the international payments mechanism by holding deposits in banks abroad, by accepting deposits of foreign banks, and by debiting and crediting the accounts as payments are made across international borders. (While international remittances may take many different channels, they, like most domestic payments, ultimately involve only a change in ownership of a bank deposit in the designated amount.) Banks reduce the risk of international transactions by traders and investors by, in effect, interposing their credit for that of individual and institutional debtors via letters of credit. By helping to maintain orderly and efficient spot and forward foreign exchange markets, banks reduce the foreign exchange risk associated with international financial obligations. Banks expedite international commerce by lending to both exporters and importers. By making international financial intermediation possible they facilitate global capital mobility.

Bankers Acceptances.   The use of drafts (also called bills of exchange) is common to effect payment for internationally traded goods. In international transactions, an importer (or the importer's bank) often must accept (agree to pay) a **time draft** or make payment on a **sight draft** drawn by the exporter on the importer's firm or bank before the importer can take possession of the merchandise. A sight draft requires immediate payment; a time draft becomes a **trade acceptance** if accepted by a business firm (the importer) or a **bankers acceptance** if accepted by a bank. Trade acceptances are generally not marketable and are likely to be held by the exporter until due. Bankers acceptances, on the other hand, are readily marketable and are often sold by exporters wishing to obtain immediate cash.

Since bankers acceptances, as short-term investments, have the same quality as bank certificates of deposit, there is a large market for these instruments. In the United States, about a dozen New York acceptance dealers buy and sell bankers acceptances at a spread ranging from $\frac{1}{8}$ to $\frac{1}{4}$ percent. Purchasers of acceptances from these dealers include banks, insurance firms, and nonfinancial corporations. Foreign investors find acceptances attractive because interest on them is not subject to withholding tax. Further, bankers acceptances originating from international transactions are not subject to state usury laws, which prescribe interest rate ceilings—an attractive aspect during high-interest-rate periods.

Letters of Credit.   Letters of credit issued by banks are of considerable importance to international trade. Bankers acceptances are often created under a letter of credit arrangement. A **letter of credit** amounts to a written promise by an importer's bank to make payment to the exporter in the event of default by the importer. For the exporter a letter of credit minimizes credit risk (provided that a strong and reputable bank is the issuer), reduces political risk (governments are loathe to jeopardize their banking system's reputation), reduces the need for credit checking, facilitates financing, and provides for immediate payment on delivery of the goods to the importer. The importer benefits by the issuing bank's becoming party to the transaction, since it provides a source of expert assistance in monitoring and ensuring exporter performance.

Foreign Exchange Trading.   The role of commercial banks in foreign exchange trading is of considerable significance in the maintenance of efficient and orderly foreign exchange markets. Bank profit on the buying and selling of foreign exchange is realized by the spread between the "bid" (buying) and "offer" (selling) prices for a given currency. Although banks sometimes speculate in foreign currencies, they generally prefer to maintain a hedged position that minimizes their exposure to foreign exchange risk.

Bank trading in foreign exchange includes transactions with nonbank customers, domestic banks, and foreign banks. Trading occurs in both the spot and forward markets. One or more individuals are designated as foreign exchange traders for a given bank. Such traders must be highly skilled, because they must make rapid judgments (most major trades are accomplished by telephone or telex) about the buying and selling of frequently volatile currencies.

Until the emergence of the U.S. multinational corporation as a worldwide phenomenon in its rate of growth and economic significance, most U.S. banks could meet their customers' needs for international banking services by maintaining international banking departments. These departments handle foreign exchange trading, international payments, and trade financing (including letters of credit). But as more and more bank customers launched extensive foreign operations, their need for the provision of bank services in their foreign locations increased. As a result, U.S. banks were led to increase greatly their overseas operations. The next section sketches selected aspects of U.S. banks' foreign operations.

OVERSEAS BANKING AND THE U.S. FINANCIAL SYSTEM

The size and strength of the U.S. banking system have caused major U.S. banks to become significantly involved in overseas banking and foreign banks to seek a share of the U.S. banking market. Both of the international operations of U.S. banks and the activities of foreign banks in the United States have had major impacts on the regulatory structure of the banking system.

Scope of Overseas Operations of U.S. Banks

During the past two decades, international banking operations have grown at a phenomenal rate. The highest rate of growth has been in multinational activities of U.S. banks. The United States, particularly compared to European nations like Great Britain, is very much a newcomer to international banking. Only since World War II, as U.S. corporations began their great wave of overseas expansion, have U.S. banks moved abroad in a significant fashion. In a sense, U.S. banks were following their largest customers abroad—customers they wished to retain. Overseas branching was also encouraged by various tax advantages and by the foreign lending constraints of the 1960s that could be avoided by foreign branches. By 1988, more than 150 U.S. banks had foreign offices (of which there were more than 750) with total assets amounting to more than $500 billion (up from about $5 billion in 1960). Roughly half of the operating profits of the ten largest U.S. banks is currently earned abroad.

Some of the most significant expansion in U.S. banks' international activities is under the purview of legislation passed early in the century. The 1919 Edge Act (an amendment to the Federal Reserve Act) authorized the Fed's Board of Governors to permit banks to establish corporations for the purpose of engaging in international or foreign banking, either directly or through the acquisition of local institutions in foreign countries. U.S. banks were thus allowed to engage in international banking activities and to acquire foreign banks by the establishment of subsidiary "Edge Act Corporations" (EACs). The latter proved not only to be a means of entry into overseas banking but also a means (albeit limited) of achieving an interstate banking presence in the domestic market.

The Edge Act permitted U.S. banks indirectly to own foreign bank subsidiaries, which they had long been prohibited from doing directly. Further, the Edge Act permitted EACs to have U.S. offices throughout the entire nation (often located in Chicago, Los Angeles, Miami, San Francisco, and Houston) to service their multinational customers, accept deposits related to foreign transactions, and refer potential new customers to the parent bank. Such offices have allowed large U.S. banks to develop an interstate network of banking services, despite the federal prohibition of interstate branching. This development was expedited when, in 1979, the Federal Reserve System excluded EACs from the interstate branching rule. Edge Act corporations may now, subject to approval by the Fed, establish and operate branches in other states. The Fed took this action under the mandate of the International Banking Act of 1978, which includes a directive to the Fed for relaxation of restrictions on EACs in order to allow them to compete more effectively with foreign banks operating in the United States (which are allowed interstate branches at home and abroad). Edge Act overseas subsidiaries are generally allowed to engage in activities common to foreign banking practice in the host country, even though such activities may be prohibited in the United States (or even to the country's own resident banks). EACs are regulated by the Federal Reserve System; the Fed governs the scope of operations of both the domestic and foreign offices and must approve all equity participations in foreign institutions.

Overseas operations of U.S. banks are notable in aggregate impact, but only a relatively small proportion of this country's banking institutions (the largest banks) are involved. Only about 1 percent of U.S. banks (approximately 150 of 14,500 banks) have overseas branches or affiliates. Many of these 150 banks have only a few relatively small branches abroad or have only "shell" branches (essentially a set of accounts in a Caribbean area or other such offshore office, where international transactions originating in the United States are recorded). Ownership of more than 80 percent of overseas branches and affiliates and 90 percent of all overseas banking assets is held by only twenty U.S. banks. As might be expected, these same banks also dominate domestic banking, holding more than 30 percent of U.S. bank assets.

Overseas branches and affiliates of U.S. banks are located throughout the world. In terms of European, Asian, Caribbean, and Latin American geographic divisions the difference in number of branches and subsidiaries is not great, but Europe (led by London) is dominant in amount of assets. Only four U.S. banks— Citibank, Bank of America, First National Bank of Boston, and Chase Manhattan—have significant branch networks in Latin America, and the total amount of assets held by U.S. banks in that region is relatively small and has changed little in the past decade. (These assets do not include the large amounts of dollar-denominated loans booked in the home offices of U.S. banks.) In Asia, U.S. banks have steadily expanded their operations in response to the region's economic expansion, its increasing trade with the United States, the growth of Hong Kong and Singapore as Eurocurrency centers, and the emergence of Tokyo as a major financial center.

Overseas operations have provided U.S. banks with both the means and the incentive to deepen and broaden significantly their international lending. In addition to traditional export and import financing and lending to U.S. multinational firms and their foreign affiliates, the foreign lending of U.S. banks now includes extensive amounts of loans to foreign local firms, foreign banks, and foreign governments and their entities. Along with increased amounts of overseas lending, a number of U.S. banks have undertaken extensive diversification programs abroad. To a large degree, such diversification was necessary for U.S. banks to compete effectively with their European counterparts, which have traditionally offered their customers a full range of financial services. A domestic base for worldwide diversification was provided in the late 1960s as one-bank holding companies provided a means for involvement in such activities as leasing, factoring, cash management, and mortgage banking. The Federal Reserve Board has generally permitted such "finance-related" activities of Edge Act subsidiaries abroad. (Foreign branches are limited to the same activities as are permitted to their U.S. parent banks.) Such large U.S. banks as Bank America, First National Bank of Chicago, and Manufacturers Hanover Trust have investment banking subsidiaries in Europe.

International Banking Facilities

A recent development in U.S. international banking is the establishment, since 1981, of International Banking Facilities (IBFs). IBFs are allowed to be established by any U.S. depository institution, Edge Act Corporation, or U.S. office of a foreign bank. IBFs are a structure (essentially just a separate set of books within an existing institution) that banks can use to conduct international banking business exempt (for the most part) from domestic regulation and reserve requirements. An IBF can accept foreign-source deposits and make overseas loans with essentially the same degree of freedom as an overseas branch. Indeed, one of the purposes of IBFs was to "bring offshore banking home." There is a great deal of irony in the need for IBFs. As expressed by one author, the "crazy quilt of U.S. banking regulation" put this country in the "extraordinary position of having to create special banking facilities to repatriate to the United States a gigantic financial market whose principal commodity is none other than our own currency."[11]

The appeal of IBFs lies in their ability to combine the attractive features of offshore deposits and lending operations with only U.S. sovereign risk. They free U.S. banks of the burden of establishing and operating offshore branches and subsidiaries. The IBF structure is relatively simple—a set of asset and liability accounts segregated on the books of a banking organization from its other assets and liabilities. IBFs are not separate legal entities. U.S. banks can now use IBFs as a base to compete in the international markets for deposits and loans. There has scarcely been a nationwide rush to do so, however; IBFs are operated mainly by money center banks. Almost half of all IBFs are operated by New York banks; California, Illinois, and Florida banks account for most of the others.

Agencies and branches of foreign banks operating in the United States have been at least as eager as U.S. banks to create IBFs. Japanese banks, which are not allowed by Japan's Ministry of Finance to establish "shell" branches in the Caribbean, have been particularly notable operators of IBFs. Of the more than

[11]Franklin R. Edwards, "The New International Banking Facility: A Study in Regulatory Frustration," *Columbia Journal of World Business* (Winter 1981), 6.

500 IBFs in existence, more than half are owned by the U.S. offices of foreign banks.

FOREIGN BANKING IN THE UNITED STATES

The level of foreign banking operations in the United States increased dramatically in the past two decades. Foreign bank assets in the United States grew from about $7 billion in 1965 to more than $600 billion by 1988 (about 20 percent of all commercial banking assets booked in the United States). Foreign banks in the United States generally focus on wholesale, commercial transactions rather than retail, consumer banking. By the late 1980s, agencies and branches of foreign banks held more than 20 percent of commercial and industrial lending in the United States. More than 250 banks from more than 65 different nations have branch and agency offices or own subsidiary banks in the United States. There are more than 500 of these branches and agencies. Further, more than 125 other foreign banks have representative offices in this country. There are more than 1000 agencies, branches, subsidiaries, Edge Act banks, and representative offices of foreign banks operating in the United States. Significant foreign bank operations are now being carried on in about a dozen states (and the District of Columbia) and are concentrated in the cities of New York, Los Angeles, San Francisco, Chicago, Miami, and Houston, New York being the major center.

The reasons for the rapid growth of foreign bank operations in the United States are similar to those accounting for the expanded overseas operations of U.S. banks. Just as U.S. banks followed multinational U.S. firms abroad, foreign banks have followed their customers into U.S. operations. Investment in the United States by foreign firms has grown enormously in recent years as a consequence of both periodic declines in the value of the U.S. dollar (when U.S. assets become relatively cheaper in terms of many foreign currencies) and a higher rate of economic growth in this country compared to most European countries. The latter factor also makes the United States an attractive arena for foreign banks to pursue new lending business. In addition to these factors, foreign banks have initiated or expanded U.S. operations in order to operate outside their home country's restrictions and regulatory constraints, to improve their access to U.S. money and capital markets, and to obtain a new source of dollars by competing for deposits. Foreign banking operations in the United States have focused primarily on the wholesale market, most retail banking activity stemming from acquisitions of U.S. banks. Foreign banks have been aggressive competitors for corporate and institutional customers, often "outbidding" U.S. banks in terms of fees, lending rates, and borrowing terms.

Asian banks, led by the Japanese, hold more than 60 percent of all foreign bank assets in the United States. More than thirty Japanese banks have a presence in the United States, and they account for more than one half of total foreign bank assets with more than $300 billion of holdings. Canadian banks are a distant second (around $50 billion), followed by Western European banks.

Regulation of Foreign Banks Before 1978

Prior to the International Banking Act of 1978, foreign banks in the United States were regulated primarily by the states in which they were chartered. Almost all foreign banks received state rather than national charters because of the requirement that all directors of national banks be U.S. citizens. Federal regulatory authority over foreign banks was essentially limited to that of the Federal Reserve Board purview over foreign bank subsidiaries under the 1970 Bank Holding Company Act. Also, foreign bank branches were not eligible for FDIC deposit insurance.

There was (and still is) a great deal of variation among the states regarding the nature and extent of regulation of foreign banking activities. As of 1978, sixteen states explicitly prohibited entry of foreign banks in any form (other than representative offices). Eighteen permitted some form of foreign activity, while the rest had no laws regarding foreign banks.[12] The states that issued foreign licenses or charters processed them in the same manner as those of domestic banks. Foreign banking corporations usually entered U.S. markets through New York or California, simply because a significant proportion of the U.S. commercial and international financial transactions occur in these states. These states and certain others were receptive to foreign banks because of the states' interest in becoming international financial centers and their concern about reciprocity for their domestic banks' foreign operations.

Foreign bank branches, agencies, and other offices were thus entirely free of federal examination and supervision and largely outside the purview of federal regulation. Of particular importance was foreign bank exemption from federal prohibition of interstate banking and investment banking activities. Congressional concern about the lack of federal jurisdiction over foreign banks operating in this country led to the passage of the International Banking Act of 1978.

The International Banking Act of 1978

The purpose of the International Banking Act (IBA) of 1978 was to establish a framework for Federal Reserve supervision and regulation of foreign banking and to put foreign banks operating in this country on the same footing as domestic banks, insofar as governmental restrictions are concerned. The IBA made all branches, agencies, and commercial lending companies of foreign banks subject to the Bank Holding Company Act and thus to Fed regulation and supervision.

---

[12]James C. Baker, *International Bank Regulation* (New York: Praeger Publishers, 1978), 43–72.

INTERNATIONAL FINANCIAL INTEGRATION

An integrated financial system is one in which geographically separated savers and investors respond to the same financial market developments (such as interest-rate changes) in financial decision making and funds flow freely in response to these market signals. For example, financial market agents in California and New York are part of an integrated (U.S.) financial system, earning very similar returns on saving and paying very similar interest rates for loans. Financial institutions operating across the fifty states serve to integrate the U.S. financial system as do the nation's money and capital markets.

The extent of *international* financial integration is considerably less than the national financial integration that exists within the United States and other economically advanced Western nations. Some nations choose to separate their financial systems from the rest of the world with various exchange and capital flow controls or regulations that limit their citizens' access to financial services outside the national borders. In addition, *information and other transactions costs* have historically been much higher for transnational financial transactions, thus impeding international financial integration. In the past 25 years, the removal of capital and foreign exchange controls by industrialized countries, the emergence of the Eurocurrency markets, and the rapid development of international banking have had the effect of achieving a much higher degree of international financial integration. In the 1980s the globalization of financial markets accelerated as information and transactions costs of international investing declined as a consequence of both technical and economic developments, further spurring international financial integration. The degree to which integration of the world's financial markets had developed was graphically illustrated by their remarkable concordance on the occasion of the October 19, 1987, "Black Monday" crash (not only in the plunge of equity values, but also in the ensuing dip in interest rates).

International financial integration is a very positive development for the world economy. In much the same way as free trade made all free-trading nations better off and an integrated domestic financial system improves national capital allocation, the world economy is enriched by the efficiency gains of financial integration. Further, an internationally integrated financial system cushions the world real economy from real shocks (like unexpected oil price hikes) as well as financial disturbances like the 1987 stock market plunge or the Third World debt crisis.

A "grandfather" clause, however, protected existing activities prohibited by this law and its amendments.

The IBA permits the Comptroller of the Currency to grant a national charter to a subsidiary or affiliate of a foreign bank if a majority of the directors are U.S. citizens. (Prior to the act, all directors had to be U.S. citizens.) Federally chartered foreign banks can now operate in all states where permitted by state law, subject to the rules and regulations of the National Bank Act. State branches and agencies may be converted to federally chartered institutions with approval of the Comptroller of the Currency.

Foreign banks engaged in retail deposit taking were made eligible for deposit insurance and, indeed, are required to have it if they are chartered in states requiring deposit insurance of domestic banks. Foreign banks were allowed to form Edge Act corporations, the regulation of which was liberalized for both foreign and domestic varieties. Foreign banks were made subject to the McFadden Act and Douglas Amendment regarding interstate branching, but existing interstate operations were "grandfathered" under the act. (A foreign bank operating in more than one state was required to declare a "home state.") Foreign banks were brought under the same restrictions as U.S. banks regarding the nonbanking activities of their affiliates. Foreign branches and agencies were required to submit federal quarterly report-of-condition reports.

Other provisions of the IBA authorized the federal regulatory authorities to issue rules and regulations necessary to carry out the act, provided for studies of foreign treatment of U.S. banks and of the interstate banking issue, and authorized the Fed to impose reserve requirements on agencies and branches of foreign banks with worldwide assets of more than $1 billion. The IBA established a competitive balance between foreign and domestic banks, although many U.S. bankers grumbled about the "grandfather" clauses in the act and various exemptions from disclosure requirements.

SUMMARY

International financial markets have been greatly broadened and deepened in recent decades by the emergence and rapid development of the Eurocurrency and Eurobond markets. Because these markets involve transactions in bank deposits located outside the nation of their currency of denomination, they offer participants the opportunity to engage in lending and borrowing outside the regulatory framework of any nation. The absence of reserve requirements and a minimum of restrictions allow Eurobanks to offer higher deposit yields and lower loan rates than domestic U.S. banks. The Eurobond market offers a similar means of avoiding regulatory constraints. The freedom that characterizes these markets is one of the principal reasons for their spectacular growth since their inception in the late 1950s.

The Eurodollar market is closely linked to domestic U.S. money markets because of the identical currency, the leading role of U.S. banks and U.S. multinational corporations in the Eurodollar market, and the relative ease with which participants in either market can switch to the other. Thus rate structure and funds availability conditions in the two markets tend to move very closely together. The Eurodollar market continues to dominate the offshore deposit (Eurocurrency) market, dollar deposits accounting for about 70 percent of total offshore bank deposits. The Eurocurrency market is dominated by interbank transactions in short-term deposits in very large amounts—essentially a "wholesale" market—but is also a significant credit source for nonbank borrowers.

The market for Eurobonds, bonds denominated in a currency other than that of the country of issue, and the Eurocredit market (intermediate-term lending of Eurocurrency) experienced dramatic growth as a result of the U.S. capital outflows control program of the 1960s. The program effectively closed the New York capital market to many foreign and U.S. multinational firms, obliging them to turn to the Euromarket for capital funds. The U.S. dollar is the predominant currency of denomination for Eurobonds and the most frequently borrowed Eurocredit currency. Thus the Eurocurrency capital market is closely linked to the Eurodollar market and the domestic U.S. capital markets.

Commercial banks play a vital role in the international financial system, facilitating both world trade and foreign investment. Most international payments are accomplished by a change in ownership of bank deposits from a resident to a nonresident or vice versa. Banks facilitate foreign trade not only by providing the payments mechanism but also by financing world trade; for this purpose, letters of credit are of special importance. Banks also dominate the foreign exchange market and contribute greatly to the efficiency of that market.

The huge increase in international trade and investment since the 1950s has spurred a corresponding expansion in international banking. Though relative latecomers to the international banking scene, U.S. banks have established an extensive worldwide network of overseas operations during this period. More recently, U.S. banks have been confronted with increasing foreign bank competition in their domestic markets.

QUESTIONS

1. "Every Eurodollar deposit is linked to a domestic U.S. deposit." Explain why this statement is correct.

2. What were some of the principal reasons for the emergence and growth of the Eurodollar market?

3. Evaluate the following statement (from an 8/30/74 editorial in the *Wall Street Journal*): "In the Eurocurrency markets there are no reserve requirements at all, which means that $1 of reserve can be multiplied endlessly—theoretically, if the banks lost all prudence, into millions of dollars of bank deposits."

4. Compare interest rate structure and behavior in the domestic U.S. money markets and the Eurodollar market.

5. Discuss the major participants in the Eurodollar market. How does their participation link the Eurodollar market and the domestic U.S. money market?

6. Why did the U.S. capital-outflows control program of 1963–1974 spur the development of the Eurobond and Eurocredit markets?

7. What are "Eurocredits"? How has one aspect of Eurocredit lending become a problem for the international financial system?

8. Describe the principal instruments of the international bond market.

9. Identify and discuss the principal activities of commercial banks in the international financial system.

10. Compare the development of U.S. overseas banking and foreign banking in the United States.

REFERENCES

Aliber, Robert Z., "International Banking: Growth and Regulation," *Columbia Journal of World Business* (Winter 1975), 9–15.

Baker, James C., and M. Gerald Bradford, *American Banks Abroad: Edge Act Companies and Multinational Banking* (New York: Praeger, 1974).

Cheng, Hang-Sheng, "International Financial Intermediation," Federal Reserve Bank of San Francisco *Weekly Letter,* (December 16, 1983), 1–3.

Chrystal, K. Alec, "International Banking Facilities," Federal Reserve Bank of St. Louis *Review* (April 1984), 5–11.

Dufey, Gunter, and Ian Giddy, *The International Money Market* (Englewood Cliffs, N.J.: Prentice-Hall, 1978).

Fieleke, Norman S., "International Lending on Trial," Federal Reserve Bank of Boston *New England Economic Review* (May/June 1983), 5–13.

———, *The International Economy Under Stress* (Cambridge, Mass.: Ballinger, 1988).

Giddy, Ian, "Why Eurodollars Grow," *Columbia Journal of World Business* (Fall 1979), 54–60.

Goodfriend, Marvin, "Eurodollars," *Instruments of the Money Market*, 5th ed., (Federal Reserve Bank of Richmond, 1981).

Grabbe, Oren J., *International Financial Markets* (New York: Wiley, 1986).

Hewson, John, and Eisuke Sakakibara, *The Eurocurrency Markets and Their Implications* (Lexington, Mass.: D.C. Heath, 1975).

Houpt, James V., "International Trends for U.S. Banks and Banking Markets," Staff Study (Washington, D.C.: Board of Governors of the Federal Reserve System, May 1988).

"International Banking," *The Economist* (March 21, 1987), 3–70.

"International Capital Markets: Securitization Strikes Back," *Barclay's Review* (August 1988), 34–37.

Khoury, Sarkis J., *Dynamics of International Banking* (New York: Praeger, 1980).

Lees, Francis A., *International Banking and Finance* (New York: Wiley, 1974).

———, and Maximo Eng, *International Financial Markets* (New York: Praeger, 1975).

Lewis, M.K., and K.T. Davis, *Domestic and International Banking* (Cambridge, Mass.: Ballinger, 1987), 216–394.

Makin, John H., and Dennis E. Logue (Eds.), *Eurocurrencies and the International Monetary System* (Washington, D.C.: American Enterprise Institute for Public Policy Research, 1976).

Mendelsohn, M. S., *Money on the Move: The Modern International Capital Market* (New York: McGraw-Hill, 1980).

Ogilvie, Nigel, "Foreign Banks in the U.S. and Geographic Restrictions on Banking," *Journal of Bank Research* (Summer 1980), 72–79.

Park, Yoon S., and Jack Zwick, *International Banking in Theory and Practice* (Reading, Mass.: Addison-Wesley, 1985).

Riehl, Heinz, and Rita M. Rodriguez, *Foreign Exchange and Money Markets* (New York: McGraw-Hill, 1983).

Ricks, David, and Jeffrey S. Arpan, "Foreign Banking in the United States," *Business Horizons* (February 1976), 84–87.

Salomon Brothers, *United States Multinational Banking* (New York: Salomon Brothers, Inc., 1976).

Sampson, Anthony, *The Money Lenders* (London: Hodder and Stoughton, 1982).

Shapiro, Alan C., *Multinational Financial Management* (Boston: Allyn and Bacon, 1989), 655–702.

Solnik, Bruno, *International Investments* (Reading, Mass.: Addison-Wesley, 1987).

Tan Chiwee Huat, "The Asian Dollar Market," in P. D. Grub, Tan Chiwee Huat, Kwan Kuen-Chor, and G. H. Rott (Eds.), *East Asia Dimensions of International Business* (Englewood Cliffs, N.J.: Prentice-Hall, 1982).

PART VII

ECONOMIC POLICY AND THE FINANCIAL MARKETPLACE

CHAPTER 26

Monetary Policy: Formulation, Implementation, and Impact

The highly significant and multifaceted role that the Federal Reserve System plays in the U.S. financial system was noted and emphasized in a number of preceding chapters. The Fed is featured prominently in this chapter, which is concerned with the Fed's primary purpose: the formulation and implementation of monetary policy. The organizational aspects of the Fed related to monetary policy are reviewed, the tools and techniques of monetary control are described and discussed, and the effects of monetary policy are assessed. The latter discussion includes treatment of various unsettled issues of monetary policy impact.

Monetary policy, the subject of this chapter, and fiscal policy, the subject of the next chapter, are the principal methods employed by the government in its attempts to achieve certain goals of economic policy. Thus the purpose of this chapter and Chapter 27 is to examine the nature of these policies and goals and the ways in which policy actions affect both the financial system and the real sector of the economy. We begin by describing the economic policy tools available to the government and explaining how they relate to economic activity. We then discuss policy objectives and some of the problems associated with their pursuit. The remainder of the chapter focuses on monetary policy.

ECONOMIC POLICY AND ECONOMIC ACTIVITY

The economic policy tools that may be employed in a market economy (such as that of the United States) may be grouped into three types: monetary policy, fiscal policy, and incomes policy. The first two policy types generally have broad effects across the economy, although certain instruments of selective impact are included among the various measures of both monetary and fiscal policy. For example, monetary policy includes (currently or potentially) various consumer credit controls and margin requirements on security purchases. Fiscal policy includes spending programs and tax measures that focus on relatively narrow segments of the economy. In general, however, monetary and fiscal policy are aimed at the aggregate level of spending in the economy, perhaps the broadest possible target for an economic policy tool.

Economic Policy and Aggregate Demand

Both fiscal and monetary policy are intended to affect aggregate demand in the economy—the total spending for goods and services. Restraining the expansion of aggregate demand is the intent of an anti-inflationary policy, since a reduction in demand for goods and services presumably dampens the tendency for prices and wages to rise. On the other hand, the stimulation of aggregate demand by policy action is presumed to bring forth an increase in aggregate supply—the quantity of goods and services produced—thus expanding employment as well as output and income.

Aggregate demand has four components: consumption, investment, net exports, and government spending (see Table 26.1).[1] **Consumption demand** is spending for durable goods (cars, furniture, appliances, and so on), nondurable goods (food, clothing, and so on), and services (transportation, entertainment, medical care, and so on). Income is the principal determinant of consumption spending, but the ratio of consumption to income (percentage of income spent on consumption) is affected in varying degrees by such factors as wealth, expectations, and interest rates.

Investment demand is composed of business spending for plant and equipment (business fixed investment), changes in business inventories, and household-sector spending for residential housing. Changes in business inventories are determined, of course, by the difference between production and sales, and though important, they account for a relatively small part of total investment spending.[2] The amount of business fixed investment is largely determined by

---

[1] Aggregate demand—in total and in its various components—may be viewed as an *ex ante* (before the fact) schedule of potential amounts of aggregate spending or as an *ex post* (after the fact) amount that was expended during some past period. *Ex ante* aggregate demand can be unequal to aggregate supply *(ex ante* and *ex post),* but *ex post* aggregate spending necessarily equals *ex post* aggregate supply—the amount sold must be equal to the amount bought.

Aggregate supply includes goods and services produced for export to the rest of the world, and aggregate domestic spending includes imports from the rest of the world. Thus exports increase the gross national product (GNP), but imports do not; that is, GNP = consumption + investment + government spending + (exports − imports).

[2] Changes in inventories constitute an "early warning" indicator of shifts in the level of economic activity. Businesses generally attempt to maintain stable inventory levels (harmonize production and sales), but their ability to do so is a function of the level of stability in the economy and/or their ability to forecast future sales. Unexpected surges in demand thus result in reduced inventories, and unexpected sales dips result in inventory buildup.

TABLE 26.1 Gross National Product and Income (Billions of current dollars except as noted; quarterly data are at seasonally adjusted annual rates) _____

Account	1986	1987	1988
Gross National Product			
1 Total	$4,240.3	$4,526.7	$4,864.3
By source			
2 Personal consumption expenditures	2,807.5	3,012.1	3,227.5
3 Durable goods	406.5	421.9	451.1
4 Nondurable goods	943.6	997.9	1,046.9
5 Services	1,457.3	1,592.3	1,729.6
6 Gross private domestic investment	665.9	712.9	766.5
7 Fixed investment	650.4	673.7	718.1
8 Nonresidential	433.9	446.8	488.4
9 Structures	138.5	139.5	142.8
10 Producers' durable equipment	295.4	307.3	345.6
11 Residential structures	216.6	226.9	229.7
12 Change in business inventories	15.5	39.2	48.4
13 Nonfarm	17.4	40.7	42.2
14 Net exports of goods and services	−104.4	−123.0	−94.6
15 Exports	378.4	428.0	519.7
16 Imports	482.8	551.1	614.4
17 Government purchases of goods and services	871.2	924.7	964.9
18 Federal	366.2	382.0	381.0
19 State and local	505.0	542.8	583.9
By major type of product			
20 Final sales, total	4,224.7	4,487.5	4,815.9
21 Goods	1,697.9	1,792.5	1,938.7
22 Durable	725.3	776.3	858.3
23 Nondurable	972.6	1,016.3	1,080.4
24 Services	2,118.3	2,295.7	2,478.0
25 Structures	424.0	438.4	447.7
26 Change in business inventories	15.5	39.2	48.4
27 Durable goods	4.3	26.6	30.9
28 Nondurable goods	11.3	12.6	17.4
MEMO			
29 Total GNP in 1982 dollars	$3,721.7	$3,847.0	$3,996.1
National Income			
30 Total	$3,437.1	$3,678.7	$3,968.2
31 Compensation of employees	2,507.1	2,683.4	2,904.7
32 Wages and salaries	2,094.0	2,248.4	2,436.9
33 Government and government enterprises	393.7	420.1	446.1
34 Other	1,700.3	1,828.3	1,990.7
35 Supplement to wages and salaries	413.1	435.0	467.8
36 Employer contributions for social insurance	217.0	227.1	249.6
37 Other labor income	196.1	207.9	218.3
38 Proprietors' income[1]	286.7	312.9	324.5
39 Business and professional[1]	250.3	270.0	288.2

(continued)

TABLE 26.1 *(continued)*

Account	1986	1987	1988
40 Farm[1]	36.4	43.0	36.3
41 Rental income of persons[2]	12.4	18.4	19.3
42 Corporate profits[1]	298.9	310.4	328.1
43 Profits before tax	236.4	276.7	306.4
44 Inventory valuation adjustment	8.3	−18.0	−23.8
45 Capital consumption adjustment	54.2	51.7	45.6
46 Net interest	331.9	353.6	391.5

[1]With inventory valuation and capital consumption adjustments.
[2]With capital consumption adjustment.

Source: Federal Reserve Bulletin, *May 1989.*

business firms' expectations of future sales volume (and thus production volume) in relation to existing capacity and inventory levels. The availability and cost of funds to finance plant and equipment expansion are also significant. The degree of sensitivity of investment spending to the interest rate—the relationship of changes in investment spending to changes in the rate of interest—is termed the **interest elasticity** of investment demand.

The demand for residential housing is viewed as quite responsive to credit conditions. Higher interest rates for mortgage credit and reduced availability of mortgage lending curtail this component of investment spending, whereas eased credit conditions stimulate it. Various demographic factors outside the purview of economic policy, such as the age composition of the population, are also critical determinants of spending for residential housing.

Total government spending is the sum of the expenditures of the federal, state, and local governments. Although the spending of all government units has significant economic impact, only federal spending is considered a fiscal policy tool aimed at the management of aggregate demand in the economy.

Monetary and fiscal policy are thus intended to affect consumption, investment, and state and local government (not federal) spending. The presumed effectiveness of monetary policy as an instrument of economic stabilization depends on a relatively stable and systematic (and thus predictable) relationship between the money supply (and perhaps various other financial variables) and the various components of aggregate demand. Increases in the money supply should stimulate aggregate demand and thus result in expanded employment and production; the reverse should happen for decreases in the money stock.

Fiscal policy affects aggregate demand via the balance between government tax collections (which withdraw purchasing power from the economy) and government spending (which injects purchasing power into the economy). When expenditures exceed tax receipts, aggregate spending increases, rippling through the economy to create additional income in some multiple of the excess of spending over taxes. Output and employment rise concurrently. The reverse effect holds for an excess of tax collections over government spending.[3] (Further discussion of fiscal policy is included in the next chapter.)

Incomes Policy

Incomes policy, essentially an anti-inflation policy, represents an attempt by government to restrain prices, profits, and wages directly rather than through the indirect mechanism of aggregate-demand restraint. Such a policy, in both its compulsory and "voluntary" variations, has been invoked on several occasions in recent decades. The perennial popularity and political appeal of incomes policy can be attributed to a number of things, including the following.

1. The fact that wage/price controls, unlike the esoteric workings of monetary and fiscal policy, are readily comprehensible to the lay public.

2. The belief that some inflationary bouts are due to "structural imperfections" in the economy that push up costs and prices in the absence of excessive aggregate demand.

3. The view of a number of professional economists that an incomes policy can restrain prices while monetary and fiscal policies (which obviously impact much more slowly on the price level) are taking hold and "wringing out" inflationary expectations.

Neither an analysis of the likely effectiveness of incomes policy nor an account of its use in this country is within the scope of this book. However, direct economic controls (of any sort) alter the pattern of resource allocation (relative to a market-determined path) to a much greater degree than do economic measures that impact more generally. Further, the "track record" of wage/price controls is rather dismal.

Economic Policy and Aggregate Supply

The point is often made that since monetary and fiscal policy impact directly on aggregate demand, changes in aggregate supply occur as a consequence of changes in aggregate demand. This aspect is of special significance for anti-inflation policies. So-called demand-pull inflation amounts to an excess of aggregate demand over aggregate supply at the existing price level; prices of goods and services rise to fill the "inflationary gap." Monetary and fiscal policies are aimed

---

[3]Whether or not these fiscal effects, independent of monetary expansion, result in sustainable increases or decreases in income is an issue of considerable debate that will be considered at a later point in this chapter.

at closing the inflationary gap by curbing aggregate demand. Unfortunately, the impact of these policies is not only on inflationary "fat" but on real output "muscle." In effect, the price of an aggregate-demand policy–induced reduction in the inflation rate is the goods and services forgone because of the policy's impact on output and employment.

So-called supply-side economics is a response to this policy dilemma. This approach to curbing inflation emphasizes tax incentives and other policy measures to increase productivity and thus total output of goods and services. The objective is to close the inflationary gap by increasing aggregate supply rather than by decreasing aggregate demand. Discussion and analysis of supply-side economics are included in the next chapter, but we will note here that, irrespective of the extent that policymakers turn their attention to aggregate supply stimulus measures, appropriate aggregate-demand policies remain important for economic stability.

GOALS OF ECONOMIC POLICY

The standard litany of economic goals is full employment, price stability, sustainable economic growth, and a "balanced" balance of payments. One of the many difficulties in "managing the economy" is the fact that monetary and fiscal measures appropriate for the achievement of one of these goals are often counterproductive to one or more of the other goals. For example, policies aimed at increasing employment and the rate of economic growth conventionally focus on monetary expansion and fiscal stimulus (increased government spending and/ or a reduction in taxes). A resulting increase in economic activity may create both inflationary pressures and balance of payments problems. The threat to price stability emerges even before the economy reaches full employment because various imperfections in the markets for productive resources cause scarcity that trigger price increases. (Once full employment of available resources is attained, any additional stimulus will result only in inflation—money income will rise but not real income.) A further potential difficulty with a policy of stimulus is that since the volume of imports increases with income, a balance of payments problem may develop as imports expand more than exports. There are other difficulties in pursuing the various goals of economic policy, and we assess some of these problems as we present a brief overview of the goals themselves.

Full Employment

The worldwide Great Depression of the 1930s was characterized by massive and unprecedented unemployment. In addition to the human suffering and shocking waste of human and material potential that this economic crisis entailed, it contributed in large measure to the chain of events that culminated in World War II. Therefore it is not surprising that full employment emerged as the paramount economic objective of the United States (and most other countries) in the postwar period. Indeed, by act of Congress (the Employment Act of 1946) the promotion of "maximum employment, production, and purchasing power" was named as a goal of government.

Full employment does not mean a zero unemployment rate; rather, it means an employment level that allows for "friction" in the labor market, such as workers changing jobs and new entrants into the labor force finding jobs. The amount of friction is in turn affected by the composition of the labor force. There is disagreement as to what level of unemployment is acceptable in the pursuit of a full-employment goal. The term **natural rate of unemployment** has been given to that level of unemployment at which the demand and supply of available labor are equal and there is neither upward nor downward pressure on the real (price-level adjusted) wage rate. There is no operational measure of the natural rate of unemployment (although some economists have estimated it to be about 6 or 7 percent for the United States). However, the concept does serve as a vehicle for the argument that government economic stimulus in the pursuit of "full employment" has frequently unleashed inflationary pressures. During the decade of the 1970s this view won enough adherents to cause the "acceptable" rate of unemployment, as viewed by professional economists, to rise. Many economists viewed the target rate of unemployment of the 1978 Full Employment and Balanced Growth Act (the Humphrey-Hawkins Act)—4 percent of overall and 3 percent for workers over the age of 20—as inflationary at the time of enactment, despite the fact that 4 percent unemployment rate had been the "full employment" bench mark for many years.[4] As indicated in Fig. 26.1, this goal has been elusive since the early 1950s.

Price Stability

Chapter 8 includes a discussion of inflation's causes and consequences, and such treatment need not be repeated here. Price stability is a goal of economic policy because both inflation and deflation have negative economic and social consequences. In recent decades, inflation has been a serious problem for most industrialized societies. The chronic, persistent nature of inflation since World War II is unique in history; previous episodes of price inflation were less enduring and generally connected to wars or other serious disruptions of the social order. (Figure 26.2 shows consumer goods price trends in the United States since 1910.) One suggested reason for the persistent and pervasive inflationary trend

---

[4]In the 1950s and 1960s, "full employment" was deemed to be achieved at a 4 percent unemployment rate. In the late 1960s the latter rate was boosted to $4\frac{1}{2}$ percent, then to 5 percent in the 1970s, and then to 6 percent in the 1980s.

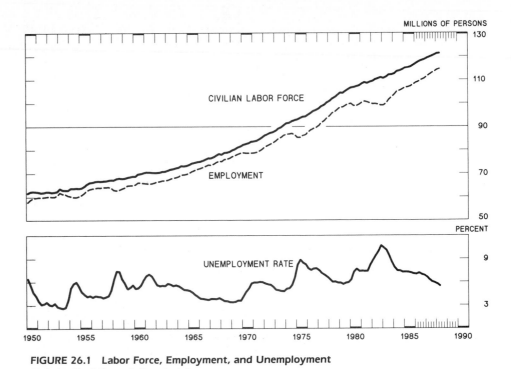

FIGURE 26.1   Labor Force, Employment, and Unemployment
(Seasonally Adjusted, Quarterly)

Source: Board of Governors of the Federal Reserve System, Historical Chart Book, *1988.*

of recent decades is efforts by central government economic policymakers to stimulate economic growth and employment. Such efforts (primarily expansionary monetary and fiscal policy) are viewed as creating excess demand for goods and productive resources and thus driving up prices of output and the costs of inputs.

Indeed, a relationship between the level of unemployment and the rate of inflation was formally noted by the eminent economist Irving Fisher in 1926. In 1958, A. W. Phillips, an Australian economist, published results of a study he had made of unemployment levels and the rate of change in money wage rates in the United Kingdom from 1861 to 1957. The term "Phillips curve" was adopted for the inverse relationship between these variables that Phillips reported. Since the money wage rate is the principal component of the cost of goods and services, the Phillips curve has often been cited to indicate the apparent tradeoff between inflation and unemployment that characterizes modern economies. According to the assumed dynamics of this tradeoff, as economic activity accelerates and unemployment declines, labor markets tighten and money wages rise, creating upward pressure on the price level. The reverse holds for economic downturns.

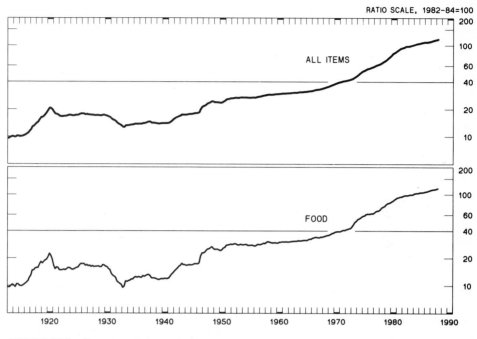

**FIGURE 26.2   Consumer Prices, all Items and Food
(Quarterly Averages)**

Source: Board of Governors of the Federal Reserve System, Historical Chart Book, *1988.*

Until about 1968, inflation and unemployment data for the United States and most industrial Western nations fitted the Phillips curve fairly well. Then the "fit" dissolved when rising unemployment and accelerating inflation began to occur together during the 1970s. (See Fig. 26.3.) As economists sought to explain the empirical breakdown in the Phillips curve relationship between unemployment and inflation, the attention of many monetarists focused on the role of inflationary expectations as a potential stumbling block for economic stabilization policy.

In his 1967 presidential address to the American Economic Association, Milton Friedman implicitly (and correctly) forecasted the demise of the Phillips curve by labeling its demonstrated unemployment–inflation relationship as a purely transitory phenomenon. Phillips's oversight, Friedman charged, was in charting the *money* wage rate rather than the *real* wage rate (the money wage rate less the rate of increase in the price level). The money and real wage rates are equivalent only in the absence of inflation, and Phillips's good empirical fit merely reflected a past prevalence of price-stability expectations among workers, Friedman asserted.

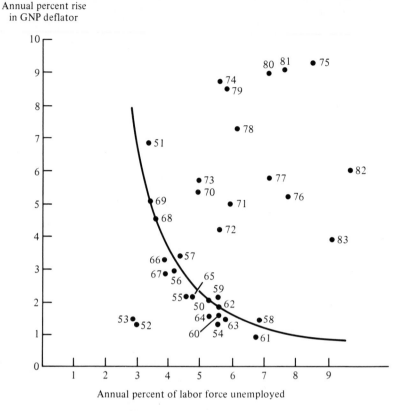

Annual percent rise
in GNP deflator

Annual percent of labor force unemployed

FIGURE 26.3   Rates of Inflation and Unemployment in the United States, 1950–1983.

Source: U.S. Department of Labor, Economic Report of the President, *various issues.*

If, as Friedman suggests, the correct Phillips curve relationship is one of real wages and unemployment, there will be, in effect, a Phillips curve for each possible price level when the money wage rate and unemployment rate are compared.[5] During periods in which workers expect the price level to rise (doubtless the state

[5]Friedman and others argue that a Phillips curve depicting real wage and unemployment rates in the long run will not be a curve at all; it will be a vertical line at the so-called natural rate of unemployment—the "full employment" level of unemployment that allows for "frictional" unemployment. The argument negates any policy significance of the Phillips curve, since it indicates that (except temporarily) unemployment is not affected by the inflation rate or vice versa. Deviations from the natural rate of unemployment occur only when employers or workers or both are fooled regarding the real wage level for the employment period, most likely because they have overestimated or underestimated the rate of inflation for the ensuing period.

of affairs during the 1970s) the actual money wage–unemployment relationship will be on a Phillips curve to the right of a Phillips curve for a period of antici-pated relative price level stability. (This result is due to the necessity for money wages to increase at the same rate as the price level if the real wage is to be constant.) Thus the tradeoff between two economic "bads"—inflation and unem-ployment—worsens during periods of inflationary expectations.

The inflation–unemployment tradeoff has been called the "dilemma model" for economic policy makers. If the scenario above is accurate, it appears that inflationary expectations can exacerbate this dilemma. One possible implication for monetary policy is that monetary stringency must be applied longer and more vigorously to check inflation, for inflationary expectations must be wrung out of the economy before the dampening of aggregate demand can have a significant impact on the tendency for wages and prices to rise. This also implies that the "price" of price stability—the real output lost as a result of monetary restraint and ensuing unemployment—will be much higher when inflationary expecta-tions have become ingrained in the economy. Public belief in the Fed's capacity and determination to curb inflation thus becomes a necessary element of mone-tary policy, and such credibility is attained by the application of monetary strin-gency "as long as it takes."

On the other hand, in regard to the public's perceptions and expectations of Fed policy, if anti-inflationary policy moves are credible, the belief that the infla-tion rate (and economic activity) will soon be slowed may result in anticipatory behavior that reinforces and speeds up the policy's effects. A plausible possibility in this instance is the observed tendency of business firms to curtail inventory growth and defer investment projects when the Fed signals that credit will be tightened as an anti-inflationary action. In this context, when the public is per-suaded that the Fed will pursue a strong program of monetary restraint that will check inflation (or when recession is the problem, it is believed that a Fed pro-gram of monetary ease will stimulate recovery), expectations effects can be viewed as a channel for the transmission of monetary policy action to the real sector of the economy. In the long run, according to this view, the proper anti-inflationary stance for the Fed is an announced policy of stable monetary growth to which the Fed religiously adheres.

Whether inflationary expectations must be slowly and painfully squeezed out of an economy or can instead be erased relatively quickly and painlessly depends on the process by which these expectations change. If the public's "forecast" of future inflation is based solely on experienced inflation (an "adaptive" process), there is no alternative to the slow and painful "wringing out" process. On the other hand, if the public is able and willing to use information other than past price level changes in forming its collective inflation forecast, inflationary expec-tations can shift very rapidly. (Granting the public this degree of sophistication and foresight has markedly interesting implications, as we consider later in this chapter.)

Thus the pursuit of price stability as an economic policy goal—particularly the curbing of inflationary pressures—while simultaneously seeking to maintain full employment and a high rate of economic growth is a difficult task. The desired rate of price change (zero or otherwise) can likely be attained by control of the rate of monetary growth, but there is no assurance that other economic goals can be concomitantly achieved. (However, many monetarists argue that such a policy approach is the best means of maximizing the probability of such joint attainment of the principal economic policy objectives.)

Economic Growth

Figure 26.4 indicates growth in the U.S. gross national product in recent years. Such growth is a measure of the rise in the material standard of living, which, if not ensuring a rise in the overall quality of life, does generally help. Economic growth is a consequence of an increase in the quantity of the factors of

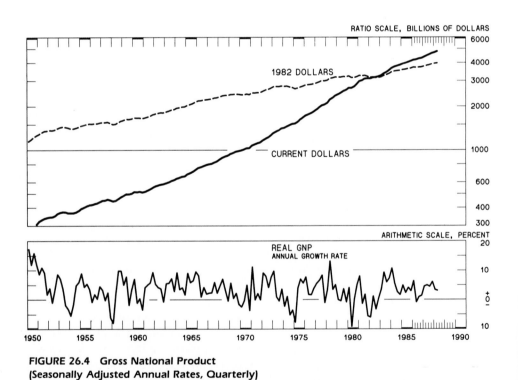

FIGURE 26.4   Gross National Product
(Seasonally Adjusted Annual Rates, Quarterly)

Source: Board of Governors of the Federal Reserve System, Historical Chart Book, 1988.

production and/or an increase in the productive capacity of these various factors.

Aggregate output may rise simply because labor, capital, or natural resources become more abundant. Output per worker, however, is likely to increase only if the latter two factors of production become more plentiful (cheaper). This aspect of economic growth is the reason for the importance of capital formulation (and its necessary conditions, saving and investment). Economic growth is also made possible by an increase in the productive capacity of a given labor supply or stock of capital. Labor becomes more productive as skills are gained and improved by training and education. Capital becomes more productive as technological improvements in the use of capital occur, or as capital is used more intensively.

Economic growth is thus a more fundamental goal than either price stability or full employment. Economic growth is facilitated by both the full employment of resources and the appropriate degree of price change (not necessarily zero). Yet these conditions, though necessary for a maximum rate of economic growth, are not sufficient. The desire and capacity of people to save, invest, innovate, and simply work hard are the basic determinants of economic growth. An efficient financial system and a rational tax system can contribute to capital formation, but the necessary ingredients include social, cultural, and political factors as well as economic conditions.

Balance of Payments "Equilibrium"

As described in Chapter 24, the U.S. transition to a floating-exchange-rate regime reduced the direct role of the Federal Reserve in maintaining the value of the dollar in the foreign exchange market. However, the Fed still intervenes occasionally to avoid violent fluctuations in the dollar's value, and the Fed's interest-rate targets are surely influenced by international economic considerations. Further, the Fed acts as fiscal agent for the Treasury in its various international transactions.

The level of interest rates in the United States relative to other countries affects the capital-account balance component of the balance of payments. If U.S. rates are relatively lower than those prevailing in other major countries, foreign private and official holders of U.S. money market instruments may sell them and invest the dollar proceeds in other countries. The resulting inflow of dollars (increased supply) to the foreign exchange market may depress the value of the dollar. On the other hand, high U.S. interest rates tend to attract foreign investment in U.S. money market instruments. As foreign investors obtain U.S. dollars for such investments, the increased demand for dollars tends to raise the dollar's value. The extraordinary surge in the dollar's strength in foreign currency markets in the early 1980s stemmed primarily from relatively high (real) interest rates in the United States.

Of critical importance to currency values in the long run is a country's **balance of trade**—its exports relative to its imports. Paradoxically, rapid growth of the domestic economy can create problems for a country's trade balance. Rising income tends to expand imports but creates no corresponding incentive for the boosting of exports (unless the economies of trading partners are expanding at a commensurate or more rapid pace).

Expansionary monetary policy may result in balance of payments problems for two reasons. As the money supply increases, interest rates tend to fall, and spending (as well as income) tends to rise. When fiscal policy measures are employed to stimulate the economy, only the resulting income increase is a potential source of a balance of payments problem, since interest rates tend to rise when taxes are cut and government spending increases (unless such measures are accompanied by expansionary monetary policy). Conversely, restrictive monetary policy aimed at curbing inflation tends to push up interest rates and lower income; both of these effects act (by attracting foreign capital and reducing imports) to strengthen the currency. Restrictive fiscal policy tends to lower income and interest rates, the former effect serving to reduce imports and the latter effect acting to discourage foreign capital inflows.

It is apparent that the pursuit of concurrent full employment, price stability, economic growth, and balance of payments equilibrium is a difficult, imprecise, and complex process. We consider next how a principal tool of such pursuit, monetary policy, is formulated and implemented. In so doing, an effort has been made to avoid repetition of the Chapter 5 treatment of the Fed's basic role and operating instruments; the reader is referred to this chapter for such description.

FORMULATION OF MONETARY POLICY

The fundamental decisions shaping monetary policy are made in the regular meetings of the Federal Open Market Committee. These meetings generally consume an entire day and occur about once a month. FOMC members are briefed on a wide range of domestic and international economic developments. Policy options and potential strategies in the conduct of open-market operations are discussed. The committee then agrees on policy guidelines for open-market operations to be conducted over the period before the next meeting of the group. A policy statement incorporating these guidelines is then drafted and presented to the Manager of the System Open Market Account, an officer of the Federal Reserve Bank of New York who is responsible for the execution of open-market operations. The statement serves as the directive for the day-to-day implementation of the Federal Reserve's operations in the securities markets.

The directives, which are not made public until about a month after each meeting, indicate the Fed's general monetary objectives over the period until the next meeting. The directives typically include a brief review of economic developments, a summary of the Committee's economic objectives, and instructions to the Account Manager for conducting open-market operations. The policy statements may seem rather vague to an outsider—policy direction is couched in phrases like "actions to moderate pressures on financial markets," "moderate growth in monetary aggregates," "fostering financial conditions that will encourage economic recovery while resisting inflationary pressures," and so forth. Further, such guides are interspersed with highly technical discussions of current economic conditions. The Manager of the System Open Market Account, however, always sits in on the FOMC meetings that produce these directives and is thus likely to know more about what the Fed wants than the statements actually say. Moreover, there is daily communication between the manager and the Board in the normal course of implementing the general policy directive.[6] The directives issued by the FOMC, along with a summary justification of FOMC actions, are made public after the next FOMC meeting. The "Record of Policy Actions of the Federal Open Market Committee" is published in the *Federal Reserve Bulletin* soon after its public release. The directive issued in February 1989 is contained in Exhibit 26.1.

Monetary Policy Targets

The ultimate objective of monetary policy measures is to impact in some desired fashion on the price level, employment and production, and/or (via its impact on these economic variables) the balance of payments. However, as we discussed above, monetary policy inevitably involves time lags before such impacts can be assessed. To adopt, conduct, and adapt the exercise of policy instruments in an appropriate and timely fashion, the Fed is obligated to employ **intermediate targets.** Potential target variables include interest rates, reserves (total reserves, borrowed reserves, and nonborrowed reserves), the monetary base (reserves plus currency in circulation), and one or more of the various monetary aggregates (measures of the money stock) described earlier.[7] Needless to say,

---

[6]The FOMC, in addition to its regular meetings, occasionally holds telephone consultations between the dates of scheduled meetings. Such sessions may result in revised instructions to the manager if warranted.

[7]The literature on this subject is rendered somewhat confusing by the plethora of terms—goals, objectives, targets, indicators, guides, etc.—that are used to describe the Fed's various bench marks of results. In this chapter the terms "goals" and "objectives" are used synonymously and refer to ultimate contributions to the economic goals cited in the chapter. The term "targets" is used to refer to economic variables that constitute intermediate impact goals. The term "operating target" is used to denote economic variables that the Fed uses to gauge its impact on "policy target" variables.

EXHIBIT 26.1 ∎
Record of Policy Actions of the Federal Open Market Committee

MEETING HELD ON FEBRUARY 7–8, 1989

Domestic policy directive

The information reviewed at this meeting suggested that, apart from the direct effects of the drought, economic activity had continued to expand at a fairly vigorous pace. The latest information on prices indicated little change in the rate of inflation from recent trends, while labor costs had continued to accelerate.

After strong gains in the fourth quarter, total nonfarm payroll employment rose sharply in January. Although some of the strength may have reflected such temporary factors as unusually mild winter weather, job gains were widespread; in manufacturing, sizable increases were registered in nonelectrical machinery, transportation equipment, and food processing. The civilian unemployment rate, at 5.4 percent, remained in the lower part of the range that had prevailed since the early spring of last year.

Industrial production rose appreciably further in December and January, with gains continuing at about the robust pace experienced in 1988 as a whole. Output of consumer goods advanced strongly, despite a somewhat slower pace of automobile assemblies over the two months, and production of business equipment picked up a bit. Total industrial capacity utilization moved higher, owing to a sizable jump in the utilization of manufacturing capacity to the highest level since 1979. Housing starts declined somewhat in December but were up substantially on balance for the fourth quarter as a whole, largely because of a strengthening in single-family construction. Multifamily starts have remained relatively flat in recent months.

Consumer spending was up considerably in the fourth quarter, capping a strong year. Spending on household durables rose vigorously in the quarter; and outlays for services again advanced at a rapid pace, reflecting big increases in expenditures for medical care, airline travel, and recreation. Consumption of nondurables advanced further, after a steep rise the previous quarter, while purchases of motor vehicles were little changed over the quarter as a whole.

Indicators of business capital spending suggested some weakening in recent months from the rapid increases evident earlier in 1988. Real outlays for business fixed investment were estimated to have fallen somewhat in the fourth quarter. Softness was fairly widespread among various types of equipment, but the most pronounced weakness was in office and computing equipment. Nonresidential construction activity picked up in December but was estimated to have been about flat on balance for the quarter; oil drilling and expenditures on commercial buildings other than offices declined further. Inventory investment in the manufacturing sector in the fourth quarter was little changed from the third-quarter pace, with much of the accumulation continuing to occur in durable goods industries where demand had been strong. At the retail level, increases in nonautomobile inventories generally kept pace with the growth in sales.

Excluding food and energy, producer prices of finished goods rose sharply in December, the rise reflecting large increases for tobacco products, women's apparel, and passenger cars. Prices for intermediate materials again increased substantially in November and December. The most notable hikes occurred in industries such as metals, chemicals, and paper products in which capacity utilization has been high. Consumer prices, reflecting more favorable developments in the food, energy, and apparel components, rose at a somewhat slower pace in November and December. Excluding food and energy, consumer prices rose in the fourth quarter at about the rate observed over 1988 as a whole. Reflecting tighter market conditions, wages and salaries, and labor costs more generally, advanced at a faster pace in the fourth quarter than was observed a year earlier.

The nominal U.S. merchandise trade deficit was slightly larger on average in October and November than it was in the third quarter. The value of imports rose as a sharp rise in the value of non-oil imports, especially from industrial countries, outweighed a drop in the value of oil imports resulting from a decline in oil prices. Increases were widespread across trade categories but were paced by a rebound in imports of passenger cars from somewhat depressed levels in the third quarter. The value of exports was little changed as a decline in agricultural exports offset a rise in nonagricultural products.

In foreign exchange markets, the trade-weighted value of the dollar in terms of the other G-10 currencies rose substantially over the intermeeting period and nearly reversed its decline of October and November. Despite the release of data indicating U.S. trade deficits that were larger than expected for October and November, the dollar climbed persistently from early December in response to perceptions of a relative tightening of monetary policy in the United States; short-term interest rate differentials moved in favor of the dollar relative to the yen.

At its meeting on December 13-14, the Committee adopted a directive calling for some immediate increase in the degree of pressure on reserve positions, with some further tightening to be implemented at the start of 1989 if economic and financial conditions remained consistent with the Committee's expectations. These reserve conditions were expected to be associated with growth of M2 and M3 at annual rates of about 3 percent and $6\frac{1}{2}$ percent respectively over the period from November through March. The members agreed that somewhat greater reserve restraint would, or slightly lesser reserve restraint might, be acceptable depending on indications of inflationary pressures, the strength of the business expansion, the behavior of the monetary aggregates, and developments in foreign exchange and domestic financial markets.

In accordance with the Committee's instructions, a firming of reserve supply conditions was carried out in two stages over the intermeeting period, although operations were complicated by continuing uncertainty about the relationship between borrowing and money market conditions. In the circumstances, open market operations continued to be conducted with a special degree of flexibility. Adjustment plus seasonal borrowing averaged somewhat more than $500 million over the period, but such borrowing fluctuated over a wide range, including a typical bulge around the year-end. The federal funds rate rose from around $8\frac{1}{2}$ percent to a little above 9 percent during the intermeeting period.

Changes in other short-term market rates were mixed over the intermeeting period. Treasury bill rates rose somewhat on balance, although less than the federal funds rate, while rates on private market instruments were generally unchanged to slightly lower. To some extent, the firming of monetary policy had been anticipated; in addition, private rates in particular were affected by the passing of year-end pressures. Bond yields declined somewhat, apparently influenced in part by the favorable effect of actual and anticipated monetary restraint on inflationary expectations. Major indexes of stock prices rose considerably over the intermeeting period.

Growth of the broader monetary aggregates weakened appreciably in January, especially M2, which apparently declined slightly after a moderate increase in December. The behavior of these aggregates appeared to reflect recent increases in short-term market rates, which in turn widened the opportunity costs of holding deposits. Those costs were accentuated by slower-than-usual adjustments in offering rates by depository institutions on most

EXHIBIT 26.1 (*continued*) ▇▇▇▇▇▇▇▇

of their retail deposits. Also, needs for deposits to fund credit growth were damped in this period. On average in December and January, growth of M2 was slightly below Committee expectations and that of M3 considerably below. M1 changed little on balance over the two months. For the year 1988, M2 expanded at a rate a little below and M3 at a rate around the midpoint of the Committee's ranges. Growth of total domestic nonfinancial debt moderated in 1988 to a pace around the midpoint of the Committee's monitoring range. The staff projections prepared for this meeting suggested that the expansion was likely to moderate in 1989 from the pace in 1988, although the adjustments related to the assumed end of the drought would be reflected in relatively strong measured growth in the first quarter. To the extent that expansion of final demand tended to remain at a pace that could foster higher inflation but was not accommodated by monetary policy, pressures would be generated in financial markets that would restrain domestic spending. The staff continued to project slower growth in consumer spending, sharply reduced expansion of business fixed investment, and some decline in housing construction. Foreign trade was expected to make a smaller contribution to growth in domestic output than in 1988. The staff antici- pated somewhat faster increases in consumer prices and also some further cost pressures over the year ahead, especially because of reduced margins of unutilized labor and other production resources.

In the Committee's discussion of the economic situation and outlook, members com- mented that the expansion in business activity was generally well balanced and that contin- uing growth was a reasonable expectation for the year ahead. Nearly all the members believed that the risks remained on the side of greater inflation and that the Federal Reserve would need to stay especially alert to inflationary developments. However, views differed to some extent with regard to the likely strength of the expansion and the degree of infla- tionary risk. Several members stressed that, in the absence of some further monetary re- straint, economic growth was likely to continue at a rate that would foster greater pressures on already strained production resources and induce more inflation. Other members gave more weight to indications of possible slowing in the expansion and to the possibility that the substantial restraint applied over the past year might be sufficient to foster sustainable expansion without increased inflationary pressures. The members agreed that the chances for satisfactory economic performance over time would be greatly enhanced by progress in reducing the federal budget deficit in order to contain domestic demands and to facilitate the process of adjustment in the nation's external balance.

In conformance with the usual practice at meetings when the Committee considers its long-term objectives for monetary growth, the members of the Committee and the Federal Reserve Bank presidents not currently serving as members had prepared specific projections of economic activity, the rate of unemployment, and inflation for the year 1989. The central tendency of these forecasts pointed to somewhat slower expansion and somewhat greater inflation than had occurred in 1988. For the period from the fourth quarter of 1988 to the fourth quarter of 1989, the forecasts for growth of real GNP had a central tendency of $2\frac{1}{2}$ to 3 percent and a full range of $1\frac{1}{2}$ to $3\frac{1}{4}$ percent. Forecasts of nominal GNP centered on growth rates of $6\frac{1}{2}$ to $7\frac{1}{2}$ percent and ranged from $5\frac{1}{2}$ to $8\frac{1}{2}$ percent. Estimates of the civilian rate of unemployment in the fourth quarter of 1989 were concentrated in a range of $5\frac{1}{4}$ to $5\frac{1}{2}$ percent with a full range of 5 to 6 percent. The projected increase in the consumer price index centered on rates of $4\frac{1}{2}$ to 5 percent and had an overall range of $3\frac{1}{2}$ to $5\frac{1}{2}$ percent for the year. In making these forecasts, the members took account of the Committee's policy of continuing restraint on aggregate demand to resist any increase in inflation pressures and foster price stability over time. They also assumed that normal weather conditions and a rise in acreage under cultivation this year would increase farm output and add around $\frac{2}{3}$ of a percentage point to the growth of GNP, an amount similar to the reduction in GNP that resulted from the drought in 1988. Excluding this swing in farm output, the central tendency of the forecasts implied considerably slower growth in output than in 1988. Finally, the forecasts assumed that fluctuations in the foreign exchange value of the dollar would not be of sufficient magnitude to have a significant effect on the economy or prices.

In the Committee's discussion of developments bearing on the economic outlook, a number of members stressed that the economy had a good deal of momentum and that there was little or no current evidence of a potential slowdown or downturn in the expansion. Indeed, some recent data, including those on employment and consumer spending, could be viewed as consistent with some strengthening of the expansion in recent months. Reports from around the country suggested a high level of business activity in many parts of the nation and at least modest improvement in some previously depressed areas. On the whole, growth in production was being well maintained, buttressed by continuing expansion in exports. Other members saw a greater potential for some softening in the rate of economic growth. They referred to sectors of relative weakness in the economy, including energy, nonresidential construction, and housing. With regard to the outlook for capital expenditures, many firms were investing in new equipment to improve their efficiency in competitive markets, but they generally continued to hold back on investments to expand production facilities. More generally, a number of members emphasized that the behavior of money, whose growth had been relatively damped for an extended period and was likely to remain so in 1989 under the Committee's targets, probably was consistent with only limited strength in spending.

A key element in the outlook for business was the extent of the improvement in the nation's external trade balance. The members generally expected further gains, at least over the year ahead, but several observed that these might be considerably smaller than in 1988, given the behavior of the dollar over the past year and assuming a steady dollar in the future. Such an outcome could have the advantage of helping to moderate potential inflationary demand pressures in the economy but at the cost and the risks associated with a continuing need to finance massive external deficits. It also was noted that substantial improvement in the trade balance at a time of increasing pressure on productive resources would require the expansion in domestic demand to slow sufficiently—perhaps more than was currently anticipated—to permit added production for exports.

Turning to the outlook for inflation, several members expressed concern that, with margins of unused labor and capital relatively low, any slowing in the growth of overall demands now in train might be inadequate to prevent some rise in the underlying rate of inflation, much less to permit progress to be made in bringing inflation down. In this view the economy's current momentum in association with a reduced availability of production resources clearly biased the economic risks toward greater inflation. A number of these members expressed particular concern about recent indications of higher labor costs, which might augur escalating inflationary pressures. Other members saw a lesser risk that inflation would intensify, at least in the absence of unfavorable developments such as a second year of drought conditions, a sharp upturn in energy prices, or a substantial decline in the foreign exchange value of the dollar. It was difficult to judge the point at which added pressures on production resources might be translated into stronger inflationary pressures, but several members observed that despite relatively vigorous economic growth the impact on the overall rate of inflation had been less than they might have anticipated earlier. Promising

EXHIBIT 26.1 (*continued*)

factors in the inflation outlook included the continuation of strong competitive pressures, notably competition from abroad that tended to inhibit efforts to raise prices, restrained monetary growth, and generally favorable inflationary expectations as evidenced by developments in financial markets. In one view, commodity prices, while still affected by the impact of the drought, might be signalling at least tentatively a downturn in the overall rate of inflation.

Against the background of the members' views regarding the economic outlook and in keeping with the requirements of the Full Employment and Balanced Growth Act of 1978 (the Humphrey–Hawkins Act), the Committee at this meeting reviewed the ranges of growth for the monetary and debt aggregates that had been established on a tentative basis in late June 1988 for the year 1989. The tentative range for M2 had been reduced by 1 percentage point to 3 to 7 percent and that for M3 by $\frac{1}{2}$ percentage point to $3\frac{1}{2}$ to $7\frac{1}{2}$ percent for 1989. The monitoring range for growth of total domestic nonfinancial debt had been lowered by $\frac{1}{2}$ percentage point to $6\frac{1}{2}$ to $10\frac{1}{2}$ percent for the year. The Committee had decided in June not to establish any range for M1.

In the Committee's discussion, a majority of the members indicated that they were in favor of affirming the reduced ranges that had been set on a tentative basis in mid-1988, while the remaining members expressed a preference for some further reductions. Members who supported the tentative ranges believed that they were fully consistent with progress toward price level stability. Indeed, the reduction of a full percentage point in the M2 range was larger than usual and would convey in this view an appropriately strong signal of the System's commitment to an anti-inflationary policy. This lower range encompassed money growth that was fully consistent under likely economic and financial conditions with continued expansion of spending but at the somewhat slower pace needed to contain inflationary pressures. A number of members also commented that the tentative ranges would provide more room in subsequent years for continuing the desirable policy of gradually lowering the monetary growth targets to noninflationary levels while also reducing the possibility that unanticipated economic or financial developments might require those targets to be raised on a temporary basis. Even though temporarily higher ranges might be consistent with progress toward price stability, a decision to raise the ranges could be misinterpreted as a weakening of the System's anti-inflationary resolve.

Other members believed that further reductions in the ranges would provide greater assurance of encompassing the potential policy responses and associated monetary growth that might be needed to resist inflationary pressures over the year ahead, should they prove to be especially strong. Such reductions would underscore the Committee's commitment to its longer-run objective of price stability, since achieving that objective would require lower money growth at some point than was indicated by the middle of the tentative ranges. Lower ranges for the broader aggregates would have midpoints that were more clearly below actual growth in 1988 and given the slow growth thus far this year, especially in the case of M2, would improve the prospects that expansion for the year would approximate the midpoints. Moreover, the upper ends of the tentative ranges, while below those for 1988, nonetheless remained appreciably higher than the rates of monetary growth that were likely to be consistent with price stability over time.

The Committee agreed on the desirability of retaining the relatively wide spread of 4 percentage points between the upper and the lower ends of the growth ranges for M2 and M3. These ranges were initially widened in 1988 in recognition of the uncertain outlook for financial markets and the economy and the extent to which the relationship between monetary growth and economic performance had varied over an extended period. In particular, the growth of M2 and its velocity had remained very sensitive to fluctuations in interest rates, reflecting in turn a tendency of depository institutions to adjust only sluggishly their offering rates on many types of deposit accounts. In these circumstances and against the background of the multiplicity of largely unpredictable factors affecting the economy and interest rates, the appropriate rate of monetary growth remained subject to considerable uncertainty and could not be projected within narrow ranges with any degree of confidence. An additional uncertainty in 1989 would be the impact of developments affecting thrift depository institutions as serious financial problems at many of those institutions moved toward resolution under the aegis of new government programs. The behavior of M2 and M3 was likely to be affected by such developments, but there was only limited basis in prior experience to gauge the extent of the impact.

The members found acceptable the tentative reduction of $\frac{1}{2}$ percentage point in the monitoring range for total domestic nonfinancial debt in 1989. As in several previous years, growth of total debt was expected to exceed that of nominal GNP. The members anticipated that the federal government would continue to place heavy demands on credit markets to finance its large ongoing deficits. In addition, the expansion of business borrowing would probably continue to be boosted by a widening financing gap and by the substitution of debt for equity in conjunction with leveraged buyouts and other corporate restructuring activities. Growth of household debt might moderate somewhat, reflecting the effect of increases in interest rates in 1988 on mortgage debt and of reduced expansion in consumer credit in association with a smaller rise in outlays on consumer durables over the year.

In keeping with the Committee's tentative decision in late June, no member proposed the inclusion of M1 among the monetary target ranges. The Committee continued to view the prospective relationship between M1 and aggregate measures of economic activity as too unpredictable to warrant reliance on this monetary measure as a guide for the conduct of monetary policy.

At the conclusion of the Committee's discussion, all but one of the members indicated that they favored or could accept the ranges for 1989 that had been established on a tentative basis in late June 1988. Against the background of the uncertainties that continued to surround the relationship between monetary growth and broad measures of economic performance, most of the members endorsed a proposal to make explicit in the directive the Committee's procedure in recent years of evaluating money growth in the conduct of policy in light of the behavior of other indicators, including inflationary pressures, the strength of the business expansion, and developments in domestic financial and foreign exchange markets.

At the conclusion of this discussion, the Committee approved for inclusion in the domestic policy directive the following paragraph relating to its longer-run policy for 1989:

> *The Federal Open Market Committee seeks monetary and financial conditions that will foster price stability, promote growth in output on a sustainable basis, and contribute to an improved pattern of international transactions. In furtherance of these objectives, the Committee at this meeting reaffirmed its decision of late June to lower the ranges for growth of M2 and M3 to 3 to 7 percent and $3\frac{1}{2}$ to $7\frac{1}{2}$ percent, respectively, measured from the fourth quarter of 1988 to the fourth quarter of 1989. The monitoring range for growth of total domestic nonfinancial debt was set at $6\frac{1}{2}$ to $10\frac{1}{2}$ percent for the year. The behavior of the monetary*

EXHIBIT 26.1 *(continued)* ▬▬▬▬▬

aggregates will continue to be evaluated in the light of movements in their velocities, developments in the economy and financial markets, and progress toward price level stability. Votes for this action: Messrs. Greenspan, Corrigan, Angell, Black, Forrestal, Heller, Johnson, Kelley, LaWare, Parry, and Ms. Seger. Vote against this action: Mr. Hoskins.

Mr. Hoskins dissented because he preferred lower ranges for the year. In his view satisfactory progress in reducing the underlying rate of inflation would require a degree of restraint over the year that would be likely to result in money growth at the low end of the tentative ranges, and he believed that the ranges adopted should be more closely centered on that possible outcome. He also felt that lower ranges were desirable at this time to underscore the System's determination to pursue an anti-inflationary policy.

In the Committee's discussion of policy implementation for the period until the next meeting, a majority of the members indicated a preference for maintaining unchanged conditions of reserve availability, at least initially, following today's meeting. Further monetary restraint might be desirable in the near future, perhaps during the intermeeting period. However, recent information had given a somewhat mixed picture of economic and price developments, and these members preferred to wait for further confirmation of inflationary pressures before additional firming of monetary policy was undertaken. Appreciable policy tightening had been implemented only recently and the impact would be felt only after a considerable lag. Monetary policy was now fairly restrictive, as evidenced for example by relatively high real rates of interest, a slightly inverted yield curve, and the slow growth of the monetary aggregates. The credibility of the System's anti-inflationary policy was quite high. Some members expressed concern that higher interest rates would exacerbate the financial difficulties of many thrift depository institutions, weaken heavily indebted firms, and in the context of a strong dollar possibly lead to an undesired upward ratcheting of interest rates in world financial markets. It also was noted that further tightening should be approached with special caution when the dollar was under upward pressure in the foreign exchange markets.

Other members indicated a preference for some immediate firming of monetary policy in light of their concerns about current and prospective inflationary pressures in the economy. In this view delaying further tightening would only worsen such pressures and could greatly increase the difficulty and ultimate cost of achieving the Committee's anti-inflationary objectives. Moreover, while higher interest rates could have adverse effects on interest-sensitive sectors of the economy, a failure to arrest and to reverse inflation would lead to even higher interest rates and greater damage over time. Some concern also was expressed that maintenance of steady reserve conditions might disappoint market expectations, with adverse repercussions in present circumstances on the credibility of the System's anti-inflationary policy and thus on inflationary expectations. Should too much restraint later prove to have been applied, it could be reversed more readily and with less lasting implications for economic performance than too little restraint, which would tend to embed inflation and inflationary expectations in the economic structure.

A number of members observed that the relatively slow monetary expansion that had been experienced in recent months—and indeed on balance for some two years—portended restraint on prices and was a welcome development. A staff forecast suggested that money growth was likely to remain damped over coming months, with both M2 and M3 growing at the lower end of the Committee's 1989 ranges. In the view of a number of members, this might be acceptable or even desirable depending on the extent of inflationary pressures being experienced in the economy. At the same time some members cautioned that a persistent shortfall from the ranges might be a cause for concern.

In the Committee's discussion of possible intermeeting adjustments in the degree of reserve restraint, members generally felt that there should be a clear presumption of some further firming if the incoming information tended to confirm expectations of growing inflationary pressures. Indeed, several members indicated that such a presumption would enable them to accept a directive that called for no immediate change in the degree of reserve pressure. Some members expressed the view that developments in foreign exchange markets might have an important bearing on the timing or even the desirability of any firming in the period ahead. More generally, the Committee agreed that consideration would need to be given to the usual range of factors that might call for a change in policy implementation, including the possibility that some easing might be warranted under certain conditions. For the immediate future, however, several stressed that any perceptions that monetary policy might be easing should be resisted.

At the conclusion of the Committee's discussion, all but two members indicated that they favored or could accept a directive that called for maintaining the current degree of pressure on reserve conditions and for remaining alert to potential developments that might require some firming during the intermeeting period. Accordingly, somewhat greater reserve restraint would be acceptable, or slightly lesser reserve restraint might be acceptable, over the intermeeting period depending on indications of inflationary pressures, the strength of the business expansion, the behavior of the monetary aggregates, and developments in foreign exchange and domestic financial markets. The reserve conditions contemplated by the Committee were expected to be consistent with growth of M2 and M3 at annual rates of around 2 percent and $3\frac{1}{2}$ percent respectively over the three-month period from December to March. It was understood that operations would continue to be conducted with some flexibility in light of the persisting uncertainty in the relationship between the demand for borrowed reserves and the federal funds rate. The intermeeting range for the federal funds rate, which provides one mechanism for initiating consultation of the Committee when its boundaries are persistently exceeded, was left unchanged at 7 to 11 percent.

At the conclusion of the meeting, the following domestic policy directive was issued to the Federal Reserve Bank of New York:

The information reviewed at this meeting suggests that, apart from the direct effects of the drought, economic activity has continued to expand at a fairly vigorous pace. After strong gains in the fourth quarter, total nonfarm payroll employment rose sharply in January, including a sizable increase in manufacturing. The civilian unemployment rate, at 5.4 percent in January, remained in the lower part of the range that has prevailed since the early spring of last year. Industrial production rose appreciably further in December and January. Housing starts declined somewhat in December but were up substantially on balance in the fourth quarter. Consumer spending advanced considerably in the fourth quarter, in part reflecting stronger sales of durable goods. Indicators of business capital spending suggest some weakening in recent months. The nominal U.S. merchandise trade deficit was slightly larger on average in October and November than in the third quarter. The latest information on prices suggests little change from recent trends, while wages have tended to accelerate.

EXHIBIT 26.1 *(continued)*

The federal funds rate and Treasury bill rates have risen since the Committee meeting in mid-December; other short-term interest rates are generally unchanged to somewhat lower. Bond yields have declined somewhat. In foreign exchange markets, the trade-weighted value of the dollar in terms of the other G-10 currencies rose substantially over the intermeeting period.

M2 and M3 weakened appreciably in January, especially M2. For the year 1988, M2 expanded at a rate a little below, and M3 at a rate around, the midpoint of the ranges established by the Committee. M1 has changed little on balance over the past several months; it grew about 4¼ percent in 1988. Expansion of total domestic nonfinancial debt appears to have moderated somewhat in 1988 to a pace around the midpoint of the Committee's monitoring range for the year.

The Federal Open Market Committee seeks monetary and financial conditions that will foster price stability, promote growth in output on a sustainable basis, and contribute to an improved pattern of international transactions. In furtherance of these objectives, the Committee at this meeting reaffirmed its decision of late June to lower the ranges for growth of M2 and M3 to 3 to 7 percent and 3½ to 7½ percent, respectively, measured from the fourth quarter of 1988 to the fourth quarter of 1989. The monitoring range for growth of total domestic nonfinancial debt was set at 6½ to 10½ percent for the year. The behavior of the monetary aggregates will continue to be evaluated in the light of movements in their velocities, developments in the economy and financial markets, and progress toward price level stability.

In the implementation of policy for the immediate future, the Committee seeks to maintain the existing degree of pressure on reserve positions. Taking account of indications of inflationary pressures, the strength of the business expansion, the behavior of the monetary aggregates, and developments in foreign exchange and domestic financial markets, somewhat greater reserve restraint would, or slightly lesser reserve restraint might, be acceptable in the intermeeting period. The contemplated reserve conditions are expected to be consistent with growth of M2 and M3 over the period from December through March at annual rates of about 2 and 3½ percent, respectively. The Chairman may call for Committee consultation if it appears to the Manager for Domestic Operations that reserve conditions during the period before the next meeting are likely to be associated with a federal funds rate persistently outside a range of 7 to 11 percent. Votes for the paragraph on short-term policy implementation: Messrs. Greenspan, Corrigan, Angell, Black, Forrestal, Heller, Johnson, Kelley, LaWare, and Ms. Seger. Votes against this action: Messrs. Hoskins and Parry.

Messrs. Hoskins and Parry dissented because they believed that a prompt move to greater monetary restraint was needed. Mr. Hoskins felt that additional restraint was desirable to put policy on a course that would lead toward longer-run price stability. Mr. Parry emphasized that inflationary pressures appeared to be intensifying as the economy had grown to a level in excess of its long-run, noninflationary potential. Both believed that any delay in implementing more restraint probably would aggravate inflationary pressures, thereby increasing the difficulty of achieving the Committee's anti-inflationary objectives and leading to even higher interest rates over time.

Source: Federal Reserve *Bulletin,* (May 1989).

changes in this intermediate economic variable should be closely linked to ulti-mate changes in output, employment, and the price level. If this is the case, the Fed can adjust its policies according to changes in target variables. At the present time the Fed ostensibly focuses on the level of bank reserves, the monetary base (bank reserves plus currency in circulation), and the money supply (particularly the M2 measure of money).

Since 1975 the Fed has been required by Congress to announce publicly its target rates of growth in monetary aggregates for the ensuing 12-month period.[8] The Fed complies by announcing its monetary growth goals in terms of an **annual target range** (minimum and maximum) of money supply expansion. In 1989, for example, these target ranges were 3 percent to 7 percent for M2 and 3.5 percent to 7.5 percent for M3. (The Fed indefinitely suspended setting growth targets for M1 in 1987 because of the volatile behavior of the M1 aggregate in recent years.) In addition, the short-run targets established by the FOMC in its monthly meet-ings are made public with about a one-month lag. For each meeting the FOMC's directive to the System Open Market Account Manager, a condensed version of the minutes of the meeting, and various policy decision notes are published a month or so later as the "Record of Policy Actions of the Federal Open Market Committee" in the *Federal Reserve Bulletin.*

The Fed's relative emphasis among the various monetary policy targets has varied over the years. Before 1970 the Fed's policy attention and procedures were essentially focused on a constellation of target variables summarized as "condi-tions in the money market." Such money market conditions included interest rates, the level of bank reserves, and the operating positions of securities dealers (including their financing costs and inventory holdings). Beginning in 1970 the Fed began to focus more attention on monetary aggregates—bank credit and the various measures of the money stock. Evidence of this shift includes the Federal Open Market Committee's adoption of explicit references to these various mone-tary aggregates in its instructions to the Manager of the Open Market Account. Further, the FOMC's instructions began to be more specific during this period, not only in regard to monetary aggregates but also in regard to their target vari-ables—the federal funds rate and bank reserves. Figure 26.5 depicts the Fed's track record in hitting its targeted growth rates for the monetary aggregates in recent years.

The Federal Funds Rate as a Policy Target

In sum, the operating-target policy for the 1970–1979 period can be charac-terized as one that focused on monetary aggregates but that sought to use the federal funds rate as a means of gauging "appropriate" changes in the money

---

[8]The Full Employment and Balanced Growth Act of 1978 requires the Federal Reserve (in the person of the Chairman) to report to Congress its objectives for monetary growth and how they will contribute to the goals of the Act.

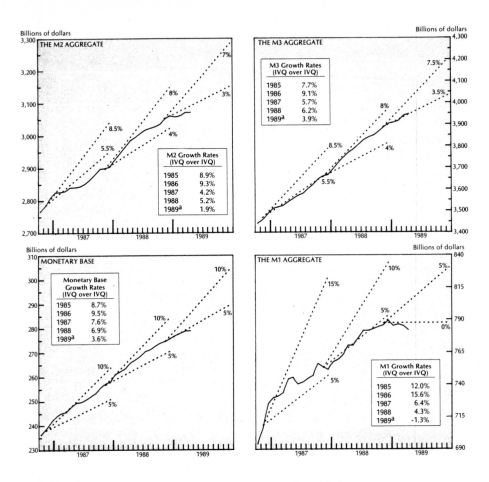

FIGURE 26.5   Growth Rates of Monetary Aggregates, 1987–1989

a. April 1989 over 1988:IVQ
Note: Last plot is April 1989. Dotted lines are target ranges for M2 and M3. Dotted lines for M1 and monetary base are for reference only.

Source: Federal Reserve Bank of Cleveland, Economic Trends, *(June 1989).*

stock.[9] The role of the federal funds rate as an "operating target" stemmed from its apparent ability to serve as an "indicator" of emerging trends in the growth

---

[9]There were variations in emphasis among target variables and changes in Fed procedures during this period. The charge made by some observers that interest rate levels were the Fed's only policy targets during this period is denied by Fed officials. The official position of the Fed is that bank reserves and monetary aggregates were the policy targets throughout this period, and the Fed's deliberate influencing of the interest rate level was only an "operating target"—a means of pursuing these policy targets.

of monetary aggregates. The funds rate is viewed as a very sensitive indicator of the degree of ease or tightness in bank reserves. The policy linkage was thus viewed as follows:

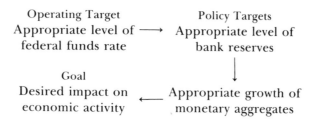

The use of the funds rate as an operating target in implementing monetary policy had a number of advantages. One advantage was relative simplicity. The Fed sought to supply or withdraw bank reserves so as to set the federal funds rate at a level consistent with the desired rate of growth in monetary aggregates. This requires, among other things, an estimate of the demand for money at different interest rates for a given level of income. Since the quantity of money demanded and the quantity supplied are equal in equilibrium, this estimate provides a means of identifying the funds rate consistent with the money supply target. This procedure does not require reliance on the monetary-multiplier link between bank reserves and the money supply and thus is not subject to its occasional shifts in magnitude. Further, money supply disturbances, such as changes in float and currency in circulation, are readily accommodated by stabilization of the funds rate.

While the funds-rate procedure avoids money market disturbances by accommodating shocks to the supply side of monetary aggregates, it also accommodates shocks on the demand side—a source of serious potential problems. Shifts in the demand for money (changes in income velocity) often signal the emergence of inflationary or deflationary economic pressures. Under the funds-rate approach, such shifts are not allowed to change interest rates. Thus the potential for rate changes to correct such trends is dissipated. This is particularly bothersome when the money demand shift is due to inflationary increases in money income, since the Fed's action in holding rates stable (supplying new reserves) "validates" inflation.[10] In general, to the extent that demand for money shifts occur when the Fed is focusing on the funds rate, the Fed will tend to over or undershoot its monetary growth goals. Indeed, the record shows that the Fed has achieved its targeted federal funds rate with a great deal more success than its monetary aggregate goals.

---

[10]The Fed's accommodation of shifts in the demand for money schedule is appropriate when a permanent change in the relation of money to income (velocity) occurs. Accommodation of a temporary change in this relation, however, will result in growth of monetary aggregates, which may be undesirable.

The Fed's Shift to a Reserve-Based Policy Procedure

The FOMC, while focusing on the funds rate, did not ignore bank reserves during the 1970–1979 period. Indeed, from early 1972 to early 1976, target growth rates were specified for RPDs—reserves available for private nonbank deposits—which consist of total member bank reserves less legal reserves for Treasury and interbank deposits. (The RPD segment of total reserves was viewed as the one most significant to the economy.) The FOMC had little success in achieving targeted RPD growth rates during this period. This lack of success was largely due to the higher priority given the funds rate (the committee was unwilling to allow it to fluctuate to a major degree), but it was also due to an apparent instability in the relationship of RPDs to monetary aggregates. The "experiment," though resulting in some useful learning experiences for the Fed, mainly reinforced the FOMC's preoccupation with the funds rate–money supply approach until 1979.

In October 1979, however, the Fed announced a change in operating procedures from the funds rate approach to a reserves-based approach. The Fed did not abandon attention to the Fed funds rate, but it significantly expanded the range (to around 5 percent) of allowed fluctuation in the rate. Part of the reason for the change was technical—the Fed's mounting dissatisfaction with the tendency of the fund-rate procedure to lead to the overshooting of money supply targets. Also of significance was the desire of Fed chairman Volcker, during a period of sharp decline in the dollar's value in the foreign exchange market, to regain international confidence in the Fed's ability and determination to control U.S. monetary growth.

The reserves-based operating procedure begins with the formulation of a targeted growth path for the money supply. The estimated demand for currency in circulation is then deducted from the money supply targets, resulting in a target growth path for deposits. The targeted deposit amounts, in turn, imply target levels of required reserves, which must be estimated for the various reserve requirement categories. In addition to required reserves, the Fed must also allow for holdings of excess reserves and required reserves for deposits that are not included in the money supply (interbank deposits, Treasury deposits, and foreign central and commercial bank deposits). The net result is a targeted growth path for total reserves. In the use of open-market operations to achieve these total-reserves targets, the Fed must (as always) consider the effects of such factors as changes in float, currency in circulation, and Treasury deposits in commercial banks.

Total reserves consist both of reserves borrowed from the Fed via the discount window and of nonborrowed reserves. The Fed must thus assume some level of borrowing in order to develop an estimate of the level of nonborrowed reserves that is to be achieved by open-market operations. The Fed's control of the discount rate provides a means of altering this "mix" of total reserves, if it chooses to do so, since the volume of borrowing is largely a function of the level of the discount rate relative to the federal funds rate.

The implementation of the new focus in Fed procedures coincided with a general tightening of monetary policy aimed at reducing the rate of inflation. In early 1980 the FOMC announced annual ranges for growth of the monetary aggregates that were below the 1979 growth targets. Such reductions in monetary growth, combined with rising credit demand and worsening inflationary expectations, resulted in high and volatile interest rates. By the end of 1980 the Fed funds rate had soared to a range of 19 to 20 percent. Despite the pressures created by these developments, the Fed generally held its course.

In the second half of 1981 the U.S. economy moved into recession, creating another source of pressure on Fed policies. By early 1982 the severity of the recession and the Fed's restrictive monetary policies had significantly slowed the rate of inflation. While unemployment reached a postwar high (and industrial capacity utilization fell to a postwar low), the rate of inflation and interest rates fell sharply in 1982, and recovery from the recession began at the end of the year.

In the 1980s the relationship between the measures of money, nominal income, and other macroeconomic variables became less stable and predictable than appears to have been the case in prior years of their measurement. Thus the Fed's attempt to focus more on simple monetary targeting was not particularly well-timed. The income velocity of M1 departed from its long-term upward trend and became much more volatile. M2 and M3 velocity also became less stable, though in a less pronounced fashion than M1.

These changes in monetary velocity coincided with a variety of financial innovations and changes in the nature and degree of financial regulation as well as an environment of more volatile interest-rate behavior. These various developments led the Fed to first de-emphasize M1 as a policy target and then cease setting target rates of growth for M1. In its operating procedures the Fed adopted a more judgmental approach in reserves targeting. (The 1979–1983 approach has been called "nonborrowed reserves" targeting, succeeded by a "borrowed reserves" procedure. The labels derive from the nature of the forecasting assumptions, but the significant difference is in the greater discretion of the latter approach.) The Fed also widened its targeted growth bands for M2 and M3 somewhat and increased its attention to various other leading indicators of economic activity patterns such as commodity prices, relative interest rates, and exchange rates. Monetary targeting remains central to monetary policy, however, since the link between the long-term rate of money growth and the rate of inflation is indisputable in the long-run.

The inherent difficulty in choosing policy targets lies in the rigor of the criteria that must be satisfied. A policy target obviously must be closely related to ultimate policy goals (preferably in cause-and-effect fashion). Changes in the policy target variable must signal subsequent (and timely) change in the economic policy goals (the former must be a "leading indicator" of the latter). The Fed must be able to control directly the target variable in a timely manner. Further, accurate data regarding the target variable must be available on a timely basis. It is not surprising that reasonable and informed observers differ on which economic variables best satisfy these criteria.[11]

THE TRANSMISSION OF MONETARY POLICY

How are the measures taken by the Fed to increase or reduce the level of bank reserves transmitted to the economy? There is more agreement on the ultimate economic effects of monetary policy than on how monetary measures bring about such effects. We will offer here an account of the various elements of the transmission process, while recognizing that there are differences of opinion as to the relative importance of these various elements. Our scenario considers open-market operations, but the effects of any policy-induced change in reserves will be essentially the same.

The chain of events triggered by open-market operations begins when the trading desk of the New York Federal Reserve Bank, acting on instructions from the Manager of the Open Market Account (who is in turn acting on much less specific instructions from the Federal Open Market Committee), executes an order. If the Fed sells securities, bank reserves will contract; if the Fed buys securities, bank reserves will expand. What happens next? The subsequent effects of a monetary policy action may be grouped into four interrelated transmission elements: (1) credit (price and availability) effects, (2) portfolio-adjustment effects, (3) wealth effects, and (4) expectations effects. (Again, these effects can be expected to ensue for any Fed policy move affecting bank reserves, although our discussion here focuses on open-market operations.)

Credit Effects

The buying and selling of securities by the Federal Reserve have an immediate effect on security prices and thus on interest rates. When the Fed buys, say, Treasury bills, their prices rise and their yields fall. Security holders are induced to sell their holdings of T-bills and acquire other securities. The prices and yields of these various other securities thus rise and fall, respectively, and the dampening effects on interest rates of the Fed's purchase spread quickly.[12] When the Fed

---

[11]See Gillian Garcia, "The Right Rabbit: Which Intermediate Target Should the Fed Pursue?" Federal Reserve Bank of Chicago, *Economic Perspectives*, (May–June 1984), pp. 15–31.

[12]The process by which the impact of the Fed's action on security prices and yields is disseminated across all financial assets is one of the "portfolio effects" described in the next section.

sells securities, interest rates tend to rise by corresponding actions in the reverse direction.

Concurrently, reserves of depository institutions are affected by the Fed's actions. A Fed purchase of securities injects new reserves into the depository system, providing a means for banks and other institutions to acquire new loans and securities. The new lending and security purchases by financial institutions augment the downward pressures on interest rates that the Fed purchase initiated. A Fed sale of securities, on the other hand, reduces reserves while tending to boost interest rates. As institutions curtail lending and sell securities to restore their positions, additional upward pressure on interest rates develops.

Note that, up to this point, the presumed effects of a Fed action are limited to the financial sector. But as consumers and business firms find the price and availability of credit altered, their borrowing and spending are affected. If interest rates have fallen and credit is more easily obtained, borrowing and spending are stimulated. If interest rates are rising and credit is tightening, consumers and business firms may curtail, cancel, or defer planned spending.

Because of various institutional limitations and financial market imperfections, the impact of more expensive (and less available) credit on the economy is rather uneven. For example, state and local governments may face statutory limitations on the level of interest rates they are permitted to pay. To the extent that lenders "ration" credit, borrowers viewed as less creditworthy (often small business firms) are more likely to be denied credit.

Portfolio Effects

The portfolio effects of the Fed's monetary policy actions stem from the kind of equilibriating portfolio selection process, as described in Chapter 15, that is presumed to characterize wealthholders' behavior. A Fed policy action changes the supply of securities held in the private sector, the quantity of money, security prices, and interest rates, and thus it disturbs the equilibrium position of wealthholders. Wealthholders respond by taking action to restore their risk–return equilibrium position. These actions include the sale or purchase of securities and spending for real (as well as financial) assets. (Note the universality of these presumed portfolio effects—all economic units hold asset portfolios, the size and composition of which are viewed as being affected by monetary policy actions.)

Consider, for example, the portfolio effects of a Fed open-market sale of Treasury bills, which drains reserves from the depository system. The purchasers of these T-bills alter the composition of their portfolios by exchanging bank deposits for the securities, and their portfolio rearrangement is unlikely to end here. Depository institutions, of course, experience immediate disturbance of their portfolio positions by the shrinkage of their deposits and reserves. They will act to restore portfolio balance by selling securities and curtailing lending. As these actions reverberate through the economy, security prices tend to fall and interest rates tend to rise, triggering more portfolio effects. Declining values of financial asset holdings and higher available yields on prospective financial asset acquisitions tend to reduce spending for real assets—business firms curtail investment spending, and consumers reduce consumption spending.

A reverse pattern of events follows a Fed open-market purchase. In this case, banks experience increased deposits and reserves, and their portfolio rearrangements involve new lending and security purchases. Throughout the economy, portfolio effects both result from and result in rising security prices and falling interest rates. Spending for real assets is stimulated as an integral part of the total pattern of portfolio adjustments.

Credit effects and portfolio effects are thus closely intertwined. The former focus primarily on the effects of interest-rate changes on borrowing and spending, whereas the latter focus on a broader framework of economic decision. Both point to similar economic effects of Fed actions, however. When the Fed reduces depository institution reserves by open-market sales of securities, an increase in reserve requirements, or reduction of its lending to depository institutions (or some combination thereof), the money supply will fall, interest rates will rise, and spending for real assets will be reduced. When the Fed increases reserves by purchasing securities in the open market, reducing reserve requirements, or increasing its lending to depository institutions (or some combination thereof), the money supply will expand, interest rates will fall, and borrowing and spending will increase.

Wealth Effects

Spending (as well as other aspects of economic behavior) is influenced by **wealth,** which is defined as the present value of all future income flows, discounted (capitalized) by some rate of interest. Income is generated by capital assets, including "human capital" (providing one's services is the means of generating income from this particular asset), other real assets, and financial assets. Since monetary policy measures can impact on wealth, it is postulated that such induced changes in wealth can subsequently affect spending and engender various other economic effects.

Expansionary monetary policy can conceivably increase apparent wealth in several ways. The stock of financial assets of private wealthholders is increased. Debt security prices increase (and perhaps market values of equities as well) as interest rates decline, raising the market value of financial portfolios. To the extent that current interest rates affect the long-run capitalization rate for future income flows, the present value of these expected future flows (which is wealth) increases. The apparent increase in wealth may induce increased consumption and investment spending.

Again, the reverse is postulated for contractionary monetary policy measures. In this case the rise of interest rates adversely affects security prices and the present value of expected future income. The decline in wealth is presumed to result in reduced consumption and investment spending.

Expectations Effects

The fact that the Fed's actions affect expectations regarding future economic developments and that such alterations in expectations influence the pattern of subsequent economic events is obvious. "Fed watching" is an everyday activity in the financial community, and statements and actions (or the absence thereof) by Federal Reserve officials are carefully monitored and widely reported. The potential significance of this phenomenon for monetary policy is apparent and is best assessed by considering how expectations effects may interact with interest rate, portfolio, and wealth effects.

The "credit effects" scenario outlined above considers only liquidity effects of a Fed action impacting on bank reserves. When reserves are increased, the liquidity effect is that of credit becoming both cheaper (lower interest rates) and more available, thus stimulating borrowing and spending. The expectations effect may partly, wholly, or more than offset the liquidity effect in terms of the impact on interest rates, as shown in Fig. 26.6 for an increase in bank reserves and the money supply. In this figure the increase in the supply of loanable funds due to new money creation is depicted as a shift in the supply schedule from S_1

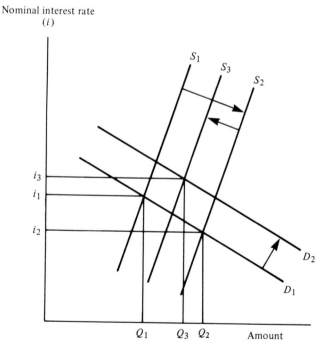

FIGURE 26.6 Liquidity, Output, and Expectations Effects on Nominal Interest Rates

to S_2. The liquidity effect ensues, the nominal interest rate falling to i_2. The demand for loanable funds schedule now shifts from D_1 to D_2.[13] Why might such a shift ensue? One reason is the output effect due to increased production and demand for money resulting from the stimulative liquidity effect. The other reason is that the increased rate of monetary growth may engender an expectations effect of increased inflation. This is likely if the market views the increased rate of monetary growth as likely to continue for a sustained period of time and to exceed growth in real output during this period. Then the Fisher effect described in Chapter 8 ensues: the demand for loanable funds schedule shifts because borrowers (anticipating inflation) are willing to pay a higher nominal rate of interest for funds.

Next, the supply of loanable funds schedule shifts to the left (to S_3) as lenders require a higher nominal interest rate for all levels of lending. The new equilibrium interest rate, i_3, is at the intersection of D_2 and S_3. In this case the combined output and expectations have outweighed the liquidity effect, and the result of the increase in the money supply is an increase in interest rates.

Obviously, the reverse of this scenario follows for a *decrease* in the rate of growth of bank reserves and the money supply. The liquidity effect would tend to raise nominal interest rates, and the output effect and the expectations effect would tend to lower them.

Changes in monetary policy may also alter expectations in a way that results in different "portfolio effects" and "wealth effects" than those described above. The fact that credit and portfolio effects are closely related means that the impact of expectations effects on credit effects will influence portfolio effects. The influence of expectations effects on portfolio effects may augment or retard the intended consequences of monetary policy action. For example, restrictive monetary policies that dampen inflationary expectations may have the effect of increasing the demand for money (due to diminished risk to its purchasing power). This effect augments the tightening of monetary policy as velocity falls. (This effect may be partly responsible for the 1980s dip in M1 velocity.)

While important for monetary policy, the nature and degree of expectations effects remain somewhat nebulous.[14] At this point, however, it is clear that the Fed has learned that its actions and pronouncements have decided impact on inflationary expectations, and monetary policy formulation and implementation

---

[13]Note that this shift represents an increase in demand for loanable funds at all interest rates, not just an increase in the quantity of loanable funds demanded as a result of the initial drop in the interest rate (which is a movement along the original D_1 schedule).

[14]The expectations effects discussed here relate only to expectations changes stemming from an announced (or perceived) sustained change in the rate of monetary growth. As such, they are distinguished from short-run market reactions to announcements of unexpectedly large increases or decreases in the money supply for a particular time period. Such changes in the quantity of money usually reflect the Fed's difficulties in day-to-day (and week-to-week) management of the money supply rather than Fed policy shifts. In these cases, announcement of an unexpectedly large weekly increase (decrease) in the money supply may cause short-term interest rates to rise (fall) as the market anticipates offsetting Fed tightening (loosening) of monetary control in the succeeding week.

have been decidedly (and perhaps permanently) affected as a result. Indeed, as we discuss below, some economists believe that expectations affect economic behavior in a way that places highly significant limitations on the degree to which any economic policy measure can influence a market economy.

UNSETTLED ISSUES OF MONETARY POLICY

There is considerable disagreement among economists about the transmission process by which monetary policy affects spending for real assets, the degree that aggregate demand is affected by monetary change, and how long it takes monetary expansion or contraction to affect policy variables. Much of this disagreement is between "monetarist" economists and Keynesian (or "neo-Keynesian") economists. Monetarists emphasize the portfolio-adjustment pattern of monetary-policy effects, whereas Keynesians attach more significance to credit effects. The underlying technical argument between these camps is also of significance for the relative effectiveness of monetary and fiscal policy, a subject addressed in the next chapter. This argument concerns how responsive the behavior of economic agents is to changes in the rate of interest in terms of demand for cash balances and spending for real assets. Monetarists generally regard the demand for money as relatively insensitive to changes in the rate of interest and regard real spending as very sensitive; Keynesians hold that the reverse is true.

THE MONETARIST–KEYNESIAN DEBATE

In general, monetarists paint a rather ambivalent picture of monetary policy. The money stock is viewed as a crucial economic variable, but discretionary management of its growth is deemed to be of dubious merit. The potency of the quantity of money, in the monetarist framework, stems from a perception that the rate of turnover of the money supply (monetary velocity) is a stable function of certain economic variables (including wealth, price level expectations, and rates of interest). Since total spending is necessarily the product of the money stock used for transactions and how many times that stock "turns over" (is used for transactions purposes), it follows that the amount of the money supply determines the amount of aggregate spending if the number of turnovers (velocity) does not shift to a significant degree.[15] (Figure 26.6 shows the historical pattern

---

[15]Recall from Chapter 4 the discussion of the "equation of exchange" that defines this argument. The Quantity Theory of Money, the monetarist credo, is a derivative of this equation. This theory holds that velocity is a function of a number of variables but is determined largely by behavioral patterns that are slow to change. Also, the relevant issue for the usefulness of monetary policy is the predictability of velocity, for which stability is a sufficient but not a necessary condition. Further, the usual preference of monetarists for a measure of "money" is M2, not M1, and M2 velocity has been a great deal more stable than M1 velocity.

of the income velocity of money for three different measures of money.) To a large degree, however, monetarists point to empirical evidence of the economic significance of the money stock, rather than a theoretical framework. Such evidence shows a close long-term relationship between the money supply, GNP, and the price level.

Though all monetarists believe that changes in the money supply impact significantly on the economy, not all monetarists favor the use of discretionary monetary policy to stabilize the economy. Milton Friedman, the best-known monetarist, contends that the historical record shows that in the long run, changes in the quantity of money affect only the price level, not real income.[16] Friedman (together with many other monetarists) believes that nonmonetary factors determine real income, that the economy has great built-in inherent stability, and that discretionary monetary policy is destabilizing. Friedman's view that discretionary monetary management does more harm than good is based on the results of his empirical investigations of lags in the effect of monetary policy—results, it should be noted, that are not consistent with those of a number of other investigators.

Since monetarists generally regard the economic system as possessing considerable inherent stability, they view economic problems as stemming largely from government mismanagement of the economy. In particular, the architects of economic policy are charged with having repeatedly attempted to push the unemployment rate below its "natural" rate (at which the real wage and labor's marginal product are in harmony) and have created inflation and inflationary expectations in the process. Specifically, inflation is viewed as the inevitable result of a monetary growth rate that is in excess of real output expansion. To halt inflation, monetarists recommend a policy of reducing the growth of the money stock until monetary expansion is in line with real economic growth. This policy will likely result in high unemployment and high rates of interest (until inflationary pressures ease), but this economic discomfort is regarded as necessary for price stability. The required duration of such distress is a function of how quickly inflationary expectations are squelched.

Monetarists regard the rate of economic growth and the level of employment as fundamentally determined by "real" factors—the quantity and quality of the labor supply, capital, and other productive resources (as well as cultural and political attributes and conditions conducive to economic expansion). Monetary policy cannot, in the long run, significantly affect these "aggregate supply" factors. If appropriate monetary policy achieves current and expected price stability, unemployment will be limited to its "natural rate." Keynesians do not regard the economy's self-stabilizing capacity with the rosy perspective generally held by monetarists. Rather, they regard government management of the economy as nec-

---

[16]See Milton Friedman, "A Theoretical Framework for Monetary Analysis," *Journal of Political Economy*, March 1970, for an account of this view, which is also described in several of the references at the end of the chapter.

essary to avoid roller-coaster economic performance. The frequent use of discretionary monetary and fiscal policy measures is viewed as necessary to maintain price stability and full employment. Further, many Keynesians consider the U.S. economic system so fraught with price, wage, and other rigidities as to require occasional resort to the "incomes policies" of wage and price control.

Few, if any, Keynesians would deny that demand-pull inflation should be countered with monetary/fiscal measures to reduce aggregate demand. But some inflationary pressures are regarded as stemming not from excessive demand but from cost-push pressures in the economy. The monetarist prescription of prolonged (if necessary) economic austerity to stop inflation and wipe out inflationary expectations is thus rejected. Further, Keynesians do not usually consider inflation (at any rate) to be as injurious as do monetarists, nor is inflation viewed as inevitably snowballing (accelerating in rate). Economic stagnation rather than inflation is held to be the principal problem of modern economies. Many Keynesians also urge that various structural problems in the economy (lack of labor mobility, concentration of pricing power, technological unemployment, and so on) be vigorously attacked by the government. (Many monetarists also worry about structural rigidities in the economy, and they would certainly add "unnecessary government regulation" to this list.) However, such recasting of the economic order in a more competitive and efficient mold, while a laudable objective, is very difficult to engineer in a representative democracy (special-interest groups benefiting from lack of competition are usually especially well represented).

Lags in the Effects of Monetary Policy

The amount of time required for monetary policy to affect such key economic variables as employment, output, and the price level is of crucial importance to its usefulness as an instrument of economic stabilization. If the lag in the economic effects of monetary policy is either unduly long or unduly variable in length, discretionary monetary policy may be destabilizing rather than stabilizing. Economic conditions can change very rapidly, and economic policymakers have often been surprised by how suddenly the current economic problem shifts from recession to inflation or vice versa.

The total time lag involved in the use of monetary policy to pursue economic objectives is often separated into the "inside lag" and the "outside lag." The **inside lag** is the amount of time it takes for the Fed to recognize the need for policy action (or change in policy), to decide what the particulars of its response will be, and to put the policy measure into effect. (The inside lag is thus sometimes divided into "recognition," "decision," and "implementation" lags.) The **outside lag** is the time period required for the policy action, working through the various transmission channels, to impact significantly on economic activity.

Both the inside and outside lags are generally assessed as being matters of months (not days or weeks, unfortunately), although how many months is a matter of disagreement. The inside lag is probably about three to six months, and the outside lag about six to twelve months, but not all observers would accept even these wide ranges.

Milton Friedman, as mentioned above, has argued for many years that the monetary policy lag is both long and variable. For this reason he views discretionary monetary policy as being more apt to destabilize the economy than to stabilize it. Friedman argues that the discretionary monetary policy, which necessarily involves Fed-engineered changes in the rate of growth of the money supply, should be replaced by a steady, unchanging rate of monetary growth. Such constant growth in the money supply would be at a rate sufficient to accommodate long-run economic growth. In effect, Friedman has more faith in the economy's inherent capacity for self-stabilization than in the ability of government policymakers to stabilize it. Most Keynesians (and many monetarists) do not share this view. They rather regard this proposal for abandonment of discretionary monetary policy as an unnecessary and counterproductive measure that would result in increased economic instability.

The Behavior of Monetary Velocity

Friedman's preference for a "monetary rule" of constant money growth, as opposed to discretionary management of the money supply, undoubtedly stems in part from his belief in the stability of the income velocity of money. If income velocity is inherently unstable, such a monetary rule would prevent the Fed from offsetting destabilizing changes in velocity (changes in the demand for money) with offsetting changes in the money stock. More generally, velocity must be either predictable—a constant or a stable function of identifiable and measurable variables—or be controllable by the monetary authorities.

Since money's income velocity is calculated as simply the ratio of nominal-dollar GNP to the money stock, assessment of its degree of stability may appear to be an equally simple task. However, such assessment hinges on which money measure is employed and how much significance one attaches to the cyclical rate of change in velocity as opposed to longer-term stability. Figure 26.7 shows the M1, M2, M3, and L income velocity through the early 1980s. Relative long-run stability in these measures of velocity was accompanied by considerable cyclical variation. Further, M1 velocity rose steadily, whereas the magnitude of M2 velocity changed little.[17] (In general, the broader the definition of money, the more stable measured velocity will be.)

Recall that money velocity and the demand for money balances amount to

---

[17]The decline in velocity measures in the early 1980s is attributed to changes in the nature of the components of these measures (particularly the advent of interest-bearing checking accounts and the money market deposit account) and to a reduction in inflationary expectations.

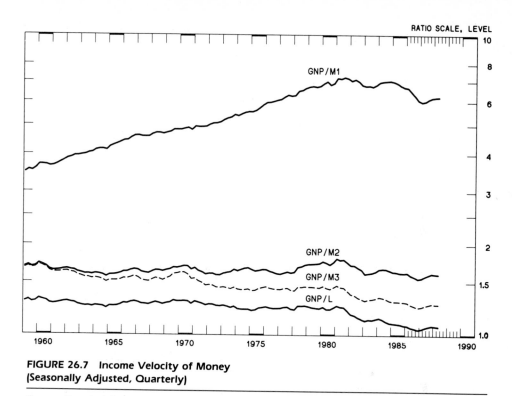

FIGURE 26.7 Income Velocity of Money
(Seasonally Adjusted, Quarterly)

Source: Board of Governors of the Federal Reserve System, Historical Chart Book, *1988.*

the same thing. An increase in the demand for money function of wealthholders corresponds to a decrease in velocity and vice versa. The principal determinants of the demand for money are believed to be income, interest rates, and expectations regarding future levels of interest rates and prices. Increased income results in increased transactions demand for money. Higher interest rates encourage "economizing" of transactions balances in order to place money in interest-earning assets. Expectations of higher future interest rates tend to discourage the purchase of interest-earning assets (encourage holding "idle" money), particularly long-term financial instruments, because the prices of such assets move inversely with interest rates. Expectations of increases in future price levels tend to encourage reductions of money holdings in favor of purchases of physical assets because holding of physical assets offers a positive yield during periods of inflation, whereas idle money balances incur a negative yield equal to the rate of price level increase.

How significant are these various variables in the determination of velocity? Milton Friedman, though postulating a demand-for-money function that includes these variables as well as others,[18] asserts that only real income is likely to be significant. Most monetarists hold this view, but nonmonetarist economists reject it. The basic economic policy issue is one that can only be resolved empirically— the extent to which velocity can rise during a period of a constant (or declining) real money stock to finance inflationary expenditures or will fall during a period of real money supply expansion and thus offset the monetary stimulus to aggregate demand.

Viewed from this perspective, it is plausible that the behavior of velocity is a potential problem for monetary policy. The supply of liquid assets has grown enormously in the United States and other advanced economies. Such growth has been coupled with a host of financial innovations that greatly facilitate the mobilizing of these liquid assets for transactions purposes. Examples include the remarkable growth in money market mutual funds that offer check-writing privileges, electronic funds transfer systems, automated clearinghouses, automated teller machines, and the emergence of ATS and NOW accounts with depository institutions and "cash management" accounts with other financial institutions. The result of these and other financial innovations is almost certain to loosen somewhat the connection between M1 and M2 "money" and the financing of aggregate expenditure by the financial system. The difficulties encountered by the Federal Reserve in the United States and the Bank of England in the United Kingdom in their respective monetary control efforts (to curb inflation) of the 1979–1982 period may have stemmed in part from such changes in the financial system.

"Rational Expectations" and Monetary Policy

One argument against discretionary monetary policy is founded on a **"rational expectations"** view of economic behavior. This view is based on the assumption that people act in their economic self-interest on the basis of all available information and the knowledge gained from past observation of economic actions and consequences.[19] Relative to monetary policy actions, it is assumed that economic units possess the ability to assess the Fed's intentions and their implications for the economy very quickly and accurately (or at least without systematic inaccuracy). Second, economic units will immediately take action to enhance or protect their own economic situation in accordance with their fore-

---

[18]Milton Friedman, "The Quantity Theory of Money—A Restatement," in Milton Friedman (Ed.), *Studies in the Quantity Theory of Money* (Chicago: The University of Chicago Press, 1956), 3–21.

[19]See Robert E. Lucas and Thomas J. Sargent, "After Keynesian Macroeconomics," Federal Reserve Bank of Minneapolis *Quarterly Review* (Spring 1979), 1–16; and Thomas J. Sargent and Neil Wallace, *Rational Expectations and the Theory of Economic Policy* (Federal Reserve Bank of Minneapolis, 1978). Lucas and Sargent are generally considered the founders of the "new classical" school of economics, which embraces rational expectations and holds a pre-Keynesian ("classical economics") opinion of macroeconomic policy.

cast of the Fed's monetary actions. Such behavior may negate the intended effects of the monetary policy measures implemented by the Fed.

Suppose, for example, that the Fed seeks to stimulate output and employment by pursuing an expansionary monetary policy. Assume that the average money wage rate does not fall and that the production function for the economy does not change (output is the same at all employment levels). In this case, monetary expansion alone (without supporting change in the supply sector) can cause output to increase only by precipitating a rise in the price level that is not accompanied by a corresponding increase in wages. In other words, expansionary monetary policy (or any policy measure limited to stimulating aggregate demand) can result in increased output and employment only by inflating prices and thus lowering the real wage. But rational expectations theory suggests that workers will anticipate the fall in their real wages that such a scenario involves and will take anticipatory action to protect their real income. Such action takes the form of demanding (through labor union representatives) higher money wages. If money wages rise concomitantly and commensurately (at the same time and to the same degree) as prices are pushed up by monetary expansion, output and employment will not change. Only prices and money wages will increase.

Similarly, a rational expectations scenario suggests that the Fed cannot affect interest rates by changing the rate of growth in the money stock. Suppose that the Fed seeks to lower interest rates by expanding the money supply, but their plan is fully anticipated by suppliers of loanable funds. Forecasting a rise in the price level stemming from monetary expansion, lenders add an "inflation premium" to interest rates. The "expectations effect" of the inflation premium offsets the "liquidity effect" (decline in interest rates due to the increase in the money stock), and interest rates do not change.

The essential lesson in the rational expectations argument is that monetary policy actions will affect real economic variables only to the extent that people are "fooled" (do not anticipate the policy and/or its effects) or, if not fooled, are unable to take measures to protect themselves.[20] There are, however, reasons to believe that one or both of these conditions often exist. The enormous complexity of modern economic systems is a major problem for professional economists, as anyone who compares economic outcomes to economic forecasts can attest. Further, relatively few economic agents possess the degree of control over their economic situation that the theory, in its extreme form, presumes. Labor and management are often committed to long-term wage contracts, lessors and lessees to long-terms leases, business firms to various long-term supply contracts, and so forth.

---

[20]Herbert Stein has said that "rational expectations is the theory that the magician cannot fool the girl in the box whom he is pretending to saw in half." See Stein's comment on Gregory Mankiw's article, "Recent Developments in Macroeconomics: A Refresher Course," *Journal of Money, Credit, and Banking* (August 1988).

"REAL BUSINESS CYCLES" AND MONETARY POLICY

In the 1980s, still another school of macroeconomic thought began to develop around the notion of "real business cycles."* A real business cycle is a fluctuation in aggregate economic activity that has its root cause in a variation (or "shock") in fundamental supply factors. An example of such a shock is a sudden upward surge in oil prices, such as occurred in 1974 and 1979. Another (less obvious) example is the remarkable rise in the value of the U.S. dollar in the foreign exchange market in the early 1980s and its even more rapid plunge in the late 1980s. Such shocks are injurious to the production process, and production is likely to fall until production techniques adjust to the altered circumstances.

There is, of course, nothing particularly novel or remarkable about these observations. But what real business cycle theorists point out is that shocks are normal and inevitable economic phenomena and that business cycles are thus also normal and inevitable. Further, real business cycles are necessary and, indeed, optimal. They are, so to speak, nature's way of adapting the economy to changed circumstances. Social welfare is best served by allowing real business cycles to run their course. It follows that countercyclical economic policy is often ill-advised and, over time, will "overstabilize" the economy to the detriment of aggregate output.

Real business cycle analysis does not necessarily suggest that all aspects of any particular business cycle are positive, that all cycles are necessarily optimal (that is, that all recessions are "good" for the economy in the long run), or that economic stabilization policy has no role. But proponents of the theory do argue that monetary policy has no significant effect on real output. The empirical evidence regarding the real business cycle hypothesis is mixed, and it remains to be seen whether the theory will give rise to a significant school of macroeconomics.

*See John B. Long and Charles I. Plosser, "Real Business Cycles," Journal of Political Economy (February 1983), 36–69; Robert G. King and Charles I. Plosser, "Money, Credit, and Prices in a Real Business Cycle," American Economic Review (June 1984), 363–380: and "Real Business Cycle Models," in Robert Barro (Ed.), Handbook of Modern Business Cycle Theory (New York: John Wiley, 1988).

Nonetheless, the rational expectations theorists have contributed a great deal to the economic policy debate by their strong emphasis on the fact that the public is not "deaf, dumb, and blind" to pending economic change and will seek to protect its economic interests in anticipation of such change. Recall the aphorism, "You can fool all the people some of the time and some of the people all the time, but you can't fool all the people all the time." Moreover, "all the people" need not be rational anticipators for the theory to hold. In the case of many workers, only their labor union leaders need to have an informed view of government economic policy plans and likely implications for prices (and many large unions employ their own economists to provide information and analysis). In the financial markets, only the major suppliers of funds (that is, institutional investors) need to possess the requisite degree of economic sophistication. Much of the macroeconomic theorizing before the 1970s ignored these facts and was couched in terms of a passive, inert public that responded according to the prescription of economic policymakers. Further, much of the ill-founded euphoria concerning the efficacy of economic policy was rooted in this premise. Neither this knee-jerk view of economic response nor the related euphoria is likely to be revived in the foreseeable future.

SUMMARY

Monetary policy is intended to impact on aggregate spending in the economy in a fashion that will contribute to the goals of full employment, price stability, sustainable economic growth, and balance of payments equilibrium. Monetary policy is conducted by the Federal Reserve primarily via its open-market operations, discount-window policies and rates, control of reserve requirements, various selective controls, and "moral suasion." Open-market operations—the most important tool—consist of buying and selling by the U.S. government in the open market. Many open-market operations are defensive in nature—designed to offset the impact on reserves of factors over which the Fed has no direct control, such as currency flows. Other open-market operations are dynamic in nature—designed to implement some particular monetary policy objective, such as an easing in credit conditions. Compared to open-market operations, the other techniques—lending through the discount window, reserve requirement changes, credit controls, and interest-rate ceilings—are relatively minor in importance.

These various monetary policy instruments impact initially on monetary and credit aggregates, security prices, and interest rates. The effects of changes in these variables are then transmitted to the real sector of the economy (affecting investment and consumption) through various "transmission" channels. These channels include credit-price and availability effects, portfolio effects, and wealth effects.

Monetary policy affects economic activity only after some time lag, part of which is administrative in nature (the "inside lag") and part of which relates to the time required for monetary measures to be transmitted to the real sector of the economy (the "outside lag"). Because of the lag in monetary policy impact, the Fed must rely on one or more intermediate "targets" to assess policy effects. At present the Fed is focusing primarily on monetary aggregates, using a targeted growth path of reserves as the intermediate policy objective, but the Fed also acts to prevent large fluctuations in the federal funds rate. During the 1970s the Fed focused on the federal funds rate as an "operating target" but shifted away from this procedure in the 1979–83 period to employ a reserves-based procedure that resulted in wide short-run fluctuations in the federal funds rate.

The record of monetary policy is somewhat mixed. As an economic policy instrument that impacts on aggregate demand, it influences aggregate supply indirectly and with a bothersome lag. When monetary policy is used to fight inflation, it depresses real as well as inflationary income, and the corresponding dampening of investment spending poses potential long-run problems for capital formation. In addition, the Fed must cope with a perennial inflation–unemployment tradeoff and the tenuous but increasingly important role of expectations in its pursuit of monetary policy. These and other problems have led to the emergence of supply-side economics and the development of a rational expectations theory of policy effects that rejects the usefulness of any aggregate-demand–focused instrument of economic stabilization. Despite these various developments, monetary policy is likely to continue its important role for the foreseeable future.

QUESTIONS

1. Discuss the concept of aggregate demand, its various components, and its relationship to aggregate supply.
2. Describe how monetary policy affects aggregate demand.
3. What are the principal goals of economic policy? In what way do they sometimes become conflicting goals?
4. What is the Phillips curve? Discuss its significance for economic policy
5. How may expectations cause inflation to accelerate? How may expectations pose difficulties for economic policy measures? Reinforce policy measures?
6. Trace the presumed sequence of effects of a monetary policy measure in terms of credit, portfolio, wealth, and expectations effects.
7. Discuss lags in the effect of monetary policy. Why do such lags necessitate the use of "operating" and "policy" targets in the pursuit of monetary policy?
8. Why is the behavior of income velocity significant for monetary policy? For Friedman's "monetary rule" proposal?
9. Compare the funds-rate and the reserves-based approaches to monetary policy and discuss the advantages and disadvantages of each.
10. Describe the rational expectations theory of economic behavior and discuss its significance for monetary policy.
11. Compare and discuss Keynesian and monetarist views of economic policy and the role of monetary control.

REFERENCES

Black, Robert, "The Fed's Mandate: Help or Hindrance?" Federal Reserve Bank of Richmond *Economic Review* (July/August 1984), 3–7.

Burns, Arthur, "The Anguish of Central Banking," *Federal Reserve Bulletin* (September 1987), 687–698.

de Saint Phalle, Thibaut, *The Federal Reserve* (New York: Praeger, 1985).

Friedman, Milton, and Anna Schwartz, *A Monetary History of the United States* (Princeton: Princeton University Press, 1963).

Galbraith, John Kenneth, *Economics and the Public Purpose* (Boston: Houghton Mifflin, 1973).

———, *Money: Whence It Came, Where It Went* (Boston: Houghton Mifflin, 1975).

Gilbert, R. Alton, "Operating Procedures for Conducting Monetary Policy," Federal Reserve Bank of St. Louis *Review* (February 1985), 13–21.

Hafer, R.W., and Joseph H. Haslag, "The FOMC in 1987: The Effects of a Falling Dollar and the Stock Market Collapse," Federal Reserve Bank of St. Louis *Review* (March/April 1988), 3–16.

Heller, Robert H., "Implementing Monetary Policy," *Federal Reserve Bulletin* (July 1988), 419–429.

Hetzel, Robert L., "The Monetary Responsibilities of a Central Bank," Federal Reserve Bank of Richmond *Economic Review* (September/October 1988), 19–31.

Judd, John P., and Bharat Trehan, "Portfolio Substitution and the Reliability of M1, M2, and M3 as Monetary Policy Indicators," Federal Reserve Bank of San Francisco *Economic Review* (Summer 1987), 5–29.

Laidler, David, "Money and Money Income: An Essay on the Transmission Mechanism," *Journal of Monetary Economics* (April 1978), 151–193.

Lucas, Robert E., and Thomas J. Sargent, "After Keynesian Macroeconomics," Federal Reserve Bank of Minneapolis *Quarterly Review* (Spring 1979), 1–16.

Mankiw, N. Gregory, "Recent Developments in Macroeconomics: A Very Quick Refresher Course," *Journal of Money, Credit, and Banking* (August 1988), 436–449.

Meek, Paul, *U.S. Monetary Policy and Financial Markets* (New York: Federal Reserve Bank of New York, 1982).

Melton, William, *Inside the Fed* (New York: Federal Reserve Bank of New York, 1982).

Meltzer, Allan, Robert Rasche, Stephen Axilrod, and Peter Sternlight, "Is the Federal Reserve's Monetary Control Policy Misdirected?" *Journal of Money, Credit, and Banking* (February 1982), 119–147.

Mengle, David L. "The Discount Window," Federal Reserve Bank of Richmond *Economic Review,* (May/June 1986), 2–10.

Mote, Larry R., "Looking Back: The Use of Interest Rates in Monetary Policy," Federal Reserve Bank of Chicago *Economic Perspective* (January/February 1988), 15–29.

Rosenbaum, Mary Susan, "Lags in the Effects of Monetary Policy," Federal Reserve Bank of Atlanta *Economic Review* (November 1985), 20–33.

Roth, Howard L., "Federal Reserve Open Market Techniques," Federal Reserve Bank of Kansas City *Economic Review* (March 1986), 3–15.

Siegel, Diane F., "The Relationship of Money and Income: The Breakdowns in the 70s and 80s," Federal Reserve Bank of Chicago *Economic Perspective* (July/August 1986), 3–15.

Stone, Courtenay C., and Daniel L. Thornton, "Solving the 1980's Velocity Puzzle: A Progress Report," Federal Reserve Bank of St. Louis *Review* (August/September 1987), 5–23.

CHAPTER 27

Fiscal Policy: Federal Taxing, Spending, and Borrowing

In this chapter we offer a description and analysis of the fiscal activities of government—taxation, expenditures, and management of the national debt—and the impact of these activities on the financial system and the economy. Various issues relating to the effectiveness of fiscal policy as a tool of economic stabilization are also assessed.

The economic and financial effects of government income, expenditures and fiscal management are considerable. Such significant impacts are ensured, if for no other reason, by the sheer magnitude of government taxing, spending, and borrowing. The fiscal year 1990 budget for the federal government amounted to almost $1.2 trillion in expenditures, more than 20 percent of the gross national product. The national debt (federal government's debt) amounted to more than $2.8 trillion in 1989.[1] Net interest payments on the federal debt exceeded $160 billion in 1989. The size of the national debt reflects, of course, the federal government's propensity for deficit spending since the 1930s. In the past 30 years the federal budget has been in balance or in surplus only twice. Table 27.1 indicates the amount of federal government receipts and expenditures and the corresponding surplus or deficit for fiscal years 1960–1988. (See also Fig. 27.1) Figure 27.2 shows the principal revenue sources of the federal government since 1950. Figure 27.3 depicts the outstanding federal debt in dollars and as a percentage of GNP since 1950.

The management of the fiscal and financing operations of the federal government is the responsibility of the U.S. Treasury. Some aspects of Treasury activities have been discussed in previous chapters, but a more detailed description

---

[1]A large portion of the gross amount of the federal debt (more than 20 percent) is held by federal agencies and trust funds. The net federal debt is held by the Federal Reserve, U.S. resident private investors, state and local governments, and foreign investors.

TABLE 27.1   Federal Government Receipts and Expenditures (Unified Budget), Fiscal Years 1960–1984 (Billions of Dollars)

Fiscal Year	Receipts	Expenditures	Surplus or Deficit
1960	$ 92.5	$ 92.2	+ 0.3
1961	94.4	97.8	− 3.4
1962	99.7	106.8	− 7.1
1963	106.6	111.3	− 4.8
1964	112.7	118.6	− 5.9
1965	116.8	118.4	− 1.6
1966	130.9	134.7	− 3.8
1967	149.6	158.3	− 8.7
1968	153.7	178.8	− 25.2
1969	187.8	184.5	+ 3.2
1970	193.7	196.6	− 2.8
1971	188.4	211.4	− 23.0
1972	208.6	231.9	− 23.2
1973	232.2	246.5	− 14.3
1974	264.9	268.4	− 3.5
1975	281.0	324.6	− 43.6
1976	300.0	365.6	− 65.6
1977	378.5	402.1	− 45.1
1978	402.0	450.8	− 43.9
1979	465.9	493.7	− 27.8
1980	520.1	579.6	− 59.5
1981	599.3	657.2	− 57.9
1982	617.8	728.4	− 110.6
1983	600.6	795.9	− 195.3
1984	666.5	841.8	− 175.3
1985	734.0	936.8	− 202.8
1986	769.0	989.8	− 220.8
1987	854.1	1,004.6	− 150.5
1988	908.6	1,064.0	− 155.4

Source: Federal Reserve Bulletin, *various issues.*

of Treasury fiscal management activities will be useful prior to an assessment of the economic and financial effects of fiscal policy and debt management.

FISCAL MANAGEMENT ACTIVITIES OF THE U.S. TREASURY

The U.S. Treasury has the responsibility for collecting taxes and other federal revenues, handling federal disbursements, borrowing the amounts necessary to finance deficit spending (also temporary shortfalls in cash flow), and refunding

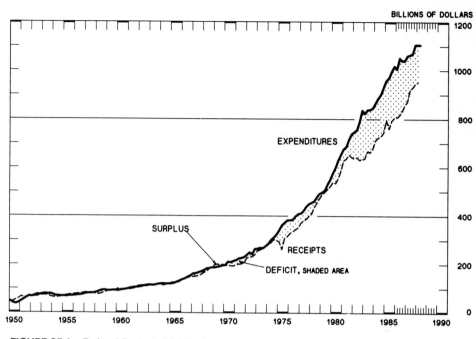

FIGURE 27.1   Federal Budget, NIA Basis
(Seasonally Adjusted Annual Rates, Quarterly)

Source: Board of Governors of the Federal Reserve System, Historical Chart Book, 1988.

the maturing portions of the federal debt. All these activities involve the Treasury's management of its deposits held with more than 13,000 commercial banks and (since 1977) savings and loan associations and credit unions, as well as its accounts with the Federal Reserve System. Most of the Treasury's cash balances are held in accounts with commercial banks called tax and loan (T & L) accounts. Transfers of funds from the T & L accounts to the Treasury's Federal Reserve accounts (with banks being forewarned of such transfers) generally occur concomitantly with federal disbursements. The Treasury uses its accounts at the Federal Reserve banks to make payments. Thus the flow of federal government payments into the recipients' bank accounts approximately corresponds to the decrease in federal deposit balances with the banking system. The intended result is minimum disturbance of aggregate bank deposits and reserves.

The avoidance of federal financing resulting in large and irregular movements of deposits out of the banking system is facilitated by the mechanics of the T & L accounts. Payments of taxes to the federal government are deposited in the T & L accounts of the banks on which the checks are drawn, thus avoiding abrupt regional (as well as aggregate) shifts of bank deposits. The T & L accounts are authorized collecting accounts for corporate income taxes, excise taxes, var-

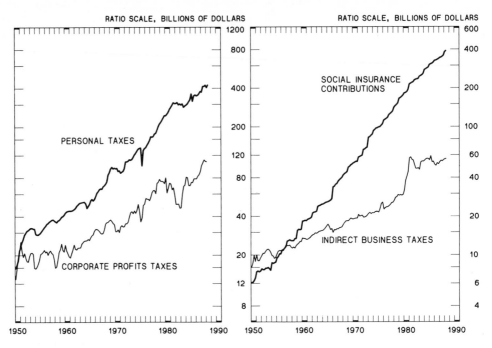

FIGURE 27.2   Federal Government Receipts, NIA Basis
(Seasonally Adjusted Annual Rates, Quarterly)

Source: Board of Governors of the Federal Reserve System, Historical Chart Book, *1988.*

ious federal withholding taxes, and unemployment insurance taxes. Taxpayers deposit funds in these accounts and receive a depository receipt, which is included with the appropriate tax form when filed as proof of payment. Further, banks acquiring new issues of federal government securities when the Treasury is borrowing can make payment by simply crediting the T & L accounts. This procedure allows banks to acquire federal securities without reducing total reserves (although excess reserves are reduced by the amount of reserves against the increase in Treasury deposits).[2]

---

[2]Until 1978, banks paid no interest on T & L deposits. This practice was long justified on the grounds that it constituted a means of compensating banks for their services to the Treasury. In 1978, however, congressional action resulted in new procedures whereby banks are directly compensated for services and the Treasury is permitted to invest funds in interest-bearing notes of depository banks. Banks can avoid paying interest on T & L account balances (currently the rate is 25 basis points less than the average federal funds rate for the week) only by remitting funds received in these accounts the day following receipt. The 1978 changes also caused most banks to begin paying for government securities by having their reserves with the Fed reduced, rather than by crediting T & L accounts.

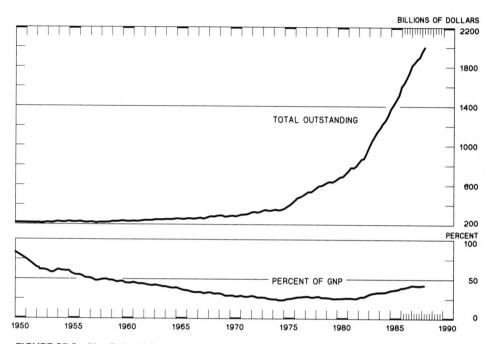

FIGURE 27.3 Net Federal Debt
(Amount Outstanding; End of Year, 1950–1951; Seasonally Adjusted, end of quarter, 1952–)

Source: Board of Governors of the Federal Reserve System, Historical Chart Book, 1988.

Treasury Borrowing

Even in years of balanced or surplus federal budgets (rare in recent U.S. financial history), the Treasury is obliged to borrow extensively. One reason is that cash inflows and outflows do not occur evenly throughout a fiscal year. As a result, the Treasury must sometimes borrow to cover temporary deficits during a year of a balanced budget. Further, maturing issues of outstanding federal government securities must be refunded by the Treasury (except on those rare occasions when the national debt is being reduced and the Treasury has a large cash surplus with which to redeem maturing debt). An issue of Treasury bills, for example, matures each week. And, of course, an excess of government spending over government revenues in a fiscal year increases the federal debt by the amount of this deficit, necessitating new Treasury borrowing in that amount.

Treasury securities include both marketable and nonmarketable issues. Non-marketable securities, which amounted to about $842 billion in 1988, are held by individuals (savings bonds), various U.S. government trust funds (including the federal employee retirement and Social Security funds), foreign governments, and state and local governments. Nonmarketable securities may not be resold. Marketable Treasury securities, which amounted to more than $1.8 trillion in 1988, include bills and coupon-bearing securities (notes and bonds) and can be resold by their holders. The composition of ownership of Treasury securities in recent years is shown in Fig. 27.4.

In refunding debt the Treasury generally offers holders of the maturing securities either a new issue of the same type of security or some alternative issue in exchange. But whether the Treasury is issuing new securities for the purpose of refunding maturing debt or the financing of a deficit, the Treasury must make a determination regarding the time to maturity of the new issue. It is in the choice of the maturity length of Treasury securities that the potential for discretionary policy action in federal debt management exists—a subject that we will address at a later point in this chapter. Aside from any policy considerations, the Treasury is likely to consider the availability of funds in various segments of the financial markets. In the case of a refunding of a maturing issue the choice is generally dictated by the maturity of the particular issue. In general, the Treasury's principal goal appears to be the minimization of interest costs on the public debt.

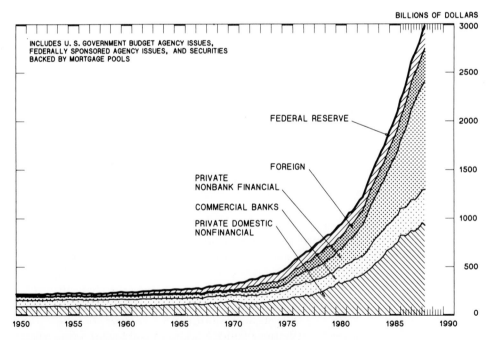

FIGURE 27.4 Ownership of U.S. Government Securities
(Amount Outstanding; End of Year, 1950–1951; Seasonally Adjusted, End of Quarter, 1952–)

Source: Board of Governors of the Federal Reserve System, Historical Chart Book, *1988.*

The Treasury has used the auction method for Treasury bill issues for many years, and in recent years it has employed this method for notes and bonds as well. The alternative to the auction method (of which there are several variations) is a subscription approach, which obliges the Treasury (rather than the market) to determine an interest rate on the subscription issue. Use of the subscription method usually involves Federal Reserve System cooperation; the Fed acts to ensure a successful subscription issue by "stabilizing" financial market conditions. (In the absence of Fed assistance a shift in market conditions could cause a subscription issue to fail.) As a practical matter, Fed intervention is also certain if the auction of Treasury issues should encounter difficulties. In general, however, the auction method poses less interference with the Fed's pursuit of monetary policy.

The Treasury has contributed to the efficiency and smoothness of operation of the financial markets in recent years by offering many of its securities on a regularly scheduled basis. Auctioned weekly are 3- and 6-month Treasury bills, and 1-year bills are auctioned monthly. The Treasury has also developed more regular cycles for its 2-year, 4-year, and 5-year notes, as well as for its bond offerings. Such regularity in Treasury offerings minimizes market disturbances and facilitates inventory management. As discussed previously, government security dealers play a very significant role in both the primary and secondary markets for Treasury securities.

Federal Lending Programs

As discussed in Chapter 11, a portion of total federal outlays is for lending programs rather than expenditures for goods and services.[3] However, these outlays affect the size of the federal deficit and affect the allocation of the economic resources in much the same way as any other federal government expenditure. There is thus little justification for not including these federal lending outlays as part of the total federal budget, as has been the practice in the past.

In an effort to make federal lending operations more efficient, the Federal Financing Bank (FFB) was created in 1973. The FFB is empowered to issue debt securities and lend the proceeds to the various federal agencies that administer the government's credit programs, although in practice it generally obtains funds by borrowing from the Treasury. Before the FFB's establishment, most federal credit agencies financed their lending operations by issuing their own securities. These agency securities, though fully backed by the federal government, lacked a well-developed secondary market and thus tended to carry greater interest costs than ordinary federal securities. The FFB's activities corrected this problem.

---

[3]This distinction is not always clearcut. Certain "loan" programs for agriculture and less-developed countries amount to outright grants, since repayment is made unlikely by various provisions of the loan agreements.

About twenty federal agencies use the services of the FFB, including the U.S. Postal Service, the Small Business Adminstration, Amtrak, the Export-Import Bank, and the Government National Mortgage Association. In 1989 FFB debt exceeded $140 billion.

Government-sponsored privately owned agencies are not eligible for FFB services and issue securities directly to the public. These agencies include the Federal Home Loan Banks, the Federal National Mortgage Association, and the Federal Farm Credit System. In 1989 the Federal National Mortgage Association had issued more than $105 billion of outstanding securities. The Federal Home Loan Banks had more than $130 billion of outstanding securities, and Federal Farm Credit System securities amounted to more than $55 billion. In total, the market for federally sponsored agency securities amounts to one of the largest financial markets in the United States, with more than $360 billion of outstanding securities.

It is difficult to evaluate the effects of these various lending programs. Many of these loans amount to subsidies in the sense that they support economic activities that would not otherwise take place. (Indeed, if the economic activity in question would otherwise be conducted, a low-interest federal loan amounts to a windfall gain for the borrower.) Such lending programs thus usually result in a reallocation of resources among the various sectors of the economy, just as federal taxing and spending do.

The policy pursued in managing the composition of the federal debt can have significant effects on the financial system and thus the overall economy, although to a lesser extent than the taxing, spending, and lending that determine its size. These effects include potential impacts on the degree of liquidity in the economy and on the term structure of interest rates. Before assessing these potential effects of debt management policy, however, a much more powerful instrument of economic policy—fiscal policy—will be examined.

FISCAL POLICY

The deliberate use of fiscal measures by governments to stimulate or restrain economic activity is a relatively recent phenomenon. Before the 1930s, belief in the capacity of government taxation and spending policies to affect aggregate economic activity was generally limited to individuals who were untrained in economics. The accepted view among professional economists was that government spending could displace private-sector spending but could not enlarge total spending in the economy. (A modified variant of this view has, indeed, enjoyed a renaissance in recent years.)

Fiscal policy was swiftly incorporated into conventional economic theory after the 1936 publication of John Maynard Keynes's monumental book, *The General Theory of Employment, Interest, and Money*. In this classic work, Keynes demonstrated a plausible scenario in which fiscal policy could impact significantly on the aggregate level of spending and employment in an economy.[4] Keynesian theory has been modified and refined over the past five decades, and the present version of what Keynes originally proposed is often labeled "neo-Keynesian" theory. The theoretical foundations of fiscal policy, however, remain firmly fixed in neo-Keynesian analysis.

Fiscal policy is essentially use of central government powers to spend, tax, and borrow in an attempt to change aggregate spending (aggregate demand) in the economy in a desired direction and magnitude. Suppose economic policy-makers wish to stimulate the economy in order to promote employment and output expansion. Either or both of two fiscal policy measures—increased government expenditures or decreased taxes—will increase aggregate demand. Stimulative fiscal policy actions result in an increase in the government budget deficit (or, much less likely, a diminished budget surplus), since government spending increases without an increase in taxes, or taxes are reduced without a reduction in government expenditures. Increased government borrowing to fund a deficit tends to push up interest rates as aggregate demand for loanable funds increases.

Fiscal policy measures aimed at curbing inflationary pressures in the economy are the reverse of the stimulative prescription. Here the objective is to reduce aggregate demand via government spending cuts, tax increases, or a combination thereof. As for the effect on the level of government borrowing, restrictive fiscal policy measures should narrow a budget deficit or create a surplus, thus exerting downward pressures on interest rates.

As a discretionary tool of economic stabilization in this country, fiscal policy has a number of implementation shortcomings. One is the inevitable time lag between recognition of a need for fiscal stimulus or restraint and action by the Congress to implement changes in federal expenditures or taxes. (This limitation does not apply to the so-called "automatic" fiscal stabilizers described in a subsequent section of this chapter.) Further, once Congress has enacted spending and tax changes and they have been implemented, it is difficult to reserve these measures. Also, there are inherent political difficulties in conducting fiscal policy. Most notably, the fiscal prescription for combating inflation—spending cuts and higher taxes—are very unattractive politically. More generally, *any* fiscal action taken by the Congress tends to affect the distribution of income in the economy (as well as aggregate income) and thus is likely to provoke political conflicts. While monetary policy, as noted in the previous chapter, also has problems of implementation, discretionary monetary policy is generally much more flexible than discretionary fiscal policy. There are also a number of unsettled issues re-

---

[4]Keynes had many predecessors (and, indeed, many successors) in the economic theorizing that is labeled "Keynesianism," "Neo-Keynesianism," and "fiscalism," but an account of the development of the theory that would give them fair credit is beyond the scope of this book. Such an account is provided by several of the references at the end of this chapter.

PRESIDENT BUSH'S FIRST BUDGET

Many political observers credited George Bush's large margin of electoral victory in November 1988 to his pledge "Read my lips—no new taxes." The new President's first budget message to Congress was faithful to his campaign pledge. The President's proposed budgets for fiscal years 1990 and 1991 included no new taxes but did include projected deficits of $94.8 billion and $64.2 billion, respectively. The new President had made campaign promises other than "no new taxes," promises that involved new federal government outlays for various programs. However, President Bush was constrained both by his "no new taxes" pledge and by the Gramm-Rudman-Hollings deficit reduction law, which mandated a budget deficit of no more than $100 billion in fiscal year 1990 and no more than $64 billion in 1991. Thus the additional spending called for in the President's budget message to carry out campaign promises in such areas as education, space exploration, health care, AIDS research, and antidrug efforts was modest in amount.

The new President's budget called for total federal spending of $1160.4 billion in fiscal year 1990 and $1211.8 billion in fiscal year 1991. Projected revenues were $1065.6 in FY 1990 and $1147.6 in FY 1991. In comparison to his predecessor's planned spending on defense, President Bush trimmed Pentagon spending by imposing a "flexible freeze" on military outlays—with such spending projected to grow at 2 percent after inflation. This action would allow more spending on social programs without increasing the deficit beyond the Gramm-Rudman-Hollings-mandated ceilings.

The adminstration's revenue and expenditure projections were based on an optimistic economic outlook; in particular, they foresaw no recession and declining interest rates. The projections also assumed that the Congress would pass President Bush's proposed cut in the capital gains tax to 15 percent and that the result would actually *increase* federal tax revenues (because of an assumed increase in capital transactions).

garding the effectiveness of fiscal policy measures in achieving significant, sustained changes in aggregate demand.

The monetarist school of macroeconomic theory generally regards fiscal policy as an ineffective tool for economic stabilization. In the view of most monetarists, fiscal policy is seen as simply effecting a division of resources between public and private sectors; high government spending and borrowing are believed to have the effect of crowding out private-sector economic activity. Certainly, such a substitution of government economic activity for private economic activity will result when government outlays expand during a period of full employment. But when unemployed resources exist and government spending increases more than tax revenues, the potential exists for an expansion of total output. In the narrow monetarist view, such growth in output can occur only if the fiscal stimulus is accompanied by monetary expansion. In the absence of the latter, many monetarists view the rise in interest rates that government deficit spending precipitates as being likely to choke off private (investment and consumption) spending in the same amount as the increase in government spending.

Coordination of Fiscal and Monetary Policy

Arguments over the relative effectiveness of monetary and fiscal policy should not be allowed to obscure the need for their integration and coordination. Effective economic policy surely requires their tandem utilization at joint, not cross-purposes.[5]

When the economy is threatened by recession, the appropriate prescription is fiscal stimulus and monetary expansion. Whether the fiscal stimulus takes the form of increased government spending or a tax cut to spur private spending, the immediate effect is to raise income. Monetary expansion checks the rise in interest rates that the fiscal measure would otherwise trigger while concomitantly stimulating economic activity through the credit, portfolio, and wealth effects described in the previous chapter.

When inflation is the policy target, both fiscal restraint and monetary restraint are in order. Again, fiscal policy can quickly impact on aggregate spending either by decreasing government outlays or by raising taxes (and thus curtailing private spending). The various effects of a tighter monetary policy also reduce aggregate spending. Fiscal restraint alone would result in declining interest rates, which would be at cross-purposes with policy, but monetary restraint checks this tendency for rates to fall.

When a balance of payments problem (a persistent deficit) must also be confronted by economic policy, the appropriate mix of monetary and fiscal measures is affected by domestic economic conditions. Monetary restraint is more effective if inflation is the current domestic problem. This is so because anti-inflationary monetary policy entails higher interest rates, which help the balance of payments problem by attracting foreign capital. When both recession and a balance of payments deficit are to be combated, expansionary fiscal policy is preferable, since it tends to raise interest rates while stimulating economic activity.

The previous chapter suggested that monetary policy has become an increas-

---

[5]Unfortunately, this has not always been the case. One example is the 1968 income tax surcharge. This tax increase (a 10 percent add-on to 1968 tax liabilities) was intended to dampen inflation, but monetary expansion continued. (It appears that the Fed overestimated the contractionary impact of the surtax and thus chose not to slow monetary growth to a significant degree.) The apparent failure of the surtax to have any major impact on spending has been hailed by some monetarists as evidence of the greater relative potency of monetary policy, but this does not necessarily follow. The emphasis on the surtax as "temporary," for example, is also likely to have contributed to its lack of impact. A more recent example is the mixture of highly expansionary fiscal policy and relatively restrictive monetary policy that characterized the 1980s.

ingly controversial tool of economic policy in recent years. The same holds for fiscal policy or, more generally, the policies pursued by government in taxing, spending, and borrowing. Deficit spending in particular has been labeled by many as the root cause of recent inflation and other economic problems. On occasion someone charges that the federal deficit has not been expansionary enough! A few of these aspects of fiscal policy are worth our attention.

Monetary Effects of Fiscal Policy

Despite frequent assertions to the contrary by politicians and the media, federal government deficits need not result in an inflationary expansion of the money supply. When the Treasury sells securities to nonbank lenders, the effect is simply the transfer of money from the lenders to the recipients of federal outlays; no new money is created. When the Treasury sells securities to banks, the effects differ somewhat depending on whether or not the banks are holding excess reserves. In either case the potential for new money creation is unchanged unless the Fed injects reserves into the banking system.

If the banks acquiring new Treasury securities are holding excess reserves, the new debt holdings simply correspond to a reduction in these excess reserves and an increase in Treasury deposits. Ownership of the latter deposits then passes to the recipients of government outlays. The outcome—decreased excess reserves and increased deposits—is not different from what the banks could have accomplished by an alternative use of their excess reserves. Nonetheless, the money supply does expand in this case by the amount of new deposits.[6]

No significant degree of monetary expansion will occur if the banks acquiring the new Treasury securities hold only negligible amounts of excess reserves, as is the present norm. In this case, purchase of federal securities by banks necessarily involves the selling of other security holdings or the reduction of outstanding loans. The latter actions result initially in a reduction in deposits, but as government spending of the borrowed funds takes place, these deposits are restored.

A multiple expansion of the money supply *will* occur if the Fed injects reserves into the banking system to "support" the Treasury's borrowing operations. The same would be true if the Treasury sold securities to the Fed (an operation that is prohibited except in emergency situations). Such a purchase of new securities by the Fed—as is the case with any purchase—would provide new reserves to the banking system in the amount of the purchase, and money creation would follow.

Thus budget deficits need not result in money creation. According to the

---

[6]The amount of new deposits will not necessarily be equal to the amount of new Treasury borrowing but may rather be some multiple thereof.

conventional view, however, they exert upward pressure on interest rates.[7] To the extent that interest rates rise as a result of federal deficit financing, private borrowing for investment purposes will be less than it would have been otherwise, adversely affecting private-sector economic growth. This "crowding out" of private borrowing by federal government borrowing has received considerable attention in recent years.

The "Crowding-Out" Effect

No borrowing entity in the United States can issue securities having less default risk than the federal government. Thus federal deficits can always be debt financed (by borrowing as opposed to money creation) up to the amount of loanable funds available. The issue is how much private borrowing is negated—"crowded out"—as the federal government secures that portion of the available supply of loanable funds necessary to finance deficit spending. In the view of most observers, debt-financed deficit spending would result in dollar-for-dollar crowding out of private borrowing in a full employment, "closed" (no foreign capital inflows) economy. In such an economy, savings available to finance government and private borrowing is at its maximum level. In effect, the federal government induces substitution by lenders of federal for private securities by bidding up real interest rates, thus crowding out interest-rate-sensitive private borrowing. To the extent that capital formation is thereby curtailed, future output of goods and services is reduced.

Such complete crowding out need not occur if deficit financing occurs when there is less than full employment. In this case the deficit spending should cause output to expand, thus generating new saving and enlarging the supply of loanable funds available to finance both public and private borrowing. Partial crowding out will take place, however, as both the increase in federal borrowing and output expansion (which increases the demand for money) act to push up real interest rates. Crowding out may also be ameliorated by foreign capital inflows as higher real interest rates in the United States attract the attention of foreign investors.

While the foregoing analysis represents the consensus view, not all economists agree that debt-financed federal deficits necessarily result in higher real interest rates (and thus some degree of crowding out). One view is that the public—recognizing that current deficits will bring forth higher taxes in the future

---

[7]Such pressure may be mitigated, as in the 1980s, by inflows of foreign capital, but this source of deficit funding is not without problems. The increased demand for dollars in foreign exchange markets that necessarily coincides with the capital inflows drives up the value of the dollar, creating problems for U.S. export and import-competing industries. Further, foreign debt must ultimately be repaid by the transfer of goods and services to foreign residents, reducing future living standards in the United States.

in order to service the increased federal debt—responds by increasing saving in the amount of the deficit. (The deficit is, in effect, the present value of the increment in future taxes.) There is little evidence to support this proposition. A less abstract argument focuses attention on whether the deficit results from increased government spending or from tax cuts. The view here is that "crowding out" occurs only when the government increases its share of total productive resources in the economy.

The crowding out issue should not be allowed to obscure a more fundamental aspect of fiscal policy—the fact that government spending uses resources that are thus rendered unavailable to the private sector. If the economy is at the point of full employment of resources, it makes no difference whether the government taxes or borrows to finance its spending—private spending will be supplanted in an amount approximately equal to government outlays. Further, unless offset by appropriate monetary policy (and unless dollar-for-dollar crowding out occurs), government deficit spending in a full-employment economy will be inflationary. Exhibit 27.1 synopsizes theoretical views of the deficit and illustrates that the economic impact of federal budget deficits remains an unsettled issue. The huge growth in the deficit in the 1980s fueled debate about the short-run and long-run effects of burgeoning deficits, both among economists and in the political arena.

The High-Employment Budget

The degree of economic stimulus of fiscal policy is generally viewed as a function of the amount of the surplus or deficit. A surplus indicates that government taxation is removing more funds from the economy than are being provided by government outlays. A deficit indicates the reverse. However, the meaningfulness of the magnitude of the deficit or surplus as a measure of appropriate fiscal stimulus is a function of the level of economic activity. This is so because the amount of most government receipts and some expenditures are determined by the level of economic activity. For example, income tax revenues decline and unemployment compensation payments increase during periods of recession. In this case a deficit will probably result, but its magnitude may be inadequate to provide sufficient stimulus to economic recovery. On the other hand, economic booms swell tax revenues while transfer payments are declining. This "induced" surplus may be inadequate to provide a fiscal policy check to inflationary pressures.

The high-employment or "full-employment" budget is meant to deal with this difficulty by separating those budget amounts that are a function of economic conditions and those that are determined autonomously. This is accomplished by constructing a hypothetical budget for each fiscal year that incorporates esti-

EXHIBIT 27.1
A Theory of Optimal Federal Deficits

Some economists have worked out a theory that attempts to find the optimal combination of deficits and taxation necessary to finance a given pattern of government spending plans. The theory of optimal deficits rests on two pillars: first, the proposition that government debt is neutral, and second, the theory of efficient taxation.

DEBT NEUTRALITY

The proposition that debt is neutral recognizes that government spending must be paid for and suggests that government debt is nothing more than a means of substituting future taxation for current taxation. If people are rational, they realize that real deficits today imply higher taxes in the future. Knowing that higher future taxes will reduce their future after-tax income, people will save more when there is a deficit to maintain and a constant level of consumption. In other words, people base their consumption plans on the present value of their after-tax income. Suppose the government were to reduce taxes by $1 billion today, issue a bond (that is, run a deficit) worth $1 billion bearing an interest rate of, say, 6 percent, and announce that it will raise taxes by $1.06 billion next year to pay the debt plus interest. Then rational taxpayers would save the $1 billion from the deficit caused by the tax cut, invest it in a bond earning 6 percent, and use the principal and interest from the bond to pay off the tax increase in the following year. By acting in this way they are better off than not saving the $1 billion today and having to consume $1.06 billion less the next year when taxes are raised. Deficits (surpluses) raise (reduce) savings, dollar for dollar, according to the theory of debt neutrality.

When debt is neutral, deficits do not raise interest rates, crowd out borrowers, reduce investment, appreciate the dollar on foreign exchange markets, or cause inflation because deficits automatically generate enough extra savings to fund the deficit.

PRINCIPLES OF EFFICIENT TAXATION

Deficits redistribute the tax burden from year to year. But is there a unique pattern of taxes better than any other? If all taxes were lump-sum (fixed amounts) in nature, then as long as debt is neutral, it would not matter how or when the government ran deficits. But what if taxes are not lump-sum, but instead are proportional income? This is where the theory of efficient taxation plays a role. As long as debt is neutral, the only consideration necessary in setting the level of deficits is the goal of minimizing the deadweight loss due to taxation. Efficient taxation requires that tax rates be set so that they are *expected* to remain constant, given forecasts of future GNP and government spending. If new information is obtained, the tax rate must be revised to reflect the new information. The new tax rate must be set such that, once again, the expected tax remains constant in the future. (More technically, the tax rate follows a random walk.) If tax rates are set efficiently, then the deficits that result are "efficient" deficits.

ALTERNATIVE VIEWS OF THE DEFICIT

There are schools of economic thought that deny the economic reasoning or the political relevance of the theory of debt neutrality. Keynesian economists believe that the economy is inherently so unstable that it needs strong doses of monetary and fiscal stimulation to remain near full employment. Keynesians recommend—among other policies—tax cuts to

EXHIBIT 27.1 *(continued)* ▬▬▬

stimulate the economy when it falls below full employment and tax increases when the economy "overheats." Keynesians assert that the improvement in well-being due to having an economy nearer full employment on average justifies the relatively minor—in their opinion—deadweight loss caused by changing the tax rate. Under Keynesian fiscal policy, budget deficits during recessions should be even *larger* than the efficient deficits calculated here, and the deficits during booms should be smaller.[a]

Other economists are more interested in using fiscal policy to stabilize inflation than they are in using fiscal policy to stabilize employment. They believe that deficits are always monetized to some extent, that is, when the government issues more debt, the Federal Reserve purchases more of it, which creates bank reserves, thus expanding the money supply and ultimately raising the price level. Monetization turns deficits into an engine of inflation. These economists recommend raising taxes or cutting expenditures to reduce inflation when the inflation rate is too high. During inflationary periods these economists recommend deficits smaller than those advocated by efficient deficit theorists.[b]

The "neoclassical" school asserts that the higher real deficits are relative to real GNP, the higher are real interest rates, which crowd out private investment: too high real deficits result in too little investment and eventually in a too small capital stock. These economists do not believe that debt is neutral and recommend that the deficit-GNP ratio be kept low, on average, in order to increase the stock. These economists agree with efficient deficit theorists that deficits should fluctuate over the business cycle and with war and peace, but they recommend that the average level of the deficit should be smaller than that advocated by efficient deficit theorists.[c]

Some balanced-budget advocates, on the other hand, are not concerned with the deficit *per se* but with the size of the government relative to the entire economy. They believe the government has a tendency to grow larger than it should and that there is less political opposition to governmental growth when government spending is financed by deficits instead of taxes. When the government is forced to pay for its spending with taxes, the government will be smaller, in their opinion. They believe that the benefits of tax stabilization are small in relation to the benefits of having less government.[d]

---

[a]For an exposition of Keynesian deficit theory, see A. Blinder and R. Solow, "Analytical Foundations of Fiscal Policy," in *The Economics of Public Finance* (Washington, D.C.: The Brookings Institution, 1974), 3–118.

[b]This traditional point of view is being defended with rigorous (though controversial) economic analysis by P. Miller, "Deficit Policies, Deficit Fallacies," Federal Reserve Bank of Minneapolis *Quarterly Review 4* (Summer 1980), 2–4, and I. Sargent and N. Wallace, "Some Unpleasant Monetarist Arithmetic," Federal Reserve Bank of Minneapolis *Quarterly Review 5* (Fall 1981), 1–18.

[c]This "neoclassical" point of view has been discussed and defended in many publications. A good example is M. Feldstein, "Fiscal Policies, Inflation, and Capital Formation," *American Economic Review,* 70 (September 1980), 636–650.

[d]This point of view is strongly argued in J. Buchanan and R. Wagner, *Democracy in Deficit: The Political Legacy of Lord Keynes* (New York: Academic Press, 1977). The authors recommend a constitutional amendment to prohibit deficit spending except during declared national emergencies. Critical evaluations of Buchanan and Wagner's work can be found in a symposium published by the *Journal of Monetary Economics 3* (August 1978).

Source: Brian Horrigan, "Sizing Up the Deficit: An Efficient Tax Perspective," Federal Reserve Bank of Philadelphia *Business Review* (May/June, 1984), 17, 23.

mates of revenues and expenditures at full employment. Actual budget expenditures are adjusted for additional unemployment compensation payments, and receipts are adjusted to reflect full employment economic conditions. The amount of the deficit or surplus of the high-employment budget provides a bench mark for assessing the fiscal impact of the actual budget on the economy. When this hypothetical budget shows movement toward a surplus or balance, the corresponding actual budget is not providing fiscal stimulus—even if the actual budget has a sizable deficit.

The federal budget deficit can also be broken down by its "structural" and "cyclical" components in a manner similar to the actual and high-employment deficit distinction. The **cyclical deficit** is calculated on the basis of departure of real GNP from its trend line in preceding years (used as a measure of average economic activity) rather than from a high employment level. The **structural deficit** is calculated on the basis of real GNP remaining on the trend line and thus represents the part of the total deficit that would prevail under normal economic conditions, that is, when the cyclical deficit is zero.

Changes in the cyclical deficit result from changes in economic activity. As the economy slows, the cyclical deficit increases as tax receipts decline and transfer payments increase. An expanding economy has the opposite effect, the cyclical "deficit" being a surplus during periods of above-average levels of economic activity. Changes in the structural deficit, on the other hand, reflect changes in tax and expenditure policy (or reflect the effects of inflation on tax collections and budget outlays when policy changes are not made to offset such effects). The large federal budget deficits of the 1980s reflect both cyclical and structural effects. The deficits of the early 1980s stem largely from the mild recession of 1980 and the very harsh recession of 1981–1982. The deficits of the mid- and late 1980s reflect large net federal income tax reductions. The structural deficit of the period explains why the longest peacetime U.S. economic expansion failed to shrink the total budget deficit back to pre-1980 norms.

"AUTOMATIC" AND DISCRETIONARY FISCAL EFFECTS

The foregoing discussion in this chapter has focused on **discretionary** fiscal policy measures—deliberate tax and spending policies of the government to stimulate or restrain economic activity. There are also certain built-in features of the economy that "automatically" react to economic events in a stabilizing fashion.

The principal built-in stabilizer is the U.S. income tax system. Since income taxes are paid as a percentage of income, it necessarily follows that tax receipts increase when aggregate income is rising and decrease when aggregate income is falling. This effect is enhanced by the fact that income tax rates are graduated, increasing as income levels increase. Thus a tendency for the economy to move into recession (declining incomes) is automatically countered by a reduction in tax payments. The reverse holds for inflationary tendencies occurring in the economy. The U.S. system of transfer payments—unemployment, welfare, and retirement benefits—also plays a role as a built-in stabilizer.

Too much should not be made of these automatic stabilizers. Tax payments increase for desired as well as undesired expansions in aggregate income, and they decrease for desired as well as undesired contractions in aggregate income. Transfer payments reduce the human cost of policies of economic restraint (which increase unemployment) and provide a built-in check against undesired economic contraction. However, in the opinion of many observers the growth in transfer payments in recent years (both new programs and increased payments in existing programs) has exacerbated the economic stabilization problem. For example, cost-of-living adjustments aggravate inflation, and generous unemployment benefits may necessitate a higher level of unemployment in order to achieve a desired degree of anti-inflationary contraction in spending. All these various aspects may result in a need for discretionary policy action.

Once implemented, fiscal policy quickly affects economic activity. The path to its implementation, however, is often long and tortuous, since fiscal policy measures require action by both the legislative and executive branches of the federal government. Even when both the President and the Congress agree on the need for a change in taxes or spending, agreeing on which taxes and which expenditures to change seldom comes easily or quickly. The fact that monetary policy must so often carry the brunt of the economic stabilization burden is less a triumph of monetarist theory than a reflection of this political reality.

Nonetheless, fiscal policy is not without a "track record." Proponents of fiscal policy point to the 1964 tax cut as evidence of its power to spur economic activity. This huge tax cut (the bill for which languished in the Congress for more than two years) did indeed mark the beginning of a long and vigorous economic expansion. (It should be noted, however, that monetary policy was also expansionary during this period, and Vietnam War expenditures provided additional fiscal stimulus.)

The 1964 tax reduction featured across-the-board income tax cuts and cuts in federal excise taxes. During the early 1960s, selective tax measures included an investment tax credit (which permits a firm to deduct from its income tax liability for a year a certain percentage of its outlays for plant and equipment during the year) and more liberal depreciation allowances for business depreciable assets.

More recent fiscal policy measures have apparently been much less successful than the 1964 tax cut. In 1968, for example, as a response to mounting inflationary pressures, the Congress (at the urging of President Lyndon Johnson) imposed a 10 percent surtax on 1968 income taxes payable. (A taxpayer who would have otherwise owed $1000 of income taxes on 1968 income now owed $1100.) The surtax apparently had little effect on inflation. Though the ratio of consumption spending to income fell somewhat, the ratio of saving to income fell more. It is likely that, insofar as consumption spending was curtailed, the surtax did slow inflation, but the impact was simply inadequate. As we mentioned previously, this is an excellent example of the need to harmonize monetary and fiscal policy, since monetary expansion continued in 1968 and thus did *not* support the surtax effect. It is also an example of the importance of accurate economic forecasting, since the Fed apparently overreacted to the enactment of the surtax, overestimating its economic impact.

Fiscal policy in the 1970s was generally expansionary because "tax reform" measures tended to lower average tax rates, and federal spending continued to grow. The Tax Reduction Act of 1975, which reduced federal taxes by approximately $23 billion, was largely a policy response to the sharp 1973–1975 recession. The stimulative effect of the 1975 tax reductions and those that followed in 1977 and 1978 were largely dissipated as inflation moved taxpayers into higher tax brackets. Then, in the early 1980s, traditional fiscal policy was supplanted by "supply-side economics" tax-cutting measures.

Supply-Side Economics

The "stagflation"—high inflation and slow economic growth—that plagued the U.S. economy (and other industrial nations) in the 1970s was not a problem that lent itself to solution by conventional fiscal policy or, for that matter, any economic policy aimed at the management of aggregate demand. So-called **supply-side economics** has emerged as a recommended policy approach aimed at increasing aggregate supply at a rate and in a manner that would serve both to check inflation and to expand employment. Much of the supply-side economic program involves fiscal measures but not in the fashion of conventional fiscal policy theory. Rather the emphasis is on both government spending reductions and tax cuts. Properly proportioned, theses two steps theoretically may change aggregate demand only slightly or not at all. The intent is to boost the output of the private sector by jointly making more resources available to it (via reducing the amount consumed by the public sector) and by increasing the aftertax return on productive effort, saving, and investment. These fiscal measures are to be coupled with the streamlining (reducing) of government regulation in a further bid to boost productivity. In addition, a strict monetarist posture is to be struck in the management of the money supply in order to reduce both inflation and inflationary expectations.

The Economic Recovery Tax Act of 1981 constituted a "supply-sider" victory for the Reagan administration (which was strongly committed to supply-side economics) and its congressional allies. Massive tax cuts for both individuals and business firms—totaling an estimated $280 billion for fiscal years 1982, 1983, and 1984—were mandated, even larger cuts being scheduled for 1985 and 1986. The efforts of the Reagan administration to pursuade Congress to curb nondefense federal spending were less successful, resulting in large budget deficits. As a matter of fact, ERTA resulted in such large deficits in the federal budget that Congress rescinded part of the tax reductions the following year (August 1982) with passage of the Tax Equity and Fiscal Responsibility Act (TEFRA) of 1982. Despite TEFRA's enactment, the federal deficits remained huge in absolute amount and, in terms of percentage of GNP, at the highest levels since World War II. Another tax hike was enacted in 1984—the Deficit Reduction Act of 1984—aimed at trimming the deficit by $50 billion per year. In 1985, Congress passed the Gramm-Rudman-Hollings Act (GRH), which mandated the elimination of federal budget deficits by the mid 1990s. As amended in 1987, GRH sets declining deficit targets for each fiscal year and specifies a procedure (a series of across-the-board spending cuts) to achieve these targets if they are not met by Congressional appropriations legislation. However, while this legislation had a significant dampening effect on federal spending, it was apparent by the end of the decade that Gramm-Rudman-Hollings was not the beginning of the end of federal deficit spending.

The Tax Reform Act of 1986

The Tax Reform Act of 1986 was not intended to deal with the budget deficit, but rather with the real and perceived shortcomings of the federal income tax system. (Intended to be "revenue-neutral"—neither hiking nor cutting income tax collections—the effect of the act was a revenue reduction of several billion dollars.) The basic thrust of the Tax Reform Act was to reduce both income tax rates and income tax deductions. A new personal income tax rate structure of two rates, 15 and 28 percent (with a de facto third rate of 33 percent holding for some individuals), was established to replace the fifteen different rates of the old system. The differential (lower) tax rate for capital gains was eliminated. A number of deductions previously allowed in the computation of personal income tax liability were eliminated, notably the deduction of nonmortgage personal interest payments and sales taxes paid. As for corporations, the top tax rate was cut from 46 to 34 percent, but a number of favorable business tax treatments were dropped (including the investment tax credit) so that the relative tax burden of the business sector increased.

While numerous individuals and business firms were dramatically affected by the Tax Reform Act of 1986, the macroeconomic effects of the act were muted. Despite some economists' warnings that the elimination of the investment tax credit and the relative hike in business taxes would lead to an economic downturn, the economy continued to expand (albeit at a moderate pace) as the act was phased into practice. As a new decade approached, the dominant dimension of fiscal policy continued to be the huge federal budget deficits, about which more will be said in the next chapter.

DEBT MANAGEMENT AS A TOOL OF ECONOMIC POLICY

The sheer magnitude of the federal debt is the primary source of its potential as an economic policy tool, separate and apart from the fiscal policy actions that gave rise to its size. Because federal securities account for such a significant proportion of total financial asset holdings of the private sector, the composition of the national debt has implications for all securities. Specifically, the maturity structure of the federal debt may affect the term structure of interest rates in the economy. Also, the allocation of the national debt between marketable and nonmarketable securities, as well as the maturity structure, has implications for the liquidity of the financial system.[8]

Figure 27.5 shows the maturity distribution of federal debt as of December 31, 1988. It is apparent that the tilt of debt management policy is toward relatively short-term debt instruments. In the case of outstanding securities the impact on average maturity is the time left to maturity, not the original time to maturity. Thus the effect of continuously maturing outstanding securities is to shorten the average maturity of the debt. In the absence of new issues of long-term securities the debt's average maturity would become progressively shorter.

The Treasury is continuously issuing securities, for both new debt and the refunding of existing debt. Thus the opportunity for restructuring the debt's maturity composition is continually available and, to the extent that debt maturity "matters," is a potentially countercyclical economic policy instrument.

The possible economic consequences of the national debt's maturity composition stem from its potential influence on the term structure of interest rates (and security prices).[9] To some extent, it is possible that a lengthening of the debt's average maturity will lower the market prices of long-term securities and thus boost long-term interest rates (relative to short-term rates). Similarly, shortening the debt's average maturity should ease long-term interest rates while raising short-term rates. The economic significance of inducing such a tilt in interest-rate structure stems from the fact that long-term rates are likely to be more significant for business and household spending than are short-term rates. Thus a countercyclical debt management policy would involve the issue of long-term securities when rising aggregate spending threatens to trigger inflationary pressures. When economic re-

---

[8]Nonmarketable Treasury issues must be held until maturity or redemption. These issues include savings bonds and notes, foreign issues, and various special issues. As of 1988, the dollar amount of nonmarketable issues accounted for about 30 percent of the gross public debt.

[9]The term structure of interest rates, as indicated in Chapter 9, is determined by a number of factors other than relative supplies of long- and short-term securities. For example, to the extent that expectations shape the yield curve, debt management policy is irrelevant for the term structure.

Federal Debt

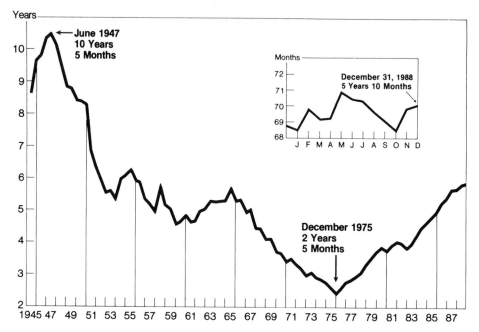

FIGURE 27.5   *Average Length of the Marketable Debt, Privately Held*

Source: U.S. Treasury Bulletin, December 1988.

cession looms, the appropriate measure would be the issuance of short-term securities by the Treasury in its new borrowing and debt-refunding operations. The latter action, by keeping the Treasury from competing with other borrowers for long-term funds and increasing aggregate liquidity, would presumably serve as a stimulus to aggregate spending.

The Federal Reserve also has the ability to influence the average maturity of outstanding federal debt because of its large holdings of Treasury securities and the frequency of its open-market operations. The Fed can alter the debt's maturity structure by purchasing securities at one point in the maturity spectrum and selling securities of a different time to maturity. An example of such an effort by the Fed was "Operation Twist" of the early 1960s, when the U.S. economy was jointly plagued by slow growth and balance of payments deficits. The Fed attempted to "twist" the interest-rate structure toward long-term rates (to spur economic growth) and higher short-term rates (to attract inflows of foreign capital and thus alleviate the balance of payments problem). Operation Twist took the form of Fed purchases of long-term federal securities and sales of short-term securities. Unfortunately for the Fed's goal the Treasury was *issuing* long-term securities during this period. Perhaps this factor and various others (the market for negotiable certificates of deposit emerged during this period) account for the relatively limited success of Operation Twist. However, the Fed's lack of success in achieving a major tilt in the yield structure adds credence to the generally accepted view that the potential for debt management to play a significant policy role is quite limited.

The capacity of debt management policy to serve as an economic stabilization tool depends on a number of economic variables that do not lend themselves to easy assessment. These include some of the factors mentioned in the previous discussion of the crowding-out issue—such as the interest elasticity of investment spending—in addition to the more fundamental issue of whether or not debt management policies can exert a significant influence (for a meaningful duration) on the term structure of interest rates. In any event it does not appear that a countercyclical debt management policy can accomplish anything that an "extra dose" of appropriate monetary/fiscal policy cannot.

The Treasury's apparent objective in debt management has generally been to minimize interest costs rather than to pursue economic policy goals. (This is not to imply that the Treasury is indifferent to economic stability; rather, it suggests that the Treasury does not view the pursuit of economic stability as one of its primary responsibilities.) Indeed, the approach to a policy of minimizing interest paid on the federal debt is exactly the reverse of a countercyclical policy. During periods of economic recession, long-term interest rates are generally low, and the Treasury thus has an incentive to issue long-term securities. When long-term rates are high during an economic boom, the Treasury minimizes long-term interest costs by issuing short-term securities. Such actions, of course, are exactly contrary to those dictated by countercyclical considerations. For this reason, few (if any) economists believe that the minimization of interest costs should be the sole objective of debt management policy.[10]

SUMMARY

It is undisputed that federal government taxation and expenditures have an enormous impact on the financial system and the economy. The federal government's ability to command and allocate huge amounts of resources makes it a dominant participant in the financial markets and the markets for goods and services. Less generally accepted is the view that the federal government can exercise its taxing, borrowing, spending, and lending powers to effectively ensure economic stability and growth.

Fiscal policy is the use of changes in federal taxes and spending as a tool of economic stabilization. Like monetary policy, it affects aggregate spending—expanding it to in-

---

[10]See Vance Roley, "Federal Debt Management: A Re-examination of the Issues," Federal Reserve Bank of Kansas City *Economic Review* (February 1978), 14–23.

crease output and employment in the economy, and restraining it when inflationary forces emerge or accelerate. Its effectiveness remains an unsettled issue among economists. Even less clear in terms of its ultimate economic effects are those fiscal measures embodied in "supply-side economics."

The management of the national debt is the task of the Treasury. Though debt management is a potential economic-stabilization policy tool, the Treasury has generally focused on an interest-rate-minimization objective in its management of the debt's maturity composition, rather than the pursuit of countercyclical policies.

QUESTIONS

1. Evaluate and discuss the following statement: "In both its operating procedures and its choice of maturities for new security issues, the Treasury attempts to minimize the financial and economic impact of its operations, thus avoiding the exercise of discretionary economic policy measures."

2. What economic relationships must exist in a significant degree for fiscal policy to have the potential for a major impact on the level of economic activity?

3. Analyze and discuss the argument that deficit spending is inherently inflationary because it results in an expansion of the money supply.

4. What is meant by the term "crowding out"?

5. Why is coordination of monetary and fiscal policies so important to an effective program of economic stabilization?

6. What is a "high-employment budget"? What is it used for?

7. In what sense is the "supply-side economics" approach to economic policy a program of fiscal measures? How does it differ from conventional fiscal policy?

8. How and why could debt management be employed as an economic policy tool?

REFERENCES

Barro, Robert, "Are Government Bonds Net Wealth?" *Journal of Political Economy* (November/December 1984), 1095–1117.

Carlson, John B., and E. J. Stevens, "The National Debt: A Secular Perspective," Federal Reserve Bank of Cleveland *Economic Review* (Autumn 1985), 11–24. Reprinted in Donald R. Fraser and Peter S. Rose (Eds.), *Financial Institutions and Markets in a Changing World,* 3rd ed. (Plano, Texas: Business Publications, Inc., 1987), 569–586.

Dew, Kurt, "The Capital Market Crowding Out Problem in Perspective," Federal Reserve Bank of San Francisco *Economic Review* (December 1975), 36–42.

Dewald, William G., "Federal Deficits and Real Interest Rates: Theory and Evidence," Federal Reserve Bank of Atlanta *Economic Review* (January 1983), 20–29.

Dotsey, Michael, "Controversy Over the Federal Budget Deficit: A Theoretical Perspective," Federal Reserve Bank of Richmond *Economic Review* (September/October 1985), 3–16.

Dumas, Charles E., "The Effects of Government Deficits: A Comparative Analysis of Crowding Out," *Essays in International Finance,* No. 158 (Princeton, N.J.: Princeton University, October 1985).

Federal Reserve Bank of Boston, *Issues in Federal Debt Management,* Conference Series No. 10, June 1973.

Friedman, Milton, and Walter Heller, *Monetary vs. Fiscal Policy* (New York, W. W. Norton, 1969).

Greenspan, Alan, "Statement to the Deficit Commission," *Federal Reserve Bulletin* (January 1989), 15–18.

Hamburger, Michael J., and Burton Zwick, "Deficits, Money, and Inflation," *Journal of Monetary Economics* (January 1981), 141–150.

Horrigan, Brian, "Sizing Up the Deficit: An Efficient Tax Perspective," Federal Reserve Bank of Philadelphia *Business Review* (May/June 1984), 15–25.

Keynes, John M., *The General Theory of Employment, Interest, and Money* (New York: Harcourt Brace, 1936).

Motley, Brian, "Ricardo or Keynes: Does the Government Debt Affect Consumption?" Federal Reserve Bank of San Francisco *Economic Review* (Winter 1987), 47–62.

Protopapadakis, Aris, and Jeremy J. Siegel, "Are Government Deficits Monetized: Some International Evidence," Federal Reserve Bank of Philadelphia *Business Review* (November/December 1986), 13–22.

Stein, Herbert, *The Fiscal Revolution in America* (Chicago: University of Chicago Press, 1969).

Summers, Lawrence H., "Debt Problems and Macroeconomic Policies," in *Debt, Financial Stability, and Public Policy* (Federal Reserve Bank of Kansas City, 1986).

Tatom, John A., "A Perspective on the Federal Deficit Problem," Federal Reserve Bank of St. Louis *Review* (June/July 1984), 5–17.

U.S. Department of the Treasury, *The Effects of Deficits on Prices of Financial Assets: Theory and Evidence* (Washington, D.C.: Government Printing Office, 1984).

Webster, Charles E., "The Effects of Deficits on Interest Rates," Federal Reserve Bank of Kansas City *Economic Review* (May 1983), 19–28.

CHAPTER 28

The Record
of Economic Policy

In this chapter we provide a brief review of the historical evolution and record of economic policy. The emphasis is on monetary policy, though fiscal policy is treated also. The time span of the discussion is from the founding of the Federal Reserve in 1913 to the late 1980s, though a greater emphasis is placed on more recent developments, since they are presumably more relevant to understanding current economic policies and problems. This review is provided not only because it is interesting and important in itself, but also because it is the base on which an assessment of the successes and failures of economic policy can be grounded and perhaps offers insights into the nature and likely effectiveness of economic policy in the future.

Economic policy as practiced today, with monetary and fiscal policy designed explicitly to stabilize the economy and to achieve broad economic goals, is a relatively recent phenomenon. The Federal Reserve was not created until 1913, and countercyclical monetary policy was not practiced until well after its founding. The notion of using the federal budget as a means to stabilize the levels of production, employment, and income through fiscal policy was not widely held until the 1930s, when John Maynard Keynes and others developed a theory that attempted to explain how fiscal policy could achieve desirable economic goals.

The present review of economic policy is divided into five subdivisions:

1. *The period from the founding of the Federal Reserve until the Great Depression of the 1930s.* During this period, U.S. monetary policy was in an embryonic stage, and fiscal policy as practiced today did not exist. Yet during this period there was considerable progress in the application of the tools of monetary policy, and open-market operations—today the principal technique of Federal Reserve monetary policy—were discovered as a weapon of monetary control.

2. *The period between the Great Depression until the end of World War II (1945).* This period marked the beginning of government attempts at countercyclical economic policy. However, it was an era in which monetary policy became discredited in the view of many, and fiscal policy became the dominant weapon of economic stabilization. Monetary policy appeared weak and ineffectual in its apparent inability to counter the greatest decline in U.S. economic history, though many monetarists would argue that monetary policy did not fail; rather, it was not tried.

3. *The period of roughly two decades between the end of World War II and the end of the economic expansion of the 1960s—a period of rapid economic growth and great faith in the efficacy of government economic stabilization policy.* Monetary and fiscal policy were both used as stabilization tools, and both seemed to work. Employment and income expanded except for short and relatively shallow recessions, and the inflation rate was very low by standards of the more recent past.

4. *The late 1960s to 1982.* This period marked the emergence of the "stagflation" problem: low rates of economic growth and high rates of inflation. Monetary and fiscal policy seemed to be ineffectual means of coping with stagflation. During this period, monetary policy appeared to be perennially in a posture of restraint aimed at countering the stimulus provided by recurring large federal deficits. For monetary policy the period was one of intense controversy over the proper targets of policy. The Keynesians favored an emphasis on interest rates, especially money market rates, and the monetarists urged the Fed to concentrate on the growth of monetary aggregates, such as the money supply and the monetary base. The influence of the monetarists grew considerably during the period, as evidenced in 1979 when the Fed publicly announced that it was changing its operating procedures in order to focus on the growth of the monetary aggregates.

5. Finally, a discussion is presented of the 1980s, reflecting the substantial economic policy shifts associated with the Reagan Administration.

FROM THE FOUNDING OF THE FEDERAL RESERVE TO THE GREAT DEPRESSION: 1913–1929

Operations of the Federal Reserve during the 1913–1929 period were not principally conducted for the purpose of general economic stabilization. This is not really surprising, since at the inception of the Fed it was not at all clear that the central bank was charged with such responsibilities, nor was it obvious what tools the Fed possessed that could be used to stabilize the economy. To a considerable extent, within broad and somewhat vague general legislative guidelines the Fed has had to determine both its functions and its techniques by itself.

How did the Fed, as the first central bank in the United States in almost 100 years (since 1836, when the charter of the Second Bank of the United States was allowed to lapse), initially perceive its proper role? An important early concern was international conditions produced by World War I (1914–1918) and its aftermath. A substantial inflow of gold occurred during the war, resulting (since the United States was on a gold standard) in an increase in prices. As shown in Figs. 28.1 and 28.2, prices increased sharply from 1915 to 1920. Figure 28.1 shows the level of wholesale or producer prices for industrial commodities, farm products, and for all commodities, and Fig. 28.2 shows the level of consumer prices (both the price level index for all items and separately for food). The Federal Reserve apparently made little or no serious effort to prevent the monetary expansion (and price inflation) resulting from the gold inflow. Given the uncertainty concerning the responsibilities of the Fed as well as the prevailing view that the economy was self-regulating under the gold standard, we can perhaps understand why the Fed did not vigorously counteract the monetary effects of the gold inflow. Further, even if the Fed had wished to contain the expansionary effect of the gold inflow on the money supply, it would have found it impossible to do so. Since banks were holding large amounts of excess reserves at the time, raising the discount rate would not have been effective. Moreover, the Fed did not then have

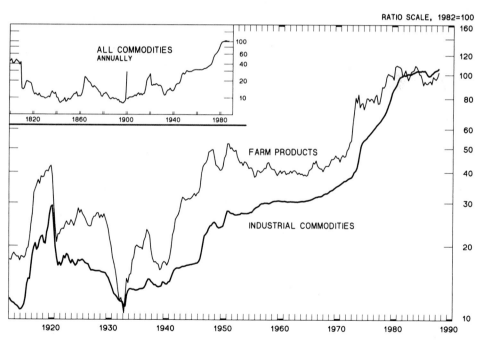

**FIGURE 28.1   Producer Prices
(Quarterly)**

Source: *Board of Governors of the Federal Reserve System,* Historical Chart Book, *1988.*

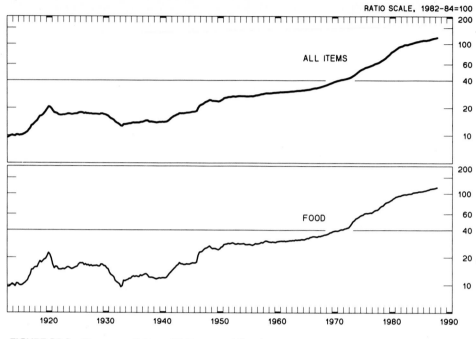

RATIO SCALE, 1982–84=100

**FIGURE 28.2   Consumer Prices, All Items and Food
(Quarterly Averages)**

Source: Board of Governors of the Federal Reserve System, Historical Chart Book, *1988.*

the power to increase reserve requirements. (This authority was not given to the Fed until the 1930s.) The only way the Fed could have reduced bank reserves would have been to sell securities, but the Fed had no securities early in the war period, and it did not choose to sell the securities that it acquired later in this period. Indeed, the technique of open-market operations and its effects on bank reserves were not yet fully understood. Instead of acting as an agent to stabilize the economy during this period, the Fed was principally concerned with facilitating the necessary Treasury borrowing associated with financing World War I.

The Fed began to employ a more aggressive countercyclical policy during the 1920s. In 1920 it raised the discount rate substantially. Yet, as can be seen by referring to Figs. 28.1 and 28.2, prices were already beginning to fall. This action led to criticism that the Fed waited too long to act and then did the wrong thing. This criticism has been aimed at the Fed on many occasions since 1920, especially in the period since 1966. There is considerable evidence that because of lags in implementing monetary policy and further lags until monetary policy changes affect the economy, the Fed often does wait too long and then does too much. It appears that this was the case in the early 1920s. The Fed maintained a high discount rate despite falling prices while attempting to stem large outflows of gold that developed as Europe stabilized after the war. During the remainder of the 1920s, however, the Fed pursued a countercyclical monetary policy more consistent with that suggested by monetary theory.

The decade of the 1920s was an important one for the development of the tools of monetary policy. At the time of the formation of the Fed it was expected that the discount rate would be the principal tool of monetary policy, as it was for other central banks throughout the world. Yet it became evident during the 1920s that open-market operations could be a very effective means of affecting economic activity. Initially, open-market operations, in terms of the purchase of securities, were employed primarily to provide interest income from security holdings to the regional Federal Reserve Banks. Yet when it was recognized that such purchases (as well as sales) had substantial effects on the amount of bank reserves, it became obvious that these purchases would have to be coordinated through the Federal Reserve System (each regional Reserve Bank was then determining its own open-market operating policy) and made consistent with overall monetary policy objectives. As a result, the Fed established in 1920 an informal Open-Market Committee made up of five of the presidents of the regional Reserve Banks.

FROM THE GREAT DEPRESSION TO THE END OF WORLD WAR II

The trauma of the Great Depression of the 1930s led to great changes in the manner in which government economic stabilization policy was viewed and conducted. Monetary policy, apparently ineffectual in countering this great economic decline, lost substantial credibility as an economic policy technique and was replaced for a considerable period by fiscal policy as the principal technique of economic stabilization. Moreover, the organizational structure of the Fed, as well as the tools under its control, was markedly altered by the banking reform legislation that emerged from the financial collapse of the early 1930s. The Great Depression undoubtedly produced a fundamental change in this nation's economic system and particularly in the role of government in the economy.

It is sometimes said that the Great Depression resulted from the stock market crash of 1929. At best this is a gross oversimplification. A more accurate interpretation would be that the business decline that began before the stock market crash was accelerated, intensified, and deepened by the financial problems and diminished-wealth effects associated with the precipitous decline of stock prices.[1]

---

[1] It is also argued that the stock market's 1929 collapse stemmed from a "forecast" of the Great Depression by market participants.

In any case, as can be seen from Fig. 28.3, industrial production fell dramatically from 1929 through 1933. Similar declines were occurring in employment and personal income. The rate of unemployment skyrocketed, reaching well over 20 percent by 1933. Personal and corporate bankruptcies multiplied, and the social fabric of the nation was threatened with disintegration. It is interesting to note, however, that, as shown in Figs. 28.1 and 28.2, prices declined sharply in the early 1930s. In fact, prices had been declining throughout much of the 1920s, though at a much slower rate. The economy stabilized in the mid-1930s as industrial production advanced, though another substantial decline occurred in the late 1930s. It was not until the massive government spending associated with World War II occurred that the economy once again attained prosperity.

The monetary policy actions taken by the Fed to stem the declining economic conditions of the 1930s were less than might have been expected. The discount rate was lowered in a number of steps beginning in 1930. Yet in 1931 the discount

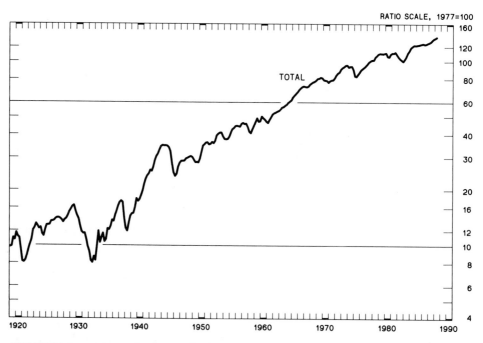

FIGURE 28.3 Industrial Production, Total (Seasonally Adjusted, Quarterly)

Source: Board of Governors of the Federal Reserve System, Historical Chart Book, *1988.*

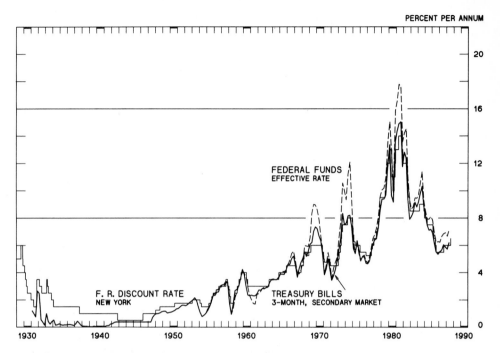

FIGURE 28.4 Short-Term Interest Rates, Money Market
(Discount Rate, Effective Date of Change; All Others, Quarterly averages)

Source: Board of Governors of the Federal Reserve System, Historical Chart Book, 1988.

rate was increased, though not to the level of 1929, as is shown in Fig. 28.4. A small quantity of government securities were purchased by the Fed, but considering the decline in borrowing by member banks, total reserve bank credit actually declined in the early 1930s. Responding to this decline in reserve bank credit, the total quantity of money also declined in the early 1930s. Further, the Fed tightened credit (raised reserve requirements) in 1936 and 1937, apparently precipitating the sharp decline in economic activity in those years.

Two questions are immediately raised by these events. First, why did the Fed pursue the policy that it did? Second, what would have occurred if it had pursued a different policy? An answer to the first question is obviously more easily offered than to the second. The Fed did not pursue an aggressive policy of monetary ease in the early 1930s because of an outflow of gold associated with the collapse of the gold standard. The Fed followed the policy that was appropriate under a gold standard—expand when gold flows into the country and contract when gold flows out. Unfortunately, such a policy necessarily relegates the domestic economy to a role subsidiary to the maintenance of the gold standard.[2] Answering the second question is, of course, more speculative. Monetarists, who place principal emphasis on the growth rate of monetary aggregates, tend to be very harsh regarding the Fed's performance in the 1930s. Indeed, in their monumental *Monetary History of the United States*, Milton Friedman and Anna Schwartz argue that the severity of the Great Depression was due, to a considerable extent, to the actions of (and inaction of) the Federal Reserve. Economists who view the economic influence of money primarily in terms of interest rate movements (interest rates were quite low throughout the 1930s) and those who place more emphasis on fiscal policy would be less inclined to fault the Fed to such a degree. Thus "Keynesian" economists would generally attach a less significant role to monetary policy during the period.

The financial collapse of the early 1930s led to numerous reforms in the economy and the financial system. Major legislative changes were enacted dealing with the operation and supervision of commercial banks. Since these changes are discussed in Chapters 5 and 12, we will not detail them here. However, relevant to our current discussion are the major reforms of the Federal Reserve System produced by legislation of the early 1930s. These reforms both increased the degree of centralization of power within the Fed and gave the Fed additional stabilization tools with which to work. By way of centralizing authority the composition of the Board of Governors was changed, the duration of each member's term was lengthened, and ex officio membership by the Secretary of the Treasury and the Comptroller of the Currency was eliminated with the intent of increasing the power of the Board relative to that of the regional Reserve Banks. This diffusion of power has created considerable difficulties within the Federal Reserve System since its founding. It was doubtless inevitable that conflicts would develop between the Board and the Reserve Banks. The Board was often at odds with the Federal Reserve Bank of New York, both because of the prominence of New York as a financial center and because the New York Fed had vigorous leadership during this period in the person of Benjamin Strong. The move toward centralizing power in the Board of Governors and thereby in Washington has continued to the present (though primarily without legislation) so that today the Board dominates the entire Federal Reserve System.

The legislative reforms of the early 1930s also produced major changes in

---

[2]The tightening by the Fed in 1936 and 1937 was apparently due to the fear that an inflow of gold in the mid-1930s (resulting from the rise of Nazism and other European political and military tension), along with excess reserve holdings by U.S. banks, would produce inflation. (It is perhaps significant to note that this argument is inconsistent with the justification for Fed actions in the early 1930s.) The Fed was also concerned in 1936–1937 about the relatively large amounts of excess reserves held by the banking system at the time.

the status and role of the Open Market Committee, until this time an informal group within the Federal Reserve System. Now the Federal Open Market Committee was established by law as comprising twelve members, the five presidents of the regional Reserve Banks and the seven members of the Board of Governors. Significantly, the Board was given a majority of the voting membership of the FOMC.

The powers of the Federal Reserve System, and especially that of the Board of Governors, were substantially increased by these legislative reforms. Most important, the Board was given the power to vary reserve requirements for member banks—today one of the three principal techniques of monetary policy but completely lacking until the early 1930s. In addition, the Board was given the authority to set maximum or ceiling rates for time and savings deposits at member banks. The Board was also given powers to set margin (collateral) requirements on loans for purchase of equity securities, as well as on loans for purchase of convertible bonds.[3]

Monetary policy appears to have played at best a neutral role in reversing the economic decline of the 1930s and at worst a strongly negative role, whereas fiscal policy was highly and properly stimulative. The expansionary thrust of fiscal policy, however, stemmed primarily from increased federal expenditures (deficit spending) aimed at reducing economic suffering rather than from a carefully planned stabilization policy. In fact, there did not yet exist a theory of using fiscal policy to moderate the swings of the business cycle. (Such a theory was offered by John Maynard Keynes in his *General Theory of Employment, Interest, and Money,* published in 1936.) Rather, the fiscal policy of large federal deficits reflected the views of President Roosevelt, his Congressional supporters, and others, who believed that the prevention of social chaos was a more pressing concern than the tradition of balancing the federal budget. It was these large federal deficits during the 1930s and throughout World War II, accommodated by monetary policy in the Fed's attempts to assist in the war financing effort, that appear to have been the principal contributions of government in restoring the economy to relative prosperity. As shown in Fig. 28.5, the federal debt (which reflects the deficit or surplus in the federal budget) began to expand rapidly in the early 1930s and continued to grow rapidly throughout World War II. These deficits helped to bring the economy back to full employment, though not without inflationary pressures—pressures that were contained during the war by price controls.

---

[3]It is interesting to speculate on whether the course of economic history would have been different if the Fed had held (and exercised) the power to set margin limits on stock market credit in the late 1920s. The orgy of speculation in the stock market might have been prevented, with perhaps a significant influence on the severity of the Great Depression. (As was pointed out above, the stock market crash did not *cause* the Great Depression, though the financial distress associated with declining stock prices undoubtedly contributed to the severity of the decline.)

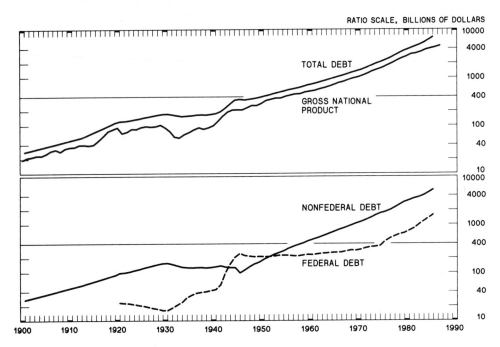

FIGURE 28.5   Debt in The United States
(Amount Outstanding; Debt, End of Year; GNP, Annually)

Source: Board of Governors of the Federal Reserve System, Historical Chart Book, 1988.

TWO DECADES OF ECONOMIC EXPANSION: 1945–1966

There was widespread concern after World War II that without the stimulus of large federal defense expenditures, the economy would sink back into depression. Fortunately, however, no such postwar depression developed. In fact, the economy advanced sharply after a short adjustment period immediately after the end of the war. Further, the 20-year period from 1946 to 1966 was one of balanced economic growth with relatively low rates of unemployment and inflation, as is shown in Figs. 28.6 and 28.7. It was a period during which economic goals were much more nearly achieved than has been the case in more recent years. It was also a period when both monetary and fiscal policy were used in countercyclical fashion with apparent success.

Despite the prosperity of the period, however, there were significant problems in the economy and in the implementation of monetary and fiscal policy. These problems may best be discussed under the following headings: the accord in 1951 between the Fed and the Treasury, the 1964 tax cut, and the problem of inflation that persisted throughout much of the period.

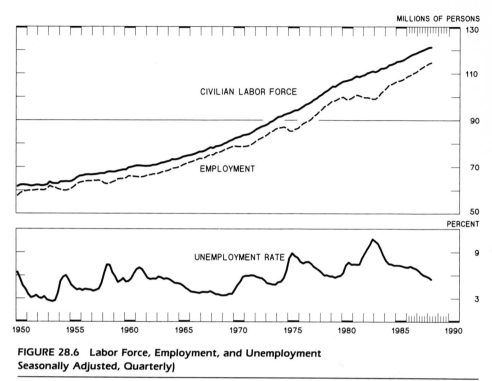

FIGURE 28.6 Labor Force, Employment, and Unemployment Seasonally Adjusted, Quarterly)

Source: Board of Governors of the Federal Reserve System, Historical Chart Book, *1988.*

The Accord

The period immediately after the end of World War II was one of substantial discord between the Federal Reserve and the U.S. Treasury. The Fed was quite concerned about the inflation that was taking place in the late 1940s. As is evident from examining Figs. 28.1 and 28.2, prices rose sharply after the end of the war. No doubt some of this inflation reflected the release of pent-up inflationary pressures created by government deficit spending during World War II but contained during that period by price controls. Part of the inflationary pressures, however, also may have reflected the rapid growth in production, employment, and income during the period. In any case the Federal Reserve wished to pursue a restrictive monetary policy to reduce these inflationary pressures.

The Treasury, though also concerned about inflation, was especially concerned about the effects of a contractionary monetary policy on the market value of the federal debt. During the war, appeals to patriotism had been made to sell federal government securities, and the Fed had made purchase of these securities risk free by pegging their prices at high levels (thereby pegging interest rates at

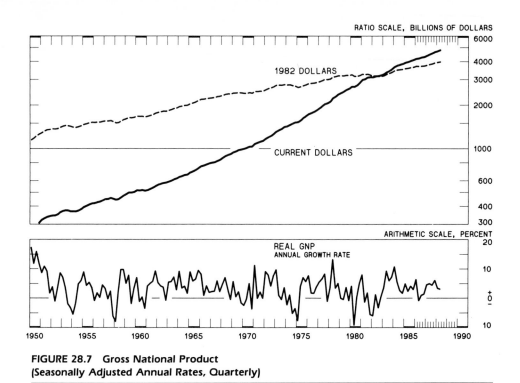

**FIGURE 28.7   Gross National Product
(Seasonally Adjusted Annual Rates, Quarterly)**

Source: Board of Governors of the Federal Reserve System, Historical Chart Book, *1988.*

low levels) via open-market purchases. Any restraint now on the part of the Fed would produce rising interest rates and falling bond prices. Investors would lose literally billions of dollars, as they had when interest rates rose after World War I. Yet if the Fed were to continue to peg the price of U.S. government securities, it could not operate a countercyclical monetary policy.

The conflict between the Fed and the Treasury continued throughout the late 1940s. But the Treasury view prevailed, with the result that the Fed was unable to implement a policy of monetary restraint. However, the increased spending associated with the Korean War and the acceleration of inflation intensified the need for a resolution of the conflict. Finally, in 1951 the Treasury and the Fed reached an accord that resulted in a joint statement issued on March 4, 1951, indicating that:

> *The Treasury and the Federal Reserve System have reached full accord with respect to debt-management and monetary policies to be pursued in furthering their common purpose to assure the successful financing of the government's requirements and, at the same time, to minimize monetization of the public debt.*

Following the accord the Fed regained its independence to pursue countercyclical monetary policy. However, it used this independence carefully in the period immediately following the accord. Interest rates rose, and bond prices fell, though the changes were modest in size. In fact, as is shown in Fig. 28.4, the interest rates began to decline in 1953 as the economy entered the first (with the exception of the immediate postwar adjustment) of a number of short recessions that would characterize the period.

Economic growth was generally quite rapid in the 1950s (although a serious recession occurred in 1958), and inflation was generally subdued. The federal budget was occasionally in deficit, though the deficits were quite small by recent standards. There was, as a result, little pressure on the Federal Reserve to accommodate fiscal policy. In fact, there was little of any type of activist fiscal policy. The Federal Reserve gradually reasserted its independence, though it did not need to take vigorous action very frequently during the period.

The 1964 Tax Cut

The reduction in federal taxes implemented in 1964 represents one of the most important examples of the use of countercyclical fiscal policy. It also, however, might represent the high-water mark in the credibility of fiscal policy as an effective stabilization device. Originally proposed by President Kennedy to "get the economy moving again," the tax cut was proposed and later enacted at a time when the federal budget was in deficit. The argument was that the tax cut would reduce fiscal drag on the economy and increase the level of production, employment, and income, and through the higher tax revenues associated with the rise in incomes, the budget would be balanced. The notion that the way to balance the budget was to reduce rather than to raise tax rates was quite novel at the time. (Economist Arthur Laffer and others have since developed this notion into a doctrine.) Implementation of such a concept represented a major victory for those who argued that the federal budget should be used as a conscious tool of economic stabilization. It is interesting to note that the arguments underlying this tax cut were similar in some ways to the "supply-side" arguments associated with the Economic Recovery Act of 1981, though the 1964 tax cut was aimed at stimulating spending generally, and the emphasis of the 1981 tax cut was on expanding saving and investment.

After a mild recession in 1960, the years from 1961 to 1965 constituted a period of particularly notable economic stability and growth. Real GNP grew at an average annual rate of 5.2 percent, and the rate of inflation never exceeded 2 percent during these years. The rate of unemployment had dropped below 4 percent by 1965. By the standards of more recent years, federal budget deficits were quite small in the 1961–1965 period—less than $12 billion totally.

Unfortunately, this happy state of economic affairs became unwound in 1966 and the following years. As U.S. military involvement in Vietnam escalated and the bill for President Johnson's ambitious "Great Society" social reforms mounted, federal spending grew by almost $60 billion in the 1966–1968 period. Since taxes were not increased, the federal deficit grew also. The federal debt grew by $20 billion in these three years. Much of this increase in Treasury debt was "monetized" by Fed open-market purchases, and money supply growth increased from an average annual growth rate of 3.5 percent in the 1961–1965 period to more than 5.5 percent in the 1966–1968 period. As economic theory predicts, the result of these stimulative fiscal and monetary policies during a period of full employment was an acceleration of inflation. By 1968 the rate of inflation was nearing 5 percent—the highest since the Korean War. Thus began a siege of inflation that persisted into the early 1980s.

Inflation

An examination of the behavior of prices in the United States since the early nineteenth century indicates that throughout U.S. economic history, extended periods of price increases have been followed by extended periods of price declines. However, until about 1940 there appeared to be no trend to this movement of prices; producer prices in 1940 were little higher than those in the early 1800s. However, beginning with World War II, and especially in the postwar period we are now discussing, this pattern appears to have changed. A persistent upward trend to prices emerged in the postwar period, one that seems to have become embedded in the economy and much more pronounced in recent years.

Thus though the U.S. economy generally performed well during the period from World War II to 1966, an unfavorable aspect of this performance was the development of an inflationary trend in the economy. The rate of inflation itself was not especially high in 1966 in relation to the inflation rate in more recent years or in comparison with the inflation rate in many other countries at the time. Yet the persistence of the inflation that developed during this period might have been of considerable importance for future developments in the economy and for the success of economic policy. Expectation of the rate of future price level changes on the part of economic participants might have changed so drastically during this period that the reaction of the economy to economic policy action might now be quite different from past years. This could account, at least partly, for the problems in implementing economic policy in more recent years.

FROM 1966 TO 1981

It appears that everything went wrong during the 1966–1981 period, when the economy became "unstuck." The inflation rate began to rise, and despite price and wage controls during some of the period (1971–1974), as well as a number of severe economic declines, the inflation rate reached levels beyond those experienced by the United States in this century (see Figs. 28.1 and 28.2). At the same time, high interest rates produced severe financial problems for many businesses. Particularly hard hit were financial institutions, such as savings and loan associations, that had large holdings of long-term, fixed-rate debt instruments, the values of which dropped sharply as interest rates rose. At the same time the trend of unemployment was sharply upward, so by the early 1980s the unemployment rate reached a level not seen in this country since the Great Depression of the 1930s.

Not only were the trends of inflation, interest rates, unemployment, and other indexes of economic performance unfavorable during this period, but the volatility in these indexes, especially in the early 1980s, was pronounced. Indeed, the great volatility of the economy in the period from 1966 to the early 1980s was one of its most distinctive characteristics. Large economic declines occurred in 1969–1970, 1974–1975, and 1981–1982. These declines sharply reduced the volume of employment and industrial production and sharply increased the amount of unemployment. These recessions were preceded or accompanied by interest rate "spikes" and by the persistence of high inflation. (The unusual combination of economic stagnation and inflation was termed "**stagflation**".) Though the recessions appeared to produce some benefit in the rate of inflation, the benefit was temporary, the inflation rate increasing to successively higher levels at each peak in the business cycle.

Some observers add together the unemployment rate and the inflation rate in order to obtain a "**discomfort index.**" By this standard the period from 1966 to the early 1980s was one of high and rising discomfort. To some extent these developments were produced by events external to the U.S. economy. The "oil shocks" of 1973 and 1979 (huge OPEC-engineered hikes in petroleum prices) certainly made the simultaneous achievement of stable prices and full employment very difficult. It must also be recognized that rising unemployment, coupled with rising inflation, was common throughout much of the Western industrial economy during this period, perhaps reflecting basic structural changes in the world economy. Such structural change could have stemmed not only from the rising cost of resources but also from growing industrial competition from less-developed economies. Yet the record of economic policy during this period was hardly distinguished.[4]

Fiscal policy, in particular, was applied in questionable fashion over much of the period. It might be expected that a period of substantial cyclical movements in the economy would produce alternating periods of surplus and deficit in the federal budget. In fact, the federal budget was in deficit almost throughout the

---

[4]It was the apparent impossibility of dealing with high unemployment and high inflation simultaneously with the conventional prescriptions for monetary and fiscal policy that led to the emphasis on supply-side economics of the Reagan Administration. The Economic Recovery Tax Act of 1981, essentially a "Reaganomics" piece of legislation, reflected this shift in the direction of economic policy.

entire period, and the federal debt grew at a rapid rate (see Fig. 28.5). Control over federal expenditures began to appear impossible after a series of Presidents whose campaign pledges had included balancing the budget were forced to admit shortly into their terms that a balanced budget was impossible (at least in their first term).

Continuing large federal deficits during periods of relatively full employment create a serious dilemma for the Fed. Suppose the Fed chooses to create sufficient reserves to allow the debt to be monetized in an effort to avert large increases in interest rates. Such a policy would likely be appropriate during times of high unemployment. But during a period of inflation, such a policy will lead to more rapid growth in the money supply and thus aggravate inflation (perhaps eventually causing interest rates to rise despite the Fed's monetary ease). Moreover, if the financial markets perceive this policy as eventually spurring higher inflation rates, they might drive interest rates up immediately through extracting a premium in current interest rates for the expected future inflation. Suppose instead that the Fed refuses to provide reserves to monetize the increased federal debt. In the short term, at least, interest rates are likely to rise sharply, bringing the Fed under substantial political pressure to ease monetary policy.

The Fed appears to have followed a somewhat erratic course in responding to this economic and political dilemma. On balance, the Fed allowed the growth of the money supply to occur at a much higher rate during the 1966–1981 period than had been the case during the period from World War II to 1966. This suggests a general policy of accommodation by the Fed of the deficits of the federal government. Yet for some short subperiods the Fed has pursued a stringent monetary policy, sharply reducing the growth of reserves.

These broad problems of monetary policy goals were compounded by intense debate over proper operating targets for implementation of monetary policy actions. It has been argued that one of the principal reasons for the erratic behavior of monetary policy, as well as for occasional excessively rapid growth of the money supply, was emphasis on interest rate targets in the conduct of open-market operations. This controversy led in 1979 to a focus on monetary aggregates as policy targets. However early experience with the new operating targets did not suggest that they were fully successful in producing their goals, and a partial retreat to broader targeting resulted.

REAGANOMICS: 1981–1988

The inauguration of Ronald Reagan as President of the United States in 1981 marked the beginning of several bold new approaches to the problems of the U.S. economy. Reagan had long advocated a reduced role for the federal government in the U.S. economy, "sound money," and balanced federal budgets. The new President was also a devotee of **supply-side economics**—the view that the key to breaking the U.S. economy out of the swamp of stagflation lay in stimulating labor productivity and capital formation via large tax cuts, deregulation, and various measures to encourage savings and investment.

Beginning in late 1980 the Fed moved to curb monetary growth sharply in an effort to halt inflation. (The inflation rate in 1980, as measured by the consumer price index, exceeded 12 percent.) In the Fed's report to Congress of February 1981 (such periodic reports are mandated by the Full Employment and Balanced Growth Act of 1978), the Fed indicated that "the principal objective for monetary policy in 1981 would be to exert continuing resistance to inflationary forces." Such resistance, of course, took the form of reducing the rate of monetary growth, and in 1981, M1 grew at a rate of only 4.7 percent (compared to 5.9 percent in 1980, 7.7 percent in 1979, and 8.2 percent in 1978).

President Reagan thus inherited a tight monetary policy but initially endorsed the Fed's tightfisted posture. As Reagan's economic program took shape in 1981, the term "**Reaganomics**" was coined to describe its mixture of slow monetary growth, federal spending cuts, and federal tax cuts. In August 1981, Congress passed the Economic Recovery Tax Act of 1981 (ERTA), the largest tax cut in modern U.S. history. It was estimated at the time of ERTA's enactment that the act would reduce taxes by about $38 billion in fiscal year 1982, $93 billion in 1983, $150 billion in 1984, and even more in 1985 and 1986. (Various ERTA provisions were rescinded in 1982 and 1984 legislation.) Although providing for broadly based tax reduction, the new law included various measures aimed at providing increased incentive for saving and investment.

At the time of the tax cut bill's enactment, the economy had already entered into its eighth postwar recession—an economic slump that was attributable largely to the Fed's policy of tight money. Because of both monetary stringency and expectations of continued inflation, interest rates remained at exceptionally high levels. Federal tax revenues usually fall significantly during economic declines, and the 1981–1982 recession was no exception. As this recession-induced decline in the tax rate was coupled with the tax reduction mandated by ERTA, federal budget deficits—current and forecast—mounted. Present and prospective pressure on available loanable funds (constrained by the Fed's monetary stringency) kept interest rates high despite the significant decline in inflationary pressures resulting from the recession. Thus the spring of 1982 found the U.S. economy mired in recession, the interest rate level extraordinarily high, and the prospect of record-setting budget deficits in the offing. The potential size of future federal deficits resulted in passage by Congress in August 1982 of a large administration-supported tax increase.

Predictions of the demise of Reaganomics were premature. As the Fed gradually eased its monetary leash and the considerable fiscal stimulus of the Reagan budgets spurred the economy, economic recovery commenced in late 1982. As economic growth resumed, inflationary forces strengthened only slightly, and a near-term return to the double-digit levels of inflation of the 1970s appeared unlikely. To what degree, if at all, these modest indications of economic renewal stemmed from supply-side stimulus is unclear. At present it appears that the ebbing of inflation was due to a considerable extent to the severity of the 1981–1982 recession (which, in turn, resulted largely from the Fed's tight money policies) and to softening of world oil prices. The economic revival in 1982 can also be attributed in part to another conventional economic policy cause—the 1981 tax cuts—as well as to a more stimulative monetary policy adopted by the Fed in mid-1982.

The cyclical trough was reached in the last quarter of 1982, following an extraordinarily large decline in real economic activity and an increase in the unemployment rate to above 10 percent. In the following months the economy moved forward rapidly. In fact, the economic recovery that began in late 1982 and was continuing through mid-1989 had two interesting and somewhat surprising dimensions. First, the economic recovery was much stronger than had been anticipated by most economic analysts. Analysts' projections were for a relatively slow recovery from the economic contraction of 1981–1982. Instead, the recovery was robust and rapid. Real economic growth spurted in 1983 and throughout 1984. As a result, the unemployment rate fell dramatically, and the economy appeared to approach capacity of labor and capital resources by late 1984 (when the pace of the economic surge slowed). The recovery was led initially by a surge in consumer spending, though by 1984 business spending for capital goods expanded dramatically. The more rapid expansion in real economic activity in the United States than in most other industrial nations of the world contributed (as did the rise in the value of the dollar as compared to most of the trading partners of the United States) to a surge in imports, with the result that the trade deficit of the United States reached unprecedented levels.

The second surprising dimension to the post-1982 expansion in economic activity was the failure of the inflation rate to accelerate. The decline in the inflation rate in the later stages of the 1981–1982 contraction and during the early stages of the recovery was perhaps not surprising, given the severity of the recession. But the inflation rate remained relatively subdued throughout 1984 and 1985, settling into the 3 percent to 4 percent range. Then, partly as the result of sharp decline in oil prices, the rate of price increases fell to less than 2 percent in 1986. Inflation rates moved back into the 4 percent range after 1986, as a result, at least in part, of the plunge in the value of the dollar that caused the prices of imported goods to rise and allowed import-competing domestic producers an opportunity to raise their own prices.

The remarkable economic expansion of the 1980s was marred by a number of problems, however. Even as the national rate of unemployment declined steadily after 1982 (to about 5.5 percent by 1989), the energy-producing and agricultural states of the nation encountered their most difficult economic conditions since the 1930s. Their problems stemmed largely from large decreases in the price of oil and agricultural products—events that helped to hold down the national inflation rate. But aside from the unevenness of the economic blessings of the 1980s, the pattern of economic developments in the period raised troubling questions about the economic future of the United States. The national debt roughly tripled in the 1980s, from about $1 trillion to $3 trillion. A decade of trade deficits turned the United States into the world's largest debtor nation, with net indebtedness to nonresidents exceeding $500 billion in 1989. The decline in the value of the dollar had proceeded to the point that international comparisons of economic conditions became unsettling to Americans; in 1989, average hourly pay in the United States had fallen behind the dollar-equivalent rates in West Germany, Japan, France, and Italy. But despite the anemic dollar, the U.S. trade deficit continued to exceed $100 billion.

Nonetheless, as the U.S. economic expansion continued into its seventh year—the longest in peacetime history—the stock market had regained all the ground lost in the Black Monday of October 19, 1987, and neither recession nor another siege of double-digit inflation appeared on the horizon. Indeed, the only reason economists found for predicting an end to the expansion in the economy was the lack of a reason to believe that the business cycle had been repealed. As for the "twin deficits" and the huge external debt, it is possible that they will spawn neither recession nor double-digit inflation, but only a quiet and unremarkable erosion of relative U.S. living standards in the future.

SUMMARY

The record of economic policy since the founding of the Federal Reserve may, though somewhat arbitrarily, be divided into five time segments. The first segment—from 1913 until the Great Depression—was characterized by only limited use of monetary policy and by the use of fiscal policy as a conscious use of the federal budget to achieve desired economic goals. The Federal Reserve was still attempting to determine the nature of its economic role and how its actions affected the financial system and the economy. The Fed did, however, engage in some countercyclical use of its techniques of monetary control during the 1920s.

The second time segment—from the Great Depression through World War II—provided a major test for economic policy. The performance of economic policy in this period was not particularly distinguished. Monetary policy came out of the period almost completely discredited, although in retrospect it appears that the failure of the Fed to effectively counter the depression stemmed not from any inherent limitation of monetary policy but from weak and misguided Fed leadership. Fiscal policy, though not yet based on well-developed theoretical grounds, became for the first time a conscious tool of economic policy. Fiscal stimulus in the 1930s was not of sufficient magnitude to move the economy back to full employment, but the huge federal outlays of World War II did accomplish this.

The third time segment—from World War II to 1966—was characterized by a substantial degree of economic growth and prosperity. Both monetary and fiscal policy were used in countercyclical fashion during this period (monetary policy being "unleashed" after the 1951 "accord" with the Treasury). In 1964 a bold and apparently successful fiscal policy experiment was mounted with a large decrease in personal and business taxes. Economic policy appeared to work during this period, giving policymakers the (false) impression that they could "fine-tune" the economy to achieve desired economic goals. Yet during this period inflation became an increasingly serious problem.

The fourth time segment—from 1966 to 1981—saw almost everything go wrong with the economy. Achievement of the desired economic goals of full employment, stable prices, economic growth, and balance in our international payments account appeared to elude the grasp of policymakers. The economy appeared unstable, with wide fluctuations in interest rates and the unemployment rate. The inflation rate reached levels unheard of in the recent past. In general, the record of economic policy left a great deal to be desired. Fiscal policy became subsumed under an uncontrolled federal budget, and monetary policy alternated between monetizing the growing federal debt and pursing a restrictive policy aimed at curbing inflation.

The fifth time segment—1981–1988—began with double-digit inflation rates, very high interest rates, and the worst recession since the Great Depression. However, after economic recovery from the recession began in late 1982, the ensuing economic expansion set a new peacetime record for longevity. It is likely that much of the economy's good performance during this period was the result of the fiscal stimulus supplied by an extraordinary surge in federal deficit spending, the national debt increasing more during the eight years of the Reagan presidency than all the cumulative deficits prior to 1981. The ill effects of the huge increase in federal borrowing included high real interest rates (although their nominal magnitudes fell from the inflation-bloated levels of earlier years) relative to historical norms. The federal budget deficit also contributed to the nation's trade deficit, which also hit record levels year after year in the 1980s and resulted in the United States becoming the world's largest debtor nation. While the nation thus had plenty of economic matters to worry about as the decade of the 1980s ended, it was nonetheless no small consolation to be ending it at full employment and a manageable inflation rate.

QUESTIONS

1. How did gold flows affect the conduct of monetary policy from 1913 to the Great Depression?

2. What role did fiscal policy play in the period from 1913 to the Great Depression?

3. What did the Fed do to counter the economic decline of the 1930s? Why?

4. What reforms in the functions and organization of the Fed were implemented in the early 1930s? Why?

5. What was the Fed-Treasury Accord? Of what significance was it?

6. Why has the tax cut of 1964 been called a victory for those who advocated using the federal budget to stabilize the economy?

7. Evaluate the conduct of monetary and fiscal policy in the period from 1966 through the early 1980s.

8. Describe and assess "Reaganomics." In your opinion, were the economic policies of the Reagan administration successful? Why or why not?

REFERENCES

Cacy, J. A., and Richard Roberts, "The U.S. Economy in 1989: An Uncertain Outlook," Federal Reserve Bank of Kansas City *Economic Review* (December 1988), 3–18.

Carlson, Keith M., "Federal Fiscal Policy Since the Employment Act of 1946," Federal Reserve Bank of St. Louis *Review* (December 1987), 14–29.

Council of Economic Advisors, *Economic Report of the President*, various issues of this annual publication.

Friedman, Milton, and Anna Schwartz, *A Monetary History of the United States, 1867–1960* (Princeton: Princeton University Press, 1963).

Galbraith, John K., *The Great Crash* (Boston: Houghton Mifflin, 1954).

Gilbert, R. Alton, and Michael E. Trebing, "The FOMC in 1980: A Year of Reserve Targeting," Federal Reserve Bank of St. Louis *Review* (August/September 1981).

Goldenweiser, E. A., *American Monetary Policy* (New York: McGraw-Hill, 1951).

McCallum, Bennett T., "Macroeconomics After a Decade of Rational Expectations: Some Critical Issues," Federal Reserve Bank of Richmond *Economic Review* (November/December 1982), 3–12.

Miller, Glenn H. Jr., "Inflation and Recession, 1979–82: Supply Shocks and Economic Policy," Federal Reserve Bank of Kansas City *Economic Review* (June 1983), 8–21.

Okun, Arthur M., *The Political Economy of Prosperity* (Washington, D.C.: The Brookings Institution, 1970).

Stein, Herbert, *Presidential Economics* (New York: Simon & Schuster, 1984).

Tatom, John A., "A Perspective on the Federal Deficit Problem," Federal Reserve Bank of St. Louis *Review* (June/July 1984), 5–17.

Thornton, Daniel L., "The FOMC in 1981: Monetary Control in a Changing Financial Environment," Federal Reserve Bank of St. Louis *Review* (April 1982).

Wallich, Henry C., "Recent Techniques of Monetary Policy," Federal Reserve Bank of Kansas City *Economic Review* (May 1984), 21–30.

POSTSCRIPT

THE FINANCIAL INSTITUTIONS REFORM, RECOVERY, AND ENFORCEMENT ACT OF 1989

As this book went to press in August 1989, Congress and the Bush administration finally reached agreement on a wide range of actions to deal with the devastated thrift institution industry. The legislation passed by Congress and signed by the President, the Financial Institutions Reform, Recovery, and Enforcement Act of 1989, was labelled a "thrift rescue" and a "thrift bail-out" bill by the media. It remains to be seen, however, if the financing plan will be adequate to deal with the vast financial wasteland created by a decade of poorly-implemented deregulation and Congressional unwillingness to deal with the steadily mounting financial problems of the nation's savings and loan associations.

The bill's estimated cost, including interest on the bonds issued to raise funds for closing and merging insolvent thrifts, was more than $160 billion. The thrift industry was to pay one-third of this cost and the taxpaying public the balance. The act included a number of provisions that seem likely to trigger a significant shrinkage of the number of thrift institutions. The more than 260 thrifts already held by regulators were to be closed or merged and another 500 or more were expected to meet the same fate in the next two years. The act required savings associations to boost their tangible capital to a minimum of 1.5 percent of assets in 1989 and 3 percent of assets by the end of 1994. At the time the bill was passed, almost one-fourth of all thrifts did not meet the 1.5 percent capital standard. In addition to the capital adequacy pressure created by the act, deposit insurance premiums were hiked dramatically. Further, the lending authority of thrifts was greatly narrowed, with thrifts being obliged to hold about 70 percent of their assets in home mortgages, other residential loans, or mortgage-backed securities. A provision of the act limited the authority of thrifts to invest directly in real estate to separately capitalized subsidiaries. The act also prohibited investment by savings institutions in corporate debt securities not of investment grade (so-called "junk bonds"), with divestiture of any existing holdings by July 1, 1994. The investment powers and permissible activities of federally-chartered and state-chartered thrifts were made uniform.

The more stringent capital requirements and narrowed lending powers mandated by the act reduced the value of a thrift institution charter. Thrifts can convert to a bank charter, but are still obliged to pay higher deposit insurance premiums than banks for five years. The act allows commercial banks to acquire healthy thrifts (banks were already allowed to buy failing ones) and place them in their branch network or otherwise meld them into banking operations. The prospects of numerous savings associations turning into commercial banks, along with the thrift industry attrition due to unprofitability, led many observers to forecast the demise of half or more of all thrift institutions. The number of savings associations had already declined from about 4600 in 1980 to less than 3000 in 1989.

The act also restructured the regulatory framework for thrifts. The Federal Home Loan Bank Board was abolished and replaced by the Office of Thrift Supervision, a bureau of the Treasury Department (as is the Office of the Comptroller of the Currency), which would charter new thrifts and regulate and supervise existing ones. The Federal Home Loan Bank system, however, remained in existence, with responsibility for overseeing it being assigned to a newly-created independent agency called the Federal Housing Finance Board. The Federal Savings and Loan Insurance Corporation was dissolved, with thrift institution deposit insurance protection being transferred to the Federal Deposit Insurance Corporation (FDIC). The FDIC will henceforth administer two separate funds—the Bank Insurance Fund and the Savings Association Insurance Fund (SAIF). The act also made explicit federal government backing of the deposit insurance guarantee, making it clear that the two funds were not the only guarantors. Further, the act created the Resolution Trust Corporation (RTC) to oversee the disposition of the assets of the failed thrifts that were closed or merged by regulators. The RTC is staffed by the FDIC, with responsibility for broad policy being exercised by an oversight board that includes the Secretary of the Treasury, the Secretary of Housing and Urban Development, and the Chairman of the Federal Reserve Board of Governors. The RTC was thus charged with the responsibility for dealing with hundreds of billions of foreclosed real estate properties and other troubled assets of defunct thrifts.

As far-reaching as the Financial Institutions Recovery, Reform, and Enforcement Act of 1989 is, the legislation is not likely to be the final chapter of the thrift crisis saga. The decade of the 1990s is likely to bring new efforts to revive the thrift industry. Further, the Resolution Trust Corporation has been given a task that is perhaps much more difficult than Congress realized, and the RTC may well need considerably more resources and more time than the act provided.

INDEX

178, 681; yield curve to forecast, 173

Interest-rate arbitrage, 576–577

Interest-rate risk, 199n; as factor in failure of commercial banks, 395n; use of swaps to manage, 524–528, 597; total risk of financial institutions and, 397–398

Interest-rate swap, 524–528; 597; see also Swaps

Interest-sensitive assets, 386–387

Interest-sensitive liabilities, 386–387

Interest-sensitivity management, 389–391

Interest-sensitivity measurement, 386–389

Intermediated financial markets, 19

Intermediation: see Financial intermediation

Intermediation services, 215

Internal financing, 488, 489

International banking: effects of, 333–336; expansion, 310, 313–314, 331; legislation permitting, 307, 309, 331–332; risk and, 336–337

International Banking Act of 1978, 603, 606, 608

International Banking Facilities, 604–605

International financial markets: for bonds, 594–599; debt problem in, 591–594; nature of, 581–589; participants in, 588–589; see also Eurocurrency market

International gold standard, 562–563

International Monetary Fund (IMF), 564–565

International monetary system, 547; exchange rate determination and, 551–562; exchange rate systems and, 562–575; foreign exchange market and, 549–551; integration of, 607; interest rate and exchange rate relationships and, 575–578; role of commercial banks in, 600–601

International trade financing, 600–601

Intrastate banking expansion, 310, 331

Inventory levels, 616n

Inverted yield curve, 157–159, 161–164, 166

Investment, 534–536

Investment bankers, 249–250

Investment banking, 50, 312

Investment companies: closed-end, 248n; explanation of, 248–249; growth in, 54

Investment demand, 616, 618

Investments: explanation of, 8; importance of, 8–9; interest rate effects on, 133–135

Jackson, Andrew, 44, 46

Jacowski, M., 310n

Japan, 587, 589

J-curve effect, 564n

Johnson, Lyndon, 678, 700

Johnson, Sylvester, 230

Joint ventures, 332

Jordan, Jerry, 70n

Junk bonds, 202–203, 452, 453

Kamphoefner, J. E., 556n

Kane, Edward, 122n

Kaufman, George, 315, 391n, 393n

Keeley, Michael, 308n

Kennedy, John F., 699

Keran, Michael W., 70n

Kessel, Reuben, 181

Keynes, John Maynard, 69, 70, 668–669, 687, 695

Keynesian economics, 69, 70, 650–651, 669, 675

King, Robert G., 656n

Klebaner, Benjamin, 41n

Kohn, Ernest, 335n

Korean War, 698

Kroos, H., 42n, 43n

L monetary measure, 62, 64, 652, 653

Laffer, Arthur, 699

Lending and yield curve, 158–159, 174

Letters of credit, 601

Leveraged buyouts, 452, 453

Leveraging, 364

Liabilities, 71, 532

Life Insurance Association of America, 542

Life insurance companies: assets and liabilities of, 243–245; bond holdings of, 446, 447; growth of, 49, 54; pension funds held by, 243–245; size and offerings of, 218; see also Insurance companies

Line, Carolyn P., 559n

Lions, 459

Liquidity preference: influence on yield curve of, 162; 164; theory of, 148–153, 162n

Liquidity premiums, 162, 180, 181

Liquidity risk, 397n

Loanable funds: demand for, 139–144; supply of, 135–139, 193; theory of, 135, 144–145, 193, 194

Loeys, Jan G., 526n

London Interbank Offered Rate (LIBOR), 525–526, 584

Long, John B., 656n

Long hedge, 513–515, 518–519

Louvre accord (1987), 568

Lucas, Robert E., 654n

Macaulay, Frederick R., 36n

McCulloch, J. H., 181

McCurdy, Christopher J., 412n, 507n

McFadden Act, 331–332, 608

MacMinn, R. D., 362n

Malkiel, Burton G., 182, 500n

Management risk, 398n

Mankiw, Gregory, 655n

Marginal rate of return, 130, 132

Market index, 363

Market segmentation: hypothesis of, 181–182; yield curves and, 164–167

Marketing function, 250

Marshall, Alfred, 67n

Martin, J. D., 362n

Martin, William McChesney, 107

Matched sale-purchase agreement (reverse repo), 110

Maturity and yield curves, 156–162

Maturity buckets, 387, 390

Maturity intermediation, 242, 384

Maturity management, 384, 397–399

Meiselman, David, 70n, 180, 181

Mengle, David L., 116n

Merrill Lynch and Co., 309, 311

Mester, Loretta J., 17n

Middle Eastern currency market, 587

Miller, P., 676n

Modigliani, Franco, 182

M1, M2, and M3 monetary measures: explanation of, 62–64; growth of, 703; velocity of, 65, 652, 653

Monetarism, 69–71

Monetarists: on fiscal policy, 670–671; on monetary policy, 649–651

Monetary base, 90–93

Monetary control problems, 118–119

Monetary growth, 187

Monetary multiplier, 78, 86, 90–93

Monetary policy, 615–616, 618; during 1930s, 692–693, 695; federal funds and, 419, 639–642; Federal Open Market Committee meetings and, 628–629; Federal Reserve's role in, 106–118; lags in effects of, 651–652, 691; monetarist vs. Keynesian views of, 649–651; monetary velocity and, 652–654; rational expectations and, 654–657; targets of, 629–639; transmission of, 644–649; unsettled issues of, 649

Monetary stringency, 108

Monetary velocity, 64–67, 652–654

715

Price volatility: duration and, 35–37; interest rate changes and, 34–35
Price volatility risk, 32
Primary deposits, 81
Primary market, 19–20, 370; for corporate bonds, 447–448; for municipal bonds, 456; for U.S. government securities, 410–412
Primary security, 10–13
Private debt instruments, 16–17
Private placement: for bonds, 447–448; for equity securities, 494
Product deregulation: commercial banks and, 326; explanation of, 306, 325; motivation for, 329; risk and, 326–328; state's role in, 307–308
Product line expansion, 314–315
Property and casualty insurance companies, 243–246; see also Insurance companies
Prudent man rule, 300, 383
Public issues of corporate bonds, 448
Public offering of stock, 493–494
Purchase-and-assumption transaction, 339, 340
Purchasing power parity, 557
Purchasing power risk, 32
Pure expectations theory, 167–171, 173, 174, 177, 180–181
Put option, 521–524

Quantity theory of money, 67–68, 649n
Quotas on imports, 573

Random walk, 369, 500n
Ratchet effect, 187n, 188
Rational expectations theory, 70, 654–657
Reagan, Ronald, 107, 702
Reagan administration, 679–680
Reaganomics, 702–705
Real assets, 4, 532–534
Real business cycles, 656
Real Estate Investment Trusts, 471–472
Real estate limited partnerships, 472
Real Estate Mortgage Investment Conduit, 482
Real Estate Settlement Procedures Act of 1974, 290
Real interest rates: determination of, 132–133; effect on savings and investment and, 133–135; explanation of, 129–132; see also Interest rates
Regulation Q, 117, 220, 222, 285–286, 309
Regulatory reform: agency, 347–349;

current system and, 346–347; proposals for, 318–321; see also Deregulation
Reinvestment rate risk, 162n, 450
Renegotiated-rate mortgages, 476, 478, 479
Repurchase agreements (Repos), 61; characteristics of 108–110, 419–420; purchasers of, 421; reverse, 420
Required rate of return, 34–35
Reserve requirements: changes in, 86, 115–117, 220; differences between Federal Reserve and state, 101; Eurodollar deposits and, 583–584; monetary multiplier and, 92–93
Reserves available for nonbank deposits, 642
Resolution Funding Corporation, 271
Retail market, 406
Retained earnings, 6, 489n
Revenue bonds, 452, 454
Reverse annuity mortgages, 476
Reverse repurchase agreements, 420
Riding the yield curve, 176–178
Right to Financial Privacy Act of 1978, 290
Risk: default, 32 (see also Credit risk; Default risk); deposit insurance and, 337–339; of financial institutions, 396–397; inflation, 32; interest rate (see interest-rate risk); liquidity, 397n; price volatility, 32; product deregulation and, 326–328; systematic, 362, 363, 366, 497; unsystematic, 362, 366
Risk intermediation, 242
Risk management, 384
Risk premium, 200
Risk-free rate, 129–130, 199
Risk-related deposit insurance premiums, 344–345
Roley, Vance, 683n
Roll, Richard, 366
Rolnick, Arthur J., 47n
Roosevelt, Franklin D., 50
Rosenblum, Harvey, 315
Runs on banks, 278–280

Salomon Brothers, 221, 542
Santoni, G. J., 504n
Sargent, I., 676n
Sargent, Thomas J., 654n
Savings: definition of, 6, 544; effect of interstate banking on, 336; explanation of, 7; flow of funds and, 534–535; importance of, 8–9; interest rate effects on, 133–135; loanable funds and, 136–137; motivation for, 130

Savings banks, 234–235, 382, 394
Savings and loan associations: crisis in, 233; deregulation of, 222, 312; explanation of, 14; interest rate increases and, 701; as mortgage lenders, 473–474; origins and growth of, 43, 52, 231; role in financial market of, 382, 394; regulatory structure for, 291–293, 297; source of funds in, 232, 234; use of funds in, 231–232
Saxon, James, 346
Schwartz, Anna, 280, 694
Schweitzer, Robert L., 337n
Search and transaction costs, 58
Seasonal credit, 112
Second Bank of the United States, 44–46
Secondary market, 20, 144, 371; for corporate bonds, 448–449; for municipal bonds, 458; for U.S. government securities, 412
Securities: federal agency (see Federal agency securities); government (see U.S. government securities; Federal Reserve's effect on prices of, 644–645; indirect, 10–12, 19; marketability of, 207; primary, 10–13; risk premium of, 199–200; selection of (see Portfolio selection); Treasury, 665–666, 672, 681, 682 (see also Treasury bills; Treasury bonds; Treasury notes); yield curves and, 174–176
Securities brokers, 249–251, 374
Securities dealers, 249–251; activities of, 405–406; financing, 406; profit sources of, 407
Securities and Exchange Commission (SEC): function of, 300–301; registration with, 495–496; on shelf registration, 448
Securities industry: origins of, 43, 44; size of, 218
Securities market growth, 54
Securitization, 219–221, 328
Security market line, 363, 364
Separately Traded Registered Interest and Principal Securities, 459
Serial bonds, 455
Shared appreciation, 465
Shared appreciation mortgages, 476
Shelf registration, 448
Shiller, Robert J., 502
Short hedge, 513–514
Sight drafts, 428n, 600
Silber, W. L., 263n
Simmons, Bruce J., 406n
Single European Act, 567
Sinking fund, 444
Sinquefield, Rex A., 196